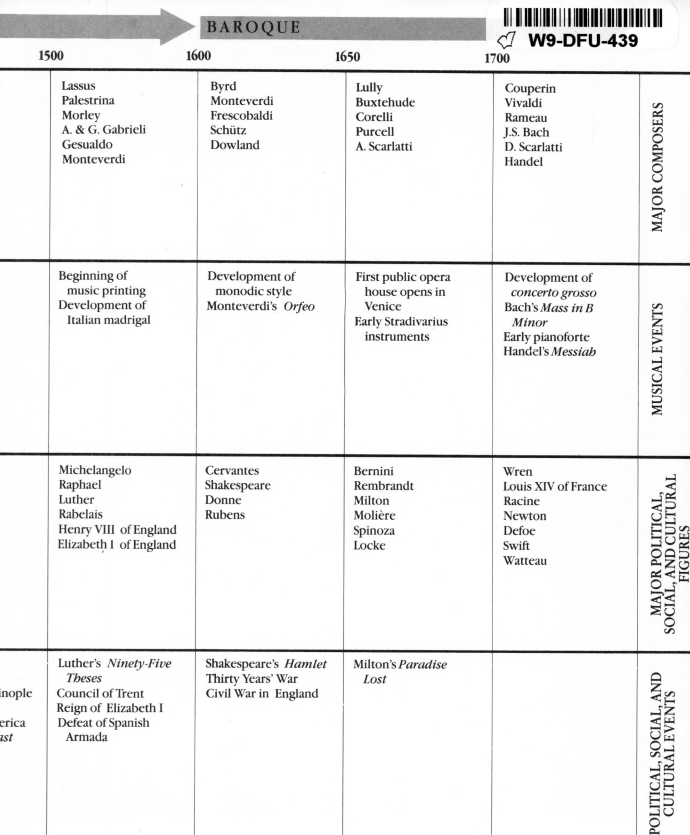

BAROQUE W9-DFU-439

| | 1500 | 1600 | 1650 | 1700 | |
|---|---|---|---|---|---|
| **MAJOR COMPOSERS** | Lassus<br>Palestrina<br>Morley<br>A. & G. Gabrieli<br>Gesualdo<br>Monteverdi | Byrd<br>Monteverdi<br>Frescobaldi<br>Schütz<br>Dowland | Lully<br>Buxtehude<br>Corelli<br>Purcell<br>A. Scarlatti | Couperin<br>Vivaldi<br>Rameau<br>J.S. Bach<br>D. Scarlatti<br>Handel | MAJOR COMPOSERS |
| **MUSICAL EVENTS** | Beginning of music printing<br>Development of Italian madrigal | Development of monodic style<br>Monteverdi's *Orfeo* | First public opera house opens in Venice<br>Early Stradivarius instruments | Development of *concerto grosso*<br>Bach's *Mass in B Minor*<br>Early pianoforte<br>Handel's *Messiah* | MUSICAL EVENTS |
| **MAJOR POLITICAL, SOCIAL, AND CULTURAL FIGURES** | Michelangelo<br>Raphael<br>Luther<br>Rabelais<br>Henry VIII of England<br>Elizabeth I of England | Cervantes<br>Shakespeare<br>Donne<br>Rubens | Bernini<br>Rembrandt<br>Milton<br>Molière<br>Spinoza<br>Locke | Wren<br>Louis XIV of France<br>Racine<br>Newton<br>Defoe<br>Swift<br>Watteau | MAJOR POLITICAL, SOCIAL, AND CULTURAL FIGURES |
| **POLITICAL, SOCIAL, AND CULTURAL EVENTS** | inople<br>erica<br>ast<br>Luther's *Ninety-Five Theses*<br>Council of Trent<br>Reign of Elizabeth I<br>Defeat of Spanish Armada | Shakespeare's *Hamlet*<br>Thirty Years' War<br>Civil War in England | Milton's *Paradise Lost* | | POLITICAL, SOCIAL, AND CULTURAL EVENTS |

FOURTH EDITION

# Music

**DANIEL T. POLITOSKE**
*University of Kansas*

**ART ESSAYS BY MARTIN WERNER**
*Temple University*

PRENTICE-HALL INC.
Englewood Cliffs, New Jersey 07632

...outh American edition first published 1988 by
...e-Hall, Inc., Englewood Cliffs, N.J. 07632
...opyright © 1988, 1984, 1979, 1974 by Prentice-Hall, Inc.

PRENTICE-HALL INTERNATIONAL, INC., *London*
PRENTICE-HALL OF AUSTRALIA PTY. LIMITED, *Sydney*
EDITORA PRENTICE-HALL DO BRASIL, LTDA., *Rio de Janeiro*
PRENTICE-HALL CANADA INC., *Toronto*
PRENTICE-HALL OF INDIA PRIVATE LIMITED, *New Delhi*
PRENTICE-HALL OF JAPAN, INC., *Tokyo*
PRENTICE-HALL OF SOUTHEAST ASIA PTE. LTD., *Singapore*
WHITEHALL BOOKS LIMITED, *Wellington, New Zealand*

ISBN 0-13-607616-5

This edition was designed and produced by
JOHN CALMANN AND KING LTD, LONDON

Designer Martin Bronkhorst
Printed in Spain by Cayfosa, Barcelona

# Contents

**8**

# Special Features

**10**

# Preface

This edition of *Music* is intended for anyone who is interested in learning how to listen to music with greater perception and understanding. Music forms a part of almost everyone's life today—so much so that it is easy to listen to it without giving it much thought. Yet by making some effort to listen carefully to what is heard and by gaining some knowledge of the many different musical styles and forms that have developed over the centuries, a person can hear more and have a far greater enjoyment of what is heard.

With this goal in mind, the present text places primary emphasis on the listening experience, encouraging the development of listening skills through a historical survey of musical styles. Although social, political, and cultural influences are mentioned for each historical period, the focus of the discussion is music itself rather than things peripheral to it. Major styles and periods of music are considered, along with their principal types and forms of composition. Representative examples are discussed, and the major composers of each style and period are presented. The focus on listening is strengthened by an accompanying record set that includes recordings of most of the works analyzed in the text.

## Organization

Music has certain basic terms and concepts that are peculiar to it, and an understanding of them is helpful, if not absolutely necessary, to most discussions of music. For this reason, Part One of the book is devoted to a survey of the fundamentals of music—melody, rhythm, harmony, texture, timbre, dynamics, form, and notation. Parts Two through Six trace major developments in music of the Western world from the Middle Ages to our own time. Part Seven examines briefly the music of four non-Western cultures and points out some of the ways in which their music differs from that of the West.

The book is organized flexibly so that it can be used in several ways. Each of the major periods in the history of Western music is presented as a compact unit that can be studied with or without the periods immediately preceding or following it. Individual chapters or sections within each period can also be selected as time and interest permit.

## Features

The revision process has made it possible to add new feature material, all directed toward enhancing the reader's understanding and enjoyment of the study of music. The development of material to strengthen the reader's aural perception of music has received the most attention, but the importance of aesthetic and pedagogical factors has also been carefully considered. In this edition, American music of a given period until the twentieth century is discussed in a discrete section at the end of each period's general coverage. It is hoped that the student will thus be better able to develop a sense of America's musical output within the mainstream of musical achievement. Since the most important twentieth-century American composers have had influence throughout the Western world, they are discussed alongside their European counterparts. For certain composers material has been added, primarily to help the student assimilate the musical discussion. This includes pertinent biographical information and summaries of overall output. More emphasis has been given to the transitions and overlappings between historical periods. Other particular features of this book can be grouped under the three headings that follow.

### Listening Material

In keeping with the book's primary goal, several items related directly to listening are included. Perhaps most important are the Listening Analyses and Listening Summaries given for each work included on the recordings. Each Listening Analysis describes in some detail the major characteristics of the content and structure of a work. In addition to the Analysis, a Listening Summary is provided which lists schematically the major points made in the analysis. Also included are thirty Listening Previews, located at the beginning of each chapter of the book, and five Cross-Period Listening Exercises that illustrate the evolution of different genres of music, such as opera, Mass, and symphony. An audio-cassette of selected pieces accompanies this book.

### Art Essays, Maps, and Illustrations

Just as words alone cannot equal the experience of listening to music, verbal references and black-and-white photographs cannot give a true picture of the fine art of the major styles in the history of music. For this reason, full-color art sections, with interpretative essays by art historian Martin Werner, are included for each period. Maps of major centers of musical activity appear where they can help in comprehension of trends in music. Reproductions of interesting scores, manuscripts, and programs help to give deeper insights into some of the music discussed.

### Coverage of Basic Material

Great care has been taken to provide a clear introduction to the elements of music, with detailed coverage of instruments, form, and style. This initial emphasis is carried throughout the text in the Listening Analyses and Summaries and in the comparison charts for music of different periods. Emphasis is placed on the most important composers and genres of each period. Other aids to the reader include chronology charts, a glossary, an index of musical compositions, a general index, and a list of the Listening Analyses and Summaries.

## Readability and the Use of Notation

Throughout this edition, care has been taken to focus on only the most important details of musical style, presenting them in a clear and interesting fashion, in terms that will be accessible to the student. Readers who have not learned to read music need not be alarmed by the many short musical examples found in the text. The examples are intended to enhance the discussions of music for those who read music and to give a general visual representation of sounds for those who do not. Ability to read music is not important to understanding the text. The main goal of the book is to stimulate the reader to listen to music, not to look at it.

## Supplements

Although not essential to the use of the text, the accompanying set of six records, directly keyed to the major analyses found in the text, can be a valuable aid to both student and instructor. Full movements are given for all instrumental works, full sections for all vocal works. A *Study Guide and Workbook* by Raymond A. Barr of the University of Miami at Coral Gables, and an *Instructor's Manual* by Maurice Legault of Southern Illinois University are also available from the publisher. The first contains study aids, self-tests, listening exercises and a series of cumulative reviews designed to place the study of specific works within a much broader framework. The Instructor's Manual features a number of diagrams that can be used in the classroom to clarify musical form.

## Acknowledgments

Kind acknowledgments and profound thanks are due to many friends and colleagues for countless suggestions and much active help. The published works of Rose Brandel and William P. Malm provided invaluable insights in the preparation of the first edition. In preparing the second, third, and fourth editions, several people graciously provided fine suggestions in their fields of expertise and to them I am grateful: J. Bunker Clark in American music, Bruno Nettl in non-Western music, Charles Hoag in later twentieth-century music, Richard Wright in jazz and popular music, Stephen Addiss in Asian music, and Alan Luecke in rock music. Sterling Murray offered many excellent ideas for numerous parts of the text. Jan Kozma, Guido Milanese, and Ann Shaw provided invaluable assistance with translations of texts of vocal music into English. Martha Minor's help in making many positive suggestions and in editorial and clerical matters is greatly appreciated. I also wish to thank the many reviewers involved in the development of all editions.

Thanks are also due to the many people at Prentice-Hall involved in each of the editions. For their help in the preparation of the first edition, I owe a special debt of gratitude to Project Editor Michael Feist and Production Editor Sarah Parker. In the preparation of the second edition, special thanks are due to Art Director Florence Silverman, Manufacturing Buyer Nancy Myers, Production Editor Eleanor Perz, and especially to the Project Editor, Stephanie Roby. For their expert and patient editorial assistance in preparing the third edition, I am very grateful to Fred Bernardi, Production Editor, and also to Anita Duncan, photo researcher. For their excellent editorial assistance in preparing the fourth edition, I offer my gratitude to Louise Bloomfield, Elisabeth Ingles and Julia Engelhardt.

# *Introduction: Listening to Music*

Music, in all its variety, is one of our most constant public and private companions. It is the sound from our dashboards, the background to our movies, the product of our stereo sets and the reason for our concert halls. Nearly everyone responds to some kind of music. Most of us can identify at least one performer or musical style that moves us emotionally. Our choices today are without limit, for technology gives us instant access to more than ten centuries of music. Even so, most of us can readily summarize our musical tastes with a simple thought: we like what we know.

In other words, we appreciate only that music that we have come to understand. We can follow a familiar piece of music with expectation, welcoming its main melodies, participating in its moments of climax and repose. An unfamiliar work is not likely to affect us so strongly, for we can only guess what its unfolding content will be.

For these reasons, one obvious way to know and love music better is through repeated exposure to specific works. Indeed, few sensual pleasures equal that of immersing oneself in an evening of old favorites, be they rock, jazz, or symphonic. But to restrict oneself to the familiar is to limit the possibilities for pleasure, and to limit them sharply. A far more adventurous way of increasing musical enjoyment is to cultivate the art of listening—the special abilities that enable a person to perceive the patterns of musical movement, the uses of musical themes, and, ultimately, the creative intentions of the composer and performer. Such abilities can heighten the enjoyment of unfamiliar works as well as familiar. For the attentive listener, they can open entire new worlds of musical experience.

An enhanced ability to listen to music is also likely to lead one to a deeper understanding of the meaning of music. Music is unique as a form of expression. Unlike traditional painting or sculpture, it is nonrepresentational. A melody can bring to mind a seascape or the death of a loved one, but it cannot represent them in an obvious way.

In this sense, music is an art without subject matter, which may be why its appeal is almost universal.

Music has often been said to convey pure emotion. Its effect on the attentive listener is, in fact, very similar to that of other emotional experiences. However, music does not express emotions in any clearly definable way. A given work may strike two listeners differently, or it may call forth different reactions from the same listener on different hearings. In this way, music closely parallels the way in which emotions are played out in our inner lives, leaving us with feelings ambiguous in content, fluid, yet strongly felt.

How does one set about listening to music more carefully, more actively? First, it is important to concentrate fully on listening, without the distraction of talking, reading, or other activity. Then, one can focus attention on the different aspects of sound, such as melody, rhythm, or harmony. Initially it is best to consider one thing at a time—for example, what are the characteristics of melody in a particular piece, what instruments are used in the performance, or how is rhythm made to be an outstanding aspect of a composition? With concentration and practice in careful listening, one becomes able to think about and analyze several aspects of musical sound in quick succession, and some closely related aspects can be considered simultaneously. Melody and rhythm, for example, can be analyzed separately, but they are really inseparable in music and are ultimately best viewed that way in listening to much music.

In that wordless state in which we think and feel, there are movement and rest, tension and release, dissonance and harmony, acceleration and retardation, intensity and dissolution. With attentive listening, one can perceive how many of these effects are created in music. Often one can even come to understand why a particular musical technique creates the effect it does. Perceptive listening can increase the level of the intellectual experience of listening, and at the same time intensify the emotional experience. Both aspects are equally important. Both contribute greatly to the potential for enjoying music.

# PART ONE

# Elements of Music

Dance, as movement, is one of the most intuitive reactions to the interplay of melody and rhythm. Many traditional peasant dances grew more sophisticated from the 16th century onwards, were stylized to become court dances and then the subjects of instrumental music, often in the form of dance suites. The Bourrée, depicted in this woodcut published in 1716, is a typical example of this development. (Victoria & Albert Museum, Crown copyright; photo Heritage of Music)

# CHAPTER 1

# *Melody and Rhythm*

*LISTENING PREVIEW Melody and rhythm are fundamental to many pieces of music in all countries and periods. Sometimes one or the other seems to be dominant, but both often work together to create a particular musical effect. Listen to a performance of a Gregorian chant, such as the Introit of the* Requiem Mass *(side 2, band 1 of the record set), and notice the prominence of the single melody with very free rhythm sung by a choir. Contrast that use of melody with the melody heard at the beginning of Bach's* Fugue in G Minor *(side 3, band 7), in which the melody is also very prominent and distinctive, but whose rhythm is heard in more regular patterns. As the opening melody and rhythm are repeated in the piece, notice how quickly they become easy to recognize because of certain recurring patterns.*

## The Basic Materials of Music

An outpouring of thoughts or emotions is not in itself artistic. It must be made accessible to another person before a work of art is created. This requires organizing, disciplining, and refining the basic material.

### Sound and time

A musical work is essentially a disciplined and refined organization of sounds. The sounds that are produced proceed chronologically—from one moment to the next. Thus, music itself may be defined very simply as *sound* organized within *time*. Indeed, the twentieth-century composer Igor Stravinsky (1882–1971) once defined music as "a speculation in terms of sound and time."

## Music vs. Noise

### Musical tones

Many a music critic has damned a new work by calling it "noise." The critic knows that we expect *musical tones* to differ from other sounds and will be shocked or disappointed when they seem not to.

All sounds are caused by vibrations of objects, which in turn produce vibrations in the air. But whereas the vibrations that create noise are random and irregular, a musical tone consists of a series of regular, evenly timed vibrations, recurring in a pattern. On an oscillograph, a device that records fluctuations in vibration, it is possible to see the difference between a *noise* such as a human scream and a musical *tone* held by a trained soprano:

Scream

Musical Tone
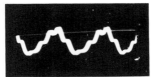

### Pitch

In a musical tone, the number of vibrations that occur per second determines a property called *pitch.* The greater the number of vibrations per second, the higher the pitch, and vice versa. Musical notation indicates specific pitches or tones by *notes,* usually oval symbols arranged on a sort of linear ladder called a *staff.* The higher-pitched notes are placed higher on the staff:

*Notes and staff*

It seems natural to think of pitches in terms of upward or downward movement. We can, in fact, actually feel music ascend and descend in space. *Ascending tones* tend to produce a feeling of expansion or excitement, as in the opening notes of "Maria," from Bernstein's *West Side Story. Descending tones,* on the other hand, suggest a downward pull that may be associated with rest, finality, or a preparation for another upward swell, as in the opening of "Swing Low, Sweet Chariot."

*Ascending and descending tones*

The beginning of the waltz "The Blue Danube," by Johann Strauss II (1825–1899), can be used to demonstrate how upward and downward movement is used in music. A graphic representation of the passage would look something like this:

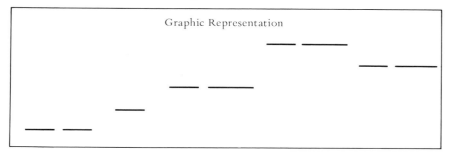

Graphic Representation

A notational representation of the same passage would look very much like a graph:

Notational Representation

Pitch notation will be discussed further in Chapter 5.

### Melody

The notes on the staff shown immediately above represent a *melody*—a succession of tones used in a meaningful way. Melody is generally the first thing people listen for in a piece of music. It is the "tune" that will be remembered long after the music is over.

Melodic lines may be characterized by upward or downward

The guitar is a good example of an instrument that can be used both to produce lyrical melodic lines and accompanying rhythms. However, its traditional use in folk music, particularly during its rise to wide popularity in the 19th century, was as an instrument played to accompany a song. Edouard Manet's painting *Spanish Guitar Player* (1861) beautifully illustrates this type of performance. (The Metropolitan Museum of Art, Gift of William Church Osborn, 1949)

**Disjunct and conjunct melodies**

movement, by both, or by hardly any movement at all. A melody in which there are large *intervals*, or distances, between successive tones is called a *disjunct melody*. Such melodies often call for great dexterity in performance; consider the difficulty many people have in singing "The Star-Spangled Banner" because of the relatively large distance between many of its pitches, the resulting wide range of the melody, and the wide vocal range needed to sing the melody. "Over the Rainbow" is another disjunct melody that is very distinctive and easy to remember because of its wide leaps. A melody that moves in small steps is called a *conjunct melody*. Such melodies are generally much easier to sing: "The First Nowell," an extremely conjunct melody, is a familiar example. In a very general sense, disjunct melodies tend to impart drama and energy, while conjunct melodies are capable of sweeter, more lyrical effects.

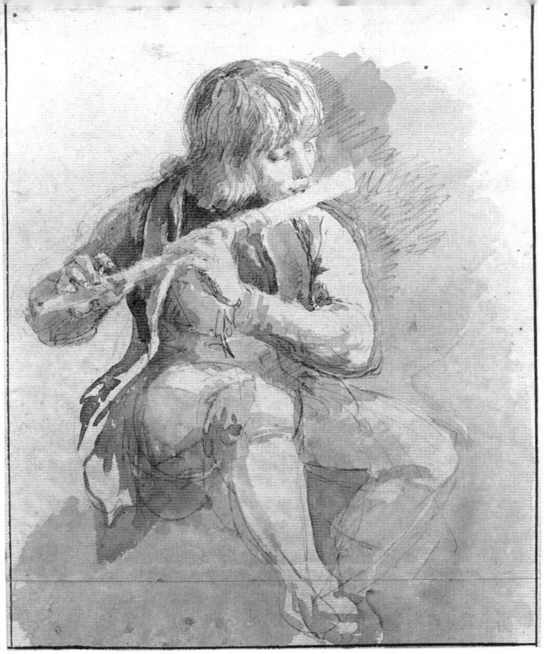

The flute is a melodic instrument of ancient origin and much used in many different cultures, both as a folk and an art instrument. This early Romantic drawing (1796) by J.G. von Dillis shows his son playing the traverse flute. (Staatliche Graphische Sammlung, Munich)

## *Melodic Structure*

As a complete artistic statement, a melody has a beginning, a middle, and an end. We are conscious of its structure much in the same way that we are conscious of the structure of a sentence. Just as the sentence's structure is understood in the reading, so is the structure of a melody understood in the listening.

Most of us actually have a very well developed understanding of music within our own culture. For example, nearly everyone can supply the last note of the following short melody, when it is sung or played:

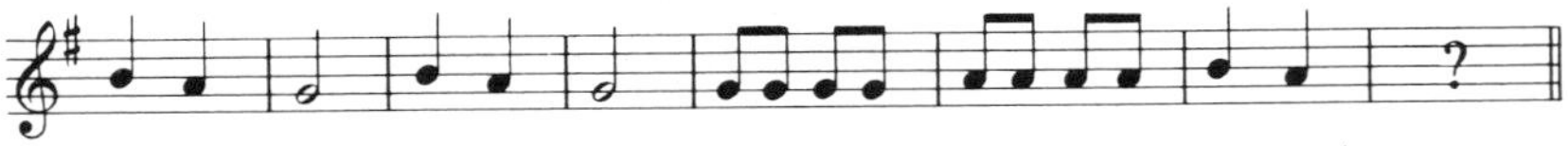


(As you have probably guessed, the last note of the melody is 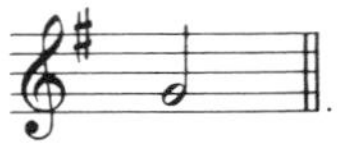.)

Moreover, most people can sense intuitively whether or not a musical work has ended. Few people, for example, would be satisfied with hearing the melody of "Yankee Doodle" without its final line.

Most people would also be dissatisfied if the second half of a melody began and ended just like the first. We expect melodies to change, to offer the *contrast* of a new material. Try singing both sentences of "London Bridge" to the same melody. They begin the same but end differently. In cases where the first part of a melody *is* repeated from beginning to end, as in "The Star-Spangled Banner," or "Eleanor Rigby" by the Beatles, the ear demands that it be followed by something new. In the former, that new material is supplied with the lines beginning "And the rocket's red glare."

Contrast

Repetition

Although change is essential, the *repetition* found in "London Bridge" and "The Star-Spangled Banner" is just as important. In fact, without any conscious effort, most of us have learned to expect a fine balance between repeated elements, which give music its basic organization, and new elements, which provide dramatic impact. This is true with even the simplest, most repetitious melodies. The repetition at the beginning of the second sentence of "London Bridge" gives the piece a unity it would otherwise lack.

Clearly, we have strong expectations about melodies. We expect a melody to come to rest on a tone that conveys finality—and our ears can supply this tone. We expect melodies to change, to offer new and contrasting material. But at the same time, we want this contrast to be balanced by a unifying repetition. Almost intuitively, we understand some of the basic structural principles inherent in many melodies.

Think about the melodic structure of the following simple melody:

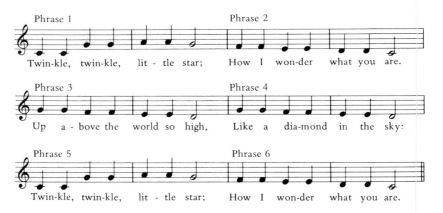

**Phrases**

Perhaps the first thing that is apparent about the melody is the fact that it is not heard all at once. Instead, we hear it in *phrases*, or melodic units, that correspond to the lines of the poem. The melodic material of this song falls into six phrases, with the second seeming to answer the first, the fourth answering the third, and the sixth answering the fifth. The phrases balance one another, and the last phrase comes to rest on the tonal center, a note that provides a strong sense of finality.

## Rhythm

When we listen for musical structure, we hear not only the upward and downward movements associated with pitch but rhythmic patterns as well. Music is, after all, organized within time. *Rhythm* is its organizing principle, and *beats* are the regular divisions of time which define rhythm. In its widest sense, rhythm is the organizing principle of the natural world and our lives also: musical rhythms were probably originally modeled after such natural phenomena as regularly recurring heartbeats, breathing, and the cycle of days and nights.

**Melodic and rhythmic patterns**

One structural factor that is immediately evident to the ear is the repetition of certain *melodic* and *rhythmic patterns*. These patterns are made obvious in "Twinkle, Twinkle, Little Star" by the repetition of words. The melodic pattern of Phrase I, for example, is repeated exactly in Phrase 5. The rhythmic pattern of these two phrases is also identical. In fact, this rhythmic pattern is repeated, even when the tonal pattern itself is varied. Though some of the phrases move upward in pitch and some of the phrases move downward, all six of them are sung to the same rhythm. You will hear this constantly repeated rhythmic pattern even more clearly if you clap the rhythm of the song.

Historians have speculated that music originated in the beating of rhythms that were used to accompany ritual. In some cultures, music still focuses predominantly on rhythms, often very complicated ones. At times, in these cultures and in our own, rhythmic patterns are played alone, with no accompanying melody. Military drum rolls are a familiar example. The rhythmic patterns of "Twinkle, Twinkle, Little Star" can be clapped without singing the melodic patterns. In most music, however, rhythmic patterns are wedded so closely to melody as to be nearly inseparable.

Consider the following example, a melody familiar to us as "America," but also the melody of "God Save the Queen," the national anthem of Great Britain:

The drum is the archetypal rhythm instrument, here played by members of the Afro-Caribbean group Osibisa. (Photo: David Redfern)

Certain patterns of long and short tones are immediately perceived by the ear. The pattern——————––, for example, is heard several times. In each case, the fourth note is longer than all the others, the fifth note shorter. In all, the——————–– rhythm occurs four times in the song, creating a distinctive, repeated rhythmic pattern.

## *Meter*

Beat
Accent

A regularly recurring pulse or beat underlies most rhythmic patterns. In "America," the beat is quite clear from the beginning. Also very clear is a recurring stress—or *accent*—on the first of every three beats. Sometimes this accent is very pronounced, sometimes less so, but it is always there. If the symbol / is used to indicate accented beats and the symbol ‿ to show weaker beats, the pattern looks like this:

| / | ‿ | ‿ | / | ‿ | ‿ |
|---|---|---|---|---|---|
| **My** | **coun - try,** | | **'tis** | **of** | **thee,** |
| / | ‿ | ‿ | / | ‿ | ‿ |
| **Sweet** | **land** | **of** | **li -** | **ber-** | **ty,** |
| / | ‿ | ‿ | / | ‿ | ‿ |
| **Of** | **thee** | **I** | **sing** ——— | | **.** |

Notice that the accented beats of the music do not always correspond with the accents in the text when it is spoken.

The pattern of accented and unaccented beats in "Twinkle, Twinkle, Little Star" is quite different:

| / | ‿ | / | ‿ | / | ‿ | / | ‿ |
|---|---|---|---|---|---|---|---|
| **Twin - kle,** | | **twin - kle,** | | **lit - tle** | | **star** ——— | **;** |
| / | ‿ | / | ‿ | / | ‿ | / | ‿ |
| **How** | **I** | **won - der** | | **what** | **you** | **are** ——— | **.** |

Triple and duple meters

The pattern of accented and unaccented beats or pulses in music is called *meter*. "America" is said to be "in three," or in *triple meter*, because each accented beat marks off a set of three equal beats. "Twinkle, Twinkle, Little Star" is in "two" or *duple meter*, because each accented beat marks off a set of two equal beats. Notice that the musical accents often coincide with the natural accents of the words as they would be spoken.

Measures

The ear perceives the beats in these songs in groups of three or two—that is, in *measures*. Having observed the formation of one measure, we expect that similar measures will follow, all in the same metrical pattern.

Most people are acquainted with the metrical patterns used in special kinds of music. A person can easily fall into step to the meter of a march—ONE-two, ONE-two. Dances are also characterized by their meters—the waltz by its sweeping ONE-two-three and the polka by its vigorous ONE-two.

Other meters are formed from combinations of the basic duple or triple patterns. Especially within the last century, musicians have made unusual deviations from the traditional meters. Tchaikovsky, in the second movement of *Symphony No. 6* (the "Pathétique"), used a meter of ONE-two-THREE-four-five, while Béla Bartók, a Hungarian composer, sometimes used measures of seven beats. "Everything's All Right" from the muscial *Jesus Christ Superstar* uses a five-beat meter, with the same ONE-two-THREE-four-five stress pattern employed by the Tchaikovsky movement. Igor Stravinsky, in *The Rite of Spring*, not only used unusual meters but also changed metrical patterns frequently to avoid a feeling of metric regularity. In much music, beats are subdivided normally into either two or three units. A meter whose beats are subdivided into two is known as *simple*, "Ba Ba Black Sheep" is in simple duple meter, and "The First Nowell" is in simple triple meter. If the beat has three subdivisions, the meter is *compound*; "Row, Row, Row your Boat" has a compound duple meter, as its "Merrily merrily" section illustrates.

One of the most delightfully surprising effects in music occurs when the meter of a work is deliberately upset for expressive purposes—that is, when an accent is placed on a normally weak beat or half of a beat. *Syncopation*, as this is called, can be obvious, as in Gershwin's "I've Got Rhythm," or it can be very subtle, as in some folk-songs, e.g. "Joe Hill." In dance music, syncopation creates a strong and distinctive rhythmic pattern. Syncopation can also be used to help propel music to the end of a phrase.

Meter organizes a composition into identical groups—measures—of strong and weak beats. Syncopation simply changes the placement of the strong accent to an unexpected beat. Aaron Copland, a modern American composer, has said: "We get the real rhythm only when we stress the notes according to the musical sense of the phrase."

**Syncopation** *(margin)*

## *Rhythmic Motion*

Just as the beauty of poetry is lost if it is read in singsong fashion, the expressive impact of music is much diminished if it is played in absolutely strict meter. In "America," for example, the amount of stress placed on notes changes from measure to measure. The strong beat in the second measure is stressed more than the strong beat in the first measure and, in the two measures that make up the line "Of thee I sing," there are four beats of nearly equal stress. The number of notes per measure and per beat also changes. In cases where there is more than one note per beat, the *rhythmic motion* is faster, as with the word "every" in the phrase "from every mountain side." Thus, in hearing music, we are conscious both of the overall meter and also of the way the rhythm plays against it for expressive purposes.

Rhythm as expressed in another art form: the distinct pulses and accents found in Umberto Boccioni's *States of Mind I, II and III* (1911) subtitled "The Farewells," "Those Who Stay," and "Those Who Go" help to underline the notion of movement versus the static. (Collection The Museum of Modern Art, New York; gift of Vico Baer)

## Tempo

**Tempo markings**

A composer often provides a marking for *tempo*, or overall speed, to help convey the character of a composition. On a musical score tempos generally appear above the opening measure, and on concert programs they are often used to identify movements. Several of the most common tempos, traditionally written in Italian, are given, with their translations, in the chart on page 29.

Other terms are sometimes added to show that the work is of a special nature. For example, the term *minuet*, or *menuetto*, indicates that a work or movement is in the manner of the traditional courtly dance of that name, that is, in a moderate tempo and in triple meter. (see Chapter 4 on musical form).

**Gradual changes of tempo**

Within a composition the tempo may be varied for expressive purposes. An *accelerando*, or gradual quickening, is often used to create excitement. A *ritardando*, or *rallentando*, a gradual slowing down, suggests rest, deliberation, or other moods, depending on the context. Often such changes in tempo are part of a larger expressive scheme that may also include changes in melody and in the loudness or softness of the music.

## Common Tempos

| | |
|---|---|
| *largo* (broad)<br>*grave* (solemn) | **very slow** |
| *lento* (slow)<br>*adagio* (leisurely) | **slow** |
| *andante* (at a walking pace)<br>*andantino* (a little faster than andante)<br>*moderato* (moderate) | **moderate** |
| *allegretto* (moderately fast)<br>*allegro* (fast) | **fast** |
| *vivace* (vivacious)<br>*presto* (very fast)<br>*prestissimo* (as fast as possible) | **very fast** |

### *Adjectives Often Used with Tempos*

*molto* (very)
*più* (more)
*meno* (less)
*poco* (a little)
*ma non troppo* (but not too much)

## Listening to Melody and Rhythm

**Side 1, Band 1**

The record set that accompanies the text gives aural examples of many of the points covered in Chapter 1. You may also want to listen to recordings of folk and popular songs to find your own examples of the following *ascending* and *descending* melodic lines, *disjunct* and *conjunct* melodies, *repetition* and *contrast*, *melodic* and *rhythmic* patterns, *duple* and *triple meter*, *syncopation*, and *tempo* changes.

# CHAPTER 2

# *Harmony and Texture*

*LISTENING PREVIEW Harmony and texture refer to the ways in which musical tones are combined. Composers in different ages arrived at different methods of combining musical sounds. Listen to Morley's "Now Is the Month of Maying" (side 2, band 8) and notice the consonant, easy-to-listen-to sound as the several voices move together during the piece. Contrast that with the opening of Stravinsky's Movements for Piano and Orchestra (side 11, band 5), in which the various instruments perform in a more dissonant, independent style.*

**Harmony**

It is not surprising that people first approached music through the pulse of rhythm and the melodic medium of song, which needs no instrument other than the human voice. Melody and rhythm have been, from the earliest times, the natural materials of nearly all the world's music. *Harmony* is a more complex phenomenon and a relatively recent one. It involves the sounding together of two or more tones with the effect of adding musical depth and richness.

The effect of harmony is most evident in those works that have both a melody and an *accompaniment*. A vocalist sings a melody enriched by the harmonies of a guitar. A pianist produces a melody with the right hand while sounding clusters of tones, or *chords*, with the left. The listener enjoys a richer experience because the melody is supported by harmonic materials.

Harmony in written music is generally thought to have begun in the ninth century when monks added a second melodic line to the original melodic line in their chants. The second line was generally parallel to the first, producing a hollow sound that still evokes images of the Middle Ages. More sophisticated forms of harmony developed in the centuries that followed. It was soon discovered that two voices pulling in opposite directions could impart more drama and interest than parallel voices, and that three or more melodies could produce an even greater effect. In later centuries, after this *polyphonic*, or "many-voiced," style of music had been developed to a very high peak, some composers began to emphasize one voice or melodic line. What had been several layers of melody became perceived as a melody with harmonic support.

Most harmony of recent centuries is *tonal*; that is, it centers around

Organ (1443) of the Catedral de la Seo in Zaragoza (Spain). (Photo: Ad Windig)

one tone or note, and it is this type of harmony we are now considering. In the twentieth century some composers have devised harmonic systems that do not center around one tone. We shall observe examples of such harmony later.

## Consonance and Dissonance

The basic unit of tonal harmony is a *chord*, three or more tones sounded simultaneously. Some chords sound pleasing and complete in themselves. The word "harmonious" is often used to describe them, but they are properly referred to as *consonant*. They suggest peace and stability. Other chords are so harsh that they may not sound "harmonious." They are unstable, and seem to demand resolution to a consonant harmony. These chords are known as *dissonant*. A good illustration of the difference is the striking two-chord opening of the *Symphony No. 1* by Ludwig van Beethoven. The first (dissonant) chord somehow reaches toward the (consonant) second chord.

Music would be unnecessarily dull if restricted to pleasing or consonant sounds. It would be seriously limited in expressing inner realities if harsher, dissonant sounds were excluded. Who has not experienced the interweaving of consonant and dissonant memories? Dissonance is as natural to music as to thought.

Although some musical sounds may be displeasing in themselves, dissonance is usually more relative than absolute. Our judgment depends on our frame of reference. A series of dissonant chords will sound harsher than a single dissonant chord moving to a consonant chord. A series of dissonances will also be received differently in the twentieth century than it would have been in the seventeenth. It will be felt differently by a student of modern music than by people familiar only with the music of the Classical period.

In much of traditional music, dissonance is used cautiously. It serves to provide conflict and contrast with consonant sounds rather than as an entity in its own right. Dissonances are not stable sounds, and they strain to be resolved; the traditional composer has usually treated them accordingly. But, as Igor Stravinsky once remarked, "Nothing forces us to be looking constantly for satisfaction that resides only in repose." Modern composers of both classical and popular music, seeking new means of musical expression, have learned to use dissonance for its own sake rather than simply as a foil to consonance.

Composers in every age have countered consonance with dissonance. Some composers of our time are particularly noted for their use of strikingly dissonant harmonies in contrast to consonant sounds. Dissonance and consonance are equally important if music is to express a full range of human emotion.

## The Elements of Harmony

### Intervals and chords

While melody refers to a single-line sequence of pitches, harmony refers to pitches that are sounded together. When two different pitches are sung together, we become less aware of their individual sounds. A composite sound is heard. The nature of the sound depends on the relationship of the two tones—that is, the interval between them, calculated by the difference between their specific numbers of vibrations per second. C to C♯ for example, is a minor second; C to D, a major second; C to E♭, a minor third, and so forth. The interval of a minor second is also called a *half step*; a major second is known as a *whole step*.

The combination of three or more tones sounded together is called a chord. The study of harmony is, in effect, the study of relationships found in intervals and chords and the way these groups of tones are wed within a musical composition.

It is clear to anyone who has ever experimented with a piano keyboard that different combinations of tones will produce different effects. When adjacent white keys are played together, the effect is somewhat harsh. In contrast, alternate white keys give a pleasing sound. Different harmonic effects are achieved as the interval between tones is increased. However, if two keys that are exactly eight white keys apart are sounded, there is a definite similarity to their sound, but little sense of harmony. The explanation behind the similar sounds in this eight-tone interval—which is called an *octave*—lies in the relationship between their frequencies of vibration: that of the higher tone in the octave is exactly twice that of the lower tone.

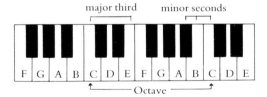

### Chromatic scale

If we count all the keys—black and white—between and including those that produce the octave, they number thirteen. However, two of these thirteen keys, the first and the last, have the same pitch name. Thus, there are twelve different tones that can be used for harmonic purposes. When the twelve tones are played in order, the result is a progression known as the *chromatic scale*. Most of our music is based, not on this scale, but on scales that use only seven of these twelve tones.

### Major scale

### Tonic note and related intervals

The best known scale in Western music—the *major scale*—is so familiar as to seem almost second nature. Any of the twelve tones of the chromatic scale may serve as the basic or *tonic note* of a major scale. The choice of the other six tones depends on the choice of tonic, because the pitch relationships—the arrangement of minor and major seconds (half steps and whole steps)—are the same in all

This detail of angels playing citterns, from Luca della Robbia's sculpture *Cantoria* (1431–40), illustrates the balance of composition and harmony of line often found in sculpture. (Florence, Museo dell' Opera del Duomo; photo: Scala)

major scales: 1, 1, ½, 1, 1, 1, ½. If, for example, the note C is the tonic, the major scale that results from this arrangement is C, D, E, F, G, A, B, C.

**Minor scale**

Another seven-tone scale prominently used in much Western music is the *minor scale*. There are several versions of the minor scale, all of which differ from the major scale in the way the intervals are arranged. Music based on a minor scale often seems more serious and somber than music based on a major scale, as we will see later in numerous examples.

In any scale, the tonic note is that which conveys rest and finality. This is the tone that the ear supplies at the end of the incomplete example on page 22.

Try singing the seven tones of the major scale (*do-re-mi-fa-sol-la-ti*) without the final tonic (*do*), and you will see how strongly the ear demands it. The seventh note pulls so strongly upward that you must supply the tonic mentally. By singing "Yankee Doodle" without the last two syllables, you can see the way the same effect operates in the realm of melody.

The tones of the major and minor scales have very specific relationships to each other. In melody these relationships are perceived as the music develops horizontally. With the addition of harmony, we perceive the relationships both horizontally and vertically. Relationships are heard between simultaneous pitches or chords as well as between consecutive notes.

### Triads

If played together, the first, third, and fifth notes of the major scale produce a consonant chord of three tones, or *triad*, that is very common in the music of our culture. This is the *tonic triad*, the most basic chord of tonal harmony. Because the lower third of the chord is major and the fifth is perfect, the chord is a major triad. Other triads can be formed by playing other alternate tones in the major scale. Thus, a triad can be made of the tones 2–4–6, 3–5–7, and so on. Chord symbols indicated with Roman numerals show the scale degree on which the triad is based. Upper case Roman numerals symbolize major triads and lower-case numerals a minor triad (a minor third and perfect fifth). The ° beside the final triad below indicates it is a diminished chord, consisting of a minor third and a diminished fifth.

| | | | | | | | |
|---|---|---|---|---|---|---|---|
| | 5 | 6 | 7 | 8 | 2 | 3 | 4 |
| | 3 | 4 | 5 | 6 | 7 | 8 | 2 |
| Scale Degrees: | 1 | 2 | 3 | 4 | 5 | 6 | 7 |
| Chord Symbols: | I | ii | iii | IV | V | vi | vii° |

Any of the tones in a triad can be duplicated in another octave, and although the chord will sound higher or lower, it will not be basically changed. In fact, the four-part harmony found in much of our music generally consists of triads with one of the tones duplicated (1–3–5–8, for example). The notes of a triad may also be arranged in different order or *inversion* (5–1–3, for example) without radically changing the nature of the chord.

What is important from a harmonic standpoint is that the different chords have different harmonic effects in a given piece of music. For convenience, chords are usually identified by the number of the scale degree on which they are based. Thus, a triad based on the first, or tonic, note of the scale is called the I chord or the *tonic chord*. Its notes are 1–3–5 of the scale. Just as the tonic note provides the melodic center toward which the music returns, the chord with this note as its basis or *root* is the harmonic center of a piece. All else in a composition happens in relation to the tonic and the tonic chord. Also important for the contrast they provide are the IV chord or *subdominant chord* (4–6–8) and the V chord or *dominant chord* (5–7–2), the only other major triads derived from a major scale.

Three chords, I, IV, and V, are enough to accompany many simple pieces. The harmonic scheme of "Yankee Doodle" is an example:

**Tonic chord**

**Subdominant and dominant chords**

| I | | I | V | I | | I V |
|---|---|---|---|---|---|---|

**Yankee Doodle went to town/ Riding on a pony**

| I | | IV | | V | | I |
|---|---|---|---|---|---|---|

**Stuck a feather in his hat/ And called it macaroni.**

Triads built on the other tones of the scale are essential to harmonic variety in music, but they usually play less central roles than the I, IV, and V chords.

### Cadences

Resolution

Authentic and plagal cadences

One of the strongest chordal relationships in Western music is that between the tonic and dominant chords. When the V chord is played, the ear strives for and anticipates the I chord. The *resolution* of the V chord to the I chord is a harmonic formula called a *cadence*. A cadence brings a musical composition, or part of it, to an identifiable close. The V–I cadence, called the *authentic cadence*, almost invariably ends the main body of a composition. A less common cadence—and a weaker one—is found in the movement from the IV chord to the I chord. This weaker IV–I cadence, called the *plagal cadence*, is often sung to the word "Amen" at the end of hymns (and is sometimes referred to as the "Amen" cadence). While the V–I cadence exerts a decisive pull from the dominant to the tonic, the IV–I cadence almost relaxes into the tonic, conveying a feeling of peace. Other cadential formulae have less feeling of finality than these.

### Changes in Tonality

Accidentals and modulations

Music based on a major or minor scale, or on any other scale that centers around a single tonic note, is said to be *tonal*. The *tonality* of a piece of music is defined by the note around which it revolves. If the tonic note is C, the tonality or *key* is C.

Listening to music based on a major or minor scale, we somehow expect to hear only the seven tones of that scale, and not the tones from some other scale. We expect the music to remain within the given tonality. When a note foreign to the scale—an *accidental*—is used, it creates a surprise. Even more surprising is a *modulation*—a shifting of the tonic and an acceptance, by the ear, of a new tonic with its new harmonic relationships.

The explanations for accidentals and modulations are rather technical and demand more theoretical background than has been developed here. However, the ear is not bound to theoretical considerations. It clearly recognizes and understands surprises in tonality, and these unexpected features of music are often among the most enjoyable and easily recognized. In the Frank Sinatra recording of "Strangers in the Night," the entire melody, as it is sung for the final time, shifts upward to a different tonic. The Beatles' song "If I Fell in Love with You" also shows a very effective use of modulation. Generally, modulation results in greater intensity. The "Liebestod" (literally "love-death") from the opera *Tristan und Isolde* by Richard Wagner (1813–1883) derives much of its transcending power from the continuous upward shifting of the tonal center—that is, from modulation. Modulation is a vital force in creating harmonic interest in nearly all types of music. "Yesterday," by the Beatles, derives much interest and

The perception of dissonance is relative, in music as much as in painting. James McNeill Whistler was one of the earliest painters to use musical titles such as Nocturne, Symphony, Variation, Arrangement etc. for his compositions. When *Nocturne in Black and Gold: The Falling Rocket* (c. 1874) was first exhibited, he was accused of "flinging a pot of paint in the public's face," but the modern viewer is unlikely to find the work the least bit outrageous. (The Detroit Institute of Art, Purchase, Dexter M. Ferry Jr. Fund)

poignancy from the modulations between major and minor keys.

A full account of modulation is given in Chapter 11, on the musical style of the Classical era, where it is most relevant.

## Texture

When a melody is accompanied by chords, the result is an interweaving of sound. Melody is the horizontal strand; the chordal harmonies are the vertical strands. This interweaving of sound layers is called *texture*. As fine or coarse threads in cloth are woven together with different techniques, so can melodies and harmonies be arranged to produce widely contrasting results.

The simplest kind of musical texture—*monophonic* texture—consists of a single melodic line without accompaniment. Sing any melody you know and the result is *monophony*. Vocal solos, as well as solo works for such instruments as violin and flute, demonstrate the many uses of monophony. So, too, does much of the music of China and Japan. It is often monophonic, consisting of finely articulated melodies, supported, at times, by rhythmic accompaniments.

*Monophony*

In many cultures, especially in the Western world, a number of different ways of combining two or more voices or parts have been developed. Some Western music, particularly of the fifteenth to eighteenth centuries, has a *polyphonic,* or *contrapuntal*, texture. Such music, known as *polyphony* or *counterpoint*, consists of several different voices. If the melodic material in the different voices is the same or very similar and one voice follows another in presenting it,

*Polyphony or counterpoint*

*The Choir Loft in St. Mark's, Venice* (1766) by Canaletto. (Hamburger Kunsthalle)

**Homophony**

**Use of chords in homophony**

**Use of arpeggios**

the texture is described as *imitative*. If the melodic material is different, the texture is *nonimitative*. With either, the result is several different layers of melody. The horizontal aspect of each voice is most important, but the several melodies sounding simultaneously contribute to the overall vertical, or harmonic, effect. If you sing "Row, Row, Row Your Boat" as a round, you will note that while each voice moves independently, the interplay between voices produces a pleasant total sound.

Not all songs can be treated in this way, however. While "Row, Row, Row Your Boat" works as a round, "America" will not. The writer of counterpoint uses special techniques to produce both strong individual melodies and a harmonious whole. Listening to counterpoint also calls for special skills in that we must follow both the horizontal and the vertical elements. However, familiarity with the music and some practice in listening to it make it meaningful. Many people find counterpoint among the most stimulating elements in music. The interplay of several melodies can, at times, express different emotional content simultaneously, and creates a musical whole much richer than the sum of its independent parts.

More common in our listening experience is *homophonic* texture, or melody accompanied by chords. In *homophony*, the melody is often heard in the highest voice, but it can appear in lower voices or be taken up by different voices in turn. While we tend to listen for the melody, the harmonic activity in the nonmelodic voices is also important.

A graphic representation of the three basic textures would look something like the examples given in the chart opposite. The arrangement of polyphonic and homophonic textures, however, may take many forms other than the simple representations given. In polyphony, the highest-pitched voice or part may enter first (as it does in the chart), or a lower-pitched voice may enter first, or all voices may begin together. In homophony, the arrangement of the chords may vary. Chords may be played with each note of melody, producing a firm vertical texture. Or chords may be played only occasionally—just on the strong beats, for example—producing a texture that is lighter and more open. Finally, the tones in a chord may be played as *arpeggios*—in succession rather than simultaneously—generally producing a more fluid texture. (Arpeggios get their name from the Italian word for harp, "arpa," an instrument which can easily play chords in their broken form.) Even the untrained eye will notice the difference in these three examples from Schumann's *Album for the Young*, a collection of piano music:

Chord with Each Note of Melody

Chords on Strong Beats

Arpeggiated Chords

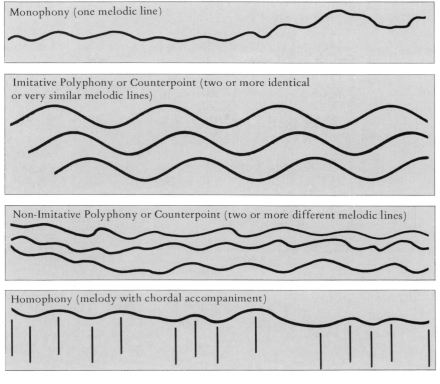

Monophony (one melodic line)

Imitative Polyphony or Counterpoint (two or more identical or very similar melodic lines)

Non-Imitative Polyphony or Counterpoint (two or more different melodic lines)

Homophony (melody with chordal accompaniment)

In Western music, texture is often more complex and varied than in the few examples given here. Moreover, it is seldom constant throughout a composition. A solo voice may be joined in counterpoint by several other independent voices, bringing about a change from monophonic to polyphonic texture. Similarly, a homophonic piano work or symphony may make use of counterpoint for greater contrast or intensity. Popular music is full of variety in its texture. "Scarborough Fair" by Simon and Garfunkel has one voice played off against another in a distinctive way, and numerous popular songs use backing vocals to reinforce or contrast with the principal voice.

**Listening to Harmony and Texture**

On the record set that accompanies the text (Side 1, Band 2), you will find aural examples of many of the points covered in Chapter 2. As musical examples are discussed in the following chapters, the characteristics of harmony and texture will be further amplified and clarified.

# CHAPTER 3

# *Timbre and Dynamics*

*LISTENING PREVIEW The choice and use of musical instruments and voices for a piece of music are always characteristic in some way of the period in which the music is composed. The relatively small size and instrumentation of the orchestra heard in Handel's* Concerto in B-Flat Major *(side 3, band 5) were typical of the early eighteenth century. The electronically synthesized sounds with solo flute heard in Davidovsky's "Synchronisms No. 1" (side 12 band 1) have been musical possibilities only since the middle of this century. Throughout music history, evolving technology has enabled composers to create new varieties of musical sound.*

## Timbre

A melody sung by folk-singer Joan Baez will sound very different when performed by the operatic soprano Beverly Sills. Although both may sing the same pitches, the quality of sound of each voice is unique. The explanation for these different qualities lies in tone color or timbre.

*Timbre* is a term used to describe the characteristic quality of the sound produced by a voice or instrument. The quality of the sound will be influenced by many factors. Among these are the material from which an instrument is made, the size and shape of an instrument or vocal mechanism, and the way in which an instrument or voice is used.

## Voices

It is very likely that the first musical instruments used were human voices. People are equipped with strings or cords that vibrate to produce both non-musical and musical sound. These are, of course, the vocal cords, found within the larynx or "voice box." After sounds are produced in the larynx, they are amplified by sounding bodies— the throat, mouth, sinus and nasal cavities.

That some voices are high in pitch and some low is common observation. Actually we are all able to produce a wide range of musical sounds by adjusting the muscles that affect our vocal cords. As muscular tension is increased, the vibrating portion of the vocal cords is shortened and a higher pitch is produced. As tension is decreased, the vibrating portion is lengthened and a lower pitch is produced.

The overall range of sounds a person can make is determined largely by the size of the person's larynx. Just as a long string produces a lower sound than a short one, so does a large larynx

Marcel Duchamp: *Sonata* (1911). The artist himself talked about the "pale and tender tonalities of this picture." (Philadelphia Museum of Art, Louise and Walter Arensberg Collection)

Voice categories

produce a lower voice. Small larynxes and shorter strings produce higher pitches. These relationships also apply to the orchestra: the double bass, a large, long-stringed instrument, produces a lower range of sounds than the much smaller violin. Among vocalists, the highest range belongs to the *soprano*. The other types of female voices, from relatively high to low, are *mezzo-soprano* and *contralto* (or simply *alto*). The three common types of male voices, from highest to lowest, are *tenor, baritone*, and *bass*. A rare male voice is the *countertenor*, an unusually high tenor or a falsetto voice that has a range similar to that of an alto.

Just as voices differ in the range of tones they can produce, so do they differ in style and quality. Sometimes this reflects cultural differences. Singing in the Western world is based largely on an Italian style—a relaxed, open-throated sound in which vowels are emphasized. In some non-Western countries, singing is based on entirely different artistic ideas. Chinese singers aim at a somewhat closed-throated sound, which seems strident or nasal to our ears. They may slide from one tone to another rather than come to rest on different tones as we do in singing Western melodies. Different cultures, then, have different methods of singing and different definitions of a beautiful vocal or instrumental timbre. Even within western culture there is a tremendous variety of standards. Bob Dylan's singing style is completely different both from an opera singer's and from other popular singers such as Joni Mitchell.

## Instrument Families

A modern symphony orchestra is made up of several different *families* of instruments, all products of centuries of development. The families are grouped according to the means by which they produce the vibrations that make musical tones: strings, columns of air, or stretched membranes, for instance. All acoustic (non-electronic) instruments belong to one family or another. We will study some non-Western instruments of the main families in Chapter 30. The most common Western instruments and their particular tone qualities are discussed below.

### String Instruments

Violin family

String instruments, or *chordophones*, produce sound through the vibration of thin strings by plucking, bowing, or strumming. The modern Western orchestra features a large section of these string instruments, the most prominent of which is the violin. The player draws a bow across the strings of this instrument or, at times, plucks the strings, a technique known as *pizzicato*. The pitch of the tone produced depends on the length, thickness, tautness, and material of the string. Each string can be pressed down, or "stopped," at any point with the fingertip and thus lengthened or shortened to produce different pitches. Instruments in the *violin family* are, from highest to

Brass Instruments: The various instruments of the brass family add brilliance and power to the modern band and orchestra more than any other single group of instruments. The relative sizes and shapes of the tuba, piccolo trumpet, C trumpet, horn, and alto, tenor, and bass trombones are shown left. (Photo courtesy of Jon Blumb)

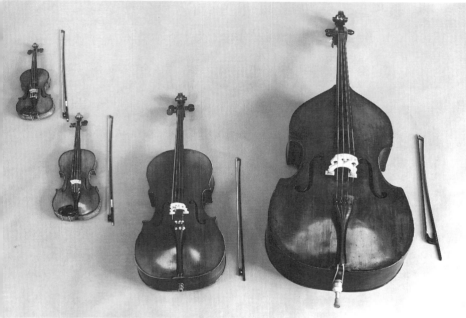

Violin Family: The instruments of the violin family are the basis of the modern orchestra. Notice the relative sizes of the violin, viola, cello, and double bass. (Photo courtesy of Jon Blumb)

Woodwind Instruments: The several different instruments of the woodwind group play important roles in the modern orchestra and band. The relative sizes and shapes of the baritone saxophone, alto saxophone, piccolo, flute, clarinet, bass, clarinet, oboe, English horn, bassoon, and contrabassoon are shown left. (Photo courtesy of Jon Blumb)

lowest in pitch, the *violin, viola, violoncello* (or *cello*), and *double bass*. The first two are positioned on the shoulder. The cello rests on the floor and is held between the knees, while the double bass stands on the floor in front of the player.

All of the bowed instruments are noted for a smooth singing tone. When the player draws the bow over the string, a nearly human tone is produced in the high-pitched instruments and a warm, vibrant sound in the lower ones. As a group they produce a homogeneous timbre of wide range and varied function. They are the basic family of instruments in the modern orchestra.

**Plucked or strummed instruments**

Other string instruments are specifically designed to be plucked or strummed. Several of these, such as the *guitar, banjo*, and *ukulele*, are familiar to us from folk music. The *lute* was a very popular instrument in early music. All have frets, or ridges, on the fingerboard against which the musician presses the strings in order to produce a given tone or group of tones.

**Harp family**

Another group of string instruments—one that seems to be represented in nearly every culture—is the *harp family*. The sizes and shapes of the many different harps vary considerably. However, they share one common characteristic: they are generally plucked.

### Wind Instruments

If the string family is the mainstay of an orchestra, the wind instruments are its main source of variety, with an immense range of tone qualities. The player of a wind instrument, or *aerophone*, produces sound by forcing breath through a tube and causing a column of air to vibrate. Wind instruments are generally made of either wood or metal. In the Western orchestra, they are divided into two families— the woodwinds and the brasses.

**Woodwind family**

Despite its name, the *woodwind family* includes both wood and metal instruments (originally all of its instruments were wooden). The woodwind tube is sometimes equipped with a flexible reed, such as the one found on the clarinet, which vibrates when the instrument is played. The air column vibrating within the instrument may be shortened or lengthened by means of finger holes or keys. By covering a hole through which air escapes, for example, the player can lengthen the column of air and produce a lower tone. This principle can be seen in the familiar song flute of elementary schools and in simple flutes found in the archeological remains of the Stone Age. Aerophones were among the earliest melodic instruments. They were relatively simple to make, requiring only a piece of hollow reed, an animal horn, or a bone.

The Western orchestra includes a number of woodwinds. The *transverse flute* (usually simply called *flute*), held horizontally and played without a reed, has a high-pitched sound capable of great variety and nuance of tone quality. The *piccolo* is simply a smaller, and thus higher-sounding, flute. The *oboe*, similar to the flute in range, has a double-reed mouthpiece that gives it a reedy nasal tone—somewhat piercing, often captivating. Other double-reed instruments, all lower in pitch than the oboe, are the *English horn* (a lower-voiced oboe), *bassoon*, and *contrabassoon*. In these instruments, sound is produced when the player blows between the mouthpiece's two very delicate, sensitive reeds. In the single-reed instruments, the *clarinet* and *saxophone*, sound is produced when the player makes the reed vibrate against the mouthpiece. The clarinet is especially impressive in the variety of its timbre. It is clear and bright in the highest part of its range, warm and full in the lower.

**Brass family**

The *brass family* includes, from highest to lowest in pitch, the *trumpet, horn* (or *French horn*), *trombone*, and *tuba*. Structurally the brasses are quite similar. Each begins with a cup-shaped mouthpiece and ends in a flared bell. Air travels through a tube that is shorter for instruments of higher pitch and longer for those of lower pitch. The length of the tube in which the air column vibrates can be increased

During the 19th century, brass bands enjoyed high popularity in the United States, both as regimental and municipal bands. This picture shows one such band in a Fourth of July celebration at Cincinnati (from *Frank Leslie's Illustrated Newspaper*, July 29 1865)

or decreased by means of valves (a nineteenth-century invention) or, in the case of the trombone, with a slide. However, changing the length of the tubing is not, by itself, enough to determine the pitch of a tone. To produce different tones with the same fingering, players must carefully adjust the muscles of their lips and the force of their breath.

The brasses can be bright or "brassy" in timbre as is typical of the trumpet, or they can be rich, mellow, and warm, as the horn usually sounds. They add considerable strength to the orchestral sound and are often used for special flourishes, fanfares, and symbolic effects. Each of the brasses may be muted to produce a nasal tone, either gentle or raucous, depending on how forcefully the instrument is played.

### Percussion Instruments

The percussion instruments take advantage of two basic performing techniques—to strike objects and to shake them. Percussion instruments include *idiophones* such as the *gong* or *cymbal*, in which the whole body of the instrument vibrates, as well as *membranophones* such as the *bass drum*, which rely on a drum head as the principal means of creating sound.

Some percussion instruments can produce a series of definite pitches. The *xylophone*, for example, which is played by striking wooden bars with mallets, can produce a wide range of tones simultaneously or one at a time. The *timpani* (or *kettledrums*) can also produce tones of definite pitch, but each drum makes no more than one tone without being retuned—that is, without a readjustment of the tension of the drum head. Many percussion instruments produce tones of indefinite pitch and are used for rhythmic or dramatic purposes. These include *snare drums, tambourines, cymbals, bass drums, maracas, tambourines*, and *gongs*.

### Keyboard Instruments

Instruments with keyboards have been very popular for several hundred years, since they are relatively easy to learn and can play both melody and harmony together. The *harpsichord* and *clavichord* were well known in the sixteenth century. On the harpsichord, a string is plucked when a key is depressed, while on the clavichord a string is struck. The sound of both instruments, especially that of the clavichord, is generally small and rather delicate. Another keyboard instrument, the *pipe organ*, reached a high point of development in the eighteenth century. It is capable of a very wide variety of sounds, which are produced by forcing air through the instrument's pipes. The organ inspired some of the grandest and most expressive music ever written for a single instrument. It was developed for use in worship, and it still fulfills a vital function in Christian services.

The piano was invented in the early eighteenth century and grad-

Percussion Instruments: These and other percussion instruments are essential to the modern band and orchestra for the great rhythmic and timbral variety they offer. Shown left are the gong, cymbals, orchestral bells (Glockenspiel), xylophone, timpani (kettle drums), snare drum, and bass drum. (Photo courtesy of Jon Blumb)

Percussion ensemble, performing a piece by the leading avant-garde composer Karlheinz Stockhausen for a video-recording at St. Giles' Church in London, 1986. (Photo: Clive Barda)

ually replaced the harpsichord as the most popular keyboard instrument. Because sound is produced when hammers strike the strings within the instrument the piano is often considered a percussion instrument. It is an instrument very commonly played by amateurs, and is found in many homes.

## The Evolution of Instruments

Musical instruments, like most other things, have changed in response to new technology. We have already mentioned the fact that the piano replaced the harpsichord in the eighteenth century. Many of the other instruments mentioned on the preceding pages have also descended from older and generally simpler forms. The modern transverse flute, for example, is the latest in a long line of simpler flutes, many of which still exist in other cultures and in our own. One early type of flute, the *recorder*, is often played in ensembles that perform music of the Renaissance and Baroque, the periods in which this instrument was prominent. *Crumhorns* and *shawms*, predecessors of modern double-reed instruments and well known in the sixteenth and seventeenth centuries, are often heard today in performances of early music.

### Older instruments

In most cases, the more modern instruments have extended the capacities of the earlier instruments. The modern metal flute can produce a much louder sound than the earlier wooden flutes, which might easily be overwhelmed in a large orchestra. The piano, unlike the harpsichord, can achieve many different levels of volume. A pianist can rapidly vary the level from very soft to very loud, while a harpsichordist must play each pitch in a passage at the same volume.

Naturally, composers today are in search of opportunities to extend musical language. One such opportunity is found in the use of electronics. In *musique concrète*, conventional sounds recorded on tape are altered electronically to produce new effects. The sound used may be music, human speech, or noises such as those heard on the street. The composer splices the tapes together and adjusts speed and volume to produce the desired effect. Even more innovative is music that is generated electronically rather than just altered by electronic means. With the use of *sound synthesizers*, entirely new and unconventional sounds can be created. Many composers of the 1970s and 1980s have made use of computer technology to create electronic music.

### Electronic and computer music

Electronic and computerized equipment offers the composer an extremely rich array of pitches and timbres that cannot be conveniently or accurately produced on other instruments. The uses of electronic sound are quite varied. In fact, in many compositions, natural and electronic music are still being combined, even as other compositions are created for computer alone.

## The Orchestra

Most of the modern string, wind, and percussion instruments discussed earlier are used in the *symphony orchestra*. Some, such as the piano, are used only in certain works. Others, such as the violin and

The New York Philharmonic Orchestra, conducted by Leonard Bernstein, in a concert at the Royal Albert Hall, London, in 1986. Founded in 1842, it is America's oldest symphony orchestra and is today one of the world's leading ensembles. (Photo: Clive Barda)

clarinet, are essential. In all, most modern symphony orchestras have about one hundred performers who play from fifteen to twenty different instruments. The possible combinations of sounds are vast in number and effect.

Just as individual instruments have changed over time, so has the orchestra. Up until about 1600, instrumental music was generally confined to individual performers or small groups of players. Small groups of listeners could assemble in one room—or chamber—to enjoy the refined, relatively soft sound of the *chamber ensemble*. Large ensembles were used only for festive or ceremonial occasions. But changes came rapidly. Two Venetian composers, Giovanni Gabrieli (1553/6–1612) and Claudio Monteverdi (1567–1643), used varied and occasionally large instrumental ensembles with voices. Composers in the seventeenth century began to specify consistently the exact instruments to play in an ensemble or orchestra, and such groups gradually came to have rather standard instrumentation.

During the eighteenth century, the size of the orchestra and the instruments in it became quite standardized, although the orchestra itself was not yet as large or as inclusive as the modern orchestra.

One of the most famous
string quartets, the Amadeus
Quartet, performing in 1967.
(Photo: Erich Auerbach)

*Orchestration*, the art of writing instrumental music to achieve a variety of effects, developed greatly over the century as the size of the orchestra grew. In the nineteenth century, the orchestra was expanded to include many different percussion instruments as well as more wind and string players.

Today's symphony orchestra includes strings, woodwinds, brasses, and percussion. The strings are generally given important melodic parts, and contribute harmonic support. The woodwinds also present melodic material, and reinforce the harmony. The brass instruments

**Seating Plan for a Modern Symphony Orchestra**

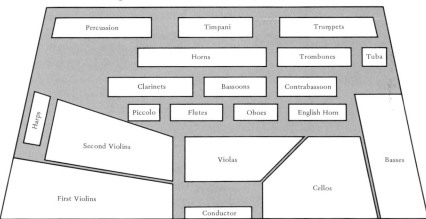

An Orchestral Score: The first page of the last movement of Beethoven's Fifth Symphony shows how an orchestral score is typically arranged. Notice that the woodwinds are at the top, the brass and timpani are in the middle, and the strings are at the bottom. (Reprinted from *Norton Critical Scores: Beethoven.* "Symphony No. 5 in C minor," edited by Elliott Forbes. W. W. Norton & Co., p. 68.)

are used strikingly in solo melodic parts, in climaxing passages, to provide harmonic support, and in music of a military nature. The percussion section functions mainly as a source of rhythmic vitality and accent, but it may also be used to create special moods and effects. Although all orchestras do not use the same seating plan, one typical seating arrangement used by orchestras is shown here (*left*).

## Dynamics

The effects created by different intensities of sound, or *dynamics*, are basic to all musical expression. In traditional music, we often first become aware of the impact of dynamic effects upon hearing very sudden changes from soft to loud, or vice versa. For some of us, the first awareness of musical dynamics is very obvious, as in the so-called "Surprise" Symphony of Franz Joseph Haydn (1732–1809). Here, the surprise is a radical change in volume, a very loud chord coming on the heels of a gentle melody. Of course, dynamic effects can also be more subtle. In any case, the level of volume that a composer specifies for a given note, chord, or section of a work is an important indication of expressive intent. Dynamic indications are often used to regulate the balance between the various voices and lines of a composition.

Dynamic markings, like many other musical terms, are conventionally given in Italian. Italian composers around 1600 seem to have been the first to mark dynamics in their music, and partly due to the quality and influence of Italian musicians, the use of markings of dynamics and tempo in Italian became common practice in following centuries. A list of the markings used most often is given in the following chart.

### Dynamic Markings

| | | |
|---|---|---|
| *pp* | *pianissimo* | very soft |
| *p* | *piano* | soft |
| *mp* | *mezzo piano* | moderately soft |
| *mf* | *mezzo forte* | moderately loud |
| *f* | *forte* | loud |
| *ff* | *fortissimo* | very loud |
| *sf* | *sforzando* | "forced," sudden stress on a single note or chord |
| *fp* | *forte-piano* | loud followed suddenly by soft |

The development of *contrast* in dynamic level is especially important in music. The famous *Bolero* of Maurice Ravel (1875–1937), for example, would sound like a simple exercise in repetition were it not for its slow and steady increase in dynamic level and its changes in orchestration. Such building up of volume is called a *crescendo* (abbreviated *cresc.*), and is indicated on a musical score by the mark ⎯⎯◁.

**Crescendo**

Of course, a crescendo can be realized on a much smaller scale than in *Bolero*. It may be heard in the single voice of the clarinet that George Gershwin (1898–1937) used to introduce *Rhapsody in Blue* and in the so-called "Funeral March" from the *Sonata No. 2 in B♭ Minor* by Frédéric Chopin (1810–1849). One of the most thrilling of all crescendos occurs in Beethoven's *Symphony No. 5*, carrying the end of the third movement into the beginning of the fourth, obviating the need for the traditional pause.

**Decrescendo or diminuendo**

As might be expected, composers have also used a gradual softening effect, or *decrescendo*, for expressive purposes. Also called the *diminuendo* (*dim.*), this effect is indicated by the mark ▷⎯⎯, which very graphically shows a fading away of sound. The diminuendo may be found within a musical work or at its end. A well-loved symphony that virtually dies away at the close is the *Symphony No. 6* (the "Pathétique") of Piotr Ilyich Tchaikovsky (1840–1893). It was much criticized when first performed because at the time symphonies were expected to come to a loud and dramatic close.

Changes in volume are often closely related to changes in melody, tempo, and orchestration. If you listen closely to your own voice, you will soon discover that as you speak more loudly and more quickly, the pitch tends to rise. Conversely, lowering the pitch of your voice generally softens it and may slow it down as well. Of course, you can speak slowly in a high pitch and quickly in a low pitch, but the opposite combinations seem more natural. In music, as in speech, increases in tempo, volume, and pitch often work together to generate excitement and climax. The frenzied dance "In the Hall of the Mountain King" from the *Peer Gynt Suite* by Edvard Grieg (1843–1907) is an excellent example. Decreases in volume, speed, and pitch may also occur together. These decreases may be used to provide contrasts to the more exciting passages or to convey a variety of melancholy or restful moods. In orchestral works, the composer's choice of instruments and tone colors is integral to the production of these effects.

## Listening to Timbre and Dynamics

The record set that accompanies the text (Side 1 Band 3) gives aural examples of the different voice categories and of many of the instruments discussed in Chapter 3. To develop a better understanding of orchestration and dynamics you may also want to listen to recordings of some of the pieces mentioned in the text. Finally, you may gain additional information by listening to one of the following records:

*The Instruments of the Orchestra* [Vanguard VSD 721–722]
*The Orchestra and Its Instruments* [Scholastic FT 3602]
Britten, *Young Person's Guide to the Orchestra* (various recordings)

The taste, style and use of musical instruments changes as much from century to century as music itself. The illustration shows a detail of the soundboard—with bridges, painted decoration and carved rose—of a 17th-century French harpsichord, a highly decorative piece of furniture indicating social status as much as a musical instrument. (Victoria and Albert Museum, Crown copyright)

# CHAPTER 4

# *Introduction to Musical Form and Style*

*LISTENING PREVIEW Even though music is an art of constant motion and changing sounds, form in music can be perceived by comparing musical ideas that have been heard throughout a composition. Repetition of musical ideas can suggest a sense of coherent structure in music, whereas contrast provided by new ideas can offer needed variety. Notice in Chopin's* Nocturne in E-flat Major *(side 7, band 1) how the memorable first melody is presented and then repeated immediately. It is followed by a contrasting melody before it is repeated again. Such repetition and contrast help one to identify form in a piece of music.*

## *Discovering Musical Form*

When listening to music, we are conscious of movement—the succession of musical events. Unless we are familiar with a piece, we cannot anticipate the course of musical events any more than we can anticipate the plot of a drama without seeing or reading it. Yet it is clear that in a musical work, as in a drama, the later action depends on or proceeds from the earlier action. We know that when the work is complete an overall design will be apparent.

The overall design of a piece of music is referred to as *form, structure,* or *shape.* It is the particular way all of the sonic elements of music—melody, harmony, tone color, tempo, dynamics—are used in combination. It is form that explains the choices of the composer— the conscious shaping of major ideas and the careful selection of detail. An awareness of form in music can make listening a more rewarding and enjoyable experience.

## *Fundamental Principles: Repetition and Contrast*

In music, the listener is confronted with an abstract, ever-changing flow of organized sound. One cannot easily explain precisely what happens in a piece of music, as one can with a drama. Instead, most listeners simply try to describe "what it sounds like." And it is true that some music really does sound like something easily described— the singing of birds or the approach of footsteps. But in describing most music, we can only relate sounds, melodies, rhythms, and so on, to other sounds, melodies, and rhythms in the composition. Thus, a melody may be identical to an earlier melody, similar to it, or quite different. These relationships can be drawn because as we listen, we become sensitive to the repetition of certain elements and the introduction of other, new material.

Repetition, providing unity and continuity, and contrast, providing variety and surprise, are the two most fundamental principles of musical form. Even simple examples such as "Twinkle, Twinkle, Little Star" show repetition and contrast to be the organizing principles.

## Outlining Form

### Motives

Form in music can be identified by giving a letter designation to each prominent musical idea and noting the order in which these ideas appear and are repeated. "Frère Jacques," for example, consists of four short musical ideas, or *motives*—the shortest units of melody. Each of the motives is presented and then repeated. The first motive, a, consists of only four notes. It is repeated before the second motive, b, is heard. After b is repeated, the third and fourth motives, c, and d, are heard and repeated in turn.

| | | | |
|---|---|---|---|
| a | Are you sleeping, | c | Morning bells are ringing; |
| a | Are you sleeping, | c | Morning bells are ringing; |
| b | Brother John, | d | Ding, ding, dong; |
| b | Brother John? | d | Ding, ding, dong. |

The order of ideas here is aabbccdd, or more simply abcd. The form uses both of the fundamental principles—repetition and contrast.

## Listening for Musical Form

Most forms can be outlined in a manner similar to that used for "Frère Jacques." Here we will consider a few of the most common forms.

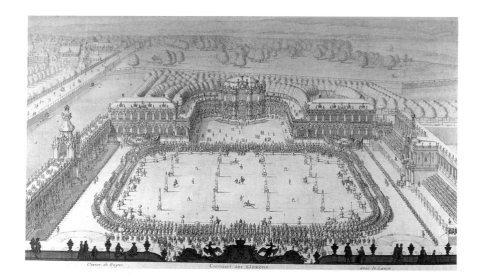

Equestrian ballet in celebration of a prince's wedding, 1719, in the court of a German Baroque castle, the Zwinger in Dresden. The music here is subservient to the occasion it celebrates, but finds powerful visual expression in the highly formalized movements of horses and riders. (Dresden: Kupferstichkabinett; photo: Sachsische Landesbibliothek, Abt. Deutsche Fotothek)

## Strophic Form

**Phrases**

**Sections**

The form of most songs is built up from phrases, longer melodic units, comparable to the lines of most poems. The phrases of "The Star-Spangled Banner," like the motives of "Frère Jacques," show the clear use of repetition and contrast. The first four phrases, a, b, c, and d, are presented and then immediately repeated. Because of the repetition, *sections* can be perceived in the song. The first four lines of the song, the first section of the song, can be labeled Section A. The next four lines are a melodic repetition of Section A, and thus can also be labeled Section A. The six lines at the end, however, are different. These lines fall into two natural groups—four short lines and two longer lines—and can be labeled Section B and Section C. The resulting form is AABC.

| Sections | Phrases | |
|---|---|---|
| A | a | Oh, say can you see |
| | b | By the dawn's early light |
| | c | What so proudly we hailed |
| | d | At the twilight's last gleaming? |
| A | a | Whose broad stripes and bright stars, |
| | b | Through the perilous fight, |
| | c | O'er the ramparts we watched |
| | d | Were so gallantly streaming? |
| B | e | And the rocket's red glare, |
| | f | The bombs bursting in air, |
| | g | Gave proof through the night |
| | h | That our flag was still there. |
| C | i | Oh, say does that star-spangled banner yet wave |
| | j | O'er the land of the free and the home of the brave? |

These four sections make up "The Star-Spangled Banner" as we usually sing it. However, there are, as you may know, three other *stanzas* of the text which are all intended to be sung to the same melody.

| Stanza: | 1 | 2 | 3 | 4 |
|---|---|---|---|---|
| | AABC | AABC | AABC | AABC |

This form is referred to as *strophic form*, in that the same music is repeated for each stanza—or strophe—of text. Many popular and folk songs are in strophic form.

## Ternary Form

In music it is also common to find an organization of sections in a three-part or *ternary form*:

"Twinkle, Twinkle, Little Star" is a familiar example of this. Here the middle section offers a melodic contrast to the first and third sections. Contrast may also be heightened by changes in mode, key, rhythm, instrumentation, dynamics, and other factors. Nearly every march that a band plays is in ternary form, as are the minuets of Haydn and Mozart. The form provides a fine sense of balance and symmetry, leaving A for the novelty of B, then returning to the pleasurable familiarity of A.

## Binary Form

Also important is two-part or *binary form*:

| A | B |
|---|---|

In this form, the second part often acts as an answer to the first. The AB form was very important during the seventeenth and eighteenth centuries and may readily be found in the works of Johann Sebastian Bach (1685–1750), Domenico Scarlatti (1685–1757), and other master composers of the period. In many pieces, each section is repeated immediately after it is presented.

## Rondo Form

A variety of *rondo forms* have developed in music of different periods, but they usually contrast one primary theme with secondary themes. The primary theme usually reappears in the tonic key, while the secondary themes are often in other keys. A typical plan might be diagramed as:

| A | B | A | C | A | B | A |
|---|---|---|---|---|---|---|

## Theme and Variations Form

Repetition and contrast are opposing principles. The composer tries to make the best use of both of them. One way is to state a musical idea and then repeat it, but to vary it in such a way that it sounds at once familiar and new. If a number of variations are put together, the result is a *theme and variations form*. A theme followed by four variations might be symbolized in this manner:

| Theme | Var. I | Var. II | Var. III | Var. IV |
|-------|--------|---------|----------|---------|
| A | $A^1$ | $A^2$ | $A^3$ | $A^4$ |

Familiar examples of theme and variations form are *Variations on the Theme "Ah, vous dirai-je, Maman"* (or "Twinkle, Twinkle, Little Star") by Wolfgang Amadeus Mozart (1756–1791), *Variations on a Theme of Paganini* by Johannes Brahms (1833–1892), the fourth movement of the *"Trout" Quintet* by Franz Schubert (1797–1828), and the second movement from Haydn's *Symphony No. 94* (The "Surprise" Symphony).

## Other Forms

**Ritornello**

**Sonata and rondo**

**Free forms**

Still other forms have been devised by composers in all ages. The music of fourteenth- and fifteenth-century French composers was influenced by poetry, and several poetic-musical forms were popular. In the seventeenth century, the *ritornello* form evolved, stressing several returns to modified versions of the opening theme. By the late eighteenth century, the complex *sonata* and *rondo* forms had been developed. Throughout the nineteenth century, forms grew ever more elaborate, while, in our own century, much freer and looser forms have come into being, often involving a seemingly free flow of sound tied together by the barest of motives. These and other forms will be discussed as they are appropriate in chronological context. Still other forms do not fall into clear sectional patterns and can be described as *free forms*. They always include some element of repetition—for example, melody or rhythm—but not in a manner that suggests clearly contrasting sections. Fantasias and preludes are usually in free forms.

## Types of Compositions

**Movements**

The many different types or genres of compositions that have been developed over the centuries can be classified in several different ways. One obvious method is to categorize them by their uses of form. Many works are based on a single form—on a theme and variations, a strophic, or a ternary form, for example. Included here are most *songs* and *marches* as well as many piano pieces. Other compositions are built up into larger, more complex structures, consisting of several relatively independent sections called *movements*, each of which may be based on a different form. Perhaps the best known multi-movement work is the *symphony*.

Compositions may also be categorized by the use of different performing groups. Works for solo instruments have been given a wide variety of names, some with extramusical associations—such as "Song of the Brook"—and some with more abstract titles—such as *étude, nocturne,* and *rhapsody. Sonatas* may be intended for one instrument or for almost any combination of instruments. Works for small groups of instruments include *duets, trios, quartets, quintets,* and so forth. Compositions for orchestra include *symphonies, symphonic poems, concertos, suites,* and *overtures.* There are *Lieder* and *arias* for individual singers and *madrigals, motets,* and *Masses* for groups of singers. Numerous combinations of singers and instruments are possible in *cantatas, oratorios,* and *operas.*

New types of compositions have evolved in every age, as have the individual forms found in movements of large works. We shall meet all of the compositional types mentioned above and others, as we examine each period of musical style.

## Change in Musical Style

Music of any given time period has certain special characteristics. As fashions in clothing change, so do tastes and styles in music. Instruments and the manner in which they are used change, and new ways of using melody, harmony, and the other elements of music are devised by at least some of the composers in every period. Consequently, new musical styles emerge.

The musical style of any period is a kind of imprecise composite of the styles of all or most of the composers of that period. Often stylistic features of music are influenced or shaped by social or political realities of the time. It is not always easy to determine which composers are typical of a particular time and which are behind or ahead of the time. Nor is it easy to give precise dates to any stylistic period, since styles of composition overlap from one historical period into the next. However, the blocks of time in the chart below can be used to outline stylistic periods in the history of Western music as they are generally regarded today. They also serve as basic divisions of this text.

| Styles | Approximate Dates |
|---|---|
| Medieval | sixth–early fifteenth centuries |
| Renaissance | later fifteenth–sixteenth centuries |
| Baroque | seventeenth–first half of eighteenth centuries |
| Classical | late eighteenth–very early nineteenth centuries |
| Romantic | middle and later nineteenth century |
| Twentieth Century | |

The Greek and Roman civilizations had highly developed musical cultures, and we know a great deal about theoretical and philosophical aspects of their music. But few actual examples of their music survive, and we are not certain how they would have sounded in their day. Thus, our consideration of music from a listener's viewpoint will begin with Western medieval music after the following summary of musical notation.

# CHAPTER 5

# *Musical Notation*

*LISTENING PREVIEW Musical notation is a collection of symbols that tells a performer the pitches to perform, how long they should be sustained, and other details of intensity, attack, and release of pitches. When we speak, we rarely stop to think of the printed appearance or spelling of words we use. Similarly, when we listen to music, we rarely pause to think of specific pitches, their durations, and their appearance on the printed page. Think of one of your favorite songs for a moment. What things come to mind while you are thinking of the song? The way the song is notated on a printed page was probably not among your thoughts. Musical notation is a very important means of communication from composer to performer, but the essence of music is not in its notation, but in its sounds and how they are interpreted. Notation is primarily a means of recording in symbols some of the most basic aspects of music.*

## The Purpose of Notation

Most people are familiar with the general appearance of musical notation, but many have never learned to "read music"—that is, to translate the written symbols into sound. Contrary to some popular opinion, however, there is no great mystery about reading music. Fundamentally, musical notation is designed to indicate just two things—the pitch and the relative duration of the musical tones.

## Pitch and Key

The pitch of a note is shown by its vertical location on a series of horizontal lines called a *staff*. The modern staff has five lines with four spaces in between. If you count the spaces above and below the top and bottom lines, this gives enough space for eleven notes. Higher and lower notes are placed on short *ledger lines* above or below the staff.

Use of Staff and Ledger Lines

High Pitches

Low Pitches

**Clef**

The actual pitch of a given note depends on the *clef,* a sign that appears at the extreme left of the staff. Most familiar is the *treble clef,* which looks somewhat like a written capital G. In fact, it is also called the *G clef,* because the tail of the clef indicates the line on which the note G is to be written:

When the treble clef is used, middle C—the C approximately at the center of the piano keyboard—is placed on the first ledger line below the staff.

The notes of the other white keys go up the staff in order following it, as can be seen in the example below.

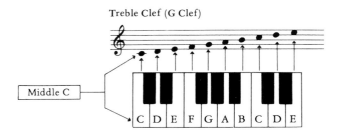

Treble Clef (G Clef)

Middle C

C D E F G A B C D E

Notes below middle C can be written on additional ledger lines further below the staff. However, if the notes are considerably below middle C, the number of ledger lines soon becomes hard to read. So, for music that consists mainly of lower notes, another clef is generally chosen—the *bass clef*. When this clef is used, middle C is on the ledger line just above the staff:

Bass Clef (**F Clef**)

C   D   E   F   G   A   B   C

Middle C

This clef is also called the F clef, because the two dots in the clef appear on either side of the line on which the note F is to be written. Middle C appears at the midpoint of the two *staves* if both are used together. If the bass staff and the treble staff are placed one below the other, with an extra space between for the ledger line of middle C, the result is the *great staff*. All the white-key notes at the center of the piano keyboard can be written on this staff without a break.

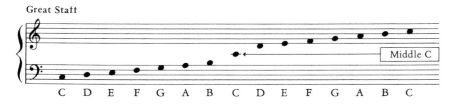

Great Staff

Middle C

C   D   E   F   G   A   B   C   D   E   F   G   A   B   C

Piano music is generally written on the great staff, with the space in the middle expanded somewhat for convenience.

Another, less common, clef—the *C clef*—is sometimes used for music with a range between those of the treble and bass clefs. The C clef can be moved around on the staff. If it is centered on the third line of the staff, it is known as the *alto clef;* if on the fourth line, the *tenor clef.* The line that passes through the middle of the clef, wherever it appears, is the location of middle C.

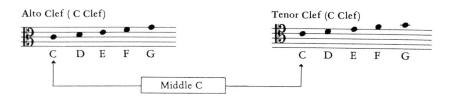

**Sharps and flats**

The black keys on the piano are shown by the use of *sharp* (♯) and *flat* (♭) signs. These signs tell the performer to raise (sharp) or lower (flat) the pitch of a particular note by a semitone or half step:

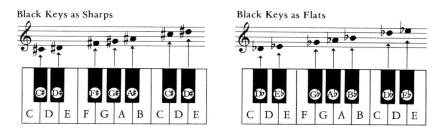

Notice that each of the black keys may represent either a sharp of the note below or a flat of the note above it. On a keyboard instrument, A♯ is the same note as B♭, F♯ is the same as G♭, and so on. As you may have noticed, there are no black keys between B and C or E and F. Since the note one half step above B is C, it follows that B♯ is the same as C on keyboard instruments. In like manner, C♭ is B, E♯ is F, and F♭ is E.

With the aid of either sharp or flat signs, the entire twelve-tone chromatic scale can be written. Using sharps the scale can be written this way:

When a particular note is to be sharped or flatted throughout a piece of music, it would be inconvenient to mark it each time it appears. For this reason, sharp and flat signs to be used throughout are placed at the left side of the staff immediately after the clef. This **Key signatures** group of signs is known as the *key signature.*

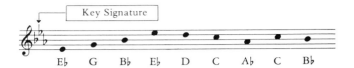

Eb    G    Bb    Eb    D    C    Ab    C    Bb

In addition to showing what notes should be sharped or flatted, the key signature also tells the performer by inference the tonic note of the scale being used and hence what scale—or *key*—the music is built upon. In the example above, for instance, the tonic note is Eb and the key is Eb major. Everyone can learn to recognize the key signatures of a few of the most commonly used keys.

Common Key Signatures

C Major       F Major       Bb Major      G Major       D Major
A Minor       D Minor       G Minor       E Minor       B Minor

**Major and relative minor scales**

As you can see, two scales, or keys, share each key signature. In each case, a *major scale* is paired with its *relative minor*. The key signatures are the same, but the tonic notes differ: the minor tonic is a minor third lower than the major tonic. This can be seen more clearly if we compare two specific scales:

Scale of F Major                          Scale of D Minor

**Major and minor modes**

The most important difference between scales in the *major mode* and scales in the *minor mode* is the arrangement of half and whole steps. All major scales have half-step intervals after the third and seventh notes. Their relative minors have half-step intervals after the second and fifth notes.

After establishing a key, composers sometimes want to use a note that is not contained in the particular key, or scale, they have chosen. If they wish to add a sharp, or flat, they write the sign to the left of that particular note. When composers wish to show that a note that would normally be sharped or flatted should be played without sharp **Natural sign** or flat, they mark it with another sign, the *natural sign* (♮). This sign can be used to cancel a sharp or flat either given in the key signature or as it occurs within a composition. Sharps, flats, and naturals are **Accidentals** called *accidentals* when used beside individual notes in music.

Use of Accidentals and Natural Signs

## Duration and Meter

The appearance of a note tells the performer not only its pitch but also the length of time the note should be held relative to the notes around it. The different durations, or *note values*, are shown below:

**Note Values**

Whole    Half    Quarter    Eighth    Sixteenth    Thirty-second    Sixty-fourth

As the names suggest, each of these note values has a duration half as long as the preceding one. If a whole note represents four beats, a half note will represent two beats, a quarter note one beat, an eighth note half a beat, and so on.

Groups of notes of smaller value are often linked together with heavy *beams* to make them easier to read:

**Use of Beams**

If a composer wants to show a duration of another length—say three beats—there are two ways to do it. Two or more notes of smaller value can be linked together with a curved line called a *tie*. If, for example, three quarter notes equal to one beat each are linked together, the performer will play just one note for three beats. A composer may also use a *dot*. A dot added to any note increases its value by half the original length. If, for example, a half note equal to two beats is dotted, the note will be held for three beats.

**Use of Ties and Dots**

Periods of silence—or *rests*—in music must also be notated for duration. The standard rest signs are shown below:

**Rests**

Whole    Half    Quarter    Eighth    Sixteenth    Thirty-second    Sixty-fourth

**Measures and bar lines**

In most music of the Western world, the beats are arranged in regular groups of equal length, often with an accent on the first beat of each group. These groups, as mentioned in Chapter 1, are called *measures*. They are divided on the written score by narrow vertical lines called *bar lines*. Sometimes the measures themselves are called bars.

A *meter signature*, sometimes called a time signature, is given next to the key signature at the beginning of the music. The meter signature is a pair of numbers, one above the other. The lower number shows which note has a value of one beat. The upper number shows the number of beats in a measure. A meter signature of $\frac{2}{4}$, for example, means that a quarter note gets one beat and that there are two beats in a measure. A meter signature of $\frac{3}{8}$ means that an eighth note gets one beat and that there are three beats in a measure. Other possible meter signatures include the following:

*Common time* ($\frac{4}{4}$) is often shown by the sign $\mathbf{C}$. A vertical line through the sign ($\mathbf{\mathbb{C}}$) indicates *alla breve*, or *cut time* ($\frac{2}{2}$), in which

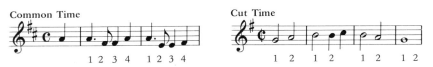

Measures with any number of beats are theoretically possible. Traditional music is usually written in measures of two, three, four, or six beats. Modern composers, however, have experimented with other measures, such as those of five or seven beats.

The absolute duration of individual notes is arrived at by determining a precise overall tempo for a given piece. Composers from Beethoven on have traditionally done this by specifying a number of beats per minute. Performers wishing to recreate the composer's intended speed use a *metronome*, a clockwork device dating from the early nineteenth century which can be set to click (or blink a light) regularly at one of a variety of speeds. The composer's exact tempo indication in a score is called a *metronome marking*.

A metronome marking of ♩ = 60, for example, means that the basic beat is a quarter note, and there are 60 beats a minute. ♩ = 44 is a slower tempo, with only 44 quarter-note beats per minute. In the first case, a metronome would be set to 60 on a calibrated scale, in the second, to 44.

Until Galileo discovered the laws applying to the movement of a pendulum in the late 16th century, small intervals of time could only be measured against the beat of the human pulse. The modern metronome, first patented in 1815—the date of manufacture of the one shown here—is essentially governed by a double pendulum and allows for the definite fixing of tempo of a musical performance. (Gesellschaft der Musikfreunde, Vienna)

The Metronome

# PART TWO

# Early Music

## Main Composers of the Medieval and Renaissance Periods (c.1150–1600)

*Léonin* (c.1163–90)
*Pérotin* (fl. 1200)
*Bernart de Ventadorn* (d.c.1195)
*Philippe de Vitry* (?1290–1361)
*Guillaume de Machaut* (c.1300–77)
*Francesco Landini* (1325–97)
*John Dunstable* (c.1390–c.1453)
*Guillaume Dufay* (c.1400–74)
*Johannes Ockeghem* (c.1410–c.1497)
*Josquin des Prez* (c.1440–1521)
*Andrea* (c.1520–86) *& Giovanni* (c.1557–1612) *Gabrieli*
*Giovanni Pierluigi da Palestrina* (c.1524–94)
*Roland de Lassus* (1532–94)
*William Byrd* (1543–1623)
*Luca Marenzio* (1553–99)
*Carlo Gesualdo* (1560–1613)
*John Dowland* (1562–1626)
*Claudio Monteverdi* (1567–1643)

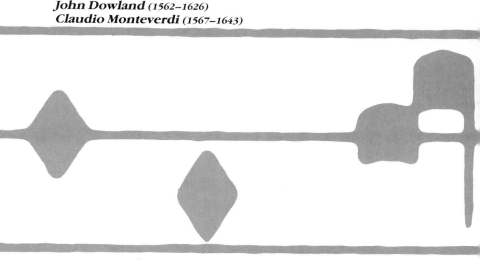

(*Above*) This 15th-century
Flemish drawing depicts St.
Cecilia, the patron saint of
music, playing an early hand-
held organ. (Musée du
Louvre; photo: Giraudon)

(*Right*) Arming of a Knight:
This miniature from the
fourteenth century shows
musicians playing the lute
and fiddle as the knight is
dressed and armed for battle.
(Bibliothèque Nationale,
Paris; taken from David
Munrow, Instruments of the
Middle Ages and Renaissance,
London: Oxford University
Press, 1976)

: puuus filz acchille

# CHAPTER 6

# *Medieval Music*

*LISTENING PREVIEW A major innovation in music of the Western world during the Middle Ages was the development of polyphony—music comprising two or more lines performed simultaneously. Early polyphony was based on and grew from Gregorian chant, as in Léonin's "Viderunt omnes" (side 2, band 3) from Paris of the late twelfth century. Identify the number of voices performing in the example and describe specifically how they interact with one another.*

## The Medieval Period

The people of fifth-century Rome did not know their empire was dying. They only knew that money kept getting scarcer and life ever more dangerous. Survival was their main concern. How were peasants to prevent barbarian bands from raiding their livestock and burning their barns? How were travelers to reach their destinations without being murdered by brigands?

The best answer lay in finding a strong protector. The feudal system gradually evolved as vulnerable peasants gained protection from a few strong landowners in exchange for working their land. The most powerful shield of all, however, was the Church. In Christianity, people found an invincible savior who, in return for their devotion, promised to lead them from the miseries of life on earth to an eternity of bliss.

The feudal system and the Church remained important throughout the Medieval period. Only in the last few centuries of the Middle Ages were these two forces to be seriously challenged. As we shall see, the growth of trade and cities, the rise of strong rulers, and schisms in the Church all helped to usher in a new period.

## General Characteristics of Medieval Music

The vast majority of the music that survives from the Middle Ages is religious, since the Church was for many centuries the home of almost all learning; apart from church music little could be written down. The music favored by the Church was vocal, incorporating most of the qualities that make any music singable. It was of limited range, mostly conjunct, and often centered around a tonic note. The harmonic system that developed over the centuries was based on eight *modes*, or scales. These were loosely derived from ancient Greek modes and would eventually evolve into the major and minor modes so widely used in later centuries. Early Church music was monophonic, but in the later centuries of the Middle Ages the Church played an important part in the development of polyphony.

As might be expected, the same general characteristics were found in varying proportions in the secular music that developed during the Middle Ages. Although the words of the texts sung might differ considerably, the religious and secular music of the Middle Ages had many stylistic points in common. Perhaps the most significant difference was the use of instruments to accompany secular songs. The use of musical instruments had been banned in the Church of the early Middle Ages, and only slowly did the Church come to accept anything but vocal music.

## Music for the Church

By the year 1000, the Church had codified its rituals into a standardized pattern of services. Earlier Jewish traditions were especially influential in their formation, and much Church music used texts from the Old Testament. Services including psalms, prayers, and readings from scripture became elaborate rituals and were held every day of the year. There were also a number of special days, often requiring even more ornate services. The great feast days of Easter, Pentecost, and Christmas were central to the church year, and hundreds of other feast days and saints' days were gradually added to the Church calendar. For these many services, singers had to learn, often without the help of musical notation, the music for innumerable psalms, responses, litanies, and antiphons.

**The Office**

In the monasteries, bells summoned the monks eight times a day to sing and pray the *Hours of the Divine Office*, a round-the-clock series of services. The first was *Matins*, celebrated after midnight. Next came *Lauds* at "cock-crow," followed by *Prime* at sunrise. These were followed by *Terce* at midmorning, *Sext* at noon, *None* at midafternoon, *Vespers* before the evening meal, and, lastly, *Compline* at nightfall, just before the monks went to bed. Vespers was one of the most musically elaborate Hours and included the famous canticle of Mary, the Magnificat. Prayers, scripture readings, and the singing of psalms and hymns were all part of the Hours of the Office.

**The Mass**

The heart of the Church rite was the *Mass*, symbolically based on the last Supper, when Christ offered his body and blood as a sacrifice. In the early centuries, Mass was celebrated only on Sundays and special days. Later, a High Mass, with many parts of it sung, often followed shortly after Terce every day of the week. A celebration of the Mass was meant to capture the human spirit through the solemn movement of the celebrants before the altar, the glowing colors of embroidered vestments and altar cloths, the incense and candlelight, bells tolling at the moment of the Elevation of the Host, and the chanting of the singers, not only from the choir stalls but also in procession, so that the congregation was surrounded by music.

**Proper and Ordinary texts**

The Mass consisted of two different kinds of texts. In the *Ordinary*, the text was always the same, even though the music might remain the same or change, depending on the needs of a particular Mass. The Masses held on Christmas and Easter, for example, had different *Proper* texts, each appropriate to the particular feast day, but the Ordinary texts were the same on both days. The parts of the Mass that were most often set to music are shown below:

## Parts of the Mass set to music

| Proper | Ordinary |
|---|---|
| 1. Introit | |
| | 2. Kyrie eleison (Lord, have mercy) |
| | 3. Gloria in excelsis Deo (Glory to God in the highest) |
| 4. Gradual | |
| 5. Alleluia or Tract; Sequence | |
| | 6. Credo in unum Deum (I believe in one God) |
| 7. Offertory | |
| | 8. Sanctus (Holy, Holy, Holy, Lord God of Hosts); Benedictus (Blessed is he that cometh in the name of the Lord) |
| | 9. Agnus Dei (Lamb of God) |
| 10. Communion | |

Detail of the Minstrel Gallery (1556) in Exeter Cathedral. English minstrels were mostly instrumentalists and are here seen playing the fiddle and harp. (Photo: Clive Hicks)

*Plainchant or Gregorian chant*

The early music written for the Mass is known as *plainchant*, or *Gregorian chant*—after Gregory I, pope from 590 to 604. No one knows if Gregory himself really wrote plainchant, but he probably organized the plain chants better than they had been. Each chant consists of a single melodic line sung by a unison choir or a soloist without accompaniment.

### Theory and Notation

*Neumes*

The chants were notated in symbols called *neumes*, a Greek word meaning "nod" or "sign." The earliest neumes were little marks that showed the relative height of pitches, and were written, without any staff, immediately above the words in a musical manuscript. Probably intended to depict the head and hand gestures of a lead singer for the direction of melodies, these neumes developed into a square notation that eventually came to represent specific pitches. A four-line staff was adopted, with a clef placed at the beginning to show the position of the note C or F. An example can be seen below.

Chants were generally built on one of eight modes or scales, the concept of which was borrowed from the ancient Greeks. The eight

*Authentic modes*

modes make use of four different scale patterns, or *authentic modes*, each of which centers on a different note called a *final* and generally spans an octave in range. The four authentic modes are:

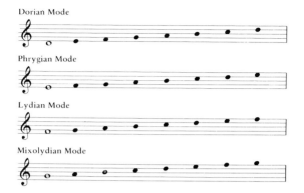

**Plagal modes**

Each of these authentic modes has a related *plagal mode*, which has the same final as the authentic mode, but has a lower range that extends about four notes below the final and five notes above it. The names of the plagal modes are formed by adding the prefix "Hypo-" to the name of the authentic mode—Hypodorian, Hypophrygian, Hypolydian, Hypomixolydian. The modes are often identified and referred to by number, usually in the following manner: 1. Dorian, 2. Hypodorian, 3. Phrygian, 4. Hypophrygian, 5. Lydian, and so forth. Chants do not always use the entire hypothetical octave range, and they sometimes exceed it. In the Renaissance period two more authentic modes, Ionian on C and Aeolian on A, were added.

**Melodic styles**

Thousands of plainchant melodies were written, and they represent a number of different styles. Some, such as the Alleluias, were very *melismatic*—that is, with a large number of notes for each syllable of text. Other chants were *syllabic*, with only one note per syllable. Still others were *neumatic*, with several notes per syllable, but not as many as the melismatic chants.

### "Introit" of the Requiem Mass

One representative example of neumatic chant is found in the "Introit" of the *Requiem Mass*, or "Mass for the Dead." The first line of the chant is given below, first in Medieval black, square notation, then in modern notation.

The VI at the beginning of the chant indicates the mode on which the music is based—in this case the sixth or Hypolydian mode. The clef at the beginning of the four-line staff shows on which line the note C will occur. Thus the chant begins on the note F, as can also be seen in the modern transcription.

## "Introit" of the Requiem Mass

**LISTENING ANALYSIS** SIDE 2 BAND 1

After a solo male voice sings the opening words, the chant is sung in unison by a male choir, without accompaniment. The Hypolydian mode is colored by the use of B♭ which makes the mode sound like the major mode. Melodic motion in the Introit is almost always by step—that is, in conjunct motion. The monophonic texture is characteristic of all chants. After the opening section, a contrasting section "Te decet hymnus" is chanted. Finally, the opening melody is repeated with the same words, "Requiem aeternam." Thus, the overall form of the Introit is ternary (ABA). The melody of the Introit is quite tuneful.

Text:

A   Requiem aeternam dona eis, Domine; et lux perpetua luceat eis.

*Rest eternal grant unto them, O Lord; and let perpetual light shine upon them.*

B   Te decet hymnus, Deus, in Sion, et tibi reddetur votum in Jerusalem; exaudi orationem meam, ad te omnis caro veniet.

*You are praised, O God, in Zion, and unto You shall the vow be performed in Jerusalem; hear my prayer, unto You all flesh shall come.*

A   Requiem aeternam dona eis, Domine; et lux perpetua luceat eis.

*Rest eternal grant unto them, O Lord; and let perpetual light shine upon them.*

**LISTENING SUMMARY**

| | |
|---|---|
| Timbre: | solo male voice intones first words; then unison male choir enters and sings chant unaccompanied |
| Melody: | mainly conjunct; limited range |
| Rhythm: | nonmetrical; no clear beat or regular accent |
| Harmony: | based on the Hypolydian mode |
| Texture: | monophonic |
| Form: | ABA |

### Hymns

Another important type of plainchant used in church services throughout Medieval Europe was the *hymn*. It is one of the oldest genres of music incorporated into Christian worship. Often based on folk melodies and set in strophic form, hymns were meant to be sung by the congregation and were therefore relatively simple to sing.

## Secular Music

### Troubadours

A new body of poetry and music bloomed in the courts of Provence in southern France toward the end of the eleventh century in the work of the *troubadours*. It was nourished by the mingling of Moorish, Oriental, and Spanish influences there, where the trade routes met. From Britain came the legends of King Arthur and of Tristan and Iseult to add their potent mystique. An early troubadour,

### Ventadorn

Bernart de Ventadorn (c. 1130–1190), once declared to his employer,

**Courtly love**

Eleanor of Aquitaine, that Tristan had never suffered for Iseult as he did for her. Such a statement was very typical of *courtly love*. Both erotic and spiritual, courtly love defied the monastic, ascetic emphasis of Christianity in other parts of Europe. It called upon men to seek a form of temporal salvation through devotion to earthly, but highly idealized, women. Typically, the troubadour sang of his adoring enslavement to an unattainable woman who was beauty and goodness incarnate. He praised her loveliness, lamented her disdain, vowed to become more virtuous for her sake, and dedicated all his knightly deeds to her. Women also wrote and sang courtly love songs, with themes paralleling those of the male troubadours.

Troubadour songs were written in the southern vernacular tongue called the *langue d'oc*. Although the songs were written down as monophonic melodies, they may often have been sung with harp, lute, or some other Medieval instrument. They are generally thought to have been in triple meter and many were in Church modes.

**Trouvères**

Flourishing a little later in northern France were the *trouvères*. They wrote in the *langue d'oïl*, the dialect of northern France, and they continued the development of monophonic songs that dealt with courtly love and other chivalrous topics. Over 2,000 poems and about 1,700 melodies have come down to us from the trouvères, including works by such famous people as Richard the Lion-hearted (son of Eleanor of Aquitaine), and Thibaut, king of Navarre.

### *Le Châtelain de Coucy: "Li noviaus tens"*

One of the most gifted of the trouvères was Le Châtelain de Coucy (1165–1203), a nobleman. Of more than a dozen of his songs that have survived, "Li noviaus tens" provides a lovely example of a trouvère song that concerns love.

**Le Châtelain de Coucy: "Li noviaus tens"**

### LISTENING ANALYSIS

In its original form, "Li noviaus tens" was written as a single modal melodic line with text and without accompaniment. It is sung here by a countertenor (a very high tenor voice). A simple, improvised accompaniment is added to the voice, in a style and by instruments that would have been used in the time of the trouvères. The accompaniment is played by alto-recorder, lute, bass rebec, and harp, and consists of repetitions of the first and fifth notes of the mode throughout the piece. The opening phrase of the song is played by the solo recorder with accompaniment by the other instruments, after which the voice enters and sings the entire melody. Emphasis is on conjunct motion, and the meter is a flowing compound duple ($^6_4$), as can be seen in the first phrase.

1. Li no - viaus tens et mais et vi - o - le - te    Et

ros - i - gnols    me    se - mont de    chan - ter,

Minstrels playing bagpipe and shawm (a woodwind instrument) accompany the funeral procession of a king, as was already widely the custom in medieval times. This illustration comes from a late 14th-century manuscript of St. Augustine's *Cité de Dieu.* (Bibliothèque nationale, Paris)

Ornaments, or short added notes, are performed by the singer at the two places marked in the melody. The tonal center of the song is C—two phrases begin with C and four of the five phrases end on C. The use of some B-flats in the melody suggests the transposed Mixolydian mode, but when B naturals are used the mode sounds like the Ionian or major mode.

The first phrase, which is rather long, is repeated immediately with new words. The third and fourth phrases are short, and the final phrase is nearly as long as the first phrase. The same melody is to be sung with all stanzas of the text (three are sung on the recording), and so the overall form of the song is strophic. The first phrase is played by the solo recorder before the second and third stanzas are sung. The text tells of bitter-sweet feelings of love and makes a number of references to nature.

Text:

Li noviaus tens et mais et violete
et rosignols me semont de chanter,
et mes fins cuers me fait d'une
    amourete
si douz present que ne l'os refuser.
or me laist Dieus en tel honor
    monter,
que cele ou j'ai mon cuer et mon
    penser,
tiegne une foiz entre mes braz
    nüete,
ainz que voise outre mer.

*The new season, the month of May, the violet and the nightingale summon me to sing and my gentle heart offers me such a sweet gift of love that I dare not refuse. May God allow me to ascend to such high honour that I might hold her once naked in my arms before I go overseas.*

Au comencier la trovai si doucete,
ja ne cuidai por li mal endurer;
mais ses douz vis et sa fresche
    bouchete
et si bel oel vair et riant et cler-
    m'orent ainz pris que m'osasse
    doner.
se ne m'i veut retenir ou quiter,
mieuz aim a li faillir, si me promete,
qu'a une autre achiever.

*At the beginning I found her so sweet that I could not believe that I would have to endure pain on her account, but her gentle face, her small fresh mouth and her beautiful grey eyes that laugh and shine took me before I could give myself. If she does not want my service as her vassal, nor to set me free I prefer to go without the solace of love, as long as she promises it to me, rather than find it with another.*

De mil sospirs ke je li doi par dete
ne me veut ele un seul quite clamer,
ne fausse Amors ne lait ke
    s'entremete,
ne ne m'i lait dormir ne reposer.
s'ele m'ocit, mains avra a garder;
je ne m'en sai vengier fors au plorer;
car cui Amors destruit et desirete,
ne s'en set ou clamer.

*I owe her a thousand sighs and she demands them all. Love, the traitor, does not allow her to let me sleep and rest. If she kills me, Love will have less captives to look after. I can only avenge myself with tears, for the one that Love ruins and strips of his resources does not know who to turn to.*

(Translation by Norman Clare)

| LISTENING SUMMARY | |
|---|---|
| Timbre: | Solo countertenor. Solo alto recorder plays the first phrase before each stanza. Lute, bass rebec, and harp provide a simple accompaniment |
| Melody: | Largely conjunct, very lyrical |
| Rhythm: | Compound duple meter, moderate tempo |
| Harmony: | Tonal center of C. Transposed Mixolydian and major modes suggested |
| Texture: | Originally a monophonic song. In this recording, the texture is homophonic, consisting of a prominent melody with a simple accompaniment |
| Form: | Strophic. Each strophe is introduced by the recorder playing the first phrase, and each strophe consists of five phrases |

## The Growth of Polyphony

### Organum

The earliest polyphony in church music seems to have been created by adding a second voice part to chant. As long as it did not obscure the meaning of the text, polyphony—or *organum*, as it was initially called—was welcomed by the Church. In the earliest, which dates from the ninth century, a second voice duplicates the plainchant melody, running parallel to it, generally three or four notes above or below.

### Tenor and duplum

At the French monastery of Saint Martial of Limoges, a leading center for all the arts in the late eleventh and early twelfth centuries, musicians sometimes extended the notes of the original chant to great length. This line was often called the *tenor*, from the Latin *tenere* ("to hold"). The added line, now called the *duplum*, became the more prominent line, because of its melismatic use of many notes against each lengthy note of the tenor. The chant thus came to serve as a foundation for a newly composed, independent melody.

### Léonin

But it was in Paris in the late twelfth century that organum reached its peak of development. The great Léonin was choirmaster at Notre Dame when the new cathedral was being built. His music, called the *Magnus liber organi* ("Large Book of Organum"), is made up of two-voiced organa for the Propers of many Masses. "Viderunt omnes" from the collection is a clear, typical example.

### Léonin: "Viderunt omnes" from Magnus liber organi

"Viderunt omnes" and the other organa in the *Magnus liber organi* make use of two different styles of two-part polyphony—*organum purum* and *discantus*. Each work begins in organum purum style. The notes of the tenor line are extremely long, changing only when the duplum—a florid melody of many notes—changes syllables. The tenor notes thus set up a strong foundation for the melismatic upper part. Eventually, however, the music changes to discantus style; the tenor notes begin to move in quicker rhythms, similar to those in the duplum. Léonin and other composers at Notre Dame were the first to specify rhythms and give a duration for each note. Rhythmic modes,

Paris was an important musical center from the middle of the 12th to the early 14th century. The Notre Dame School of Music comprised composers such as Léonin and Pérotin, both choirmasters at the cathedral, which was being built during this period. (BBC Hulton Picture Library)

analogous to the melodic/harmonic modes, were established to organize metrical patterns.

## Léonin: "Viderunt omnes"

Léonin's "Viderunt omnes" has two voice parts, the upper sung by a solo countertenor and the lower by several male voices. The lower line is borrowed from the Gregorian chant "Viderunt omnes," the Gradual for the Mass for Christmas Day, which is presented in longer note values. The music clearly shows both the organum purum and the discantus styles. The first section of the chant moves from the initial use of organum purum style to discantus, as is shown in the example below. Finally, at the very end, monophonic chant is heard.

Text:

| | |
|---|---|
| Viderunt omnes fines terrae salutare Dei nostri. | *All the ends of the earth have seen the salvation of our God.* |
| Jubilate Deo omnis terra. | *Rejoice in God all lands.* |

**LISTENING SUMMARY**

| | |
|---|---|
| Timbre: | solo male voice sings top line; several male voices sing bottom line |
| Melody: | bottom line borrowed from Gregorian chant and presented in sustained then slowly moving notes; new top line much more active |
| Rhythm: | compound duple meter with triple rhythms |
| Texture: | two parts, changing to monophonic near the end |
| Form: | first section changes from organum purum style to discantus style for the beginning of the word "omnes"; organum purum style returns to complete the setting of the word "omnes"; monophonic chant returns with the text "fines terrae …" |

**Pérotin**
While Léonin had preferred the organum style, his successor Pérotin made more use of discantus style. Although Pérotin did write elaborate three- and four-part organa of his own, as well as *conductus*

(serious or sacred songs not based on Gregorian chant), he devoted much of his time to revising and shortening Léonin's works. He pruned long organum passages and often replaced them with new passages written in discantus style.

Pérotin's successors continued to stress the use of discantus. They also followed Pérotin in writing music with three and four parts. New words were sometimes added in the upper voices, often as a commentary on the original words retained in the tenor line. The complexity and richness of sound were gradually increasing. Out of this process, a new type of composition was born. This was the *motet*, from the French *mot*, or "word." The motet was based on a tenor that was usually borrowed from chant. Over time, the voices in the motet became more and more independent. Each had its own melody, its own words, and at times its own rhythmic mode.

As the thirteenth century closed, the motet became freer in structure. Tenor and upper lines were borrowed from secular songs as well as from plainchant. Two French secular texts often appeared together over a tenor from plainchant. In general, music was being written and performed out of more aesthetic considerations and was less directly tied to worship.

The evolution of the motet reveals in miniature what was happening to society in general. With the growth of cities and the increasing power of regional and national secular leaders, Church musicians began to look beyond the confines of the Church. They began to think that they might find something of value in the temporal world.

**Motet** *(margin note)*

## Music of the Fourteenth Century

In 1324, while the papacy was in its "Babylonian captivity" at Avignon, Pope John XXII issued a bull, or papal order, in which he expressed his concern over the growing elaboration of Church music. Things had gone so far, he said, that excitement was replacing devotion as the object of the singing. Worship was hindered rather than helped. Therefore he directed that, at least in the Divine Office and the Mass, modern decorations such as polyphony and secular melodies must be eliminated. Plainchant was the only proper music for the Church's worship.

But this proclamation went largely unheeded. The Church had lost a great deal of its earlier power. Amid such calamities as the Hundred Years' War, peasant uprisings, and the catastrophic outbreak of bubonic plague known as the Black Death, the divisions within the Church were increasing. Furthermore, the new style was too popular to be suppressed.

### France

Ars Nova
Vitry
Rhythmic
innovations

The term *ars nova* ("new art") was used by Philippe de Vitry (1290–1361) in the title of his treatise of c.1322, describing the new and profoundly different characteristics of style in music of the fourteenth century. Among them was an important development in rhythm. Until the late thirteenth century, almost all music was in triple meter, the

Medieval Instruments: This fourteenth-century Italian manuscript shows a number of the instruments popular in the late Medieval period. Perhaps the most interesting is the early organ in the center. The other instruments, clockwise from the upper left, are a viol, a psaltery, a mandola, clappers, trumpets, kettledrums, a shawm, a bagpipe, and a jingle drum. (Courtesy of the Biblioteca Nationale, Naples)

*tempus perfectum*, or "perfect time." Three was a number widely revered for mystical reasons, particularly its association with the Holy Trinity. Duple meter was viewed as imperfect. Vitry observed, however, that triple and duple had now become equally acceptable. Another rhythmic innovation of the time was *isorhythm*, the repetition of one rhythmic pattern throughout a work. The rhythm was sometimes combined with a repeated melodic pattern. In cases where the two elements were of different lengths, the result was a complex mixture of rhythm and melody.

The fourteenth century also saw a general increase in rhythmic complexity. Composers of motets began to change rhythms frequently. Musicians, following the directions given by time signatures, had to be ready to change from a pulse of two beats to a pulse of three while holding their own against the other lines, which were making similar shifts at different times.

Polyphonic settings of the Mass—the Ordinary rather than the Proper—also occupied composers in the fourteenth century. They made use of new as well as older styles. Kyries, Glorias, and other

# The Medieval Sense of Beauty

*Abraham's Hospitality and the Sacrifice of Isaac.* 6th-century wall mosaic, San Vitale, Ravenna.

***Early Medieval Art*** An emphasis on spirituality was found in all the arts of the early Medieval period, an impetus that began in the declining centuries of Roman civilization. While paganism had stressed the reality of physical existence in this world, the Judeo-Christian tradition thought of the world to come. It is remarkable how closely the history of early Christian art paralleled this changing concept of reality. The general and persistent artistic tendency was toward dematerialization and abstraction. In the glowing San Vitale wall mosaic, little sense of bodily weight or structure is felt beneath the conventionalized drapery. The drama of Abraham's sacrifice is contrasted with the world of simple absolutes and eternal order in which Christ is depicted in the apse of the church.

***Late Medieval Art*** By the end of the Medieval period, secularism, capitalism, and worldly pleasure began to replace the early emphasis on spirituality. Yet painting and sculpture, particularly in northern Europe, continued to be permeated by religious feeling, now increasingly personal, introspective and mystical. The miniature seen here in a fourteenth-century music manuscript displays the refined, mannered style that was so typical of the period. The scene is painted in a lovely decorative manner. Equal attention is paid to the figures and to the initial. The colors are bright and cheerful. There is a curious and typical late Medieval mixture here of fact and fantasy. There seems to have been no concern with relating the size of the figures to the space they occupy or to each other. A sense of religious mystery hidden beneath the surface of reality continues to be felt.

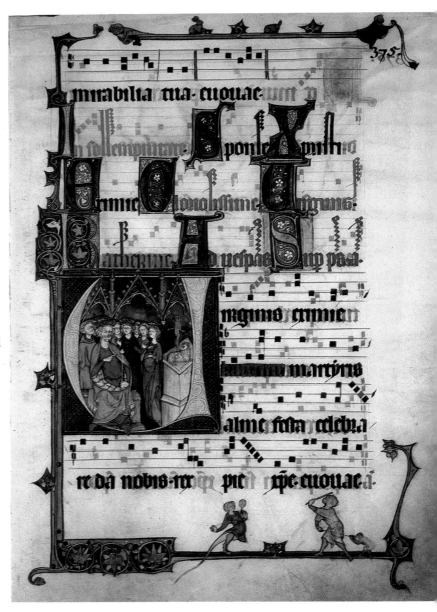

Page from the Beaupré Antiphonary. 14th century. Oxford, Ashmolean Museum.

# The Renaissance Sense of Beauty

***Individual Creativity*** For both composers and artists, the Renaissance brought a glorification of individual creativity. Geniuses such as Michelangelo restlessly drove themselves toward heroic, often unattainable goals. Two concepts central to much of Michelangelo's work are embodied in the statue *David:* titanic yet human energy driven by divine inspiration. The work is enormous in size, approximately eighteen feet high. The subject, sternly aware of the approaching enemy, face and muscles tense with defiance, represents not only the biblical David but also the ideal of freedom for the Italian city of Florence. Renaissance artist and historian Vasari compared the statue to ancient sculptures of gods and athletes, saying it had "stolen the thunder of all statues, whether modern or ancient, Greek or Latin."

Matthias Grünewald: *The Incarnation*, left panel of the Isenheim Altarpiece. c. 1510—15. Colmar, Musée Unterlinden (photo Giraudon).

***The Renaissance in the North*** In the painting and sculpture of northern Europe, Renaissance humanism was fused with theology. Grünewald's *Incarnation* makes use of many of the lessons of Italian art, but the vision remains essentially Medieval. Intense light fills the panel, and the colors are iridescent, almost unearthly. The possibilities of color and light as an expressive force are explored in the service of the presentation of the enduring truths of Christianity.

Michelangelo: *David*. 1501—4. Florence, Accademia (photo Scala).

**The Italian Renaissance**  In the Italian cities where the Renaissance began, great emphasis was placed on humanism—on human values and the ideals of Classical Greece and Rome. Raphael's *School of Athens* is probably the most complete and perfect pictorial statement of humanistic ideals achieved during the High Renaissance. All the compositional elements—the majestic architectural setting, the effortless sense of three-dimensional space, the massive yet active figures and their balanced symmetrical placement—achieve that quality of severe harmony ever since associated with the Renaissance.

Raphael: *School of Athens*. 1509–11. Stanza della Segnatura, Vatican, Rome.

parts of the Ordinary seem as a rule to have been written independently of one another. The earliest complete polyphonic Ordinary known to have been written by one composer is the *Messe de Nostre Dame* ("Mass of Our Lady") by Guillaume de Machaut (c. 1300–1377). Though sacred music formed only a small part of Machaut's output (and the work of his contemporaries), the *Messe de Nostre Dame* is one of the most widely known works of the fourteenth century.

Machaut

Machaut, a priest, poet, and civil servant, was also an important French composer. He was born in Champagne of a noble family. After ordination as a priest, he became secretary to King John of Bohemia and followed him on his military campaigns. At the same time, he also held honorary positions with churches at home in France. Throughout his life, Machaut maintained close connections with several royal families, writing poetry and music for them when he was able to do so. His secular music was generally written in one of four popular musical forms—*rondeau, virelai, ballade,* and *lai*—all based on poetic forms. In fourteenth-century France, music and poetry were so closely related that they were considered separate facets of the same lyric art. Many of Machaut's secular works were written as vocal solos to be accompanied by two or three instruments. Others were monophonic, possibly with improvised accompaniment.

Secular 14th-century French forms

### *Machaut:* "Douce dame jolie"

Virelai

The lovely *virelai* "Douce dame jolie" shows Machaut's monophonic vocal style to best advantage. The lyrical quality that is typical of many of his songs is clearly evident in this one.

## *Machaut:* "Douce dame jolie"

**LISTENING ANALYSIS**                                   SIDE 2, BAND 4

Originally written as a simple, monophonic song, "Douce dame jolie" is sung in this recording by a group of singers in unison. Instruments are added to enhance the timbre of the piece—vielle (fiddle) and soprano recorder to play parts of the melody, and lute to play repetitions of the tonal center throughout the performance. The melody is in the Dorian mode and includes a mixture of conjunct and disjunct motion, helping to give it a strong character. The meter is duple, and the syncopated rhythms are very engaging and instantly identifiable. The musical form of the virelai falls into an AbbaA pattern, with large letters indicating repetitions of music and text. The performance on this recording may be diagrammed as follows:

| Voices & Instruments | Instruments alone | Voices & Instruments |
|---|---|---|
| **A b b a A b b a** | **A** | **A b b a A b b a A** |

Section A

1. Dou - ce   da - me   jo - li - e,   pour
4. He - las!   et   je   men - di - e   d'es -
5. Dou - ce   da - me   jo - li - e,   pour

Dieu ne pen - ses mi - - e que nulle ait
pe - rance et____ d'a - i - - e; dont ma joie
Dieu ne pen - ses mi - - e que nulle ait

sig - nou - ri - e seur moy fors vous seu - le - ment.
est fe - ni - e, se pi - te ne vous en prent.
sig - nou - ri - e seur moy fors vous seu - le - ment.

Section B

2. Qu'a - des sans tri - che - ri - e____ chie - ri - e____ vous
3. Tous les jours de ma vi - e____ ser - vi - e____ sans

ay et hum - ble - ment vi - lein pen - se - ment.

(*Above*) Minnesingers playing transverse flute and fiddle. This early 14th-century miniature comes from the Manesse'sche Liederhandschrift, one of the most important surviving manuscripts of this type of music. (Universitätsbibliothek, Heidelberg)

**Text:**

A  Douce dame jolie,
   pour Dieu ne penses mie
   que nulle ait signourie
   seur moy fors vous seulement.

B  Qu'ades sans tricherie chierie
   vous ay et humblement
B  tous les jours de ma vie
   servie
   sans vilein pensement.

A  Helas! et je mendie
   d'esperance et d'aie;
   dont ma joie est fenie,
   se pite ne vous en prent.

A  Douce dame jolie, pour Dieu ne
   penses mie que nulle ait signourie
   seur moy fors vous seulement.

*Sweet lady of my delight, I pray you, never dream that anyone rules over me save only you.*

*For without deceit would I cherish you and humbly serve you all my life without evil thought.*

*But alas! Here I am, a beggar, pleading for hope and help; for my joy is all ended unless you have pity on me.*

*Sweet lady of my delight, I pray you, never dream that anyone rules over me save only you.*

**LISTENING SUMMARY**

Timbre:  solo male voice; recorder, vielle, drum, and finger cymbals not indicated in score
Rhythm:  duple meter with syncopation
Harmony: based on a Church mode
Texture: monophonic
Form:    virelai (ABBAA)

(*Right*) Guillaume de Machaut was probably the most prolific composer of the 14th century. This miniature portrait tells the story of his inspiration: Nature orders him to write new songs and offers the help of three of her children—Sense, Rhetoric and Music. (Bibliothèque nationale, Paris)

## Italy

During the fourteenth century, Italy was torn by numerous political and religious problems as well as plague. But Italian musicians reacted by making joyful, serenely sensuous music. In this age of Dante, Giotto, Petrarch, and Boccaccio, people seemed to regard art as a refuge of sanity in a world gone mad. Everyone, gifted amateurs as well as professionals, played and sang to make leisure hours more lovely. Three poetic-musical forms were especially popular: the *madrigal*, the *caccia*, and the *ballata*.

**14th-century Italian forms**

The *madrigal* was a poetic form with texts that involved love or the beauty of nature. Written for two or three voices, the upper voice(s) presented melodic material over the slow-moving lower voice. The *caccia* was a work in which two upper voices entered separately singing the same melody in *exact imitation* of each other—in the same way that rounds are sung today. These voices were heard over another, slow-moving lower voice. Texts included hunting calls, shouts, and birdcalls, all set to elaborate melodies.

**Exact imitation**

Toward the end of the fourteenth century, the *ballata*, similar to the French virelai, was also much heard in Italy. The works of Francesco Landini (1325–1397), the best-known Italian composer of the period, include several fine examples of the ballata. Though blinded by a smallpox attack in his youth, Landini achieved fame as a poet and a virtuoso on the portative organ, besides writing around 140 ballate and several other secular works.

**Landini**

An idealized depiction of Emperor Maximilian I (1459–1519) among his instrumentalists (note the harp, organ, drums, and virginal in the foreground.) An ardent humanist, Maximilian I became an enthusiastic patron of the arts, greatly enlarging his Vienna court orchestra and thus setting the pattern for secular, royal or noble, patronage of composers and orchestras for the next 300 years. (Österreichische Nationalbibliothek, Vienna)

# CHAPTER 7

# *Renaissance Music*

*LISTENING PREVIEW Polyphony became increasingly complex in the fifteenth and sixteenth centuries as composers sought new ways to combine several voices in a piece of music. At the same time, composers became more and more concerned about sensitive, expressive ways to set words to music. In Josquin's "Absalon, fili mi" (side 2, band 5), notice the careful use of imitation as each voice enters with essentially the same melody that opened the work. Describe the aspects of the musical sound that help reflect the sorrowful text in which David mourns the death of his son Absalom.*

## The Renaissance Period

The Renaissance marked a transition from a style of life that was predominantly religious in orientation to one much more secular. Life on earth, rather than the afterlife, became the focus of human endeavor in all spheres of achievement. No longer were the people of western Europe guided solely by a mystical acceptance of divine authority. Instead, they turned to reason and scientific inquiry. To learn, to measure, to understand the structure of reality was the passion of the Renaissance as education was gradually freed from the confines of the church and religious orthodoxy. The modern sciences of astronomy and anatomy began. Voyages such as those of Columbus, Vasco da Gama, and Magellan were launched to explore new oceans and new lands. New techniques and instruments for navigating and mapping were developed. Printing using movable type was invented. Artists concerned themselves with proportion and perspective. The age of anonymity was at an end. Individual creation, epitomized by the prophetic science and artistry of Leonardo da Vinci, was glorified. The philosophical basis of this creative climate came to

Humanism

be known as humanism.

The times were changing politically and economically as well. After the Hundred Years' War (1337–1453), the Church lost much of its grip on the people's purses and imaginations. Money and political power were now held by merchants, princes, and monarchs, as well as the Church.

The Renaissance came early to Italy, whose people, at home on the soil of the ancient Romans, set out to recapture the "golden age" of classical antiquity. The rulers of Italian city-states, such as the Medici of Florence and the Sforzas of Milan, and the powerful dukes of

Burgundy sought to show off their wealth by building splendid palaces that reflected the balance and proportion of the classical style. Renaissance princes gathered huge entourages, including composers and performing musicians, to attend them at home and to travel with them wherever they went.

New musical styles that we associate with the Renaissance evolved in the early fifteenth century in the works of Burgundian and English composers. Even though musical styles continued to change, music of much of the fifteenth and all of the sixteenth centuries is generally thought of as the Renaissance in music.

## General Characteristics of Renaissance Music

Music was skillfully woven into nearly every aspect of court life. Private religious services, meals, processions through the city, leavetakings, and homecomings all called for accompaniment by elegantly dressed performers. Special occasions, such as weddings, jousts, hunts, masquerades, funerals, and wars, required larger forces. All the trumpeters in the area would hurry to welcome a visiting prince or noble bride.

Music was thus an important part of daily life in the Renaissance. Instrumental and vocal music was widely heard, but vocal music is much more important in the notated music that has survived. Melodies, generally very singable ones, were often used in counterpoint. Four different voice parts became standard, and the use of imitation became increasingly popular. Harmony was still based on the Church modes, which were used with increasing ingenuity and freedom. While some of the types and forms of music used in the Middle Ages continued in use, a number of new ones evolved as composers sought new ways to express themselves.

## New Developments in Polyphony

As we have seen, Medieval polyphony was most often performed by soloists, each singing a different vocal part. The number of parts was generally two or three, and they were confined to a fairly narrow range of pitches. Within this range, the melodic lines often crossed. Thus it was necessary to make the different parts contrast as much as possible. The parts were given contrasting melodies, rhythms, and sometimes texts, so that the listener could tell them apart. Voices or instruments were often chosen for their contrasting timbres, again to make it easier to hear the different parts.

**Wide use of four-part polyphony**

In the early fifteenth century, however, each part of a polyphonic work came to be sung by more than one voice. This added greater depth to the sound of polyphony. By the mid-Renaissance, four parts had become the normal number for a polyphonic work, resulting in very full-sounding harmonies. With these changes came an expansion of the overall range of the vocal parts. Melodic lines crossed much less often, as each part tended to have its own range. The same thematic material was frequently assigned to all the voices, so that a piece was more like a conversation among equals.

Chapel Musicians: Singers and instrumentalists perform together from a choir book. The music might have been a motet or a Mass movement. (New York Public Library Picture Collection)

Plainchant continued to be used as a basis for new compositions. A phrase of chant might still be used in the tenor, with the note values lengthened. However, the phrase might appear in the top voice as well or even wander from line to line, taking on new rhythmic identities in each line.

The use of *imitation* became very prominent. A theme would be stated first by one voice, then repeated, either exactly or with modification, by the other voices. Even when it underwent numerous changes, the theme acted to unify the piece.

The attitude toward dissonance changed greatly during the Renaissance. Much of the dissonance in Medieval music resulted from the fact that compositions were often built up in layers. A composer began with one complete line, usually a tenor taken from plainchant, and wrote another line, a duplum, to go with it. Later the same composer or someone else would add a third line, relating it to the tenor according to certain rules, but paying little attention to the duplum. This process caused some extraordinary dissonance.

**Careful use of dissonance**

In the fifteenth century, however, composers began to treat dissonance more systematically. Renaissance composers generally worked out all the lines at once and thus had greater control over all of them. For most composers, harmonies grew richer than those of the Medieval period, which were mostly byproducts of two or more melodic lines sounded simultaneously. At the same time, consonance became the norm. Dissonance became a special effect, to be used before cadences, at dramatic moments, and, in general, on weak beats. It could occur on strong beats, but only with careful preparation followed by resolution. Thus, it became both less common and more important.

The relationship of music to words changed greatly during the Renaissance. In the Middle Ages, texts were generally fitted to music with little or no regard for the musical possibilities implied by the words. In contrast, a Renaissance composer was usually very alert to the general spirit and mood of a text, choosing a mode, melodic materials, and rhythms as appropriate to the text as possible. Words or phrases were often sensitively developed with *text painting*. The phrase "rise up," for example, might be set to an ascending scale. The word "death" might be sung to a dissonant chord.

*Text painting*

This new concern for words also helped free rhythm from the repeated designs of the Middle Ages. The trend seems to have begun with the music of the fourteenth century. During the next hundred years, rhythm became more varied and spontaneous. Duple meter became very popular, and duple and triple meters could be combined in one piece. Syncopation and other complex rhythms were freely mixed with simpler patterns.

## Religious Music

In the fifteenth century, the motet changed gradually from a work that had both secular and religious aspects to one that was mainly religious. The Mass and the motet, sharing a common musical style, were the most important types of religious music during the Renaissance. With the Reformation in the early sixteenth century, hymns became very important in the newly Protestant areas of Europe.

## Religious Music of the Early and Mid-Renaissance

Dufay

The lives of Renaissance composers reflected both the new glorification of the individual and the large variety of activities open to the talented. The career of Guillaume Dufay is in a number of ways typical. Born about 1400, Dufay began as a choirboy at the cathedral of Cambrai in northern France. As a young man, he appears to have gone to Italy to spend a few years at the Malatesta court; a number of his early works are dedicated to the family. In 1428 he joined the papal choir, where he stayed for a number of years. Afterward, his travels are difficult to trace, but he spent some time in Florence and Savoy. He died at Cambrai in 1474, widely respected and loved.

Dufay wrote a number of polyphonic Ordinaries of the Mass, each set as a complete cycle. In his Masses, he generally used plainchant for the tenor, writing two lines of polyphony above it and one line below it. The two lower lines, with longer note values, were probably played on instruments. Dufay chose melodies from a number of sources. He was among the first to use secular tunes in his Masses, borrowing melodies from *chansons*—secular songs with French texts.

Ockeghem

The leading composer of the next generation was Johannes Ockeghem (c. 1410–c. 1497). He was trained at the cathedral of Antwerp

# Comparison of Medieval and Renaissance Music

| Elements | Medieval Music<br>6th – early<br>15th centuries | Renaissance Music<br>15th – 16th centuries |
|---|---|---|
| Melody | Generally conjunct and singable<br>Narrow range | Generally conjunct and singable<br>Wider range |
| Rhythm | Rhythm of chant free or in recurring patterns<br>Triple time in 13th century with duple time accepted in 14th century<br>Isorhythm and other complex rhythms in 14th century | Metric patterns not emphasized in religious vocal music but clear in many secular works<br>Generally less complex than in 14th century<br>Bar lines devised in 16th century |
| Harmony | Usually based on 8 Church modes<br>Freer use of dissonance | Church modes expanded to 12<br>Careful use of dissonance |
| Texture | Monophony very important<br>Polyphony for 2, 3 and 4 voices by end of period | Polyphonic music for 4 voices standard; 5 or more voices often used in 16th century<br>Wide use of imitation<br>Some homophony |
| Timbre | Notated music mainly vocal<br>Small choirs sang monophonic chants<br>Polyphonic music generally sung by soloists<br>Instrumental music quite important | Notated vocal music still most important<br>Small choirs sang polyphonic religious music<br>Secular music for soloists and small ensembles<br>More music written specifically for instruments |
| Important Forms | Free vocal chant forms<br>Free and fixed poetic forms for secular music<br>Strophic songs and hymns | Fixed poetic forms gradually replaced by freer, imitative forms<br>Strophic songs and hymns |
| Important Types of Compositions | Plainchant settings of parts of the Mass<br>Motet (secular and religious)<br>Secular songs<br>Instrumental dances | Polyphonic settings of parts of the Mass<br>Motet (mainly religious)<br>Secular songs<br>Instrumental dances<br>Instrumental pieces such as the ricercar |

and began his career in the service of Duke Charles I of Bourbon. Some time later he entered the service of Charles VII of France. He seems to have worked at the French court all his life, although he is known to have traveled from time to time. He had a splendid singing voice and was admired for being a very good, pious man. His music is characterized by a firm rhythmic energy and long phrases that overlap one another, frequently avoiding cadences. He wrote at least thirteen Masses, one of which is the earliest existing polyphonic Requiem Mass. In his Masses, he made prominent use of borrowed thematic material and imitation, both canonic—that is, exact—and free. His motets and chansons also show his excellent mastery of all compositional techniques of his time.

Josquin

The works of Josquin des Prez (c. 1440–1521) represent the height of musical achievement in the mid-Renaissance. Josquin may have been a student of Ockeghem. His adult career took him all over Europe. In Italy, he served at the Sforza court in Milan and with the Papal choir in Rome. In France, he had contact with Louis XII. He returned to Italy and was chapel master at Ferrara for a number of years. He spent his last years as a canon at the collegiate church of Condé. Josquin's early works show a mastery of compositional techniques. During his years in Italy, his compositions became more facile and ·eloquent, and he wrote Masses, motets, and chansons that represent a high point of each genre. He used imitation to unify his music more thoroughly than anyone had before, passing material from voice to voice so that each one had an equal part in the musical process.

The Masses of Josquin are works of beautifully controlled counterpoint which were created with a variety of techniques that incorporated borrowed melodic material from plainchant and other sources. His motets are based on a wide variety of religious texts, and the expressive, often dramatic phrases seem to have given him inspiration for wonderful creativity in all aspects of his music.

Portrait of Josquin des Prez, published in 1611. (British Library)

### Josquin: "Absalon, fili mi"

The motet "Absalon, fili mi" provides a lovely example of the manner in which Josquin wrote an appropriate musical setting for an expressive text. The words are David's statement from the Old Testament as he mourns the death of his son Absalom. The text is divided into three phrases by Josquin, and each is set in turn to four-voice counterpoint that is sometimes imitative and at other times free. The four parts are tenor, two baritone, and bass, and thus the overall tessitura of the motet is very low.

## Josquin: "Absalon, fili mi"

**LISTENING ANALYSIS**

SIDE 2, BAND 5

The first line of the text "Absalon, fili mi, fili mi, Absalon" ("Absalom, my son, My son, Absalom") is set to a phrase in imitation, as each voice in turn, starting with the top voice and proceeding down to the bass, sings the same phrase but at a pitch a fifth or fourth lower each time; the entries of the voices are one or two measures apart. Such an imitative process, called a "point of imitation," occurs several times in the motet. (The recording is a semitone lower than the music example given here.)

After the first point of imitation, the text is repeated several times, but usually with freer imitation or independent melodic lines. The second and third lines of text are set similarly to imitative and nonimitative contrapuntal lines. Beginnings and endings of phrases often overlap among the voices, and thus the effect of a long, uninterrupted contrapuntal flow of music is created.

The third and last phrase of text, "Non vivam ultra, sed descendam in infernum plorans" ("Let me live no longer but descend to hell, weeping"), is striking for its unexpected sonorities within the Mixolydian mode, and for the text painting with an imitated, descending line on the word "Descendam." The final chord without a third is typical of Josquin's works and suggests an empty feeling that is appropriate to the word "plorans" ("weeping").

Text:

| | |
|---|---|
| Absalon, fili mi, fili mi, Absalon! | *Absalom, my son, my son, Absalom!* |
| Quis det ut moriar pro te, fili mi Absalon. | *Oh that I had died for you, my son Absalom.* |
| Non vivam ultra, sed descendam in infernum plorans. | *Let me live no longer but descend to hell, weeping.* |

> **LISTENING SUMMARY**
>
> Timbre: small four-part choir, unaccompanied
> Rhythm: duple meter
> Harmony: based on Church mode
> Texture: contrapuntal and imitative
> Form: free, evolving from points of imitation and nonimitative counterpoint

## Music of the Reformation

The Reformation, which aroused sixteenth-century Europe to such bloody strife, was an attempt to make liturgical and political changes and to end corruption in the Catholic Church. Leaders of the Reformation proclaimed that each person had a right to confront God directly in an essentially private act of worship. These same leaders believed that Latin should no longer be the sole language of worship. Consequently, Protestants in each country developed their own forms of church service making use of the language of the country.

*Luther*

Martin Luther (1483–1546), one of the key figures at the beginning of the religious revolution, had a great love of music. He was very familiar with the music of the Catholic Church. He also sang, played instruments, and admired Josquin des Prez above all other composers. Luther knew the power of music to sway souls. To him music was an invaluable part of Christian education and of daily life, for, he said, "The devil hates and fears music .. and flees [it] as much as he does theology." In keeping with his belief that worship is an individual's act, Luther wanted his congregations to have music they could sing themselves. Thus the hymn—or *chorale*—became very important in his services. Chorales were monophonic hymns at first, though they later came to be harmonized and used as the basis of other new compositions, much as earlier composers had used chant.

*Chorale*

Luther himself may have written some of the most famous chorales of the Lutheran church. Among the most famous is the adaptation of Psalm 46, "Ein' feste Burg ist unser Gott" ("A Mighty Fortress Is Our God"). Music for the Lutheran services was also adapted from Latin chants, which were translated into German and arranged for the congregation to sing.

Other Protestant leaders were less enthusiastic about the use of music in church services. John Calvin (1509–1564), for instance, subscribed to Saint Augustine's suspicion that music was not altogether wholesome. He barred polyphony and instruments from his church services, as had the early Catholic Church. Congregational singing of psalms was, however, greatly encouraged.

*Council of Trent*

With the so-called Counter-Reformation the Catholic Church, in turn, initiated a number of reforms designed to reawaken religious fervor and purify Rome's spiritual leadership. At the Council of Trent (1545–1563), some attempts were made to control polyphony. One faction wanted such "scandalous noise" banned from the services on the grounds that it obscured the sacred texts. But princely music patrons objected. Special performances of polyphonic masterpieces finally persuaded the council that polyphony should remain as long as the text was clearly presented.

## Religious Music of the Late Renaissance

### Lassus

The new awareness of words found among Renaissance composers had a major effect upon the motet and the Mass as well as upon secular music. The motets of Roland de Lassus, known also by the Italian form of his name, Orlando di Lasso (1532–1594), are almost a compendium of expressive devices used to display words with great feeling. Lassus also wrote Masses and a number of secular songs. Flemish by birth, he was one of the most popular composers of the age, and his career was active and international in scope. At an early age he entered the service of Ferdinando Gonzaga with whom he traveled to Italy and Sicily. He spent his youth in various Italian households. After a brief stay in Antwerp, he went in 1556 to the court of Albert V of Bavaria, in Munich. A few years later, he was made *Kapellmeister* (chapel master), and he stayed there for the rest of his life. He became the most celebrated musician of his day.

### Palestrina

Lassus' great contemporary Giovanni Pierluigi da Palestrina (c. 1524–1594) was one of the most skilled Italian composers of the later sixteenth century. Most of his music was written for the Catholic Church, and expresses many of the ideals of the Council of Trent. Palestrina spent his career in the churches of Rome. From 1571 until his death, he led the Cappella Giulia of Saint Peter's Basilica and bore the honorary title of *maestro compositore* (master composer) of the papal chapel. He wrote over 100 Masses and 375 motets, which include many models of beautifully conceived counterpoint. He handled dissonance carefully, avoided chromaticism, and sculpted his lines so that rising and descending curves balanced each other. His music represents a classical peak of late Renaissance style. It is essentially conservative, reflecting the ideas of the Counter-Reformation in its purity, abstraction, and clear presentation of sacred texts.

### Palestrina: "Kyrie" of the *Missa brevis*

The "Kyrie" of Palestrina's *Missa brevis* ("Short Mass") provides a good example of many aspects of his music. It is in three sections that correspond to the three phrases of text.

## Palestrina: "Kyrie"

**LISTENING ANALYSIS**                                   SIDE 2, BAND 6

At the beginning, a melody of strong character is presented in imitation by all voices, that is, at a "point of imitation."

The meter is duple, although the rhythmic flow does not accentuate duple patterns. Throughout the first section, as well as in the succeeding two sections, one can hear the overlapping of phrases, a fluid flow of rhythm, and a sublime sense of balance and proportion that are characteristic of much of Palestrina's music. The first section closes with a strong, clear cadence.

The second section, Christe eleison, is based on different melodic material. The third section introduces more new melodic material, but in a triple meter.

The overall form of the three sections may then be diagrammed as ABC. The entire movement conveys a sense of great serenity.

Text:

| | | |
|---|---|---|
| A | Kyrie eleison; Kyrie eleison; Kyrie eleison. | *Lord, have mercy; Lord have mercy; Lord, have mercy.* |
| B | Christe eleison; Christe eleison; Christe eleison. | *Christ, have mercy; Christ, have mercy; Christ, have mercy.* |
| C | Kyrie eleison; Kyrie eleison; Kyrie eleison. | *Lord, have mercy; Lord, have mercy; Lord, have mercy.* |

Opening Theme in Four-Part Imitation

**LISTENING SUMMARY**

Timbre:  small four-part choir, unaccompanied
Rhythm:  duple meter in the first two sections; triple meter in the last section
Harmony:  based on a Church mode
Texture:  contrapuntal and imitative
Form:  ABC; each section is based on different melodic material

**The Venetian School**

Although Palestrina's Rome was a major center for composers of music for the Catholic Church in the years after the Reformation, other areas developed styles of their own. Venice, in particular, developed a style that reflected the city's importance as a center of trade and culture, and its love of ceremony, grandeur, and colorful display. The Venetian style of music, which had its origins in the music written for services at Saint Mark's Basilica (San Marco), used groups of singers and instruments. This was a radical departure from Counter-Reformation theory and Roman practice, which used the more austere unaccompanied style. In Venice high, middle, and low voices, strings and wind instruments were all used together to create contrasting masses of sound. St. Mark's could accommodate two widely separated choirs, each with an accompanying instrumental ensemble. This encouraged the use of *antiphony*—music in which two or more performing groups alternated with each other in one

**The Gabrielis**

work. This style was the specialty of the Gabrielis, Andrea (c. 1520–1586) and his nephew Giovanni (c. 1557–1612). By the end of the century, similar styles were adopted in other European courts and cathedrals where the facilities were large enough.

**Byrd**

The English counterpart of Lassus and Palestrina was William Byrd (1543–1623). He wrote easily in any style he chose. He was somewhat conservative by nature, and primarily a composer of church music. Although a devout Catholic, he was loyal politically to the Protestant queen, Elizabeth I (who in 1575 granted him a monopoly for music printing in England, to be shared with his teacher Thomas Tallis, c. 1505–1585). He thus wrote church music in both English and Latin. His English services are rich in texture and rhythmic play. Some are quite long and elaborate, as if to indulge the queen's fondness for pageantry. His three Latin Masses are brief but superbly constructed, with long lines unwinding over a subtle but powerful pulse.

# Secular Music

**Music as entertainment**

During the late fifteenth century, music-making occupied much of the same time and energy that we today spend with radio, television, films, newspapers, and magazines. People in the upper and middle classes were expected to develop a considerable amount of musical skill. Music helped fulfill their need to do something well, to communicate, and to express themselves. After dinner a family and their guests would tune their instruments, get out part books, and read through the latest madrigals or chansons.

**Music printing**

The art of printing music from type both encouraged and chronicled this state of affairs. It began in 1501 when Ottaviano dei Petrucci (1466–1539) of Venice issued the *Odhecaton* ("Hundred Songs"), the first of his almost sixty books of music. His books were exquisite, but his printing technique was complicated and expensive. Over the years, printing methods improved. Soon publishers were supplying not only editions for churches and private collectors, but also part books and anthologies for the growing middle class.

At first the demand was mostly for vocal music. Secular forms evolved rapidly with the new excitement over music's poetic expres-

# PARTHENIA

## or

## THE MAYDENHEAD

of the first musicke that

ever was printed for the VIRGINALLS.

## COMPOSED

By three famous Masters: William Byrd, Dr: John Bull, & Orlando Gibbons,

Gentilmen of his Ma:ties most Illustrious Chappell.

Dedicated to all the Masters and Louers of Musick

Ingrauen

by William Hole.

for

DORETHIE EUANS.

Cum

Priuilegio.

siveness. In the sixteenth century, during the reign of the French King Francis I, there was a fruitful intermixture of French and Italian music. French poets were turning to a simpler, more colloquial verse form, and a new style of French chanson evolved in the sixteenth century. The new chansons were shaped by the stanzas and rhyme schemes of the poems on which they were based. The chansons were usually strophic in form and homophonic in texture, with some use of imitative counterpoint.

**Italy**

Italian music came to greater prominence in the sixteenth century. Two trends—one literary and the other musical—culminated in the sixteenth-century Italian madrigal. The *frottola*—a chordal, syllabic, part song—was gradually supplanted by the madrigal, which had nothing in common with the fourteenth-century pieces of the same name. In their earliest form, the sixteenth-century madrigals were, like the chansons of the same period, shaped by the stanzas and rhymes of the poems on which they were based. Later composers, however, rejected this reliance on poetic form and used other creative devices to shape their madrigals.

16th-century Italian madrigal

By the middle of the sixteenth century, madrigals were fast becoming the most popular secular music in Italy. They were generally written for five voices, all sharing equally in the work. The texts usually concerned love—intense, erotic, and painfully ecstatic—and great use was made of text painting.

Marenzio and Gesualdo

The madrigals of Luca Marenzio (1553–1599) and Carlo Gesualdo (1560–1613) represent a high point of the genre in the late sixteenth century. Their works are highly expressive because of their effective use of text painting and harmonic innovation. Gesualdo, an Italian prince, was perhaps the most unorthodox of Renaissance composers, juxtaposing chords that seemed completely unrelated to each other. His madrigals possess power and a strange beauty, and often make dramatic use of chromaticism. His life, too, had highly unorthodox moments: he assassinated his first wife and her lover.

Monteverdi

The madrigals of Claudio Monteverdi (1567–1643) both epitomize the genre and point beyond it. He also wrote some of the first operas. Monteverdi's music as a whole forms a transition from the Renaissance to the early Baroque styles of music. Since his operas belong to his later style, those works will be discussed in Chapter 9. Even in his early books of madrigals, which are in the conventional style, his dramatic flair is evident.

*Title page of Parthenia (1612/13), the first collection of keyboard music published in England; it includes works by William Byrd. (British Library)*

### *Monteverdi:* "Si ch'io vorrei morire"

Monteverdi's madrigal "Si ch'io vorrei morire". ("Yes, I would like to die"), from the fourth of his eight books of madrigals, reflects his skill in setting an impassioned love text. Each phrase is set uniquely so as to match each thought with the appropriate music.

**Monteverdi: "Si ch'io vorrei morire"**

**LISTENING ANALYSIS**

Text painting can be found in the opening phrase, which speaks of death ("morire") in descending melodic lines:

Opening Phrases

The homophonic, five-voice texture is typical of many Italian madrigals of the period, and presages the early Baroque style. As each phrase of text is presented it is with new musical material, often homophonic in texture, but sometimes contrapuntal and imitative. More text painting occurs later in the madrigal when the rising pitches with "Ahi car'e dolce lingua" ("Ah, dear, sweet tongue") aptly underscore the intensity of that line of text. The first setting of "deh stringetemi fin chi'o venga meno" ("press me, crush me, make me nothing") fittingly descends from a high pitch level to a low, quiet one. The madrigal includes a strong sense of drama with contrast of high and low pitches, and of chordal and contrapuntal writing. At the end, the first phrase of text and music returns and gives a strong sense of unity to the madrigal after the rather free structure of the previous phrases.

Text:

| | |
|---|---|
| Si ch'io vorrei morire | *Yes, I would like to die,* |
| hora ch'io bacio amore | *now that, at last, O Love,* |
| la bella bocca del mio amato core. | *I kiss the lovely mouth of her whom my heart desires.* |
| | |
| Ahi car'e dolce lingua | *Ah, dear, sweet tongue,* |
| datemi tant' humore | *give me such humors of thine* |
| che di dolcezz' in questo sen m'estingua. | *that on this breast I may perish for very sweetness and cease to be.* |
| | |
| Ahi vita mia, a questo bianco seno | *Life of my life, against thy white breast* |
| deh stringetemi fin ch'io venga meno. | *press me, crush me, make me nothing.* |
| Ahi bocca, ahi baci, ahi lingua torn' a dire | *Ah, mouth—ah, kisses—ah, tongue, come back to me that I may say,* |
| si ch'io vorrei morire. | *"Yes, I would like to die."* |

**LISTENING SUMMARY**

Timbre:   five-part, mixed, vocal ensemble, unaccompanied
Rhythm:   basically duple meter but quite free
Harmony: based on a Church mode
Texture:  homophonic and contrapuntal; some use of imitation
Form:      free, with repetition of first phrase at end

## The Evolution of the Secular Song

To a large extent the secular song offers a means of gauging the temper of an era. It will become popular if it offers something meaningful to the people of the period.

Listen to the secular songs of four different periods – either those listed below from the record set that accompanies the text, or others that are available.

| | | |
|---|---|---|
| **Medieval:** | Le Chatelain's "Le Noviaus Tens" | **Side 2, Band 2** |
| **Renaissance:** | Monteverdi's "Si ch'io vorrei morire" | **Side 2, Band 7** |
| **Romantic:** | Schubert's "Das Wandern" | **Side 7, Band 3** |
| **Modern:** | Beatles – any selection | |

What specific musical qualities make it possible to identify the first two selections as Medieval and Renaissance? What musical qualities establish the latter two selections as more recent works?

In what ways can each of the four selections be seen as a reflection of the social and historical setting in which they were created?

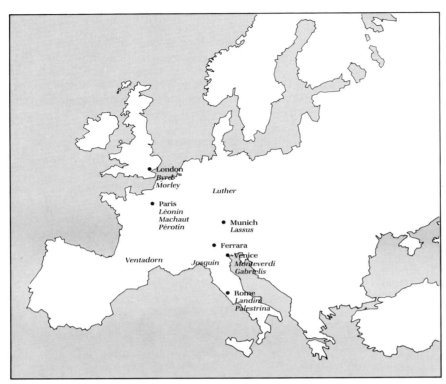

London
Byrd
Morley

Luther

Paris
Léonin
Machaut
Pérotin

Munich
Lassus

Ferrara

Venice
Monteverdi
Gabrielis

Ventadorn

Josquin

Rome
Landini
Palestrina

Major Medieval
and Renaissance
composers

Eventually, Monteverdi's experiments carried him away from madrigals written in the Renaissance style to madrigals for one or two voices with instrumental accompaniment.

## England

**English madrigal**

As the madrigal was beginning to give way to different forms in Italy, it reached a new peak in England. Both music and literature were included in the vogue for things Italian during the reign of Elizabeth I. Italian madrigals began to circulate among the gentry about 1560. Singing madrigals became enormously popular, and English composers began to write their own. William Byrd and Thomas Morley (1557–1602) were among the most popular composers of English madrigals.

**Morley**

The English were influenced by Italian styles but found in them a way to honor their own language. During Elizabeth's reign, English poetry and music flourished side by side. William Shakespeare (1564–1616) was the supreme poetic and dramatic figure of the time. Poems used as madrigal texts express a wide range of moods, from pastoral gaiety and bawdy mirth, through the sorrow of unrequited love, to despair and the longing for death. The words are illustrated through the use of every contrapuntal, chordal, rhythmic, and harmonic device then available.

**Ballett**

Other related forms were also developed. One was the *ballett*, a rhythmically regular composition, simpler than the madrigal and usually homophonic. Most balletts can easily be recognized by their "fa-la-la" refrains. Morley wrote a number of balletts, including "Now Is the Month of Maying."

*Morley:* "Now Is the Month of Maying"
Morley's ballett is written for five voice parts in typical chordal style.
The text refers to many light-hearted aspects of spring.

**Morley: "Now Is the Month of Maying"**

**LISTENING ANALYSIS**                                            SIDE 2, BAND 8

The music for each of the three stanzas is the same, making the piece strophic
in form. The opening melodic phrase is in the highest voice part and is
harmonized by the other voices. The melody moves mostly by step and reveals
the sprightly nature of the entire piece. It is followed by a fa-la-la phrase.

First a Section

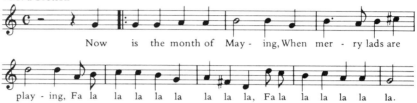

This opening *a* section of music and text is then repeated. Then a *b* section is
heard, with a new melody and a closing fa-la-la phrase. It is then repeated. The
stanzas are thus in aabb form, and the following overall musical form of the
ballett results:

| I | II | III |
|------|------|------|
| aabb | aabb | aabb |

Text:

I   a   Now is the month of Maying,
       When merry lads are playing,
       Fa-la-la . . .
    b   Each with his bonny lass
       Upon the greeny grass,
       Fa-la-la. . .

II   a   The spring, clad all in gladness,
       Doth laugh at winter's sadness,
       Fa-la-la . . .
    b   And to the bagpipes' sound
       The nymphs tread out their ground.
       Fa-la-la . . .

III   a   Fie then, why sit we musing,
       Youth's sweet delight refusing?
       Fa-la-la . . .
    b   Say, dainty nymphs, and speak,
       Shall we play barley-break?
       Fa-la-la . . .

**LISTENING SUMMARY**

Timbre:   five-part, mixed, vocal ensemble, unaccompanied
Rhythm:   duple meter
Harmony: major mode
Texture:   homophonic
Form:     strophic, with each stanza in aabb form

Ayres      Solo songs or *ayres* with lute accompaniment were also fashionable
in England. The *lute,* an early string instrument, was rather widely

known and used in the sixteenth century. Generally it was used, not only to support the singing voice, but as an equal partner with the voice. Lute songs were often very emotional, and in some the text was in a declamatory style. Some ayres by John Dowland (1562–1626) might appear morbid if they were not so beautiful. His famous "Lachrymae" ("Flow, My Tears") opens with a four-note descending motive associated with death.

*Dowland*

# Instruments and Instrumental Music

*Consort*

Renaissance instruments were classified as *haut* (loud) and *bas* (soft), and were grouped in families, or *consorts*. Flutes were often used, both in the transverse and recorder forms. The recorders came in several sizes from the tiny *sopranino* to the giant *contrabass*, which an adult had to play standing up. Other wind instruments included the *cornetto, shawm, trumpet*, and *sackbut*.

String instruments used were *viols, lutes, guitars*, and other instruments of similar form. *Drums, bells*, and *cymbals* of different sizes added percussive color. A polyphonic piece could be played either by instruments of the same consort—just recorders or just viols, for example—or a piece could be played by a *broken consort*—a mixture of recorders, viols, lutes, or other instruments.

*Pavane and galliard*

Dance music was very important for instruments. A favorite dance of the period was the *pavane*. A slow, stately processional dance in duple meter, it was generally paired with the *galliard*, a quick, leaping dance in triple meter. Dancing the galliard called for great skill. Musically, the pavane and the galliard were often rhythmic variations of the same tune.

Many early instrumental works were simply transcriptions of vocal music. Madrigals, for example, were often played on the lute or on whatever instruments might be at hand. Byrd published some of his solo songs with accompaniments for viol consort. Lute music and lute songs were especially popular over all of western Europe.

*Ricercar, fantasia, and canzona*

It was natural, when adapting a vocal piece to keyboard or lute, to replace the long notes, which these instruments could not sustain, with groups of shorter notes. In this way, instrumental music gained independence from its vocal models. The *ricercar* was an imitative, contrapuntal piece that seems to be a counterpart of the motet. The *fantasia* also used imitation, but in a freer style, as its name suggests. The *canzona*, originally a chanson for instruments, kept the rhythmic style and sectional structure of the chanson.

Though these pieces were often played by lute or consort, they were perhaps most prominent as works for keyboard instruments. Both the *organ* and the *harpsichord* were important in Renaissance music. Organ music, especially in Germany, became more and more elaborate. The harpsichord was the instrument for amateurs, and the music written for it remained somewhat simpler. Both the organ and the harpsichord, and the music written for them, were much more extensively developed in the Baroque period.

PART THREE

# *Baroque Music*

## *Main Composers of the Baroque Period (c.1600–1750)*

**Girolamo Frescobaldi** *(1583–1643)*
**Heinrich Schütz** *(1585–1672)*
**Johann Hermann Schein** *(1586–1630)*
**Jean-Baptiste Lully** *(1632–87)*
**Dietrich Buxtehude** *(c.1637–1707)*
**Arcangelo Corelli** *(1653–1713)*
**Giuseppe Torelli** *(1658–1709)*
**Henry Purcell** *(1659–95)*
**Alessandro Scarlatti** *(1660–1725)*
**François Couperin** *(1668–1733)*
**Antonio Vivaldi** *(c.1675–1741)*
**Jean-Philippe Rameau** *(1683–1764)*
**Domenico Scarlatti** *(1685–1757)*
**Johann Sebastian Bach** *(1685–1750)*
**George Frideric Handel** *(1685–1759)*

# CHAPTER 8

# *Introduction to Baroque Musical Style*

*LISTENING PREVIEW One of the most striking innovations in music of the early seventeenth century was an emphasis on music for solo voice accompanied by a keyboard instrument and often a low-pitched string instrument that played the bass line. This style became an integral part of many types of compositions and was used with great effect in early opera. Listen to "Tu se' morta" (side 2, band 9) from Monteverdi's opera* Orfeo *and notice the emphasis on melody in the voice supported by a chordal accompaniment played on the organ. Try to identify the musical effects used to underscore Orfeo's lamenting the death of his beloved Euridice.*

## The Baroque Style

The word "Baroque" is used today to refer to a style in the arts—in music, a style and period that encompasses the seventeenth and first half of the eighteenth centuries. As is true of most historical periods, there are really no specific dates that mark the beginning and end of the Baroque period. Renaissance styles continued well into the seventeenth century; the beginnings of the Classical style can be found in some works created before the middle of the eighteenth century.

## The Term "Baroque"

The origin of the term "Baroque" is uncertain. Possibly it derives from the Portuguese word *barroco*, an irregularly shaped pearl. Or it may have come from the Italian word *baroco*, a far-fetched syllogistic argument. Or perhaps it came from the name of a sixteenth-century Italian painter, Federigo Barocci.

Ceremonial music at the coronation of Louis XIV at Reims Cathedral, France, in 1654. Today, Louis XIV embodies the image of the absolute monarch of the period, delighting in fêtes, spectacles, and royal balls, all of which called for special music composed to suit the tastes of the ruler. In France, music became virtually a state monopoly. (Bibliothèque nationale, Paris)

Whatever its origins, when the term was first applied to art and music, it was not intended as a compliment. Not until well into the nineteenth century did people begin to see the Baroque age as something other than a period of artistic decadence following the Renaissance. In 1888 German art critic Heinrich Wölfflin wrote positively about the art of the seventeenth century. Other critics in turn took up the idea that there might be something good in Baroque style. Since then there has been a major reevaluation of the period, and today the works of Baroque artists and composers are thought to be among the finest in the history of the Western world.

## Life in the Seventeenth Century

Music at night, performed by Leipzig students (engraving published in 1729) who had formed a so-called "Collegium musicum." As most of the rising urban middle classes were excluded from music performances at court, the formation of musical associations such as this became very popular in the 18th and 19th centuries. This particular group was taken over by J. S. Bach in 1729 and performed during church services on Sundays, as well as at concerts and other secular events.

Europe in the seventeenth century was deeply affected by the aftermath of the Reformation. Politically, socially, and intellectually, both the Protestant Reformation and the Catholic Counter-Reformation left their mark. In a sense, the Reformation can be seen as the culmination of a long struggle between church and state. Through the Middle Ages the Catholic Church had helped unify Europe. It had also served at times as a check on the power of secular rulers. During the Renaissance, however, secular rulers grew stronger and the authority of the Catholic Church weakened. With Luther's call to reform, secular rulers all over Europe saw their chance to weaken papal power even further. By becoming Protestants, they could gain control over the churches within their lands. By remaining faithful to Rome, they could bargain with the pope, receive concessions for their support, and thus also gain greater control. Many of the bitter religious battles fought in the sixteenth and seventeenth centuries were motivated as much by the politics as by theology.

The seventeenth century also brought major increases in commercial activity and in the power of the middle class. Throughout the sixteenth century, European trade networks had expanded. Spain and Portugal had begun the exploitation of the wealth of the New World. They were joined, in the seventeenth century, by the other nations of western Europe. Merchants and bankers, of course, figured largely in all of this and prospered by it. It was no accident that the two countries that came to dominate European trade—the Netherlands and England—were also those in which the commercial middle class was strongest.

Yet perhaps the most striking feature of the age was the growth of absolute monarchy. While asserting their right to rule unhampered by religious authority, national and regional rulers also tried to get rid of the traditional "liberties" of the nobles and the free towns. In their desire to gain control over all aspects of government, they did their best to put an end to the customary prerogatives of council and popular assembly. Sometimes they failed. In England, for example, the absolutist policies of Charles I led to the revolution of the 1640s and the execution of the king. But the rulers rarely failed completely.

The absolutist state par excellence was France. The monarchy acquired an unprecedented amount of control over national life. France became the model for absolutists everywhere. Louis XIV, the "Sun King" who ruled from 1643 to 1715, was the symbol of monarchy for over half a century. French became the language of culture and diplomacy, and the French court at Versailles became the literary and artistic center of Europe.

Finally, the century was a time of greatly expanding horizons. As colonization of the New World increased, the scientific exploration begun in the Renaissance also reached a peak. Kepler and Galileo confirmed and extended earlier findings in astronomy. Leeuwenhoek with his microscope probed worlds too small for the naked eye.

Newton formulated the law of gravity, and Descartes and other philosophers established new ways of thinking about the world, in the light of the discoveries made since the Middle Ages.

### Art and Music

Art and music also reflected the search for knowledge and understanding. The period saw the work of several masterful painters, including such disparate artists as El Greco, with his strange, distorted figures, and Rembrandt, with his intense, dramatic presentation of a commonplace world. Architects exchanged the balanced, straight lines of the Renaissance for massive, curved shapes with a multiplication of detail. In music, earlier rules of rhythm and harmony were ignored as composers tried to create a new style.

People today, viewing the art of the Baroque age, are often struck by the overt emotionalism found in many of the works. One explanation for this lies in the *doctrine of the affections* derived in part from Latin and Greek principles of rhetoric. In the seventeenth century, it was widely believed that various emotions—fear, anger, love, joy, and others—were caused by an imbalance of fluids in the human body. Both internal and external sensations were thought capable of stimulating the flow of these fluids and bringing about changes in a person's emotional state. The resultant emotions were known as affections, and the theory was thus called the doctrine of the affections. Works of art and music were rationally conceived to embody a

Doctrine of the affections

St. Thomas's Church and School in Leipzig, where Bach took charge of the post of Kantor in 1723, a post in which he remained for the rest of his life. It brought with it general responsibility for musical life in the city, a task he took very seriously. (Leipzig Historical Museum)

particular emotion, so they could "move the affections" and stimulate one mood or another. A movement could be unified by presenting basically one emotional state.

The new style did not begin everywhere at once, nor did it develop in the same way in all countries. In music the theories that gave birth to the new style were shaped in Italy around the beginning of the seventeenth century. The creative center remained there for many decades, but France and Germany also made major contributions and rose to great musical prominence. Music in countries such as France and Spain, where the fashions of the court were dominant, differed in some ways from the music in countries such as England, where the middle class were strong. The church music in Roman Catholic countries differed in some ways from the church music in the Protestant states to the north. Nevertheless, music took on certain new characteristics of style that distinguished it from the music of the Renaissance and the music of the Classical age that was to follow. To understand the Baroque style, we must first consider certain theoretical changes made early in the period.

## Melody and Rhythm

### Camerata

In the late sixteenth century, a group known as the *Camerata* met at the home of Count Giovanni de' Bardi (1534–1612), a wealthy gentleman of Florence. The members of the group were mainly interested in the revival of ancient Greek drama. In the course of their research, they came to the conclusion that the Greeks had not merely recited the words of their plays but had sung them as well. Obviously, the elaborate polyphony of the late Renaissance, with its interplay of melodic lines, could not be used in the revival of the Greek plays. The audience would scarcely be able to distinguish the words, let alone the emotions of the characters. What was needed was a style in which the music would be subordinate to the text in its expression of ideas and emotions while advancing the action of the

### Stile rappresentativo

play. From this need grew the *stile rappresentativo*—the representative, or theatrical, style.

### Monody

The most important characteristic of this style was *monody*—that is, the use of one principal melody, with a simple chordal accompaniment. In the Renaissance, the ideal musical sound was created by a number of voices, all singing different lines of approximately equal importance. The new approach concentrated melodic interest in one voice, usually the highest, with an accompaniment supporting it. Monteverdi called his new technique the *seconda prattica* ("second practice"), in contrast to the older *prima prattica* ("first practice").

The earliest music written in the *stile rappresentativo* called for a musical declamation of the text in accordance with the natural rhythm of the words. The melody would be fairly simple, but in places where great affective expression seemed to be needed, the singer could add

### Ornamentation

*ornamentation*—elaborate melodic embellishments.

Many of the ornamental devices developed in the Baroque age are still used today. One is the *trill*, generally shown by the symbol ⌣ or the abbreviation *tr* placed above a note. This shows that the note is to be played in rapid alternation with the note just above it. A *turn*, shown by the sign ∞, is slightly more complicated. It consists of a group of notes that "turn around" the main note. An arpeggio, shown by the sign ⌡ at the left of a chord, indicates that the notes are to be played one after another rather than all together.

Because of the wide use of ornamentation, the consistent beat of the music was sometimes interrupted. To accommodate a flurry of extra notes, the beat would have to slow down, speeding up again only when the singer returned to the basic melody. Herein lay another important departure from the *prima prattica*. In Renaissance music, an even rhythmic flow was fundamental. In the new style, greater rhythmic flexibility was required. Still, instrumental pieces of the Baroque period show a new definition and standardization of rhythm: time signatures and measures separated by measure bars came into standard use.

**Freedom and standardization of rhythm**

With the *stile rappresentativo* came a growing interest in individual performance. The solo singer was becoming popular even before the advent of monodic music, but the importance of expression in the new style made soloists especially valuable. And the new music gave these soloists full opportunity to display their skill. Many types of ornamental flourishes were added to the melody. Sometimes these flourishes were indicated by the composer. More often, however, they were simply added by the performer.

**Recitative and aria**

Gradually the *stile rappresentativo* developed into two different kinds of vocal compositions. The first, the *recitative*, kept the early emphasis on musical declamation, free rhythm, and fairly simple melody. The second, the *aria*, was a composition with regular rhythm, more elaborate melody, and often with ornamentation.

**Bel canto style**

Soon after 1630, the *stile rappresentativo* itself was further reshaped into a style sometimes called *bel canto*. In this style, the use of ornamentation in the aria decreased. The result was a simplification of harmony and rhythm leading to a smooth, flowing melody. A third type of vocal composition, the *arioso*, was also introduced. More melodic than the recitative, it was less rhythmically regular and active than the aria.

**Arioso**

**Sequence**

In both vocal and instrumental melodies, *sequence* came to be used prominently in Baroque music. The same melodic motive was repeated at different pitches, clarifying and unifying a long melodic line. A simple use of sequence occurs in "My Country Tis of Thee" at the words "Land where my fathers died, Land of the pilgrims' pride."

## *Harmony and Texture*

##### Major-minor harmony

The early Baroque interest in the monodic style was paralleled by the development of major-minor harmony. In Renaissance music, harmony resulted from the interplay of polyphonic lines with, of course, some concern for harmonic progression. Renaissance harmony was based on the relationship of intervals within the Church modes. Certain intervals were recognized as giving consonant sounds, while others were noted for their dissonance. Composers made use of these consonant and dissonant sounds to get the harmonic effects they wanted. Toward the end of the Renaissance, however, the modern concept of key within the major-minor system began to emerge. Baroque harmony codified principles of harmonic progression in the major and minor modes, and harmonic considerations came to dominate other aspects of music, such as counterpoint, to a great degree. In short, the role of harmony in Baroque music came to be of great, central importance in music. These newer attitudes toward and uses of harmony were described by Jean-Philippe Rameau (1683–1764) in his famous *Traité de l'harmonie* (Treatise on Harmony) of 1722.

##### Altered use of dissonance

The use of dissonance changed correspondingly in the seventeenth century. Renaissance composers had been very careful about dissonance. Too much of it could easily have upset their delicately balanced modal harmony. But Baroque composers, with the security of a strong tonal center, could be more adventurous. Harmonic experimentation was thus an important feature of the early Baroque, within the framework of major-minor tonality.

##### Chordal progression

One result was the idea of *chordal progression*—the sense of one chord leading on to the next. As already noted, a dominant chord creates a pull toward the tonic. Other chords have other effects. They may serve to begin, lift, suspend, or close a piece of music. Major-minor harmony thus gives music a much stronger sense of inner dynamism than did the older modal harmony.

The use of the new harmony also added richness through the process of modulation—the changing of the tonal center of a piece. Once a particular note was established as the tonal center, new interest could be created by changing the center. Modulation was a basic compositional tool in the Baroque age and has remained so for tonal music ever since. It is valuable because it provides an important resource for harmonic variety. A melody first stated in the key of C major, for example, will sound quite different when repeated in the key of G major. Modulation also helps to make longer compositions possible because changes of key contribute to a balance between the elements of repetition and contrast and thus help to sustain the interest of the listener.

##### Equal temperament

With the use of modulation came the introduction of the system of

This portrait, dating from c. 1746, shows Johann Sebastian Bach toward the end of his life. (British Library; photo: John Freeman & Co)

**Basso continuo**

**Figured bass**

tuning known as *equal temperament*. The early Greek modes that formed the basis for the Church modes were based on intervals discovered by Pythagoras. The steps and half steps in the modes were not, in most cases, of precisely equal length. This unevenness caused problems when performers wanted to shift keys. The problem was especially acute with keyboard instruments, where the steps and half steps are of predetermined length. Thus, there was a move to equalize the steps so that all instruments could play as well in one key as in another. This tampering with tradition met with heated opposition from many quarters, but eventually the equal-tempered, or well-tempered, scale proved so useful that it became standard. Bach's *Well-Tempered Clavier*, a series of keyboard pieces in all keys, was written partly to show the advantages of the new tuning.

The musical texture that resulted from the emphasis on monody, tonal harmony, and affective expression was quite different from that of the Renaissance. As indicated, the monodic style, a distinctly homophonic style, stressed one principal melody with supporting harmony in the other parts. The harmonic support was generally supplied by two instruments. One—usually a harpsichord or an organ—played a chordal accompaniment, while the other—a low melodic instrument such as the viol, cello, or bassoon—reinforced the bass line of the chords. This type of harmonic support, played continuously under the melody, came to be known as *basso continuo*.

Composers adopted a form of shorthand notation for the accompaniment that came to be known as *figured bass*. The chords were not written out. Instead, composers wrote out only the melody and the bass line, placing over or under the bass notes numbers that indicated the type of chord to be played.

Figured Bass

The keyboard accompanist "realized" the bass by adding the appropriate notes. In the example above, the 6 under the note E calls for a chord made up of the note E and the note a sixth above it; counting the note E as the first note, the sixth note is C. The triad was usually completed by adding the fifth to the chord, in this case, G. The number of notes doubled and the spacing of the chord was left up to the performer.

The use of figured bass saved time for the composer. It also let the performers share in the creative process, giving the music a greater sense of spontaneity than would have been possible if all the parts had been set. The effect in this respect must have been similar to that of good jazz or rock improvisation, even though the style of music was of course very different.

Homophony was a feature of much Baroque music, instrumental and vocal. But while in vocal music homophony became very prominent, in instrumental music polyphony remained very important. There were at least two reasons for this. Instruments can usually handle more complex music than can the human voice; they generally have a wider pitch range, can change notes faster, and can jump wide intervals more easily. Also in purely instrumental music, there is no need to keep the melody simple so that words can be understood. Baroque composers soon realized that affective expression in instrumental music need not be merely copied from vocal styles. As instrumental music grew more important over the course of the Baroque period, polyphony also found its way back into vocal music.

**Imitative counterpoint**

A number of existing polyphonic techniques were further developed at this time. One of the most important was *imitative counterpoint*, in which the same theme is repeated by different voices, either exactly or with variations. Imitative counterpoint, already common in the Renaissance, was important in some of the major compositional forms, such as the fugue, that arose in the Baroque period.

## *Timbre*

A major development in the seventeenth century was the raising of instrumental music to equal status with vocal music. This was made possible in part by technical improvements in the instruments. It was also encouraged by the desire to stimulate the affections. The search for emotional expression led to a growing awareness of the potential of different instruments. It was realized that each instrument had its own characteristic tone, timbre, range, and flexibility. One was better suited to a certain purpose or mood than the others. Thus in the seventeenth century, composers started to write music with specific

**Instrumentation**

*instrumentation*—that is, with specific parts assigned to particular instruments. They also arranged their own and each others' works for different instrumental groups.

**Major instruments**

While some instruments were being improved, other new instruments were being developed. The *violin*, for example, was developed in northern Italy after long experimentation. With its wide range and variety of dynamic possibilities, it offered a perfect medium for the Baroque spirit. It was often used by Italian composers such as Arcangelo Corelli and Antonio Vivaldi, whose works still form an important part of the violin repertory. Some of the violins produced in the Baroque age are still regarded as the finest in the world. Bearing the names of makers such as Antonio Stradivari (1644–1737), or of the Guarneri or Amati families, they sell for thousands of dollars and are the treasured possessions of the world's great violinists.

# *The Baroque Sense of Beauty*

Gianlorenzo Bernini: *Ecstasy of St Theresa.* 1645–52. Cornaro Chapel altar, Sta Maria della Vittoria, Rome.

***Overt Emotionalism*** Baroque art, like Baroque music, began in Italy. As a definable style within the seventeenth century, it was the child of the Catholic Counter-Reformation. The Catholic Church supported an art exciting, dramatic, dynamic, and sensuous—an art that would appeal not to the intellectual and cultivated few, as in the Renaissance, but to the broad masses of the people. Baroque artists succeeded in making transcendental events seem real, religious experiences direct, complete, and emotionally satisfying. A high point in Baroque emotionalism can be seen in Bernini's sculpture for the chapel of Santa Theresa in the church of Santa Maria della Vittoria. With amazing vividness, Bernini's work captures the delightful anguish of the nun's swoon in the presence of the angel, who is about to thrust the fire-tipped dart of Divine Love into her bosom. The saint's heavy drapery, the soft flesh of her face and that of the angel, the evanescent distentions of the clouds are interpreted so convincingly that the physical limitations of stone are overcome.

The Hall of Mirrors, Versailles, begun 1678.

***Opulent Interiors*** Opulent is perhaps the most descriptive word for the interior designs favored in both secular and religious buildings throughout the Baroque period. The Hall of Mirrors of Louis XIV's Palace of Versailles furnishes an outstanding example. The French tended to avoid the movement and emotion generally associated with Baroque art in favor of clarity, symmetry, and uniformity, qualities that in no way inhibited the splendid richness of effect achieved by the enormous paintings covering the vault, the green marble pilasters, and the arched mirrors they frame. In Germany, interior design was far less restrained than in France. Indeed, one finds an almost Medieval extravagance of feeling culminating in interiors such as that of Sanssouci. In this late Baroque interior, powerful and dynamic Baroque curves have developed into more sprightly and delicate rhythms, and warm, rich Baroque colors have given way to even more evanescent color harmonies.

The Palace of Sanssouci, Potsdam: the Concert Room. 1740s (photo Bildarchiv Preussischer Kulturbesitz).

Rembrandt: *Self-Portrait with Easel*. 1660. Paris, Louvre (photo Scala).

**The Dutch Bourgeois Style**   In the Baroque age, Holland was distinguished from the rest of continental Europe by her liberal bourgeois institutions and Calvinist religion. To a degree unmatched elsewhere, patronage rested with a large ascendant middle class. Rembrandt van Rijn, the giant of Dutch painting, shared with his contemporaries their devotion to the middle-class domestic life around them, but while other Dutch painters were primarily concerned with the external physical aspects of their subjects, Rembrandt was interested in their inner spiritual experiences. In particular, Rembrandt found that the motion of light through space and across physical forms could be used to express feeling and sentiment. In the self-portrait seen here, he created a very real image of a flesh-and-blood, sensuous being, and then combined this intensely realistic description with a new, expressive, spiritual pattern of light and dark.

***Late Baroque and Rococo Styles***   In the eighteenth century, the Baroque style in both art and music developed into a style known as Rococo, the musical aspects of which will be discussed in Chapter 11. In painting and sculpture, there was no sharp break in continuity but rather a shift in emphasis from the austere and ponderous to the relaxed, agreeable, and elegant. Rococo painters showed little interest in the Catholic Church's ecstatic visions of the saints. Instead they wished to delight the eye, to caress the senses. In the *Mandolin-Player*, Watteau transformed the heavy, dynamic figure of the Baroque into the slender, graceful creature with her instrument. Small-scaled, delicate, and lyrical, Watteau's paintings present a vision of a world filled with beautiful ladies and devoted lovers gliding through wistfully atmospheric parks and woods, a world of silks and satins, a world devoid of pain and ugliness.

Jean-Antoine Watteau: *The mandolin-player.* c. 1720. Paris, Louvre.

Like the violin, the *organ* was well suited to Baroque taste. It had great sonority, a wide range, and a huge capacity for dynamic contrast. Composers in many countries wrote music for the organ, but the heights of the genre were reached in Germany, where the instrument acquired a full set of pedals. This made possible the combination of powerful bass notes and vigorous upper-register sound that we associate with such composers as Dietrich Buxtehude and Johann Sebastian Bach. Organs, because they were so expensive to build, were generally public instruments in churches and were, then as now, associated mostly with church music.

Other major keyboard instruments of the Baroque age were the *harpsichord* and the *clavichord*. The harpsichord, a plucked-string instrument, lacked the sustained tone of the organ, but it had a precision and brilliance greatly suited to the music of the time. In France it replaced the lute as the most popular solo instrument. In Germany it was favored for fast-moving compositional forms such as the fugue. The clavichord, an ancestor of the modern piano, was much softer in volume than the harpsichord and was more of a chamber instrument.

**Other instruments**

Other common instruments, which began to assume their modern form during this time, were the *viola, violoncello, flute, oboe, bassoon, trumpet, horn,* and *trombone*.

With the concern for specific instrumentation came a greater standardization of ensembles. No longer was it enough to gather a number of players and pass out parts. The instruments had to be the right ones for the music. Thus, the makeup of ensembles was closely related to the types of compositions that developed during the period.

**Beginning of the orchestra**

Small orchestras, too, began to take shape; they were used to accompany singers in operas, and for purely instrumental works. Monteverdi's opera *Orfeo*, produced in 1607, called for an accompanying group of about forty instruments, mostly strings. Such groups were very far removed from the later orchestra, but they contributed to its development.

## Types of Compositions and Form

While some types of Renaissance compositions, such as the Mass and the motet, continued to be used in the Baroque period, a number of new types of vocal and instrumental music were developed. *Operas, cantatas,* and *oratorios* were important new vocal works. *Sonatas, concertos, suites* and *fugues* were major new instrumental works.

**Multi-movement works**

Many of these works were divided into movements, with similar or different forms for each movement. Numerous forms were used in the Baroque age, and the most important of them can be seen in the chart on page 124. The simplest of these forms—*binary* and *ternary*—were discussed in Chapter 4. Two formal principles especially characteristic of the Baroque period—*ritornello* and *fugue*—will be considered in Chapter 10.

**Ritornello and fugue**

One of the earliest pictures of a conductor, dating from c. 1720. Note that he is holding rolled-up sheets of music rather than the baton which is now customary. It is only since the 19th century that the importance of the conductor's role is recognized. (Germanisches Nationalmuseum, Nürnberg)

## Contrast and the Concertato Style

As we have seen, the homophonic, basso-continuo texture of Baroque music was already quite distinct from the interwoven, equal-voice texture of Renaissance polyphony. Another important element in Baroque music was supplied by the idea of *contrast*. Contrast of different sounds was a device with obvious potential for affective expression. Composers explored it with ingenuity and enthusiasm. This led to the development of the *concertato style*, a very important aspect of much seventeenth-century music.

The word *concertato* seems to be derived from the verb *concertare*, which originally meant "to compete" and later "to collaborate." These meanings are both implicit in the concertato style, in which performing groups played or sang in alternation with one another. The alternating sounds might be those of a large ensemble against a small one, chorus against chorus, single performer against ensemble, or chorus against ensemble.

We have seen the beginning of this style in the music of Venice in the sixteenth century. The Gabrielis experimented with a variety of possible contrasts, such as choruses of different overall ranges, or a full chorus against a solo quartet. Giovanni Gabrieli, in his works written for Saint Mark's, sometimes used several small choirs that

(*Opposite*) This organ (1732) in the famous Austrian monastery church of Melk exemplifies one of the main characteristics of the Baroque style: a strong, clear structure half-buried in rich and elaborate ornamentation. (Photo: Ad Windig)

# Comparison of Renaissance and Baroque Music

| | Renaissance Music 15th – 16th centuries | Baroque Music 17th – first half of 18th centuries |
|---|---|---|
| *Elements* | | |
| Melody | Generally conjunct and singable | Conjunct and disjunct Frequent ornamentation Much use of sequence |
| Rhythm | Steady rhythmic flow Metric patterns not emphasized in religious vocal music but clear in many secular works | Free rhythm in recitative Steady, driving rhythms and clear meters in many vocal and instrumental works |
| Harmony | Based on 12 Church modes Careful control of dissonance | Based on major-minor system Greater use of dissonance |
| Texture | Polyphony, often imitative, for 4 or more voices Some homophony | Polyphony, often imitative, important in vocal and instrumental works Homophony also used frequently |
| Timbre | Notated music mainly vocal but some instrumental works Small choral groups Small instrumental ensembles | Instrumental music much more important than before Small choral groups Small orchestra of strings, winds, and continuo Soloists important in vocal and instrumental works |
| Important Forms | Imitative forms Strophic songs and hymns | Binary, ternary, ritornello, and fugue Development of multi-movement works |
| Important Types of Compositions | Mass and motet Secular songs Instrumental dances Instrumental pieces such as the ricercar | Mass and motet, often with instrumental accompaniment Opera, cantata, and oratorio Sonata, concerto, fugue, and suite |

contrasted with one another. Later composers imitated him where they had the space and resources to do so. Writers of the day commented with awe on the intensely emotional and dramatic effects created by such music.

*Terraced dynamics*

The use of contrast appears also in the *terraced dynamics* of the Baroque age. These were sudden sharp changes in dynamic level. Terraced dynamics formed a natural part of the concertato style, but also owed something to the limitations of keyboard instruments. Neither the harpsichord nor the organ was capable of the kind of gradual dynamic shading found in the later piano.

## Colonial American Music

Concurrent with the development of the Baroque style in European music was the emergence of an American musical tradition, at first based largely on the English music brought by the colonists in the early seventeenth century. Among the tunes they sang and played were hymns, psalms, ballads, and dances. Early musical development was strongest in the New England colonies, where much of the music was religious. The fact that the music was considered religious did not, however, mean that it was always solemn. The *Ainsworth Psalter*, which the Pilgrims brought with them in 1620, contained a number of metrical translations of psalms, some of which were set to tunes in the style of lively dances.

*Early religious music*

American religious music, isolated from steady contact with its English roots, developed in a fundamentally European but yet distinctive way. This specifically American quality was perhaps less perceptible in the growing urban centers of the East Coast than in the rural and western regions. In fact, by the end of the seventeenth century, religious music in America could be roughly divided into two parallel traditions—one urban, the other rural.

In many congregations relatively few tunes were used in singing psalms and hymns, because many people could not read music. Some individual singers would add spontaneous improvisation to make the act of singing more interesting. A result was that such psalm singing sounded rather poor much of the time. This style of performance came to be called the "usual" manner of singing.

While this practice continued in some remote areas in the late seventeenth and early eighteenth centuries, reforms were sought by some. Church members were encouraged to learn to read music, and when they did they were able to sing a greater number of hymns with more accuracy and uniformity. This was called the "regular" style of singing. It gradually took over in the populous East, and the "usual" style continued in use in isolated areas of the South and West.

A musical culture was thus a part of colonial life in America. It was to develop and grow extensively in the later eighteenth and nineteenth centuries, but it was usually quite close to the European styles from which it sprang.

Farinello Napolitano
famoso. autore d'opere...
...di...el. ... d'. ... ...anno 1724
...da me ... . ... Mar. 1724

# CHAPTER 9

# *Baroque Vocal Music*

*LISTENING PREVIEW Vocal music of the Baroque era was often very ornate and difficult to perform. Handel, for example, wrote a number of impressive choruses in his oratorio* Messiah *that require great skill from both the singers and instrumentalists. In the chorus "For unto Us a Child Is Born" (side 3, band 2), lengthy, quickly moving phrases are given to all the performers. Notice and describe how Handel builds to a climax with his use of voices and instruments at the text "And His name shall be called Wonderful! Counselor! The Mighty God! The Everlasting Father! The Prince of Peace!"*

## General Trends in Vocal Music

**Early composers of monody**

As we have seen, the Baroque style of vocal music began with the Italian interest in monody—that is, an emphasis on one principal melody rather than on the contrapuntal interweaving of several melodies characteristic of the Renaissance. Since the monodic style grew out of an interest in the revival of ancient drama, it is not surprising that it was soon used in Baroque dramas.

One of the earliest Baroque composers of monody was Giulio Caccini (1546–1618), who was a singer as well. In the opera *Euridice* (1600), which he wrote with Jacopo Peri (1561–1633, also a singer) the *stile rappresentativo* crystallized. In fact, *Euridice* is commonly regarded as the first surviving opera. It contains airs, choruses, dances, and recitatives upon which later operas and other Baroque vocal compositions were to be built. But early operas bear little resemblance to the eighteenth- and nineteenth-century operas which are those most often performed today. Our general discussion of the characteristics and conventions of opera is therefore part of the examination of the Classical era, which saw its great flowering as a musical-dramatic genre (see Chapter 16).

In Italy, castrati sang female as well as some male parts in Baroque operas. They had a particularly thorough training and enjoyed highest esteem within the musical community throughout Europe. This caricature, drawn in Rome in 1724 by Pierleone Ghezzi, shows the most famous castrato of his time, Carlo Broschi Farinelli, in a female part.

Caccini had contact with members of Giovanni de Bardi's Camerata in Florence, and he felt it important to explain to his contemporaries the theory underlying his new style. This he did in the foreword of *Le nuove musiche* ("New Music"), published in 1602; his treatise soon became a veritable handbook on monody. The technique, as Caccini saw it, called for a solo voice supported by instrumental accompaniment only loosely connected to the vocal part. Over a basso continuo, often made up of sustained low tones, the melodic line proceeded through both consonances and dissonances. Dissonance was vital to a vocal style that tried to approximate speech. It was subject to only one restriction: that each new bass note be consonant with the first melodic note sounded with it. The following notes of the melody could be dissonant to the bass note, until the bass note changed. Thus, in the monodic style, composers found a way to blend the rhythms, melodies, and harmonies of speech with those of music. Caccini used his new technique particularly in the dialogues of his operas.

The use of the monodic style and the compositional devices that it involved had an effect on many of the vocal works of the period. The eight books of madrigals written by Claudio Monteverdi between 1587 and 1638 neatly illustrate the progression from Renaissance to Baroque music. In attempting to present the text of his madrigals more convincingly, Monteverdi permitted dissonance to appear even on strong beats without previous preparation—if the emotive quality of the work called for it. In his later madrigals he reduced the number of vocal parts from five to three or fewer and added a basso continuo. In these madrigals for few voices, the polarization of bass **Continuo madrigal** and soprano began to occur. This novel style, with free dissonance and accompaniment, was called the *continuo madrigal*. In time it

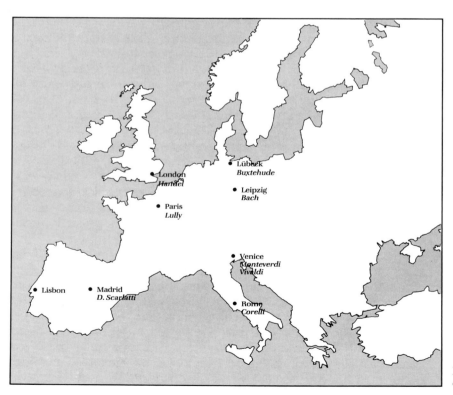

**Major Baroque composers**

evolved into the vocal-instrumental chamber works characteristic of the Baroque period.

Other types of vocal music were also vitally affected by the rise of the monodic style and the transformation of the madrigal. Monteverdi's innovations were part of a general shift from the four- and five-part polyphonic works of the Renaissance toward the vocal styles of the seventeenth century. Baroque vocal music used the solo voice more prominently than was common before his time. Monodies and other types of chamber music, such as the secular cantata, gradually took over the popularity that had once belonged to the madrigal. Even the Mass declined in importance, while the oratorio and the sacred cantata, which permitted greater freedom in musical and poetic organization, became prominent.

## Opera

One of the most important inventions of the early seventeenth century was the special combination of drama and music that came to be known as *opera*. It was at least partly derived from certain secular dramatic amusements of the sixteenth century. Its staging, for example, was borrowed from contemporary theater and its poetry from the Italian pastorale, a poem on a highly idealized rural subject which was set to music.

## Early Development

The earliest Florentine operas, among them *Euridice* and Jacopo Peri's *Dafne* (1597), were largely monodic. Instrumentation and melody were both subordinated to clear rendering of natural speech. Counterpoint did not have as large a role as in earlier music. Only at the end of crucial scenes did early composers of opera vary their monody by introducing songs or choruses, with more elaborate music, and often with dancing.

In early operas, the stage action was highly stylized. They presented abstractions of emotions rather than the feelings themselves. Operas were originally small-scale staged events, often on mythical subjects, intended as diversions for aristocratic patrons. Composers often found ways to compliment their noble employers in the course of the opera. Later opera evolved into a much larger, more elaborate spectacle, as will be seen in Chapter 16. But operas of all ages have one common element: they are staged works in which most or all of the text is sung rather than spoken.

## Monteverdi: Orfeo

Claudio Monteverdi spent many years in the service of the Duke of Mantua. After the Duke's death, he became music director of St. Mark's, Venice, and stayed there for thirty years until his own death in 1643. Monteverdi wrote only vocal music. In addition to the eight books of madrigals there are twelve operas and many religious works, including the magnificent *Vespers* of 1610. Some of the operas were written while he was at Mantua, but he also wrote some during the time he worked at St. Mark's. Monteverdi's madrigals had already

Portrait of Monteverdi, published on a title page the year after his death in 1643. (Music Division, Library of Congress, Washington DC)

displayed his interest in monody, and with it and other techniques he enriched the style of early operas. His *Orfeo* (1607) followed the general outlines of earlier operas. The story upon which the opera was based was one used in many early works. Taken from Greek mythology, it concerns Orfeo's descent into hell to rescue his beloved Euridice. Although the story was a common one, Monteverdi's opera was dramatically and musically far more sophisticated than any of the earlier operas. His score called for a large number and variety of instruments, many of which were specifically designated. He also included some purely instrumental passages for variety and color. The monodic vocal passages were enhanced by considerable variety in melodic writing. Monteverdi's expressive melodies and sensitive setting of text indicated his great concern for these aspects of music. He even wrote out the ornaments and variations for some of the solo parts. His scores were at times extremely complex, as in one aria in the third act in which each of the six stanzas had a different orchestral accompaniment.

### *"Tu se' morta"*

An excellent example of Monteverdi's expressive monody is Orfeo's lament "Tu se' morta," a recitative-like solo in monodic style in the opera's second act. Having just learned that Euridice has died of a snakebite, Orfeo at first despairs. He then summons his courage and resolves to travel to the land of the dead to retrieve her, or failing that, to stay there with her. Monteverdi's music mirrors these emotions faithfully.

*Monteverdi: "Tu se' morta" from Orfeo*

**LISTENING ANALYSIS**                                          SIDE 2, BAND 9

Orfeo's despair is captured in the somber accompaniment and in the faltering rhythm of the opening phrases. Then the music moves ahead with greater assurance, reflecting Orfeo's decision to follow Euridice. The musical setting of the text is syllabic, that is, one note per syllable of text, typical of monody. Monteverdi took great care to be sure that the words were appropriately set to music and that they be understood. The solo tenor voice of Orfeo is accompanied by basso continuo, consisting here of organ and lute. The meter is duple, the tempo slow, and expressive rhythmic interruptions help to emphasize certain thoughts in the text. The mode is largely minor throughout the piece, matching the somber mood of the words. The form is free as the text is presented with no major repetitions of melody.

Throughout the piece, Monteverdi made effective use of *chromaticism*, introducing notes that were not part of the scale. In the last phrase, the chromaticism becomes particularly striking as it is associated with the idea of departure.

Last Phrase

Monteverdi also used a considerable amount of text painting in Orfeo's lament. In the last phrase, note the melodic descent to *terra* ("earth"), and the melodic ascent to *cielo* ("heaven"), continuing even higher to *sole* ("sun"). Thus the melody as well as the rhythm is tied as closely as possible to the text.

Text:

| | |
|---|---|
| Tu se' morta, mia vita, ed io respiro? | *You are dead, my life, and I breathe?* |
| Tu se' da me partita | *You have left me,* |
| Per mai piu, mai piu non tornare, ed io rimango? | *Never, never more to return, and I remain?* |
| No, no, che se i versi alcuna cosa ponno | *No, no, for if my songs can take effect* |
| N'andro sicuro a piu profondi abissi, | *I shall go surely to the deepest abysses,* |
| E intenerito il cor del Re de l'ombre | *And having softened the heart of the dreaded king* |
| Meco trarroti a riveder le stelle: | *I'll bring you back again to see the stars;* |
| O se cio negherammi empio destino | *Or if this is denied me by cruel destiny,* |
| Rimarro teco in compagnia di morte. | *I shall stay with you in the company of death.* |
| Addio, terra: addio cielo. e sole, addio. | *Farewell earth; farewell sun and heaven.* |

English translation by Denis Stevens, President Accademia Monteverdiana, for Musical Heritage Society. Copyright 1968, Accademia Monteverdiana.

---

**LISTENING SUMMARY**

| | |
|---|---|
| Timbre: | tenor voice accompanied by basso continuo of organ and lute |
| Melody: | use of expressive leaps and chromaticism; some use of sequence |
| Rhythm: | $\frac{4}{2}$ meter; slow tempo; closely tied to text; expressive interruptions |
| Harmony: | mainly minor mode; begins in G minor, modulates to D minor at the end |
| Texture: | monodic homophony (melody with chordal accompaniment) |
| Form | free, continuous unfolding of text with no clear sectional divisions |

**Recitative and aria**

By the middle of the seventeenth century, a distinction between recitative and aria was developing. In recitative the melodies were usually simple with many repeated notes, while the rhythm tended to follow the flow of the words. Music in the recitatives was generally subordinate to the text, which was used mainly for dialogue and to advance the action of the plot. In arias the melodies were much more elaborate and interesting. A clear meter prevailed, and emphasis was placed on the music instead of the text, which usually commented repeatedly on action that had taken place or was about to take place.

**Types of recitatives**

Baroque composers made use of two different types of recitatives. The first, accompanied only by continuo, was called *recitativo secco* ("dry recitative"). The second, accompanied by a larger instrumental ensemble, was called *recitativo accompagnato* ("recitative accompanied" [by a larger segment of the orchestra]). The second type was usually used for more dramatic moments.

**Types of arias**

Arias were generally of several types. The earliest, the *strophic-bass aria,* was predominant in the years before 1630. It had a number of consecutive stanzas, the melodies of which were varied over a repeated bass line. In the 1630s a second type, the *ostinato aria,* appeared and was subsequently used for many years by Purcell and other composers. The ostinato aria set a lengthy melody over a short, constantly repeating bass, the *basso ostinato* ("obstinate" or "stubborn" bass), in the accompaniment. A third variety, the *da capo aria,* became the favorite of most composers between 1650 and 1750. It was made up of three sections. After the second section, the words *da capo* ("from the beginning") or *d.c.* were written in the score, indicating that the first section should be repeated. This repeat was usually embellished with improvisations.

Many of the formative developments in opera began in Florence. By 1630, however, Rome had become a center of opera. From Florence and Rome, opera spread to other Italian cities, and later to other countries. The world's first public opera house opened in **Venetian opera** Venice in 1637, marking the emergence of this genre as entertainment for a broad audience. Monteverdi was the first important composer of operas in Venice. He wrote many of his finest operas, including *Il Ritorno d'Ulisse in patria* ("The Return of Ulysses to His Native Land", 1641) and *L'Incoronazione di Poppea* ("The Coronation of Poppea", 1642), after becoming music director at St. Mark's.

## The Neapolitan Style

In Naples a new style of opera was arising in the late seventeenth century. While the mature Venetian style made use of counterpoint and often gave important musical material to the orchestra, the Neapolitan composers adopted a much more homophonic style in which the vocal melody was clearly dominant. In the early eighteenth century, the Neapolitan style superseded the Venetian. It soon dominated not only Italian opera but that of all Europe except France.

The person generally regarded as the founder of Neapolitan opera **Scarlatti's operas** was Alessandro Scarlatti (1660–1725). His early works were very much derived from Venetian composers, but by 1700 he had adopted a style with prominent, well defined melody, supported by homophonic accompaniment. Scarlatti played an important part in the standardization of the Italian overture. Scarlatti's operas are perhaps most noted for their da capo arias, lyrical and virtuosic Italian melodies, and general elegance.

Because the early comic episodes were soon eliminated from serious Neapolitan opera, it is not surprising that an entirely independent form, *opera buffa,* or "comic opera," appeared in Italy soon after **Opera buffa** 1700. In the early eighteenth century, the two types existed side by side with little influence on each other. Opera buffa generally presented humorous or farcical subjects, often about the everyday lives of common people. Its music was simple, and performances were usually given by untrained singers and semiskilled actors. Not surprisingly, opera buffa was, in its early stages, regarded as low-class

Destruction of Armide's Palace, from Lully's opera *Armide*, first performed in Paris in 1686; stage design by Jean Bérain. In both France and Italy, the aspect of opera as spectacle was much emphasized in the late 17th century. Accordingly, the architecture of operatic décor and machinery reached previously unseen heights. The floating boat in the foreground, the collapsing palace in the center, and the descending devils at the top of this drawing amply illustrate the designer's amazing technical capabilities. (Bibliothèque nationale, Paris)

entertainment. Later, however, it was gradually transformed into a highly regarded art form in the works of Mozart and other composers. The tradition of comic opera was also developed in other European countries during the eighteenth century.

## The French Style

Long before the spread of comic opera to countries outside Italy, serious opera had reached the rest of Europe. Only in France, however, did it develop a distinctly non-Italian style. The French opera was largely the creation of Jean-Baptiste Lully (1632–1687). Lully was Italian, but established himself as the court composer to

Louis XIV of France. In his royal patron's service, he set out to make opera a dramatic medium of as much dignity as the contemporary theater which was at a particularly high level, thanks to the talents of Corneille, Racine, and Molière.

*Lully's operas*

Since Lully's operas were designed first of all to please the king, nearly all of their music was refined, stately, and somewhat pompous. They typically began with a two-part French overture, an orchestral form Lully himself devised. This opened with a slow, majestic section and was followed by a quicker section in imitative counterpoint. Arias were shorter, simpler, and less numerous than their Italian counterparts and avoided virtuosic effects. A number of scenes involved such things as processions, pastoral interludes, dances, triumphs, funerals, and combats. Many of these were barely relevant to the rest of the action and served mainly as eye-pleasing spectacles. Orchestration was generally more colorful than in the Neapolitan opera.

The French operatic style, as first conceived by Lully, lasted with few changes through the eighteenth century, as can be seen in the works of Jean-Philippe Rameau. He modeled his music on Lully's but he favored the Neapolitan da capo aria and used the orchestra more contrapuntally.

## Opera in England

Opera developed in England during the seventeenth century, influenced largely by earlier court entertainments such as the masque, which included dialogue, songs, dances, and instrumental music. It was Henry Purcell (1659–1695) who perhaps did the most to bring English opera to a level of greatness. Purcell, the organist of the Chapel Royal in London, wrote music for plays such as *King Arthur*

*Purcell's opera*

and *The Fairy Queen* and one opera, that is, a work in which the entire text is set to music—*Dido and Aeneas* (1689). Many aspects of *Dido and Aeneas* are worthy of comment, including the sensitive setting of the English text and the emphasis placed on choral music and dance. Influence from the Continent can be seen in the use of the French overture and the fact that the dialogue is sung in recitative. The arias present intense ideas, both textually and musically, as in Dido's famous lament, "When I am laid in earth." The chorus is featured prominently in the opera and is given delightfully surprising rhythms and charming moments of text painting. Purcell's dramatic genius reached its greatest heights in this brief masterpiece.

*Handel*

George Frideric Handel (1685–1759) was a remarkably cosmopolitan composer. Early in his career, he spent a few years in Italy, where he learned to appreciate the melodic and homophonic styles then current. This influence can be seen in his many operas, written in the Italian style. After a brief return to Germany, he visited England and, on his second visit in 1712, decided to settle there. While he continued to write operas, Handel came more and more under the influence of English music. Conceding to English taste, he wrote a number of oratorios, which added greatly to his popularity in England both with the court and with the general public, since they reached a wider audience than did his operas. Although best known, in his own time and today, for his vocal music, Handel also wrote many instrumental works. He went blind in 1753 but remained active musically to within days of his death.

Handel's operas During the years he lived in England, Handel was the leading composer of operas. Between 1712 and 1741, he wrote thirty-six operas, which show a thorough mastery of the Neapolitan style he had learned during his time in Italy.

### *Handel:* Julius Caesar

*Julius Caesar* is an effective example of Handel's mature *opera seria.* Written in London and based on a libretto by Nicola Francesco Haym, it was first performed in 1724. The plot concerns Caesar's conquest of Egypt and his affair with Cleopatra. The opera is in three acts, which include a succession of alternating recitatives and da capo arias, with each two-part scene devoted to the expression of a single effect. The opera opens with a two-part French overture, even though the language and most other characteristics of the opera are Italian. Castrato singer Handel's use of the *castrato singer*—a male soprano or alto—in the role of Caesar is one overtly Italian trait. Cleopatra's role is for a female soprano. Her aria "Da tempesta" ("By the tempests") in Act III is an especially vivacious example of the many da capo arias in the opera. The text presents a simile between a ship in a storm that arrives safely at port and a suffering heart that finds comfort. The opening A section is Allegro, is in the major mode, and is based on very dramatic melodic material. The contrasting B section is quieter and shifts to the minor mode. While both sections require virtuosity from the singer, the repeat of the A section is traditionally embellished further by the singer, making it extremely difficult, dramatic, and impressive.

The great popularity of Italian opera in London declined in the 1730s, and in his later years Handel turned to the oratorio. His great flexibility, creativity, and facility are among his many notable traits.

## *Cantata*

Opera was by no means the only important Baroque contribution to vocal music. As monodic music became more and more popular in the early seventeenth century, Italian composers began to use the new style in other types of compositions. Many of these shorter monodic pieces with varying formats were called *cantatas.* The word was first used to indicate simply that the pieces were to be sung, and it did not imply any specific structure or content.

Italian secular cantata By the middle of the seventeenth century, the Italian secular cantata had become more or less standardized. It consisted of recitative and aria sections for one, two or possibly three voices and continuo. The works were designed largely for virtuoso display in a chamber setting. Their lyrics generally described a single situation or recounted a brief,

Three leading singers of their time, the castrati Gaetano Berenstadt (*right*) and Senesino (*left*) and the soprano Francesca Cuzzoni during a performance, believed to be of Handel's opera *Flavio*. (Raymond Mander and Joe Mitchinson Theater Collection)

uncomplicated narrative.

Throughout the seventeenth century, the evolution of musical style in the Italian cantata paralleled that of opera, especially because many composers were writing both types of compositions. The importance of the recitative declined somewhat, and, particularly in the cantata, the length of arias increased while their number declined.

**Early composers**   The first of many important cantata composers during the middle part of the century were the Romans Luigi Rossi (1597–1653) and Giacomo Carissimi (1605–1674). Both were extremely prolific: three hundred and seventy-five cantatas by Rossi and one hundred and fifty-five by Carissimi survive. Among those composers who continued the tradition was Alessandro Scarlatti, who wrote more than six hundred **Scarlatti's cantatas**   such works. By Scarlatti's time the cantata had been standardized. It consisted of an introductory sinfonia followed by a pattern of alternating recitatives and arias. The Neapolitan style, which Scarlatti perfected, called for precise declamation in the recitatives, lyricism in the arias, and great virtuosity.

**German sacred cantata**   The German sacred cantata resulted from a blending of the Italian monodic style and polyphonic vocal styles. Heinrich Schütz (1585–1672), a pupil of Giovanni Gabrieli and, briefly, of Monteverdi, is generally thought to have been the first to use Italian techniques to compose cantata-like works suitable for the Lutheran service. **Schütz**   Schütz's study of recitative enabled him to unite German texts with appropriate music in such works as *Psalmen Davids* ("Psalms of David," 1619). From the Italians, he also learned the use of basso continuo, the idea of contrasting sections, and the value of melodic invention. Although he used the monodic style in many of his works,

Performance of a German Cantata: The orchestra played an important part in the German sacred cantata, just as it did in most other vocal works of the Baroque period. The engraving at the left shows the orchestra required for one early eighteenth-century cantata. The conductor is standing in a key position between the basso continuo instruments, facing the chorus. (Reproduced by permission of the British Library Board)

including the *Kleine geistliche Konzerte* ("Small Spiritual Concertos," 1636), much of his writing was highly contrapuntal. His *Cantiones sacrae* ("Sacred Motets," 1625), for example, are for four voices and continuo. This happy union of German counterpoint and Italian monodic methods, initiated by Schütz, greatly influenced the vocal works of later composers.

**Buxtehude's cantatas**    The cantatas of Dietrich Buxtehude (c. 1637–1707) make use of a variety of texts and musical styles. In many of his works, Buxtehude used a distinctive chorale-variation scheme, in which each stanza of a chorale, or congregational hymn, served as the basis for elaboration by voices and instruments. Much of his church music was performed at public concerts after the services. The use of chorales in Buxtehude's cantatas was part of a traditional Lutheran concern for the words in the religious services.

The cantatas of Joahnn Sebastian Bach (1685–1750) are acknowledged today as the greatest body of such works. Bach and Handel were by far the finest composers of late Baroque vocal music, and were two of the leading instrumental composers also. Unlike Handel, Bach made his career entirely in Germany. Yet he absorbed the influences of other national styles, Italian and French particularly, and his own works pointed the way to later developments.

## Johann Sebastian Bach

Bach came from a musical family, and several of his own sons became composers in turn. Born in the small town of Eisenach, Bach lived in Germany all his life, holding various posts as violinist, organist, and music director. In 1723 he settled in Leipzig, where he served as director of the choir at Saint Thomas' Church, as well as a teacher of singing and Latin in the church's school. Married twice, he had twenty children, only ten of whom survived infancy. In his own lifetime he was much admired for his exceptional talents as an organist and improviser, but his compositions failed to achieve wide acclaim. Most of his works were written to fill specific needs. He wrote instrumental music for the court functions at Cöthen, choral music (cantatas, motets, and masses) for the services at Leipzig, and keyboard works for the instruction of his own children. The neglect of most of his works for more than a century after his death would probably not have surprised Bach, though their later revival might have. Yet, as later generations have seen, the quality of even his most routine compositions is astounding. Indeed, Bach wrote masterpieces in almost all the different types of Baroque music.

**Bach's cantatas**

Bach was the acknowledged master of the German cantata. He wrote nearly three hundred cantatas between 1723 (the year he received the Leipzig post) and 1750. The works included both religious cantatas and secular cantatas, for soloists and chorus accompanied by a small orchestra or ensemble.

A large number of Bach's religious cantatas had both solo and choral movements. The choral movements were generally performed by a group of eight to twelve singers and an instrumental ensemble of eighteen to twenty-four instruments—string instruments, wind instruments, timpani, and continuo. Bach's unsurpassed melodic and harmonic abilities are very apparent in his cantatas, with their expressive recitatives, profound solos, and superb counterpoint. He generally began with a chorus, which sometimes incorporated an instrumental *sinfonia*. This was followed by five or six movements of alternating recitatives and arias. The cantatas usually ended with a harmonized chorale.

### Bach: Cantata No. 80

The *Cantata No. 80,* "Ein' feste Burg ist unser Gott" ("A Mighty Fortress Is Our God"), is a fine example of Bach's religious cantatas. It was written to commemorate the Reformation and was first performed in 1724. The music calls for soloists, four-part chorus, and an orchestra of violins, violas, cellos, trumpets, oboes, timpani, and continuo with the organ used as the keyboard instrument (the trumpets and timpani may have been added to the score by Bach's son Wilhelm Friedemann [1710–1784]). The work has eight movements:

1. Opening movement for chorus and orchestra
2. Aria (duet) for soprano and bass accompanied by oboe, violins, viola, and continuo
3. Recitative for bass and continuo
4. Aria for soprano and continuo
5. Chorale for unison chorus accompanied by orchestra
6. Recitative for tenor and continuo
7. Duet for alto and tenor accompanied by oboe, violin, and continuo
8. Closing four-part harmonization of the chorale for chorus

The congregation may have joined in singing the chorale melody in the last movement.

## *Bach:* Cantata No. 80

**LISTENING ANALYSIS**                                      SIDE 3, BAND 1

### *First Movement*

The opening movement of *Cantata No. 80* shows Bach's mature contrapuntal style to great advantage. The four choral parts are soprano, alto, tenor, and bass. The small orchestra includes parts for violins, viola, cello, bass, trumpet, oboes, timpani, and basso continuo. The mode is major throughout most of the movement; the meter is quadruple, and the tempo is moderate. The phrases of the chorale melody are the basis for nearly all the melodic material. The first phrase is introduced by the tenors and violas and then imitated by the other voices of the chorus in succession. These voices, like the tenor, are doubled by instruments of the orchestra. The source of Bach's opening melody is clear if we compare it with the first phrase of the chorale:

First Phrase of Chorale

Ein' fe - ste Burg ist un - ser Gott

Opening Tenor Phrase of Cantata

Ein' fe - - - ste Burg ist un - ser Gott
[A mi - - - ghty Fortress is our God]

The rest of the chorale is presented in a similarly elaborated fashion. Bach's genius as a composer can be heard in the brilliant use of imitative counterpoint with each of the phrases. After each phrase is treated contrapuntally, a final, unornamented presentation of the phrase is heard in canon, that is, in exact imitation, between the winds (trumpet and oboe) and the continuo (organ and string bass). The result of the entire movement is a grand, imitative work for chorus and orchestra that grows directly, phrase by phrase, from the structure of the chorale.

Text:

| | |
|---|---|
| Ein' feste Burg ist unser Gott, | *A mighty fortress is our God.* |
| ein' gute Wehr und Waffen; | *a bulwark never failing;* |
| er hilft uns frei aus aller Not, | *our helper he amid the flood* |

| die uns jetzt hat betroffen. | *of mortal ills prevailing.* |
| Der alte boese Feind | *For still our ancient foe* |
| mit Ernst er's jetzt meint, | *doth seek to work us woe;* |
| gross Macht und viel List | *his craft and power are great,* |
| sein grausam Ruestung ist, | *and, armed with cruel hate,* |
| auf Erd' ist nicht seinsgleichen. | *on earth is not his equal.* |

**LISTENING SUMMARY**

| | |
|---|---|
| Timbre: | four-part choir, small orchestra of violins, violas, cellos, bass, trumpets, oboes, timpani, and organ continuo |
| Melody: | based on chorale melody |
| Rhythm: | duple meter; moderate tempo |
| Harmony: | mainly major mode; begins in D major, modulates most significantly through the keys of A major and B minor, ends in D major |
| Texture: | imitative counterpoint |
| Form: | based on chorale melody |

## Oratorio

*Laude*

*Cavalieri*

The term *oratorio* (literally "place of prayer") was first used for a chapel in Rome where, during the late sixteenth century, popular religious services were often held. A common feature of these services was the singing of *laude*—allegorical "conversations" between God and the soul, heaven and hell, or other similar participants. Some laude were very simple, while others were more elaborate, amounting almost to sacred operas. The earliest major work that has survived is the *Rappresentazione di anima e di corpo* ("Representation of Soul and Body") (1600), by Emilio del Cavalieri (c. 1550–1602). Closely resembling the contemporary operas of Caccini in its elaborate staging, the *Rappresentazione* is often considered more an opera than an oratorio. Similar compositions enjoyed modest popularity until the middle of the century, when Carissimi produced the first works that were indisputably oratorios.

## Early Oratorios

Italian oratorios such as Carissimi's *Jepthe* (c.1649) were sacred works with long narrative texts in Latin or Italian. They were generally presented without scenery, costumes, or action. A narrator's part was often included to outline the dramatic action. As in operas and cantatas, structure was derived from the juxtaposition of recitatives, arias, and choruses. Instrumental accompaniments were also used. The oratorio differed from the opera not only in that it was generally not intended to be staged but also in its greater use of the chorus for narrative and dramatic purposes.

In Germany the most important composers of oratorios included Schütz, best known for *Die sieben Worte Jesu Christi am Kreuz* ("The Seven Last Words of Christ"), and Bach. But probably the greatest of all oratorio composers was Handel, whose works include *Israel in Egypt* (1739), *Saul* (1739), *Judas Maccabaeus* (1747), and *Messiah*, his most famous work.

## Handel's Oratorios

In all of his oratorios, *Messiah* among them, Handel followed the general structure of the Italian prototype but expanded it to suit the needs of the text and implied drama. Although the subjects are religious, Handel's treatment of them is clearly intended for presentation in a public concert hall, not a church. His works began with instrumental overtures and then proceeded with recitatives, arias, ariosos, and choruses. The great emphasis on attractive and often elaborate melody in his arias was inspired by the Italian style. Yet his choral technique, which incorporated elements from a number of different vocal styles, departed considerably from the Italian practice in the use of imitation with occasional homophony.

Handel's oratorios, and his other vocal works as well, frequently demand great virtuosity from both singers and instrumentalists. His melodic phrases are often long ones based on scales and arpeggios. There is also a liberal use of melodic sequence. A fine balance is maintained between contrapuntal and homophonic textures. Imitation is generally very important in his choruses, but for contrast important words and climaxes are often set homophonically, giving greater dramatic impact.

This anonymous drawing is believed to show Handel (*far right*) conducting an oratorio rehearsal. Originally, his oratorios were performed by quite small ensembles and it was only from the late 18th century onwards that massive choirs and huge orchestras were employed for performance of his works. (British Library; photo: John Freeman & Co.)

Handel used word-painting and other methods of musical representation to enhance the drama and excitement of his choruses. His imaginative use of the chorus is perhaps the greatest single feature of his oratorios. Handel made the chorus a participant in and commentator on the action, but also a vehicle for emotional expression. No composer since has given the chorus greater range—or greater music. Many composers after him, including Haydn and Mendelssohn, were influenced by his choral style. And many of his choral works, *Messiah* chief among them, are today performed regularly throughout the world.

## Handel: Messiah

Handel's *Messiah* was written in 1741, in the amazingly short period of twenty-four days, and was first performed the following year in Dublin. It is divided into three parts: the first dealing with the birth of Jesus, the second with his death and resurrection, and the third with the redemption of humanity. The music consists of a French overture, recitatives, arias, and choruses. It was first performed by a small chorus and a small orchestra made up of string instruments, wind instruments, timpani, and continuo.

Musical styles in Handel's *Messiah* range from the conventional da capo aria to freer structures using the ritornello technique. In these later movements, a main theme returns throughout, either in complete or shortened versions. The choruses of the work include some of Handel's best choral writing and are widely known and loved throughout the world. Few pieces of music surpass the "Hallelujah Chorus" in musical and dramatic intensity, or in popularity. Its strong homophonic opening creates a profound effect, while its judicious mixture of contrapuntal and homophonic textures gives it great contrast and interest.

---

**LISTENING ANALYSIS**                                                    SIDE 3, BAND 2

The chorus "For Unto Us a Child Is Born" occurs in the first part of *Messiah* and is the climax of this section. It begins somewhat differently from the "Hallelujah Chorus." In both choruses, the orchestra first presents the opening theme. In this chorus, however, the voices then enter imitatively, beginning with the sopranos. The result is a superb contrapuntal section based on the opening theme:

First Theme

For un-to us a child is born; un-to us a son is giv-en, un-to us a son is giv-en,

The mode is major, the meter quadruple, and the tempo moderately fast. The continuation of this opening theme features a long, melismatic passage of sixteenth notes that requires considerable agility and virtuosity of the singers. Handel borrowed this opening theme from one of his secular compositions, typical of the many times he borrowed from his own music.

A new theme is introduced with the next phrase of text:

Second Theme

And the government shall be   upon   his   shoul                                    der

The music then builds to a climax with the text "and his name shall be called Wonderful! Counselor!"—the last words of which are set chordally for emphasis. During the remainder of the chorus, the two themes are alternately and simultaneously developed in brilliant fashion. The chordal setting of "Wonderful! Counselor!" returns three times, each time creating an impressive climax. The orchestra brings the movement to a close with a ritornello, or repeated statement, of the first theme, in the original key.

Text:

> *For unto us a child is born; unto us a son is given;*
> *And the government shall be upon his shoulder,*
> *And his name shall be called Wonderful! Counselor!*
> *The Mighty God! The Everlasting Father! The Prince of Peace!*

**LISTENING SUMMARY**

| | |
|---|---|
| Timbre: | four-part choir, small orchestra of string instruments, wind instruments, timpani, and continuo |
| Melody: | first theme begins declamatory, but changes to melismatic; second theme features uneven rhythms |
| Rhythm: | quadruple meter; moderately fast tempo |
| Harmony: | major mode; begins in G major, modulates to D major and C major, ends in G major |
| Texture: | alternating imitative and homophonic sections |
| Form: | ritornello, with alternating imitative and homophonic sections |

## Mass

With the growing interest in secular compositions and the fact that much of the new religious music was designed for use in Protestant churches, the Mass became a relatively less important type of music. Those composers who worked for the Roman Catholic Church still produced unaccompanied polyphonic works much in the style of the late Renaissance Mass. Often, however, they sought ways to achieve new color in their work, some by writing Masses for very large numbers of different vocal parts. Others, especially in Germany, began to use orchestral accompaniment in their Masses.

Like many other musical works, settings of the Mass became longer and more elaborate in the Baroque period. Composers often divided the music for the longer parts of the Ordinary into contrasting sections or movements. The texts of the Gloria and Credo were particularly subject to such division. In many cases, chorus and soloists alternated in the various sections. Mood, tempo, key, and other musical characteristics changed as well.

The Lutheran Church in Germany continued to use parts of the Latin Ordinary, but polyphonic choral settings were generally written only for the Kyrie and Gloria. This kind of shortened setting was called a *Missa brevis* ("short Mass"). (The Baroque Missa brevis should be distinguished from the Roman Catholic Missa brevis of the late Renaissance, which was a relatively short and simple setting of all five parts of the Ordinary.) In Bach's Masses, we find the culmination of the Baroque Mass: four settings entitled *Missa brevis* and one setting of the complete Ordinary, the *Mass in B Minor*.

*Missa brevis*

Bach's Masses

## Bach: Mass in B Minor

Bach's *Mass in B Minor* is one of his greatest accomplishments. Unlike his own settings of the Passions and Handel's oratorios, this Mass is not a dramatic work. Its greatness lies in its grandeur and profound emotional expression. It presents a rich variety of musical ideas that combine to form a sublimely convincing, cohesive whole, even though the several sections of the Mass were not composed in order. Some were rearrangements of earlier works. It is doubtful that Bach ever even heard a complete performance of the Mass.

The score of the Mass calls for a relatively small orchestra of violins, violas, flutes, oboes, trumpets, timpani, and continuo. Single instruments and small groups of instruments are often used in a solo capacity. Solo voices are also featured from time to time, but the chorus sings the bulk of the music.

The five parts of Bach's Mass—the Kyrie, the Gloria, the Credo, the Sanctus, and the Agnus Dei—cover a wide range of moods, making use of a number of different techniques. The first Kyrie, for example, uses imitative counterpoint and a strong rhythmic flow to express the supplication of the words "Kyrie eleison" ("Lord, have mercy"). The section of the Credo dealing with the crucifixion uses an ostinato bass and chromaticism to intensify the idea of Christ's suffering. Because of the grand scope and wealth of ideas in *Mass in B Minor*, a thorough study of it is time-consuming but very rewarding. Here we will examine the Sanctus. Although only a part of the entire work, it offers an excellent example of many of the characteristics of the work as a whole.

---

**LISTENING ANALYSIS**                          SIDE 3, BAND 3, SECTIONS A,B,C

Bach divided the text of the Sanctus into several large musical sections:

- A  Sanctus: six-part chorus and orchestra
- B  Pleni sunt coeli: six-part chorus and orchestra
- C  Hosanna: eight-part chorus and orchestra
- D  Benedictus: tenor solo and orchestra
- C  Hosanna (exact repeat)

Section A   The first section of the Sanctus opens with all voices proclaiming the text chordally in $\frac{4}{4}$ meter. Many of the beats in the section are subdivided into three parts—or *triplets*—as seen in the opening theme:

Opening in First-Soprano Part

Sanc - tus, sanc - - tus, sanc - - tus
[Ho - ly, ho - - ly, ho - - ly]

Several voices present mostly conjunct lines together in triplet rhythm, moving contrapuntally within the basic homophonic texture. The effect is one of great solemnity.

**Section B**   With the text "Pleni sunt coeli," a contrasting section begins. The meter changes from duple to triple, and an important new theme is presented by the tenors. This theme has a distinct character because of the repeated notes at the beginning, the large rising interval that follows, and the use of the melisma of sixteenth notes for the word "gloria." These rapidly sung notes emphasize the word, while contributing to the strong sense of constant rhythmic motion and overall lightening of mood:

Second Theme in Tenor Part

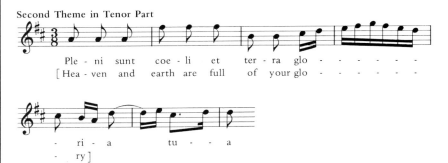

Ple - ni sunt coe - li et ter - ra glo - - - - - -
[Hea - ven and earth are full of your glo - - - - - -

- ri - a tu - - a
- ry]

After the tenors complete the theme, the other voices in turn imitate it, entering alternately on the tonic and the dominant. All voices continue the imitative development of the theme throughout this magnificent fugal section.

**Section C**   The Hosanna that follows is quick and vivacious, very appropriate to the spirit of the text. It begins chordally, with the eight-part chorus declaiming the text in a clear manner. The chorus is divided into two four-part choruses which are used in contrast to one another in much of the movement. After the declamatory beginning, imitative counterpoint follows, with the altos of the first chorus introducing an elaborate, quickly moving theme that is imitated by the sopranos, basses, and tenors in turn. The declamatory statement of "Hosanna" then returns in the second chorus to accompany the continuing counterpoint of the first chorus. The two choruses then reverse roles in presenting the materials once again. They continue to develop the materials, touching on a number of different keys before returning to the original tonic of D major for the emphatic close of the movement.

**Section D–C**   The Benedictus, by contrast, shows Bach in one of his most lyrical and contemplative styles. It is scored for an unspecified solo instrument (probably either transverse flute or violin), solo tenor, and continuo. The closing Hosanna is an exact repetition of the first Hosanna.

Text:

| | | |
|---|---|---|
| A | Sanctus, sanctus, sanctus Dominus Deus Sabaoth, | *Holy, holy, holy Lord God of hosts,* |
| B | Pleni sunt coeli et terra gloria tua. | *Heaven and earth are full of your glory.* |
| C | Hosanna in excelsis. | *Hosanna in the highest.* |
| D | Benedictus qui venit in nomine Domini. | *Blessed is he who comes in the name of the Lord.* |
| C | Hosanna in excelsis. | *Hosanna in the highest.* |

**LISTENING SUMMARY**

Timbre:     six- and eight-part chorus; small orchestra of string instruments, wind instruments, timpani, and continuo

Melody:     different themes for each of the four sections

Rhythm:     Section A in quadruple meter, slow tempo, with beats subdivided into triplets; Sections B and C in $\frac{3}{8}$ and $\frac{3}{4}$ meters, moderately quick tempo; Section D in $\frac{3}{4}$ meter, slow tempo

Harmony:    Sections A, B, and C predominantly in D major; Section D predominantly in B minor

Texture:    Section A contrapuntal within basically homophonic texture; Sections B and C contrapuntal; Section D contrapuntal and homophonic

Form:       ABCDC

## The Evolution of the Mass

Through the centuries, musical settings of the Mass have continued to play an important part in religious services. There has, however, been a trend, most notably in the last two centuries, to write Masses for performance in the concert hall as well as in the church.

Listen to musical settings of the Mass from five different periods – either those listed below from the record set that accompanies the text, or other selections.

| | | |
|---|---|---|
| **Medieval:** | Introit of the Requiem Mass | Side 2, Band 1 |
| **Renaissance:** | Palestrina's Kyrie of the *Missa brevis* | Side 2, Band 6 |
| **Baroque:** | Bach's Sanctus of the *Mass in B Minor*, First Section | Side 3, Band 3 |
| **Classical:** | Haydn's *Nelson Mass* | |
| **Romantic:** | Verdi's *Requiem* | |
| **Modern:** | Bernstein's *Mass* | |

What musical qualities are most strongly contrasting in the first four works? What musical qualities establish the latter two selections as more recent works?

In what ways can each of the selections be seen as a reflection of the period in which it was composed?

AVDITVS.
L'OVYE.

Chamber music as performed
in an elegant Paris household
during the first half of the
17th century: this ensemble
consists of two singers, a
lutenist, a boy singer, and a
bass player. (British Library;
photo: John Freeman & Co.)

# CHAPTER 10

# *Baroque Instrumental Music*

*LISTENING PREVIEW Although vocal music continued to be prominent throughout the Baroque era, instrumental music reached a new, great height of maturity and complexity. One of the most important new types of instrumental music was the fugue written for keyboard instruments. Many fugues were written for the organ, perhaps the most intricate and artfully constructed instrument of the period. Listen to Bach's* Fugue in G Minor *for organ (side 3, band 7) and notice how clearly each presentation of the opening theme can be heard. Identify the characteristics of that theme that help make it so distinctive.*

## The Rise of Instrumental Music

Italy was the main source of musical ideas during the early seventeenth century. We have already noted the rise of the *stile rappresentativo*, with its emphasis on textual clarity and expressiveness. Also Italian were the increasing use of dissonance and the rejection of counterpoint typical of those early years.

In the later seventeenth century, the influence of France became almost as important as that of Italy. This was the period of Louis XIV and royal absolutism in France, and music, like the other arts, was closely bound to the state and the interests of the court. This was the age, too, when major-minor harmony became fully established. Dissonance was somewhat reduced and highly controlled. In Italy the exuberance of the *stile rappresentativo* was being contained. Experimentation was subdued, counterpoint reappeared, and instrumental music was emerging from its long subordination to vocal music.

By about 1690, the main theoretical developments were complete and a number of important new types of compositions had taken shape. Instrumental music was now clearly as important as vocal. Italian and French influence spread to other countries, notably Germany, where some of the greatest keyboard music was written. The affections tended to be intellectualized—thanks, perhaps, to French rationality and systematization. The rules and standards developed during the earlier years of the period were thoroughly accepted. In Germany, as we have seen, Bach wrote masterpieces in almost all the different types of Baroque music. But even during Bach's lifetime, some composers were seeking newer styles. While the Baroque style was at its height, elements of the Classical style were emerging.

The Baroque is one of the most important eras in musical history, primarily because of the contribution it made to the development of diverse types of instrumental music. Those it inherited from the Renaissance were perfected, and important new ones were developed.

## Sonata

The gradual development of instrumental music from its vocal roots is well illustrated by the *sonata*. The Baroque sonata can be traced back to the *canzon da sonar* ("played song"), an instrumental song of the late Renaissance, and beyond that to the early French vocal part song, the *chanson*. At first the canzon da sonar simply imitated the contrapuntal texture of the chanson, with as many different parts as the composer wanted. But with the new monodic style came a preference for canzone of only a few parts. This led eventually to the *trio sonata*, which despite its name was a work for four instruments: two melody instruments playing over a basso continuo. Also popular was the *solo sonata*, written for one melody instrument and basso continuo. As with vocal forms, the sonata was developed mainly by Italian musicians.

**Trio and solo sonatas**

At first the term "sonata" meant only that the music was wholly instrumental. It did not signify any particular compositional form. Some of the early canzone da sonar had ten or more sections of music. These were generally set in contrasting style with long sections in imitative counterpoint alternating with shorter homophonic sections. In time, the number of sections decreased, and the remaining sections grew longer, taking on the character of full-scale movements. It was with this later type of composition that the term "sonata" came to be most often associated. There were *sonate da chiesa* and *sonate da camera*—sonatas for church and for chamber.

**Church and chamber sonatas**

At this time, the musical term *da camera* had a much broader meaning than it does today. Music "of the chamber" was not yet limited to ensemble music in which each part is played by a single instrument. Rather, the term *da camera* referred to any music written for neither the church nor the stage. Naturally, though, since *camera* music tended to be played in private homes rather than public halls, a small ensemble was generally used. Thus, the term "chamber music" acquired its present meaning. The sonata da chiesa, on the other hand, performed in church, often called for a larger ensemble, two or more instruments doubling each part to give the necessary volume.

**Corelli**

Both church and chamber sonatas were widely popular in the late seventeenth century. It was Arcangelo Corelli (1653–1713) of Bologna who brought the compositional form to perfection. Widely traveled, Corelli achieved great fame as a violin virtuoso. As might be expected,

Domenico Scarlatti went to Spain in 1729, where he stayed until his death in 1757. He is seen in this group portrait of the Spanish royal household in the musicians' gallery, together with the castrato Farinelli. (Calcografía Nacional, Real Academia de Bellas Artes de San Fernando, Madrid)

Other composers of sonatas

Sonatas for one instrument

Domenico Scarlatti

most of his published works, including his sonatas, contain prominent parts for violin. From 1681 to 1707, he published four sets of trio sonatas—two for church and two for chamber. At the same time, he published one set of solo sonatas, equally divided between church and chamber. His church sonatas were usually written in four movements, alternating from slow to fast. The chamber sonatas were generally made up of an introductory movement and three or four dances, also alternating between slow and fast.

In addition to being used by virtually every Italian composer of the late Baroque, the trio sonata was also popular elsewhere in Europe. Henry Purcell in England, François Couperin (1668–1733) in France, and Dietrich Buxtehude in Germany all wrote notable trio sonatas.

A number of Baroque composers were also writing sonatas for a single, unaccompanied instrument. This type of composition was brought to perfection in the sonatas written by Bach for unaccompanied violin and unaccompanied cello. However, the most prolific writer of sonatas for solo instrument was undoubtedly Domenico Scarlatti (1685–1757), who wrote over six hundred sonatas for the harpsichord, an unmatched display of creativity. He himself was a harpsichord virtuoso and helped lay the foundation for modern keyboard technique. His sonatas were written in the character of exercises, using a wide variety of techniques, one at a time. Each is a one-movement work, although they seem to have been intended to be played in pairs.

## *Scarlatti:* **Sonata in C Major, K. 159**

The *Sonata in C Major,* K. 159 offers a vivacious example of Scarlatti's sonatas for harpsichord. (K. stands for Ralph Kirkpatrick [1911–1984], a cataloguer of Scarlatti's works.)

### LISTENING ANALYSIS                                    SIDE 3, BAND 6

Typical of Scarlatti's sonatas, the work is divided into two sections. Each section is repeated, and so the resulting form is AABB.

**Section A**    The brisk opening theme clearly establishes the key of C major in $\frac{6}{8}$ meter:

Opening Theme

This theme and its continuation are the melodic and harmonic basis for Section A. During the section, however, a modulation to the key of G major, the dominant of C, takes place. After the section ends, in the key of G major, the section is repeated.

**Section B**    Typically Section B should start in G major. But Scarlatti departs from the usual here and suggests C minor without firmly establishing it. The section begins with a variant of the opening theme. Later in the section, the opening theme itself returns firmly in C major and, with its continuation, brings the section to a close. Like Section A, Section B is then repeated.

### LISTENING SUMMARY

Timbre:     harpsichord
Melody:     strong melodic material with many repeated notes
Rhythm:     $\frac{6}{8}$ meter; tempo Allegro
Harmony:    mainly major mode; first section begins in C major, modulates to G major; second section suggests C minor, modulates to C major
Texture:    homophonic
Form:       binary (AABB)

Although trio and solo sonatas were most common, sonatas were also written for three or more melody instruments over a basso continuo throughout the Baroque period. Toward the end of the period, the solo sonata became decidedly the most popular, heralding the transition to the solo and duo sonatas of the later eighteenth century—works for one or two instruments. The sonata was also an ancestor of several other types of compositions developed later in the century, including the symphony.

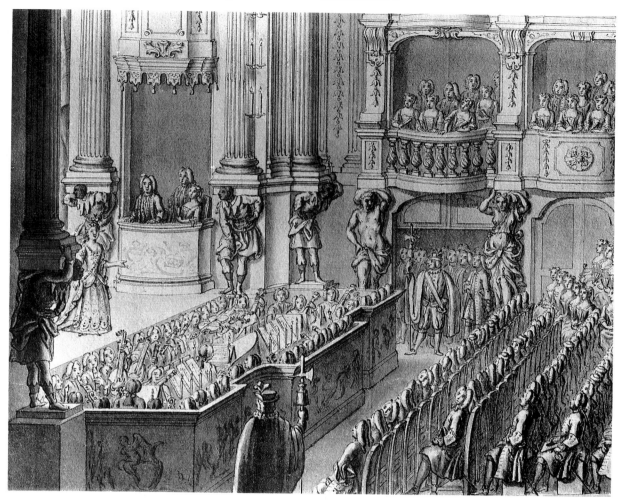

## *The Orchestra*

*(Above)* The orchestra of the Dresden opera house during a performance in 1719. During the Baroque period, court orchestras such as this would not only play at the opera but also at public functions, as well as performing concerts for the ruler's pleasure. (Dresden: Kupferstichkabinett; photo: Sächsische Landesbibliothek, Abt. Deutsche Fotothek)

The development of the orchestra, like that of new harmonic concepts, took place gradually. In 1600 it was uncommon for a composer to indicate specific instrumentation in a composition. By 1750 most composers did give specific instrumentation. The years in between were filled with experimentation and the exploration of new musical ideas about the use of different instruments.

The *concertato* style, with its stress on contrasting timbres, encouraged the writing of music suited to the characteristics of particular instruments. The trend became more marked as the *concertato* style evolved toward the concerto styles of the late Baroque. Solo instruments also began to acquire their own music. This was true not only for the keyboard instruments but also for the violin and various wind instruments. The solo music undoubtedly influenced the way these instruments were used in ensembles as well.

The creation of professional orchestras, employed by nobility or by important towns, encouraged composers to write for specific instruments. Now composers could be sure that the instruments they wanted would be present. One of the earliest of the professional **Lully's orchestra** orchestras was *Les Vingt-quatre violons du roi* ("The Twenty-four Strings of the King"). It was established by Lully at the French court in the mid-seventeenth century. As the name indicates, this was at first mainly a string ensemble. By the end of the century, however, a number of wind instruments had been added—flutes, oboes, and horns. Similar orchestras were soon organized throughout western Europe. Since French styles of the late seventeenth century were widely imitated, Louis XIV's orchestra was bound to have had an influence on orchestras and orchestral writing elsewhere.

By the middle of the eighteenth century, the small Baroque orchestra was fairly standardized. The string section and the basso continuo were frequently joined by two flutes, two horns, two oboes, and two bassoons. The basso continuo was generally made up of a harpsichord, organ, or lute—playing the harmony as indicated by a figured bass—and a low, melodic instrument such as the viola da gamba, cello, or bass—reinforcing the bass line. Casual instrumentation had definitely been left behind, and the small orchestra was an important, established aspect of musical life.

## Concerto

One of the most important types of works for small orchestras to emerge during the seventeenth century was the *concerto*, and Corelli was one of the most successful early composers of this genre. It was carried to a high point of development during the first half of the eighteenth century.

A number of characteristics of music of the period merged in the concerto. One was the idea of contrast between large and small groups. The use of homophony was also important in the development of the concerto and was in fact one of its early distinctions. Finally, the combination of several short sections in a single composition, already encountered in the sonata, achieved a new unity and power in the concerto.

**Concerto grosso** The *concerto grosso* ("large concerto"), the earliest true concerto, had one of its earliest developers in Corelli. In a group of works published in 1714, but probably written around 1682, Corelli set a small group of performers against a much larger ensemble. The small group, known as the *concertino*, was generally made up of two violins and continuo—a group that typically played trio sonatas. The larger group, known as the *ripieno* ("full"), also had a basso continuo as well as additional string instruments and occasional wind instruments. The term *tutti* ("all") was used to refer to all of the instruments in the two ensembles combined.

Corelli's concerti grossi were often little more than sonatas divided between large and small groups. He made little effort to differentiate

A bassoon-maker's workshop; engraving dating from 1698. As with other instruments, technical improvements to the bassoon were beginning to speed up considerably from this period. (Städtische Kunstsammlungen, Augsburg; photo Heritage of Music)

between the music written for the two groups and even used descriptive adjectives also applied to the sonata, calling his concertos *da chiesa* or *da camera* (*for church* and *for chamber*). He also used the structural forms that had been developed for the church and chamber sonatas. His church concertos were especially conservative, with five or more movements, much like the many sections of the older sonatas. However, the slow movements in these concertos were often very short, acting as transitions between the more important fast movements.

**Torelli**

More important than Corelli in the perfection of the concerto's compositional form was Giuseppe Torelli (1658–1709) of Bologna. His earliest concertos, published in 1692, were orchestral works of several movements with occasional solo passages for violin. Pursuing

**Solo concerto**

this innovation, he soon evolved the *solo concerto*, in which a single instrument, rather than a small group of instruments, is set against the ripieno.

Ritornello form

In his solo concertos, Torelli made a distinction between the music for the ripieno and the music for the solo parts; logically, he often used more contrapuntal material in the ripieno. He also began the use of the *ritornello* principle, or form, for both solo concertos and concerti grossi.

Following this principle, the ripieno passages are a return—ritornello—to the opening theme in modified forms. The solo passages, on the other hand, offer changes from or elaborations of the opening theme. Ritornello depends very much upon the use of major-minor harmony, since all the inner statements of the theme are in different keys. The opening theme is first stated by the ripieno in the tonic. In the ritornelli, a variety of keys can be used. This, in turn, makes it possible to have longer movements and a more complete working out of the musical idea. At the end of a movement, the final ritornello returns to the initial key, thus unifying the work. The simplified diagram below shows a typical ritornello pattern:

| **Ripieno** | **Solo** | **Ripieno** | **Solo** | **Ripieno** | **Solo** | **Ripieno** |
| --- | --- | --- | --- | --- | --- | --- |
| **Tonic Key** ⟶ | | **New Keys** | | | | ⟶ **Tonic Key** |

Using longer, fuller movements, Torelli began to write concertos of just three movements: generally, allegro—adagio—allegro. In keeping with Baroque tastes, the allegro movements were the most lengthy; the adagio movements was often much shorter than the other two. Torelli also used certain internal devices that became standard in later concertos. These included a steady, driving rhythm, the use of strong patterns of triads to set the initial key, and the introduction of the ritornello by a series of three "hammerstrokes" on the tonic and dominant chords. This last device seems to have been borrowed from the fanfares of trumpet sonatas, which were very popular in Bologna at the time.

## Vivaldi

All of these new developments in Baroque music culminated in the works of several master composers, the most important of whom were Antonio Vivaldi (c. 1675–1741), Bach, and Handel. Vivaldi, a priest, taught music at a school for orphaned and illegitimate girls in Venice. Though a violinist himself, he wrote solo concertos for almost every available instrument and concerti grossi for many combinations of instruments. Vivaldi built on Torelli's structure of a solo concerto but added some elements of his own. He made the adagio movements as important as the allegro movements. He liked programmatic music and often introduced such things as imitations of bird calls or rippling brooks in his solo passages. This, of course, gave him a chance to make use of the marvelous virtuosity in which he excelled, both as a composer and as a performer. But all of these flights of fancy were held together by a firm adherence to the ritornello

Portrait of Antonio Vivaldi. The sheer vigor and inventiveness of his instrumental music make him a highly popular composer even today. (British Library; photo: John Freeman & Co.)

principle. He also used precise themes and vigorous rhythms derived from a driving, insistent beat. The elements that developed in the solo concerto were transferred to the concerto grosso as well. They were used by Vivaldi in the more than four hundred and fifty concertos he wrote in the first half of the eighteenth century.

Though Vivaldi wrote both sacred and secular vocal music (including a setting of the Gloria that is often performed) his greatest achievements were in the field of instrumental music, particularly concertos. His *Four Seasons, Op. 8, No. 1–4* (1725) is an outstanding collection of four solo concertos for violin, works that clearly show his mature skill. Accompanying the solo violin in each work is a chamber orchestra (the ripieno) made up of two violin parts, viola, and continuo. Vivaldi tried to associate the concertos—"Spring," "Summer," "Autumn," and "Winter"—with the general and specific moods of each season.

**Four Seasons**

The abbreviation "Op." in the title of Vivaldi's concerto stands for "opus," the Latin term for "work." Since early Baroque times, com-

**Opus numbers**

posers and publishers have catalogued especially instrumental compositions by opus number. Usually opus numbers were assigned chronologically by composers to their works. A set of multiple compositions of the same type sometimes shared the same opus number; hence "Op. 8, No. 4" is the fourth violin concerto of Opus 8. Later composers usually assigned only one work to each opus number.

## Vivaldi: Winter Concerto in F Minor, Op. 8, No. 4

In the *Winter Concerto*, Vivaldi's attempt to associate music and seasonal events can clearly be heard. At times, the music seems to suggest whirling wind and, at other times, the chattering of teeth. The work also shows many other characteristics of Vivaldi's concerto writing. It consists of three movements—Allegro non molto, Largo, and Allegro. The keys of the movements are F minor, Eb major, and F minor. The brighter major mode and unusual key relationship of the second movement offer sharp contrast with the first and third movements.

### LISTENING ANALYSIS                                    SIDE 3 BAND 4

*First Movement: Allegro non molto; Ritornello Form*

The first movement of the *Winter Concerto* opens quietly with the ripieno instruments entering one at a time. Repeated notes gradually build into a dissonant chord progression that creates great tension. After the ripieno chordal statement, the solo violin enters with a quick theme based on arpeggios, repeated notes, and scales:

First Solo Passage

**Use of sequence**

The ends of the phrases in the solo violin part are twice punctuated by the opening chordal materials of the ripieno. Then solo violin and orchestra join in repeated notes, which suddenly quicken with greater intensity. The solo violin proceeds with the continuo in fast rhythmic motion, presenting several motives and scales. A longer solo for the violin follows. It is made up of a lengthy phrase played three times in descending *sequence*. After this the orchestra returns with quickly repeated notes. Soloist and orchestra briefly continue a rapid dialogue. Then the repeated notes return in the orchestra, building to a dissonant chord progression before the resolution. This last orchestral part is a modified, more elaborate version of the first orchestral part. The movement makes use of the ritornello form, with the returns of the opening repeated-note material in different keys and in the tonic at the close.

Above the solo violin part in the score, short descriptions are occasionally written about human reactions to winter weather, such as shivering in the cold, being chilled by the wind, and so forth. These comments were probably intended to create an appropriate frame of mind for the performers.

**LISTENING SUMMARY**

| | |
|---|---|
| Timbre: | solo violin; ripieno made up of string orchestra with continuo |
| Melody: | ripieno theme uses many repeated notes; solo passages use arpeggios, repeated notes, scales, and sequence |
| Rhythm: | duple meter; tempo Allegro non molto; slow rhythmic motion at first, then faster |
| Harmony: | mainly minor mode; begins in F minor, modulates to C minor and Eb major, ends in F minor |
| Texture: | mainly homophonic |
| Form: | ritornello |

### Second Movement: Largo

*Use of pizzicato*

The slow second movement in the major mode is, in effect, an exquisite aria for solo violin, accompanied by ripieno group. The accompanying violins are played *pizzicato*—that is, with the notes produced by plucking rather than by bowing. The melody in the solo violin is especially lovely and memorable. It includes very effective use of melodic sequence. The key of Eb major is fresh and unexpected, after the key of F minor in the first movement. The movement is in a two-part form (AA′); the first part modulates to the dominant key of Bb major, and the second modulates back to Eb major. A note in the score mentions the comforts of being inside by a warm fire.

### Third Movement: Allegro

The last movement returns to a fast tempo and to F minor, the key for the first movement. It begins with an extended violin solo before the ripieno group enters. Throughout the movement the soloist and ripieno present and develop material alternately and simultaneously. Repeated notes and melodic sequence are again prominent. The movement closes dramatically with a great flourish of rhythmic activity in all instruments. Comments in the score allude to various aspects of winter, such as riding or walking on ice, sliding on a frozen pond, and the happiness that such activities can bring.

## Other Concertos of the Late Baroque

Vivaldi's influence on eighteenth-century music, even into the Classical period, was enormous. Bach, in particular, was much taken with his work and transcribed a number of Vivaldi's concertos so that they could be played on keyboard instruments, either alone or with orchestral accompaniment. Bach's own concertos, both the famous *Brandenburg Concertos* (1721) and the solo violin concertos, show Vivaldi's influence, albeit transformed and deepened by Bach's own genius. One interesting variation in Bach's concertos is the use of wind instruments as well as string instruments in the concertino of the concerto grosso. His *Brandenburg Concerto No. 2*, for example, uses a concertino of trumpet, flute, oboe, and violin.

*Handel's concerti grossi*

Handel also wrote a number of notable concertos. The twelve

concerti grossi of his *Op. 6* (1739) are splendid examples. Each uses two violins and a cello in the concertino. The six concerti grossi of his *Op. 3* (1734) are more varied, in that, like Bach, Handel used wind instruments as well as string instruments in the concertino.

**Handel: Concerto in B♭ Major, Op. 3, No. 1**

Handel's *Concerto in B♭ Major, Op. 3, No. 1* is in three movements: Allegro, Largo, and Allegro. The first and third movements use two oboes and one violin as the concertino. The solo instruments in the second movement are two flutes, one oboe, and two violins. In this concerto, two bassoons join the continuo, as is typical in Baroque music when high-pitched wind instruments are used.

---

**LISTENING ANALYSIS**                                           SIDE 3 BAND 5

### *First Movement: Allegro; Ritornello Form*

The first movement of the *Concerto in B♭ Major* uses the ritornello principle. The first theme, presented by the ripieno of violins, violas, and continuo, returns in partial form and once in nearly complete form during the movement. This strong theme opens with two descending arpeggios, followed by a motive in descending sequence, and closes with a scale:

Opening Ripieno Theme

The solo oboes present a second theme, after which the solo violin presents a third theme. Both themes offer considerable contrast to the opening ripieno theme in that they are generally quite conjunct. As these themes are repeated and extended, the opening motive of the first theme returns a number of times while several different keys are explored. Toward the end, the opening ripieno theme returns in the original tonic key to close the movement.

**LISTENING SUMMARY**

| | |
|---|---|
| Timbre: | concertino of two oboes and one violin; ripieno made up of string orchestra and continuo with two bassoons |
| Melody: | first theme presented by ripieno made up of descending arpeggios followed by motive in descending sequence; second theme presented by oboes; third theme presented by solo violin |
| Rhythm: | duple meter, tempo Allegro |
| Harmony: | mainly major mode; begins in B♭ major, modulates most significantly to F major, ends in B♭ major |
| Texture: | mainly homophonic |
| Form: | ritornello |

### *Second Movement: Largo*

The second movement moves to the key of G minor and slow tempo.

The contemplative mood of the movement contrasts well with the brighter tone of the first movement. Contrast is also found in the fact that the concertino now contains two flutes as well as one oboe and two violins. The movement is in a ternary form.

### Third Movement: Allegro

The last movement features the original concertino of solo oboes and violin. There is also a return to a quick tempo. Somewhat unexpectedly the final movement does not return to the major key of the first movement; rather, it is in the minor key of G minor—the key of the second movement. This last movement is relatively brief and brings the concerto to an effective close.

As a whole, the *Concerto in B♭ Major* offers a fine example of Handel's fresh, vivacious style. Concerti grossi such as this work were a vital aspect of musical life in the early eighteenth century.

## Fugue

The *fugue* represents the most mature form of imitative counterpoint, having eclipsed, by the end of the seventeenth century, the ricercar from which it evolved. Fugues could be written for any solo instru-

George Frideric Handel, c. 1748/49. (British Library; photo: John Freeman & Co.)

**Subject**

**Episodes**

ment, or instrumental or vocal groups, but the form is primarily associated with keyboard music. The basis of a fugue is a melody called the *subject*. This melody is stated in the beginning by a single voice, then taken up in succession by the other voices. Statements of the subject may be separated by sections of freely invented counterpoint called *episodes*. These are often built upon a motive from the subject and elaborated with scale passages. The form of the fugue is based essentially on the alternation of statements of the subject and episodic passages.

The supreme master of the fugue was Johann Sebastian Bach. Both of the two volumes of his *Well-Tempered Clavier* (1722, 1744) contain a prelude (introductory piece) and fugue in each of the twelve major and twelve minor keys. The works represent a skillful probing of the fugue's potential, while demonstrating Bach's limitless imagination.

Bach's manuscript score of the Fugue in E minor. The tenth fugue in the second volume of Bach's *Well-Tempered Clavier* has only three voices. The highest voice enters first, the second highest at the very end of the first line, and the lowest enters at the beginning of the third line, all of which can be clearly seen in Bach's manuscript (MS. 35021). *(Reproduced by permission of the British Library Board)*

### Bach: Fugue in G Minor

Bach's *Fugue in G Minor,* written for organ, is a classic example of fugal structure—perhaps too classic to be typical. No two fugues by Bach or by any other composer are structured exactly alike. The *Fugue in G Minor,* however, is a fine model of most characteristics of Bach's keyboard fugues.

**LISTENING ANALYSIS**                                                    SIDE 3, BAND 7

**Exposition**

In the first part, the *exposition,* the subject begins with an outlining of the G minor triad. The subject itself is divided into two parts. The first part, in two measures, begins and ends with relatively long notes. The second part changes to quicker rhythmic motion.

Subject

There are four voices in the fugue. Each of the voices presents the subject—the highest voice entering first, the lowest last—all in exact imitation. These four statements of the subject, which make up the exposition, begin alternately on the tonic G and the dominant D. Those statements of the subject on the dominant are usually called *answer*. After presenting the subject, each voice continues with a *countersubject*, or secondary melody, which is characterized in this fugue by a trill. Just before the third statement of the subject, a short episode occurs—a brief section, based on the subject, but not including a complete statement of the subject.

**Countersubject**

Countersubject

Answer

The structure of the exposition is perhaps clarified by the following diagram. Note that the exposition is broken by a short episode.

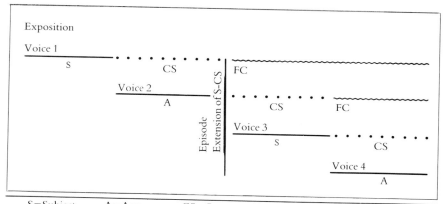

S=Subject    A=Answer    CS=Countersubject    FC=Free counterpoint

When the exposition is completed, an episode follows, briefly developing a motive from the subject in sequence. In the middle part of the fugue, the subject appears again four times, each time preceded and followed by an episode. The most prominent keys in this section are the contrasting ones of B♭ major and C minor.

Near the end, there is a modulation back to G minor. The subject is then presented for the ninth and final time, in the tonic key by the lowest voice.

---

**LISTENING SUMMARY**

| | |
|---|---|
| Timbre: | organ |
| Melody: | begins disjunct, then becomes more conjunct; the subject is in two parts and is followed by a countersubject; episodes characterized by use of sequence |
| Rhythm: | C meter; moderate to moderately fast tempo |
| Harmony: | mainly minor mode; begins in G minor, modulates to B♭ major and C minor, returns to G minor, ends with G major chord |
| Texture: | monophonic at beginning, then contrapuntal; homophonic in the final cadence |
| Form: | fugue |

---

*The Art of the Fugue* (1748–9), Bach's last work, is made up of eighteen canons and fugues. All are based on the same subject and arranged in order of increasing complexity. Included in the music is a four-note motive that, in German names of pitches, spells out the composer's name (in German, H = B natural and B = B♭).

Bach's great accomplishments as a composer are acknowledged by numerous composers of the nineteenth and twentieth centuries who have used this motive in their compositions to pay homage to Bach.

## Other Types of Compositions

Besides the sonata, concerto, and fugue, a number of other important instrumental compositions were developed during the Baroque age. Prominent among them were the following compositions for solo keyboard instrument or for orchestra.

### Sinfonia and Overture

Rather than implying any particular style, the term *sinfonia* was generally used to refer to the orchestral introductions or interludes written for vocal works such as operas or cantatas. Monteverdi wrote a sinfonia for his opera *Orfeo*. Rossi used the name for the introduction to an orchestral suite. Bach prefaced a number of his cantatas with sinfonias.

Over the course of the seventeenth century, two distinct forms of overture emerged—one in Italy, the other in France. The *French overture* was largely the creation of Lully, whose influential position at the court of Versailles made him a major arbiter of musical taste. The

French overture and Lully

earliest example of its use was in Lully's ballet *Alcidiane*, written in 1658. The French overture had two sections. The first section was slow, homophonic, and majestic in style, with an emphasis on uneven rhythms. The second section was fast moving, although still serious in character, and frequently began with some form of imitative counterpoint. This section often ended with an *allargando*, or slowing down, which might contain a repetition of the rhythm or theme of the first section. In later compositions, this closing passage was sometimes expanded into a third section.

French Overture

| Uneven rhythms | Imitative |
|----------------|-----------|
| Slow | Fast |

Italian overture and Alessandro Scarlatti

The development of the *Italian overture* was a major contribution of Alessandro Scarlatti, the father of Domenico. It had three sections: fast—slow—fast. The first section made some use of imitative counterpoint. The second and third sections, however, were in simpler homophonic style. The Italian overture, with its three sections, was still another progenitor of the Classical symphony.

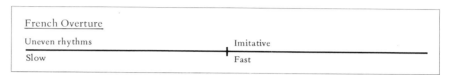

Italian Overture

| Imitative | Homophonic | Homophonic |
|-----------|------------|------------|
| Fast | Slow | Fast |

## Suite

A *suite* is made up of a number of movements, each like a dance and all in the same key or related keys. Its history offers a good example of Baroque internationalism. The characteristic style of the individual dances was established largely in France, but the formal organization of them into a musical entity, the suite, was a German contribution.

Suites for solo instruments

The French dances were written for solo instruments, at first the lute and then the harpsichord. They were published in sets that included an *allemande*, a *courante*, a *sarabande*, and a random variety of other dances. Each set was thus a collection of short pieces, many of them separately titled and generally unified only by being written in the same key. Couperin wrote a large number of *ordres*, or suites, for harpsichord. Each was made up of several loosely connected short pieces, sometimes more than twenty. These were highly stylized, very graceful compositions, with delicate melodies, rich embellishments, and touches of wit.

Couperin's ordres

Suites for ensembles
Schein

Initially departing from the French preference for solo composition, German composers at the beginning of the seventeenth century wrote suites for ensembles. An important collection of suites was published in 1617 by Johann Hermann Schein (1586–1630). Entitled *Banchetto musicale* ("Musical Banquet"), it contained twenty suites written in five parts for viols. Schein, unlike his French contemporaries, limited the number of dances in his suites. Each suite has a combination of slow and fast dances: a *padouana* (*pavane*), a *gagliarda,* a *courante,* and an *allemande.* In some suites, a single melody is used, with variation, for all the dances; in others, different melodies are added.

**Bach's suites and partitas**

The power and expressiveness of German suites, for ensemble and later for solo instrument, surpassed that of their French models. There are few compositions that can rival the "Air" from Bach's *Suite No. 3 in D Major* in somber, profound beauty of theme and texture. Bach also wrote three *partitas* (another name for the suite) for violin. These are among the most magnificent solo works ever created for that instrument. The complexity and grandeur of the "Chaconne" of the *Partita No. 2* is unparalleled.

**Structure of solo keyboard suites**

By the late Baroque, the solo keyboard suite had become relatively standardized. The first movement, the *allemande,* was written in moderately fast duple meter. Beginning with a quick upbeat, it made use of short running figures. The second movement, the *courante,* was often based on the theme of the first movement. The French version was generally in moderate $\frac{6}{4}$ time. The Italian version—the *corrente*—was a faster, more homophonic dance in $\frac{3}{4}$ time. The third movement, the *sarabande,* was a slow movement in triple meter, written in a dignified style, and often more homophonic than the earlier movements. It was sometimes followed by an ornamented version of the same dance called a *double.* The final movement, the *gigue,* was a lively, quick-paced dance in $\frac{6}{8}$ time, often written in imitative counterpoint. Occasional variants of this scheme might include an opening movement or other dances inserted between the standard movements. The form of most of the dance movements was binary, similar to the structure of Scarlatti's sonatas.

## Toccata

The *toccata,* a form of prelude, dates back to the lute music of the early sixteenth century. In the Baroque period, it became a vehicle for keyboard instruments, particularly the organ. While showing a performer's virtuosity, toccatas are meant to convey a sense of improvisation. They are marked by irregular rhythms, sudden sharp changes of texture, and a relentless drive of scalelike passages, turns, trills, and other ornamentation. With its exuberant, dramatic nature, the toccata is a wonderful example of the Baroque spirit.

**Frescobaldi**

Girolamo Frescobaldi (1583–1643) was an early composer of toccatas. His pieces are made up of loosely connected sections that are rich in musical ideas and allow for great display of virtuosity. Since the toccata was clearly intended to be a performer's showcase, it is not surprising that it reached the height of its development in Germany, where composers could take full advantage of the advanced state of organ construction. Froberger created toccatas that were somewhat more controlled than Frescobaldi's. His works served as models for Buxtehude and Bach, whose toccatas, written in a somewhat more elaborate style, were often coupled with fugues.

# PART FOUR

# *Classicism in Music*

## *Main Composers of the Classical Period*

**Christoph Willibald Gluck** *(1714–87)*
**Carl Philipp Emanuel Bach** *(1714–88)*
**Johann Stamitz** *(1717–57)*
**Franz Joseph Haydn** *(1732–1809)*
**Wolfgang Amadeus Mozart** *(1756–91)*
**Ludwig van Beethoven** *(1770–1827)*

# CHAPTER 11

# *Introduction to the Musical Style of the Classical Era*

*LISTENING PREVIEW The orchestra came to be somewhat larger and more standardized in instrumentation in the later eighteenth century. Although still small in comparison to nineteenth-century orchestras, it was capable of a wide variety of sounds and effects. Listen to the first movement of Haydn's Symphony No. 94 in G Major (side 4, band 1) and identify the principal groups of instruments that you hear. Observe any changes in the choice and use of instruments from the works of Bach, Handel, and Vivaldi in the early eighteenth century.*

## The Classical Style

The Classical style in music of the late eighteenth and early nineteenth centuries brought the repudiation of the complicated, somewhat mannered style of music heard in the Baroque age. Instead there was a demand for simpler music that would appeal to a wider audience. Different ages, of course, have different sensitivities and, consequently, different ideas about human nature. The musical language that developed in the middle and late eighteenth century is capable of addressing itself to many aspects of human nature, but it was grounded in the sensitivities of its own time. In order to understand the music of the Classical style more fully, we must know something of the age itself.

## Life in the Late Eighteenth Century

(*Left*) Wolfgang Amadeus Mozart, aged 7 and his family. (British Museum; photo: John Freeman & Co.)

The early decades of the Classical era correspond roughly with what has been called the Age of Reason. The period was marked by a new interest in the improvement of the human condition, through natural science, technology, and social philosophy. Benjamin Franklin stands as a symbol of a generation that concerned itself with the practical fulfillment of the individual and with the individual's relationship to the social state. No longer was it taken for granted that the Church or an absolutist monarch would determine the course of history.

The middle class grew stronger as technology laid the basis for the Industrial Revolution. The age of Haydn, Mozart, Schubert and Beethoven was also that which produced the first steam engine, the cotton gin, and the spinning jenny. Armed with the Newtonian laws of physics, people began to feel themselves increasingly in control of their universe—the explorers of their own immense capacities. Immanuel Kant attempted nothing less than a definition of the possible limits of human knowledge in his *Critique of Pure Reason* (1781). Diderot and other French philosophers worked to assemble this diverse knowledge in the ambitious *Encyclopédie*. In 1776 Adam Smith published *The Wealth of Nations*, the first systematic treatment of political economy. Political theorists on both sides of the Atlantic began to address themselves to the problem of monarchy: the growth of individualism had brought a strong challenge to the idea that monarchs ruled by divine right. The American Declaration of Independence proposed that all people were equal in the eyes of their Creator. Everywhere people seemed to glimpse the possibility of social improvement. Middle-class wealth and aspirations demanded that art and music should be available to non-aristocratic amateurs in the home and public concert hall as well as the Church.

The Age of Reason soon passed into the Age of Revolution. As early as 1762, the French philosopher Jean Jacques Rousseau wrote that "Man is born free but everywhere is in chains." And, indeed, a reasoned examination of eighteenth-century society often seemed to lead to a rejection of that society in all its inequities and to a glorification of life in a more natural state—or at least to the belief that people did have certain "natural rights." The breakdowns of traditional authority and the growing confidence in human abilities presaged the late eighteenth-century revolutions in America and France. It also heralded an individualism that would soon undergo far-reaching development.

## Art and Music in the Middle and Late Eighteenth Century

In the middle of the eighteenth century, a preference for classic simplicity in both art and music emerged. In part, this indicated a revolt against the complexity of Baroque styles. But the trend to simplicity also reflected other influences, among them the archeological excavations at Pompeii and Herculaneum. With the excavations came a revival of interest in Greek and Roman art forms, outstanding for their symmetry and simple grandeur.

Since the arts of ancient Greece and Rome are termed 'Classical,' the eighteenth-century interest in these art forms is sometimes called "Neoclassicism" ("New" or revived Classicism). Architects, painters, and sculptors made direct use of Classical ideas. Buildings resembling those of ancient Greece and Rome sprang up in England and France, and even in the American colonies. Thomas Jefferson, when ambassador to France, traveled through Italy, gaining from Classical models

inspiration that he would later use in the designs of Monticello and the University of Virginia. The architect Jacques Ange Gabriel made Classical additions to the palace of Versailles. The painter Jacques Louis David chose Greek philosopher Socrates and Roman statesman Brutus as subjects. The classic ideals of reason and proportion were the ideals of the age.

In music, however, there was little to revive. Although our knowledge of Greek music theory is extensive, few examples of music have survived, and we have no idea how even these few pieces sounded in their own time. The musical style that coincided with the Neoclassic movement is today called Classical rather than Neoclassical because it was not an actual revival of earlier music. The music is related only in spirit to ancient art. "Serenity, repose, grace, the characteristics of the antique works of art, are also those of Mozart's school," wrote Robert Schumann (1810–1856), who admired the Classical style.

In both the art and the music of the Classical age, a high degree of order and symmetry is readily seen. This order and relative predictability says much about the taste of the people in the second half of the eighteenth century. However, the Neoclassical revival was a brief one—almost a fad. And the rational order of the period was in many ways illusory. The industrial and political revolutions of the time were soon to belie the social and cultural tenets of the Age of Reason, even though the new political order represented the belief that reason and rationality could change history.

## The Emergence of the Classical Style in Music

**Bach's Sons**

Every so often a generation inherits an art form so fully developed, a style so richly articulated, that it seems as if nothing new need be said. A predicament very like this faced the sons of Johann Sebastian Bach, three of whom were composers in their own right. Wilhelm Friedemann Bach (1710–1784), Carl Philipp Emanuel Bach (1714–1788) and Johann Christian Bach (1735–1782) had seen in their father's works the fullest achievement of the Baroque. They might also have recognized elements in the work of less gifted contemporaries that were inevitably to bring the style to its demise. In fact, by the middle of the eighteenth century, the mature Baroque style had begun to fall from popularity even as some of its greatest masterpieces were being written. It was criticized for its extravagance and for its self-serving sophistication. Even the elder Bach was criticized at times for not having written in a simpler, more natural idiom. There had been a general change in sensibility, and with it came a demand for a new means of expression.

**Rococo style**

This change was not confined to musical taste but, rather, represented a growing rejection of court society and the arts that it had favored. The late Baroque, especially that decorative courtly aspect of it known as the Rococo, had gloried in the ornamental, the pretty, the pleasantly artificial. Artisans carved innumerable scrolls on the arms and legs of ordinary furniture. Painters put cherubs in the corners of ceilings and seashell designs in the moldings. So, too, did musicians improvise decorations at every performance. Many composers left their melodic lines bare to accommodate these playful ornamentations. Music, like the other arts of the period, sought to imitate and entertain. The audience was to be charmed rather than moved deeply. In some ways, the Rococo music of the early eighteenth century can be seen as a transitional stage. Based on Baroque principles, the music departed from the Baroque in its extreme emphasis on elegant ornamentation. The works of François Couperin provide numerous examples of the style.

**C. P. E. Bach**

Around the middle of the eighteenth century, Carl Philipp Emanuel Bach played an important part in the creation of a new style, which came to be known as the "expressive" or "sensitive" style, or *Empfindsamer Stil*. The new style rejected the polyphonic complexities of the Baroque in an attempt to present emotions more freely. It permitted the expression of a variety of moods within a single movement, introducing different themes with corresponding harmonic and rhythmic changes. Thus there evolved a series of changes in the musical language of the mid-eighteenth century.

**Empfindsamer Stil**

The music in the early Classical style was simple and disarmingly original. Composers found themselves with new expressive tools and considerable freedom to use them in new ways. They were encouraged to use dynamic effects as never before. They were free to experiment with rhythmic contrasts and develop highly original melodies. Yet, even with all these new freedoms, the aim was to write simple, well-proportioned works. Composers recognized the fact they must discipline their material and shape each work into an ordered, unified whole.

Attitudes toward the new music varied greatly. By some the composers in the new style were hailed as "romantics," people of great and noble sentiment. By others they were taunted for the easy tears their melodies provoked and for the part they were playing in the breakdown of the old Baroque order. Haydn, the first great figure of the new age, was described by one of his elders as a mere "scribbler of songs." It seemed to some that romantic musing was replacing many years of solid polyphonic tradition.

When we listen to the works of the new composers—C. P. E. Bach, Haydn, and Mozart—we cannot help but feel historically removed from their audiences. To us the music sounds like the epitome of reason, not of sentiment. It is full of wit, grace, and balance. The composers are not those whom we would call "romantic." In fact, the term "Romantic" is now used to refer to a later generation—composers such as Chopin and Liszt, who seemingly rebelled against the very style now under discussion. What this suggests is that the terms used to describe music are relative and historical rather than absolute.

**Classical-Romantic continuum**

As has been noted, the musical style that succeeded the Baroque, the style now called Classical, began to emerge in the middle of the eighteenth century. But it was not called Classical until the nineteenth century when it, too, was replaced by a movement more romantic than itself. Suddenly composers such as Haydn and Mozart had to be distinguished from those who continued their tradition in a more passionate vein. Over the years, there had been a gradual increase in experimentation. Composers began to use musical language in increasingly personal ways. By the nineteenth century, the Classical style had become more flexible, intense, and "romantic." The style that finally emerged—the Romantic style—was not a revolt against the Classical style but rather an expansion of it. It is thus possible to speak of a *Classical-Romantic continuum*, with order increasingly tempered by subjectivism in diverse ways.

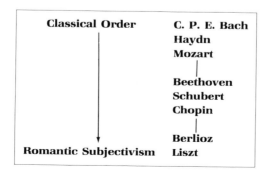

Only after the Classical style had been superseded by the Romantic did it become common to speak of a "classic" beauty, an earlier standard of excellence against which the art of music could be measured. This standard is found in the works of Haydn, Mozart, Schubert, and the early works of Beethoven.

## Melody and Rhythm

In the late eighteenth century, melody took on a dominant role in both instrumental and vocal music. The strong, prominent bass line of the Baroque gave way to a bass line that was wholly subordinated to the melody. When we recall a Classical work, it is usually the main melody—or theme—that we remember first. New emphasis came to be placed on the originality and expressive nature of melody. Composers often used melody as a means of conveying mood. They might use a disjunct melody to enhance the dramatic sense of a fast movement. A conjunct melody might be used to bring sweet composure to the slow movement that followed. The emotional potential of melody was widely explored.

The significance of this change may be seen by comparing the Classical and Baroque styles. Many Baroque melodies were made up of the repetition of small melodic patterns or motives. The challenge to the composer, particularly in the contrapuntal instrumental music, lay not simply in the creation of a melodic line but as much in the arrangement of several lines, layer upon layer. The horizontal independence of the different parts meant that each part had its own particular melodic movements. The melodic climaxes of the several parts did not always coincide. In the music of the Classical period, however, there was much more likely to be a single melodic line that could clearly be felt to rise and fall.

Classical music also differed from that of the Baroque in its linear organization of melodic material. One of the forces that gives a Classical work its sense of unity is, oddly enough, the way it is divided. The polyphonic works of the Baroque age strove for continuous momentum—for a smooth, uninterrupted flow. With Classical music, however, phrases of more regular length tend to appear, and a sense of proportion is cultivated. Often a motive will begin a theme, and an answering motive of the same length will complete it. In **Phrase structure** Classical music, as in simple folk songs, melody is often organized into phrases of regularly recurring length.

A phrase is a short segment of melody, comparable to a line of poetry, that progresses toward a temporary pause or conclusion. "Twinkle, Twinkle, Little Star," which was well known in the late eighteenth century as "Ah, vous dirais-je, Maman," begins with two phrases that exactly balance one another:

The first movement of Mozart's *Symphony No. 40 in G Minor* also begins with two balanced phrases, the second of which complements or answers the first:

Moreover, each phrase is made up of three presentations of the same rhythmic motive.

The organization of music into phrases that are clearly heard is one of the chief characteristics of the Classical style. At the beginning of the period, phrases were sometimes patterned closely on folksongs. This in itself was a radical departure from Baroque melodies. The era of Rousseau's "noble savage" and a new interest in simplicity and nature among aristocratic society made folk music a permissible influence for the first time. Phrases were often four measures long, following the typical folksong pattern. As compositions became more sophisticated, the length was varied. Mozart's phrases are sometimes irregular, but they are carefully proportioned to the needs of the composition.

The changes in the use of melody and phrase structure in the Classical style could hardly fail to bring about changes in the use of rhythm. Baroque music seemed almost to propel itself, evenly and continuously. Seldom were there any marked changes in the overall rhythmic pattern. In a Classical work, however, the phrase structure

**Rhythmic variety** punctuates the melody, resulting in a rhythmic variety much greater than that found in Baroque music.

In addition, the new prominence of melody encouraged a reassignment of rhythmic chores. While all the different parts in the contrapuntal music of the Baroque age helped to generate the rhythmic impulse, Classical music could afford the luxury of one part that was primarily melodic. Thus, in Classical music, we hear a melodic line in which the rhythm is variable, often supported by a more regular accompaniment. The rhythms of the melody could play against the more steady metrical accompaniment, adding to the expressiveness of the piece.

The use of rhythm in Classical music was also influenced by the tendency to show contrasting moods within a work or movement. Often more than one type of rhythmic activity would be used. There might, for example, be a change in tempo or a change from an active to a calm passage.

Despite this rhythmic variety, music in the Classical style is generally characterized by steady meter and a regularly recurring pulse. At the same time, however, a gradual trend toward more varied and complex rhythms and more experiments in meter can be heard.

## *Harmony and Texture*

Harmony is the structural basis of Classical music. While specific harmonic relationships had become very important in Baroque music, they took on even greater importance in the Classical style, and the structural use of harmony became a fundamental part of almost all long works. Because specific harmonic devices and techniques are such a vital part of Classical music, some further discussion of harmony is important here.

The introduction to harmony in Chapter 2 explained the harmonic uses of three important triads: the tonic (I), subdominant (IV), and dominant (V) chords, all major triads based respectively on the first, fourth, and fifth tones of the scale. Of these, the tonic and dominant chords are the most important. The dominant chord, particularly when heard at the end of a composition, produces in the listener a strong anticipation of the tonic chord. The dominant chord introduces tension, which is resolved with the tonic chord.

This pattern can be seen in the accompaniment to numerous Classical melodies. It is most easily heard in a well-known song such as "Twinkle, Twinkle, Little Star." The tonic, subdominant, and dominant chords provide a pleasing harmonic accompaniment to the melody.

| Twinkle, twinkle, little star, how I wonder what you are. | | | | | | | |
|---|---|---|---|---|---|---|---|
| I | I | IV | I | V | I | V | I |

Note the order in which the chords appear. The phrase begins and ends with the tonic chord. The middle is accompanied alternately by all three chords. The phrase ends with the dominant chord leading to the tonic.

If, in singing "Twinkle, Twinkle, Little Star," we were to choose the note C for our tonic, we would be singing in the key of C major. A move from the tonic chord to the dominant chord in this key is simply a move from the triad based on C to the triad based on G:

I and V Chords in C Major

Within the composition, the move from the tonic to the dominant chord will be perceived as movement from a stable position to one of tension or expectation.

If we had chosen not C but G as our tonic, in order to sing the melody at a higher pitch, we would be in the key of G major. The I chord would begin on G, and the V chord would be based on D:

I and V Chords in G Major

The triad based on G would give a feeling of stable home position, while the triad beginning on D would introduce conflict.

## Modulation

Use of modulation

The I–V–I pattern is enough to provide harmonic structure for many brief songs. However, it would soon prove boring in a longer work. Therefore, in many longer compositions of the Classical period, there is a modulation, from the tonic key to the dominant key and back again to the tonic. If the beginning of a composition is in the key of C major, the middle part is likely to be in the key of G major. The final part will generally return to the key of C major just as a melodic line generally returns to the tonic. The effect is much the same—a feeling of finality. The organized use of modulation, already seen in the Baroque period when major-minor harmony was developing, was of prime importance to the Classical composer.

A question that logically arises upon first consideration of key change is this: how do we know, for example, that it has modulated from the key of C major to the key of G major rather than simply moved from the I chord to the V chord of the key of C? How can we *hear* such a modulation?

The answer is that when the music modulates from one key to another, new tones are introduced, and the central note or tonality of the music changes. The seven notes in the key of C major are not quite the same as the seven notes in the key of G major. Different keys use different tones from the twelve tones of the chromatic scale.

We can see why this is so by examining the scales of C major and G major on the piano keyboard. First, look at the scale of C major:

Scale of C Major

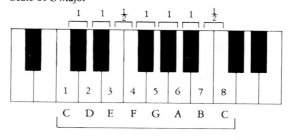

In the scale of C major, there are whole steps between most of the notes. Half steps fall between tones 3 and 4 and between tones 7 and 8. Every major scale has the same pattern of whole and half steps. The half steps always fall after the third and seventh notes. The piano is basically "in the key of C," which means that it is built to play the C major scale without any black keys. In all other major scales the pattern of whole and half steps can be followed only if one or more black keys are used. In the G major scale, for example, a black key will be needed for the seventh note of the scale:

Scale of G Major

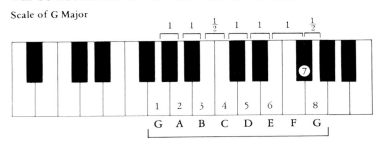

As noted in Chapter 5, the use of black keys is shown by the sharp or flat signs in the key signature:

**Related keys**

Clearly the key of G major, with only one sharp, is more similar to the key of C major than is the key of E major, which has four sharps, or the key of D♭ major, which has five flats, or any other key with more than one note change. The notes of the closely related keys of C and G major are exactly alike except for the F♯. Thus, when music modulates from C major to G major, only one note changes. If, however, the music were to move from the key of C major to that of E major, more than half the notes would be new. It would present somewhat of a shock to our ears if a composer did this directly. Generally such a change will not be direct. Instead it will be made by passing through a series of related keys.

In Classical music, modulation from the original or home keys to a key based on the dominant of the original key becomes an ever-present dramatic force. Often the modulation is gradual, beginning with the first phrase but not firmly established until somewhat later. Sometimes it is abrupt and witty, as in some of Haydn's surprise effects. Like rhythm, modulation became more daring and experimental in the later Classical period, with more striking and more frequent changes, often between unrelated keys.

**Minor keys**

While the same pattern is used for all the keys of the major mode, a different arrangement of half and whole steps is used in the minor mode. The character of the major mode, and of music based on it, is generally considered "bright," while that of the minor mode is often more somber. The minor keys thus offer composers additional choices for modulation and tonal contrast.

**Relative majors and minors**

A key in the minor mode shares the same key signature with a related major key; for example, three flats are in the key signature of C minor and E♭ major. For this reason, E♭ major is said to be the *relative major* of C minor. Likewise, C minor is the *relative minor* of E♭ major. This means that the two keys are closely related and that their relationship can be easily exploited through modulation. A work might begin in C minor, modulate to E♭ major, and return to C minor. This often happens in Classical music. If a movement opens in a major key, it is likely to modulate to a major key based on its dominant. But if it opens in a minor key, it is likely to modulate to the relative major. In the latter case, there may be a change of mood since the minor may have a characteristically sad or wistful effect that can be effectively contrasted with the brighter major key.

**Changes in texture**

Along with the increasing use of modulation came changes in musical texture. As the Classical style emerged in the mid-eighteenth century, the texture of music tended to be homophonic and less complex than before. In the late eighteenth and early nineteenth centuries, however, when musical forms grew longer and more elaborate, counterpoint began to be used somewhat more often. In many cases, homophonic and contrapuntal textures were used in the same composition or movement. The juxtaposition was important in achieving contrast and variety. While sparse textures were often characteristic of music for solo instruments, the expanding orchestra was capable of producing increasingly dense textures.

**Arrangement of Instruments of the Orchestra for Late Eighteenth-Century Music**

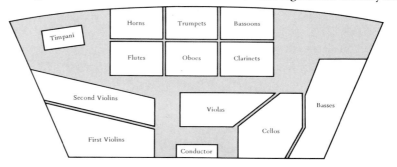

# Timbre and Dynamics

**Classical orchestra**

The Classical period saw the standardization of the orchestra in the form we know today. The usually modest instrumental groups of the Baroque age were surpassed by orchestras of ever-increasing size. By the late eighteenth century, orchestras sometimes had thirty to forty players. The orchestra was dominated by the string section, which was given most of the melodic material. In the woodwind section could be found two flutes, two oboes, two bassoons, and, by the end of the century, the newly developed clarinet. The brass section could include two trumpets and two horns, and the percussion section generally had two timpani. Composers took advantage of the variety and capabilities of instruments available by writing melodies with specific instruments in mind. They exploited tone color as a means of contrast more than had been done before.

One of the largest and most famous of the early Classical orchestras developed at the German court of Mannheim, under the leadership of Johann Stamitz (1717–1757), a talented violinist and composer. All who heard the orchestra were awed by its size and discipline. Especially impressive was its mastery of dynamic effects. The Mannheim orchestra is sometimes credited with having created the crescendo, but it can more accurately be described as the first group to have shown what a strong effect a controlled increase of volume could have on an audience. Equally fine, if less spectacular, was the orchestra's performance of both sudden and sustained decrescendos. The ensemble playing of the Mannheim orchestra impressed many, including Mozart.

The modern symphony orchestra is somewhat larger than that of the Classical age, but the balance of instrumentation is similar to that found in the earlier orchestra. The plan on page 179 shows the arrangement that would likely be used by a modern orchestra playing a symphony by Haydn or Mozart.

Coincident with the development of the Classical orchestra was the rise in prominence of the piano. Invented before 1700 by Bartolomeo Cristofori of Florence, it is properly and was originally called the *pianoforte*, because the pianist, unlike the harpsichordist, could vary the dynamic level of individual notes and chords by the amount of pressure with which the keys were struck. Thus sforzandos, crescen-

The electoral palace at Mannheim, 1725. Carl Theodor, Elector until 1799, was one of the most enlightened patrons of music in his time. (Städtisches Reiss-Museum, Mannheim)

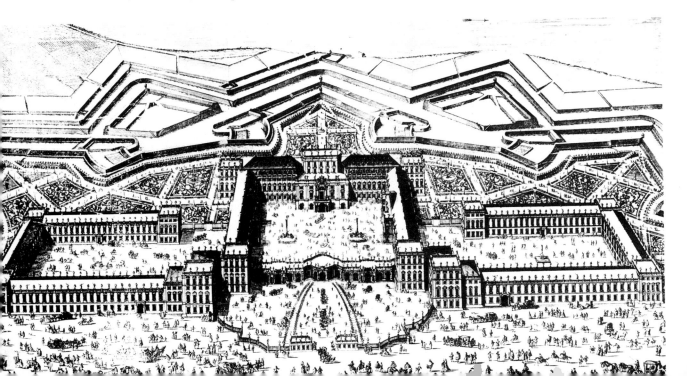

dos, and decrescendos could be produced at will. In the late eighteenth century, the piano gradually replaced the harpsichord as the favorite keyboard instrument.

Vocal music continued to be important in the late eighteenth century, though instrumental music seems generally to have received greater attention from composers. The new and simpler esthetic was applied to vocal forms. Music for solo voices and choirs was written by nearly all composers of the period, much of it with specified instrumental accompaniment.

### Types of Compositions and Forms

In the middle and late eighteenth century, a number of new types of music developed. Instrumental music became even more prominent than it had been in the Baroque age. *Sonatas* were written for all available instruments, and the term *sonata* took on new characteristics and meaning. Other types of chamber music were written for many different combinations of instruments, with the *string quartet* by far the most popular work for chamber ensemble. The *solo concerto* was very popular, as was a new type of composition, the *symphony*. Vocal music included *songs, operas, Masses,* and *oratorios*.

*Sonata cycle*

Particularly characteristic of Classical instrumental music was the so-called *sonata cycle*, a sequence of three or four movements, each cast in a specific form. A number of important Classical works are sonata cycles: the sonata for piano, the symphony for orchestra, the concerto for soloist and orchestra, and many small ensemble works such as the string quartet. All have the typical three or four movements cast in a variety of similar or different forms.

Performance of an opera (c. 1775) on a Turkish subject at the Esterházy court theater in Hungary. Prince Nikolaus I Esterházy engaged Joseph Haydn as court composer and conductor; this appointment lasted from 1762 until 1790 (the year of the Prince's death). Throughout Nikolaus I's reign, musical life at his court was extremely lively. (Deutsches Theatermuseum, Munich)

# Comparison of Baroque and Classical Music

| Elements | Baroque Music 17th and first half 18th centuries | Classical Music Last half of 18th and early 19th centuries |
|---|---|---|
| Melody | Frequent ornamentation Much use of sequence Phrases often lengthy and irregular | Melodies built on motives and short phrases Phrases often very regular in length |
| Rhythm | Free rhythm in recitative Steady, driving rhythm and clear meters in many works | Continued use of free rhythm in recitative Clear meters Greater rhythmic variety within a movement |
| Harmony | Major-minor system Use of modulation, usually to closely related keys | Major-minor system Increased use of modulation as structural basis, to closely related and sometimes distantly related keys |
| Texture | Polyphony, often imitative, important in many works Homophony also used frequently | Homophony most important but continued use of polyphony, often within basically homophonic works Imitative counterpoint less important than before |
| Timbre | Instrumental and vocal music both important Small orchestra, with continuo | Instrumental music more prominent than vocal Larger, more differentiated, standardized orchestra |
| Important Forms | Binary, ternary, ritornello, and fugue Development of many multi-movement works | Sonata, rondo, theme and variations, ternary, and binary Many multi-movement, especially four-movement, works |
| Important Types of Compositions | Older types such as the Mass and motet New types such as opera, cantata, oratorio, sonata, concerto, fugue, and suite | Older types such as the Mass, oratorio, opera, solo concerto, and unaccompanied sonata Many instrumental works based on sonata cycle: symphony, concerto, sonata, and string quartet |

**Sonata Form**

The sonata cycle should not be confused with the sonata, a work for one or a few instruments, or with the *sonata form*, a newly developed musical form. Sometimes called the *sonata-allegro form*, the sonata form provides an elaborate and lively structure for individual movements of sonata-cycle works. It was generally used as the form of the first movement and sometimes for other movements as well, in various types of works, including the solo sonata. The sonata form is divided into three basic sections: the exposition, the development, and the recapitulation. Sometimes a slow introduction precedes the exposition which is usually of a quicker, contrasting character.

## Sonata Form

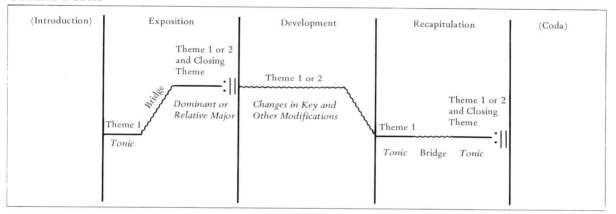

Exposition

The *exposition*, or opening section, of a movement written in the sonata form "exposes" the first theme in the home key. After the listener becomes familiar with this primary material, a harmonic transition, or *bridge* or *transition* passage, takes place. The music modulates to a contrasting key—generally to the key of the dominant or, if the first theme is in a minor key, to the relative major. In the contrasting key, new material may be presented—perhaps several themes, unified mainly by the fact that they are cast in the same key. In some cases, however, the first theme reappears immediately after the bridge and is then followed by a second theme. The exposition closes with a cadence in the second key. Generally the entire exposition is repeated so that the initial musical ideas are heard again. The repetition is indicated by the sign :‖ at the end of the section.

Bridge or transition

Development

In the *development* section, the thematic material of the exposition undergoes a number of changes and musical excitement increases. New and sometimes distant keys are explored with frequent modulations. The themes of the exposition are presented in new ways. They may be broken into motives and recombined, with alterations in timbre, harmony, rhythm, or dynamics. Momentum and intensity generally increase throughout the section.

Recapitulation

Tension is pleasurably resolved in the final section, the *recapitulation*, beginning with a return to the home key and the first theme.

Although the section recapitulates material from the exposition, it is not identical to it. While the same thematic material is presented, a contrasting key is generally not firmly established. Though brief excursions to another key may take place, all themes from the exposition are usually played in the original tonic key. At the end of the recapitulation, a repeat sign often appears, indicating that the development and recapitulation should be repeated as a unit (few performers actually do so in modern performances). Some move-ments in sonata form conclude with a *coda* that affirms or reaffirms the ending.

Coda

Any description of the sonata form is a result of generalizations about compositions already written. Descriptions can merely attempt to capture in words the characteristics of this important Classical form. Individual composers naturally deviated from the model, being more concerned with the immediate expression of musical ideas than with a rigidly followed plan form. Although a general pattern was followed, no two works are exactly alike in form. The form grew out of the material, as is always the case in a living, changing style.

## Rondo Form

The *rondo form* was also much used by Classical composers, fre-quently for final movements. In the rondo form, a primary theme, which almost always appears in the tonic, alternates with two or more themes of secondary importance, which are in different keys. Thus, a typical five-part rondo form might be diagramed in this fashion:

| A | B | A | C | A |
|---|---|---|---|---|

This form can be expanded by the addition of another repetition of the B and A themes.

The rondo form is similar to the Baroque ritornello form in that it alternates between a beginning theme and other lesser themes. It differs from the ritornello form in a number of ways. Perhaps most important is that in the rondo form the first theme almost always reappears in the tonic, while with the ritornello form it may return in other keys. Partly for this reason, the contrasting sections are generally more obvious in the rondo form.

## Sonata-Rondo Form

*Sonata-rondo form* appears in some works of the later eighteenth century, perhaps most often in last movements of multi-movement compositions. As the name suggests, it incorporates aspects of both sonata and rondo principles. Characteristics of the two forms are combined in different ways by composers of the period. A favorite plan was to cast a movement basically in a sonata structure but to have the first theme return periodically in the tonic key, typical of the rondo form. Less frequently used than the sonata form, it was a result of the manner in which a composer used themes and keys.

Antonio Canova: *Pauline Borghese as Venus.* 1808. Rome, Galleria Borghese (photo Scala).

**Neoclassicism**   In art, as in music, a desire for a new means of expression arose toward the middle of the eighteenth century. This yearning for a new and "pure" style, coinciding as it did with the excavations at Herculaneum and Pompeii, culminated in a style based on Classical Greek and Roman models. Philosophers and revolutionaries sought precedents in the republics of ancient Athens and Rome, and it was almost inevitable that Classical art, with its sobriety, its idealization of and obedience to rational rules, would also strike a responsive chord. Based in part on early republican fervor, Neoclassical styles outlived the French Revolution and provided the basis for the Empire style of Napoleon Bonaparte's reign. This late style can be seen in Canova's statue of Napoleon's sister Pauline Borghese. Following a Greek prototype, Canova presented his subject as Venus Victorious. Head and body are idealized, while the clear, cold outline imparts the character of ancient relief.

Jacques Louis David: *The Death of Socrates*. 1787. New York, Metropolitan Museum of Art (Catharine Lorillard Wolfe Collection).

***The Work of David*** Jacques Louis David was one of the first painters to use Classical themes as metaphors of modern life. An ardent republican, he became the virtual dictator of French art in the years after Napoleon's rise to power. In his heroic *Death of Socrates*, Rococo lightness and evanescence are displaced by austere configurations intended to evoke lofty thoughts—thoughts of self-sacrifice and moral elevation. Each of the figures is carefully set apart from his neighbor by David's sharp, icy, relief-like drawing and restricted, uniform colors. Elements of dress and setting are treated, however, with an almost scientific exactitude. David's attempt to create a synthesis of Classical idealism and direct observation had a major influence on early nineteenth-century art.

**English Portraiture** English painters of the Classical age were less influenced by republicanism than by the growing power and wealth of both the English nobility and merchant class, a wealth that created a great demand for portraiture. The seventeenth-century Flemish painter Van Dyck had established a standard of refined portrait painting in England that subsequent English painters sought to emulate. Sitters expected to be flattered and shown at their very best. They wished to look both elegant and aristocratic. Gainsborough, in his *The Honourable Mrs. Graham*, preserved the Vandyckian tradition. Posed full-length in rich brocade beside a column and before a landscape background, the young woman is the very model of grace and breeding. Because of his feeling for color and quiet sensitivity to personality, Gainsborough was able to elevate the rather pedestrian art of portraiture as it was practiced in eighteenth-century England to the level of high art.

Thomas Gainsborough: *The Honourable Mrs. Graham.* 1775. Edinburgh, National Galleries of Scotland.

***Romantic Tendencies*** One of the great individualists of nineteenth-century art, Spanish master Francisco Goya did most of his work some years before the Romantic movement coalesced around French painter Delacroix in the 1820s. Goya saw his country ravaged by Napoleon's soldiers and witnessed the growing poverty and moral decay following the withdrawal of the French forces. During these years he withdrew from the confusions of Madrid to a small house across the river. Its walls he covered with his "black paintings." To paint them he employed the materials he could still find in a ravaged land— lamp black, earth brown and white—yet these nightmare visions of subhuman, devil-worshiping monsters glow with an eerie, almost unnatural light. *Saturn Devouring his Children* is particularly hypnotic. Glorying in mindless fury, Saturn cannibalizes the horribly mangled body of a tiny man. Outlines are rough and colors dominated by a deathly black. It is an art wrenched from the depths of the subconscious.

Francisco Goya: *Saturn devouring One of his Children.* 1820–23. Madrid, Prado.

**Binary Form**

The use of *binary form* (AA' or AB) continued to be important in works of the later eighteenth century. Second movements of multi-movement compositions, in slow or moderate tempos, sometimes make effective use of binary form.

**Ternary Form**

The ternary form (ABA), already observed in earlier music, is prominent in music of the Classical style. Like the rondo, Classical ternary forms became more standardized expansions of their Baroque predecessors. Clear examples will be seen in the minuet and trio, and later in the scherzo and trio of the symphony.

**Theme and Variations Form**

Composers in the late eighteenth and early nineteenth centuries used the theme and variations form often and with great imagination. Its basic principles will be observed in music of this period.

**Other Forms**

The ritornello and fugal forms of the Baroque age gradually lost the importance they once had, although aspects of them were incorporated into music of the Classical period. Both Mozart and Haydn wrote magnificent fugues as part of their Masses. Composers occasionally broke away from the standard forms mentioned here and experimented with a few other hybrid variants of them.

**Music in Eighteenth-Century America**

Singing schools

While musical styles in western Europe were the most highly developed and sophisticated in the Western world in the eighteenth century, some very important developments were taking place in the New World at the same time. A significant development in early music in this country—the *singing school*—began around 1720. Itinerant singing masters traveled from town to town conducting series of weekly sessions and often making an additional profit by selling the necessary songbooks. The musical sessions generally climaxed in a public concert in which the local singers sang in parts. The music taught at the singing schools usually included psalms, hymn tunes, anthems, and fuguing tunes, which included short, imitative sections.

Billings

Prominent among composers of music for the singing schools was William Billings (1746–1800). A self-taught composer who abandoned a career as a tanner to devote himself to music, Billings conspicuously lacked technical sophistication and made no effort to acquire it. Among his works are a number of fuguing tunes, relatively simple, three- or four-part works that feature imitation in much the same way it is used in fugues. Another Yankee tunesmith was Daniel Read (1759–1836). His fuguing tune "Sherburne," originally published in 1785, appears below in shape-note notation. It is taken from the *Sacred Harp*, a book of religious songs that is still used today, after having appeared in many editions, attesting to the long life of this repertory in some areas of the United States.

The system of singing from shape notes was a continuation of the singing school movement in the South and West in the nineteenth

"Sherburne" from the *Sacred Harp*. This fuguing tune in shape-note notation is typical of a long tradition of such religious songs found chiefly in the southeastern part of the United States.

**Fasola and shape-note notation**

century. Its predecessor in England and America in the seventeenth and eighteenth centuries was a system of sight-singing known as *fasola* because it used principally those three syllables—fa, sol, and la; the syllable mi was used for the leading tone. The fasola system led in the early nineteenth century to the invention of *shape-note notation*, in which four notes of different shapes—generally triangular, round, oblong, and diamond-shaped—were used to show relative pitches in a melody. A major scale, notated with appropriate note shapes, would be sung as: fa sol la fa sol la mi fa. The object was to enable a middle-class congregation to read music without spending much time learning how. Shape notes were much used in the rural South in the nineteenth century, largely in popular collections of hymns and anthems. Today shape-note singing is still avidly pursued by a number of small groups in the South.

In the East, a "better music" movement began around 1800. Greater adherence to European standards of church music was urged. Lowell Mason (1792–1872) was the most important leader of the movement. He established "normal schools" for music to instruct teachers in the better aspects of European musical styles, including how to sing. Mason was as much an entrepreneur as an artist. He used advertising techniques to attract audiences and quite frankly wrote his music in a style to suit the current fashion. He introduced improved teaching methods and compiled a number of song collections including *The Boston Handel and Haydn Society Collection of Church Music*. Mason was also important in popularizing hymns based on music adapted from European master composers. He is generally considered to be the father of public school music education in this country.

**Secular folk music**

A secular folk tradition was brought to America by the earliest settlers. Songs originally brought from England changed their contours a bit, picked up new words here and there, and soon became comfortably American. They were passed on informally from one singer or fiddler to another at barn raisings, on the trail, or around the fire on winter nights, changing as they went—sometimes greatly, sometimes scarcely at all. In some parts of the United States, notably the remote southern Appalachian region, many of these tunes have survived in common use up to the present day. Tracing their evolution from their English or Scottish origins is one of the fascinating elements in the study of American folklore.

While folk music soon became part of the American tradition, composed music long remained fundamentally European in style. Throughout the colonial period, music outside of the folk tradition **European influence** was dominated by European composers, European teachers, and European performers. This is not to say that Americans were uninterested in concert music. In fact, the late eighteenth century was a time of increasing musical interest and activity throughout what would soon be the United States. Amateur composers studied European works, and books of music instruction were published. Public concerts grew in popularity, and impressive, expensive pipe organs were built in many city churches. Philadelphia and Charleston became the chief music centers of the era. By 1762, the Saint Cecilia Society, the first major musical society in the New World, had been established in Charleston. Many professionally trained musicians arrived from Europe after the Revolutionary War to work as teachers, performers, and composers.

An influential group of amateurs, including Thomas Jefferson and Benjamin Franklin, had much to do with introducing the works of such European composers as Haydn and Mozart to the Eastern Seaboard. Jefferson hoped to create a cultural center at his Virginia home, Monticello. Franklin was not only a lover of music but an amateur composer and the inventor of an improved type of glass harmonica that inspired several works by Mozart. Francis Hopkinson (1737–1791) was one of the earliest native-born American composers of secular music. Hopkinson wrote several large works as well as a number of songs, the best known of which, "My Days Have Been So Wondrous Free" (1759), is the earliest surviving song by an American.

Many types and styles of folk music were widely known and greatly loved in eighteenth-century America. Concert music was heard with greater frequency. Works by European composers were often performed, but also compositions by native American composers were increasingly heard. People who were very busy building a new country and society also found time to enjoy music.

# CHAPTER 12

# Symphonies of Haydn and Mozart

*LISTENING PREVIEW The symphony came to be one of the most important types of instrumental compositions in the later eighteenth century. Haydn was extremely innovative and imaginative in the development of the symphony. Mozart's symphonies were influenced by a number of Haydn's ideas, but they also include many fresh, new approaches to content and structure. Mozart's late symphonies show very striking use of dramatic contrast. Listen to the first movement of his* Symphony No. 40 in G Minor *(side 4, band 4) and identify the musical techniques through which dramatic contrast is achieved.*

## Development of the Classical Symphony

### Antecedents of the symphony

The *symphony* of the late eighteenth century drew upon, and was influenced by, a number of earlier musical developments. The three-part Italian overture of the Baroque age suggested the overall fast–slow–fast plan of movements. The Baroque suite provided the concept of independent movements within a large work, as well as the minuet, a compositional form often chosen for the symphony's third movement. The binary form, which had been used in many Baroque sonatas, played an important part in the development of the sonata form of the Classical age—the form on which the first movement of most symphonies was based. These and other subtler influences were important in the development of the Classical symphony—a sonata cycle for orchestra.

The orchestra and the symphony were both undergoing significant development in many different parts of mid-eighteenth-century Europe; Mannheim, Berlin, and Vienna were among the most prominent centers of activity. But it is in the works of Franz Josef Haydn (1732–1809), a major pioneer of the Classical style, that the growth of the symphony from a short work of simple style to a longer, more sophisticated work can most clearly be seen. Many of his symphonies are quite light and very direct in style; others are considerably more serious. Many were written for the diversion of a small circle of aristocrats rather than for the general public. What is perhaps more surprising is the great number of Haydn's symphonies—more than

### Haydn

Joseph Haydn; engraving after the portrait (c. 1770) by Ludwig Guttenbrunn. (Österreichische Nationalbibliothek, Vienna)

one hundred and four. Most later composers wrote fewer than ten.

**Structure of the symphony**

While some of Haydn's early symphonies have only three movements, four movements soon became the standard number. The tempos of the four movements were generally fast, slow, moderate, and fast. The first movement of one of Haydn's mature works, or of a symphony written by one of his contemporaries, was almost invariably in sonata form, sometimes preceded by a slow introduction, which often contrasted dramatically with the exposition that followed it. The second movement was generally in binary or sonata form but sometimes in theme and variations form. It tended to be more lyrical and contemplative in mood. The third movement was usually a stylized minuet and trio in ternary form. The last movement was generally in a quick sonata or rondo form but sometimes in a sonata-rondo form that combined features of both forms. Often the mood here was whimsical and lighthearted.

## Haydn's Symphonies

Haydn was born and raised in a small village, and his earliest musical exposure was to the traditional folk music of rural Austria. Throughout his career he maintained a strong and genuine attachment to folk music, and many of his symphonies testify to its influence on him.

Haydn received some musical education as a choirboy of St. Stefan's Cathedral in Vienna, but he left that position when his voice changed. He then had to spend several precarious years as a freelance musician and teacher, learning composition in the process. In 1761 he became assistant music director at the Esterházy estate in Hungary. He served first under the patronage of Prince Paul Anton Esterházy and later under that of his brother Prince Nikolaus, who was an amateur musician. Because the principal music director was old, Haydn took over the direction of his patron's orchestra. His duties were broad and varied, including the administration of the musicians' salaries and wardrobes as well as the supervision of their moral behavior. But most important, Haydn was expected to write music—a great deal of music—for the many social events at the Esterházy palace.

In eighteenth-century society, Haydn's position was really no more prestigious than that of a gardener, housekeeper, or other skilled servant. And yet it offered a number of real advantages. Haydn had at his command an excellent group of singers and players. He had the use of fine musical facilities, including an opera house. Because of the patronage system, he enjoyed economic security in a time when the financial position of the artist was otherwise precarious. Of course, the advantages could be outweighed by disadvantages if patron and composer had incompatible ideas about music. In this regard, Haydn was in many ways quite fortunate to be working for the Esterházy family—patrons who expected him to compose works in the latest style. Even though he was a servant, his music achieved an international reputation.

The compositions Haydn wrote for the Esterházys were very origi-

An early 19th-century glass, showing a street in Vienna. Compared to Paris and London, the imperial capital of Vienna in the late 18th and early 19th century was commercially and politically still fairly quiet. As the breath of enlightenment swept through the city, music and theater flourished. Unobtrusively, a musical revolution was taking place. (Photo:Werner Forman Archive)

**Garden front of the Esterházy palace, the "Hungarian Versailles" where Haydn was employed. (British Library; photo Heritage of Music)**

nal. He was a champion of new forms, an innovator in modulation, the acknowledged master of surprise, and yet his music was both logical and coherent. Early attempts at fresh melody, harmony, and phrasing developed under Haydn into the perfect balance of the Classical style.

Haydn's music drew on the folksongs of his native Austria and on the dance music of the Baroque. He was one of the first composers to develop themes in the Classical sense and to exploit the enormous power of modulation and changes of tonality for dramatic purposes. Haydn and his contemporaries were able to prepare for and suggest the dramatic development of an entire work in the musical relationships of its opening phrases.

**The London Symphonies**

Prince Nikolaus died in 1790. Haydn left the Esterházy court, and soon traveled to London. The height of his symphonic art is nowhere more apparent than in his *Symphonies No. 93–104*, written not for the Esterházys but for British impresario Johann Peter Salomon (1745–1815). In 1791 Haydn, already well known throughout Europe, was commissioned by Salomon to write and conduct a series of symphonies to be performed in London. These have come to be known as the "London" or "Salomon" Symphonies. At this point in his career, Haydn had gained a degree of freedom from the Esterházys and had moved to Vienna. There he had become very friendly with Mozart, and had been in contact with the young Beethoven. Clearly he was the master of an important new style of music. And yet Haydn was not insensible to the beauty of Baroque music. Upon hearing the London orchestra that was to present his new works to the world in a performance of the works of past masters, he was deeply moved. "Handel is the master of us all," he is reported to have said. It was not by chance that after he left London he devoted his last years to sacred music, notably six remarkable settings of the Mass and *The Creation*, an oratorio that is still frequently performed. He agreed to compose one religious work a year for Prince Nikolaus Esterházy II. The English visits had proved as important to Haydn's later development as the Esterházy experience was to his middle years.

**Haydn's other works**

Haydn wrote in many specifically Classical forms, and seems astonishingly prolific by today's standards. He wrote about 108 symphonies, around 70 string quartets, 200 other chamber works, and 60 keyboard sonatas besides 20 operas and several cantatas, oratorios, and concertos. Such was his prestige in his own time that a tune he wrote became the Austrian national anthem. (It is the theme of the slow movement of his "Emperor" string quartet, Op. 76, No. 3, which we will study in Chapter 15.) Haydn symphonies often begin orchestral concerts today, while many of his chamber and choral works are also frequently heard. We will study different aspects of Haydn's music in later chapters.

## *Haydn: Symphony No. 94 in G Major ("Surprise" Symphony)*

Haydn's *Symphony No. 94 in G Major* was first performed in London, on March 23, 1792. It was an immediate success—especially the second movement, which included the "surprise" that gave the work its name. The *London Diary* called it "simple and profound," great praise for a work in the Classical spirit. In our own time, the symphony continues to be widely appreciated and often performed.

The symphony is in four movements. It is scored for pairs of flutes, oboes, bassoons, horns, trumpets, and timpani, in addition to the string parts.

**LISTENING ANALYSIS**                                             SIDE 4, BAND 1

*First Movement: Adagio cantabile—Vivace assai; Sonata Form*

**Introduction**

The first movement opens with an introduction that readily evokes a pastoral setting—a sense of peaceful countryside that is never long absent from Haydn's music. The introduction is marked Adagio cantabile (slow, in a singing style) and is in triple meter. The woodwinds and strings alternate in presenting the opening material. The strings then play a chromatic passage that ends on the dominant, to lead to the tonic key for the exposition.

**Exposition**

The first theme, in G major and marked Vivace assai (very, very fast), is a vivacious, folklike melody introduced by the first violins.

First Theme

The final note in the theme is marked *forte* ("loud"). At this point the violins are joined by the full orchestra, which presents a loud rhythmic pattern in the lower register:

/◡◡◡◡. This rhythmic pattern, accompanied by a whirling figure in the violins, creates a generally rousing effect.

The music moves toward a repeat of the first theme with a delightful prefatory phrase that will be heard many times in the movement:

Prefatory Phrase

First Theme

After this phrase, and just before the return of the first theme, the orchestra comes to a full stop.

When the first theme reappears in the violins, it is again followed by the full orchestra. But this time the rhythmic pattern and the theme are somewhat different. They are part of a bridge passage by which the music modulates to a new key—that of the dominant, D major.

After the new key is established, a quick series of scale passages is played by the violins and flutes. The second theme is then heard. It is marked *dolce* ("sweet") and is somewhat more lyrical than the first. The large-interval dips in the later measures have an especially pleasing effect.

Second Theme

The exposition closes with a short scale figure and repeated notes. Haydn indicated that the exposition should then be repeated. The introduction and exposition may be summarized as follows:

| Introduction | Exposition |
|---|---|
| Adagio | Vivace assai |
| | Scales Theme II    II    Scales |
| Tonic | Theme I    I    Dominant |

**Development**

The development section opens with a variation of the first theme:

Variation of First Theme

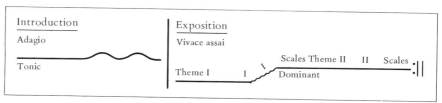

A series of modulations and dynamic changes help to create the dramatic tension so characteristic of development sections. Scales, arpeggios, and repeated notes are all heard in turn as familiar musical ideas reappear in a new context.

**Recapitulation**

The recapitulation begins with the first theme returning clearly in the home key. After a passage based largely on scales and motives from the first theme, the first theme returns again and is momentarily developed. After a brief pause, the first theme is again repeated. The second theme then returns briefly, also in the home key. The movement comes to a close with a short scale passage and a strong, repeated cadence.

### LISTENING SUMMARY

Timbre:    orchestra of moderate size: string section and pairs of flutes, oboes, bassoons, horns, trumpets and timpani
Melody:    first theme most prominent in the movement; second theme more lyrical
Rhythm:    introduction in ¾ meter; tempo Adagio cantabile (slow, singing style); rest of movement in $\frac{6}{8}$ meter, tempo vivace assai (very, very fast)
Harmony:   mainly major mode; begins in G major, modulates most significantly to D major; ends in G major
Form:      sonata form preceded by slow introduction

**Haydn: Symphony No. 94 in G Major ("Surprise" Symphony), Second Movement**

### LISTENING ANALYSIS                                           SIDE 4, BAND 2

*Second Movement: Andante; Theme and Variations Form*

The second movement of the "Surprise" Symphony is marked Andante ("moderate") in contrast to the very quick tempo of the first movement. There is also a dynamic contrast between the vigorous final chords of the first movement and the first notes of the second movement, which are marked *piano* ("soft"). Finally, the second movement is in C major, providing a tonal contrast to the first movement in G major.

It was the second movement that immediately charmed London audiences with its use of a beautifully simple theme in a masterful theme and variations form. The first phrase of the theme is built mainly of triads. The first motive, in fact, uses nothing but the I chord of the key of C. The second motive is based on a $V^7$ chord (G–B–D–F).

The rest of the theme is nearly as simple. The first two phrases, each four measures long, are shown below. Note that the second phrase begins like the first but ends differently. The last note of each phrase, however, is the same—the dominant. The phrases are labeled a¹ and a² because they begin so similarly.

Phrases a¹ and a²

These phrases are first played softly by the violins. They are then repeated, even more softly. It is at the end of this repetition that the famous *ff* chord is heard. The chord is a V chord that needs to be resolved or answered, and it is indeed answered, in perfect balance, by another sixteen measures. Like the first sixteen measures, these are made up of two four-measure phrases played twice. The answering phrases are shown below, slightly simplified.

Note that the last phrase ends on the tonic note C, conveying a sense of finality and rest.
The theme then is made up of eight phrases arranged in the following order:

**Theme**

| Part: | A | | | | B | | | |
|---|---|---|---|---|---|---|---|---|
| **Phrase:** | a¹ | a² | a¹ | a² | b | c | b | c |

Variations

From this simple material, Haydn created a series of delightful variations. In the first variation, the second violins play the theme. After they complete the first motive, the first violins enter lightly with a countermelody. The quick, conjunct notes of the countermelody are full of Classical charm and grace.

This part of the variation, the first half of the theme, is repeated. Then phrases b and c, the second half of the theme, are presented, also with a countermelody in the first violins.

In the second variation, the music moves to the key of C minor. The first phrase of the theme is boldly presented by the woodwinds and strings without any harmony or elaboration. The use of the minor mode creates a dramatic effect.

Variation 2 : Minore

As the variation unfolds, the first half of the theme undergoes a modulation to the relative major key. It is then repeated. The second half of the theme does not appear at all in this variation. Instead, there is additional development of the first phrase. A unison passage then leads to the next variation without pause.

The major mode is firmly reestablished at the beginning of the third variation. This variation presents the theme in a new 2:1 rhythm—two notes are played for every one note in the original theme.

Variation 3

The repeat of Phrase a$^1$ omits the 2:1 rhythm and is accompanied by a countermelody in the flute and oboe. Sometimes paralleling the movement of the theme, sometimes departing from it, this countermelody has a colorful, lilting effect. The second half of the theme then appears in varied form and is repeated, with the flute and oboe continuing to play a prominent countermelody.

In the fourth variation, the music generates an excitement that propels the movement to its close. The variation starts with a 3:1 rhythm, with three notes in the accompaniment for every one note of the theme. If you think "ONE-two-three" for every note of the theme, you can reproduce this rhythmic effect for yourself:

Variation 4

1-2-3 1-2-3  1-2-3 1-2-3     1-2-3 1-2-3  1-2-3 1-2-3

As the theme is played to this rhythm, it undergoes additional changes. Most notably in the opening phrase of the variation, *ff* chords are sounded on normally weak beats. Then, a new variation of the first part of the theme is heard. The original melody is recast in an uneven or dotted rhythm to produce an interesting new effect.

Additional Variation of Theme in Variation 4

*p dolce*

What were formerly two notes of the same pitch and duration have become two notes of different pitch and unequal duration, and yet the theme remains recognizable. The second half of the theme is presented more dramatically, first with a 2:1 rhythm and then with a 3:1 rhythm.

**Coda**

The movement ends with a coda that is a work of art in itself. It consists of an extension of the fourth variation and a phrase from the theme. The treatment of this material produces a feeling of suspense followed by resolution.

**LISTENING SUMMARY**

Timbre: orchestra of moderate size: string section, and pairs of flutes, oboes, bassoons, horns, trumpets, and timpani

Melody: based on the tonic and dominant chords; phrase structure very symmetrical; melody easily identifiable in the varied guises it takes

Rhythm: $\frac{2}{4}$ meter, tempo Andante (moderate); use of 2:1, 3:1, and dotted rhythms as means of variation

Harmony: mainly major mode; C major through most of the movement, C minor and E♭ major in the second variation

Form: theme and four variations followed by a coda

### Third Movement: Allegro molto; Minuet and Trio; Ternary Form

**Minuet**

The third movement of the "Surprise" Symphony opens with a minuet that reflects the folk dances of the Austrian countryside. The music is strongly metrical, as is typical of most dances. The opening theme begins in G major and is played by full orchestra:

Opening Theme

The triple meter and moderately quick tempo are characteristic of the minuet.

The opening theme is followed by a short motive, first played by flute and violins, and growing in volume as other instruments join in. This first, short section is then repeated. A second section begins with a new melody and then returns to the opening theme. This section is also repeated.

**Trio**

The minuet is followed by a *trio* of contrasting quieter character and instrumentation. Though, typically, the trio involves more than three instruments, it is not so fully orchestrated as the rest of the movement. Bassoon and violin share the presentation of a new theme.

**Minuet**

After the trio is completed, the minuet returns. Thus the movement is in typical minuet and trio form:

| A | B | A |
|---|---|---|
| **Minuet** | **Trio** | **Minuet** |

The minuet and trio exemplifies the most common use of ternary form in early Classical symphonies. Here and in the minuets of later composers, the court or country dance is transcended. It becomes idealized, not meant for actual dancing, except perhaps for that which takes place in the imagination of the listener.

### Fourth Movement: Allegro molto; Sonata-Rondo form

**Sonata-rondo form**

The movement, in G major, is basically in sonata form, but the music frequently returns to the first theme in the tonic key. Haydn and his contemporaries are noted for combining aspects of sonata and rondo forms, particularly in the last movements of their symphonies.

**Exposition**

The tempo of the fourth movement is very fast, and the rhythm is at first quite dancelike in spirit. The first theme is full of impetuous energy. Its first part is introduced by the first violins.

Beginning of First Theme

The first violins and flutes repeat the first part of the theme. A second, complementary phrase follows, after which there is a return of the first part of the opening theme, but with a different ending. The opening theme group can therefore be viewed as: Ia a b a′. Following, there is a bridge emphasizing rapid scale passages in the violins and elements of the first part of the theme, in which the dominant key of D major is established. A second theme appears in this new key, followed by quick scales and arpeggios in the violin.

**Development**

The first theme then returns in the original key, a characteristic of rondo form. But immediately thereafter occurs development of elements of the theme, through fragmentation and changing keys. Development continues after the first theme returns again in G major: G minor and other keys are used briefly in the development.

**Recapitulation**

After the development, a recapitulation of the first and second themes is heard in the home key. The movement ends with a brilliant coda. Its last measures offer yet one more surprise—a stark change in dynamic level, from soft to very loud.

**Coda**

## Mozart's Symphonies

It was probably in 1781, eleven years before the performance of the "Surprise" Symphony, that Haydn first met the young musician whom he later acknowledged as the greatest composer of his time: Wolfgang Amadeus Mozart (1756–1791). Though Mozart was quite young when they met, he had already done much to command the attention of serious musicians. He had been in the public eye since the age of six, when he performed with his father and sister at the court of Empress

Maria Theresa of Austria. The career of this "boy genius" and his development in the later years of his short life represent another great chapter in the history of the Classical style.

Mozart was born into a very musical Austrian family. Like the young Bachs, he had a brilliant teacher in his father, Leopold Mozart, a court musician who devoted much of his time to the musical education of his son, and eventually gave up his own career to manage the child's performances. Wolfgang Mozart traveled throughout Europe, performing, improvising, and composing. Meanwhile, he was absorbing the musical atmospheres of the countries he visited, many of which would influence his later compositions.

Early in his career, Mozart accepted a position as a court music director to the archbishop of Salzburg, and thus it seemed that he was destined to follow the path laid out by both his father and Haydn. However the patronage system was ultimately to prove unbearable to him. This was partly because of his temperament and partly because historical changes created alternatives to this relationship.

**The musician as a public artist**

As we have seen, the Classical period coincided with the rise of a strong middle-class culture. No longer was music restricted to the church or reserved for the aristocracy. By the end of the eighteenth century, it was possible for impresarios such as Salomon to arrange public concerts. It was at least theoretically possible for well-known composers to support themselves by giving concerts, teaching, accepting commissions, and publishing some of their own works. The commercial world could not, however, offer the security of the patronage system. After a heady period of success due to the immense popularity of several of his operas, Mozart's years as an independent artist—years in which he wrote operas, a number of symphonies and concertos, and a great variety of chamber works—were marked by financial insecurity.

**Mozart and Haydn**

The two greatest composers of the Classical period could not have been more different as individuals. Haydn was a careful craftsman who worked out his musical ideas laboriously. He had a long, stable life within the patronage system, and his music echoes his native Austria. Mozart was traveled and cosmopolitan, impractical in everyday affairs, and prepared to sacrifice the security of the patronage system for professional freedom. He composed spontaneously, often in his head, and could carry on a conversation while writing his music down. (In only thirty-five years he wrote over 600 pieces of music.) Haydn had a hero's funeral: Mozart was buried in a pauper's grave.

**Mozart's music**

Mozart's music has elements of the styles he had heard on his early travels: light, Italianate homophony is fused with the noble polyphony of the German Baroque and with aspects of French music also. His music can be full of Classical grace and charm, yet simultaneously evoke dark, dramatic undercurrents that at times surprised his audience in his own time.

Mozart's works span the whole range of Classical achievement, and

With the decline of noble patronage of music and the steady rise of the urban middle classes, concerts open to the public – mostly in the form of subscription concerts – would become more and more common in the 19th century. This picture is of the inauguration in 1788 of the Felix Meritus Society's concert hall in Amsterdam. (Bildarchiv Preussischer Kulturbesitz)

his genius left its mark on all types of music of his day. Among his other fine works for orchestra are his 27 piano concertos and 5 violin concertos. His greatest operas are masterpieces of dramatic art, psychological insight, and the portrayal of emotion in music, as we'll see in Chapter 16. His contribution is well summed up by one critic, who said simply, "Mozart *is* music."

Mozart's earliest symphonies were, like Haydn's earliest symphonies, relatively short and simple. His later symphonies were much longer and more complex. It was during six weeks in the summer of 1788, under great financial stress, that Mozart completed his last three symphonies, all of which have come to be regarded as masterpieces. They are the *Symphony No. 39 in E♭ Major, Symphony No. 40 in G Minor,* and *Symphony No. 41 in C Major.* The last is also known as the

"Jupiter" Symphony. These three symphonies show Mozart at the height of his achievement. All—especially *Symphony No. 40 in G Minor*—speak with an emotional urgency that is highly romantic. In fact, in Mozart's last works, the beginning of the movement toward the Romantic style can already be seen. The works have the order and control of the Classical age, but they seem to reach out with the passionate yearning of the Romantic style for what is beyond them.

**Köchel**

When Mozart died at the age of thirty-five, the scope of his work was neither known nor fully appreciated. It remained for a later musicographer, Ludwig von Köchel (1800–1877), to draw up a chronological list of Mozart's works so that later musicians and audiences could make reference to them. (Similar lists have been drawn up for other composers. After all, there may be a number of "Symphonies in C" written by any one composer.) Each of Mozart's compositions now bears a number from the Köchel list. The *Symphony No. 40*, for example, bears the designation "K.550," or Köchel Number 550.

**Mozart: Symphony No. 40 in G Minor, K. 550**

The style of Mozart's mature symphonies, and indeed that of the late eighteenth century in general, is exemplified in the *Symphony No. 40 in G Minor*. No one work can be typical of all the work done by any one composer. Yet a number of general and specific characteristics of Mozart's late symphonies are beautifully evident in this work.

The symphony is in four movements. It is scored for one flute, pairs of oboes, clarinets, bassoons, horns, and the usual string section. The clarinets were added by Mozart in a second scoring.

Mozart: autograph manuscript of the opening of Symphony No. 41 in C major (1788), the "Jupiter Symphony" (Deutsche Staatsbibliothek, Berlin (East); photo: Bildarchiv Preussischer Kulturbesitz)

## Mozart: Symphony No. 40 in G Minor, K. 550, First Movement

Exposition

**LISTENING ANALYSIS**

### First Movement: Allegro molto; Sonata Form

This symphony, the second of the three that Mozart wrote during the summer of 1788, is perhaps the most "romantic" of all of Mozart's symphonies. Nevertheless it is strictly Classical in its form and development. The drama of the entire symphony is somehow latent in the three-note motive at the beginning of the exposition:

Opening Motive

Both the pitch and the rhythm of the motive are significant. The change in pitch—the interval between the first two notes—is very small. There is just the half step fall from E♭ to D. The rhythm also contributes to the sense of an abrupt fall. The short-short-long rhythm of two eighth notes followed by a quarter note combines with the tonal pattern to give a sense of a rapid fall onto the third note. In all its simplicity, this motive is the basis for the first theme and for much of the movement that follows.

The first theme is played by the violins above a soft, chordal accompaniment played by the lower strings. The accompaniment establishes the tonic key of G minor, while the theme itself hovers around the dominant and subdominant, never once coming to rest on the tonic. This accounts in part for the sense of mysterious agitation evoked by the music at the opening of the movement:

Phrases a and b

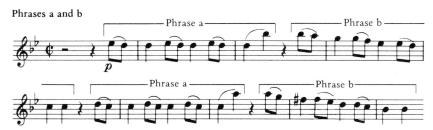

An examination of the phrases at the beginning of the movement shows that the third and fourth phrases repeat the first two—in sequence, one step lower. After this, a new, answering phrase is heard:

Phrase c

It, too, is repeated. The theme ends with the strings playing a series of emphatic chords that end in an abrupt halt.

The beginning of the theme is then repeated, leading without pause into the bridge. The modulation is completed, with a new short motive and scale passages. After a brief pause, the calmer, flowing second theme appears in the key of B♭ major, the relative major of G minor. The theme begins with a descending chromatic phrase played by the violins.

It is answered by a woodwind phrase that draws the melodic line down even farther. The rhythmic motion in this theme is slower than it was in the first, helping to give the music a more lyrical feeling. The theme is repeated by flute, clarinet, and violins, almost as if in conversation. In an extension of this repetition, tension builds with a crescendo that leads to the closing section.

The closing section of the exposition begins with the clarinet playing the opening motive. The motive is passed back and forth between clarinet and bassoon, and then played forte by the first violins. The exposition ends with the first motive, followed by a strong, clear cadence. Mozart indicated that the exposition should be repeated.

**Development**

In the development, the opening motive and the first theme undergo substantial transformation. After a feeling of suspense has been established in the opening chords, the first theme is repeated in descending sequence by the high strings. Repetitions of the theme are altered in a number of other ways. The theme is, for example, played in the low register of the basses. At one point, the theme is reduced to insistent, obsessive repetitions of the opening motive:

Repetition of Opening Motive

In some of the alterations, the rhythm of the opening motive is retained while the tonal pattern is varied, sometimes inverted—that is, turned upside down. Toward the end of the development, the theme is passed imitatively between the strings and the woodwinds as tension builds. The section ends with a descending line played by flute and clarinets, a transition that returns beautifully to the home key of G minor.

**Recapitulation**

The recapitulation begins with the first theme in the home key. This section differs from the exposition in two important ways. The bridge is extended, and the second theme is played in the tonic key of G minor rather than in the relative major—Bb major. Because the second theme is now heard in the minor instead of the major key of the exposition, it takes on a new and more tragic character. The movement ends with a closing section built on the familiar first theme.

**LISTENING SUMMARY**

Timbre:   orchestra of moderate size: string section, one flute and pairs of oboes, clarinets, bassoons, and horns
Melody:   first theme, and especially its three-note motive, dominates much of the movement; second theme conjunct, chromatic, and more lyrical
Rhythm:   duple meter; tempo Allegro molto (very fast)
Harmony:  mainly minor mode; begins in G minor, modulates most significantly to Bb major, ends in G minor
Form:     sonata form

### Second Movement: Andante; Sonata Form

As in most sonata cycles, the second movement presents an emotional contrast to the first. It is marked Andante and set in the key of Eb major, a key that is rather unexpected and therefore very fresh sounding. In this particular symphony, the second movement is written in the same form as the first—sonata form.

The two contrasting aspects of Mozart's mature works—Classicism and Romanticism—are readily apparent in the second movement. The work is the epitome of Viennese grace; the polite voices of flute, clarinet, and strings play well-turned phrases, giving the music an air of sophisticated charm. Yet at times a sense of urgency seems to take over, and the music becomes more dissonant and more forceful.

**Exposition**

The expressive contrast is suggested even in the opening bars of the movement. The first motive is played sweetly and evenly by the violas. The second violins join in, then the first violins, and at each joining the sweet melody becomes more overcast with tension. At the end of the first phrase, the calm, even, rhythmic motion turns into a hesitant dotted rhythm that foreshadows things to come. A rising two-note figure is played assertively here and later. The second theme, in Bb major, then enters, with a sweet question-and-answer sound, returning the music and the listener momentarily to the world of Viennese grace.

**Development and recapitulation**

The development begins with the first theme heard now in a more somber and intense form. It is followed by material from the second theme. The recapitulation is particularly creative in its subtle review of the earlier material.

## *Mozart: Symphony No. 40 in G Minor, K. 550, Third Movement*

**LISTENING ANALYSIS**                                    SIDE 4, BAND 4

### *Third Movement: Menuetto Allegretto; Minuet and Trio; Ternary Form*

The third movement is a minuet and trio in ternary form. The minuet, which opens the movement, returns to the key of G minor, while the trio is in G major.

The opening theme disrupts the clear triple meter typical of the minuet, featuring instead a very prominent use of syncopation. A clear triple meter is played in the accompaniment, but attention is directed to the more rhythmically active melody, which is cast basically in a duple meter and sounds dark and dramatic.

Phrases a and b

The phrase structure of the opening theme is asymmetrical. Two phrases of three measures each are followed by one phrase of five measures and another of three. The unpredictability of the melodic structure adds considerable interest and an unsettled feeling. Interest is also added by the change from G minor to the relative major mode at the beginning of the second section of the minuet. Both sections are based on the same thematic material and both are repeated.

**Trio**

The trio, set in G major, features a lyrical melody that offers contrast to the more abrupt opening theme. Like most other trios, it is more thinly orchestrated than the minuet. Solos are scored for flute, violins, and horns, and in some phrases wind instruments appear in duet. The trio is divided into two sections, and each section is repeated. After the trio, the minuet is repeated, as usual.

**LISTENING SUMMARY**

| | |
|---|---|
| Timbre: | orchestra of moderate size: string section, one flute, and pairs of oboes, clarinets, bassoons, and horns |
| Melody: | first theme of strong character; second theme more lyrical |
| Rhythm: | $\frac{3}{4}$ meter (duple meter suggested momentarily by syncopation in first theme); tempo Allegretto (moderately fast) |
| Harmony: | minor and major modes; G minor dominates in minuet; G major in trio |
| Form: | ternary (ABA) |

*Fourth Movement: Allegro assai; Sonata Form*

Finale

The fourth movement, or *finale*, is in sonata form. It is cast in the home key of G minor and played Allegro assai (very fast).

Exposition

The movement opens with a G minor arpeggio—that is, the notes of the tonic chord, played one by one. This rising pattern, sometimes called the "rocket" motive, is played softly by the first violins and answered loudly by the full orchestra:

First Phrase of First Theme

The first phrase of the theme is heard four times before the second phrase enters. The latter starts with a descending motive but ends with a version of the first phrase. It is then repeated. After the theme has been presented, a bridge including rapid scales leads to the contrasting key of B♭ major and the second theme. The exposition ends with material from the second phrase of the first theme.

Development

The rapid-fire development section is particularly appropriate in a finale. The dramatic rocket motive of the first theme is developed extensively, with the different instruments of the orchestra repeating it in turn in a complex contrapuntal dialogue. Imitation of the rocket motive and of a short scalar motive is especially effective. Frequent modulations at a rapid tempo add to the increasing excitement.

Recapitulation

At the beginning of the recapitulation, the exhilarating first theme is heard again. The second theme, now in the home key, also returns.

Coda

This time it has a wistful, even tragic, sound. A brief, powerful coda elaborates on the final cadence and brings the symphony to an end.

Other late symphonies of Haydn and Mozart follow the same general format seen in these two works. There are, of course, many new, interesting, and, at times, surprising ideas in each symphony. An exploration of other symphonies of Haydn and Mozart can provide many hours of great pleasure.

# CHAPTER 13

# Symphonies of Beethoven: Classicism and Beyond

*LISTENING PREVIEW The first movement of Beethoven's* Symphony No. 5 *is well known the world over. It is one of the most powerful musical statements of the early nineteenth century. Listen to the opening section of the first movement (side 5, band 1) and describe those characteristics of the music that create a strong sense of energy.*

Ludwig van Beethoven (1770–1827) grew up in the German city of Bonn. His father, a court singer under the patronage of Elector Maximilian Friedrich, was a man of artistic temperament but no great talent.

Young Beethoven received a little general education. He began his musical career as assistant organist at the Elector's court, where he immersed himself in performance and composition. When the Elector decided to establish an orchestra, Beethoven was quick to see possibilities in this new medium.

By 1792 Bonn had grown too small for Beethoven's ambition. In that year he left for Vienna to study with the masters. Although Mozart was now dead, Haydn was not. Count Waldstein, one of Beethoven's early sponsors, paid tribute to the masters in a letter to him: "You are going to Vienna in fulfillment of your long frustrated wishes...you will receive the spirit of Mozart from the hands of Haydn."

Beethoven took up residence in Vienna during the aftermath of the French Revolution. The French king, Louis XVI, had been taken into custody, and the Elector of Bonn would soon lose a sister, Marie Antoinette, to the guillotine. Austria and Prussia, the oldest of enemies, were united in a struggle against the new French Republic—a struggle that they were, at least in the short run, to lose. French troops were soon to march through Austria. Aristocrats would stream

Portrait sketches of Beethoven by Johann Peter Lyser. Beethoven's way of life foreshadowed future developments in that he was never in anyone's employ and proud of it; he demanded respect for the sake of his talent and managed to receive it during his lifetime. The cultural-historical figure of the artist as hero was born. (Bildarchiv Preussischer Kulturbesitz)

like refugees into Vienna. The old social order was weakening to the point of chaos. It was natural in such an environment that there would be changes in the aspirations of young composers such as Beethoven. It was also natural that social attitudes toward these people would change. No longer could they be considered simply the servants of the upper class.

Beethoven was among the first musicians of common background to mix with the aristocracy on his own terms. He felt that talent was his nobility, and it was credential enough. Though intermittently sponsored by various princes, Beethoven deferred to no one. He seems to have had absolute confidence in his own standards, moral, social and musical. Although he studied with Haydn, he later said that he gained little from his lessons. Beethoven was fierce in his insistence on originality as the mark of the true artist.

In his life and music, the figure of Beethoven reaches beyond the Classical style. Before he was thirty, he was suffering from incurable deafness. His resulting isolation from society turned him into a romantic figure; and his strong convictions that music and art were moral forces and that artists should be idealists helped to further the Romantic movement in music.

Beethoven's nine symphonies are far fewer in number than those of Haydn or Mozart. Yet they are as lengthy or longer than the later works of both of his famous predecessors. Beethoven continued to use Classical forms in his symphonies, but he expanded them beyond their previous limits in many ways. A typical, late symphony of Haydn, for example, lasts about twenty-five minutes, while Beethoven's *Symphony No. 3* is nearly twice that long. Beethoven's first symphonies reflect the Classical spirit perfectly. His Third, Fifth, and Sixth symphonies, however, while still Classical in their basic orientation and structure, have an unprecedented vitality and intensity. They play an important part in the gradual transition from the Classical style to the Romantic. Differences in Beethoven's earlier and later symphonies are sometimes attributed, in part, to his emotional despair and triumph over his increasing deafness.

In his later symphonies, Beethoven generally included more melodic material than he had in his earlier, shorter symphonies. Sections within movements often take on new significance. The development of motives and themes becomes more intense. In movements written in sonata form, development often takes place, not just in the development section, but in other sections as well. In fact, codas often serve as second development sections.

Beethoven also added new elements to the timbre of the symphonic orchestra. The trombone, for example, makes its symphonic debut in his Fifth Symphony. Solo and choral voices are heard in the last movement of the Ninth Symphony. Strings remain basic in Beethoven's orchestra, but wind instruments take on ever more important melodic roles.

**Periods of Beethoven's work**

For stylistic reasons Beethoven's compositions are often classified as belonging to his "early," "middle," or "late" period. His first two symphonies are early works; Nos. 3–8 are from his middle period (1802–1814), and the Ninth Symphony is a major work from his late period. Several piano sonatas, three piano concertos, and a set of string quartets are also early works. Into his middle period fall his only opera, *Fidelio* (1803), more string quartets and piano sonatas, overtures, incidental music, a violin concerto, and two more remarkable piano concertos. One other gigantic work stands beside the Ninth Symphony in his final period: the *Missa solemnis in D Major* (1823), a setting of the Mass which Beethoven himself regarded as his finest work. It contains some of the most difficult choral music ever written and, like the Ninth Symphony, is a statement of universal faith. After these enormous works, Beethoven returned to the smaller form of the string quartet. His final compositions of this type are unrivalled in their powerful and personal expressiveness.

## The Symphony as an Emotional Program

**The Sixth Symphony**

In his desire to make the symphony accommodate vast emotional schemes, Beethoven greatly expanded Classical forms. Yet at the same time, he brought a new unity to the work as a whole. He was the first to write symphonies in which a single motivic idea reappeared in each movement. What had been a cycle of contrasting movements now became a unified emotional program—somewhat similar to the kind of chronological progression found in literature. An extreme example, Beethoven's *Symphony No. 6* (the "Pastoral"), has movement titles that sound like chapter titles in a novel:

1. Awakening of Pleasant Feelings upon Arriving in the Country; Allegro ma non troppo
2. Scene by the Brook; Andante molto mosso
3. Peasants' Merrymaking; Allegro
4. The Storm; Allegro
5. Shepherd's Hymn of Thanksgiving after the Storm; Allegretto

**The Third Symphony**

While the "Pastoral" Symphony draws quite clearly on the imagery of the countryside, a different kind of inspiration may be seen in *Symphony No. 3* (the "Eroica"). Originally conceived as a tribute to Napoleon, the work is generally associated with the concept of heroism. The monumental first movement is followed by the traditional slow movement, in this case a funeral march. The third movement is a vivacious *scherzo*, that is, a light, quickly moving compositional form that gradually replaced the traditional third-movement minuet. The finale is frankly exuberant, as if the hero has come full circle to victory. The four movements thus convey a succession of emotions. They do not literally trace the career of any one person but instead express Beethoven's feelings about any person of great and heroic nature. Napoleon, as it happened, was not to prove worthy of the tribute. When news came that the great hope of the French

Beethoven: Opening page of the autograph manuscript of his Symphony No. 5 in C minor, op. 67 (1808). (Staatsbibliothek Preussischer Kulturbesitz, Berlin (West), Musikabteilung; photo: Bildarchiv Preussischer Kulturbesitz)

Revolution had crowned himself Emperor, Beethoven changed the dedication. The man he had seen as a hero had become, it seemed, just another despot. Even so, Beethoven later decided to restore Napoleon's name to the symphony.

## Beethoven: Symphony No. 5 in C Minor

Beethoven's *Symphony No. 5*, possibly the most popular of all symphonies, first began to appear in the composer's musical sketchbooks during the years 1801 and 1802, soon after the completion of the "Eroica." *Symphony No. 4*, in a lighter, more idyllic vein, was finished before the Fifth. It stands as an emotional relief between the Third and the Fifth symphonies. A later composer, Robert Schumann (1810–1856) described it as "a slim Greek maiden between two Norse giants." The Third and the Fifth symphonies were conceived during a period of great inner conflict, after Beethoven first learned that he was going deaf. His own great personal loss seemed to have given him a greater understanding of the enormity of human suffering.

The emotional power of the Fifth Symphony is thus in some ways a reflection of the strength of Beethoven's own spirit. That Beethoven should have gradually lost his sense of hearing, so crucial to his work as a composer, has always seemed one of the cruelest ironies in the history of music. It also seems almost miraculous that his compositions did not cease when his hearing did. Beethoven's genius, however, does not lie in the fact that he was a deaf composer. Musicians in all ages have claimed to compose music "in their heads." Few, if any, have had orchestras at their elbows, and all have had to generate symbols for sound on paper. For Beethoven, deafness did not present so great a problem to his art as it did to his spirit and to his relationship with the world. "My affliction causes me the least trouble in playing and composing, the most in association with others," he wrote in a letter dated 1801. In another document, a will or testament to his brothers, he wrote, "I must live like an exile; if I venture into company a burning dread falls on me, the dreadful risk of letting my condition be perceived." For this reason, and on the advice of a physician, Beethoven retired in 1802 to the quiet village of Heiligenstadt. From his letters at this time, we know that he succumbed to periods of intense misery, but the creative force within him was coupled with his will to live. "I will take Fate by the throat," he wrote. "It shall not wholly overcome me." Such was the determination that gave birth to the Fifth Symphony.

The work is in four movements and the third movement proceeds with a transition immediately into the fourth. The orchestra consists of the string section, plus pairs of flutes, oboes, clarinets, bassoons, horns, trumpets, and timpani. Trombones (three of them) make their first appearance in symphonic music in the fourth movement.

---

**Beethoven: Symphony No. 5 in C Minor, *First Movement***

**LISTENING ANALYSIS**

### First Movement: Allegro con brio; Sonata Form

The symphony opens authoritatively, with a motive that is undoubtedly the most famous in all symphonic literature. The basic, unifying rhythm of the first four notes immediately establishes the mood of the entire work:

Opening Motive

When asked for an explanation of this compelling motive, Beethoven answered, "Fate knocking at the door." It is unlikely that he meant that the music literally reproduced such a sound. He was more likely to have been using the words figuratively—making reference to the energy conveyed by the motive, a force similar to the remorseless energy that to him seemed the essence of fate. Beethoven used the motive with a single-mindedness appropriate to such an interpretation. In the course of the first movement, the motive is stated, restated, and very creatively changed while still keeping some prominent aspect of its original melodic or rhythmic form. It is heard in the other movements as well, bringing new unity to symphonic writing. Yet even with this constant reassertion of the initial motive, the symphony is characterized by frequent emotional changes. In fact, the opening motive itself is transformed into a statement of heroic defiance and finally into a celebration of strength. It was appropriate that this motive was used as the theme of BBC radio in London during the Second World War: its four notes symbolized a commitment to victory.

The most significant characteristic of the opening motive is its rhythm—three short notes of equal duration followed by a much longer note. The relative length of the fourth note is varied even at the outset. In the second statement of the motive, presented in descending sequence, the final note is held for two measures rather than one:

First Two Statements of Opening Motive

The entire first theme is based upon the opening motive. As the theme unfolds, the motive is tossed quickly from one section of instruments to another:

First Theme

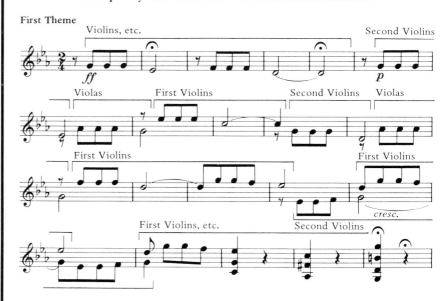

Note that it is primarily the rhythm of the motive that is stated and restated. The melodic pattern is varied for dramatic purposes. When the violas enter, the motive is played in sequence one tone higher. However, the interval between the last two notes of the motive has been shortened. In other places the interval is larger. Sometimes the third note of the motive is lowered on its way to the fourth note. In the answering phrase, the pattern is inverted.

Out of the simple rhythm of the opening motive, Beethoven was thus able to create a very dramatic first theme. Repetition, sequence, and tonal variation all play important roles. The material is so perfectly ordered, the alterations so integral to the dramatic structure, that we may not even be conscious that the motive has been altered.

After the first theme comes to a loud and abrupt end, the opening motive is immediately stated again by the entire orchestra. Then the string instruments, one by one, carry the motive downward into the range of the cellos and the double basses. The melody returns to the violins, and once again the motive is carried to the lower register. When the melody again returns to the violins, they begin a driving upward passage marked with sforzandos. The music alternately rises and descends as momentum and tension build.

At the end of this energetic passage that emphasizes descending arpeggios, a bridge prepares for a modulation to the key of E♭ major, the relative major. With a major key having been introduced, we might expect some change in emotional coloring. Significantly, the change of key coincides with a variation of the original motive, which serves as an introductory fanfare to the second theme.

Variation of Opening Motive

The altered motive, sounded by the horns, does indeed seem brighter than the original motive. It is also extended to include two additional notes.

The second theme begins with a gentle, lyrical phrase of only four measures. It is shown below, immediately following the altered motive of the bridge passage. The rhythm of the original motive is heard in the accompaniment played by the lower strings.

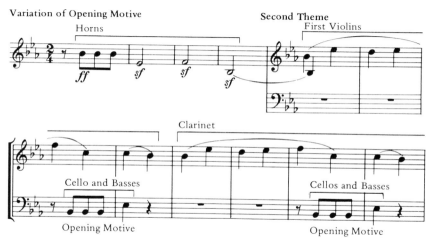

The lyrical phrase takes on a new urgency when it is repeated by the clarinet and the flute. It is then extended by a complementary phrase in the violins in rising sequence. As the rhythm of the basic motive reasserts itself again and again, the music rises to a crescendo, at the peak of which a strong closing theme emerges:

Closing Theme

This theme is immediately repeated, reinforcing its closing function. The rhythm of the basic motive then returns, and the exposition ends with a feeling of great power. Beethoven indicated that the exposition should be repeated.

Development

The development begins with the first motive played by horns and clarinets. The strings answer, reducing the motive to the very smallest of intervals. After this, different groups of instruments play the first motive imitatively in rising

The heroic image of Beethoven, bronze bust by Franz Klein, c. 1812. From c. 1798 onwards, Beethoven noticed he was slowly but steadily going deaf. By 1814, he could not hear himself play the piano because of this affliction. Yet he wrote his most innovative and impressive pieces of chamber music a few years before his death in 1827.

sequence. They are accompanied by the lower strings playing in descending sequence. At the climax of the development section, the rhythm of the basic motive is pounded out by the full orchestra. The fanfare that preceded the second theme is then heard, answered by an impatient staccato passage. The latter part of the development is remarkable for a number of reasons—the suspense created by its harmonies, the momentary absence of the motive, and the slower rhythmic motion. In the final measures of the development, Beethoven has succeeded, perhaps better than any other Classical composer, in making us anticipate the return of the first theme. An almost physical participation is demanded. We feel the music braking and then straining through a series of eighth notes to the fourth note of the opening motive. When the goal is reached, the relief is overwhelming:

**End of Development**

**Recapitulation**

The recapitulation begins at the end of the passage shown on page 218, with the sounding of the opening motive. It goes on to review the earlier material but is interrupted after the first statement of the theme by a brief oboe solo. Momentarily, we are released from the driving rhythms that characterize the rest of the movement. However, the opening motive soon returns and is followed by the second theme, which is introduced this time by the bassoons. The closing theme follows, as expected, and the recapitulation ends with the return of the first motive. The movement, however, continues with an extensive

**Coda**

coda. In its varied presentations of the opening motive, the coda equals the intensity and scope of the development section. It even introduces a new melodic motive that is rhythmically similar to the opening motive. The movement ends with very loud and powerful chords.

The former three-part structure of the sonata form has changed in this work to a four-part structure: exposition-development-recapitulation-coda. In effect, the coda has taken on the character and function of a second development section.

### LISTENING SUMMARY

| | |
|---|---|
| Timbre: | moderately large orchestra of string section, and pairs of flutes, oboes, clarinets, bassoons, horns, trumpets, and timpani |
| Melody: | opening motive of primary importance; first theme built upon variations of opening motive; second theme more lyrical; closing theme begins with conjunct motion, becoming more disjunct |
| Rhythm: | $\frac{2}{4}$ meter; tempo Allegro con brio (fast with spirit); rhythm of opening motive is heard repeatedly |
| Harmony: | mainly minor mode; begins in C minor, modulates most significantly to E♭ major, ends in C minor |
| Form: | sonata form with a coda |

## *Beethoven: Symphony No. 5 in C Minor, Second Movement*

### LISTENING ANALYSIS

SIDE 5, BAND 2

#### *Second Movement: Andante con moto; Double Theme and Variations Form*

The second movement is slower and mostly calmer in spirit, set in the contrasting key of A♭ major. Although basically in theme and variations form, it bears little resemblance to the theme and variations movement in Haydn's "Surprise" Symphony. Beethoven's work is more complex and lacks the clearly sectionalized series of variations found in the earlier work.

**Themes**

There are two important themes in the movement, each of which undergoes considerable development. The first, marked *dolce*, is reflective in spirit. It is played by the cellos and violas, accompanied by basses playing pizzicato:

First Theme

The first theme continues with woodwinds playing longer notes. The full orchestra then brings the first theme to a close.

The second theme combines the familiar rhythms of the opening motives of this movement and the opening movement.

Second Theme with Rhythm of Opening Motives

**Variations**

Throughout the movement both themes undergo changes in dynamics, tempo, and harmony. Each is played to a variety of accompaniments and by different groups of instruments. Most of the variations center on the first theme. The theme is broken into smaller and smaller units, as if a more careful reflection on the matter would reveal greater complexity. There is also a sense of growing mastery as the lilting rhythm of the original theme becomes more even and secure. The opening measures of the first two variations of the first theme illustrate these changes:

First Theme: Variation 1

First Theme: Variation 2

**Coda**

The third variation of the first theme is followed by a coda played at a slightly faster tempo. It is based on motives heard earlier in the movement and ends with a cadence played by the full orchestra.

**LISTENING SUMMARY**

| | |
|---|---|
| Timbre: | moderately large orchestra |
| Melody: | two themes, both subject to variation; first theme has many dotted rhythms; second theme has more even rhythms |
| Rhythm: | $\frac{3}{8}$ meter; tempo Andante con moto (moderate with motion); rhythm of first movement's opening motive recurs in the second theme |
| Harmony: | mainly major mode; begins in A♭ major, modulates to C major and A♭ minor, ends in A♭ major |
| Form: | theme and variations with a coda |

**Beethoven: Symphony No. 5 in C Minor, Third Movement**

**LISTENING ANALYSIS**

*Third Movement: Allegro; Ternary Form (ABA')*

One of the important changes made in the Classical symphony in Beethoven's time was the replacement of the third movement minuet with a scherzo. A scherzo ("joke" or "trifle" in Italian) is generally in the triple meter of the minuet, but tends to be lighter and quicker than the earlier dance movement. Beethoven did not use the term "scherzo" for the third movement of *Symphony No. 5* and the movement does differ in several respects from a typical scherzo; even so, it is often called a scherzo. The organization is that of the typical scherzo—ternary, or ABA—but only the B section has some of the scherzo's lighter spirit. This is hinted at in the choice of keys. The A section is in the home key of C minor, while the B section is in C major.

**Section A**

The movement opens with an ominous dialogue between low- and high-register strings. Cellos and double basses enter first, playing the opening phrase of the first theme, a phrase that begins with a rising arpeggio. This phrase is balanced by an answering phrase played by the first violins. The minor key and the very soft dynamics contribute to the foreboding mood of the theme:

First Theme

After the first theme is developed in a second exchange, the short-short-short-long rhythm of the first movement's opening motive suddenly recurs in the second theme of the third movement. Confined largely to a single tone, it is more insistent than ever. It thus offers an extreme contrast to the hesitant theme that opened the movement. The second theme is played very loudly by the horns and is then taken up by the full orchestra and expanded:

The rest of the A section alternates between the two contrasting themes. It ends with a burst of violin activity, accompanied by offbeat chords in the woodwinds.

**Section B**

The B section that follows is somewhat in the spirit of the typical scherzo. It begins with double basses and cellos lumbering away at the bottom of the orchestra in the key of C major. A delightful imitative passage follows as the theme moves upward. Violas, second violins, and first violins are heard in turn. The mood is one of exuberant playfulness. The first half of the section is then repeated, after which cellos and basses hesitantly present the theme again for another round of imitation. This half is also repeated, softly and with changes. Pizzicato cellos and basses lead back to the minor key with an air of quiet mystery.

**Section A**

The A section is then repeated. But this time the second theme is hushed and its rhythm is much less insistent than it was at the beginning of the movement. This creates a feeling of suspense and anxiety, as does the sound of the violins, played pizzicato or at times softly bowed. Suspense is further heightened by a quiet tapping of the timpani, played under the final statement of the first theme. The timpani part begins with the rhythm of the second theme, which soon turns into continuously repeated notes. Above these the violins present a lengthy passage that finally resolves to the tonic as the music moves without pause to the triumphant opening of the finale—one of the most exciting moments in music.

**LISTENING SUMMARY**

| | |
|---|---|
| Timbre: | moderately large orchestra |
| Melody: | first theme begins with rising arpeggio; second theme stresses repeated notes; third theme is lighter and quicker than the first two |
| Rhythm: | $\frac{3}{4}$ meter; tempo Allegro (fast); rhythm of the first movement's opening motive recurs in the second theme. |
| Harmony: | mainly minor mode; C minor in Section A; C major in Section B |
| Form: | ternary (ABA') |

*Beethoven: Symphony No. 5 in C Minor, Fourth Movement*

**LISTENING ANALYSIS**                                        SIDE 5, CONTINUATION OF BAND 3

*Fourth Movement: Allegro; Presto; Sonata Form*

With the opening chord of the finale, Beethoven establishes the brilliant key of C major and the symphonic debut of the trombone. The opening is joyful, suggesting a kind of spiritual rebirth. Perhaps it was for the sake of this effect that Beethoven chose to end the symphony in C major rather than in the original key of C minor. The first three notes of the opening theme are simply the tonic chord of C major, which conveys an immediate feeling of security and strength. The continuation of the theme is also distinctive, as it uses quicker, detached notes, then an uneven rhythmic motive, and finally a scale passage that includes melodic sequence.

First Theme

The orchestration of the first theme, and of the movement as a whole, is especially colorful. Two other newcomers to the symphony orchestra, the piccolo and the contrabassoon, are used for special dramatic purposes. The contrabassoon provides harmonic support along with the cellos and basses, while the piccolo adds brilliance at the top of the orchestral range.

The first theme is followed by a second, also in C major:

Second Theme

After the second theme, there is a modulation to the key of the dominant, G major. Another theme then appears in the new key. In this theme, the rhythm of the symphony's opening motive adds to the general feeling of exhilaration.

Third Theme

Following a repetition of the third theme, scale passages signal the beginning of the closing section. In this section, a final theme is presented and repeated.

**Closing Theme**

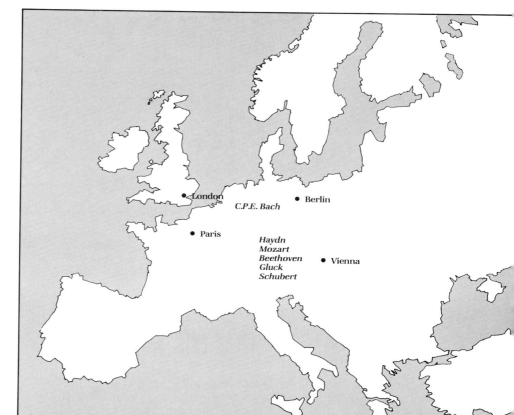

The exposition ends with a strong cadence. As in the first movement, Beethoven indicated that the exposition should be repeated.

**Development**

The development is a virtuoso display characterized by dynamic contrasts, rapid modulation, and the fragmentation and recombination of earlier motives. There is also an unprecedented return to material from the third movement. Its second theme, one of several based on the rhythm of the symphony's opening motive, is heard once again, stated as it was heard in the final portion of the third movement—which resolved into the first theme of the finale. This time the resolution signals the beginning of the recapitulation.

**Recapitulation and coda**

The recapitulation reviews the material from the exposition in the original order. A long coda follows, integrally fashioned from the thematic materials of the movement; the second, third, and closing themes are extensively developed. The conclusion of the symphony is marked Presto (as fast as possible), and it moves with powerful and inevitable pressure to the final unison C that closes the symphony.

**Major Classical Composers**

# Sinfonie

mit Schluß-Chor über Schillers Ode: „An die Freude"

für großes Orchester, 4 Solo- und 4 Chor-Stimmen,

componirt und

SEINER MAJESTAET dem KÖNIG von PREUSSEN

FRIEDRICH WILHELM III.

in tiefster Ehrfurcht zugeeignet

von

# Ludwig van Beethoven.

125tes Werk.

Eigenthum der Verleger.

Mainz und Paris,

bey B. Schotts Söhnen. Antwerpen, bey A. Schott?

**LISTENING SUMMARY**

| | |
|---|---|
| Timbre: | moderately large orchestra, with added piccolo, contrabassoon, and trombones |
| Melody: | four themes, as illustrated above |
| Rhythm: | duple meter; tempo Allegro (fast) through most of the movement, Presto (very fast) at end of movement; rhythm of the first movement's opening motive recurs in different forms |
| Harmony: | mainly major mode; begins in C major, modulates most significantly to G major, ends in C major |
| Form: | sonata form with coda |

Beethoven wrote only four more symphonies after the Fifth Symphony. *Symphony No. 6*, as we have seen, is a celebration of the pleasures of country life. *Symphony No. 7* is a powerful, romantic work on a large scale; *Symphony No. 8* is a complement to it— relaxed, joyful, and strong, with more obvious adherence to Classical principles. *Symphony No. 9*, like *No. 3* and *No. 5*, is an artistic milestone. A colossal work, it ends with a finale in which the words of Schiller's "Ode to Joy" are sung by four soloists and a large choir. It is one of the strongest statements of brotherhood, faith, serenity, and strength that a composer has ever made. Never before had vocal forces been used in a symphony, and not until decades later did other composers attempt it.

**Schubert's symphonies**

Beethoven's younger contemporary, Franz Schubert (1797–1828), was another major composer of symphonies in the early nineteenth century. In his nine symphonies, one can hear the change from Classical directness to greater length and complexity. In other types of music Schubert declared himself a romantic, turning to miniaturist forms such as the Lied for much of his output. He died the year after Beethoven, having had a very short but extremely productive musical career.

*(Left)* Title-page of the first edition of Beethoven's Symphony No. 9, op. 125, dedicated to Friedrich Wilhelm III, King of Prussia, the "Choral Symphony." (Bildarchiv Preussischer Kulturbesitz)

Concerto
a Cembalo obligato
Con Stromenti.

CHAPTER 14

# *Concertos of Mozart and His Contemporaries*

*LISTENING PREVIEW Mozart's concertos are some of his most vibrant and powerful works because of their masterful use of well balanced and proportioned contrast. He found in the piano a nearly ideal partner for the orchestra, and he exploited this partnership in his numerous keyboard concertos. Listen to the opening sections of his* Piano Concerto No. 17 in G Major *(side 6, band 1) and notice those characteristics of the piano part that enable the piano to contrast and blend with the orchestra.*

## Development of the Classical Concerto

The Classical concerto, a work of several movements, is essentially a musical confrontation between solo instrument and orchestra. A violin concerto, for example, contrasts the sound of the solo violin with the larger sound of the orchestra as a whole. A small number of Classical concertos do include more than one solo instrument. Mozart wrote a concerto for two pianos, and Beethoven, a "triple concerto" for violin, cello, and piano. However, most works call for a single solo instrument playing in alternation with the entire orchestra.

In the Classical concerto, the soloist enters like the hero of a drama. The opposition of one against many is a familiar theme in all the arts. In music the concept is never more prominent than in the concerto. The finest Classical concertos combine a sense of proportion and order with a focus on individual creativity and expressive power that would be carried much further by Romantic composers.

## Origins of the Concerto

A subscription concert (1777) at the Zurich "Concert Hall Society." The "orchestra" consists of 2 flutes, 2 violins, 2 horns and 1 cello, with a harpsichord (Zentral-bibliothek, Zurich)

The solo concerto of the Classical period developed from the Baroque concerto. As we have seen, the concerto grosso of the Baroque age contrasted a small group of instruments—the concertino—with a larger group—the ripieno. It was not very long before a number of Baroque composers were also writing concertos for solo instrument and a small orchestra. The earliest of the Baroque solo concertos were for violin, written by virtuoso violinists. Vivaldi wrote numerous concertos for solo violin and orchestra, as well as a considerable number for cello, viola d'amore, flute, oboe, and bassoon, also accompanied by orchestra. Bach also wrote two concertos for solo violin and orchestra, one for two violins and orchestra, and several for harpsichord and orchestra. Handel is well known to organists for his concertos for organ and orchestra. These Baroque works naturally had a major influence on the solo concertos of the Classical age.

The concerto, like the Classical style in general, was also influenced by Italian opera. In the Italian aria, one singer emerged from the larger company to present a melody. The solo aria thus lent a certain dramatic force to opera. Classical composers were quick to apply this principle to instrumental works, particularly to the concerto. It is no coincidence that Mozart, the most prolific and accomplished of Classical concerto writers, was also the most successful composer of Classical operas.

### Relationship Between Soloist and Orchestra

Although the Classical concerto opposes a single instrument to many, it nevertheless sets up a fair and equal contest. The orchestra can attain a greater dynamic level as well as a greater variety of tone color and texture. Soloists, on the other hand, can dazzle an audience with their expressiveness and virtuosity. Indeed, concertos offer soloists special opportunities to do just that. During certain passages, generally toward the end of a movement, the orchestra remains silent while the soloist indulges in what sounds like a spontaneous expression—the

*Cadenza*

*cadenza*. These difficult-sounding, usually fast-moving passages were

at first meant to be improvised by the performer, who was in many cases the composer of the work. Mozart and Beethoven were famous for the cadenzas they improvised during performances of their piano concertos. Many such cadenzas are lost to us, but some were written down for the benefit of students and other performers. Gradually, it became the custom to compose, rather than improvise, the cadenza. Yet the passages still retain a spirit of improvisation and exuberant breaking away from the orchestra in pursuit of personal expression.

Yet as noted above, even the most virtuosic soloist does not draw all the attention. The orchestra provides much more than mere accompaniment. In fact, it is often the dominating force. It usually announces the first theme, for example, and always follows the soloist's cadenza to give a final, affirmative musical statement. Sometimes the soloist accompanies the orchestra or enters into the fullness of the orchestral sound, momentarily giving up individuality. More often there is give-and-take as soloist and orchestra engage in musical dialogue, presenting melodic material in imitation of or contrast to one another, and simply exchanging parts. The one and the many are of equal musical importance.

## Structure of the Classical Concerto

A Classical concerto is almost always made up of three movements, and it has a number of characteristics of the sonata cycle. As in the symphony, there is a contrast in tempo between the different movements—the most common tempo pattern is fast-slow-fast.

The first movement of the Classical concerto is generally first-movement concerto form, which includes some traits of the Baroque concerto's ritornello principle and some of the Classical sonata form. The first movement usually has an opening statement or ritornello for orchestra alone (similar to an exposition in sonata form but without a key change), a second expository section for soloist and orchestra (very much like an exposition in a symphony with a major change of key), a section of dialogue between soloist and orchestra with numerous key changes, and a recapitulation of the opening ritornello for soloist and orchestra. The soloist tends to present more elaborate versions of the themes stated during the orchestral ritornello and often adds at least one new theme as well.

The second movement may take one of several different forms. It is generally slow, lyrical, and spacious, permitting a great deal of elaboration on the part of the soloist.

The third movement often has traits of the sonata and rondo forms, and is occasionally in theme and variations form. It tends to be lively and dancelike in character. Often the soloist's part is especially virtuosic, and some final movements even incorporate cadenzas.

The contrast between movements and the structural uses of theme and tonality are important in the Classical concerto. However, the overall design depends just as much on the creative interplay between soloist and orchestra.

*(Left)* The Prussian king Friedrich II with his orchestra. Like other enlightened rulers of his time, he was an accomplished amateur musician. J.S. Bach wrote his *Musical Offering* for him, based on a theme supplied by the king, who was also a composer. (Bildarchiv Preussischer Kulturbesitz)

**Mozart's Concertos**

Perhaps more than any other Classical composer, Mozart was remarkable for the great number and quality of his concertos, the composition of which remained important to him throughout his creative life. Supposedly, it was a piano concerto that Mozart presented to his father at the age of four. By the age of nine, he had written concerto arrangements of a number of J. C. Bach's works. The concerto continued to engage his energies in the few short decades left of his life. In all Mozart wrote more than forty concertos—for orchestra and piano, violin, horn, clarinet, bassoon, flute, and harp, and several other combinations of wind instruments.

**Mozart: Piano Concerto No. 17 in G Major, K. 453**

More than half of Mozart's concertos are for piano. The piano of Mozart's time was more limited in dynamic capacity, and finer and more crystalline in tone, than the modern piano. These qualities undoubtedly influenced the way he used the instrument.

One of his best piano works is the *Piano Concerto No. 17 in G Major*, K. 453, written in 1784. It is scored for an orchestra of moderate size, including strings, flute, two oboes, two horns, and two bassoons. (Later concertos would include parts for clarinets, trumpets, and timpani as well.)

---

**LISTENING ANALYSIS**                                    SIDE 6, BAND 1

*First Movement: Allegro; First-movement Concerto Form*

The first movement of Mozart's *Piano Concerto No. 17* includes an orchestral ritornello, an exposition for piano and orchestra, a bravura section for piano and orchestra, and a ritornello or recapitulation. It is characterized by a lively marchlike rhythm.

Orchestral ritornello

The orchestral ritornello opens with a lilting theme in the first violins, reinforced by woodwind figurations in the accompaniment:

First Theme

This is followed by a second theme, played forcefully by the full orchestra:

Second or Transitional Theme

In a symphony, we would now expect to hear a bridge to the dominant key followed by the restatement of the first theme or the presentation of another theme. In the first section of the concerto, however, a third theme is presented in the tonic key—in this case, the key of G major. After some preparatory scales and arpeggios, we hear this theme, a restless, thoughtful statement played by the strings:

Third Theme

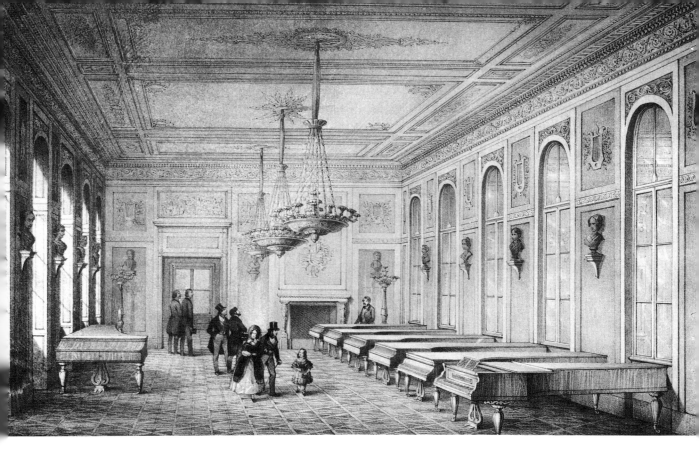

Concert hall in the Streicher piano factory, Vienna (first half of the 19th century). The Streichers were close friends of Beethoven and shared his ideas about the technical development of the piano in accordance with composers' needs. (Österreichische Nationalbibliothek, Vienna)

Solo exposition

The third theme is repeated with slight variation by the woodwinds. Then a modulatory passage leads to the closing theme, still in the tonic key.

Closing Theme

The orchestral ritornello draws to a close with forceful chords played by the entire orchestra.

At the beginning of the solo exposition, the piano enters easily with a rising passage that flows into the first theme. As is typical in the Classical concerto, this theme is now elaborated by the soloist, but still in the tonic key of G major. The woodwinds participate in the first theme, just as they did at the beginning of the movement when it was played by the violins. The second theme is then played by the orchestra, with the piano adding a decorative passage of its own. Then piano and orchestra modulate to the dominant key of D major before the piano introduces a new theme, here called the *piano theme*:

Piano Theme

This playful melody is first played by the piano alone. A rhythmic string accompaniment is then added, and finally the theme is taken over by the woodwinds. The third theme from the first exposition follows the piano theme, still in the key of D major. It is first played by the piano with a light, rhythmic accompaniment in the strings. Then the woodwinds present the theme, while the piano plays an accompaniment. The solo exposition comes to an end with a review of some of the earlier material, including the second theme.

**Third section**
The third section begins with a lengthy passage of piano arpeggios in a bravura style played against the woodwinds. A motive from the piano theme is then developed, mainly by the piano in dialogue with itself. The section is only lightly accompanied by the orchestra.

**Recapitulation**
The recapitulation or ritornello returns to the first theme, played, as in the opening, by the first violins in the original key of G major. This time, however, the piano enters quite early, before the second theme. The recapitulation also includes the piano

**Cadenza**
theme and the third theme, played in that order by the soloist. Mozart wrote a cadenza for this movement, and it is often performed by the soloist, although some pianists prefer to devise their own cadenzas. It is followed by a final statement of the closing theme by the orchestra.

**LISTENING SUMMARY**

Timbre:    solo piano; orchestra of moderate size; string section, flute, pairs of oboes, bassoons, and horns
Melody:    five themes, as illustrated above
Rhythm:    ¢ meter, tempo Allegro
Harmony:   mainly major mode; begins in G major, modulates most significantly to D major, ends in G major
Form:      first-movement concerto form, with some characteristics of ritornello and sonata forms; a cadenza appears at the end

## Diagram of First Movement

| Orchestral Ritornello | | | |
|---|---|---|---|
| Theme I | Theme II (Transitional Theme) | Theme III | Closing Theme |
| Tonic | | | |

| Solo Exposition | | | | |
|---|---|---|---|---|
| | | Piano Theme | Theme III | Closing Theme |
| Theme I | Theme II | Dominant | | |

| Third Section | |
|---|---|
| Arpeggios in Piano | Motive from Piano Theme Developed |

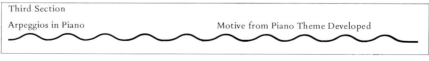

| Recapitulation (or Ritornello | | | | | |
|---|---|---|---|---|---|
| Theme I | Theme II | Piano Theme | Theme III | Cadenza | Closing Theme |
| Tonic | | | | | |

## *Second Movement: Andante; Free Rondo Form*

The lyrical quality of the themes and the modulations to a variety of keys contribute to the sensitive, sentimental mood of this movement.

**First theme**

The first theme is played by the strings. (This, incidentally, represents the strings' only major contribution to the movement.)

First Theme

Note that the theme closely resembles the third theme of the first movement. Thus it already seems somewhat familiar. The first theme is immediately followed by new material in the woodwinds. A lightly scored orchestral dialogue ensues.

**Second theme**

After a melancholy second theme has been presented, the piano enters very simply with the first theme. As is customary, the soloist elaborates upon the theme. In the course of the movement, the first theme returns three more times, usually in the tonic but once in the dominant. The influence of ritornello and rondo forms can thus be **Other themes** seen in the movement. A number of new themes are also heard, as well as elaboration of previous material. The music modulates through numerous keys, sometimes quite suddenly. Mozart also wrote **Cadenza** a cadenza for this movement, played just before the final statement of the first theme, and it is a masterpiece in itself.

### *Third Movement: Allegretto; Presto; Theme and Variations Form*

The finale is a delightful theme and variations with a Presto coda. In this movement Mozart used many of the usual means of variation—which we encountered in the second movement of Haydn's "Surprise" Symphony. At the same time, the music presents the concerto's characteristic interplay between soloist and orchestra.

**Theme**

The theme is divided into two parts, each consisting of two four-measure phrases. It is presented by flute and violins accompanied by the lower strings:

Both parts of the theme are repeated, as indicated by the repeat sign :‖. Thus the theme has the following organization:

| Part | 1 | | | | 2 | | | |
|---|---|---|---|---|---|---|---|---|
| **Phrase** | a | b | a | b | c | b′ | c | b′ |

Variations

As noted above, the theme is first stated by the orchestra. The piano enters in the first variation. Indeed, it dominates Part 1 of the first variation, generally playing two notes for every one in the string accompaniment. In Part 2 the piano part is imitated by the violins.

In the second variation, solo and orchestral parts are more equally balanced. In the first statement of Part 1, the piano accompanies the woodwinds, now playing three notes to every one of theirs. The piano part thus gains emphasis by moving faster than the orchestra, and speeds up as the movement becomes more intense. Piano and violins take up the melody as Part 1 is repeated. The repetitions of Parts 1 and 2 now offer new materials.

The third variation opens with a woodwind dialogue. The piano takes over as Part 1 is repeated. Part 2 begins with the woodwinds, and the variation ends with the piano dominating once again.

The fourth variation is in the minor mode. Syncopation is heard, first in the winds and then, as Part 1 is repeated, in the piano. A similar pattern emerges in Part 2, which ends with an exciting forte.

The major mode returns in the fifth variation. The section begins with the orchestra playing vigorous descending scales. The piano enters as Part 1 is repeated. The melody is played by the left hand under an exhilarating trill played by the right hand. In Part 2, the orchestra returns with loud ascending scales. The piano joins in as Part 2 is repeated. Its chromatic scales add greatly to the dramatic energy.

Coda

The movement ends with a long coda, marked Presto, written in comic-opera style. This rousing section develops new material while returning several times to the original theme. The music ends good-naturedly by reclaiming the original theme in the final measures.

## Other Composers of Concertos

Haydn's concertos

Haydn and other Classical composers, including Haydn's brother Michael, also wrote a number of important concertos. The works were for a variety of instruments—violin, cello, flute, oboe, trumpet, horn, harpsichord, and piano. Most often they were written for a single solo instrument, but occasionally two instruments were featured, as in Haydn's *Concerto in F Major for Harpsichord, Violin, and Strings* (by 1766). Haydn's concertos, along with Mozart's, played an important part in bringing the Classical concerto to its mature compositional form.

Beethoven's concertos

Beethoven infused the concerto with even greater drama and

expressiveness. In his concertos as in his symphonies, the development of the Classical-Romantic continuum can clearly be seen. His early concertos are very close in style to those of Mozart and Haydn; his later concertos, however, are changed considerably from the works of the earlier composers.

Beethoven's most significant concertos are the five he wrote for piano and the one he wrote for violin. Classical clarity and precision are especially characteristic of the early piano concertos, which maintain the basic compositional form of earlier concertos. The last piano concertos and the violin concerto, while still in three movements, are much freer in structure and demand even greater virtuosity from the soloist than do the earlier works. For example, the piano alone plays the opening notes of *Piano Concerto No. 4 in G Major* (1805–6). The opening orchestral statement of the Classical concerto is omitted altogether. The increased importance of the solo part was to become a feature of Romantic concertos.

Beethoven's study (1827) in the Schwarzspanierhaus, Vienna, the last of his many residences. The Broadwood piano, given to him by British admirers in 1817, can be seen in the foreground. (Österreichische Nationalbibliothek, Vienna)

String Quartet; silhouette, c. 1790. The string quartet was much cultivated in Vienna's musical life in the late 18th century. In Haydn's, Mozart's and Beethoven's quartets this trend was brought to its full fruition. (Furstlich Oettingen-Wallerstein'sche Bibliothek und Kunstammlung, Schloss Harburg)

CHAPTER 15

# *Chamber Music of Haydn, Mozart, and Beethoven*

*LISTENING PREVIEW Chamber music was very popular in aristocratic circles of the eighteenth and nineteenth centuries. It was written for small groups of performers, usually one player per part and performed in some sort of intimate environment. The string quartet came to be a highly favored instrumental group for chamber music in the later eighteenth century. Listen to the first movement of Haydn's* String Quartet in C Major *(side 6, band 2) and notice how extremely well the instruments blend with one another, yet how each of the four instruments is prominently featured at different times. Which of the instruments is generally most prominent? What specific characteristics of the music and of the instrument contribute to its prominence?*

## The Nature of Chamber Music

The late eighteenth century, which saw the mighty achievement of the symphony, was no less distinguished in its perfection of works for very small groups of musicians. Amateur and sometimes professional musicians gathered in middle-class homes and the drawing rooms of the well-to-do. Small groups also performed out-of-doors—in the gardens of summer estates, in the streets, and even in the gondolas that traveled the waterways of Venice. Large repertoires of music were written for a variety of small instrumental groups.

*Chamber music* is generally defined as music written for a small group of performers with only one player to a part and without a conductor. In a broad sense, the definition of chamber music also includes music written for only one or two performers. Orchestral music, by contrast, involves whole sections of instruments that play in unison except during rare solo passages.

**String ensembles**

Works for small groups of string instruments were popular. The most common type of composition was the *string quartet*, a work for four instruments—first violin, second violin, viola, and cello. *String trios, string quintets, string sextets*, and so on, were also written, but they were considerably less popular than the quartet. At times another instrument, such as the piano, was added to a string trio or quartet, resulting in a *piano quartet* or *piano quintet*. Such an ensemble was named for the unusual instrument in it.

The piano played a major role in much of Classical chamber music, especially in the development of the sonata. *Classical sonatas* were generally written for one instrument—the piano—or for another instrument and the piano.

As has been noted, chamber music differs from orchestral music in two obvious ways—in the small number of players involved and in the use of one player for each part. More important, however, are the differences in conception and effect. A symphonic orchestra is capable of grand and impressive sound as well as great contrast in timbre and dynamics. A chamber work, on the other hand, is economical in its means of expression. In a string quartet, the listener can usually follow the voices of the different instruments simultaneously, as the texture is often clear and transparent. Limited in variety of timbre and texture, the work achieves its effect through the ever-changing dialogue of its instruments. The small scale of the performing forces permits a very personal, intimate expression.

**Sonatas**

## Development of the String Quartet

The earliest standardized chamber groups were those that played the Baroque trio and solo sonatas (described in Chapter 10). As music became more melodically dominated in the Classical sense, and as middle parts were written to be played by string or wind instruments, the use of basso continuo declined. One major result was the string quartet, made up of two violins, one viola, and one cello.

At first the lower strings were limited to accompaniment, in deference to the Classical taste for homophony. The violin was invariably the melody instrument. All parts were kept simple enough to be played by amateurs. Indeed, the earliest quartets were written more for the enjoyment of the players than for an audience.

## Structure of the String Quartet

The overall structure of the string quartet, and of most other works for small string ensemble, is very similar to that of the symphony. All of the works are based on the concept of the sonata cycle, and all eventually came to have four movements. The forms of the individual movements in the string quartet are usually the same as those found in the symphony.

The similarities found between the symphony and the string quartet are not surprising when we consider the common history of both compositional forms. Haydn wrote a number of short "symphonies" for the small group he directed at the Esterházy palace. At the time, no one thought it necessary to define these works as either symphonies or chamber works since neither these types of composition nor the ensembles had yet been fully developed. Nevertheless, it was through Haydn that the string quartet, the most important type of

Title page of Mozart's set of six string quartets dedicated to Haydn and published in 1785, The two composers became close friends, despite the age difference of 24 years. Whilst Mozart regarded Haydn as almost a father figure, the latter was full of admiration for the younger composer's innovative works. (British Library)

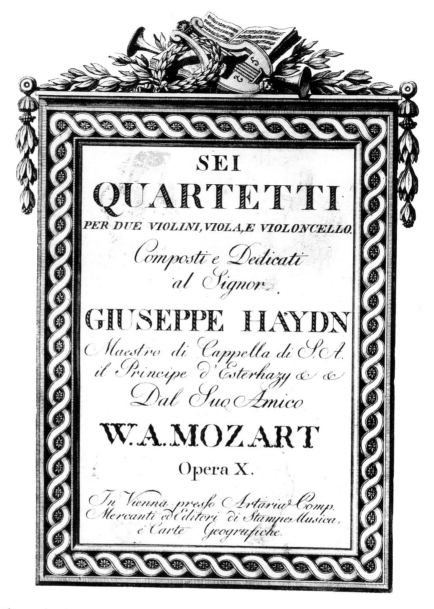

Classical chamber music, took definite form. The symphony itself grew into a work for a larger, well-defined group of players.

## Haydn's String Quartets

Many of the early string quartets, including some by Haydn, were called *divertimenti*—music for entertainment. Gradually, however, Haydn's string quartets, and those of other composers as well, came to serve more serious musical purposes. Haydn developed the lower voices, making them more independent and interesting. In fact, he sometimes used contrapuntal textures within an essentially homophonic framework. In this way music for the string quartet was able to derive strength not only from Classical use of melody and harmony but also from the growing independence of voices.

**Haydn: String Quartet in C Major, Op. 76, No. 3 ("Emperor")**

Independence of the four string parts is clearly apparent in the *String Quartet in C Major, Op. 76, No. 3.* By 1797 when the quartet was written, Haydn had reached full maturity as a composer, having written his last symphonies and countless other works. But he was still to write many important compositions, and the six string quartets of Op. 76, among the last of his more than seventy quartets, are significant works. They were dedicated to Count Joseph Erdödy, a patron of Haydn and also of Beethoven.

The *Quartet in C Major*, the third in the set, is one of Haydn's finest works. It is in the traditional four movements. The first movement is marked Allegro and is in sonata form. The subtitle "Emperor" comes from the melody of the second movement, a theme with four variations based on the Austrian national anthem "God Save Our Emperor Franz" that Haydn had written earlier. The third movement is a minuet and trio, and the last movement is a quick movement in sonata form.

| **LISTENING ANALYSIS** | SIDE 6, BAND 2 |

### First Movement: Allegro; Sonata Form

Exposition
The exposition opens in C major with a sprightly theme comprised of several different motives, two of which are used extensively in the movement. The opening two-note motive and the opening five-note motive are frequently used for development.

First Theme, First Violin Part

two-note and
five-note motives

The five-note motive is repeated after the first phrase by the viola and is accompanied by a rising scale in uneven rhythm. This uneven rhythm, not always with a scale passage, will prove to be very important throughout much of the movement. It is used with the modulation to G major that soon follows. When the new key is reached, the beginning of the theme is repeated again but continued differently than before. Soon a second theme appears in the first violin, over a very quick, steadily repeated chord pattern in the lower strings.

Second Theme

The mode soon turns from major to minor. Then a surprising shift to E♭ major accompanies a repetition of the first theme, but the G major smoothly and quickly returns. The second theme returns once more, serving as a closing theme. The transition that leads to the repeat of the exposition briefly features imitation of the opening two-note motive between the high and low strings.

Development
After the exposition is repeated, the development opens in G major with the opening five-note motive, accompanied by the scale in an uneven dancelike rhythm.

The key changes quickly as versions of the two- and five-note motives are imitated and extended. The second theme is also heard in imitation. About halfway through the development section, the five-note motive, followed by an extension of it and featuring the uneven rhythm, is heard over two pedal tones, E and B, that are repeated until near the end of the section.

Recapitulation

The recapitulation begins with the complete first theme in the tonic key, C major. The uneven rhythm returns also while a modulation is suggested, but a new key is not clearly established. The second theme returns in C major. Following this is a brief development of the two-note motive in an increasingly quick tempo, after which the second theme returns again to close the movement.

## Haydn's String Quartet in C Major, Op. 76, No. 3

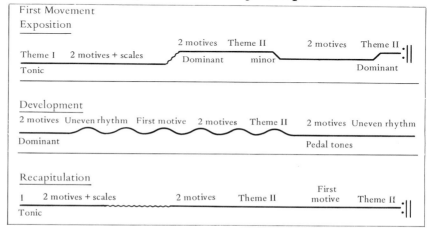

---

### LISTENING SUMMARY

Timbre:    string quartet: 2 violins, viola, cello
Melody:    2 themes; beginning of the first theme has an important 2-note motive and a 5-note motive
Rhythm:    duple meter; tempo Allegro
Harmony: begins in C major and modulates to G major in the exposition; several keys in the development; C major in the recapitulation
Form:      sonata form

### SecondMovement

The second movement is marked *Poco adagio cantabile* (rather slowly in a singing style), and is a theme with four variations. The melody of the Austrian national anthem is played by the first violin in G major, accompanied in a simple fashion by the other strings. The form of the theme is somewhat unusual in that it is made up of *five* four-measure phrases. The first phrase is presented and then repeated exactly; the third phrase is different; the fourth phrase is also different and it is repeated as the fifth phrase: a a b c c.

The same phrase structure is clearly maintained in each of the four variations that follow.

In variation 1, the second violin plays the melody while the first violin plays a more quickly moving countermelody. In variation 2, the theme is in the cello, a countermelody is heard in the first violin, and harmonizing parts fill out the other two voices. In variation 3, the theme is in the viola, and the other three parts weave counterpoint around it. Variation 4 presents the theme in the first violin, harmonized in a chordal style in the other parts. The final cadence is extended for a few measures and comes to rest with a fitting "Amen" cadence.

### Third and Fourth Movements

The third movement is a minuet and trio that returns to the key of the first movement, C major. The melodies of the minuet and trio contrast strongly with each other, and the change to the minor mode for the trio further heightens the contrast. The Finale, marked *Presto*, moves to C minor and is in sonata form. The movement is vivacious and engaging. C major returns for the coda and the final statements of the main theme.

## Mozart's String Quartets

In his twenty-three string quartets, Mozart built upon the traditions established by Haydn, to whom he dedicated six compositions in this genre. His mature quartets gave more equal emphasis to all four instruments, as the parts written for viola and cello became more demanding. The works as a whole gradually became longer and more complex.

## Beethoven's String Quartets

Beethoven chose the string quartet for the expression of some of his most profound, personal, and difficult musical ideas. His first six quartets, opus 18, are in the tradition established by Haydn, but with Beethoven the quartet became less and less a medium for the amateur. As in his sonatas and symphonies, Beethoven approached the quartet with little concession to the limitations of players or audience. Especially in his last quartets, the demands on both are extraordinary. Beethoven tended to use the quartet as a medium for experimentation, and greatly expanded its Classical form; his Quartet Op. 131, for instance, is in seven movements. The result was often confusing to his audiences. In some ways, his middle and late quartets were too modern for their time, yet one of their most striking features is the reappearance of contrapuntal techniques derived from late Baroque style. Op. 133 is a gigantic fugue for string quartet. Since Beethoven's day, a number of other composers have also chosen to introduce their most experimental ideas in quartets and other chamber works. Small ensemble pieces lend themselves well to such experimentation. The tonal relationships are especially clear and the musical ideas may be closely followed.

This engraving (1769) by Daniel Chodowiecki shows a chamber performance of (probably) a cantata, the performing group comprising 2 violins, 1 viola, 1 singer, 1 harpsichordist, and a cellist. (Bildarchiv Preussischer Kulturbesitz)

## Schubert's String Quartets

The string quartets of Schubert, though written for amateurs, aptly show many of the changes in musical style typical of the early nineteenth century. A lyrical quality is very often prominent in Schubert's works, to a greater degree than in the quartets of Beethoven. Schubert's best known chamber work is his *Piano Quintet in A Major* ("The Trout," 1819). It is written for piano and an unusual string quartet that consists of violin, viola, cello, and string bass. The fourth of five movements is a theme and variations movement based on Schubert's charming song *Die Forelle* (The Trout).

## Development of the Classical Sonata

The sonata of the late eighteenth century, a work for one or two instruments, is in some ways a composite of the many different types of sonatas popular in the Baroque age. At the same time, it is not completely like any of the earlier works. Like the trio and solo sonatas of the Baroque age, it is a work of several movements of contrasting character. Like Scarlatti's sonatas for unaccompanied harpsichord, it stresses the sound of a keyboard instrument. Not surprisingly, the popularity of the Classical sonata paralleled the growing importance of the piano as a solo instrument. By the late eighteenth century, the sonata for piano and another instrument, generally the violin, had become a very popular form of home entertainment. Baroque influences were important in shaping the Classical sonata, but the work had been molded into something completely new by the late eighteenth century.

## Structure of the Classical Sonata

Just as the Classical symphony is a sonata cycle for orchestra, the Classical sonata is a sonata cycle for piano, or for piano and another instrument. The number of movements in the cycle is usually three or four. The first movement is usually in sonata form, sometimes preceded by a slow introduction. The second movement may be in one of several forms, mainly sonata, ternary, or theme and variations form. In a four-movement work, the third movement is generally a minuet and trio, while the last movement is in rondo or sonata form. Sonatas with only three movements generally omit the minuet.

## Major Composers of Sonatas

Haydn's most important works for piano are sonatas. Mozart too wrote sonatas for solo piano and sonatas for piano and violin. In the early years of the nineteenth century, Franz Schubert also emerged as a major composer of solo piano sonatas as well as of other types of piano works. While many of their works are of fine quality, it is in the thirty-two piano sonatas of Beethoven that the epitome of the genre is reached. His works form a bridge between Classical and Romantic styles and foreshadow many later nineteenth-century developments.

## Beethoven: Piano Sonata in C Minor, Op. 13

One of Beethoven's finest and best-loved works is the *Piano Sonata in C Minor, Op. 13* (the "Pathétique"), which was published in 1799, quite early in his career. The work is in three movements.

## The Evolution of Keyboard Music

The music written for keyboard instruments has been affected perhaps as much by changes in technology as by changes in musical style. The compositions that were written for the harpsichord of the Renaissance and Baroque ages differed significantly from those that were written for the piano of the Classical age, in large part because of the technical differences in the instruments. Virtuosic possibilities continued to increase with the perfection of the piano in the early nineteenth century, and the twentieth century brought even more options with the use of electronics and other new technological devices.

Listen to works written for keyboard instruments in four different periods—those listed below from the record set that accompanies the text, or other selections.

| | | |
|---|---|---|
| **Baroque:** | Scarlatti's *Sonata in C Major*, K. 159 (for harpsichord) | **Side 3, Band 6** |
| **Classical/ Romantic:** | Beethoven's *Sonata in C Minor, Op. 13*, Third Movement (for piano) | **Side 6, Band 3** |
| **Romantic:** | Liszt's *Hungarian Rhapsody No. 6 in D flat Major* (for piano) | **Side 7, Band 2** |
| **Modern:** | Selection from Cage's *Sixteen Sonatas and Four Interludes* (for prepared piano) | |

What are the most notable differences in the musical qualities of the various instruments? In what ways do the composers seem to have taken advantage of the different technical capacities of their instruments?

### *First Movement: Grave; Allegro di molto e con brio; Sonata Form*

The first movement begins with a slow, ominous introduction. This contrasts dramatically with the remainder of the movement, which is marked Allegro and cast in sonata form. The structure of the sonata form is clear, made so to some degree by the return of the slow introductory material between the exposition and the development, and again after the recapitulation. Dramatic contrasts of mood, theme, key, and dynamics are striking in the movement. Also, the work places considerable technical demands on the pianist. The dramatic and expressive qualities of the movement are much greater than in works of a generation before.

### *Second Movement: Adagio cantabile; Rondo Form*

The second movement is marked Adagio cantabile and placed in the contrasting key of A♭ major. The first theme is one of Beethoven's most lyrical:

First Theme

**Second and third themes**    The melody is repeated immediately with a new accompaniment.

Later in the movement, two other themes are presented in contrasting keys. Each of these is preceded and followed by the first theme in the movement's tonic, or home, key—A♭. The movement is thus in rondo form with a brief coda. An outline of the arrangement of themes is shown below:

| Section: | A | A | B | A | C | C | A | A |
|---|---|---|---|---|---|---|---|---|

## *Beethoven: Piano Sonata in C Minor, Op. 13, Third Movement*

**LISTENING ANALYSIS**

### *Third Movement: Allegro; Rondo Form*

The third movement is in the sonata's home key of C minor. It opens with a vivacious theme in duple meter:

First Theme

Two contrasting sections are later heard in different keys. In the B section, after a brief transition that modulates, a new theme made up of flowing scale lines is heard in the relative major key. After a brief change to minor, a slower theme with a chordal accompaniment is presented. Shortly thereafter, the first theme returns in the original tonic key of C minor. A third section, C, moves to another major key, A♭, with a disjunct and syncopated theme. The end of the section features quick arpeggios before the first theme returns again in the tonic key. Another return of the B section, this time in C major, and a final statement of A in C minor complete this fully developed rondo form.

| **Section:** | A | B | A | C | A | B | A |
|---|---|---|---|---|---|---|---|

**LISTENING SUMMARY**

| | |
|---|---|
| Melody: | Section A includes a vivacious theme that includes some sequence; Section B features a flowing, scalar theme and a slower theme; Section C includes a disjunct, syncopated theme |
| Rhythm: | ¢ meter; tempo Allegro |
| Harmony: | mainly minor mode; A sections in C minor; first B section in E-flat major; C section in A-flat major; second B section in C major |
| Form: | rondo (ABACABA) |

As a group, Beethoven's piano sonatas reflect the composer's overall development. The earliest ones are Classical, modeled on works of Haydn. The sonatas of Beethoven's middle period break new ground in using the piano expressively, and depart from some of Classicism's formal restrictions. A good example of this innovation is his *Piano Sonata in F Minor Op. 57*, called the "Appassionata" (1804–5). The late sonatas are among the most innovative and difficult works in this genre from the early nineteenth century.

*(Left)* Chamber musicians; drawing, dating from the late 1760s, by Thomas Gainsborough. (British Museum; photo Heritage of Music)

# CHAPTER 16

# *Vocal Music of the Late Eighteenth Century*

*LISTENING PREVIEW Opera was one of the main courtly and popular entertainments of the late eighteenth century, and Mozart was one of the most brilliant composers of opera at that time. Listen to the opening duet from Mozart's* Marriage of Figaro *(side 6, band 5). It features Figaro, who is measuring the dimensions of the bedroom he will share with Susanna after their forthcoming marriage, and Susanna, who is admiring her new hat. Mozart gave them contrasting melodies that reflect their different activities. Describe the two melodic ideas, giving particular attention to the ways in which they contrast with each other.*

While new types of instrumental works are perhaps the most important legacy of Classical music, vocal music also received considerable attention from the major composers of the period. The types of vocal music developed in the Baroque period continued in use, and no important new types were devised. Nevertheless, some of the most beautiful—and enduringly popular—musical creations of the Classical age are in the realm of vocal music. Operas, Masses, and oratorios were all common, but it is in opera that the freshest and most vital creations are to be found.

We have seen that operas of the early Baroque age were simple and stylized sung dramas. By the time Handel was writing operas, they were intended for public performance and had clear divisions between arias and recitatives. But the opera as we know it today, a complex interplay of musical and dramatic elements, was a creation of the Classical age and a fulfillment of many earlier forms. Our consideration of the unique nature of opera can be best applied to those written during and after the late eighteenth century, when the genre reached a high degree of sophistication.

The original costume design
(1791) for Papageno in
Mozart's opera *The Magic
Flute*; illustration from the
libretto by Emanuel
Schikaneder. (British Library)

## The Special Nature of Opera

Opera has long enjoyed a reputation as the grandest and most glamorous of musical compositions. It is entertainment on a large scale. A combination of music and theater, opera draws upon the resources of an orchestra, vocal soloists, a chorus, and in some cases a ballet company as well. As a mixture of different musical media, opera appeals to an audience on a number of different levels.

## The Conventions of Opera

In order to enjoy opera, a person must be willing to accept its imaginative aspects as well as a number of conventions that have developed to suit the particular needs of the art form. Every art form has certain customary ways of representing the real world. These often grow out of the natural characteristics and limitations of the medium. Most of us find it easy to accept the portrayal of a boundless, rolling landscape on the flat surface of a painting. Movie audiences easily accept the insertion of sentimental music during even the most private of cinema love scenes. Molière is admired for casting his dialogue in rhymed couplets. The long soliloquies that Shakespeare gives some characters are quite beyond the inclinations of normal people, but they create profound dramatic moods and effects. In short, most of us are willing to grant each of these art forms its own necessary methods.

The conventions of opera can be accepted in much the same way if they are recognized and understood. Most basic is the fact that much or all of the text is sung rather than spoken. This is only one of many ways in which opera differs from spoken drama. In a play the author has ample opportunity to reveal the complexities of the plot, develop characters, and depict action on all levels. In an opera, where music is the main means of expression, the plot and the characters are often condensed and stylized. The texts of most operas are rather short and sketchy, since singing the text, often with repetitions of it, takes far more time than simply speaking it. When Beaumarchais' play *Le Mariage de Figaro, ou La folle journée* ("A Day of Folly"), for example, was made into an opera (Mozart's *Le nozze di Figaro*, or "The Marriage of Figaro"), many of the comic complications had to be left out. In some operas strenuous physical actions must be limited because singers cannot perform them and sing at the same time. Nonetheless, words and actions are amply conveyed, reinforced, and elaborated in the musical score. Music provides the context in which the plot and characters must be judged.

If reasons behind the conventions of opera are understood, some of the unnatural happenings in opera may seem more acceptable. It is clearly unnatural for a woman to sing loudly while she lies on her deathbed. This kind of action would be difficult to accept in a play. But in an opera, it may be necessary for the singer to complete certain climactic phrases if the aria is to make sense as a *musical* expression of the character's situation or feelings. At times she must do this even if the drama itself is not thereby improved. The audience accepts it as a convention of opera. Similarly it accepts the fact that characters who are called upon to take swift action will nevertheless repeat their thoughts four or five times if the music demands it. Some conventions of plot are accepted purely for reasons of expediency. It is difficult to believe that superficial disguises will prevent sworn lovers from recognizing one another, but this occurs often in the plots of comic operas and in some plays. None of these unrealistic devices need detract from the enjoyment of opera. Opera, through its music, introduces an entirely different dimension of reality.

Because it is a musical medium, opera is able to reach expressive depths that are beyond the scope of ordinary drama. Music intensifies the portrayal of the plot, characters, and their emotions, thus compensating for the often sketchy text. Few spoken words of love can compare with the great love arias of opera. Nor can the terror and suspense conveyed by music be easily duplicated by words alone. It is music's unique expressiveness that explains the impact of opera as theater.

## The Materials of Opera

Opera's basic appeal seems to lie in the expressive intensity of the music. Much additional interest, however, derives from the relationships among opera's many different elements: soloists, ensembles, choruses, orchestra, text, and visual staging. The composer must reconcile and integrate all of these competing elements into an artistic whole.

### Solo voices

The operatic heroine is almost always a soprano, the highest voice. There are several different types of soprano voice, ranging in timbre and style from the light and lyrical to the full-bodied and dramatic. One of the most exciting voices is that of the soprano singing in a *coloratura* style, that is, with great virtuosic display of high notes, trills, arpeggios, and other ornaments. *Lyric* and *dramatic* sopranos sing other types of roles and music. The former type is usually a light voice singing melodic and gracious music; dramatic sopranos have a heavier quality, and their music and characters are often more intense. A soprano is often a heroine offstage as well as on—the famous *prima donna* ("first lady") traditionally adored by the opera-going public.

Some female parts are written for the slightly lower and heavier voice of the mezzo-soprano or for the even lower voice of the contralto. A soprano's servant, rival, or older relative is often cast in a lower range to provide contrast. In operas where all female parts are scored for sopranos, composers generally differentiate among them in style of composition.

Male roles generally fall into three ranges—tenor, baritone, or bass. At times, however, parts for young men, especially aspiring young suitors, may be cast as mezzo-soprano parts and played by women in disguise—these roles are called "trouser" or "pants" roles. The tenor is the highest of the usual masculine ranges and is often the protagonist or lover. Important male parts may also fall to the lower-voiced baritone. The bass, the very lowest of voices, may be cast as an older man, an authority figure such as a king or a priest, or a villain. The composer of opera has wide latitude in the choice of male roles and ranges. As in the choice of female voices, the main objective is to provide dramatic variety.

The soloists sing both arias and recitatives. In arias the action generally stops while the singer comments upon it. The music is of central interest. In recitatives, however, the action is likely to continue. *Recitativo secco* (accompanied by continuo) is heard most often, while *recitativo accompagnato* (accompanied by more instruments) is generally reserved for more dramatic moments.

**Choruses and ensembles**

In opera the composer uses not only soloists but also choruses and small ensembles that perform duets, trios, quartets, and so on. In an ensemble two or more characters may join in a single melodic line, expressing shared feelings. Or they may sing back and forth, completing the melody between them. There are also ensembles in which different characters harmonize a single melody. In some cases several characters will sing different melodies expressing different emotions. The composer's skill at portraying several characters and emotional states simultaneously, and relating them to one another musically, can make such ensembles wonderfully exciting. They are often high points in the opera. This increase in musical activity generally coincides with a dramatic crisis.

In many operas a chorus is used to present a larger mass of vocal sound. During a wedding party or a military scene, for example, a large number of singers may enter to form the chorus in front of which the principal soloists appear. The chorus may participate in the action or comment upon it in the manner of ancient Greek drama.

**Orchestra**

Soloists, ensembles, and choruses are accompanied by an orchestra, usually located in a pit in front of the stage. The composer varies the orchestration in accordance with the mood and action on the stage. A large military scene may call for dramatic use of the complete orchestra, a bedroom scene for a much lighter instrumentation. In addition to accompanying the singers, the orchestra may be called upon to support the dramatic action with various sound effects—thunder and lightning, bird songs, trumpet calls, the music of a shepherd's pipes. The orchestra also performs independently, opening the opera with an overture and in some cases presenting preludes to individual acts. Other orchestral passages may function as interludes or as accompaniment to dance. The size of the opera orchestra has varied from one period to another. In the seventeenth century, it was usually quite small, in the eighteenth century, a little larger, and in the nineteenth century, larger still.

**Libretto**

The text or script of an opera is called the *libretto* ("little book"). Generally it is poetic in form. In most cases the author, or librettist, derives the material from a play, a story, or a historical account. It must then be structured to meet the special demands of opera.

The libretto is clearly an important component of opera, second only to the musical score—some would say, equal to it. For operas in foreign languages, librettos are usually published with English translations, which may be read before seeing the performance. Even without a translation, the basic events of an opera can usually be understood through its music and visual action, especially with the aid of a *synopsis* of the plot that is usually included in the program.

*Synopsis*

Although opera can give pleasure through its libretto and music alone, and operas are sometimes performed unstaged in concert halls, the full experience is not complete without the visual elements—the costumes, scenery, and staging. Opera is, after all, theater. It draws on the theatrical arts of costume, scenic design, lighting, and choreography. The importance of the visual element can be seen in the budget of the Metropolitan Opera of New York. A typical production costs thousands of dollars for the staging alone.

*Scenery and staging*

To an audience that does not understand the language of the libretto, clarity of staging can be especially important. Characters may use gesture and visual effect to help convey aspects of the plot. Some of the finest moments in opera are produced by a powerful combination of visual and musical effects. In Mozart's *Don Giovanni*, for example, the protagonist goes down to hell as flames and smoke envelop the stage and voices from the underworld promise eternal torture. Staging is of crucial importance to the theatrical art of opera.

To bring an opera successfully to life demands a well-blended realization of all these elements. The singers must do justice to both their musical and their dramatic functions. The orchestra must be clearly heard, and its contribution to the dramatic meaning must be clear, yet it cannot overbalance the singing or obscure the words. The staging has to bring out the meaning of the text but cannot get in the way of the music.

*Operatic performance*

As vital as the singers and orchestra to operatic performance are the *conductor* and *stage director*. The conductor balances the orchestral and vocal forces and coordinates the orchestra, which cannot see or hear much of the singers on stage. Molding the singers' different interpretations into a musical whole is another aspect of the conductor's role. The stage director ensures that the opera is theatrically effective and that the meaning of the music is projected through the stage action.

## Opera in the Late Eighteenth Century

Haydn, Mozart, and Beethoven all wrote operas—Beethoven only one. Christoph Willibald Gluck (1714–1787), born in Bohemia and later active in Vienna and Paris, was an important composer of opera in the early Classical style. The works of these four composers brought new direction to both the serious and comic opera traditions.

## Serious and Comic Operas

German-speaking composers were masters in the composition of opera in the late eighteenth century, a change from earlier periods in which Italian and French opera had been pre-eminent. Their works generally fall into two categories, *opera seria* and comic opera, the latter including *opera buffa* and *Singspiel.*

**Opera seria**

*Opera seria* ("serious opera" in Italian) was inherited from Baroque composers and continued as a prominent type of opera of the late eighteenth century in the works of Gluck and Mozart. The operas tended to be highly stylized, with subjects that were almost always heroic, generally concerning the gods and heroes of ancient times.

As the Classical spirit took hold, reformers attempted to make the opera seria simpler and more emotionally direct. Gluck sought to abolish "useless and superficial ornament," and expended his efforts "in the search for simple beauty instead." He felt that music should always serve and support the text and drama in opera, as he illustrated in his *Orfeo ed Euridice* (1762). Gluck's works enjoyed considerable success with audiences, and the ideas they contained had great influence on serious opera.

Mozart wrote two major serious operas, *Idomeneo* (1780–81) near the beginning of his operatic career and *La clemenza di Tito* ("The Mercy of Titus") at the end. But it is mainly for his comic operas that he is remembered today and for these same operas that he was honored in his own time.

**Opera buffa**

*Opera buffa* ("comic opera" in Italian) is fast paced and humorous, full of frivolity, practical jokes, and comic confusion. The very term *buffa* suggests the buffoonery that characterizes it. But opera buffa is also capable of great melodic beauty. Especially in the works of Mozart, the music brings out a new underlying seriousness and sensuality, which are skillfully interwoven with the traditional humor. *The Marriage of Figaro* and *Don Giovanni* are notable for their fusion of comic and serious elements. It is mainly this that distinguishes Mozart's works from the more formalized comic operas of his contemporaries.

**Singspiel**

*Singspiel* ("song play" in German) was also a popular form of comic opera in the late eighteenth century. In it the dialogue is spoken rather than sung in recitative, resulting in a simpler presentation closer to our own musical comedies. Two of the finest works in the genre are Mozart's *Die Entführung aus dem Serail* ("The abduction from the Seraglio," 1782) and *Die Zauberflöte* ("The Magic Flute," 1791).

As has been noted, all the major Classical composers wrote at least one opera. Haydn wrote a number of them, but they were produced on a small scale and were not generally performed outside the Esterházy court. Beethoven wrote only one opera, a serious moral drama entitled *Fidelio* (1805–6, revised in 1814). Alongside the work's noble ideals are some delightful lighter moments, with magnificent music throughout. Mozart, however, was the most successful operatic composer of the three. It is to him that we turn for a greater understanding of the comic opera of the period.

## Mozart: The Marriage of Figaro

Two of Mozart's most important operas are comic operas in the opera buffa style: *Le nozze di Figaro* (1786), which translates into "The Marriage of Figaro," and *Così fan tutte* (1790), which may be loosely translated as "Thus Do They All." (The "all" is feminine!) Mozart's *Don Giovanni* (1787) is in a special category of its own, since it prominently combines both buffa and seria traits.

Mozart's first opera buffa was based on a play by the French writer Beaumarchais (1732–1799), a work entitled *Le mariage de Figaro* or *La folle journée*. The play was the second of a trilogy, following *Le barbier de Seville* ("The Barber of Seville"), which was the basis for another opera written thirty years later by Gioacchino Rossini (1792–1868). Both *The Barber of Seville* and *The Marriage of Figaro* focus on the adventures of Figaro, the servant or valet of a Spanish noble, Count Almaviva.

*Da Ponte's libretto*

The librettist for *The Marriage of Figaro* was Lorenzo da Ponte (1749–1838), theater poet at the court of Emperor Joseph II in Vienna. In converting the play of Beaumarchais into a workable opera, he reduced the number of characters from sixteen to eleven and did some rather significant editing of content. The play had satirized the

Title page of the program of Beaumarchais' play *Le Mariage de Figaro*, first presented in Paris in 1784. Two years later, Mozart's opera appeared with Italian text by Da Ponte. (Bettmann Archive)

upper classes and their relationship to the servant class—a topic particularly threatening to aristocrats at a time when revolutionaries were about to overthrow the government of France. To get clearance for Mozart's opera, da Ponte had to assure the Emperor that he had "cut anything that might offend good taste or public decency at a performance over which the sovereign majesty might preside." And to a great extent he had. Mozart's opera takes full advantage of the cleverness of Beaumarchais' plot but it largely discards the play's political implications. In the play and opera, though, the challenge to a corrupt aristocracy is clear.

Plot synopsis

The opera concerns the impending marriage of Count Almaviva's valet Figaro to the Countess's maid Susanna. The plot revolves around a series of comical confusions—suspected lovers jumping out of windows, hiding in closets, and so forth. But essentially there are three major dramatic conflicts. First, the Count is bent on making love to Susanna, as feudal custom allowed, if possible before her wedding takes place. Second, a former rival of the Count, Bartolo, has an old grudge against Figaro and so wishes to prevent his marriage. Bartolo is in league with the Count's housekeeper, Marcellina, who has loaned Figaro money and has a contract stating that Figaro shall either repay her or marry her. Thus the Count, Bartolo, and Marcellina all wish to postpone or prevent Figaro's marriage for personal reasons. The third conflict involves the young page Cherubino. Seemingly in love with love itself, Cherubino especially adores the Countess, whom he woos with original love songs and other attentions, all of which enrage the Count.

Jealousies lead to a number of comic deceptions. However, at the end, all major problems are pleasantly resolved. Figaro, who had been separated from his parents at birth, proves to be the son of Marcellina and Bartolo. Upon learning that she is Figaro's mother, Marcellina drops her demands, embraces her long-lost child, and determines to marry Bartolo at this late date. Susanna and the Countess ultimately thwart the Count in his amorous designs. Susanna arranges to meet him in the garden, but it is the Countess, disguised as Susanna, who keeps the rendezvous. Figaro, however, has not been told of the deception planned by Susanna and the Countess. Seeing the woman he believes to be his sweetheart with the Count, he is so angered that he seeks out the Countess to tell her of her husband's infidelity. But the "Countess" is, of course, Susanna in disguise. When Figaro recognizes this, he proceeds to make advances to his disguised bride-to-be, feigning infidelity. For this he is boxed on the ears and thus reassured of Susanna's love and purged of his jealousy. The Count and the Countess are similarly reconciled. As for Cherubino, everyone seems to be in a good-natured conspiracy to protect him from the Count's wrath. Early in the opera, the Count dispatches him to the army, but he returns in secret. He reappears toward the end of the play disguised as a young girl, in the company of his new beloved, Barbarina. The opera ends with the ringing of wedding bells. A day of torment and folly has been resolved in the happiness of love.

### Overture

The overture to *The Marriage of Figaro* sets the mood for the entire opera. It is in abridged sonata form, without a development section. The orchestra includes the usual string section and pairs of flutes, oboes, clarinets, bassoons, horns, trumpets, and timpani.

**Mozart: The Marriage of Figaro, *Overture***

**LISTENING ANALYSIS**

SIDE 6, BAND 4

The exposition begins with a lively theme in D major. It consists of two parts, the first of which (Ia) is a quiet, conjunct line presented by the strings and bassoon in unison.

The second part of the theme (Ib) includes a mixture of conjunct and disjunct motion, features the wind and string instruments together, and grows to a loud dynamic level.

After the opening theme is repeated, a series of scales and other rapid figuration are used to effect a modulation to A major, which is confirmed by a strong cadence followed by a brief pause. A less active second theme is presented and repeated in the new key.

It is extended with a number of arpeggios and short scales. Violins and bassoon then present a third or closing theme which is immediately repeated.

A transition based on a conjunct motive in rising sequence helps to change the key back to D major. Instead of a development section, the first theme is heard in the original key, signaling the beginning of the recapitulation. The thematic material from the exposition is presented in a manner similar to the way it appears in the exposition, except that the second part of the first theme is not repeated and the second theme is presented in the tonic key of D major. After the closing theme a quick, conjunct line in the violins begins a coda that brings the overture to a fitting, firm conclusion. The overture may be diagramed as follows:

| Exposition |
| --- |
| Theme Ia b Ia b Trans. Theme II Theme II Closing Theme |

| Transition |
| --- |

| Recapitulation |
| --- |
| Ia b Ia Trans. Theme II Theme II Closing Theme |

| Coda |
| --- |

**LISTENING SUMMARY**

Timbre:     orchestra of moderate size: string instruments, wind instruments, and timpani
Melody:     three major themes
Rhythm:     C meter; very fast tempo
Harmony:    major mode; begins in D major, modulates most significantly to A major for second theme; recapitulation returns to D major
Form:       abridged sonata form with no development section

*Mozart: The Marriage of Figaro, "Cinque… dieci" from Act I*

SIDE 6, BAND 5

**LISTENING ANALYSIS**

| Characters in Act I: | Susanna, maid to Countess | soprano |
| --- | --- | --- |
| | Figaro, valet to Count | baritone |
| | Bartolo, doctor from Seville | bass |
| | Marcellina, Bartolo's housekeeper | soprano |
| | Cherubino, a page | mezzo-soprano |
| | Count Almaviva | baritone |
| | Basilio, music teacher | tenor |

*Act I*

Duet: Figaro and Susanna

Act I begins with an orchestral statement of the two main themes in the duet, "Cinque, dieci." Figaro, a baritone, is heard first, singing a series of very deliberate motives that are part of a theme played by the first violins as he measures the bedroom that he will soon share with Susanna. We hear him call out the measurements, "cinque" ("five"), "dieci" ("ten"), and so on.

First Theme

Susanna, a lyric soprano, enters, trying on a hat and contributing a new melodic idea, a tuneful, quickly moving melody that contrasts with Figaro's straightforward presentation.

Second Theme

O - ra si ch'io son con - ten - ta

After a few moments of the two themes together, Figaro notices Susanna and her hat and joins in the melody as the music modulates to the dominant D major. Here, as before, the music offers a close reflection of the actions of the characters. As the two continue to share the melody, the music modulates back to and closes in G major.

Text:

Figaro (misurando):
  Cinque ... dieci ... venti
    ... trenta ... trentasei
    ... quarantatre ...

Susanna (guardandosi nello specchio):
  Ora si' ch'io son contenta;
    sembra fatto in ver per me.
  Guarda un po', mio caro Figaro,
  guarda adesso il mio capello.

Figaro:
  Si, mio core, or è più bello;
    sembra fatto in ver per te.

Figaro e Susanna:
  Ah, il mattino alle nozze vicino
  quanto è dolce al tuo/ mio tenero sposo,
  questo bel capellino vezzoso
  che Susanna ella stessa si fè!'

*Figaro (measuring):*
  *Five ... ten ... twenty*
    *... thirty ... thirty-*
    *six ... forty-three ...*

*Susanna (inspecting herself in the mirror):*
  *Now I'm really satisfied*
    *with it; it looks quite*
    *as if it were made for me.*
  *Look here a moment,*
    *Figaro darling,*
  *just look at this cap of mine.*

*Figaro:*
  *Yes, sweethart, it's*
    *much prettier now;*
  *it really does look made for you.*

*Figaro and Susanna:*
  *Ah, with the day of our*
    *wedding so near*
  *how sweet to you/me*
    *tender husband*
  *is this darling little cap*
  *that Susanna made herself!*

**LISTENING SUMMARY**

Timbre:   soprano and baritone; orchestra of moderate size: string and wind instruments
Melody:   first theme (Figaro's) built on short motives; second theme (Susanna's) more lyrical
Rhythm:   ₵ meter: Allegro
Harmony:  major mode; begins in G major, modulates most significantly to D major, ends in G major
Form:     free form based upon the alternation of two themes.

The first duet is followed by a recitative passage in which Susanna and Figaro discuss their prospective bedroom. Susanna does not like the room, though Figaro is proud of his new quarters. It is nearly the best room in the house—situated between those of the Count and Countess. He points out how convenient it will be in the next duet.

Duet: Figaro and Susanna

The second duet, "Se a caso madama la notte ti chiama," begins with Figaro explaining to Susanna, "If at night your mistress should ring, you would quickly answer the call; and if the Count should ring for me, it would be equally convenient." Figaro expounds these advantages in the bright key of Bb major. Susanna switches to the minor mode, expressing her fears that Figaro might be sent on some errand and the Count appear at her door. Repeatedly Figaro tries to hush this line of thought, but he is finally caught by Susanna's mood. Figaro and Susanna share the same melodic material in this duet. The orchestral accompaniment is simple but effective, at times emulating the different bells of the Count and Countess for ironic effect.

The duet is followed by a recitative in which Susanna tells Figaro of the Count's designs as they have been conveyed to her by her singing teacher, Don Basilio, the Count's mouthpiece. The Countess then rings for Susanna, and she leaves Figaro alone and angry on the stage.

Cavatina: Figaro

In the *cavatina*—or short lyrical song—that follows, "Se vuol ballare" ("If You Feel Like Dancing"), Figaro voices his belief that "two can play at this game": he can deceive and outwit the Count. The opening section is couched ironically in the style of a minuet, a dance for aristocrats. As Figaro gains in aggressive spirit, the meter changes from the moderate $\frac{3}{4}$ of the opening to a quick $\frac{2}{4}$. Thus the A and B sections of the cavatina are differentiated for dramatic purposes. The song ends with a restatement of the A section followed by a vigorous coda in $\frac{2}{4}$ at a Presto tempo. Figaro is determined to protect his interests.

As Figaro leaves, Bartolo and Marcellina enter. In recitative they discuss their plot to force Figaro to marry Marcellina. Bartolo wants revenge against Figaro, the man who had once spoiled Bartolo's own chances of marrying the Countess. (Rossini's opera *The Barber of Seville*, based on an earlier play by Beaumarchais, tells *that* story.)

Aria: Bartolo

After Marcellina exits, Bartolo, a bass, explains his motives in a strong aria, "La Vendetta," that immediately characterizes the man. The aria is marked Allegro con spirito and alternates between a number of different melodic ideas, much as a man in Bartolo's situation might alternate between rage at his past failures and visions of future revenge. While Bartolo takes himself very seriously, Mozart's music suggests that he is a *basso buffo*, a comic bass. The use of bass voices in comic roles was an eighteenth-century innovation for opera, and one at which Mozart excelled. At the end of the aria, the music returns to the opening melody, which is heard this time with a dramatic orchestral accompaniment that adds more to Bartolo's pretentious and overblown image.

As Bartolo leaves the stage, Marcellina and Susanna enter. Each shares with the audience some cutting remarks about the other, in recitative, before they face each other, in a duet.

**Duet: Marcellina and Susanna**

At the beginning of the duet, "Via resti servita," the two women engage in sarcastic politeness. Marcellina is heard first, saying to Susanna, "To greet you, my lady, I'm honored supremely." The allegro interchange soon degenerates into a kind of name calling. Each woman imitates the other musically and quite often in gestures as well. The orchestra adds to the fiery exchange, playing a triplet accompaniment against the duple meter of the vocal parts. At the end, Marcellina exits angrily, leaving a laughing Susanna as the apparent victor.

Susanna comments again on Marcellina, in recitative, as Cherubino enters. The page is upset because the Count, finding him with the gardener's daughter Barbarina, has dismissed him. Cherubino, who believes he is in love with the Countess, takes one of her gloves from Susanna and covers it with kisses. He then offers to sing Susanna a love song of his own composition.

**Aria: Cherubino**

In his aria, "Non so più," Cherubino, a mezzo-soprano in a trouser role, comments on his love for women in general. "I can't give you a good explanation," he says of his state of mind, and then proceeds to describe the day-dreams of beauty that absorb him. The aria is in an allegro tempo, with a rapid accompaniment suggesting the vitality of adolescence. It moves from a quick melody made up of short motives (Section A) to a contrasting melody that begins with a rising line (Section B). The original melody returns (Section A), and is followed by a melody that is at first quiet and thoughtful with an airy woodwind accompaniment, then dramatic (Section C). The aria slows to a dejected adagio as Cherubino concludes that if no one else will listen, he will talk to himself about love.

Much comic activity takes place during the recitative that follows. The Count knocks at the door, whereupon Cherubino hides behind a chair. The Count begins to make advances to Susanna but is interrupted by the approach of the singing teacher, Basilio. Not wanting to be discovered alone with Susanna, the Count hides behind the chair just as Cherubino nimbly jumps into its seat. Susanna covers Cherubino with a dressing gown as Basilio enters. Basilio, it turns out, is looking for the Count in order to tell him of Cherubino's attentions to the Countess. Upon hearing this, the Count leaps into view, and all three join in a trio.

**Trio: Count, Basilio, and Susanna**

The trio, "Cosa sento? Tosto andate" ("What's That? Go at Once!"), is marked Allegro assai and involves the quick interplay of three different voices: baritone, tenor, and soprano. Susanna's part is the most rhythmically active. At one point, she becomes faint but recovers abruptly when the men rush to seat her in the chair where Cherubino is hiding. In the course of the trio, the Count and Basilio assure Susanna that they mean no harm. Basilio apologizes for spreading the rumor about Cherubino, but the Count is still annoyed on this score. While telling the story of Cherubino and the gardener's daughter, he accidentally uncovers the hidden Cherubino. The trio ends with the wily Basilio singing quick eighth notes against the dotted rhythms of the frightened Susanna and the angry Count.

Chorus

After a short recitative, Figaro enters carrying a white veil and accompanied by peasants strewing flowers. During the chorus that follows, Figaro praises the Count for having earlier abolished the feudal custom that would have given him sexual rights to his female servants before their marriages. The presentation is a mixture of choral singing and recitative, humorously ironic in tone.

In the recitative that follows the chorus, Cherubino is saved from disgrace. But he is told that he must leave nevertheless. The Count makes him a captain and dispatches him to a regiment in Seville.

Aria: Figaro

In the rousing final aria of the first act, "Non più andrai" ("No More"), Figaro tells Cherubino that he must now put aside his romantic ideas and court finery. He must get on with the business of being a soldier. The music is appropriate to Figaro's advice—a $\frac{4}{4}$ march theme, embellished with trumpets and other military effects, alluding to Cherubino's future in the army and to his social status. The aria is in rondo form—ABACA. The invigorating thematic material of the A section closes the first act. Again there is a measure of irony as Figaro sarcastically extols the glories of war.

### Acts II, III, and IV

The acts that follow continue to develop and then resolve the complex plot. Mozart's music seems to match each dramatic situation and nuance. The Countess, for example, is given stately and flowing music very appropriate to her nobility in her famous aria "Dove sono?" ("Where Are Those Wonderful Moments?"), with its moderate rhythms and soaring lyrical melody. The vocal ensembles in the last three acts are exceptionally sensitive and complex in structure and emotional content. The characters are given rhythms and themes particularly indicative of their moods or actions. Throughout the opera, the music adds meaning to the text in ways both obvious and subtle. It can even reveal to the audience psychological truths about the characters that the text disguises.

## Other Types of Vocal Music

Oratorios and masses

Composers in the late eighteenth century were attracted to sacred vocal music, particularly the oratorio and the Mass. Haydn wrote two important oratorios that are still frequently performed—*The Creation* (1796–8) and *The Seasons* (1799–1801). Both demonstrate the influence of Handel on Haydn's choral style. In addition, he wrote a number of Masses, the most famous of which is the *Mass in D Minor* (1798), known commonly as the "Nelson" Mass. The later Masses employ an orchestra, but were intended for church performance.

Mozart's Masses are among his most dramatic works. They range

First Vienna performance of Haydn's oratorio *The Creation*, 23 March 1808. The composer is seated left of center in the foreground. (Bildarchiv Preussischer Kulturbesitz)

from short, simple works to several that are very lengthy and ornate, the latter group including the well-known *Requiem Mass* upon which he was working when he died. The work was completed by Franz Xavier Süssmayr (1766–1803), who had been a student of Mozart. His other great sacred work is the *Mass in C Minor* (1782).

Beethoven's sacred vocal works include two Masses and an oratorio, *Christ on the Mount of Olives* (1803). The *Missa solemnis in D Major* is one of his greatest achievements. A work of grand symphonic proportions, it was intended to be performed as concert music rather than as liturgical music.

The six Masses of Schubert were intended to be performed as liturgical compositions, and they include some exceptionally lovely lyrical melodies as well as some very effective dramatic moments. The Masses of Schubert, Mozart, and Haydn are still performed today in southern Germany and Austria as liturgical music during the celebration of the Mass.

During the Classical period, sacred vocal works took on some of the structural and stylistic characteristics of the symphony. As with so many aspects of Classical music, Haydn led the way. Generally large works, they were usually written for a chorus of moderate size, soloists, and an orchestra of small or moderate size. The liturgical sections of the Mass became longer and were usually subdivided into musical sections of considerable length. Solos became as elaborate as those found in operas of the day. Choral sections were also, at times, very elaborate and demanding. The Mass and the oratorio were truly the religious counterparts of the opera, symphony, and concerto of the period.

# PART FIVE

# *Romanticism in Music*

## Main Composers of the Romantic Period

*Carl Maria von Weber* (1786–1826)
*Giacomo Meyerbeer* (1791–1864)
*Gioacchino Rossini* (1792–1868)
*Gaetano Donizetti* (1797–1848)
*Franz Schubert* (1797–1828)
*Vincenzo Bellini* (1801–35)
*Hector Berlioz* (1803–69)
*Mikhail Glinka* (1804–57)
*Felix Mendelssohn* (1809–47)
*Frédéric Chopin* (1810–49)
*Robert Schumann* (1810–54)
*Franz Liszt* (1811–86)
*Richard Wagner* (1813–83)
*Giuseppe Verdi* (1813–1901)
*Jacques Offenbach* (1819–80)
*César Franck* (1822–90)
*Anton Bruckner* (1824–96)
*Bedřich Smetana* (1824–84)
*Louis Moreau Gottschalk* (1829–69)
*Johannes Brahms* (1833–97)
*Alexander Borodin* (1833–87)
*Camille Saint-Saëns* (1835–1921)
*Mily Balakirev* (1837–1910)
*Georges Bizet* (1838–75)
*Modest Mussorgsky* (1839–1881)
*Peter Ilych Tchaikovsky* (1840–93)
*Antonin Dvořák* (1841–1904)
*Jules Massenet* (1842–1912)
*Edvard Grieg* (1843–1907)
*Nikolay Rimsky-Korsakov* (1844–1908)
*Gabriel Fauré* (1845–1924)
*John Philip Sousa* (1854–1932)
*Edward Elgar* (1857–1934)
*Giacomo Puccini* (1858–1924)
*Hugo Wolf* (1860–1903)
*Isaac Albéniz* (1860–1909)
*Gustav Mahler* (1860–1911)
*Edward Macdowell* (1861–1908)
*Claude Debussy* (1862–1918)
*Frederick Delius* (1862–1934)
*Richard Strauss* (1864–1949)
*Jean Sibelius* (1865–1957)
*Erik Satie* (1866–1925)

# CHAPTER 17

# *Introduction to Nineteenth-Century Romanticism in Music*

*LISTENING PREVIEW The Romantic style in nineteenth-century music is characterized in part by an emphasis on both small and large performing groups, and by very short and very long pieces. Listen to the* Nocturne in E-flat Major *by Chopin (side 7, band 1) and the opening section of* Danse macabre *by Saint-Saëns (side 8, band 3). Whereas the differences between the two examples are immediately striking, both have very expressive, subjective qualities. Try to describe the musical characteristics of each composition that contribute to its expressivity.*

## The Romantic Movement

**Opposite** Intimate music, performed outdoors by a small group of instrumentalists in the early evening twilight, striving for the ideal: this trio (drawn by G.P.Zwinger in 1807) playing flute, violin and guitar, captures the true spirit of Romanticism in music. (Stadtbibliothek Nürnberg)

Romanticism is not so much a style of art as a way of perceiving and dealing with the world. Its outstanding characteristic is its stress on the individual and on subjective feeling. Because of this subjective emphasis, the Romantic movement is difficult to define in general terms. While some Romantic artists placed faith in utopias to come, others saw the past, particularly the Medieval period, as the ideal age. Some sought truth in the life of the common people, in rural settings and in the urban creations of the Industrial Revolution, while others sought escape in exotic dreams and fantasy. Although most gloried in the beauty of nature, others feared its awesome power. Many artists derived inspiration from their own countries' cultural heritages, while others aspired to more universal visions. These many impulses, all a part of the Romantic spirit, exerted a major influence on the minds and imaginations of the people of the nineteenth century.

The Romantic movement developed partly out of the upheavals of the preceding era. By the end of the eighteenth century, during the

lifetimes of Haydn, Mozart, and Beethoven, revolutionary social and political events had changed the whole of Europe. With these changes came a slow and gradual evolution in artistic sensibilities. In both art and literature the winds of change blew much earlier than in music. As early as 1774, with Classicism in music not yet at its peak, Johann Wolfgang von Goethe (1749–1832) wrote his morbidly introspective novel *The Sorrows of Young Werther*. Such blatant emotionalism would not appear in music for another half century.

## Life in the Romantic Age

Romanticism originated in a desire to change the world for the better—to build upon the debris of the old Europe a structure that would reflect the beauty of the natural world and the nobility of humanity. Among the earliest expressions of Romanticism were the writings of Jean Jacques Rousseau, who stressed individual enjoyment as the highest goal in life. Well before Rousseau's *Social Contract*, eighteenth-century rationalism had challenged the two great bastions of traditional authority, the divine right of the monarchy and the church that had upheld it. Where years of enlightened skepticism had provided revolutionary tinder, early Romantic impulses furnished the spark. Revolution followed.

The relatively quick success of the American Revolution found no parallel in Europe. There the French Revolution was merely the dawn of a seemingly endless cycle of democratic revolutions and repressive reactions, in great empires and small states alike. Nevertheless, with each swing of the pendulum, with each additional shock to the old order, the middle class gained new power and confidence. It became clear that, despite repeated setbacks, a new order had begun.

Equally important to the rise of the middle class was the Industrial Revolution, which gathered momentum throughout the nineteenth century. Wealth, for so long a matter of privilege, now became more closely tied to productivity and thus more widely distributed. What the middle class was progressively gaining in the various democratic revolutions, it was consolidating in the economic and social spheres.

These new social alignments inspired a great deal of study and theorizing. The early socialists hoped to be able to shape revolutionary events to bring about utopia. A few of these theorists held notions as whimsical and fantastic as the wildest creations of Romantic art. Karl Marx was more sober in his blueprint for a working-class revolution, *The Communist Manifesto* (1848). The novels of Charles Dickens, though laced with humor, also took a hard look at Europe's social ills in the industrial age. All of this interest in the workings of middle-class society eventually led to the science of sociology.

Other scientific advances opened new frontiers as well. Archeological and historical investigations fed the Romantic fascination with the past. Charles Darwin tied this interest in the past to the Romantic love of nature in his *Origin of Species* (1859), which set evolutionary theory upon firm footing. Meanwhile, horizons were expanding everywhere. The colonization by industrial Europe of large parts of the world had introduced exotic products, unusual works of art, and previously unexplored modes of feeling. The Romantic century was one of accelerating change and ceaseless novelty.

## Literature, Art, and Music in the Romantic Period

### Position of the artist

As society changed in the early nineteenth century, so did the role of the artist and the relationship of art to society. Romantic authors and artists became severe critics of society and its institutions. As a result, art seemed to oppose what it had once served—the class structure. The artist of the Romantic period achieved unprecedented artistic and social independence, rejecting the limitations of patronage and substituting the ideals of social conscience and individualism. Literary and artistic creation became much more intertwined, since both aspired to similar ideals. Many Romantic composers were also prolific writers, and William Blake (1757–1827) was both artist and poet.

Meanwhile an audience for the new style was slowly forming. It was no longer a refined aristocracy or a religious congregation using art and music to intensify devotion but was now an unsophisticated, sentimental public valuing art mainly as entertainment and insisting that it be available and accessible, both in public and in the home.

### The Romantic hero

To the Romantic era we owe the still popular conception of the artist as hero. The Romantic hero, and thus the Romantic artist, often appeared as a prophetic loner, weighed down by a burden of sensitivity and individualism. Misunderstanding, loneliness, and suffering were the lot of Romantic heroes. They not only tolerated isolation but gloried in it, hoping to expose by their own eccentric and sometimes shocking behavior the moral hypocrisy of the age. Endowed (by themselves and their public) with an intrinsic nobility, idealism, and honesty, they seemed to transcend the conventional ideas of good and evil that bound the average person.

This highly charged atmosphere of individualism produced art with heavily subjective qualities. Emotional forces predominated. States of feeling were accorded greatest importance, even though they were sometimes difficult to convey in a clear and straightforward manner. Mystery and ambiguity, fantasy and fear were all integral parts of Romantic expression. While the Classical style had emphasized objective, impersonal qualities—balance, clarity, and reason—the Romantic style emphasized subjective, personal forces. Even love was conceived more as a state of the individual than as a relationship between two people. Romantics tended to describe their own infinite longing for a loved one rather than the attainment of any real partnership. Artists sought to overwhelm and be overwhelmed rather than to establish a pleasant equilibrium between themselves and their audiences.

Second only perhaps to the theme of Romantic individualism was the theme of nature. The Romantics saw nature, not merely as a passive background, but increasingly as an animate thing that, in its many different moods, symbolized human emotions. It could be

Tunisian ensemble with original instruments at the Paris World Fair, 1878. Exoticism was an important trait in Romantic music. Whilst, in the 18th and early 19th centuries, musical influences from foreign travels would be reflected principally in operas as local color, later composers could hear foreign musicians at events like world fairs.

gentle and soothing or mysterious and violent. To many Romantics, nature represented an ideal of freedom, an environment in which people could act naturally and give free rein to their impulses, where their liberated imaginations could develop limitless possibilities.

Romantic artists also showed keen interest in exotic themes, places, and ideas. They found inspiration in Oriental and African work and in foreign legend and mythology. The nineteenth century's fondness for the strange and different—Coleridge's use of opium and his poetic ecstasies about faraway and ancient happenings, for example—is sometimes regarded as an attempt to avoid the harsh realities of a Europe in turmoil. However, it must also be understood as part of the general Romantic tendency to emphasize the fanciful, to exalt the workings of the imagination, and to belittle the products of reason so universally admired during the greater part of the eighteenth century. The as-yet-undiscovered unconscious was perceived in dreams and visions and had an important role in Romantic creation.

The Romantic era was marked, too, by a general curiosity about the supernatural. There developed, especially among the German transcendentalists, an interest in mysticism that, in its attempt to transcend the limits of time and space, was not unlike the exoticism found in Coleridge's works.

**Romantic literature**

Literature was the first of the arts to embrace fully the Romantic movement. In Germany the poet who most strongly exemplified Romanticism was Goethe. In *The Sorrows of Young Werther* and later in *Faust*, Goethe embodied for his age the ideal of the melancholy hero. Werther, a passionate aesthete, pursues his own ruin in an impossible love affair. Faust, an erudite scholar and a symbol of Classical learning, finds beauty in horror and pain. He sells his soul

Lord Byron in Albanian dress; portrait by Thomas Phillips. Byron spent much of his adult life in the Mediterranean, and died during the Greek War of Independence in 1824. (National Portrait Gallery, London)

for youth, knowledge, and power, with tragic consequences.

In England the Romantic movement produced an important group of poets, among them Blake, Byron, Wordsworth, Coleridge, Keats, and Shelley. Byron himself was almost an archetypal Romantic hero— captivating, emotional, ridden by passion and guilt. In Byron we also find the wittier side of Romanticism. His *Don Juan* is a brilliant satire of eighteenth-century attitudes and manners. The romantic absorption with nature is nowhere better shown than in the work of Wordsworth, to whom "the meanest flower that blows can give/Thoughts that do often lie too deep for tears." The romantic attraction to the supernatural is perhaps most powerfully expressed in Coleridge's *Rime of the Ancient Mariner.*

Victor Hugo was the leading figure of French Romanticism in literature toward the middle of the nineteenth century. He was a prolific writer of poetry, novels, and plays. A number of his works were the sources of inspiration for musical compositions.

Romantic painting

Romantic painters derived many of their themes from Romantic literature as well as from the more general impulses that influenced all the arts of the period. Many Romantic painters saw their work as a reaction against "Classical artificiality" and took great interest in "nature." Landscape paintings copied natural settings as the ideal. The use of simple peasants as subjects, rather than refined aristocrats, reflected the growing interest in the common people.

Painters, sculptors, and architects sought inspiration where they could find it—in the revival of older styles, especially the distant Gothic style, and in innovation. A number of new subjects and techniques were tried. The bizarre, the horrible, and the supernatural particularly fascinated some painters, as can be seen in Henry Fuseli's *The Nightmare*. New techniques, such as broader brushstrokes, generally lent themselves less to the representation of objective reality than to the expression of subjective emotion. Artists also displayed a developing social conscience, as seen in the late works of Goya.

The chief exponent of Romanticism in French painting was Eugène Delacroix, whose friendship with the composer Chopin and the poet Baudelaire strongly influenced his work. Aiming at an emotional "poetic truth" instead of simple accuracy of detail, Delacroix's paintings throb with sensuality, cruelty, and a splendor that seems at variance with his declared intention to be "natural."

**Romantic music**

Music of the Romantic period was inspired, to an unprecedented degree, by painting and poetry. Yet at the same time, it contributed certain qualities to Romanticism that were unobtainable in any other medium. Music is perhaps the most Romantic of all the arts. Alone, without words or pictures, music can suggest the mystery and ambiguity of human emotion. The poet Sidney Lanier wrote that "Music is love in search of a word." And, indeed, music does go forth in search of the inexpressible. In the Romantic period, music was an especially appropriate medium for the artist who wished to express a longing for love, for beauty, for the infinite.

The music of the Romantic period is marked by new purposes and new drives, but the style itself was created with the basic tools inherited from the Classical age. The Romantic style in music was not one of revolution against what had preceded it, but instead a continuation and extension of the Classical style—thus, the Classical-Romantic continuum. Composers devised little that was really new in a musical sense, but rather they continued to develop the melodic, rhythmic, and harmonic materials of an earlier age.

Although certain Romantic traits in music can be seen in the late eighteenth century, it was in the early decades of the nineteenth century that Romantic characteristics became truly dominant. They were expressed in a great variety of ways in all genres of music through the rest of the nineteenth century.

## Melody and Rhythm

**Lyrical melodies**

Romantic composers emphasized melody to an even greater extent than had their predecessors. The music of the Romantic period typically contains inspired lyrical melodies rather than those logically developed out of small, disjunct motives. Melodic phrases are generally longer and more irregular than those of the Classical period, and can be extremely chromatic.

Many Romantic melodies, even those used in instrumental works, are songlike in character. Folk music inspired many composers who found in it ties to nature and to their nations' cultural past; thus folk melodies were widely used. In instrumental music, melody with accompaniment often served to express the infinite yearning of the Romantic. Many Romantic works, both vocal and instrumental, are characterized by a melody that begins haltingly and then slowly builds to great fervor, a technique that we have already seen in the third movement of Beethoven's Fifth Symphony.

While many Romantic melodies are rather simple, others are quite complex—filled with chromaticism, disjunct motion, and ornamentation. Melodies calling for great virtuosity abound in the operas and concertos of the period. Many melodies are gradually changed or transformed in their repetitions in a work, at times to a point that the original form is barely recognizable.

**Rhythmic experimentation**

Rhythm, like melody, in Romantic music varies from the simple to the complex. In much of the music, the rhythm conforms to an established meter and to regular four- or eight-measure phrases. However, elongated melodies frequently disrupted such regular patterns. Romantic composers also experimented with new meters and rhythmic patterns. Thus, the rhythm of the Romantic style is at times more varied and complex than that of the eighteenth century. In a desire to suggest emotional conflict, Romantic composers often played one kind of rhythmic pattern against another—a steady duple rhythm against a triple, for example. Changes of rhythmic pattern and meter within a movement became increasingly common during the nineteenth century.

## Harmony and Texture

**Harmonic experimentation**

Harmonic practices of the nineteenth century evolved directly from those of the Classical style, but the role harmony played received a radical shift of emphasis. In Romantic music, tonality is not only a means of logical structure but also a way of achieving striking emotional effects. The rich possibilities offered by changes to remote keys are fully exploited. Minor and major keys are strongly juxtaposed, and seldom-used keys are brought to new prominence, in part as a result of the improved technology of instruments. Key changes occur ever more rapidly until finally, in the work of Wagner, we find a continuous modulation that is a perfect metaphor for the endless ardor of the Romantic period.

Romantic harmony also makes increasing use of chromaticism— that is, of tones (or accidentals) that are not in the scale upon which a passage is based. In Classical music, at least before Beethoven, accidentals tend to appear as surprising touches or as part of a predictable change of key. In the music of the Romantic period, chromaticism takes on increasing importance. Frequent accidentals disrupt an expectation of key, introducing a kind of uncertainty that seems to reflect the character of the period as well as the passions of the Romantic composers.

As chords were increasingly embellished with accidentals and modified in the course of key changes, music became more dissonant. Ultimately dissonance became not only a means to final resolution but an integral part of Romantic expression. Certain chords once used simply to facilitate key changes became more and more useful in their own right as expressive devices for composers, and gradually they became more acceptable to Romantic audiences. One suspects that the very discovery of new dissonances—always a shocking matter in music—must have gratified the rebellious Romantics.

By the end of the Romantic period, the great use of chromaticism and dissonance had seemingly exhausted the possibilities of the major-minor system of harmony and thus opened the way for the development of new harmonic systems. Within these new systems, twentieth-century composers have continued to explore and expand the use of dissonance.

*Changes in texture*

Romantic texture was not subject to the amount of experimentation that Romantic harmony was, yet some changes can be seen. In the music of the period, harmony and melody often work closely together to convey the primary emotional idea of the work, leading to a basically chordal texture. Many Romantic composers, however, looked

*Influence of Bach*

with special interest at the works of J. S. Bach, and contrapuntal passages or sections are not uncommon in their work. In general, the availability of an enlarged orchestra and more complex harmonies contributed to a denser, more complicated texture in Romantic music.

# Timbre and Dynamics

In the Romantic period, music was most often written for very small or very large groups. The proliferation of solo works, especially for the piano, was in many ways an expression of the individualism of the age. So too was the enthusiasm for virtuoso performance. Duets and chamber ensembles were also common.

*Larger orchestra*

The composer of instrumental music was able to rely on a larger orchestra, enriched by a number of instruments that were either newly developed or newly added to the orchestra: piccolo, clarinet, trombone, tuba, English horn, contrabassoon, and harp. Several new percussion instruments were introduced for dramatic purposes, and every part of the orchestra was enlarged. Berlioz and others helped to expand the techniques of orchestration, making possible broad, kaleidoscopic effects and rapid changes of timbre. The orchestra itself was becoming a virtuoso's instrument. The Romantic era saw the emergence of a new type of performing artist: the symphonic conductor. Mendelssohn and Berlioz were both pioneers of conducting; Liszt, Wagner, and Mahler continued the trend.

Choruses likewise grew greatly in number and size in the Romantic period. Choral societies with hundreds of members appeared in Europe and the United States: Boston's Handel and Haydn Society was founded as early as 1815.

Although military and town bands of wind and percussion instruments had existed in previous centuries, there was a major increase in the number of bands in the nineteenth century. This was due in part to improved technology in wind instruments. Of great importance was the fact that valves were added to brass instruments, allowing them to play chromatically and in every key. Until the

# Comparison of Classical and Romantic Music

| Elements | Classical Music Late 18th and Very Early 19th Centuries | Romantic Music Remainder of 19th Century |
|---|---|---|
| Melody | Often built on motives and short phrases<br>Phrases often very regular in length, balancing one another | Often very lyrical<br>Phrases often longer and less regular in length |
| Rhythm | Clear meters except in recitative | Meters sometimes changed within movements<br>Greater variety of meters and rhythmic patterns |
| Harmony | Major-minor system<br>Great use of modulation as structural basis | Greater use of cross-rhythms<br>Major-minor system<br>Expanded use of both modulation and chromaticism for functional purposes and expressive ends in themselves |
| Texture | Homophony most important but continued use of polyphony, often within basically homophonic works | Homophony and counterpoint both used<br>Texture often quite dense, especially in works for large groups |
| Timbre | Standardized orchestra, without continuo<br>Small instrumental ensembles, especially string quartet, also prominent | Continued growth of orchestra<br>Large choirs and bands<br>Small ensembles still prominent<br>Solo performer important<br>New emphasis on tone color as means of expression |
| Important Forms | Sonata, rondo, theme and variations, ternary, and binary<br>Many multi-movement works | Forms of Classical period used and expanded freely in a variety of ways<br>Many multi-movement works |
| Important Types of Compositions | Older types such as the Mass, oratorio, opera, solo concerto, and sonata<br>Many instrumental works based on sonata cycle: symphony, concerto, sonata, and string quartet | Types of compositions from Classical period, often expanded<br>Newly developed symphonic poem and solo song cycle<br>Small forms developed for solo instrument, especially piano |

twentieth century, however, few composers wrote serious works for bands.

**Greater use of dynamics**

Technical improvements also brought greater dynamic flexibility, and with the expansion of the orchestra the dynamic range increased as well. Not surprisingly, dynamic changes became a very important part of Romantic music. In all types, both gradual and sudden changes are used, with effects ranging from very subtle to very dramatic.

## Types of Compositions and Form

Romantic composers developed a number of new types of compositions, almost all of which were marked by the emotional qualities of the period. They also made use of most of the types of compositions popular in the late eighteenth century, altering them to suit the needs of their own age. Virtually no new forms were developed by Romantic composers; instead they altered Classical forms to fit the Romantic mood.

## Shorter Compositions

**Piano pieces**

Many of the new types of compositions developed during the Romantic age were intended specifically as vehicles for lyric and dramatic expression. Among them were several short piano works, including *nocturnes* ("night pieces"), *études* ("studies"), *impromptus, ballades*, and a variety of stylized dances. Such works generally focused upon the presentation of a single mood, or possibly a change of mood, ranging from pure whimsy to despair. The piano became increasingly popular in the Romantic age, and the amount and variety of music written for it grew greatly throughout the century.

**Lied and chanson**

On a comparable scale in the vocal field was the song—*Lied* (pl. *Lieder*) in Germany, and *chanson* (pl. *chansons*) in France. Like the short piano work, the song reflected the Romantic's desire to convey intense lyric emotion. It also reflected the deep interest of the Romantic composer in literature. Songs were often organized into *song cycles*, a number of songs with one unifying theme.

## Longer Compositions

The sonata cycle was still the basis for most large, multi-movement instrumental works throughout the nineteenth century, but it differed in many ways from the sonata cycle of the Classical period. Composers often varied the number and order of movements, while compositions themselves became longer and more grandiose.

The symphony continued as a major work for orchestra, although composers sometimes added extramusical associations to it, making it *programmatic*. The solo concerto, often for piano or violin and orchestra, generally retained its basic Classical structure and often called for virtuosic display. Chamber music for various ensembles, especially the string quartet, continued to be written, and the sonata for solo piano, or for piano and one other instrument, remained popular. Like the symphony and the concerto, chamber works generally were based on Classical models freely altered to suit the needs of the new style.

## Program Music

Program symphonies and symphonic poems

The Romantic aspirations towards integration of different arts are strongly apparent in the *program symphony* and the *symphonic poem* of the period. Composers generally related these works to extra-musical elements such as poetry or painting through a written description or program. While the program symphony generally follows the sonata-cycle structure, the symphonic poem, or tone poem, is a one-movement work. Among the most famous examples of program symphonies are two of Berlioz' works, the *Symphonie fantastique* (1830) and *Harold in Italy* (1834), a work based on Byron's famous poem. Well-known symphonic poems are Liszt's *Les Préludes* (1848) and Richard Strauss's *Don Quixote* (1896–97).

Overtures and incidental music

At times the *overture* also became a type of program music. Generally serving as an introduction to an opera or play, it was sometimes conceived independently. Overtures such as Tchaikovsky's *Romeo and Juliet* (1869) reflect the dramatic work with which they are associated much in the same way that a cinema theme—another type of program music—does today. A considerable amount of

THE WORKS of the Right Honorable LORD BYRON. Vol. I.

CHILDE HAROLD,

NAY, smile not at my sullen brow,
Alas! I cannot smile again;

The Romantic Hero in Literature: In "Childe Harold," Byron embodied all the melancholy and disillusionment of the Romantic hero caught up in an age not of his choosing. The poem follows the hero's travels through Europe, recounting tales of earlier ages. (Culver Pictures)

*incidental music*, meant to be performed during the course of a play or other entertainment, was also written during the Romantic period. The triumphant march to which so many newlyweds leave the altar was originally written by Mendelssohn as incidental music for Shakespeare's *A Midsummer Night's Dream*.

## Choral Music and Opera

Religious music and opera were also important during the Romantic period. The Mass, beginning in the eighteenth century, increasingly took on symphonic dimensions. Both the Mass and the oratorio became somewhat more secular, longer, and more imaginative. Opera flourished as never before under the genius of such composers as Wagner, Verdi, and Puccini. Romantic composers intensified opera, gradually deleting the recitative in favor of more elaborate music and blurring the distinctions between arias and ensembles, often to heighten the realism of their works. Frequently the spectacle became more splendid and elaborate, and the use of stage effects and of the chorus more imaginative. Composers of opera explored many fresh aspects of expression in their music and drama. By the end of the Romantic period opera had become the field where literary, visual, and musical arts were most successfully combined.

## Form

Romantic composers trusted more to the validity of emotion than to any rules of form. They valued spontaneity and were not averse to presenting their compositions as products of fleeting inspiration. Compositions of the period bear such titles as "Musical Moment," "Fantasy Pieces," and "Reverie," directing attention to the supposedly spontaneous nature of their composition.

Spontaneous composition had, of course, been appreciated in Classical works. Part of what impressed the early audiences of Mozart and Beethoven was their ability to improvise on a theme. This kind of

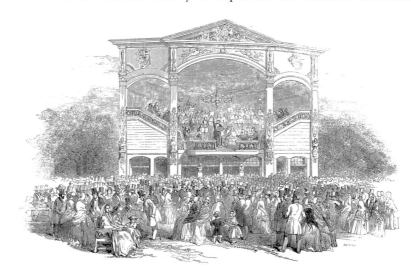

The 19th century brought the establishment of innumerable orchestral societies and a phenomenal growth in the number of public concerts given. This midcentury engraving is of a well-attended outdoor concert at Surrey Zoological Gardens. (Culver Pictures)

improvisation depended upon an understanding of formal principles and a creativity in using them. To Romantic composers, however, spontaneity seemed to demand a release from principles and a relaxation of Classical forms.

The late works of Mozart and Beethoven clearly demonstrated that Classical forms could be used for effective Romantic statement. New forms were thus not essential, and as has been noted, Romantic composers developed virtually none. Instead they based their works on Classical forms, putting them to new uses.

**Use of Classical forms**

Short compositions for piano were generally sectional, often binary or ternary in form. Songs, too, were cast in these forms and were frequently strophic. As the century progressed, the early reliance upon Classical forms turned toward freer, less traditional structures.

Works based on the sonata-cycle continued to use the same forms—theme and variations, ternary, rondo, and sonata forms. But Romantic composers seemed more interested in lyrical content and timbre than in form. Increasingly, form developed from the composer's use of musical ideas, whereas previously the use of ideas had been, to a much larger extent, governed by form. In many instances the sonata form became an argument between contrasting themes or motives as well as between different tonalities. Thematic development was somewhat less rigorous than before. The length and expressiveness of Romantic melodies worked against attempts to break them down, recombine them, or otherwise alter them in development. Romantic melodies begged not so much for development as for repetition. Recapitulation sections were often used, not primarily to repeat the initial material, but to give it a new and more tragic presentation.

In the hands of Romantic composers, Classical forms became looser and freer so that greater scope might be given to melody and the play of emotion. Clarity of form thus became less and less important, losing ground to the emotional intensity of the period as a whole.

## Trends in Nineteenth-Century American Music

**Orchestras and choral societies**

During the nineteenth century, the eighteenth-century trend toward musical sophistication accelerated in America, with the constant influences of so many aspects of the arts from western Europe. The first orchestras were founded, often in association with choral societies. One of these, the Handel and Haydn Society of Boston, was established in 1815, and another, the New York Philharmonic Society, was established in 1839. The success of the new orchestras often depended on the flamboyance with which they were presented to the general public. "Monster" concerts, with hundreds of instrumentalists and singers, were attended by audiences numbering in the thousands. Extravagant displays of this sort were good publicity and helped to encourage the development of our modern symphony orchestras.

**Thomas**

The person most responsible for the rise of the symphony orchestra in America was Theodore Thomas (1835–1905), who joined the

New York Philharmonic Society as conductor in 1879. Until then, the Society had been a cooperative venture run by the players and generally performing only a very limited repertory of familiar works. Under Thomas, business affairs were taken out of the hands of the musicians and given over to a full-time manager—an arrangement that was to become typical of the complex symphonic corporations of the twentieth century. At the same time, Thomas himself, as a conductor, asserted more and more control over the music. He organized new types of concerts, sometimes featuring solo performers, and expanded the repertory, adding new vocal, chamber, and orchestral works. In 1891 he accepted an invitation to go to Chicago. Citizens there were eager to have a symphony orchestra of their own—preferably bigger and better than that of their eastern rival. The money for salaries and a concert hall was raised by public subscription, and under Thomas's direction the Chicago Symphony Orchestra became one of the nation's major orchestras.

Despite the growing American interest in serious music, the ruling style continued to be European throughout the nineteenth century. True, there were hints of a developing national style. But even with the growing number of music conservatories and performing groups at home, the majority of American composers continued to receive their training in Austria, Germany (especially the Leipzig Conservatory founded by Mendelssohn), or other European music centers. Such practice continued, in fact, up until World War I.

**Foster**  As the nineteenth century progressed, nationalistic elements slowly began to make themselves felt in American music. Stephen Foster (1826–1864) wrote a number of sentimental ballads in the Romantic tradition, but he is far better remembered for his songs associated with blackface minstrel shows of the period. The works were for white audiences and are far from authentic black music. Foster spent most of his life in Pennsylvania and visited the south only once, and that was after he had already written most of his songs. However, even if not ethnically correct, the songs had a freshness and an "American" quality that was appealing to many middle-class families. The songs also inspired, through their popularity, an interest in their sources.

**Gottschalk**  Another composer who made use of distinctively American elements was Louis Moreau Gottschalk (1829–1869), a virtuoso pianist from New Orleans. Some of Gottschalk's music was written in an exotic Romantic style, a style that he managed well enough to achieve considerable success in Europe, making him virtually the only American of his day to do so. Even Chopin was impressed by his virtuosity as a pianist. Gottschalk's works, although basically European in style, contain many traces of Caribbean rhythms and other rhythms learned in the lively intercultural crossroads of his native city.

**Sousa**  The marches of John Philip Sousa (1854–1932) show another aspect of the American character in music. Director of the Marine

Band from 1880 to 1892, Sousa later organized his own band and toured the United States, Canada, and Europe, winning great acclaim for his stirring, inspired marches. Many of them, especially "Semper Fidelis" and "Stars and Stripes Forever," are still played by bands today.

**MacDowell**
Perhaps the prototypical American composer of the period was the German-trained Edward MacDowell (1860–1908), a man once regarded as America's greatest composer. At the age of fifteen, he left America to study in Paris and later Germany, and established himself there as a successful pianist and composer before returning to the United States in 1888. Throughout his career, he was a strong supporter of American nationalism, and he was a noted teacher. Yet his music, in its lack of any folk, religious, or Afro-American elements, seems not to reflect his own nationality.

Following a style very much within the German-Austrian Romantic tradition, MacDowell wrote music for orchestra, chorus, piano, and solo voice. Among his early works are a number of program symphonies with highly personal content and two piano concertos with a Grieg-like breadth and power. As he grew older, his compositions became smaller and more precise. He abandoned orchestral music after 1896 and near the end of his short creative life devoted most of his time to writing quaint and lively piano pieces. These late works, including *Woodland Sketches* and *Fireside Tales*, were generally brief character pieces—miniatures of evocative delicacy.

Other American composers turned to very different styles. Some were attracted by French and Russian musical developments, particularly by Impressionism and Russian nationalism. Stimulated, perhaps, by the latter movement, a number of American composers undertook for the first time a serious study of the American folk tradition. A concern for contemporary affairs also made itself felt in a number of works.

The rise of the fashionable bourgeois "salon" prompted composers in the mid-19th century to compose music suitable both for salon performance by the composer himself, and for international distribution in printed form, following the enormous rise in music publishing since the beginning of the century. This title page of "Musical Recreations" shows a piano virtuoso encircled by educated ladies interested in both painting and music. (Österreichische Nationalbibliothek, Vienna)

# CHAPTER 18

# *Piano Music: Chopin and Liszt*

*LISTENING PREVIEW The piano is one of the most expressive and dramatic of all instruments because of its capability of sounding a wide spectrum of dynamic levels and because of the multitude of special effects that can be created with it. These qualities made it a very attractive instrument to many composers and performers in the nineteenth century. Listen to the opening section of Liszt's* Hungarian Rhapsody No. 6 in D-flat Major *(side 7, band 2) and notice the contrasts between loud and soft passages. Identify those characteristics of the piano's sound and technical capabilities that are not possible on other instruments.*

## Directions in Piano Music

In the nineteenth century, music for the piano developed into a brilliant, dramatic, and lyrical showcase for virtuoso performance. While earlier composers for solo piano had devoted themselves largely to the sonata, Romantic composers often preferred shorter pieces with less well-defined structures. Nocturnes, études, impromptus, ballades, and a variety of dances all lent themselves to the capturing of a definite mood. Romantic composers were also likely to choose descriptive titles and programs for their works rather than the simple key designations used by earlier composers.

*Classical piano music*

The changes took place gradually, within the artistic framework of the Classical-Romantic continuum. Haydn's piano works were sonatas or divertimentos, denoted only by key signature—*Sonata in C Minor*, for example. Mozart's major piano compositions were also sonatas, with titles similar to those used by Haydn. Beethoven's sonatas, however, were occasionally given subtitles such as "Tempest," "Appassionata," and "Moonlight," and he wrote a number of other piano works as well, including bagatelles (literally "trifles"). Franz Schubert was also a major composer of sonatas as well as shorter pieces, such as waltzes, minuets, impromptus, and *moments musicaux*. The piano music of Beethoven and Schubert thus forms a bridge between Classical and Romantic styles, foreshadowing many developments in the later nineteenth century.

By the time of Robert Schumann (1810–1856) and Felix Mendelssohn (1809–1847), the sonata no longer dominated solo piano literature. With Schumann we encounter collections of short "character" pieces with descriptive, even fanciful, names: *Carnaval, Fantasiestücke* ("Fantasy Pieces"), *Kinderszenen* ("Scenes from Childhood"), and *Waldszenen* ("Forest Scenes"). Individual pieces bear even more explicit titles. In *Waldszenen* (1848–49), for example, we find pieces whose German titles can be translated as "Hunter on the Watch," "Solitary Flowers," and "Bird as Prophet."

Composers in the later nineteenth century continued to develop new ideas and techniques in piano music. Johannes Brahms (1833–1897) wrote short pieces and sonatas that rank among the finest written for piano, but they were more abstract than Schumann's piano pieces. Others such as Edvard Grieg (1843–1907) in Norway, Isaac Albéniz (1860–1909) in Spain, and Sergei Rachmaninoff (1873–1943) in Russia demonstrated by their outstanding works that the piano was the most international and admired instrument of the age. All the main aspects of the period's music—nationalism, literary associations, fantasy, and exoticism—were incorporated into the piano repertory.

Thus, although Romantic composers continued to write piano sonatas and to draw upon an inheritance of fugue, variation, rondo, and dance, they also developed a new literature for piano—a literature featuring short lyric or dramatic pieces. Today the short piano piece of the nineteenth century is a very important part of the repertory of all pianists.

## Chopin's Piano Music

Perhaps more than any other composer, Frédéric Chopin (1810–1849) established the piano as a voice of Romanticism. He wrote almost exclusively for solo piano, learning to exploit its expressive resources to great advantage.

Chopin was born in 1810 near Warsaw of a Polish mother and a French father. Although he was passionately attached to his native land and drew heavily from its musical traditions, he spent most of his life in self-imposed exile. When Russian troops overran Warsaw in 1831, Chopin, then on tour in Austria, decided not to return. He lived the greater part of his adult life in Paris, though his will specified that his heart be returned to Poland for burial.

Paris was a music-loving city, and in 1831, when Chopin arrived there, piano music was at an all-time fashionable high. Competition between leading pianists and teachers was widespread and very spirited. Social events were often organized around piano performance, with the solo concert becoming ever more popular. The pianist became the star of the salon, and the theatrics of piano playing often caused women in the audience to swoon. Celebrated performers were greeted with the hero worship and hysteria that have more recently been associated with rock idols.

Into this environment came twenty-one-year-old Chopin, a former

Chopin in 1847, at the age of 37; portrait drawing by Franz Winterhalter. At this time, Chopin had just separated from his extraordinary lover, the woman writer George Sand. (John Freeman & Co.)

child prodigy who had already written numerous works and performed with much success in Warsaw and Vienna. He immediately impressed Parisian society with his original style of performance and composition. He appeared regularly in the salons of intellectuals and artists. However, he seldom performed in public concert, in part because he had not the strength to play forcefully. His technique was delicate and sensitive, filled with fine nuances and melodic shadings.

**Legato**　　Chopin treated the piano as a singing instrument. His melodies are often characterized by a smoothly connected—or *legato*—style. Such a style had always been natural to singing and was easier to achieve on the piano after the development of the sustaining pedal (often mistakenly called the "loud" pedal).

**Rubato**　　Chopin made extensive explorations of the uses of pedal and legato playing. He also used *rubato*, a technique in which small displacements in rhythm are introduced for expressive purposes. Rubato literally means "robbing"—in music, robbing time value from one note and giving it to another. The technique allows the pianist to linger on a chosen note, perhaps the high climactic note of a phrase, and then make up the time lost by playing the next notes more quickly.

Repetition of theme is an important means of organization in Chopin's music. Even in short pieces such as nocturnes and mazurkas, the main theme appears several times, alternating with one or more secondary themes. With every repetition, the main theme gains in intensity—in part because of the repetition and in part because the theme is varied. The variations may include such things as increased ornamentation, dynamic change, rubato, and syncopation.

Chopin's use of harmony exploits effectively the harmonic language he inherited. Decorative chromaticism is used very expressively to embellish repetitions of melodies. Stable tonal areas modulate to expected or to surprising new tonalities, to provide variety and to create desired effects or moods.

In listening to music of the Classical style, we expect to hear a logical development of themes and an opposition of large tonal areas. In listening to Chopin, we are more likely to hear a repetition of melody and accompaniment, with intensity achieved through subtle variation and surprise. His method of composing was closely related to improvisation, and this sense of spontaneity comes across clearly in his works, even though he labored greatly over details when actually writing his music down.

### Nocturnes

#### Field

Among Chopin's most celebrated works are his *nocturnes,* or night pieces. The nocturne, one of the earliest of the new solo piano pieces, was conceived by Irish pianist John Field (1782–1837), a composer who wrote exclusively for the piano. Basically it is mood music, reflecting the subjective feelings of an artist at night. Most of Chopin's nocturnes are ardent works characterized by a long, lyrical melody set over a chordal or arpeggiated accompaniment. They do not have any particular formal characteristics as a group, though varied repetition of melody is typical. Fantasy, agitation, melancholy—all the feelings of the night are represented. The nocturne was apparently well suited to Chopin's own needs. Karasowski, his biographer, notes that he "generally improvised in the dark, frequently at night.... Then would he bury himself in the theme heart and soul, and develop from it tone-pictures full of lofty inspiration and ... poetry."

### Chopin: Nocturne in E♭ Major, Op. 9, No. 2

The second of Chopin's nocturnes, the *Nocturne in E♭ Major,* is one of the best known. It was written in 1833 when the composer was twenty-three years old. Like most of the other nocturnes in *Op. 9,* it is made up of a number of sections. A main theme alternates with a secondary theme until both are superseded by a third theme.

The main theme, heard at the opening of the work, is a slow, graceful melody played over fluid, chordal accompaniment. The theme is almost instantly memorable because of its strong emphasis on its central tonality Eb, its moderate rhythmic flow in $\frac{12}{8}$ meter, and its strong character deriving from a good balance of conjunct and disjunct melodic motion.

Main Theme

The accompaniment is very steady, with a bass note at the beginning of each measure followed by two successively higher chords. This pattern ceases only during the brief cadenza at the end of the work.

After the first presentation, the main theme is immediately repeated, this time with ornamentation. A second theme follows, beginning in the dominant key of Bb and returning quickly to Eb for a repetition of the main theme, now more highly ornamented. This time the notes of the melody are approached chromatically by half steps. The opening of the main theme, which was at first conveyed by means of only six notes, now requires fourteen. After a repetition of the second theme, the main theme reappears, even more intensely ornamented. We can see Chopin's skill as a composer by comparing the climactic last measure of the main theme as it undergoes progressive ornamentation:

Changes in Last Measure of Main Theme:
First Presentation

Second Presentation

Ornament  Added

Third Presentation

Sixteenth Notes Changed to Thirty-second Notes

Fourth Presentation

Syncopation Added

**Third theme**

This fourth and final presentation of the main theme is again in the tonic key. Following it, a third theme is presented and repeated with ornamentation. It functions somewhat as a coda and remains in the tonic key. The form of the entire piece can be outlined in the following manner:

| A | A′ | B | A″ | B′ | A‴ | C | C′ |
|---|----|---|----|----|----|---|----|

**Cadenza**

A short cadenza follows, played in the upper register by the unaccompanied right hand. It builds to a crescendo and then subsides to pianissimo as the accompaniment returns for the final quiet measures.

**LISTENING SUMMARY**

Melody:     three themes, one in each section; the first theme, the most prominent and important, is very lyrical; the other two themes are also lyrical and are closely related to the first in rhythm and overall contour

Rhythm:     $\frac{12}{8}$ meter; tempo Andante

Harmony:   mainly major mode; begins and ends in E♭ major, with several modulations

Form:       AA′BA″B′A‴CC′

## Études and Preludes

Among Chopin's earliest works are two important collections of *études,* or studies. Each was written to illustrate and develop a specific technical skill. The first, *Étude in C Major, Op, 10, No. 1,* for example, involves the playing of arpeggios over a wide span in the right hand. It is a brilliant piece that calls for great virtuosity. The constant arpeggios in the right hand are accompanied by a slowly moving bass line that supports the chords and helps in modulation to related keys.

Taken as a whole, the études cover a large part of nineteenth-century piano technique. Though written partly as exercises, they are musical masterpieces and have become popular concert works.

In addition to his collection of études, Chopin also wrote a series of twenty-four short *preludes,* each with its own idea or mood. Briefer than the études, the preludes show Chopin's pianistic art in miniature.

## Dances

**Mazurkas**

Particularly brilliant was Chopin's use of the dance forms of his native Poland. Among his works are more than fifty examples of the *mazurka,* a Slavic dance in $\frac{3}{4}$ meter, with exotic rhythmic touches of Eastern Europe. The works range in spirit from exultation to lament. In them Chopin conveys both pride in his homeland and passionate

**Polonaises**

sorrow for Poland's loss of freedom. The *polonaise,* a heroic dance of

**Waltzes**

ceremonial importance, was also the basis for several of Chopin's works. The *Polonaise in Ab* (1842) and the *Polonaise-Fantasie* (1845–46) are grand patriotic statements on a virtuoso scale. Chopin also wrote fourteen *waltzes,* somewhat lighter in spirit than the polonaise and imbued with great charm. Many of his dance pieces are often played by amateur and professional pianists today. The generalized nationalist sentiment of the Polish dances are the closest he ever came to adding an extra musical message to his work—even though his friends were some of the most celebrated literary and artistic figures in Paris.

## Ballades, Scherzos, and Sonatas

Among Chopin's other works for piano, perhaps the most important are his ballades, scherzos, and sonatas. The *ballade* is essentially a narrative piece for piano, though the literary narrative or epic on which it is based need not be indicated by the composer. Chopin, in fact, did not indicate the inspirational sources of his ballades. Particularly popular is his *Ballade No. 1 in G Minor.*

The *scherzo,* originally a movement of the sonata cycle, was treated by Chopin as a work in itself. His four scherzos are the first Romantic examples of this genre as a full-scale independent piano composition. Like most other works by Chopin, the scherzos have a spontaneity and improvisatory quality about them, due in part to the free ornamentation added to repeated themes.

The last two of Chopin's three piano sonatas are the longest and perhaps the most complex of his works for solo piano. The *Sonata in Bb Minor* (1839) is the best known. The improvisatory, expansive nature of the work creates the impression that the lyrical and virtuosic aspects of Chopin's melodic and harmonic materials are much more significant than the Classical forms into which they are freely cast.

## Chopin's Legacy

When Chopin died of tuberculosis at the age of thirty-nine, he was one of the most revered artists of his day. A great number of his works are still performed regularly today, many of them considered as indispensable parts of pianists' repertories.

Aurore Dudevant (1804–1876), the cigar-smoking novelist and feminist better known by her pen name George Sand, lived with Chopin for many years. She summarized his gift particularly well: "No musical genius has appeared so full of deep poetic feeling as Chopin. Under his hand the piano spoke an immortal longing. A short piece of scarcely half a page will contain the most sublime poetry." Chopin did not need large forms to express this longing. He found the perfect creative medium in the short piece and in the lyric voice of the piano.

## Liszt's Piano Music

Of very different talent and temperament was Franz Liszt (1811–1886), another great performer and composer of piano music in the Romantic period. Chopin's pieces were for the salon, small in scale, delicate,

The 13-year-old Liszt as a child prodigy at the piano in 1824. By all accounts, Liszt was one of the greatest pianists who ever lived. (Österreichische Nationalbibliothek, Vienna)

and intimate; Liszt's piano works were for the concert hall, on a larger scale than his contemporaries had believed possible. Liszt was blessed with great physical strength and a fiery, egotistical disposition. His piano technique was the talk of Europe, as were his many flamboyant love affairs. Throughout his long career, Liszt was pursued by women and surrounded by a veritable cult of students intent on learning the style of their master. Characteristically he refused to accept payment for teaching because "neither God nor the Emperor accepted gifts." As teacher, composer, pianist, lover, and individualist, Liszt had a powerful influence on the music and the Romantic imagination of his time.

    Liszt was born in Hungary to a family in the service of the

Esterházys. Like Chopin, he gained early recognition in Vienna and then settled in Paris. Although apparently not a child prodigy, he early developed a great facility for sight reading and improvisation. His memory was phenomenal. After hearing a piece of music only once, he could generally reproduce all or most of it at the keyboard. These gifts helped him become one of the foremost arrangers of orchestral scores for piano. And his insatiable appetite for literature of all kinds contributed to his success as a composer of program music.

It was at the piano, however, that Liszt made his reputation. Much of his style as a composer can be explained by his playing technique. Liszt was above all a virtuoso pianist—and, some would add, a showman. An important influence on his life was the great violin virtuoso Niccolò Paganini (1782–1840), whom Liszt heard in concert in 1831. He saw no reason why the piano could not attain the virtuosic heights of Paganini's violin. He therefore wrote, and played, works of dazzling difficulty—works that demanded a certain theatricality of performance or, in the words of one observer, a "great tossing of the hands." Liszt's performances were unquestionably marked by theatrics but also by incomparable finesse and power.

**Paganini's influence**

While Chopin generally wrote in an economical fashion, drawing on the very special resources of the piano, Liszt composed in a resplendent orchestral manner. His works, on the average, take in a larger part of the keyboard than do the works written by his contemporaries. More notes sound simultaneously. Ornamentation

Manuscript page from Liszt's *Soirées de Vienne*. Even the untrained eye can recognize the difficulty of the music Liszt wrote for his *Soirées de Vienne* ("Evenings of Vienne"). The passage shown is marked *Vivace*—that is, very fast—and requires considerable agility in the right hand. (The Granger Collection) occurs on many levels. Liszt made piano transcriptions of a number of works, including Beethoven's symphonies, Bach's organ fugues, and excerpts of music-dramas by a then little known contemporary, Richard Wagner. He was thus experienced in creating the various orchestral sounds, loud and soft, on the piano. This writing of transcriptions, however, did much more than encourage experiments in piano timbre. Long before the advent of recordings, it made symphonies and other orchestral works accessible to audiences in places that could not sustain a full orchestra.

Liszt wrote a wide variety of works for solo piano, including several collections of highly imaginative and virtuosic études, the renowned *Sonata in B Minor* (1852–53), numerous character pieces (including the large cycle of pieces called the *Années de pèlerinage* ("Years of Pilgrimage")), ballades, scherzos, and dances. He is well known, too, for his rhapsodies, works which are not profound but which show many aspects of his style in an appealing, popular mode.

**Rhapsodies**

The *rhapsody* is one of the most romantic of musical works. It has no set form, aside from the free use of sections, relying instead primarily on the artist's subjective organization. Generally the rhapsody is dramatic or heroic in tone and rich in emotional color. It is usually scored to achieve a large sound and is commonly written for piano or orchestra.

Liszt's nineteen *Hungarian Rhapsodies* were written after the composer's trip to Hungary in 1838. Receiving news of severe flooding in his native land, Liszt crossed the Danube and was received as in triumph by his countrymen. In appreciation and patriotic pride, he wrote a series of rhapsodies through which he hoped to convey "certain states of mind in which are condensed the ideals of a nation."

The rhapsodies were based on the gypsy music that was commonly heard in the towns and countryside of Hungary. All of the works make use of some characteristics of dance and folk material. One, the *Hungarian Rhapsody No. 15 in A Minor,* is based on a traditional march tune of the Hungarian army, the *Rákoczy March.* In places Liszt attempted to imitate gypsy instruments, particularly the *cimbalom,* a string instrument played with hammers.

Caricature of Liszt in later years as a piano virtuoso, possibly drawn by George Sand. (Bibliothèque Nationale, Paris; photo Heritage of Music)

Most of the rhapsodies are technically very difficult to play. They are characterized by extreme dynamic contrasts and luxuriant ornamentation. Typical are the repetition of difficult melodic figures, the use of octaves, rapid scales and arpeggios, and other colorful effects for which Liszt was famous. The variation and development of themes provide many occasions for virtuosity—wonderful technical displays that have all the feeling of true improvisation. In these respects, the rhapsodies are typical of a great number of his other piano works.

**Liszt: Hungarian Rhapsody No. 6 in Db Major**

Changes of mood and texture are frequent in Liszt's rhapsodies. In most of the works, quick dancelike material is contrasted with melancholy gypsy airs.

### LISTENING ANALYSIS

Such contrasts can readily be found in the *Hungarian Rhapsody No. 6 in Db Major*; different melodic materials occur in contrasting tempos and keys. The four large sections that make up the piece can be outlined thus:

| Section A | Section B | Section C | Section D |
|---|---|---|---|
| **Tempo giusto**<br>**(At a fitting tempo)** | **Presto**<br>**(Very fast)** | **Andante**<br>**(Moderate)** | **Allegro**<br>**(Fast)** |
| **Db Major** | **C# Major** | **Bb Minor** | **Bb Major** |

**Section A**    In the first section, pounding chords in the left hand accompany a hesitant dancelike melody in the right. Syncopation is strongly apparent throughout, and the section ends with a brief flourish that travels quickly up and down the keyboard.

**Section B**    The quickly moving second section also makes use of syncopation. Its tempo provides bright contrast to the slow motion of the preceding section.

**Section C**    The third section is set in the key of Bb minor, the relative minor of the key used in the first section. Marked *Quasi improvisato* (somewhat improvised), this section evokes the slow, haunting quality of a gypsy violin. Its improvisatory character stems from its slow tempo, expressive melody, unusual rhythmic patterns, and apparent lack of clear meter.

**Cadenza and section D**    A brief, clashing cadenza links the third section to the final section, which offers a vehicle for Liszt's dazzling virtuosity. The section begins with a rather simple conjunct melody that is presented several times with ever-increasing complexity. The conjunct melody and its repeated notes are clearly reminiscent of the Hungarian cimbalom. Toward the end, scale passages, arpeggios, great chords, and a presto tempo make one feel that the limits of technical virtuosity and showmanship have been reached.

### LISTENING SUMMARY

Melody:    different themes in each of the four sections; all marked by a folklike quality

Rhythm:    $\frac{2}{4}$ meter; tempos in four sections are slow-fast-slow-fast; specific tempos are shown above

Harmony:    mainly major mode, with third section in minor mode; specific keys are shown above

Form:    ABCD

Liszt made notable contributions to Romantic orchestral literature and wrote several sacred and secular choral pieces, although they are rarely heard today. He excelled in large-scale composition and, not surprisingly, ignored chamber music as a medium. His personality embodied many paradoxes. He was an unconventional man who had affairs with many women, but was nevertheless strongly religious and took holy orders in 1865. He was a flamboyant virtuoso and showman, yet he championed the works of struggling composers such as Wagner long before a receptive public existed for them.

CHAPTER 19

# *The Art Song: Schubert and Schumann*

*LISTENING PREVIEW The combination of the expressive qualities of the piano, of poetry, and of lyrical and dramatic melodies performed by a singer resulted in the rise of the solo song accompanied by the piano to a great peak of popularity in the nineteenth century. The accompanied song proved to be an ideal vehicle for the emotional, subjective thoughts of many composers. Listen to Schumann's "Widmung" ("Dedication") (side 7, band 4) and notice the exuberant mood created as the singer extols praises of his beloved. Identify the characteristics of the music that contribute to its highly spirited style. What is the particular contribution of the piano accompaniment?*

## *The Growth of the Art Song*

Art songs

In the nineteenth century, an abundant new literature developed for the solo voice with piano. These works are known, in a general sense, as *art songs*. In France the *chanson* was very important in the works of many composers. In German-speaking countries, the development of the *Lied* (pl. *Lieder*) was particularly intense. The compositional form of Lieder allowed for a variety of lyric expression on a dramatic, if limited, scale. Like most other songs, the Lied combined a poetic text with music, but it derived its special characteristics from the German Romantic movement of the early nineteenth century. Because of its great literary and musical significance, the Lied will be considered in some detail.

Schubert's influence

The Lied found its first major champion in Austrian composer Franz Schubert. Although Mozart and Haydn had written many attractive songs, most of their works had resembled either arias or folk songs. Beethoven also wrote songs, most notably his song cycle *An die ferne Geliebte* ("To the Distant Beloved," 1815–16), the first song cycle of the nineteenth century, but his larger vocal and instrumental works are of much greater significance. It was Schubert who first treated the Lied as a major vehicle of musical expression.

Developments in the piano

There are several reasons for the sudden, immense development of the Lied at the beginning of the nineteenth century. One important factor was the continued development of the piano. Compared with earlier pianos, the instrument for which Schubert composed was quite rich and warm in tone. The early nineteenth-century piano was capable of a lovely singing tone sustained by a new pedal technique. Able to perform a variety of tasks—to blend in with and complement the voice, to add lyrical and dramatic support to it—the piano provided an ideal accompaniment. Composers were quick to make use of this innovative timbre. So were the many middle-class families who, having acquired a piano, wanted songs with piano accompaniment. This new role of the piano as the center of amateur vocal performance did much to promote the nineteenth-century emphasis on song.

German poetry

The growth of Lieder was also encouraged by the outpouring of lyric poetry that began in Germany in the late eighteenth century. Not until the time of Beethoven could the Germans boast of a poetic literature equal to that which had long existed in England and Italy. But in the latter part of the eighteenth century, a number of important writers came to the fore—most notably Johann Wolfgang von Goethe and Friedrich von Schiller (1759–1805). Heinrich Heine (1797–1856) was another great lyric poet, born in the same year as Schubert, whose poems were set by many composers. Poetry and music thus flourished together in the climate of early German Romanticism. Goethe, Schiller, Heine, and many other German poets of the early nineteenth century were nearly as important to the development of the Lied as the composers whom their work inspired.

## Characteristics of the Lied

Structure

Lieder are truly compound art forms. Literary nuances deeply influence the music, while the music enhances, and more fully 'realizes,' the emotional implications of the poetic lines. Lieder thus vary in structure according to the emotional requirements of the poems on which they are based. Some, such as Schubert's "Erlkönig" ("The Elf King"), are freely structured. Others, such as Schubert's "Gute Nacht" ("Good Night") or "Die Forelle" ("The Trout"), are in modified strophic form: the same basic melody and accompaniment are repeated, with some modification in each stanza of poetry.

Piano and voice

Just as the Lied is a partnership between poetry and music, so also is it a partnership between piano and voice. For the first time, the piano part is as important as the vocal line. The melody, of course, is presented mainly by the singer. But the pianist provides much more than accompaniment. Many Lieder begin with a piano introduction that sets the mood and establishes the basic rhythm, key, and thematic idea. As the song progresses, the piano may contribute solo passages that are integral to the artistic design, and the end of the Lied is often played by the piano alone. Although the piano sometimes simply duplicates the melodic line, it usually has a part that is different from the melody and of equal significance. In most cases, the piano provides, in the words of the musicologist-critic Paul Henry Lang, "the soil from which the vocal flower grows."

## Schubert's Lieder

*Above* Schubert and friends during an excursion to an Austrian country village, c. 1825. Schubert (seated, center foreground) watches the violinist, whose playing clearly seems to have an effect on other people in the picture as well. (Gesellschaft der Musikfreunde, Vienna; photo: Österreichische Nationalbibliothek)

The Romantic concept of the hero was virtually incarnated in Franz Schubert (1797–1828). His life was marked by almost unbelievable creativity but also by much suffering—poverty, ill health, loneliness, and lack of public recognition. He was apparently subject to great extremes of emotion, and though he was undoubtedly a disciplined craftsman, there are numerous anecdotes attesting to the almost spontaneous creation of his greatest works. He is said to have written as many as seven songs in a single day. And he is thought to have been a composer by instinct, a natural talent who chose to sing of natural things—the brook, the field, the moonlit countryside, the experience of love. Like the Romantic poets Byron, Keats, and Shelley, he died a young man. But his genius seems to have been that of youth. He had completed over half of his more than 600 songs by the time he was nineteen.

## Pictorial Writing in Schubert's Lieder

Gretchen am Spinnrade

Schubert's Lieder are filled with pictorial writing—with musical sounds that are meant to represent the sounds and feelings of life itself. Such writing generally appears in the piano part. A river, for example, might be indicated by a gently flowing arpeggio or a lover's despair by dissonant chords in the minor mode. In "Gretchen am Spinnrade" ("Margaret at the Spinning Wheel"), written when Schubert was seventeen, the sound of the wheel is suggested by a revolving, rapid treble part played over a heavier punctuating rhythm that represents the treadle. The song, based on a scene from Goethe's *Faust,* expresses Margaret's deeply disturbed feelings over Faust's 'unholy courtship.' As her thoughts become more erotic, the wheel speeds faster, then comes to an abrupt stop at the memory of Faust's kiss. The revolving treble part is then heard again as Margaret returns to her work. Throughout, the piano part contributes greatly to the force of the song.

The use of the piano part varies from work to work, ranging from obvious imitation of natural sounds to very subtle interpretive effects. The sound of horses' hooves is suggested with great dramatic effect in a number of Lieder. The wind, the music of an organ grinder, the falling of rain or teardrops—all lend themselves to imitation in the Lied. At times the effects are even subtler. In the song cycle *Die schöne Müllerin* ("The beautiful Maid of the Mill"), the piano part at times represents the brook that the young miller follows in search of his beloved.

In Schubert's works, and in other German Lieder, the melody works with the accompaniment to convey the ideas and the emotional changes involved. Schubert's "Erlkönig" offers a good example. The

**Title page of the first edition of Schubert's "The beautiful Maid of the Mill" (c. 1830). (British Library)**

song, in free form with some repetition, is based on a ballad by Goethe that deals with the legend that anyone who sees the elf king inevitably dies. The piano introduction suggests hoofbeats as a father and his sick child ride at night through a dark forest. Vocal line and accompaniment differentiate the four voices of the poem—narrator, father, child, and elf king. The fright of the child, who sees the elf king, and the reassurances of the father, who does not, are vividly portrayed in the minor mode. The child's terror is further conveyed through the dramatic use of dissonance and the rising pitch of the child's cries. The voice of the elf king is smooth and seductive. At the end of the song, the galloping piano figure slows as the father arrives home with the boy dead in his arms. "Erlkönig," written when Schubert was only eighteen years old, is a powerful demonstration of the way in which text and music can work together to enhance a work of poetry. It has remained one of his most popular songs.

## Schubert: Die schöne Mullerin

Schubert wrote two song cycles, both on cycles of poems by Wilhelm Müller (1794–1827): *Die schöne Müllerin* (1820) and *Die Winterreise* ("The Winter's Journey") (1827). In *Die schöne Müllerin* the young apprentice searches for his beloved and confides many of his personal thoughts and feelings to the brook. He finds his heart's desire at last in the miller's daughter, but his love is rejected. In the end he finds peace only in the brook.

### "Das Wandern"

The cycle includes twenty songs that provide a broad range of mood, style, and technique. The opening song, "Das Wandern" ("Wandering"), introduces the young miller as he extols the pleasures and advantages of wandering.

---

**LISTENING ANALYSIS**                                           SIDE 7 BAND 3

"Das Wandern" is a superb example of a strophic song by Schubert. Major mode and a moderate tempo, a good speed for walking, are established by the piano before the voice enters. Throughout the song the piano part has arpeggios in the right hand and more slowly moving roots of chords in the left hand.

The voice enters with a melody that is quite disjunct. It is in duple meter, at a comfortable walking tempo. After its first statement, it is immediately repeated.

The third phrase is new and moves by step. The fourth phrase is also new and ends the melody quietly but firmly. The piano closes each stanza with the same four-measure phrase it played at the beginning of the song. The music for each stanza may thus be outlined:

Piano intro. Phrase a a b c Piano intro.

The other four stanzas of the poem are set to the same music, and thus the form of the song is strophic. While the words of each stanza are different, they are generally descriptive of what the wanderer sees as he sets off on his trek, so the music fits all of the stanzas quite well.

Text

| | |
|---|---|
| Das Wandern is des Müllers Lust, Das Wandern! | *Wandering is the miller's delight, wandering!* |
| Das muss ein schlechter Müller sein, | *He must be a very poor miller* |
| Dem niemals fiel das Wandern ein, Das Wandern. | *Who never felt like wandering, wandering* |
| Vom Wasser haben wir's gelernt, Vom Wasser! | *From the water we learned this, from the water!* |
| Das hat nicht Rast bei Tag und Nacht, | *It does not rest by day or night,* |
| Ist stets auf Wanderschaft bedacht, Das Wasser. | *But is always wandering, the water.* |
| Das sehn wir auch den Rädern ab, Den Rädern! | *We see it also in the mill-wheels, the mill-wheels!* |
| Die gar nicht gerne stille stehn, | *They never want to be still,* |
| Die sich mein Tag nicht müde drehn, Die Räder. | *They nor I never tire of the turning, the mill-wheels.* |
| Die Steine selbst, so schwer sie sind, Die Steine! | *The stones even, as heavy as they are, the stones!* |
| Sie tanzen mit den muntern Reihn | *They join the cheerful round dances* |
| Und wollen gar noch schneller sein, Die Steine. | *And want to go even faster, the stones.* |
| O Wandern, Wandern, meine Lust, O Wandern! | *Wandering, wandering, my delight, wandering!* |
| Herr Meister und Frau Meisterin, | *O master and mistress,* |
| Lasst mich in Frieden weiter ziehn Und wandern. | *Let me go my way in peace and wander.* |

In the remaining nineteen songs of the cycle one finds numerous references to the lovely things in nature—flowers, the brook—and to deep love. The cycle ends with a lilting lullaby of the brook to the lover. Its softly running waters offer consolation for his rejection by the beloved. Throughout the cycle Schubert shows his vast creativity in melodic invention and his great ingenuity for writing delightful accompaniments that match the words and melodies so well.

## Schubert's Last Lieder

Schubert wrote a number of songs that were later collected in a volume entitled *Schwanengesang* ("Swan Song"). The collection, however, is not as Schubert intended it to be, for he died before it was complete. In fulfillment of a last wish, he was buried at the side of Beethoven.

## Schubert's Other Works

Though his lyrical melodies and profound accompaniments mark Schubert as a Romantic composer, he was far closer than Chopin or Liszt to the Classical tradition. In addition to his dances and other short piano pieces, he wrote piano sonatas which are Classical in structure. Not surprisingly, he also wrote much chamber music, including many string quartets, a masterful string quintet, and the well known Piano Quintet in A Major ("The Trout," 1819). His nine symphonies, of which the last two are acknowledged masterpieces, and six Masses are other major works. But Schubert's greatest vocal achievements are his songs. For his last years he suffered from the syphilis which eventually killed him at age 31; his creative life was shorter even than Mozart's. Yet his accomplishments in the field of song were a great influence on later Romantics. His songs, symphonies, and chamber and piano works have an enduring place in concert programs.

## Schumann's Lieder

A second great composer of Lieder, Robert Schumann (1810–1856), was born in Germany, when Schubert was in his teens. In many ways, Schumann, like Schubert, lived the legend of the Romantic artist. His career was marked by great creativity and emotional torment.

The young Schumann had an irrepressible passion for literature (his father was a bookseller), music, and all things beautiful. His activities were somewhat of a trial to his widowed mother, who hoped that he would eventually practice law. Schumann did study law, but the discipline does not seem to have suited his temperament.

He was, in his mother's words, "a young and inexperienced man who lives but in a higher sphere and will have nothing to do with practical life." After a long inward battle, Schumann abandoned his legal studies and committed himself totally to music. For instruction he went to a leading piano teacher in Leipzig, Friedrich Wieck (1785–1873).

Wieck was apparently under no illusions about his pupil. Though perceiving that Schumann had considerable talent and imagination, he also noted his pupil's overconfidence and his impatience with "dry

Robert and Clara Schumann;
relief portrait, 1846.
(Bildarchiv Preussischer
Kulturbesitz)

cold theory"—attitudes both typically Romantic. Wieck recommended as a model student his own daughter Clara (1819–1896), a prodigy at the piano whose accomplishments spoke well of her father's methods. Schumann, however, lacked Clara's patience with technique and soon turned from piano performance to composition. He also tried music criticism, becoming editor of the *Neue Leipziger Zeitschrift für Musik* ("The New Leipzig Journal for Music"). As the son of a bookseller and an inveterate reader, he proved highly successful in his editorial role. Criticism and composition flowed readily in a period of feverish work.

In 1835, when Schumann was twenty-five years old, he became conscious of a profound love for Clara Wieck, now sixteen years old. She herself had apparently admired Schumann from the first time he set foot in her father's house. Wieck, however, objected to the proposed marriage between his daughter and his pupil. Although he liked Schumann, he saw in him a basic instability of temperament. He also wished his daughter to marry a man wealthy enough to sponsor her concert career. At this point, Clara was already becoming a well-known artist, and Schumann was but an enthusiastic young composer. For several years before their marriage, Schumann and Clara were kept apart by Wieck. It was during this period and in the early years of his marriage that Schumann wrote some of his greatest lyric works—both Lieder and piano compositions.

## Schumann: "Widmung"

Widmung ("Dedication"), was written in 1840, the year of Schumann's marriage. It was, of course, a dedication to Clara. The song is based on a poem by Friedrich Rückert (1788–1866), a German poet who was a contemporary of Schubert. The text specifically and intensely lists the different ways in which one's beloved is important.

### LISTENING ANALYSIS

SIDE 7, BAND 4

**Section A**

The song is in $\frac{3}{2}$ meter and in the major mode. Its form is ternary, or ABA'. Section A begins with a piano introduction, a rushing arpeggio that sets the emotional tone for the entire piece. This is followed by the opening melody, which rises as it enters. The first two phrases are shown below:

Opening Melody

Du mei-ne See - le, du mein Herz,    du mei-ne
[ You are my soul,    you are my heart,    you my

Wonn',    o du mein Schmerz
delight,    and you my pain ]

The melody in the second phrase soars even higher than that in the first. The music then modulates briefly to the subdominant to produce an ardent, new effect. Only at the end of Section A, the end of the first stanza of the poem, does the music return to the home key.

**Section B**

In Section B, the music jumps quickly to an unexpected key, E major, effecting a sharp change of color. The piano arpeggios heard in Section A disappear, and in their place we hear a steady succession of chords in triplets. The melody is rhythmically slower, with notes of longer duration. The effect is one of almost religious awe, which accords well with the poetic text with its references to peace, heaven, and self-realization through love. Intensity is achieved through quietness, an effective means often used in small lyric works.

**Section A′**

The A′ section returns to the first melody and key. The last part of the section, however, differs both in melody and in harmony. The work itself ends, as it began, with piano arpeggios.

Text:

A  Du meine Seele, du mein Herz,
   Du meine Wonn', o du mein Schmerz,
   Du meine Welt, in der ich lebe,
   Mein Himmel du, darein ich schwebe,
   O du mein Grab, in das hinab
   Ich ewig meinen Kummer gab!

*You are my soul, you are my heart,*
*You my delight, and you my pain;*
*You are my world in which I live,*
*And you my heaven in which I soar;*
*You are my grave wherein I ever*
*Buried all my grief!*

B  Du bist die Ruh', du bist der Frieden;
   Du bist vom Himmel mir beschieden.
   Dass du mich liebst, macht mich mir wert,
   Dein Blick hat mich vor mir verklärt,
   Du hebst mich liebend über mich,
   Mein guter Geist, mein bess'res Ich!

*You are my rest, you are my peace,*
*You were allotted me by heaven;*
*That you love me gives me my worth;*
*Your glance transfigures me in my own eyes;*
*You, loving, raise me up above myself,*
*My good spirit, my better I.*

A′  Du meine Seele, du mein Herz,
    Du meine Wonn', o du mein Schmerz,
    Du meine Welt, in der ich lebe,
    Mein Himmel du, darein ich schwebe,
    Mein guter Geist, mein bess'res Ich!

*You are my soul, you are my heart,*
*You my delight, and you my pain;*
*You are my world in which I live,*
*And you my heaven in which I soar;*
*My good spirit, my better I.*

| | |
|---|---|
| Timbre: | baritone and piano |
| Rhythm: | $\frac{3}{2}$ meter; tempo Innig, lebhaft (fervently, lively) |
| Harmony: | major mode; A sections in A♭ major, B section in E major |
| Texture: | homophonic; arpeggiated piano accompaniment in A sections; chordal piano accompaniment in B section |
| Form: | ternary (ABA′) |

**Other works by Schumann**

"Widmung" was written in the period of Schumann's most glorious musical outpouring. From these years dates some of his greatest chamber music—notably the three string quartets in *Op. 41* and the *Piano Quintet, Op. 44.* The song cycle *Frauenliebe und Leben* ("Woman's Love and Life") was also written during this period. In eight songs, the cycle traces the experiences of a woman, from love at first sight through engagement, marriage, childbirth, and widowhood. The final song, describing bereavement, ends with a piano coda that brings back material from the first song, a unifying technique that would be adapted by other composers.

Schumann's songs take us one stage deeper into Romanticism than Schubert's. Many are explicitly autobiographical, as is much of his piano music. (He even depicted his own personality in piano music, creating two imaginary characters, Florestan and Eusebius, to represent opposite sides of his nature.) Many of his piano works are full of literary associations. Besides his piano music and songs, he wrote four symphonies, concertos for piano, cello, and violin, chamber music, and choral pieces. He completed one opera and left another unfinished. In all his music he attached less importance than Schubert to structural discipline.

Despite his accomplishments as a composer and the emotional and artistic partnership he enjoyed in his marriage, Schumann grew less and less able to deal with the world. In 1854 he attempted suicide by throwing himself into the Rhine and was taken to an asylum, where he died two years later.

## Later Composers of Lieder

**Brahms' Lieder**

Johannes Brahms (1833–1897), a close friend of both Robert and Clara Schumann, was also a major composer of Lieder, as well as of piano, chamber, orchestral and choral works. Among his most notable Lieder are his folk-song arrangements, other single songs in a wide variety of styles and moods, and his masterful *Vier ernste Gesänge* ("Four Serious Songs," 1896).

**Wolf**

Another, very innovative composer of German Lieder was Hugo Wolf (1860–1903), who wrote the bulk of his work in the late 1880s. Wolf's songs are generally thought to mark the culmination of the German Romantic Lied. As a composer, Wolf was noted for his highly expressive and frequently chromatic writing, and for his extremely sensitive, careful settings of text. (He, too, spent the end of his life in an asylum.)

**Mahler and Richard Strauss**

In the works of later German composers, among them Gustav Mahler (1860–1911) and Richard Strauss (1864–1949), the Lied was carried far beyond its earlier Romantic form and style and developed in a number of new and different directions. Gustav Mahler, for example, scored some of his Lieder for orchestral accompaniment and incorporated their melodies (sometimes with the words) into several of his symphonies. *Das Lied von der Erde* ("The Song of the Earth," 1908) by Mahler is a symphony in six movements, with texts sung by solo voices in each movement. (Mahler's songs will be considered further in Chapter 23.) Richard Strauss also set many songs for voice and orchestra. Their works are outstanding examples of lyric and dramatic songs of the late nineteenth and early twentieth centuries.

## The French Art Song

Berlioz, Fauré, Debussy, and Ravel

The art song also developed in France and other countries during the nineteenth and early twentieth centuries. France acquired a great literature of art songs by such composers as Hector Berlioz (1803–1869), Gabriel Fauré (1845–1924), Claude Debussy (1862–1918), and Maurice Ravel (1875–1937). Most French poetry of the period is less intensely introspective, though no less fine, than German poetry. Some of the favorite poets were Charles Baudelaire and the Symbolists Paul Verlaine and Stéphane Mallarmé. The musical style of these composers is consequently somewhat lighter and less consciously profound. Their works show the sensitivity and elegance so often found in French music and are another very significant part of the art song repertory.

# CHAPTER 20

# *Symphony and Concerto in the Romantic Period*

*LISTENING PREVIEW The symphony continued to be a favorite type of orchestral music with composers and audiences in the nineteenth century. Many composers wrote symphonies based on purely musical ideas, as had Haydn, Mozart, Beethoven, and Schubert. Brahms' four symphonies show a number of influences of his predecessors, yet his works include many fresh, original ideas as well. Listen to the opening section of the first movement of his* Symphony No. 3 *(side 7, band 5) and notice the short, opening motive and its returns in the section. What function do these repetitions of the motive fulfill as they appear with or in alternation with the other thematic ideas?*

## Trends in the Symphony

In their development of the short piano piece and the song, Romantic composers were very innovative. In fact, they created a new tradition. But innovation was not the sole characteristic of the period. In their symphonic works, most Romantic composers chose to follow earlier forms, building on the mighty achievements of the past.

The roots of the Romantic symphony can be found in the late works of Haydn and Mozart, in a number of the symphonies written by Beethoven, and in the symphonic works of Schubert. As a composer of Lieder, Schubert owed little to his predecessors; in his symphonic writing, however, he was greatly influenced by them. He admired Beethoven and openly used certain of his works as models for composition. Like Beethoven, Schubert was a transitional figure whose works can be placed somewhere near the center of the Classical-Romantic continuum. His music shows certain Romantic tendencies—an emphasis on lyrical melody, for example, and a freer use of Classical forms—but his style was in many ways Classical.

Schubert's symphonies

Schubert's symphonies, like the symphonies of Beethoven, are an epilogue to the Classical era and a prologue to the Romantic. Nine

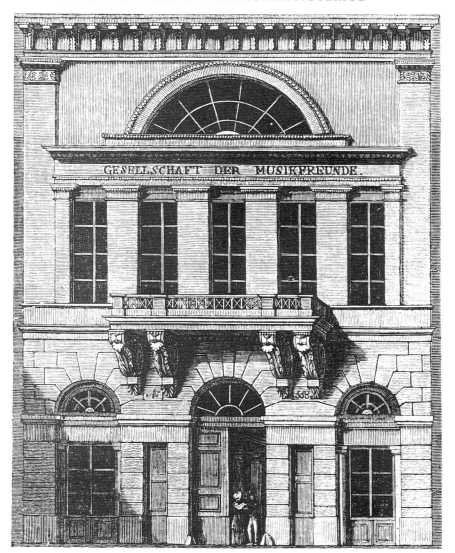

First building of the Gesellschaft der Musikfreunde (Society of the Friends of Music), Vienna, founded in 1812. Much of Vienna's musical life—both in terms of concerts and of teaching—in the 19th century centered around this institution. The Society possesses numerous very valuable manuscripts by all the leading Classical and Romantic composers who lived in Vienna, including Brahms who was the orchestra's principal conductor from 1872 until 1875. (Österreichische Nationalbibliothek, Vienna)

complete works survive, the greater number written before he was nineteen years old. The last, the *Symphony in C Major* (1825–28), is recognized as one of his finest. The most popular of his symphonies, however, is the so-called "Unfinished" Symphony, which he began in 1822 but never completed. Only two movements of the work were finished. The first movement, marked Allegro moderato, is in sonata form. The second movement, marked Andante con moto (moderately with motion), is in modified sonata form with no development section. The third movement, of which we have only ten measures, was to have been a scherzo.

The value of Schubert's symphonic achievement was not recognized in his own time. In fact, Schumann discovered the manuscript of the C Major Symphony in 1839, and this led to the work's first performance (conducted by Mendelssohn)—eleven years after its composer had died. As music critic Donald Tovey has remarked, "The tragedy of Beethoven's deafness needs no comment; but the history of the arts is full of tragedies not less pathetic and far less inspiring to the imagination.... Schubert, who was not deaf, never heard his own mature orchestral music at all."

Program symphony

In the years after Schubert's death, the symphony remained one of the major types of music for orchestra, although it underwent many changes. Some composers, especially Liszt and Berlioz, sought a new basis for symphonic writing. The result was the program symphony. The works were based in a general way on the Classical symphony, but they derived much of their logic and inspiration from literary or other artistic works rather than from purely musical ideas.

Abstract symphony

There was, however, another trend, characterized by a more traditional approach. "Abstract" symphonies, that is, symphonies organized around purely musical ideas, as the symphony in the late eighteenth century had been, were written by Mendelssohn (1809–1847) and Schumann in the second quarter of the century and by Brahms and Tchaikovsky (1840–1893) later in the century. These Romantic traditionalists believed that the Classical sonata cycle was capable of expressing their musical thoughts.

Symphonies of Mendelssohn and Schumann

In the symphonies of Mendelssohn and Schumann, Classical forms are apparent but fresh melodic and harmonic ideas strain against them. Several Romantic composers revered the Baroque masters, and used their contrapuntal techniques with the enriched timbres of a large symphony orchestra and the harmonic innovations of their own era. Mendelssohn and Schumann were both deeply influenced by Baroque music. Of Mendelssohn's five symphonies, the two subtitled "Scottish" (1842) and "Italian" (1833) are excellent works that are still frequently heard today. Even though these symphonies have descriptive titles, they are not programmatic in nature. Schumann's four symphonies are also noted for their rather clear use of Classical forms, but with expressive themes and harmonies that are more Romantic in style. Unlike the composers of program symphonies, Mendelssohn and Schumann avoided subjective organization in their larger works, although their writing itself was often subjective in spirit. Their symphonies retained Classical forms for Romantic ideas.

Characteristics of the abstract symphony

Although the composers of abstract (or "absolute") symphonies still wrote themes based on motives, they gave prominence to lyrical melodies. They used a variety of rhythms; steady and very regular rhythmic patterns were often suddenly disrupted by irregular patterns. Major-minor harmony underwent great exploration; the system was so thoroughly and freely used that many composers felt its resources were exhausted by the end of the century. Chromaticism became more evident and remote key relationships were more often exploited. Composers made extensive use of certain chords with added tones—chords that soon became typical of Romantic harmony. One such chord is the dominant chord with an added ninth, which is both dissonant and pleasing, suggesting a bittersweet quality. In the Classical period, such chords, when used at all, had been thoroughly integrated into the harmonic structure. In Romantic music, they were generally used for themselves rather than as part of a progression, and sounded conspicuously, to produce striking harmonic effects. At times they were not resolved as expected.

Texture in the symphony of the Romantic age became increasingly dense, and the range of dynamics expanded greatly. Contrasts in timbre as well as contrasts in melody were frequently stressed. Classical forms, though respected, were treated more freely than before. Brahms, for example, in the last movement of his *Symphony No. 1,* omitted a formal development section and instead incorporated extensive development into the exposition and recapitulation. Occasional changes were also made in the overall sonata cycle. Schumann, like Beethoven, wrote a symphony of five movements rather than four. And Tchaikovsky ended his *Symphony No. 6* with an intense Adagio lamentoso instead of the traditional quick finale.

The changes that nineteenth-century composers made in the symphony are in large part attributable to the dictates of the Romantic spirit. These composers did not feel compelled to adhere to the Classical ideals of balance and proportion when to do so would prevent them from expressing their own emotions and musical ideas. Some emotions, after all, are disproportionate and unbalanced. In emphasizing the individuality of their musical ideas, nineteenth-century composers brought many new ideas to the symphony.

Many characteristics of the abstract symphony of the Romantic age were, of course, already present to some degree in Beethoven's works. Among other things, his writing shows increasing chromaticism and modulation to remote keys as well as a tendency to alter form for expressive reasons. As we have observed, his *Symphony No. 6* has five movements and his *Symphony No. 9* features a chorus and soloists. Moreover, Beethoven used a large orchestra, presaging the even larger ones that would be available to his successors.

The Romantic symphony was not, however, just an extension of the ideas of Beethoven and Schubert. The intense thematic development found in Beethoven's works appears somewhat less frequently in Romantic symphonies. Melodies often undergo repetition and variation rather than development in the Classical sense. We hear a melody again and again in changing context—perhaps altered in harmony, timbre, and texture. Somewhat less often do we hear it broken down into its constituent motives, recombined, and inverted as we did in Beethoven's *Symphony No. 5.* The concentrated development process of the Classical style became, in a general sense, less essential in the symphonic works of the Romantic style.

Brahms at the piano, drawing (1911) by Willi von Beckerath, who made many sketches of the composer during the last decade of his life.

## Brahms' Symphonies

Of those Romantic composers who followed the tradition of Beethoven and Schubert, it was perhaps Johannes Brahms (1833–1897) who achieved the finest synthesis of Classical ideal and Romantic spirit. One of the most beloved of Romantic composers, he was born five years after Schubert's early death and spent his childhood in a run-down section of the north German city of Hamburg. His father was a musician who played a number of instruments in settings ranging from street and tavern to the city's philharmonic orchestra. He agreed to let his son play in a local orchestra, but the boy showed a strong preference for the piano instead and, ultimately, a talent much greater than his father's.

Under the guidance of an expert teacher, Johannes learned quickly. At the age of ten, he appeared publicly in an ensemble; at thirteen he played in tavern dance bands; at fifteen he began to give solo concerts. But Brahms was only a minor performer in a country rich with virtuosos. As a young man, he turned his attention to composition, producing among his first works a number of piano sonatas and songs.

Brahms' career was furthered by his association with several prominent musicians. Among them were, most notably, Eduard Reményi, the Hungarian violinist with whom Brahms toured in 1853, and

Joseph Joachim (1831–1907), another violin virtuoso who, like Brahms, was much interested in composition. It was through Joachim that Brahms was introduced to Robert and Clara Schumann. Schumann was greatly impressed by Brahms' work and character. In his influential *New Leipzig Journal for Music,* he predicted that the young man would "give us the highest ideal expression of our time." Although Schumann's prediction was premature, it proved accurate in the end.

Brahms' early works, mostly for the piano, were much influenced by compositions of Schubert and Schumann. Some works may reflect the conflict that Brahms experienced as a resident in the Schumann household; although within a Classical framework, his music often has a highly personal content and style. Brahms developed a deep love for Clara, whom he admired both as a woman and as an artist. That she was fourteen years his senior hardly mattered, but that she was the wife of his friend and sponsor caused him an emotional anguish that is readily apparent in his letters and compositions. Nonetheless the two of them maintained a close and enduring friendship.

Brahms wrote only four symphonies, all late in life after he had achieved recognition for his songs, chamber music, and choral writing. He agonized painstakingly over the symphonies, conscious of Beethoven's weighty works. His first symphony contains an allusion to Beethoven's Ode to Joy in its final movement.

## Brahms: Symphony No. 3 in F Major

*Symphony No. 3 in F Major* may well be the most Romantic of Brahms' symphonies. The opening motive (F-Ab-F) is supposedly associated with his motto *frei aber froh* ("free but happy"). The symphony was written in 1883 and performed in Vienna and Berlin in the following year, evoking much praise and controversy.

The work is in four movements. The orchestra includes pairs of flutes, oboes, clarinets, bassoons, a contrabassoon, four horns, two trumpets, three trombones, two timpani, and strings.

---

**LISTENING ANALYSIS**  SIDE 7, BAND 5

*First Movement: Allegro con brio; Sonata Form*

**Exposition**

The symphony begins with the winds playing the opening motive: F-Ab-F.

Opening Motive

The Ab is an accidental, for it does not occur in the key of F major. An Ab does appear in the key of F minor, however, and its momentary presence here results in the kind of ambiguity that is common in Romantic music: Is the mode major or minor? The motive returns several times in the movement and helps to articulate the form.

A firm sense of F major is established in the first phrase of the opening theme. The phrase, played in octaves by the violins, is made up almost entirely of the notes of the F major triad. The opening motive is heard in the accompaniment, played by the bass instruments in notes of longer duration. In the second phrase of the first theme, the tonal ambiguity once again becomes acute, as a shift in tonality is suggested.

First Theme

F　C　A　G　F　C　A♭ G　F　D♭ A♭ G　F　B

The fluctuation of mode and key and the marking *passionato* ("passionately") at once suggest the Romantic nature of the work.

After a new and brief theme that dissolves into quick arpeggios, the music modulates gently through the key of D major to the key of A major, one key melting into another. The next important theme is very lyrical and thus provides effective contrast with the more dramatic first theme. The meter changes from $\frac{6}{4}$ to $\frac{9}{4}$ here, giving the melody a flexible rhythmic quality that is generally characteristic of this work and other compositions of Brahms. A change of tone color also enhances this theme. It is lightly orchestrated, with the melody in the clarinets and a pizzicato accompaniment in the lower strings.

Second Major Theme

The closing section of the exposition is introduced by a return to the opening motive and $\frac{6}{4}$ meter; scales and arpeggios are featured. Rising chromatic scales bring the exposition to a close. Following Classical tradition, Brahms indicated that the exposition be repeated.

**Development**　In the development, both of the major themes are heard, altered by new contexts and contrasting tone colors. The second theme, once a graceful, flowing melody, is now played in an agitated manner by cellos, violas, and bassoons. The first motive is reiterated by the horns in a succession of keys, and the first theme is played quietly and tentatively, leading into the recapitulation.

**Recapitulation**　The opening motive then boldly reappears to announce the recapitulation. In this section the thematic materials from the exposition are restated and further developed. The recapitulation is followed by a coda, which is also announced by the **Coda** opening motive. It is based largely on the first theme, which is further developed. The movement ends with a final, quiet statement of the opening motive and the first phrase of the first theme.

### LISTENING SUMMARY

| | |
|---|---|
| Timbre: | large orchestra of string instruments, wind instruments, and timpani |
| Melody: | opening motive and two major themes as illustrated above |
| Rhythm: | $\frac{6}{4}$ meter (felt sometimes as triple and sometimes as duple) and $\frac{9}{4}$ meter; tempo Allegro con brio (fast with spirit) |
| Harmony: | fluctuates between minor and major modes, predominantly F major and F minor; frequent modulations; some chromaticism |
| Form: | sonata form with lengthy coda |

### Second Movement: Andante; Ternary Form

Section A

The second movement, in C major, begins with a lovely, songlike theme, marked *semplice* ("simply"). It is played by a solo clarinet and accompanied by the second clarinet and bassoons.

**First Phrase of First Theme**

Brahms was fond of the mellow sound of instruments of the middle register, such as the clarinet, horn, and cello, which give a melancholy quality to many of his works. Three phrases follow, each of which begins like or is similar to the first, but then proceeds differently. The first has a different ending; the next begins on a higher pitch and continues with some other changes; the last is extended and ends differently. The close of each phrase is affirmed by the appearance of the strings. Then the entire orchestra repeats the theme and elaborates on it, creating a joyous, pastoral effect.

Section B

A second theme, marked *espressivo dolce* ("sweetly expressive"), is announced by clarinet and bassoon at the beginning of the middle section. After an initial statement that confirms the new key of G major, the theme continues and modulates to D major, and then back to G major.

**First Phrase of Second Theme**

Section A

The woodwinds continue to be featured prominently throughout this section, with the strings sometimes doubling them or more often accompanying them.

Some development of the themes takes place before the original key of C major reappears with the return of the first theme. It is now accompanied by quadruplet and triplet rhythms. A coda closes the movement, and at its end, the theme, played again by the clarinet, is reaffirmed in its original simplicity and followed by a series of quiet chords.

### Third Movement: Poco allegretto; Ternary Form

Section A

The third movement, like the second, is ternary in form, following the traditional treatment of the third movement. The movement is in C minor and begins with a restless lyric melody played by the cellos:

**Beginning of First Theme**

Like a number of other nineteenth-century symphonic themes, this theme has been used in our own times as the basis for a popular song. It is repeated and expanded, then repeated again before the close of the section.

**Section B**

**Section A**

The middle section begins in Ab major and contains two themes, both of which are colored with some expressive chromaticism. With a return to C minor, the opening section is repeated, but it is reorchestrated to produce a new effect. The first theme, originally stated by the cellos, is now played in turn by horn, oboe, and violin. After a

**Coda**

short coda, the movement ends quietly.

### Fourth Movement: Allegro; Modified Sonata Form

The finale begins in the key of F minor, the key suggested at the opening of the symphony. The sonata form of the movement is modified by not having a middle section devoted to development. Considerable development does, however, take place in the course of the exposition, especially in the recapitulation, and in the coda.

**Exposition**

The first theme is a conjunct melody played *sotto voce* ("in an undertone") by strings and bassoons. It is then taken up in an expanded form by flute and clarinet.

**Beginning of First Theme**

Contrast is provided by a stately second thematic material that has more harmonic than thematic identity. It is introduced by clarinets, bassoons, and strings.

**Beginning of Second Thematic-Harmonic Material**

After it has been heard, a portion of the first theme reappears dramatically in the lower strings and bassoons. Then, after a modulatory passage stressing dotted rhythms, another theme enters.

**Beginning of Third Theme**

Played first in C major, this bright theme is soon carried into the minor mode. Such changes of mode are frequent in this particular movement and characteristic of the Romantic symphony in general.

A final theme brings the exposition to a climax.

Beginning of Final Theme

**Recapitulation and coda**

The beginning of a development section is soon stopped as the first theme returns quietly in the tonic key of F minor, seemingly to begin a recapitulation. It is followed, however, by considerable development of motives and themes from the exposition. The development section has been virtually moved to this position between the first and second themes in the recapitulation. The coda that follows begins in the key of B-flat minor and features the first theme accompanied by triplet and quadruplet rhythms. The second theme then reappears, and the opening motive of the first movement is recalled. The symphony ends as it began with the use of both major and minor modes of the F scale. The cumulative effect is one of great emotional contrast unified by the genius of the composer.

## Brahms' Other Works

Brahms, like other Romantics, was deeply conscious of the traditions of earlier music. He made notable contributions to every type of music except Mass and opera. In addition to the symphonies and overtures, he wrote two piano concertos (1858, 1881), a violin concerto (1878, for Joachim), and a double concerto for violin, cello and orchestra (1887), all of which are masterpieces and are regularly performed. Brahms paid particular attention to chamber music, not a popular form for the more radical Romantic composers. His *Piano Quintet, Op. 34a* (1864) and *Clarinet Quintet, Op. 115* (1891) are outstanding examples. He also made a study of folksong, and wrote many vocal and choral works that include folksongs. Lieder and partsongs based on folksongs are typically melancholic in tone, with piano accompaniments less descriptive than Schubert's but no less rich. His best known choral work is *A German Requiem* (see Chapter 22). He wrote many shorter choral pieces on sacred and secular texts.

Brahms died ten years after the composition of *Symphony No. 3.* The population of Vienna lined the streets as his cortege passed by. And in his home city of Hamburg, where he had long been denied recognition, the flags were flown at half staff. Brahms has remained one of the most popular of all Romantic and post-Romantic composers. Today when schoolchildren learn the names of the great composers, they are told of the "three B's": Bach, Beethoven, and Brahms—the Baroque master, the Classical master, and the Romantic who was so profoundly inspired by both of them.

# The Romantic Sense of Beauty

**Middle-Class Values and the Art of Protest** Essentially hardheaded and pragmatic in most spheres of life, the dominant middle class of the early Romantic period valued music and art that prettified and sentimentalized existence. Isabey, in his portrait of his wife, perfectly summarized the accepted taste of his time. We are shown a pretty, self-assured young woman, but we learn nothing of her emotions or the darker side of her nature. To many Romantic artists, however, art served as a means of protest, and some devoted their art to social comment.

Isabey: *Portrait of Madame Isabey.* Paris, Carnavalet Museum (photo Giraudon).

Eugène Delacroix: *Women of Algiers*. 1834. Paris, Louvre.

***Exoticism*** Early in the nineteenth century, the Newtonian idea of a rational universe began to yield to Wordsworth's vision of existence as dark and inscrutable. The Romantic world was one in which the mystery of nature and the primacy of feelings were dominant. Romantic painters were drawn to Rousseau's ideas about the beauty of nature and the goodness of humanity, corrupted not by instinct but by institutions. Artists yearned for the faraway, the exotic and uncorrupted, the "primitive." In 1831, one of the greatest of the Romantic painters, Delacroix, was overjoyed when presented with the opportunity to travel in North Africa. Everywhere he went he made sketches and watercolors. *Women of Algiers* is one of a number of later paintings in which the artist recalled and romantically transformed the images of his travels. Delacroix's delight in the brilliance of natural light and color in many ways prefigured the optical investigations of the Impressionists a generation later.

***Landscape Painting*** Romanticism brought a strong emphasis on natural appearance. The more Romantic artists became enamored of nature, the more they were compelled to confront the problem of recording optical truth. This is nowhere more true than in the art of English painter Constable, whose fascination with nature's fugitive moods and phases transformed the character of landscape painting. Like Wordsworth, Constable saw a connection between intimacy with nature and oneness with God. He found great moral significance in nature, and in this regard and in the poetic feeling expressed in his canvases he was very much a Romantic. Yet his use of broken color and loose brushwork to capture the most subtle and transient aspects of nature are equally expressive of the nineteenth century's growing interest in unalloyed realism.

John Constable: *The Leaping Horse*. 1804–5. London, Victoria and Albert Museum.

J.M.W. Turner: *The Slave Ship (Slavers Throwing Overboard the Dead and Dying, Typhoon Coming On)*. 1839. Boston, Museum of Fine Arts (Henry Lillie Pierce Fund)

**The Work of Turner** Unlike Constable, Turner was interested not in the normal or serene but in the dramatic, the titanic, the visionary. Rather than Wordsworthian, his imagination was Byronic. Though *The Slave Ship* is rooted in the reality of the cruelties of the slave trade, Turner here was essentially interested in using his understanding of natural phenomena to express the sublime. He made light the very essence of his painting. Details nearly disappear. There is only a dazzling radiance filling the work, obscuring form with its tiny specks in the face of the uncontrollable, incomprehensible processes of nature.

## Tchaikovsky and his Symphonies

The Russian Peter Ilyich Tchaikovsky (1840–1893) was a composer who revered the Classical tradition yet produced works that are in their deepest essence Romantic. Like Brahms, he based his symphonic works on Classical forms, altering and changing them to give expression to Romantic ideas.

*Rubinstein's influence*

Tchaikovsky's life was roughly contemporary with that of Brahms. However, he was geographically far removed from the world of Brahms, Liszt, and their colleagues. The imperial city of Saint Petersburg, where Tchaikovsky spent his youth, was dominated by its own native virtuoso, the pianist Anton Rubinstein (1829–1894). It was at Rubinstein's conservatory that Tchaikovsky studied piano and composition and made contact, musically speaking, with the Western world.

*Nationalistic Russian composers*

For although there was at this time a nationalistic Russian group of composers—including among its members Alexander Borodin (1833–1887), Modest Mussorgsky (1839–1881), and Nikolai Rimsky-Korsakov (1844–1908)—the conservatory itself was distinctly international in spirit. As a student there, Tchaikovsky became familiar with Classical German symphonies, Italian opera, and song and dance styles from all over Europe. His own music, while it reflects a Russian folk heritage, is generally international in intent, apart from an early nationalist period of composition.

Tchaikovsky has always been widely admired for his melodic gift. The melodies from his ballet scores—*Swan Lake* (1875-6), *The*

*Peter Tchaikovsky (seated, center right) with his brothers (Tchaikovsky House, Klin; photo: Novosti Press Agency)*

Neapolitan dancers from Act III of the ballet *Swan Lake*. The photograph shows a scene from the Moscow production of 1895 choreographed by Marius Petipa. (Victoria & Albert Museum, Crown copyright).

Symphony No. 4

*Sleeping Beauty* (1889), and *The Nutcracker* (1891–2)—are dearly loved by many. Also well known are his first piano concerto and his *Romeo and Juliet* (1869) and *1812* (1880) overtures. *Romeo and Juliet*, like many Romantic works, was inspired by Shakespeare. "None but the Lonely Heart," a perennial favorite, is one of the many songs he composed.

As a composer, Tchaikovsky greatly admired Mozart and Beethoven. His own *Symphony No. 4* (1877–78) was modeled on Beethoven's *Symphony No. 5* and opens with a bold motive similar to that of the older work. However, in Tchaikovsky's work, the unfolding of long and often lyrical melodies takes precedence over the thorough development of the opening motive. Unlike Brahms, he was not primarily interested in structure and motive development. His music is overtly emotional with a strong emphasis on lyrical melody and dramatic effect.

## Tchaikovsky: Symphony No. 6 in B Minor

**First movement**

*Symphony No. 6*, generally regarded as Tchaikovsky's most impo[rtant] symphony, was written in his last year, after a highly suc[cessful] American tour. It is scored for a large orchestra of string a[nd] instruments with timpani. The symphony opens with a somb[er] followed by a tempestuous first movement marked A[llegro] troppo and based loosely on sonata form. The second theme, a lyrical descending melody, is one of the most familiar in all symphonic literature:

**Second Theme**

**Second movement**

The second movement, marked Allegro con grazia, begins with a lilting tune in the unusual meter of $\frac{5}{4}$. So graceful in its opening, this movement gradually builds to a sense of pressing inner conflict.

**Third and fourth movements**

The third movement, Allegro molto vivace, is a brisk march that seems to express resolution or courage. The resolution of the third movement, however, is soon placed in tragic perspective by the Adagio lamentoso of the final movement. Thus instead of concluding triumphantly in the Classical manner, Tchaikovsky's last symphony ends in a despair that has seldom been equaled in literature, art, or music. Nine days after its first performance, its composer was dead by his own hand. Threatened with public exposure as a homosexual, he poisoned himself, with the encouragement of several peers.

## Other Composers of Romantic Symphonies

**Franck and Bruckner**

In many ways, the works of Brahms and the later works of Tchaikovsky represent a high point in the composition of Romantic symphonies. Yet a number of composers writing during and after the time of Brahms and Tchaikovsky also contributed greatly to the tradition of the abstract symphony.

The Belgian composer César Franck (1822–1890), for example, is remembered for his skillfully executed *Symphony in D Minor,* the only one he wrote. The ten symphonies of Anton Bruckner (1824–1896), an Austrian, are notable for their length and depth and for the large orchestra they require. Bruckner was a church organist and a profoundly religious composer. His symphonies have a religious weight and solemnity, and at times a mystic quality. His religious feeling also found expression in many sacred choral works. His symphonies were for a long time seldom performed, and are not as immediately accessible as Tchaikovsky's greatest symphonies. Recently, however, they have begun to attract a wider public.

**Mahler**

Mahler, like fellow Austrian composer Bruckner, also composed ten symphonies—works on a large scale which will be discussed in Chapter 23.

**Dvořák**

Still another important Romantic composer of symphonies is Dvořák, a Czech. His work will be discussed later in connection with the nineteenth-century nationalistic movement in music.

## The Romantic Concerto

Like the symphony, the concerto underwent a transformation during the nineteenth century. Both virtuosic display and melody became more important. Chromaticism and movement between remotely related keys were heard more frequently. The orchestra was generally larger, and the works, though usually still in three movements, tended to be longer. As in the symphony, Classical forms were still used, but more freely. The balance between soloist and orchestra was often manipulated for dramatic effect, but the solo virtuoso was almost always more important than the orchestra, whose chief role was to accompany the soloist. Mendelssohn, for example, omitted the orchestral ritornello in the first movement of his *Violin Concerto in E Minor* (1844), bringing in the soloist almost at once. Perhaps in response to Romantic individualism, virtuoso elements were increasingly emphasized.

Many composers of symphonies and piano music also wrote concertos. Chopin wrote two concertos for piano, in F minor and E minor (both 1830). Schumann wrote three, one each for piano (1845), cello (1850) and violin (1853). And Liszt wrote three for piano. Brahms' concertos have been mentioned earlier in this chapter; the beautiful *Violin Concerto in D Major*, remains one of the most popular of all concertos. Other important works include Tchaikovsky's *Piano Concerto No. 1 in B♭ Minor* (1875) and *Violin Concerto in D Major* (1878), Grieg's *Piano Concerto in A Minor* (1868, revised 1906–7) and Dvořák's *Cello Concerto in B Minor* (1895).

## Tchaikovsky: Violin Concerto in D Major

One of the best known concertos for violin from the nineteenth century was written by Tchaikovsky in two weeks in 1878. The work met with much criticism at the time. Several famous violinists complained that the soloist's part was so difficult that it was virtually unplayable. But the work later became very popular and today holds an important place in the violin repertory.

The work is in three large movements. It is scored for pairs of flutes, oboes, clarinets, bassoons, four horns, two trumpets, two timpani, strings, and solo violin.

### First Movement: Allegro moderato; Sonata Form

**Introduction and exposition**

The first movement is set in the key of D major and organized in loose sonata form. It opens with a brief introduction by the orchestra led by the first violins. The solo violin then enters and, after a few prefatory measures, presents the first theme:

First Theme

The theme is imitated briefly by the orchestral violins, and then it is extended and embellished by the soloist. A confrontation between orchestra and soloist follows, with terse orchestral chords opposing the solo violin's virtuoso scales and arpeggios. A second theme, marked Con molto espressione, is then announced by the soloist. In the material that follows, both themes are ornamented and broken up. The soloist occasionally plays two-note chords by *double stopping*—that is, by playing on two strings at a time.

**Double stopping**

**Development**

The development begins with a repetition of the first theme played by flutes and strings over a rousing rhythmic accompaniment by the wind instruments. The music is shown below in simplified form:

Repetition of First Theme

In the course of the development, the theme is set to new accompaniments, fragmented, and otherwise transformed. The development, which began in the key of A major, changes key frequently. At the climax of the movement, the soloist plays an elaborate cadenza, written out completely by Tchaikovsky, filled with double stops, arpeggios, and scales, and ending in the customary fashion with an extended trill.

**Cadenza**

**Recapitulation and coda**

The orchestra then returns for the recapitulation. A coda, marked Allegro giusto, gives the soloist additional opportunity to display technical mastery.

### Second Movement: Andante; Ternary Form

**Section A**

The second movement, in G minor, is labeled Canzonetta to suggest its songlike quality. After an introductory passage by winds and horns, the soloist enters softly with a melancholy, folklike melody:

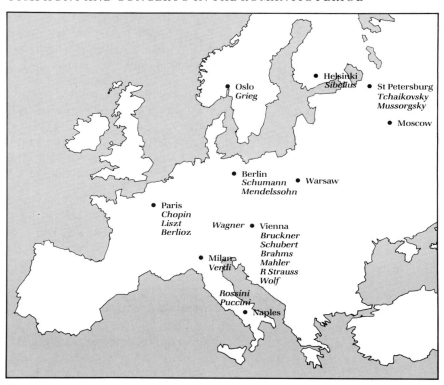

Major Romantic Composers.

It is accompanied by muted strings. After the solo violin completes the theme, it is briefly treated contrapuntally by the flute and clarinet.

**Section B**    The second theme follows in E♭ major, introduced forte by the solo violin. It is repeated and extended, still by the soloist, with sparse accompaniment by the orchestra.

**Section A**    The soloist then reintroduces the first theme, ornamented and developed against countermelodies in the flute and clarinet. The introductory material reappears, suggesting repetition but leading instead, without a break, into the last movement.

## Tchaikovsky: Violin Concerto in D Major, *Third Movement*

Introduction, cadenza, and first theme

**LISTENING ANALYSIS**                    SIDE 8, BAND 1

### Third Movement: Allegro vivacissimo; in Modified Rondo Form

The finale, cast in a modified rondo form (ABCA′B′C′A″), begins in A major, the dominant of D major—the home key of the concerto. To establish the new key, Tchaikovsky chose to open with a unison motive in A by the entire orchestra.

After a brief orchestral introduction and a cadenza for the solo violin, the soloist presents the vivacious first theme in the key of D major. The theme is based on a short figure that Tchaikovsky took from a traditional Russian folk dance.

First Theme

This energetic theme is spun out against a light accompaniment in strings and woodwinds. It is then repeated.

**Second theme**

A second theme is then introduced by the soloist in the key of A major. Like the first, it is based on Russian folk music.

Second Theme

The second theme is varied by strings and horns and by the soloist.

**Third theme**

A third, slower theme in the minor mode is then presented in dialogue fashion by solo oboe and clarinet, which are later joined by cello and bassoon.

The third theme is followed by the reappearance of the first theme in the original key of D major, which is in turn followed by the second and third themes, now in new keys. Finally the opening theme is heard a third time, this time developed in a manner designed to bring out the virtuoso capacities of the soloist. After a final burst of virtuosity from the soloist, the orchestra brings the work to a close with a resounding cadence.

The full brilliance of the orchestra is displayed throughout the movement, both in solo exchanges and in more densely orchestrated passages. The tempo increases as the work progresses—an increase often found in a finale.

**LISTENING SUMMARY**

| | |
|---|---|
| Timbre: | solo violin and large orchestra of string instruments, wind instruments, and timpani |
| Melody: | three themes; first two themes based on Russian folk music; third theme very lyrical |
| Rhythm: | $\frac{2}{4}$ meter; tempo Allegro vivacissimo (fast and very lively) |
| Harmony: | mainly major mode; begins in A major, modulates through several keys, ends in D major |
| Form: | modified rondo (ABCA′B′C′A″) |

Music for the orchestra, with or without instrumental soloists, underwent very extensive and enormously varied development in the nineteenth century. The size and tonal variety of the orchestra provided the composer with the great contrasts in color and intensity he needed. Orchestral music had become one of the most important aspects of music of the century.

# CHAPTER 21

# Program Music: Mendelssohn, Berlioz, and Saint-Saëns

*LISTENING PREVIEW A number of composers in the nineteenth century associated nonmusical ideas, sometimes in narrative form, with their instrumental compositions. Although such works could not literally "tell a story," musical sounds and moods were clearly linked with descriptive events and ideas printed in a concert program. Listen to the fourth movement of the* Symphonie fantastique *by Berlioz (side 8, band 2), and notice the very colorful, forceful use of the orchestra. Try to imagine what specific, nonmusical idea Berlioz associated with the music. Then look at the program note, given in the following chapter, that Berlioz wrote for the fourth movement. The difference between your thoughts and those of Berlioz shows that purely instrumental music cannot communicate specific verbal thoughts—such ideas can only be conveyed with the spoken or written word, even though the mood and expressive power of the music may have evoked for you an atmosphere similar to what Berlioz had in mind.*

## The Development of Program Music

*Opposite.* "Faust accosting Marguerite," from a set of lithographs (1828) by Eugéne Delacroix, illustrating a French edition of Goethe's *Faust.* The Faustian theme of a man who sells his soul to the devil inspired many Romantic composers to write either operas or program music, Berlioz and Liszt among them. (British Library; photo: John Freeman & Co.)

The nineteenth century was a time of very close relationships between the arts. The first Romantic works had been literary. Now poets, painters, and composers were drawn to the same themes and often to each other in a community of shared interests. In the time of Haydn and Mozart, musical composition had been a craft to be exercised by specialists working for patrons. The patron had been assumed to be a person of culture. But in the nineteenth century, the composer, like the artist in general, became a kind of cultural hero. The leading composers of the period were generally well educated, conversant with many different artistic media. Schumann, Liszt, Berlioz, Saint-Saëns, and Wagner were all accomplished writers and critics as well as composers. Wagner and Berlioz even wrote some of their own librettos. Most Romantic composers worked and socialized with painters, poets, actors, and dramatists. Schubert spent his years of poverty in the company of poets. Chopin lived with one novelist, Liszt with another. And Berlioz, in love with the works of Shakespeare, married a leading Shakespearean actress of the time. In their art and in their lives, composers strongly identified with the literary movements of nineteenth-century Europe. For them, this followed logically and emotionally from the principle that music was a means to express nonmusical ideas.

Characteristics of program music

During the nineteenth century, an increasing number of symphonies and other works were inspired by literary, or even pictorial, ideas. To further their expressive aims, composers often supplied verbal descriptions given to the listeners in concert programs, indicating the origin of their works—sometimes describing the very feelings and events to which the music alluded. The music was purely instrumental, yet it was closely associated with nonmusical ideas.

It was Liszt who coined the term "program music" to define pieces with a narrative or descriptive content. An example can be found in Berlioz' symphony *Harold in Italy*. The title of the symphony indicates the work's literary basis: Byron's famous poem *Childe Harold*. The titles of the individual movements call forth even more specific associations. The first movement, for example, is entitled "Harold in the Mountains: Scenes of Melancholy, Happiness, and Joy," and the second movement, "March of Pilgrims Singing Their Evening Hymn." The symphony includes a solo viola part that is often prominent, but not elaborate enough for the work to be considered a concerto.

References made in some program music allude to real or fancied experiences of the composer. Indeed, those experiences and feelings are at the essence of program music, which is frequently associated with events and subjective or emotional reactions. In Beethoven's *Symphony No. 6,* the titles of the movements refer to a succession of pastoral scenes that the composer apparently experienced or imagined—"Awakening of Pleasant Feelings upon Arriving in the Country," "Scene by the Brook," and so forth. But Beethoven stressed that even his pictorial titles were not meant to be merely descriptive, that they referred more to the feelings inspired by landscapes than to descriptions of the landscapes themselves. The *Pastoral Symphony* was seized on as a model by several Romantic composers.

A program may also relate music to the visual arts. Mussorgsky, in *Pictures at an Exhibition,* expressed the nationalistic character of the painter's work while suggesting that the composer himself was viewing the exhibit. Or, less concretely, a composition's program may simply evoke the occasion it was written to commemorate. Brahms' *Academic Festival Overture* suggests, in content as well as title, the event at which it was performed; the work contains a number of allusions to old school songs. Tchaikovsky's *1812 Overture* celebrates with musical imagery the Russian victory over Napoleon.

Whether or not a work is programmatic depends, in part, on the artistic inclinations of the composer—or how willing the composer was to specify the content of the work. Tchaikovsky's *Symphony No. 6* was originally to be titled "A Programmatic Symphony," but Tchaikovsky later decided not to specify the program. The music is so expressive that the absence of a program has never detracted from the work's accessibility. Conversely, Richard Strauss at first declined to give in detail the program of his symphonic poem *Till Eulenspiegel.* However, his public demanded a written guide to the work, and in listening we can be very much influenced by the program Strauss eventually did supply.

Although programmatic works differ in the extent to which they rely on their association with nonmusical ideas, it is generally true that familiarity with these ideas can help the listener follow one aspect of the musical design. One can certainly enjoy Tchaikovsky's *Romeo and Juliet* without being familiar with the Shakespearean plot, for the music itself is dramatic and very appealing. Yet if we know Shakespeare's play and the manner in which the overture relates to it, the listening experience is much richer. This is, in part, because the appearance of themes is governed not purely by musical organization but also by the ideas of the story. The opening theme in Tchaikovsky's *Romeo and Juliet,* for example, alludes to a specific character, Friar Lawrence; the theme reappears whenever Tchaikovsky wanted to evoke the idea of the friar. An examination of the musical structure alone will not tell us this. Similar examples of literary or pictorial influence on musical structure can be found throughout many works of program music. In most cases, however, these programmatic elements loosely coexist with traditional musical forms. While the Romantic composer found in program music alternatives to the strict and purely musical designs of the Classical period, the forms of the earlier age were seldom abandoned entirely.

*Types of program music*

The program music written during the Romantic era includes *concert overtures* and *incidental music* for theater, *program symphonies*, and *symphonic poems*, as well as short piano works. Thus except for the symphonic poem, which was a creation of the nineteenth century, Romantic composers were merely applying a new logic based on extramusical ideas to preexisting Classical structures.

## Overtures and Incidental Music

One of the important inspirations for program music was the theater. It seemed natural to Romantic composers to relate music to the plots and characters of drama. For this purpose, the overture proved eminently useful.

As we have seen, the overture was originally a one-movement orchestral work played before the first act of an opera or oratorio. Its function was to set the mood for the work to follow, either in a general way or by presenting some of the themes from the work. Although these overtures were thus, in their conception, closely tied to larger works, several of them later began to appear in the concert repertory as independent works. Overtures by Mozart, Rossini and Beethoven were often performed independently.

**Concert overtures**

As opera overtures began to achieve independent concert status, composers in turn began to think of them as independent works, or as *concert overtures*. Such an overture could simply draw upon the imagery, plot, and characters of a dramatic work. It need not be performed as part of an opera or other theatrical event. Most of the independent concert overtures of the Romantic age were based on plays, but some were written to illustrate poems or to mark special occasions. Mendelssohn's *Calm Sea and Prosperous Voyage,* based on two of Goethe's poems, Brahms' *Tragic Overture,* and Tchaikovsky's *1812 Overture* are examples of concert overtures that have no direct connection with theater. Concert overtures are generally cast in sonata form, usually quite tightly organized and often related to dramatic material.

**Incidental music**

While the nineteenth century saw the growth of the independent concert overture, it also encouraged the writing of music to accompany performed drama. Such music is called *incidental music* because it is incidental to the drama. It may appear between the acts, in ballroom scenes and chamber scenes, and in other stage situations in which music might realistically be heard.

Composers have occasionally written both an overture and incidental music for a single drama. Beethoven did this for Goethe's *Egmont,* although only the overture remains popular today. Perhaps the best known overture with incidental music is that written by Mendelssohn for Shakespeare's *A Midsummer Night's Dream.*

## *Mendelssohn: A Midsummer Night's Dream*

Felix Mendelssohn (1809–1847) was one of the most influential composers of the early nineteenth century. Born to a wealthy and cultured family, he was raised in considerably more fortunate circumstances than many composers and artists. His grandfather was a noted Jewish philosopher, his father a banker. Felix and his sister, raised as Protestants, were exposed to all the cultural and social advantages of nineteenth-century Germany—readings from the classics, visits to Goethe (who befriended Mendelssohn while the composer was still a boy) and other artists, and travels through Europe. Mendelssohn was precocious as a composer: by the age of fourteen he had written thirteen symphonies and many smaller works. As a young man, he was physically attractive and socially irresistible. He was a kind of hero to a whole generation of struggling Romantics. He was, however, quite different from the Romantic stereotype of a struggling, isolated artist.

Mendelssohn was an incredibly versatile artist. He was a renowned conductor and administrator; in fact, he earned his early reputation by organizing a revival performance of Bach's *Saint Matthew Passion.* When only twenty-six he became conductor of the famous Gewandhaus Orchestra in Leipzig; and seven years later he founded the Leipzig Conservatory, for a time the best in the world. Mendelssohn was also a gifted pianist, violinist, organist, and critic. He was respon-

"Oberon, Titania and Puck with Dancing Elves," scene painted by William Blake in c. 1800 from Shakespeare's *A Midsummer Night's Dream.* (Tate Gallery; photo: Bildarchiv Preussischer Kulturbesitz )

sible for furthering the careers of a number of other composers whose reputations eventually outshone his own (Beethoven, Schubert, and Schumann among them). As a composer, he was a traditionalist aspiring to the Classical style in music. He nevertheless caught the growing spirit of Romanticism, as can be seen, for example, in his *Songs Without Words,* a collection of short piano pieces.

Romantic influences are also apparent in *Fingal's Cave* (1830, revised 1832), the overture he wrote after a visit to the Hebrides islands of Scotland, which can be related to the rocky coastline and the sea. And Romantic feeling permeates the overture and incidental music he wrote for *A Midsummer Night's Dream.* The overture was written in 1826, when Mendelssohn was only seventeen years old, a student at the University of Berlin. The incidental music was written later, when he was thirty-four, at the request of the King of Prussia, who was planning a production of Shakespeare's comedy. Although there are thirteen musical incidents, only three—the "Scherzo," "Nocturne," and "Wedding March"—have achieved any independent popularity. The overture and the three most popular incidental pieces are sometimes presented in concert as a suite. In some performances, the "Intermezzo" and "Finale" are also included. The complete incidental music includes parts for soloists and chorus, setting portions of the Shakespeare text. Even when performed independently of the play, Mendelssohn's music conveys much of the beauty and charm of Shakespeare's immortal comedy.

### *"Overture"*

Exposition

Despite its strong programmatic basis, Mendelssohn's "Overture" is in the sonata form typical of most concert overtures. The music that opens the piece evokes the spirit of the forest fairyland with four

Concert at the Gewandhaus, Leipzig, in 1845. At this time, Mendelssohn was principal conductor of the Gewandhaus Orchestra, one of the most famous of its time. (Bildarchiv Preussischer Kulturbesitz)

sustained woodwind chords proclaiming the meeting of Oberon and Titania, king and queen of the fairies. This light music continues in a theme played by woodwinds and violins. A lyric second theme is then heard portraying the human lovers. A contrasting group, the comic tradesmen, is characterized by a theme in the violas. Finally there is a loud bray from the ophicleide, a deep-voiced precursor of the tuba: Bottom the Weaver has found his head transformed into that of an ass. The exposition is program music at its finest.

**Development, recapitulation, and coda**

The development, in its energetic, imaginative use of earlier materials, captures the fantastic activity of the woodland elves and fairies. The recapitulation begins with the four sustained woodwind chords of the opening and ends with a coda integrally fashioned from the various themes. At the very end, we hear once again the four chords that began the work. The magical quality of the play is captured marvelously in the delicate music.

### "Scherzo"

One of the most popular of the original thirteen pieces is the "Scherzo," written to be played before the opening of Act II. It begins with a high-pitched lively theme associated with Puck. The theme is presented by the woodwinds:

The movement, with its lively yet light character, is an excellent example of the style and spirit of a scherzo.

### "Nocturne"

Mendelssohn's "Nocturne" has also remained popular. The music is associated with the pairs of lovers who, bewitched by Puck's flowery potion, lie sleeping in the depths of the forest. When performed with the drama, the "Nocturne" is played between Acts III and IV. The horn presents the opening melody, a quiet theme both tender and heroic:

Horn Theme

### "Wedding March"

By far the best known of all the incidental music Mendelssohn wrote for *A Midsummer Night's Dream* is the "Wedding March." It was conceived as an accompaniment to the several marriages that form the happy ending of the play, and today, outside the theater and the concert hall, it continues to be played at the conclusion of numerous traditional wedding ceremonies. The music begins with a trumpet fanfare followed by the jubilant main theme:

Main Theme

The "Wedding March" also includes contrasting sections suggestive of the different loves that are realized in the course of the play—mortal and immortal, royal and common. Brass and woodwind timbres are emphasized, adding greatly to the festive mood.

## Mendelssohn's other works

Mendelssohn wrote five symphonies in his mature years, some of which bear descriptive titles though they are not programmatic. Other enduring works are his oratorio *Elijah* (1846) and the lyrical violin concerto. But the burden of his success in his own time may have shortened his life—he was only thirty-eight when he died. Romantic in spirit but Classical in their clarity of form, Mendelssohn's works place him towards the middle of the Classical-Romantic continuum.

## The Program Symphony

While the concert overture was an updated version of a Classical form, the program symphony marked a striking departure from its eighteenth-century counterparts. A program symphony, as well as the abstract symphony, came to employ vast orchestral forces and sometimes lasted for an hour or more, while a typical Classical symphony lasted about thirty minutes or less. Program symphonies could contain more (or fewer) than the usual four movements. But most importantly, they derived some of their musical structure from the nonmusical elements by which they were inspired.

We have seen that Beethoven, in his *Symphony No. 6*, set an early precedent for the program symphony. The notion was later taken up by the Romantic composers as a means of developing symphonic literature in a new direction. The most successful composers of the new program symphonies were Berlioz and Liszt. As a symphonist, Berlioz is chiefly remembered for *Harold in Italy* (1834) and the *Symphonie fantastique*. Among Liszt's works are the *Faust Symphony* (1854) and *A Symphony after Dante's Divine Comedy* (1856).

## Berlioz: Symphonie fantastique

Hector Berlioz (1803–1869) embodied most of the features of the Romantic artist. He was not encouraged to study music by his parents, and never learned to play the piano with any proficiency, though he did learn to play the flute and guitar. He became more interested in grand forms and the sonic possibilities of large groups of instruments than in miniaturist forms suitable for the piano.

Berlioz' relatively modest early musical education allowed him to see music differently from any of his contemporaries. To him, music was associated mainly with church services and local festivals—in other words, it belonged to public occasions, and essentially dramatic ones at that. Such music was almost always strengthened by its nonmusical associations. Later, Berlioz realized that a more subjective nonmusical program would enhance the qualities of the music that have come to be regarded as Romantic.

Berlioz also saw music as a product of diverse instruments, each with its decidedly individual character and sound. Forced to bypass the usual piano training, Berlioz came to understand much better than his peers the distinctive effects of different instruments. He was soon to use this understanding to achieve bold new sounds in orchestration, contrasting unprecedented volume and grandeur with passages of the greatest delicacy.

At the age of eighteen, Berlioz settled in Paris, ostensibly to begin his education in medicine. But it was soon clear that music was his proper field. He was especially drawn to opera, and often, after attending a performance, he spent many hours studying the score in the library of the Royal Conservatory. By 1826 he had entered the conservatory as a student.

One of the passions of Berlioz' early Parisian career was Shakespeare, whose works he first encountered in 1827 at a performance of *Hamlet*. The power of the English drama impressed him deeply, as did the resident company's leading lady. Berlioz fell madly in love

This caricature by Gustave Doré shows Berlioz as a conductor; it was published in 1850. The orchestral and choral requirements for some of Berlioz' works were enormous. (Bibliothèque Nationale, Paris; photo: Heritage of Music)

with the Ophelia he saw, an Irish actress named Harriet Smithson. He pursued her for many years, at first in imagination and later in reality. In the early stage of his passion, he even arranged private concerts at his own expense, largely so that the woman he loved would hear of his "fame."

Berlioz began to conceive of a grand symphony to be entitled *Episode de la vie d'un artiste* ("Episode from the Life of an Artist"). In it, he said, "the development of my infernal passion is to be depicted." While working on his symphony, he heard rumors of Harriet Smithson's supposed relationship with her manager and fell into a great fit of agitation. It was in this mood that he developed the plan of his *Symphonie fantastique* ("Fantastic Symphony"). It was premiered in December, 1830, the year of a political revolution in France with which Berlioz sympathized. The audience—which included Liszt—responded favorably, though several of Berlioz' novel techniques shocked listeners. With this performance his music began to wield an influence on subsequent nineteenth-century music. Immediately afterwards, he left for Rome (engaged, but not to his beloved Ophelia): after many failures, he had won the coveted Prix de Rome by deliberately writing a piece in an academic style simply to please the judges. In Rome he revised portions of the *Symphonie fantastique*.

On his return to Paris, a series of romantic coincidences led him straight to Harriet Smithson. Till then he had never even met the actress, but he deviously arranged for her to be present at a performance of the new symphony. In due course the pair were married, only to separate after a few years.

The program of the *Symphonie fantastique* is quite detailed, so much so that it offended many of Berlioz' musical contemporaries. However, it captured the imagination of the public, acting, as historian Jacques Barzun has pointed out, rather like a "promotional aid." Berlioz revised the program notes several times (at one point ordering that nothing but the names of the movements should appear), and various versions have survived. The symphony is organized in five movements, and Berlioz' notes relate quite readily to the music.

The program develops a series of strong Romantic contrasts. The hero, deep in an opium-inspired dream, has visions ranging from one extreme to another; his mind paints images both wild and poetic. Although the program centers on Berlioz' passion for Harriet Smithson, it presents an artistic rather than an autobiographical conception of the affair.

**Use of the idée fixe**

The work is filled with the association of musical ideas and extramusical images, the most basic of which is found in the *idée fixe* ("fixed idea," or recurrent theme). Berlioz' *idée fixe* represents the beloved throughout the symphony. First heard after the introduction as the opening theme of the exposition, the theme recurs in various forms in all five movements, ending up as a disreputable dance tune. The theme has many typically Romantic melodic traits: it is quite long, includes slow and fast rhythmic motion, and is not strongly metrical. Its musical function was to unify and lend coherence to this huge work. It was a bold innovation, and had many echoes in later Romantic compositions. The initial form of the *idée fixe,* played by flutes and violins, is shown below.

Idée fixe

Romantic traits—unrestrained passion, fascination with the diabolical, and depiction of nature—are as evident from Berlioz' program as from the music itself. The following version of the notes is most frequently quoted.

### *Program of Berlioz'* Symphonie fantastique*

**Introduction:**

A young musician of extraordinary sensibility and abundant imagination, in the depths of despair because of hopeless love, has poisoned himself with opium. The drug is too feeble to kill him but plunges him into a heavy sleep accompanied by weird visions. His sensations,

---

*Symphonie fantastique* by Hector Berlioz, program notes from Eulenburg Pocket Score (E 422). Reprinted by permission of Ernst Eulenburg, Ltd., London. Bracketed material added to show position of the *idée fixe.*

emotions, and memories, as they pass through his affected mind, are transformed into musical images and ideas. The beloved one herself becomes to him a melody, a recurrent theme [the *idée fixe*] which haunts him continually.

**First Movement:** *Reveries, passions*: First he remembers that weariness of the soul, that indefinable longing, that somber melancholia and those objectless joys which he experienced before meeting his beloved. Then, the volcanic love with which she at once inspired him [the *idée fixe*], his delirious suffering, his return to tenderness, his religious consolations.

**Second Movement:** *A ball*: At a ball, in the midst of a noisy, brilliant fête, he finds his beloved again [the *idée fixe*].

**Third Movement:** *In the country*: On a summer evening in the country he hears two herders calling each other with their shepherd melodies. The pastoral duet in such surroundings, the gentle rustle of the trees softly swayed by the wind, some reasons for hope which had come to his knowledge recently—all unite to fill his heart with a rare tranquility and lend brighter colors to his fancies. But his beloved appears anew [the *idée fixe*], spasms contract his heart, and he is filled with dark premonition. What if she proved faithless? Only one of the shepherds resumes his rustic tune. The sun sets. Far away there is rumbling thunder—solitude—silence.

**Fourth Movement:** *March to the scaffold*: He dreams he has killed his loved one, that he is condemned to death and led to his execution. A march, now gloomy and ferocious, now solemn and brilliant, accompanies the procession. Noisy outbursts are followed without pause by the heavy sound of measured footsteps. Finally, like a last thought of love the *idée fixe* appears for a moment, to be cut off by the fall of the axe.

**Fifth Movement:** *Dreams of a witches' sabbath*: He sees himself at a Witches' Sabbath surrounded by a fearful crowd of specters, sorcerers, and monsters of every kind, united for his burial. Unearthly sounds, groans, shrieks of laughter, distant cries, to which others seem to respond! The melody of his beloved is heard [the *idée fixe*], but it has lost its character of nobility and reserve. Instead, it is now an ignoble dance tune, trivial and grotesque. It is she who comes to the Sabbath! A shout of joy greets her arrival. She joins the diabolical orgy. The funeral knell, burlesque of the *Dies irae*. Dance of the Witches. The dance and the *Dies irae* combined.

**Use of the orchestra** The orchestra required for the *Symphonie fantastique* is unusually large. It includes piccolo, two flutes, two oboes, English horn, two clarinets, four horns, four bassoons, two trumpets, two cornets, three trombones, two ophicleides, two timpani, snare drum, cymbals, bass drum, bells, two harps, and strings. The orchestration, extraordinarily sensitive and colorful, impressed even the severest critics of the day.

Berlioz used unusual combinations of instruments, and greatly contrasting registers and tone colors. This symphony was the first to use such effects for dramatic expression; the score is filled with very specific directions about dynamics and other aspects of performance.

Berlioz was widely recognized as a master of orchestration. His sensitivity and concern for the best use of different instruments are evident in an impressive treatise he wrote on the subject.

**First, second and third movements**

Despite its originality in sound and conception, the *Symphonie fantastique* is formally based on Classical models. The first movement ("Reveries, Passions"), preceded by a slow and lengthy introduction, is in a free and expanded sonata form. The second movement ("A Ball") is a waltz organized in ternary form with an introduction and coda; the *idée fixe*, now in triple meter, appears in the contrasting middle section. The third movement ("In the Country") is also in a free ternary form, with an introduction and coda. The mood is quiet and pastoral, heightened to a degree by the use of solo oboe and flute. Yet, at the end, distant thunder effects from the timpani add a darker dimension.

**Berlioz: Symphonie fantastique, Fourth Movement**

**LISTENING ANALYSIS**                                    SIDE 8, BAND 2,

*Fourth movement*

The fourth movement ("March to the Scaffold") is in duple meter and in the key of G minor.

Berlioz claimed he wrote this movement in a single night. Here for the first time in the symphony all the brass and percussion instruments are sounded. An ominous series of rolls on the timpani, alternating with a short motive in the bassoons, introduces the movement. The first theme is based on a descending G minor scale and has a hesitant, faltering quality about it.

Beginning of First Theme

After several repetitions, expanded with changes of colorful orchestration, a second theme is heard. It is presented boldly and confidently by the winds.

Beginning of Second Theme

It is repeated immediately. Then the entire first part of the movement with introduction, first and second themes is repeated. After the repetition, the second theme is extended and repeated twice more with full orchestra. The first theme then returns in G minor, hesitantly at first and then more dramatically with full orchestra. An inversion of the theme and a passage of dotted notes brings the movement to its climax. A solo clarinet begins to play the *idée fixe*, but a crashing chord by the full orchestra cuts it short (the fall of the axe). The last measures, a short coda, change abruptly to a G major chord repeated boldly over rolls in the snare drum and timpani. The resulting form of the movement is: Introduction A B A' B'ext. A" Coda.

**LISTENING SUMMARY**

Timbre:     Very large orchestra used in a very colorful manner
Melody:     Two main themes; *idée fixe* appears at the end
Rhythm:     C meter enhanced with a variety of rhythmic patterns
Harmony:    Mainly G minor and B♭ major; G major at the end
Form:       Intro. A B Intro. A′ B′ ext. A″ coda

**Fifth movement**

The last movement ("Dream of a Witches' Sabbath") is built freely in sections, with music based on a number of themes including the *idée fixe*, in a style that suggests the witches' dance and the chant "Dies irae" ("Day of Wrath"), the sequence from the Medieval Mass for the Dead. The bells are prominent in this movement in association with the "Dies irae" which Berlioz not only quotes but parodies. The work is thus based in many ways on earlier precedents, but Berlioz' use of irregular phrases, subtleties of timbre, and innovative harmonies obscures the form.

The *Symphonie fantastique*, first performed in 1830, was unique in its own time and somewhat disturbing to many members of the Parisian audience. One negative critic wrote that "the audience thought it was having a nightmare during the whole performance." The harmonies, at times very chromatic, were received with some surprise by early audiences. The wealth of orchestral sound may have seemed overwhelming to some of the audience in 1830. And the use of the "Dies irae" in a witches' sabbath was decidedly shocking. Even today the work has a great freshness and originality of sound.

## Berlioz' Other Works

*Harold in Italy*, another program symphony, was written in 1834. But Berlioz' dramatic impulses soon led him to write works for more than just the orchestra. *Romeo and Juliet* (1839) is a dramatic symphony for chorus, soloists and orchestra; and *The Damnation of Faust* (1845–46), a "dramatic legend" after Goethe, also used vocal forces. His *Grande Messe des morts* ("Great Mass of the Dead," or Requiem Mass, 1837) is written for an extremely large orchestra, four brass bands, chorus, and soloist. He also wrote several operas (*Les troyens* or "The Trojans," 1856–58, is the greatest of these).

Berlioz' genius and originality give him a unique place in musical history. His *Memoirs* provide a fascinating and often humorous description of the musical life of the period. His influence was felt strongly by Liszt and Wagner, and by several Russian composers.

## The Symphonic Poem

**Tone poem**

Relatively few program symphonies were written in the Romantic period. Many composers were drawn instead to a new and shorter form, the symphonic poem, or as it is sometimes called, the *tone poem*. The symphonic poem is essentially a program symphony in one movement. Its evolution was more from the concert overture than from the program symphony.

The symphonic poem shares many characteristics with the concert

Concert at the newly built Trocadero in Paris during the 1878 World Fair. On the stage, an orchestra, chorus, organ and a piano can be seen. The idea of large orchestras playing for mass audiences had first been promoted in France at the time of the 1789 revolution. (Bibliothèque Nationale, Paris; photo: Heritage of Music)

Liszt's symphonic poems

overture. Both are one-movement orchestral works often based on literary ideas. In fact, some composers used the term overture for works that might just as well have been called symphonic poems. Mendelssohn, for example, designated as overtures some works that Liszt would probably have termed symphonic poems.

Despite the ambiguous distinction between the two types of compositions, however, a few general differences can be found in most of the works. The symphonic poem is generally more loosely structured than the concert overture, and may or may not be directly related to a narrative sequence. It is thus a more flexible, expressive vehicle.

The creator of the symphonic poem was Franz Liszt, who in 1848 completed *Les Préludes*, the first work of this type. It was originally intended as part of a larger work. After it was completed, however, Liszt decided to present it as an independent composition. Finding a similarity of mood and spirit between the music he had written and the poems in Lamartine's *Méditations poétiques*, Liszt produced his own version of one of the poems as a program for the work. The program begins with a question, "What is our life but a series of preludes to that unknown song of which the first solemn note is sounded by death?" It then goes on to describe the different emotional states of the human spirit.

*Les Préludes* is organized in sections, with different dramatic or emotional states portrayed musically in each. Expressive lyrical melodies allude to love. Blustering chromatic activity is used to suggest a storm. And a relaxed pastoral melody relates to nature at its best. In the final sections, the love themes are transformed into exciting martial figures to portray self-realization. The work is based on solid musical principles. It is thematically unified, with much of the material spun out of the three-note motive that opens the first phrase of the introduction.

**Other composers of symphonic poems**

The symphonic poem was an ideal vehicle with which to express orchestrally the nationalist sentiments of many composers. Several added to the repertory of symphonic poems in the later nineteenth century. Among them are Bedřich Smetana (1824–84) with his cycle of six symphonic poems entitled *Má Vlast* ("My Native Land"), dating from the 1870s, which includes the well known "Moldau;" Tchaikovsky; Richard Strauss (1864–1949); Paul Dukas (1865–1935); Jean Sibelius (1865–1957); and Camille Saint-Saëns, who wrote several notable works in this genre.

## Saint-Saëns: Danse macabre, Op. 40

Camille Saint-Saëns (1835–1921) was one of the leading French composers of the late nineteenth century who further developed the symphonic poem. His early talent and sophistication were remarkable. He was a versatile composer of many types of works—operas, symphonies, concertos, and keyboard and chamber music—and he wrote poetry, plays, and books. He also championed other Romantic composers including Schumann, Wagner, and Fauré. Several symphonic poems number among Saint-Saëns' compositions, notably *Danse macabre* from 1874.

The *Danse macabre* is a dramatic and tuneful work that has quick, popular appeal. It was originally a song, a setting of a poem by Henri Cazalis. In the orchestral score appears a quotation from the poem, the part that tells of death dancing and playing his violin. A translation of the entire poem follows:

> *Zig, zig, zig,*
> *Death is striking a tomb with his heel in cadence.*
> *Death is playing a dance tune on his violin at midnight.*
> *The winter wind blows, and the night is dark.*
> *From the linden trees come moans.*
> *White skeletons move across the shadows, running and*
>     *leaping in their shrouds.*
>
> *Zig, zig, zig, each one gives a tremor,*
>     *and the dancers' bones rattle.*
> *Hush! they suddenly leave off dancing, they jostle one*
>     *another, they flee—the cock has crowed.*

*(From the Bagar-Biancolli Concert Companion)*

Caricature of Saint-Saëns by Gabriel Fauré. (Bibliotheque Nationale, Paris)

The orchestra is large and colorful—piccolo, pairs of flutes, oboes, clarinets, and bassoons, four horns, two trumpets, three trombones, tuba, xylophone, timpani, triangle, cymbals, bass drum, harp, and strings.

**Saint-Saëns: Danse macabre, Op. 40**

LISTENING ANALYSIS                                                SIDE 8, BAND 3

The work begins with the harp striking the note D twelve times to symbolize the arrival of midnight. Soon a solo violin enters, playing on the open strings, but with the E string tuned to an E♭. An unusual tuning of a string instrument such as this is called *scordatura*. The introductory motive suggests that Death is tuning his violin.

Here, a triple meter is established. As the first theme is heard in G minor on the flute, it is clear that the music is a waltz.

*Scordatura*

Beginning of First Theme

After the repetition of the first theme, the second major theme, also in G minor, is played by the solo violin:

Beginning of Second Theme

It is repeated immediately. The first theme then returns and is slightly developed. The second theme returns and ends with a modulation to D major, followed by another appearance of the first theme. The xylophone becomes prominent at that point. A fugal exposition of the second theme occurs in G minor, and thus the theme is developed further.

A third theme is then heard; at first it seems strangely familiar, and then it becomes clear that it is the "Dies irae" from the Requiem Mass, cast in a disguising waltz meter in the key of A major.

Beginning of Third Theme

First Section of "Dies Irae"

Di - es  i - rae,  di - es  il - la,  Sol - vet  sae - clum
[Day of  wrath,  that  day  will  resolve  time

in  fa - vi - la,  Tes - te  Da - vid  cum Si - by - la.
in  ashes,  David  as witness with the Sibyl.]

In this middle section, the third theme is repeated with a broader orchestration. The second theme returns in B major, accompanied by the harp, and is repeated several times. The first theme reappears, and the two themes are heard several more times as they are developed. Death's tuning motive returns briefly. A climax is reached with the return of G minor as the two themes are presented simultaneously. The tempo increases to create greater intensity. But then a solo oboe suggests that the dance is over (the cock crows). Several brief phrases are played by the solo violin as the work comes to a quiet conclusion.

**LISTENING SUMMARY**

| | |
|---|---|
| Timbre: | Very large orchestra; solo violin used prominently |
| Melody: | Three main themes, the third a mutation of "Dies irae" |
| Rhythm: | $\frac{3}{4}$ meter—a waltz |
| Form: | Free ternary (ABA′) |

Besides *Danse macabre,* Saint-Saëns is best remembered for *Le carnaval des animaux* ("The Carnival of the Animals"), a chamber piece written in 1886, his great Symphony No. 3—Organ Symphony (1886), and his opera *Samson et Dalila* (1877), based on the Old Testament story. "Le cygne" ("The Swan') from *The Carnival of the Animals* is played very frequently today, though Saint-Saëns forbade performances of it during his lifetime for fear of hurting his reputation as a serious composer.

**Strauss**
The symphonic poem continued to be a major genre for orchestra in the very late years of the nineteenth century. It reached its greatest heights in the works of Richard Strauss (1864–1949). *Tod und Verklärung* ("Death and Transfiguration," 1888–9) and *Also sprach Zarathustra* ("Thus Spake Zarathustra," 1896) are works related to philosophical programs. *Till Eulenspiegel* (1895) and *Don Quixote* (1897) have more narrative programs, and *Ein Heldenleben* ("A Hero's Life") and the *Sinfonia domestica* are autobiographical. Most of these works were written in the late 1880s and 1890s. The symphonic poem, being so heavily dependent on programmatic content, did not outlive the Romantic era which gave birth to it. However, many symphonic poems continue to thrill concert audiences.

The later compositional efforts of Strauss were concentrated on opera, a genre in which he wrote a number of great masterworks. In his final creative years he returned to more Classical, less complicated forms. Strauss stated in 1935 that his career was governed by a principle that was of great importance to him: "My whole life belongs to German music and to an indefatigable effort to elevate German culture." He remained dedicated to his personal goal until his death.

Design for the opening scene of Richard Wagner's opera *Das Rheingold*, first performed as part of the cycle *Der Ring des Nibelungen* at Bayreuth in 1876. Wagner's stage works required elaborate machinery to create special effects. How the Rhine Maidens were made to "swim" on stage can be seen on page 362. (Victoria & Albert Museum, Crown copyright)

# CHAPTER 22

# *Opera and Choral Music of the Nineteenth Century*

*LISTENING PREVIEW Many composers of the nineteenth century were very successful in combining music with drama, taking good advantage of closely associating these two arts. Listen to the recitative "E strano!" and the first section of the following aria "Ah, fors' è lui" from Verdi's opera La Traviata (side 8, band 4), in which the heroine Violetta first excitedly muses about having found her true love in the recitative, and then more calmly contemplates the concept of her new-found love in the aria. What specific musical characteristics help underscore these two contrasting moods of Violetta?*

## Opera

Opera flourished during the nineteenth century as composers continued to find stimulating opportunities to associate words with music. Librettists and composers gave free rein to their imaginations, and a number of exciting innovations took place. In general, Italian opera stressed the vocal aspect of the form, while German opera concentrated more on mood and setting, with the orchestra having a more prominent role.

### Influence of Mozart and Beethoven

Two pre-Romantic operas, Mozart's *Don Giovanni* and Beethoven's *Fidelio*, were important precursors of the Romantic opera. *Don Giovanni*, written in 1787, two years before the fall of the Bastille, depicts one man's violent struggle with supernatural powers. Don Giovanni, the cruel deceiver and seducer of a long succession of women, is the prototype for a number of characters found in later Romantic operas. The emphasis on supernatural effects, the tremendous contrast between conflicting principles, and the dramatization of

*Opposite:* The world's operatic composers, seen as a "garden of harmony" by a French cartoonist in the mid-1870s. Jacques Offenbach, holding a score of his satirical operetta *Orpheus in the Underworld*, and Verdi, riding ahead on his bicycle, leaving behind even his latest score *Aida*, are clearly center stage. Everyone else, including Wagner (to the right, in a hat), is a mere bystander. (British Library; photo: John Freeman)

the conflict are all elements that were soon to be identified with the Romantic movement. Another major forerunner of Romantic opera, Beethoven's *Fidelio*, was written between 1805 and 1814, after the composer's thorough search for appropriate subject matter. The opera, based on an actual event that took place during the French Revolution, deals with the selflessness, bravery, fidelity, and heroic humanitarianism of the rebels. The music in *Fidelio* is often explosive, and, in combination with the drama of good against evil, it creates an intense emotional effect. Beethoven's work thus broke away from the usual style of eighteenth-century opera and heralded the opera of the Romantic era.

In the following sections, discussion will focus on the three national styles of opera most prominent in the Romantic period—French, Italian, and German. All of the styles owe something to the works of Mozart and Beethoven, though they developed in very different directions; and all offer certain innovations.

## French Opera

Since the days of Gluck, Paris had been the center of European opera, and it remained so through the first half of the nineteenth century. During the early years of the French Revolution, opera seemed especially suited to the propaganda needs of the new leaders. Huge public spectacles were held, with spectacular choral sections and "hymns" written to be sung by the audience as well as by performers. After the Revolution, operas with historical subjects and large numbers of singers remained popular, and the awakened appetite for spectacle contributed to the development of the style that came to be known as *grand opera*.

## The Development of Grand Opera

Grand opera was essentially the creation of three people—Louis Veron (1798–1867), Eugène Scribe (1791–1861), and Giacomo Meyerbeer. Veron, a businessman, was the director of the Paris Opera during the early 1830s. Scribe wrote librettos, and Meyerbeer was the composer. The three wished to concentrate their librettos on topics that dealt with early Western history or modern times. The operas they produced were serious, spectacular, and heroic, with events inevitably unfolding on a huge scale. Plots were often based on current events, and local settings were frequently used.

Meyerbeer's operas

Giacomo Meyerbeer (1791–1864), perhaps more than any other composer, determined the direction in which grand opera would evolve. It was only fitting in cosmopolitan Paris that a German Jew who had gone to Venice to study the Italian style should create operas that would be regarded everywhere as eminently French. Meyerbeer's works are based on the extravagant romanticizing of history and call for a profusion of scenery and effects. His *Robert le Diable* ("Robert the Devil"), first produced in 1831, was a smashing success—in part because it provided the shock effect demanded by the public. The opera offers an example of the extravagant music and

theatrical performances the French were flocking to at the time.

Another important grand opera, indeed one of the foremost French operas of the entire century, was Berlioz' five-act masterpiece *Les troyens* ("The Trojans"), written in the late 1850s. Berlioz himself wrote the libretto. The story concerns monumental events—the fall of Troy and the fate of the Trojans. Its many large choral and ballet scenes are characteristic of grand opera. The first part, dealing with the capture of Troy, was never even produced in Berlioz' lifetime.

**Berlioz' Les Troyens**

## Comic and Lyric Styles
Offenbach's operas

*Opéra comique*, with dialogue generally spoken, was also popular in nineteenth-century Paris. Of the many composers writing in this style, Jacques Offenbach (1819–1880) was one of the most successful. His style, sparkling and light yet satirical, was to influence the development of comic opera and operettas throughout Europe. Offenbach's tremendous popularity may be attributed in part to his revival of eighteenth-century vaudeville humor as well as to the cleverness of his librettos and the lucidity and conciseness of his music. He satirized all that he disliked in grand opera. He also made fun of traditional opera themes, particularly in his *Orphée aux Enfers* ("Orpheus in the Underworld," 1858) and his *La Belle Hélène* ("Helen the Beautiful," 1864). Elsewhere he parodied Medieval legend and satirized contemporary politics.

**Lyric opera**

Toward the middle of the century, *lyric opera* developed as a compromise between serious, elaborate grand opera and the lighter *opéra comique*. Two major composers of lyric opera were Ambroise Thomas (1811–1896) and Charles Gounod (1818–1893). Gounod's *Faust* (1859) is one of the most popular of all French operas. Its colorful plot, taken from Part I of Goethe's drama, and tuneful melodies have endeared it to countless listeners. Though the events of these operas are serious, they contain less pageantry than was the rule for grand opera, with more characterization of and interplay between principal roles.

## Bizet: Carmen

A peak of opera composition in France was reached by Georges Bizet (1838–1875) in his opera *Carmen*. This powerful work, written in the last year of the composer's life, differs from earlier Romantic opera in that much of its text is in prose rather than poetry. Oddly enough, despite the tragic love story that forms the plot, *Carmen* was first designated as an *opéra comique*, as the dialogue in it was originally spoken. Its Spanish setting and "exotic" music testify to the typically Romantic interest in foreign subjects that was widespread in France at the time. The characters and scenes are quite realistic; the music is colorful and concise.

The story is set in Seville and revolves around the beautiful, sensuous gypsy Carmen, who works in a cigarette factory. Don José, a corporal, loves Carmen intensely, but she rejects his love and turns to Escamillo, a toreador (bullfighter). In the end, the heartbroken José stabs Carmen to death.

Bizet's music seems to capture the essence of the passionate tale and all of its nuances. The melodies vary from the disarmingly lyrical to the powerfully dramatic. Rhythms from Spanish dances appear occasionally and help to create the Spanish flavor of the work. The moderately large orchestra plays an important role, providing the singers with colorful and vibrant support.

The Prélude presents two important melodies that appear later in the opera: the famous "Chanson du toréador" ("Toreador Song") and the "Fate" theme (heard at several crucial times during the opera and finally at Carmen's death). In the opera iself, Carmen sings several memorable arias, notably the "Habanera," the "Seguidilla," and the "Chanson bohème" ("Gypsy Song").

Célestine Galli-Marié, the first Carmen. (The Bettmann Archive/BBC Hulton Picture Library)

### 'Chanson bohème'

The 'Chanson bohème,' sung by Carmen at the opening of the second act of the opera, aptly displays some important aspects of the heroine's personality. Carmen sings exuberantly of the pleasures of gypsy life while her friends dance with abandon. The tempo is moderately fast in triple meter, and the minor mode seems especially appropriate to the gypsy mood.

After a substantial orchestral introduction that features a main theme accompanied by pizzicato strings, Carmen sings her opening melody of the aria:

**Beginning of Opening Melody**

The aria is strophic in form, with three stanzas of text. Each stanza ends with Carmen's friends joining her in a vivacious "Tra-la-la" in the major mode. The effect of the change from the minor mode to the major at the end of each stanza followed by the change back to minor at the beginning of the next stanza is quite striking, accentuating the impulsive abandon of the gypsy women. Musically the second and third stanzas differ only slightly from the first.

Percussion instruments, particularly tambourine, triangle, and cymbals, are increasingly prominent as the aria proceeds. With the final "Tra-la-la," the tempo begins to increase, growing faster until the orchestra closes with a repetition of the opening material in a breathless whirl of sound and dance.

## Late Romantic Style

**Operas by Saint-Saëns and Massenet**

By the late nineteenth century, Paris was no longer the center of European operatic activity, but a number of French composers continued to write very expressive works, generally lyric in style. *Samson et Dalila* (1877), a biblical work by Camille Saint-Saëns (1835–1921), was very popular. The lyrical sentimentality of Jules Massenet (1842–1912) made him one of the most popular opera composers of his time. His great interest in sensual love poetry is shown clearly in *Manon*, an opera based on an eighteenth-century tale of romance. Massenet's work brings us to the close of the late Romantic style in French opera and into the twentieth century.

## Italian Opera

In Italian opera of the early nineteenth century, music was strongly dominant over drama. Melody, supported by colorful instrumentation, harmony, and rhythm, formed the single most important aspect of opera. Recitatives and arias were still clearly separated in the traditional way, although recitatives were increasingly accompanied by the orchestra rather than by basso continuo. As the century progressed, Italian opera changed, becoming both more cosmopolitan and more national in character. The change began with Rossini, continued with Donizetti and Bellini, and reached a climax with Verdi.

## Early Romantic Operas

### Rossini's operas

Romanticism was somewhat less evident in the early years of the nineteenth century in Italy than in France or Germany. Indeed, opera was the only field in which Romanticism manifested itself strongly in Italian music. Some Romantic traits can be found in the operas of Gioachino Rossini (1792–1868), whose life and influence spanned the first half of the century. The texture of Rossini's music is light, and his melodies, often sung with coloratura ornamentation, are very catchy and appealing. He also caught the public's imagination with lively rhythms and his fine talent for building dramatic excitement in both comic and serious contexts.

Rossini presented his comic opera *Il Barbiere di Siviglia* ("The Barber of Seville") in 1816. It was based on the first play in Beaumarchais' trilogy, of which the second was the basis of Mozart's *The Marriage of Figaro*. Rossini's opera was soon celebrated throughout Europe. His *Otello* (1816), based on Shakespeare's play, was also popular until an opera of the same name was presented by Verdi in 1887, totally eclipsing Rossini's version. Rossini's last opera, *Guillaume Tell* ("William Tell"), first produced in Paris in 1829, established him as an important composer of grand opera. After the great success of *William Tell*, the thirty-seven-year-old Rossini retired, and for the remaining thirty-nine years of his life, he wrote no more operas. Only two major works, a *Stabat mater* (1832) and the *Petite messe solennelle* ("Little Solemn Mass," 1863), emerged from his later years, together with a large quantity of light vocal and instrumental music which he referred to as "sins of my old age."

### Donizetti's operas

The most important figures in Italian opera between Rossini and Verdi were Donizetti and Bellini. Gaetano Donizetti (1797–1848) was a prolific extrovert who created operas that were both dynamic and exciting. He felt it was quite all right to interrupt an aria with dialogue in order to keep it in close touch with the plot. His melodies tended to be ornate, and he used ensembles and choruses to build volume and color. His *Don Pasquale* (1843), an opera buffa, is one of the brightest operatic gems of the age. The "mad scene" from *Lucia di Lammermoor* (1834) includes some of Donizetti's most elaborate and difficult writing for solo voice.

### Bellini's operas

Vincenzo Bellini (1801–1835) leaned toward a quieter, more contemplative style. His melodies are somewhat more expressive and delicate than Donizetti's, his harmonies subtle and varied. He was a meticulous, painstaking perfectionist, which may be one reason why we have fewer operas by Bellini than by Rossini or Donizetti. Another reason is, of course, his very short life. *Norma* (1831) exemplifies not only Bellini's insistence that the aria retain the central position in the opera but also his belief that strong dramatic scenes, carefully chosen, could be most effective.

## Verdi's Operas

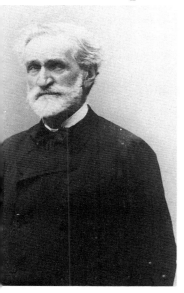

Portrait of Verdi, aged 83. (Giancarlo Costa)

The name of Giuseppe Verdi (1813–1901) has come to stand, not only for the career of a single composer, but for a whole type of opera. Verdi's music cannot be considered apart from his personality and situation in life. Verdi was a patriot, closely associated with Italy's midcentury struggle for nationhood, and his nationalism strongly influenced his work. Far from conforming to the Romantic stereotype of the isolated artist, Verdi became a symbol of Italian aspirations to independence from Austria with his opera *Nabucco*. Even his name was seized on as a political slogan: it was an acronym for "Vittore Emmanuele Re d'Italia" ("Victor Emanuel II, King of Italy"), the first king of unified Italy. Verdi became a member of the first parliament. Many of his earlier operas have to do with revolutionary conspiracies. His singers voiced stirring appeals on behalf of freedom and democracy. For him nationalism could not help but express itself in music.

All of Verdi's mature works, with the exception of his very last opera *Falstaff* (1893), were serious in mood, since comedy was hardly appropriate for the kinds of questions he wished to raise. His desire for naturalness led him to stress believable characters and the human voice. Orchestra and scenery are nearly always secondary. Scenes are short and intense, and any spectacle serves a dramatic purpose beyond being a showpiece.

Verdi's operatic career developed in a careful, continuous fashion. *Nabucco* ("Nebuchadnezzar"), a biblical opera presented in 1842, was his first real success. *Macbeth* (1847) was the other important opera written early in his career. It seemed especially melodramatic to conventional Italian audiences, for whom the mere portrayal of murder and witches on the stage was a shocking breach of custom.

The second phase in Verdi's development featured three major operas: *Rigoletto, Il trovatore,* and *La traviata.* Written between 1851 and 1853, all were inspired by well known plays. *Rigoletto* (1851) was inspired by Victor Hugo's *Le roi s'amuse* ("The King Is Enjoying Himself"); its protagonist is a hunchbacked court jester. Two of the arias from the opera have become especially well known: "Caro nome" ("Dear Name") and "La Donna è mobile" ("Woman Is Fickle").

*Il trovatore* ("The Troubadour"), first presented in 1853, was based on a play by the Spanish author Antonio García Guitérrez. The great variety in the opera's plot and music can be attributed in part to the influence of Meyerbeer: Verdi had spent much time in Paris on visits, and had lived there for two years. Azucena, the gypsy mother, is one of the many exotic characters that intrigued Verdi's audiences.

# *Verdi:* La traviata

Verdi's *La traviata* ("The Courtesan"), which first appeared in 1853, was based on Alexandre Dumas' *La dame aux camélias* ("The Lady of the Camellias") and, like the novel, is supremely sentimental. Violetta, a courtesan, falls in love with Alfredo, a young man of respectable family. Violetta and Alfredo live together for a time, but at his father's pleading she nobly leaves him to save the good name of his family. Her health, already frail, breaks under the strain, and Alfredo returns to her just as she dies of consumption in the last act of the opera.

Verdi's opera *La Traviata* was first performed in Venice in 1853. It was not initially a success, but this soon changed, as the publication of this piano score—published for people wishing to play the music at home—indicates. (The Bettmann Archive)

### "Ah, fors' è lui" *and* "Sempre libera"

Upon first realizing her love for Alfredo, Violetta sings one of the most famous arias from any opera: "Ah, fors'' è lui" ("Ah, Perhaps It's He").

LA TRAVIATA

Libretto di Francesco Maria Piave

MUSICA DI

GIUSEPPE VERDI
Cavaliere della Legion d'onore

RIDUZIONE PER PIANOFORTE A QUATTRO MANI
DI
LUIGI TRUZZI

OPERA COMPLETA

Prezzo Fr. 30 —

REGIO STABILIMENTO TITO DI GIO. RICORDI

MILANO - NAPOLI

FIRENZE, Ricordi e Jouhaud. - TORINO, Giudici e Strada. - MENDRISIO, Bustelli-Rossi.

**LISTENING ANALYSIS**

The aria is in two large sections, an aria and *cabaletta*, a concluding section in a quick tempo. The aria begins with the words "Ah, fors' è lui" and the cabaletta with the words "Sempre libera" ("Always Free"). Brief recitatives precede each of the sections.

In the recitative preceding the first section, Violetta muses on the possibility of having found her true love. These thoughts carry her into the first section of the aria. Two themes are heard, both in triple meter at a moderate tempo. The first theme, in the minor mode, is halting and disjunct, as Violetta contemplates the mystery of love. The second theme, in the major mode, is more lyrical and conjunct, as the thought of love overcomes her; it is the same melody Alfredo has sung to her in the preceding scene when he told her of his love for her.

First Section: First Theme

First Section: Second Theme

The orchestra provides a light accompaniment throughout. The entire first section is repeated with a second stanza of text.

Then, suddenly, in a brief recitative, Violetta comes to her senses, realizing that she is committed to her present life, and decides to enjoy life as it is. The recitative ends with very elaborate scale passages.

In the second section of the aria, "Sempre libera," Violetta enthusiastically anticipates the continuation of her life as a courtesan. The tempo is fast, the music in the major mode:

Second Section: First Theme

Over a simple, chordal accompaniment, the vocal fireworks multiply, abounding with scales, sequences, and high notes. At points of climax, the singer, following tradition, usually slows the tempo slightly for expressive purposes. For a moment, Violetta hears Alfredo serenading her outside the window, echoing the lovesong theme from the first part of the scene; but she is undaunted and repeats the section, vowing to remain free.

Text:

Violetta (sola):

Recitativo:

È strano! È strano! In core
Scolpiti ho quegli accenti!
Saria per me sventura un
serio amore?;
Che risolvi, o turbata anima
mia?
Null'uomo ancora
t'accendeva—O gioja
Ch'io non conobbi, esser
amata amando!
E sdegnaria poss'io
Per l'aride follie del viver
mio?

Aria:

Ah, fors' è lui che l'anima
Solinga ne' tumulti
Godea sovente pingere
De' suoi colori occulti!
Lui che modesto e vigile
All'egre soglie ascese,
E nuova febbre accese,
Destandomi all'amor.
A quell'amor ch'è palpito
Dell'universo intero,
Misterioso, altero,
Croce e delizia al cor.

Recitativo:

Follie! follie! Delirio vano è
questo!
Povera donna, sola,
Abbandonata in questo
Popoloso deserto
Che appellano Parigi,
Che spero or più? Che far
degg'io! Gioire,
Di voluttà ne' vortici perir.

Violetta (alone):

*Recitative:*

*How strange! How strange! His words*
*Are burned upon my heart!*
*Would a real love be a*
*tragedy for me?*
*What decision are you*
*taking, O my soul?*
*No man has ever made*
*me fall in love. O joy,*
*Which I have never known—loving,*
*to be loved!*
*And can I scorn it*
*For the arid follies of my present life?*

*Aria:*

*Ah, perhaps he is the one*
*Whom my soul,*
*Lonely in the tumult, loved*
*To imagine in secrecy!*
*Watchful though I never knew,*
*He came here while I lay sick,*
*Awakening a new fever,*
*The fever of love.*
*Of love which is the breath*
*Of the universe itself—*
*Mysterious and noble,*
*Both cross and ecstasy*
*of the heart.*

*Recitative:*

*Folly! All is folly! This is*
*mad delirium!*
*A poor woman, alone,*
*Lost in this*
*Crowded desert*
*Which is known to men as Paris,*
*What can I hope for?*
*What should I do? Die*
*In the whirlpool of*
*earthly pleasures!*

Aria:

    Sempre libera degg'io
    Folleggiare di gioja.
    Vo' che scorra il viver mio
    Pei sentieri del piacer.
    Nasca il giorno, o il giorno
        muoia,
    Sempre lieta ne' ritrovi.
    A diletti sempre nuovi
    Dee volare il mio pensier.

*Aria:*

    *Forever free, I must pass*
    *Madly from joy to joy.*
    *My life's course shall be*
    *Forever in the paths of pleasure.*
    *Whether it be dawn or*
        *dusk,*
    *I must always live gaily*
    *In the world's gay places,*
    *Ever seeking newer joys.*

**LISTENING SUMMARY**

Timbre:    soprano; large orchestra of string and wind instruments

Melody:   several different themes that demand great skill to perform; range is wide; melody in the second section is especially elaborate

Rhythm:   first section—$\frac{3}{8}$ meter, tempo Andantino (moderate); second section—$\frac{6}{8}$ meter, tempo Allegro brillante (fast and spirited)

Harmony:  first section—F minor changing to F major; second section— begins and ends in A♭ major

Form:     binary (AB) with a recitative preceding each section

## Later Operas of Verdi

After *La Traviata*, Verdi embarked on a brief and rather unsatisfactory association with Parisian opera. He was commissioned to write two operas in French, *Les vêpres siciliennes* ("Sicilian Vespers") in 1855 and *Don Carlos* in 1867. The first opera was based on the 1282 massacre of the French invaders in Sicily. The second was loosely based on a drama by Schiller about the Spanish court. In it Verdi dealt very effectively with the emotional power of freedom, love, and misery.

In 1871, with the appearance of *Aïda*, Verdi reached the pinnacle of his career. The occasion was festive. Cairo had a new opera house, and Verdi had been commissioned to write an opera for the opening of the Suez Canal. The opera is unusually effective in its unity of drama and music. In the arias, choruses, ballets, processions, and marches of *Aïda*, Verdi combined aspects of the grand opera of France with the best of Italian opera. The arias "Celeste Aïda" ("Celestial Aïda"), sung by the hero Radames, and "Ritorna vincitor" ("Return Victorious"), sung by Aïda, are among Verdi's finest.

Verdi's *Otello* appeared in 1887 and is one of the most outstanding serious operas produced in Italy during the nineteenth century. The libretto is, of course, based on Shakespeare's play. In none of Verdi's earlier works were the various musical pieces so intimately connected with one another as in *Otello*. Chromaticism and a relatively free treatment of tonality are important harmonic features of the music.

Verdi's *Falstaff*, produced in 1893, had the same rejuvenating effect on opera buffa that *Otello* had on opera seria. Now approaching eighty, Verdi was growing cynical about the human condition, and he satirized it strongly in *Falstaff*. The work is one of the greatest comic operas in all of opera, a perfect wedding of text and music. It is a fine credit to Verdi's genius and an appropriate culmination of his great career.

### Verismo and the Works of Puccini
#### Mascagni and Leoncavallo

Puccini (left) with Luigi Illica, co-librettist of *La Bohème*; photograph, early 1894. (Giancarlo Costa)

Three important Italian composers who continued the Romantic tradition in the late nineteenth and early twentieth centuries were Mascagni, Leoncavallo, and Puccini. Many of their works belong to the movement known as *verismo*, or "realism," which made use of subject matter based on everyday events and the lives of the common people. This had literary counterparts particularly in the works of the French author Gustave Flaubert (1821–1880), and was part of the general Romantic interest in ordinary citizens. Pietro Mascagni (1863–1945) is best known for his *Cavalleria rusticana* ("Rustic Chivalry," 1890), a notable and often performed example of the verismo style. Ruggiero Leoncavallo (1858–1919) is also remembered for an opera in the realistic style, *I pagliacci* ("The Clowns," 1892). *Cavalleria rusticana* and *I pagliacci*, both relatively short works, are often presented together.

The works of Giacomo Puccini (1858–1924) represent a variety of subjects and styles. His interest in exotic subjects can be seen in two of his most popular operas: the "Japanese" *Madama Butterfly* (1904) and the monumental "Chinese" *Turandot*. By comparison, *Tosca* (1900) is set in the Italy of his own day. *La bohème*, first presented in 1896, also has a European setting—the Latin Quarter of nineteenth-century Paris.

### Puccini: La bohème

Realism is evident in *La bohème*. As a whole, the opera provides an excellent example of many aspects of Puccini's style.

The tale revolves around Mimi, a poor and pretty young seamstress, and Rudolfo, an equally poor young poet. The opera centers on various experiences in the Bohemian lives of the two young people and their friends. Mimi and Rudolfo soon fall in love, but in true Romantic fashion Mimi dies of consumption in the last scene, leaving Rudolfo heartbroken.

#### "Che gelida manina"

Soon after they meet, Rudolfo helps Mimi to look for a key she has dropped. Their hands touch in the search, and Rudolfo comments on the coldness of her hands. The aria "Che gelida manina" ("What a Cold Little Hand") is a declaration of love in duple meter and the major mode. It has two sections, the first of which starts with a simple series of repeated notes. Typically, then, the melody becomes more active and expansive:

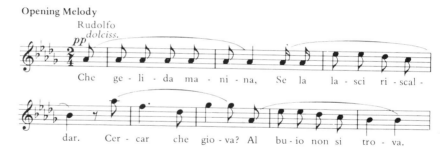

Opening Melody

Rudolfo
dolciss.

Che ge-li-da ma-ni-na, Se la la-sci ri-scal-

dar. Cer-car che gio-va? Al bu-io non si tro-va.

In the course of the first section, Rudolfo asks Mimi to stay while they look for the key—which he has already found and slipped into his pocket.

In the second section, there is a modulation and a meter change as Rudolfo tells Mimi he is a poet. The section builds to a dynamic climax with the orchestra providing strong support. The aria is highly expressive and lovely. It is followed immediately by an enchanting aria sung by Mimi in which she introduces herself to Rudolfo.

In this aria and in others, Puccini's gift for writing beautiful, lyrical melodies can clearly be seen. His text settings are nearly always syllabic, without scales and arpeggios. His melodies and their supporting orchestration often evoke a strong emotional response in the listener. The music seems to capture the very essence of late Romantic Italian opera, with its superb melodies, chromatic harmony, and interest in the common people. Puccini's work helped to close an era.

Scene from Act III of Puccini's *La Bohème*; postcard published at the time of the opera's first production in Turin, 1896. (Giancarlo Costa)

## The Evolution of Opera

In the Classical and Romantic styles, opera reached its height as a form of public entertainment. To a great extent, the works of those eras were written not only to present fresh musical ideas but also to capture the public imagination and in many cases to achieve box-office success. This has been much less true in our own age, in part because of the competition of so many other forms of public entertainment.

Listen to selections from the operas of four different periods—those listed below from the record set that accompanies the text, or other selections.

| Baroque: | Monteverdi's *Orfeo*, "Tu se' morta" | Side 2, Band 9 |
| Classical: | Mozart's *The Marriage of Figaro*, "Cinque, dieci" | Side 6, Band 5 |
| Romantic: | Verdi's *La Traviata*, "Sempre libera" | Side 8, Band 4 |
| Modern: | Berg's *Wozzeck*, any selection | |

What musical qualities make it possible to identify the first three selections as Baroque, Classical and Romantic? What musical qualities suggest that the last selection is of a more recent era?

In what ways can each of the selections be seen as a reflection of the social and historical setting in which it was created?

## German Opera

More than in any other country, Romanticism in Germany was ideological. Nationalism there was of such universal political significance that it could hardly but affect the whole of German culture. The violent potential in both Romanticism and nationalism found a fertile medium in German opera. Opera was not enshrined in tradition in Germany as it was in Italy. The close interaction in Germany between Romantic music and literature made opera a natural crossroads of German Romantic expression. Opera developed more radically there than anywhere else in Europe, and had a far-reaching influence, through Wagner, on both theater and symphonic music.

Patriotic and Medieval legends were a major source for Romantic artists, especially in Germany. Superstition, fantasy, and the supernatural were also frequently introduced. These themes were particularly evident in the librettos of German operas. Another Romantic trend, the glorification of the common people, was also very important in German operas during the Romantic period. Most Romantic operas had scenes of village life which incorporated folklike melodies if not actual folksong.

German Romantic opera had its first great flowering under the leadership of Carl Maria von Weber (1786–1826). Weber was already an experienced conductor by the time he began to write opera. His *Der Freischütz* ("The Marksman") was written in 1821 and proved a

Weber's Der Freischütz

Whilst the designs for the world première (Berlin, 1821) of Weber's opera *Der Freischütz* were purely classical, this highly imaginative decor for the Wolf's Glen scene of the Weimar production in 1822 bears all the hallmarks of Romanticism. (Staatliche Kunstsammlungen, Weimar)

masterpiece. It is a story of good and evil, of Germanic Christianity versus barbaric paganism. The heroes seem to fit in naturally with the wonderfully merry villagers and bucolic setting, while the villains ultimately find they have no place in the rural society. Among the most admirable scenes are the hunters' and bridesmaids' choruses, the songs and dances of the peasants, and the supernatural "Wolf's Glen" scene. The last is a very impressive example of melodrama, with spoken dialogue, accompanied by and alternating with the large, colorfully used orchestra.

**Melodrama**

Two features of German Romantic opera stand in sharp contrast to the Italian style as Verdi was refining it. Mood, atmosphere, setting, and symbolic content take precedence over characterization and human conflicts. Accordingly, vocal melody is of lesser importance in projecting the message of the work. The orchestra is no mere accompaniment but part of the fabric of the drama, and the significance of its music is thus increased. Wagner's music-dramas provide excellent examples.

## Wagnerian Opera

Nineteenth-century Romantic opera reached a climax in the work of Richard Wagner (1813–1883). He began writing opera at the age of twenty. In his late twenties he wrote his first major opera, *Rienzi*, a grand opera in the Meyerbeer tradition.

A turning point in Wagner's evolution was reached in 1843 with *Der fliegende Holländer* ("The Flying Dutchman"). This was not a grand opera, but a story from legend concerning the workings of supernatural forces countered by redemption, very much in the German Romantic tradition. From then on, Wagner was to use only myths, legends, and German history as sources for his opera plots. Heinrich Heine's version of a German legend supplied this plot, and the result was a truly German opera. The story concerns a Dutchman condemned to roam the seas forever. At last he is released from his bond with the devil through the love of a woman. The orchestration is very colorful and the role of the orchestra is expanded. The melodies are frequently tuneful, and the characters well conceived. The impact of the entire work is quite forceful.

In Wagner's *Tannhäuser* (1845), the grand opera trappings of *Rienzi* were combined with the idea of redemption used in *The Flying Dutchman*. The Medieval knight Tannhäuser enjoys the licentiousness of Venus' realm and then unsuccessfully seeks forgiveness from the Church. The pure love of the heroine Elizabeth finally redeems his sin. The ensembles, choruses, ballets, and crowd scenes no doubt contributed to the opera's great popularity. The various arias and ensembles are still clearly separated from one another, but not as strictly as in Wagner's previous works. The music is also more chromatic than that in Wagner's earlier operas.

*Lohengrin*, Wagner's next major work, was first performed in Weimar in 1850 under the direction of Liszt. (Wagner, exiled to Switzerland for his radical political views, could not attend.) It was based on a tale taken from German folklore, but the emphasis was placed on questions of religion and philosophy. The knight Lohengrin is a symbol of divine love, while Elsa depicts that portion of humanity incapable of strong faith. Crucial to the plot is the "forbidden question": Elsa must never doubt Lohengrin by asking his name or country. The use of recurring themes and motives, a technique he had used before and one that was to become one of his trademarks, is extended here. Particularly important are the motives for Lohengrin and for the "forbidden question." By this time, Wagner had abandoned the clear distinction between aria and recitative. Choruses are

**This is the machinery enabling the Rhine Maidens (see illustration, page 346) to swim. The technique for creating this illusion is borrowed from the Baroque tradition of Italian and French opera. (Nationalarchiv der Richard-Wagner-Stiftung/ Richard-Wagner-Gedenkstätte, Bayreuth)**

very prominent and often directly involved in the action. In order to achieve a more restrained and subtle instrumental effect, Wagner often chose to use sections of the orchestra in small mixed groups. Surprisingly in a work that followed *Tannhäuser*, there is relatively little chromaticism. However, certain tonalities take on an added dimension by being identified with specific characters, a practice Wagner was later to extend over huge musical structures.

**Wagner's theoretical writings**

By 1849 Wagner had begun to formulate new theories about the integration of music and drama. He set forth his thoughts and opinions in several books. *Art and Revolution* (1849) and *Opera and Drama* (1851) explained his political philosophy and its relationship to his music, thus providing a rationale for his later compositions. In *The Art-Work of the Future* (1849), he proposed that all artistic aspects of a dramatic work be united to form a *Gesamtkunstwerk* ("unified art work"), that is, a work of art that successfully balances all artistic components of a musical-dramatic composition. He also believed, unlike Verdi, that the orchestra should carry a larger share of the musical burden than the human voice. Harmonic schemes should be conceived on a grand scale, he insisted, so that they might unify entire musical dramas and groups of musical dramas. Wagner's philo-

**Leitmotivs**

sophical writings also called for the extensive use of *Leitmotivs* ("leading motives")—that is, of melodic and rhythmic motives associated with a particular person, thing, or idea that would be heard in the orchestral accompaniment.

**The Ring Cycle**

Wagner's *Opera and Drama* was primarily an apologia in which he explained many musical and philosophical tenets found in his greatest work, *Der Ring des Nibelungen* ("The Ring of the Nibelung"), a cycle of four operas written over a period of twenty-two years from 1852 to 1874: Wagner wrote the librettos in reverse chronological order, then composed the music from the earliest to the latest opera. The four operas in the cycle are *Das Rheingold* ("The Rhine Gold"), *Die Walküre* ("The Valkyrie"), *Siegfried*, and *Götterdämmerung* ("The Twilight of the Gods"). Two separate tales from Nordic mythology are combined. The plot of the complete cycle is very complex, involving gods, humans, giants, and dwarves. All are involved in a struggle to rule the world, a struggle that revolves around the possession of a ring made from Rhine gold. Those who possess the ring illicitly are subject to a terrible curse. Final redemption comes only when the ring is returned to the river at the end of the cycle.

**Wagner: Die Walküre**

The second opera in Wagner's Ring cycle, *Die Walküre*, represents most aspects of Wagner's mature style. The plot concerns Wotan, the chief god, and his children: nine daughters, the Valkyries, born to the earth-goddess Erda; and a son and a daughter, Siegmund and Sieglinde, born to a mortal woman. The Valkyries are warriors whose main task in life is to take dead heroes to Valhalla, the hall of the gods. In the opera Siegmund and Sieglinde, separated as children, meet again as adults. They fall in love and run away from Hunding, Sieglinde's husband. Brünnhilde, Wotan's favorite Valkyrie daughter, tries to help them in their escape, much to her father's displeasure. Siegmund is killed, and Sieglinde is hidden in the forest, where she will later bear a son, Siegfried, the hero of the next opera of the cycle.

The harmony in *Die Walküre* is rather chromatic, with frequent and sometimes rapid modulation from one tonality to another. Melodic phrases are often long and of irregular length. Form is quite free and fluid within an act. The old concept of recitative and aria is gone completely. For the most part, the music flows continuously without a clear separation into sections. The text is set syllabically and is seldom repeated. Virtuoso display rarely occurs in the singers' parts. Wagner wedded text and music carefully, never permitting the music to overwhelm the drama. Though the opera has an epic quality, the depiction of passions—Siegmund's and Sieglinde's love or Wotan's wrath, for example—through the orchestral music is extremely intense. Natural elements, such as storm, moonlight, and the advent of spring, are fused with the emotional content of the drama and represented very aptly in Wagner's music.

### *"Der Ritt der Walküren"*

At the beginning of Act III, the famous "Der Ritt der Walküren" ("The Ride of the Valkyries") is heard as the warrior goddesses assemble on a mountaintop after Siegmund's death. The very large orchestra is used in a most dramatic and flashing manner.

## Wagner:Die Walküre,*"Der Ritt der Walküren"*

| LISTENING ANALYSIS | SIDE 9, BAND 1 |

The challenging Valkyrie Leitmotiv boldly emphasizes disjunct motion and minor mode as it is played by horns and bass trumpets:

Valkyrie Leitmotiv

As the Valkyries assemble, one of them, Gerhilde, begins to sing their call, a very disjunct and dramatic motive:

Opening Vocal Motive

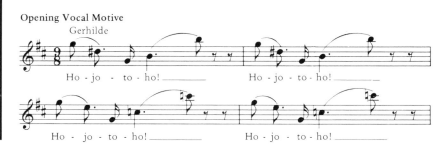

The entire scene is very colorful—vocally, orchestrally, and visually. The structure of the music is quite free, based on repetitions of the above motives. Text:

| **Gerhilde:** | **Gerhilde:** |
|---|---|
| Hojotoho! Hojotoho! | *Hoyotoho! Hoyotoho!* |
| Heiaha! Heiaha! | *Heyaha! Heyaha!* |
| Helmwige, hier! | *Helmwige, come here!* |
| Hieher mit dem Ross! | *Come here with your horse!* |

**LISTENING SUMMARY**

| | |
|---|---|
| Timbre: | soprano; large orchestra of string, wind, and percussion instruments |
| Melody: | two motives prominent, one from orchestral introduction, one from vocal part |
| Rhythm: | $\frac{9}{8}$ triple meter, tempo Lebhaft (lively) |
| Harmony: | B minor moving to B major |
| Form: | free, built largely on repetition of two motives |

After the Valkyries have gathered on the mountaintop, Wotan joins them. Then the sisters leave Brünnhilde and Wotan alone, and Wotan tells Brünnhilde of his great displeasure with her for having helped Siegmund and Sieglinde. After considerable discussion, Wotan decides to punish Brünnhilde by putting her to sleep inside a ring of fire, from which she will be awakened only by a hero brave enough to penetrate the fire and win her. Wotan bids a moving farewell to his beloved child and summons the fire to surround her; the opera ends as the flames rise higher and higher.

During the two decades in which he was concerned with the composition of the Ring Cycle, Wagner also wrote two other immensely powerful and successful operas: *Tristan und Isolde* and *Die Meistersinger von Nürnberg* (1862–67). Vastly different in character, both works illustrate certain aspects of Wagner's mature style.

## Wagner: Tristan und Isolde

Wagner's *Tristan und Isolde* is a tragic epic about love, despair, and death. It was written between 1857 and 1859, when Wagner was in love with Mathilde Wesendonk, the wife of a close friend (for whom he also composed his only song cycle, a setting of five of her poems). The Celtic legend of a faithful knight, magically enamored of his lord's wife, provided the basic material for the opera.

The dramatic significance of the plot is conveyed primarily through the music, which is in Wagner's most mature, richly chromatic style. Text and music are so well combined as to seem almost inseparable. Isolde's famous "Liebestod" ("Love-Death"), sung at the end just before she expires on her beloved Tristan's dead body, is a superb example. The entire work is continuous and symmetrical, without division into distinct arias and ensembles.

Philosopher and poet as well as composer, Wagner is shown here at the keyboard, surrounded by a circle of friends. (Picture Collection, New York Public Library: Astor, Tilden and Lenox Foundations)

## Wagner: Tristan und Isolde, Prelude

*Prelude*

Wagner often used the term "prelude" instead of the term "overture" for the music that introduced his operas. The Prelude to *Tristan und Isolde* is one of his most famous compositions. Built largely on short motives, it is highly chromatic and moves so easily and quickly from one suggested key to another that traditional major-minor harmony seems to have disappeared.

SIDE 9, BAND 2

### LISTENING ANALYSIS

In the opening measures two brief motives are dovetailed to make the opening melodic and harmonic material.

As the Prelude unfolds, the motives are frequently repeated, changed, and extended. Several other motives appear in the course of the work, but they seem to emerge from previous material and share certain characteristics, such as a predominance of melodic motion by step, rather than being placed in contrast or opposition to previous material. Tonality and modality are ambiguous and gently changing through much of the Prelude. Because of the nature and use of the thematic material and tonality, the form of the Prelude is quite free and evolutionary. The Prelude is such a successful and harmonically intriguing work that it is often performed by orchestras in concert.

| **LISTENING SUMMARY** | |
| --- | --- |
| Timbre: | large orchestra of string, wind, and percussion instruments |
| Melody: | largely motivic; almost all motives very conjunct |
| Rhythm: | $\frac{6}{8}$ meter; tempo Langsam und schmachtend (slow and yearning) |
| Harmony: | very chromatic; suggests keys without strongly confirming them |
| Form: | free, built from repetition of several motives |

Wagner's only comedy, *Die Meistersinger von Nürnberg* ("The Mastersingers of Nuremberg"), was staged in 1868 in Munich. The opera revolves around the conflict between conservative tradition, embodied by the mastersinger guild of the story, and the modern creative attitude toward art. In the young singer whose innovations offend the guild, Wagner was to some extent portraying himself. *Die Meistersinger* includes four main arias as well as ballets, choruses, and ensembles.

The staging of his operas was so important to Wagner that he designed a special theater for their presentation. Funds were made available for its construction by the young King Ludwig II of Bavaria who was Wagner's patron. The theater was built in Bayreuth, Germany, and is still in use today. The large orchestra needed for Wagner's operas—including for one opera eight horns, five tubas, four trumpets, and four trombones, plus strings, woodwinds, and percussion—sat in a huge orchestra pit extending far under the stage. This design made possible a better blend of orchestral sounds and a better balance of singers and orchestra.

Wagner's last opera, *Parsifal*, was completed and performed at Bayreuth the year before he died. The opera concerns the legend of the Holy Grail. The music displays strong emotional intensity, orchestral flair, complicated and subtle harmonies, and extreme chromaticism.

Wagner continued to compose until his death. The many Wagner cultists and, indeed, most of Europe mourned his passing. He had profoundly influenced the culture of his age and at the same time embodied its aspirations, values, and style.

## Choral Music

The chorus in the nineteenth century, like the orchestra, grew to immense proportions, with some choruses including hundreds of singers. Its newest role was as a participant in works that were chiefly symphonic in nature, though explicitly choral works continued to be composed. The chorus was, in effect, an added element in the timbre of the nineteenth-century symphonic orchestra. After Beethoven, Berlioz, Liszt, and Mahler all made use of choruses in this way.

*Short choral works*

Shorter secular works for chorus—often accompanied by piano or small instrumental ensemble—also received a great deal of attention during the Romantic period. Works by Schubert and Brahms, among others, became a part of the growing choral repertory. Brahms' folk songs are particularly charming.

**Large choral works**

Larger choral works were generally based on traditional types of compositions, mainly the Mass and the oratorio. Beethoven's two long Masses, with soloists, chorus, and orchestra, foreshadowed the later course of Mass composition in many ways. A number of composers followed his lead, writing for even larger groups of performers and expanding their works to ever greater lengths. Berlioz' *Grande messe des morts* is a monumental work in every way. The music captures the many moods of the text in a very dramatic and colorful fashion.

The late Romantic composer Anton Bruckner (1824–1896) wrote many liturgical choral works for both unaccompanied and accompanied chorus. Several make very effective use of contrapuntal texture combined with rich Romantic harmony. He also wrote three large-scale, mature choral works: Masses in D Minor and F Minor (1864, 1868) and a *Te Deum* (1884). These were not intended specifically for church performance.

Many of the Masses written in the nineteenth century were written for the concert hall rather than for the church. Many, in fact, are far too long for use in a church service. In the liturgical texts, particularly in those of the Requiem Mass, composers found a drama and excitement that inspired music quite incompatible with liturgical uses.

**The Requiem Mass**

The Requiem Mass proved an especially attractive vehicle for a number of Romantic composers. Bruckner and Liszt each wrote one *Requiem*. Brahms wrote *Ein deutsches Requiem* ("A German Requiem," 1868), a work that used not the traditional Latin text, but rather a sequence of psalm paraphrases in German arranged by the composer himself. Highly expressive yet controlled, it is one of the most sincerely hopeful, warmly Romantic religious compositions of the century. In his *Requiem*, Brahms did not resort to bombastic choral and orchestral techniques but relied instead on his mature melodic and harmonic style. Verdi's *Requiem* (1873), unlike Brahms', does make use of the traditional Latin text. The work is very dramatic, filled with great contrasts. The musical style resembles that of the operas of his middle period and seems most fitting for the text.

**Oratorios**

The oratorio found favor with many Romantic composers. Mendelssohn's two oratorios—*Saint Paul* (1836) and *Elijah* (1846)—are quite frequently performed today. Both acknowledge the influence of Handelian style. Another important Romantic oratorio, Berlioz' *L'enfance du Christ* ("The Childhood of Christ," 1850–54), is a quietly engaging work that subtly and almost tenderly gives musical expression to the nativity theme. At the very end of the century, the English composer Edward Elgar (1857–1934) revitalized the oratorio with his depiction of death and life beyond in *The Dream of Gerontius* (1900).

The increased size of the nineteenth-century choruses and orchestra added greatly to the expressive potential of choral music. A great number of very appealing and engaging choral works were written during the nineteenth century, and they form a major part of the repertory of choruses to the present day.

# CHAPTER 23

# *Nationalism and Late Romanticism*

*LISTENING PREVIEW Nationalism came to be an intense and obvious characteristic of much music of the nineteenth and twentieth centuries. Can you think of pieces of music that you have heard that have brought their country of origin to mind? What specific aspects of the works reminded you of their national origin? Play the "Hoe-Down" from* Rodeo *by Copland (side 10, band 5). What specific aspects of this work might make you suspect that it was written by an American composer?*

## Nationalism in Music

National styles of music became quite distinct during the nineteenth century in the same music that is described as Romantic. In all parts of Europe, a number of nineteenth-century composers wrote works that directly reflected their homelands in a variety of ways, and their music is referred to as nationalistic.

National contrasts in musical style began as early as 1600. Before that there had been little recognition of distinct, national musical traditions in written music. Most of the new techniques that were developed locally in the pre-Baroque era had tended to be adopted with reasonable speed by the other composers of western Europe.

After 1600, as the spirit of political nationalism grew stronger and more important, distinct national styles became increasingly prominent. The seventeenth-century Italian developments of monody and opera were strongly resisted in France. The French court countered with its own type of opera, a style based on the works of Lully and other French composers. Before long, composers from other countries felt the need to choose between Italian and French methods. In particular, both the Spanish and the Germans tended to imitate the Italian method.

Throughout the seventeenth century, France and Italy were regarded as the primary sources for new music. In the eighteenth century, Germany and Austria moved into prominence. The works of the German Baroque composers were, however, still rather inter-

Folk dances and their music became a major source of inspiration to mid- and late 19th-century composers who sought to give their music a particular national character. Many of them actually went to the countryside to collect and note down the traditional music of rural people. This engraving by Gustave Doré depicts a Spanish folk dance. (Heritage of Music)

national in style, continuing to show certain French or Italian characteristics. By the middle of the century, with the emergence of Haydn as a figure of international importance, music in Germany and Austria had gained a strong identity of its own. Mozart and Beethoven reinforced the musical leadership of that area of Europe, and by the end of the eighteenth century, Germany and Austria had become the predominant musical force, especially in instrumental music.

With the Romantic period came an unprecedented nationalism in musical styles. Many composers consciously sought new ways to make their music pointedly and obviously representative of their own countries. The trend continued into the twentieth century, with rivalries in music and the other arts paralleling political struggles. Nations possessing strong musical traditions vied with one another for influence, while countries which had less strong musical traditions and which were perhaps even more concerned with national identity, tried to develop their own musical styles.

## Characteristics of Nationalistic Music

The nationalistic music of the nineteenth century generally focused upon the presentation of particular sounds characteristic of a nation's or region's folk music. This was especially true of Central European nations and Russia, but not so true of France or Germany, on whose musical traditions other countries had until then leaned heavily. At times, this could be accomplished by stressing a single musical element—melody or rhythm, for example. More often, however, several musical elements were combined to create the particular national flavor desired.

Folk melodies

As might be expected, the melodies of nationalistic music were commonly inspired by folk songs. The composers of earlier ages, especially the composers of the Baroque age, had generally ignored peasant music or at best had parodied it. Among earlier Classical composers only Haydn had consistently used folk music as a resource. Romantic composers, however, found that the once-slighted music possessed certain qualities that could readily be used to develop national styles. Among the most significant of these qualities was the use of unusual intervals, short phrases, and a relatively narrow range. Brahms, Grieg, and Mussorgsky were only a few of the many composers who made liberal and adventurous use of the folk melodies of their respective lands.

National dances and rhythms

National dances and their characteristic rhythms were often used by composers. The polonaise, for example, strongly reminiscent of its native Poland, was unforgettably used by Chopin. Nineteenth-century composers also experimented with rhythm, foreshadowing the twentieth-century desire for rhythmic innovation and excitement. Intrigued by unusual folk-song rhythms, composers sometimes wrote in irregular meters.

Harmony

Harmony, already a major preoccupation of nineteenth-century composers, was greatly affected by the new interest in folk music. When scholars and composers began the serious study of peasant works, they soon found that the harmonies of many songs were far from simple. Scales and harmonic progressions often departed from accepted major-minor norms. Experimenting with these characteristics, a number of composers developed new scales quite different from the traditional scales of the major and minor modes. Throughout Europe the search for new national idioms led composers to cast aside many time-honored rules of progression and dissonance and to replace them with novel harmonic systems.

National opera plots and program music

Opera plots or programmatic associations in instrumental music were also used to suggest nationalistic orientation. Such suggestions were primarily verbal, but they were often linked to musical ideas that were nationalistic. Mussorgsky's *Boris Godunov* and many other operas borrow from the history of the composers' nations for their stories.

National instruments

Some composers wrote for instruments typical of their native lands, or at times imitated sounds and styles of nationally oriented instruments. Liszt's imitation of the cimbalom on the piano has already been mentioned. The guitar came to be very closely associated with and important to Spanish music. Thus, the use of the guitar or techniques typical of it, such as strumming figurations, on another instrument or in the orchestra, were used to suggest a Spanish spirit.

## Nationalistic Music in Russia

The currents of nationalism flowed with special strength in Russia. Long isolated from the rest of Europe by distance and the centuries of Tatar domination, Russia had developed quite differently from the

West. Peter the Great (1672–1725) and some of his eighteenth-century successors, impressed by Western science and military power, tried to make up for lost time, imposing Western ways by imperial fiat. But in so doing, they sowed the seeds of deep division within Russia itself. A long ideological struggle began between those who believed that Russia's only hope lay in Westernization and those who rejected such Westernization as a betrayal of the nation's soul. In the nineteenth century, the conflict became acute. Music and literature were among the chief battlegrounds.

Mikhail Glinka (1804–1857) was one of the earliest composers of Russian nationalist music. As a young man, he visited western Europe, where he heard the works of Mozart and Beethoven and became enthralled with Italian opera. Returning to Russia in 1834, he began a serious career as a composer. Although he wrote a number of orchestral pieces and chamber works, his best known and most influential works were his two operas, *A Life for the Czar* and *Russlan and Ludmila.*

Glinka's *A Life for the Czar*, first presented in 1836, follows the grand opera of France very closely in style and development. Innovative aspects are found, however, in the choral numbers and dance scenes, both of which deliberately use Russian folk melodies and

**Glinka**

Saint Petersburg, Russia's gateway to the West, was a major center of the music controversy between nationalists and Westernizers —a controversy that escalated with the establishment of Rubinstein's "international" conservatory in 1862. (Picture Collection, The New York Public Library: Astor, Tilden and Lenox Foundations)

rhythms to portray peasant life. The introduction and the finale are folk choruses, suggesting that Glinka intended his first opera to express the heroism and devotion of all Russians rather than of a single hero.

Glinka's next opera, *Russlan and Ludmila* (1842), was based on a fairy-tale romance by the Russian poet Alexander Pushkin. The new opera differed from the preceding one in its even greater use of folk material, employing a wide variety of dances, melodies, and rhythms.

**The Russian Five**

After Glinka a group of younger composers, sometimes called "The Mighty Handful" and "The Russian Five," tried to give musical expression to their intense national feelings. Mily Balakirev (1837–1910), César Cui (1835–1918), Alexander Borodin (1833–1887), Modest Mussorgsky (1839–1881) and Nikolai Rimsky-Korsakov (1844–1908) were united more by their general furthering of Russian influence on their art than by any common style. Other Russian composers, Rubinstein and Tchaikovsky among them, had adopted the mainstream French, Italian, and German styles as their own. The Five saw this leaning to the West as a danger to be resisted, and avoided Western influence in their music.

## Mussorgsky

In many ways the most important composer of the Five, and certainly the most original, was Modest Mussorgsky (1839–1881). The only one of the Five never to visit the West or even to leave Russia, Mussorgsky identified strongly with the peasants of his native land. He also took great interest in Russian folklore. He held military and civil service positions for much of his life, composing in his spare time. He was prone to nervous disorders and was debilitated by bouts of alcoholism. In the course of a short, rather Bohemian life in Saint Petersburg, Mussorgsky wrote a number of different types of works, the most successful of which were his songs and operas. Striving for a realistic rendering of human speech in music, Mussorgsky wrote works of intense dramatic quality that represented character and feeling with unusual vividness. The result was a musical language dominated by speech, declamatory rather than lyrical.

Of his *Boris Godunov* (1869, 1872–73), one of the great operas of the nineteenth century, Mussorgsky wrote: "I explore human speech; thus I arrive at the melody created by this kind of speech, arrive at the embodiment of recitative in melody.... One might call this a melody justified by sense." To his speechlike melody he added bold dissonances and adventurous harmonies. Rimsky-Korsakov made an extensive revision of Mussorgsky's *Boris Godunov*, and for years his version was the one heard most often. Today, however, the merits of Mussorgsky's own work are once again recognized. The story concerns a historical figure, and was adapted from a poem by Alexander Pushkin (1799–1837). In a sense, however, the entire Russian people are the subject. The chorus and Russian characters surrounding Tsar Boris are extremely important.

Portrait of Mussorgsky (1881), painting by Ilya Repin. (Moscow, Tretyakov Gallery; photo: Novosti Press Agency)

## Mussorgsky: Pictures at an Exhibition

Ravel's orchestration

*Pictures at an Exhibition* was originally written for piano in 1874 but is best known in a version orchestrated later by the French composer Maurice Ravel (1875–1937). The music is based on an exhibition of paintings by the Russian artist and architect Victor Hartmann, a friend of Mussorgsky. A kaleidoscope of orchestral colors, massive chords, and a wide range help to convey the many different emotions evoked by the paintings. The work, a succession of movements each relating to a specific painting, is an excellent example of program music inspired by the visual arts. At the beginning of the work and between a number of the movements, the "Promenade" is heard, during which the composer or listener walks mentally from picture to picture. Acting as a sort of musical excursion between paintings, it constitutes yet another programmatic aspect of the work. The function of the "Promenade" and the variety of movements can be seen in this list of their titles:

| | |
|---|---|
| Promenade | Ballet of the Unhatched Chicks |
| The Gnome | Two Jews, One Rich and the Other Poor |
| Promenade | Promenade |
| The Old Castle | The Market at Limoges |
| Promenade | Catacombs |
| Tuileries | The Hut on Fowl's Legs |
| Bydlo (A Polish Oxcart) | The Great Gate of Kiev |
| Promenade | |

Russian folk-style design of a clock in the form of Baba Yaga's Hut, theme of the penultimate movement of Mussorgsky's *Pictures at an Exhibition*, by Victor Hartmann. (The Bettmann Archive/BBC Hulton Picture Library)

The large, richly colorful orchestra comprises piccolo, two flutes, three oboes, English horn, two clarinets, bass clarinet, two bassoons, contrabassoon, four horns, three trumpets, three trombones, tuba, timpani, triangle, cymbals, snare drum, bass drum, tam-tam, tubular bells, xylophone, rattle, whip, celesta, two harps, and strings.

**LISTENING ANALYSIS**                                                      SIDE 9, BAND 3

### "Promenade"

The opening movement is marked *Allegro giusto, nel modo russo* ("At a fast but fitting tempo, in the Russian manner"). It is based on a theme that is typically Russian in its harmonic suggestions and frequent changes of meters, first played by a solo trumpet:

Beginning of theme of the "Promenade"

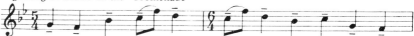

The theme is repeated and harmonized by the brass section. Two more brief exchanges between the solo trumpet and brass section follow as the theme is extended. Then the strings enter as the thematic material is further expanded. The music modulates through several keys to F major, and then back to Bb major before the last statement of the opening theme, heard in a broadly harmonized setting.

**LISTENING SUMMARY**

Timbre:   very large orchestra of string, wind, and percussion instruments (the work was originally written for piano)
Rhythm:   changing meter; tempo Allegro giusto (fast but fitting)
Harmony:  major mode; begins in Bb major, modulates to F major, ends in Bb major
Form:     free, as the first theme evolves into other thematic material, then returns at the end

**LISTENING ANALYSIS**                                                 SIDE 9, BAND 3 cont.

### "Gnomus"

The first episode of *Pictures at an Exhibition* is a movement entitled "Gnomus" ("The Gnome"), after a painting of a limping dwarf. The music is characterized by rapid changes in rhythmic motion and meter, chromatic harmony, ambiguity of key, and the minor mode. The opening seven-note motive, with its abrupt, wide-interval skips, is suggestive of the dwarf's jerky gait. The motive is heard several times. A second two-note motive grows into an ominous theme in Eb minor, which is repeated. The opening motive returns briefly. A third, ponderous thematic idea is presented and is interrupted several times by the opening motive. A series of trills in the bass register accompanies the return of the second motive with which the movement closes.

**LISTENING SUMMARY**

Timbre:   very large orchestra of string, wind, and percussion instruments
Melody:   several different motives and themes
Rhythm:   $\frac{3}{4}$ and duple meters; tempo Allegro vivo (fast and lively), slowing down in some sections
Harmony:  minor mode; basically Eb minor with much chromaticism
Form:     free, with the opening two motives returning several times

The final movement, based on Hartmann's design for the city gates of Kiev, the ancient capital of the Ukraine, is the most grandiose of all. Its music seems to capture the spirit of Russian tradition.

Ravel's orchestration of Mussorgsky's piano work was particularly brilliant. It changed a piece that is very effective as a piano solo into a work that is even more striking.

## *The Music of Bohemia*

Bohemia, part of modern Czechoslovakia, had once been an independent kingdom but in the nineteenth century was merely a province of the great Austro-Hungarian Empire. Restive under what they increasingly regarded as foreign domination, the Czechs began to take an interest in their native music as a form of artistic expression. The first collection of Czech folk songs was published in the 1820s, and the earliest Czech opera was presented in 1826.

Czech peasant music was somewhat more like conventional Western music in rhythm and harmony than were the folksongs of Russia. Nevertheless, the music offered definite possibilities as the basis for a distinctive art music. The composer who first perfected the union of native Czech music with the traditional art music of western Europe was Bedřich Smetana (1824–1884). Many of his works are, like Wagner's and Verdi's, nationalistic in choice of subject matter rather than in the use of peasant materials. His comic opera *The Bartered Bride* (1866), which later became the Czech national opera, does not include any folk songs at all. The opera does, however, deal with village characters and peasant life. It contains numerous choral and dance numbers, such as polkas and furiants, with a pronounced Czech flavor; the rhythmic, harmonic, and melodic style is largely Western.

Smetana's cycle of six symphonic poems from the 1870s, *Má Vlast* ("My Native Land"), uses traditional methods of construction in creating a national music. The cycle, most famous for the second poem "Vltava" ("The Moldau"), named for one of the country's main rivers, was conceived as an epic of the Czech people.

Another Czech composer, Antonín Dvořák (1841–1904), made much greater use of native folk music. Influenced in many ways by Brahms, and to a lesser extent by Smetana, Dvořák blended the traditional rhythms and colors of Western music with those of Slavic dances and songs. From 1892 to 1895 he was director of the National Conservatory in New York. While there, he wrote the *Symphony No. 9* "From the New World" and the *"American" Quartet, Op. 96* (both 1893) along with works without national references. Despite their sources, both his nationalist and American-inspired works are firmly in the Western European tradition exemplified by Brahms. His *"American" Quartet* makes use of the pentatonic, or five-note, scale he discovered in folk music. His first set of *Slavonic Dances* (1878) aroused a general European interest in the peasant tradition even though all the melodies were in fact his own.

*Smetana*

*Dvořák*

## The Music of Spain

*Albéniz*

Toward the end of the nineteenth century, there was a revival of interest in traditional Spanish music, again associated with a renewed interest in national folk songs and dances. Isaac Albéniz (1860–1909), the first important figure in the movement, began as a composer of light Romantic music. However, a period of residence in Paris heightened his awareness of the music of his native land. Between 1906 and 1909, he wrote a collection of twelve piano pieces called *Iberia* that achieved remarkable effects in their idealization of traditional Spanish dances. Each of the pieces alternates a dance rhythm with a vocal refrain to evoke the spirit of a particular place in Spain. While *Iberia* does show the influence of non-Spanish composers, some aspects of the music are so reminiscent of that quintessentially Spanish instrument, the guitar, as to leave no doubt where Albéniz' heart really lay.

*Falla*

Another composer who looked to the Spanish musical heritage was Manuel de Falla (1876–1946). In his *Nights in the Gardens of Spain* (1916), a composition for piano and orchestra, Falla endeavored to evoke the very spirit of his native land. Much of the music is derived from the rhythms, modes, and ornamentations of Andalusian Spain. Of all his works, perhaps the best known is *The Three-Cornered Hat* (1917–19), a ballet based on a witty tale of a philandering official and a virtuous peasant wife.

Manuel de Falla (center) and the choreographer Léonide Massine, photographed in 1919 at the Fountain of Lions in the courtyard of the Alhambra in Granada, Spain, at the time of the staging of *The Three-Cornered Hat*. (The Bettmann Archive/BBC Hulton Picture Library)

## The Music of England

### Elgar

In the late nineteenth century, a number of English composers, most notably Edward Elgar (1857–1934), brought their country back to a degree of importance in musical composition. Not since Henry Purcell in the late seventeenth century had a native-born English composer achieved a major, international reputation. Late nineteenth-century English composers did not at first achieve a clearly defined English style. Elgar, for example, was strongly influenced by both Brahms and Wagner; his *Enigma Variations* (1899) and his famous *Pomp and Circumstance Marches* (1901–07) show many characteristics of style found typically in the works of late Romantic, Germanic composers. Though he never consciously employed English folk melodies, some of his music can readily be identified as English.

### Vaughan Williams

With the early twentieth-century works of Ralph Vaughan Williams (1872–1958), however, England could finally boast of a major composer who consciously tried to shape native materials into a contemporary style. In a book called *National Music* (1934), Vaughan Williams wrote: 'Art, like charity, should begin at home. If it is to be of any value it must grow out of the very life of [the composer] himself, the community in which he lives, the nation to which he belongs." Thus Vaughan Williams sought in English folk music a source of inspiration for his own music. He worked as both a collector and a harmonizer of folk tunes, often building entire movements out of melodic lines rooted in folksong. He did this by avoiding extensive use of counterpoint, traditional modulations, and motivic development. Instead he used unusual and parallel chord progressions and a basically homophonic texture.

Among the works by Vaughan Williams that depend most clearly on folk elements is the *English Folk Song Suite* (1923), written for band and later arranged for orchestra. The composition differs from most such works in that it avoids dance tunes entirely. Another popular work by Vaughan Williams is *Fantasia on Greensleeves*, based on the well known English melody.

## The Music of Scandinavia

### Grieg

The Norwegian composer Edvard Grieg (1843–1907), after early attempts at writing in the German symphonic style, became a leading figure of the nationalistic movement in Scandinavia. His interest in creating truly Norwegian music is very much apparent in his two *Peer Gynt Suites* (1876), which were originally presented as incidental music for Ibsen's drama about the adventures of a young Norwegian peasant. The well known section "In the Hall of the Mountain King" dramatically exemplifies the energy of Grieg's music.

Grieg was also a master of songs and short piano pieces. In both types of compositions, he used techniques characteristic of Norwegian peasant music. His scales often waver between major and minor, with frequent pentatonic tendencies—qualities derived from Norwegian folk music. His ten books of *Lyric Pieces*, a series of short works for piano, demonstrate his ability to create typical "Norwegian" effects through the use of folklike tunes and harmonies, linked with descriptive titles that included national references. His most often performed work is the *Piano Concerto, Op. 16* (1868, rev. 1906–7).

Sibelius

One of the most important nationalist composers of the late nineteenth and early twentieth centuries was Jean Sibelius (1865–1957) of Finland. In his earliest works, Sibelius adopted a Scandinavian rather than a specifically Finnish outlook. Encouraged by a group of artists around him, however, he developed an intense interest in the *Kalevala*, the main body of Finnish myth and folklore.

Sibelius in c. 1888, about four years before the completion of his first major work, the choral symphony *Kullervo*, which is based on the Finnish national epic *Kalevala*. (The Embassy of Finland, London; photo: Heritage of Music)

It was folklore, not folk music, that was to prove the main inspiration for his nationalistic works. In the years that followed, he made very little direct use of the techniques or melodies of Finnish folk music in his own compositions. Yet the *Kalevala* myths inspired him to create his own unique mythological-romantic style. It was a style that incorporated much of the color and ambience of Finnish folk music.

Sibelius's symphonic poems probably reveal, better than any of his other works, his deep commitment to Finnish mythology. At the age of twenty-seven, he presented his first major symphonic poem, *Kullervo*, for soloists, chorus, and orchestra. A long work in five sections, rich in contrasting moods and timbres, it is patterned rather roughly on the life of Kullervo, one of the *Kalevala* heroes.

In 1899, when Finland was still under the domination of the Russian Empire, the Finns undertook a great patriotic celebration to support the freedom of their press, which they felt to be endangered. Included in the festival was a series of "Tableaux from the Past" depicting six crucial scenes in the history of the Finnish people. Sibelius provided extensive musical accompaniment, the finale of which received no special attention at the time but later achieved fame under the title *Finlandia*. Probably his most popular composition, *Finlandia* is a work of great fervor, power, and energy. Contrasts of theme, rhythm, and key distinguish the various sections. The first section seems to express the unrest of Finland under a hated foreign rule. The last section, notable for its hymnlike melody, became a rallying song for the nationalistic aspirations of the Finnish people.

Beginning Theme of Last Section:

## Late Romanticism

Musically the late nineteenth century was marked by a number of conflicting tendencies. As we have seen, there were composers in all parts of Europe who were seeking particularly nationalistic styles. The nationalistic aspirations, in and of themselves, were not contrary to Romanticism. Much nationalistic music of the period was indeed Romantic in spirit, but some abandoned the true Romantic style. And, as we shall soon see, a number of other composers were also seeking new styles, not for nationalistic reasons, but rather because they believed new means of expression were needed.

Not all composers, however, were ready to forsake the Romantic style. As the nineteenth century drew to an end and the twentieth began, characteristics recognized as Romantic remained prominent in the works of many composers, especially in the works of Germanic composers. This late Romantic, or post-Romantic, style can be traced, to some degree, down to our own day.

## Late Romanticism in Germany and Austria

In the works of the late Romantic composers of Germany and Austria—Wagner, Mahler, Bruckner, and Richard Strauss—the Romantic impulse became intensified and exaggerated. For some time subjective expressiveness, freed from many Classical restraints, had been leading to increased orchestral size and variety and consequently to a denser texture. Also prominent in the late Romantic style were innovative harmony and the expansion of traditional types of compositions such as the symphony. Lyrical melody and rhythmic variety remained important, as did the early Romantic custom of looking to literature and the visual arts for inspiration.

**Influence of Wagner**

A number of German composers continued to build extensively on mid-nineteenth-century harmonic practices. Many followed Wagner in placing particular stress on chromaticism. Some, in fact, saw the use of chromaticism as the only way to develop fresh sounds in musical language.

**Mahler's symphonies**

Gustav Mahler is perhaps best known for his ten symphonies, the last of which he did not live to complete. The symphonies were written for an orchestra that was large even by Romantic standards. Mahler's music is highly subjective and eclectic in style, drawing inspiration from many different periods and genres. Numerous and prominent wind instruments, chamber elements, his own songs, choruses, and vocal solos all appear in his symphonic works. In Mahler's *Symphony No. 8 in E♭ Major* (the "Symphony of a Thousand"), a work written in 1906 and 1907, two choruses and eight soloists augment the extremely large orchestra. The symphony is in two long movements and lasts about ninety minutes; the first movement is based on the Medieval hymn "Veni creator spiritus" ("Come, Holy Spirit") and the second on the ending of Part II of Goethe's *Faust*. A vast array of themes and timbres create effects ranging from delicacy to bombast. Simple songlike passages written in a single key are often juxtaposed with others that are extremely chromatic. His complete mastery of orchestral effects and his reverence for Beethoven and Wagner are clearly heard in his music. Mahler's symphonies are among the first orchestral works from the turn of the century, and they are highly esteemed by orchestras and audiences. In recent years particularly, his works have been received with great enthusiasm.

Gustav Mahler at the Vienna State Opera house. Since 1897, he had been director of this prestigious establishment but resigned in 1907, the year this photograph was taken. (British Library; photo: John Freeman & Co.)

Throughout his creative life he was active as a conductor, one of the most highly regarded of his time. His most prestigious positions were at the Vienna Court Opera, the Metropolitan Opera, and the New York Philharmonic.

**Mahler's songs**

Mahler was also a superb writer of songs. Most of his songs are accompanied by orchestra, and thus he combined the concepts of the Lied with symphonic music. The songs in his *Des Knaben Wunderhorn* ("The Youth's Magic Horn," 1888–1902) and *Kindertotenlieder* ("Songs on the Death of Children," 1901–04) show a wide variety of style and technique, all making effective use of the lyric and dramatic capabilities of the voice and orchestra. His earlier song cycle *Lieder eines fahrenden Gesellen* ("Songs of a Wayfarer") was written in 1884, but the accompaniments were not orchestrated until the mid–1890s. The four songs show clearly Mahler's fine use of the voice and orchestra in enhancing the texts that Mahler himself wrote.

## *Mahler:Lieder eines fahrenden Gesellen*
### First Song

The first of the four songs reflects sadly on the wedding of the singer's beloved to someone else. The text alludes frequently to elements in nature, integrating them with the singer's inner world, and closes in deep sorrow. The mood changes radically, though, with the second song of the cycle.

### Second song

**LISTENING ANALYSIS**                                           SIDE 9, BAND 4

"Ging heut Morgen über's Feld" ("This Morning I Went across the Field"), the second song in the cycle, begins with a bright text about a morning walk. The lines ring with exuberance until, at the end, the intense sorrow of the preceding song returns with unexpected force. Many characteristics of Mahler's style can be found in this song. The orchestra is used with great vitality in support of the solo voice. The form is highly modified strophic, with changes in the setting of each stanza of the text. Duple meter and the major mode characterize the lyrical melody that begins the first stanza:

Opening Melody

Although this theme also opens the second and third stanzas, the continuation is quite different each time. In addition, the third stanza is introduced by a marked change of key.

The last, very short stanza also emphasizes the beginning of the first theme. But the stanza closes in a melancholy mood that matches the sorrow of the text. Mahler used the melody of this song as the main theme of the first movement of his first symphony.

Text:

| | |
|---|---|
| Ging heut Morgen über's Feld, | *Walked through the field this morning;* |
| Thau noch auf den Gräsern hing, | *Dew was still on the grass;* |
| Sprach zu mir der lust'ge Fink: | *The merry finch, he spoke to me:* |
| "Ei, du! Gelt? | *"Hey, you! Isn't it true?* |
| Guten Morgen! Ei, Gelt? Du! | *Good morning! Hey, don't you think so, you!* |
| Wird's nicht eine schöne Welt? | *Won't it be a lovely world?* |
| Schöne Welt? | *Lovely world?* |

Zink! Zink!
Schön und flink!
Wie mir doch die Welt gefällt!"

*Tzink! Tzink!*
*Lovely and lively!*
*How the world does please me!"*

Auch die Glockenblum' am Feld
Hat mir lustig, guter Ding',
Mit den Glöckchen,
Klinge, kling, klinge kling,
Ihren Morgengruss geschellt:

*The bluebell also, in the field,*
*Merry, in the best of moods,*
*With her little bells,*
*Ring-a, ring, ring-a, ring,*
*Rang out to me her morning*
*greeting:*

"Wird's nicht eine schöne Welt?
Schöne Welt?
Klinge! Kling! Kling! Kling!
Schönes Ding!
Wie mir doch die Welt gefällt!"
Hei-ah!

*"Won't it be a lovely world?*
*Lovely world?*
*Ring! Ring! Ring! Ring!*
*Lovely thing!*
*How the world does please me!"*
*Hey-ah!*

Und da fing im Sonnenschein
Gleich die Welt zu funkeln an;
Alles, Alles, Ton und Farbe
gewann!
Im Sonnenschein!
Blum' und Vogel, gross und klein!
Guten Tag! Guten Tag!
Ist's nicht eine schöne Welt?
Ei, du! Gelt? Ei, du! Gelt?
Schöne Welt!

*And then in the sunlight*
*The world began to sparkle;*
*All things gained in tone and color*

*In the sunlight.*
*Birds and flowers, big and small—*
*Good day! Good day!*
*Isn't it a lovely world?*
*Hey, you! Isn't it true? Hey, you! No?*
*Lovely world!*

"Nun fängt auch Glück wohl an?!
Nun fängt auch mein Glück wohl
an?!
Nein! Nein! Das ich mein',
Mir nimmer, nimmer blühen
kann!"

*"And now bliss begins as well?*
*And now my bliss begins as well?*

*No! No! What I've in mind*
*Can never, never bloom for me!"*

### LISTENING SUMMARY

| | |
|---|---|
| Timbre: | baritone and large orchestra |
| Melody: | the same lyrical theme opens each strophe |
| Rhythm: | duple meter; moderate tempo of a walking speed |
| Harmony: | major mode; third stanza is set in a new key; more chromaticism toward end |
| Form: | highly modified strophic |

Third and fourth songs

The third and fourth songs in the cycle explore other aspects of unhappy love in ways both subtle and intense. Mahler, like many other composers in the latter part of the nineteenth century, was always very careful to match the mood of the text with appropriate musical ideas. Exact repetition of themes and sections is therefore rarely found. The music at the very end of the final song reappears in the third movement of Mahler's *Symphony No. 1 in D Major* (1889, revised 1893) as a restful interlude in a macabre funeral march.

**Strauss's Operas**    Richard Strauss, noted not only for his symphonic poems but also for his operas, followed in the tradition of Wagner. His works show a familiarity with Classical and earlier Romantic techniques, but his writing, like Mahler's, expands in all directions beyond them. In opera, particularly in *Salome* (1905), he wrote luxurious, chromatic counterpoint for a very large orchestra. His mixture of chromatic and nonchromatic harmony produced spectacular effects. In some of his later works, he expanded chromaticism almost to the point of denying the major-minor system entirely.

**Schoenberg**    The early works of the Viennese composer Arnold Schoenberg (1874–1951) belong very much to the late Romantic movement. Schoenberg wrote in a contrapuntal, chromatic style and easily rivaled Wagner and Strauss in his expressive ambition. His *Gurrelieder* ("Songs of Gurre," 1901), for example, calls for a huge orchestra, six soloists, and four choruses. The prominence of chromaticism in the *Gurrelieder* points toward Schoenberg's later efforts to develop an entirely new harmonic system—the twelve-tone serial technique, which will be discussed in Chapter 27.

Alexander Scriabin;
lithograph by J. Pasternak.
(British Library; photo: John
Freeman & Co.)

# The Late Nineteenth-Century Sense of Beauty

Claude Monet: *Water Lilies.* 1917. St-Etienne, France,
Musée d'Art et d'Industrie.

**Impressionism**   Impressionism in painting, a precursor of Impressionism in music, was an attempt to present only that which was subjectively visible at a given moment in time. Impressionist artists tried to exclude references to the past as well as any moralization or idealization. The result, in the works of Monet and his followers, was a new manner of portraying nature. Canvases were covered with continuous and overlapping strokes of pure or nearly pure color quickly applied in an attempt to find the equivalent of sunlight glare and transparent shadow. In Monet's *Water Lilies* the broad brushstrokes blur and soften the clarity of objects, and the dazzling brilliance of the hues disallows any convincing sense of depth.

Pierre-Auguste Renoir: *Luncheon of the Boating Party.* 1881. Washington D.C., Phillips Collection

Impressionist painters also delighted in depicting the everyday events of ordinary life. In his *Luncheon of the Boating Party* Renoir expresses most vividly and appealingly the sheer joy of being alive on a beautiful day by the river, with pleasant companions and good food.

***Post-Impressionism*** A number of artists soon became disenchanted with what they perceived as Impressionism's shallow objectivity and ephemeral nature. In seeking a more solid and durable style, Seurat made use of a new technique of paint application that has generally come to be known as Pointillism. In *A Sunday Afternoon on the Island of La Grande Jatte*, the confetti-like application of paint preserves Impressionism's freshness and brilliance of color within a structure of formal, nearly abstract beauty.

Georges Seurat: *A Sunday Afternoon on the Island of La Grande Jatte.* 1884–86. Courtesy of the Art Institute of Chicago (Helen Birch Bartlett Memorial Collection).

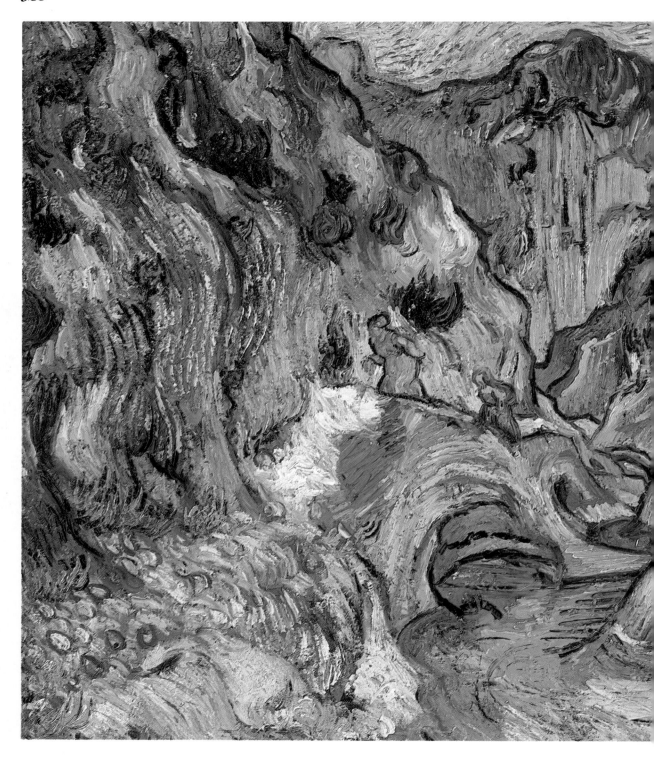

Van Gogh, a very different artist in both style and temperament, explored art's ability to communicate heightened states of emotion. In *The Ravine*, he demonstrated his special gift, using color and directional brushstrokes to express human passions. Exaggerating optical reality, he made paint reveal his exaltation before nature.

Vincent van Gogh: *Ravine*. 1889. Boston, Museum of Fine Arts (Bequest of Keith McLeod).

Paul Cézanne: *Mont Sainte Victoire seen from Les Lauves.* 1902–4. Philadelphia, Museum of Art (George W. Elkins Collection).

Cézanne also sought an aesthetic vision beyond that of Impressionism. In works such as his *Mont Sainte-Victoire* series, he concerned himself with what might be called the architecture of picture making, the creation of a balanced and unified universe. He relinquished all effort to capture changing atmospheric conditions. Instead, light becomes a generalized brightness. The landscape takes on the character of a serene, austere, balanced mathematical equation.

Another great innovator who followed on from the Impressionists was Paul Gauguin. His work was strongly Symbolist in flavor, often with a visionary element. This portrait of the cellist Schneklud typifies his style, with its blocks of strong color and its firm, uncompromising outlines. Much of Gauguin's work was influenced by the art of Japan, newly imported to Europe, which enjoyed a vogue toward the end of the century.

Paul Gauguin: *The Cellist (Portrait of Upaupa Schneklud).* 1894. Baltimore, Museum of Art (Given by Hilda K. Blaustein in memory of her husband Jacob Blaustein).

***Sculpture in the Impressionist Period*** A sculptor of great genius appeared toward the close of the nineteenth century—Auguste Rodin. Like the Impressionists, he explored the reality of nature as it was revealed by light falling upon surfaces. Rodin worked his surfaces with a touch alive to the most delicate nuances of plane, catching the ephemeral alterations of the body as it shifted in the light. As seen in his statue of Balzac, his art is one of emphatic exaggeration. Features are suggested in an almost sketchlike manner, yet the force and vigor of the great novelist emerge overwhelmingly.

Auguste Rodin: *Monument to Balzac.* Paris (photo Giraudon).

Late portrait of Edward
MacDowell with his wife.
(The Bettmann Archive/BBC
Hulton Picture Library)

## Late Romanticism in Other Countries

### Fauré

Romantic styles continued to be developed by composers in other countries as well. In France the works of Gabriel Fauré (1845–1924), though considerably more sublimated and restrained than the works of the late Romantic composers in Germany, nevertheless seemed to embody the spirit of French Romanticism. His songs are settings of the French Symbolist poets and are unsurpassed in their sensitivity to the nuances of the texts. His *Requiem Mass* and instrumental works also show his great skill in creating lovely, singable melodies accompanied by unusual and sometimes chromatic harmony.

### Rachmaninoff and Scriabin

Composers in Russia, including some already discussed as nationalists, were also part of the later Romantic tradition. Sergei Rachmaninoff (1873–1943) continued a strongly Romantic style, especially in his piano concertos. Alexander Scriabin (1872–1915), on the other hand, was among the most progressive of late nineteenth-century Russian composers. His compositions blend earlier Romantic forms and techniques with a harmony that often forsakes triadic and major-minor structures.

### Sibelius and MacDowell

Composers in many other countries also espoused a late Romantic style. Sibelius' symphonies and his *Finlandia* are prominent instances. In the United States, Edward MacDowell (1861–1908) was perhaps the most important of a group of late Romantic composers. His *Woodland Sketches* (1896) are still known to many piano students, and his piano concertos are occasionally heard in concert.

**Beyond
Romanticism**

As we have seen, chromaticism, used with ever greater freedom within the major-minor system of harmony, was one of the most important aspects of style among late Romantic composers. Two general lines of development from it can be observed in music about 1900. Many composers continued, even down to the present, to use some type of major-minor harmony in free and imaginative ways. Others, beginning in the last decades of the nineteenth century, rejected the system and worked out new means of harmonic organization. Subsequent chapters will show how these general trends manifested themselves in music.

PART SIX

# *Early Twentieth-Century Music*

## *Main Composers of the Twentieth Century*

*Alexander Scriabin* (1872–1915)
*Ralph Vaughan Williams* (1872–1958)
*Gustav Holst* (1874–1934)
*Sergei Rachmaninoff* (1874–1943)
*Arnold Schoenberg* (1874–1951)
*Charles Ives* (1874–1954)
*Maurice Ravel* (1875–1937)
*Manuel de Falla* (1876–1946)
*Béla Bartók* (1881–1945)
*Igor Stravinsky* (1882–1971)
*Anton von Webern* (1883–1945)
*Edgard Varèse* (1883–1965)
*Charles Tomlinson Griffes* (1884–1920)
*Alban Berg* (1885–1935)
*Sergei Prokofiev* (1891–1953)
*Walter Piston* (1894–1976)
*Paul Hindemith* (1895–1963)
*Roger Sessions* (b. 1896)
*Henry Cowell* (1897–1965)
*George Gershwin* (1896–1937)
*Francis Poulenc* (1899–1963)
*Duke Ellington* (1899–1974)
*Aaron Copland* (b. 1900)
*Louis Armstrong* (1900–71)
*Michael Tippett* (b. 1905)
*Dmitri Shostakovich* (1906–75)
*Olivier Messiaen* (b. 1908)
*Elliott Carter* (b. 1908)
*Samuel Barber* (1910–81)
*Vladimir Ussachevsky* (b. 1911)
*John Cage* (b. 1912)
*Benjamin Britten* (1913–76)
*Milton Babbitt* (b. 1916)
*Luciano Berio* (b. 1925)
*Pierre Boulez* (b. 1925)
*Earle Brown* (b. 1926)
*Hans Werner Henze* (b. 1926)
*Karlheinz Stockhausen* (b. 1928)
*George Crumb* (b.1929)
*Krysztof Penderecki* (b.1933)
*Mario Davidovsky* (b. 1934)

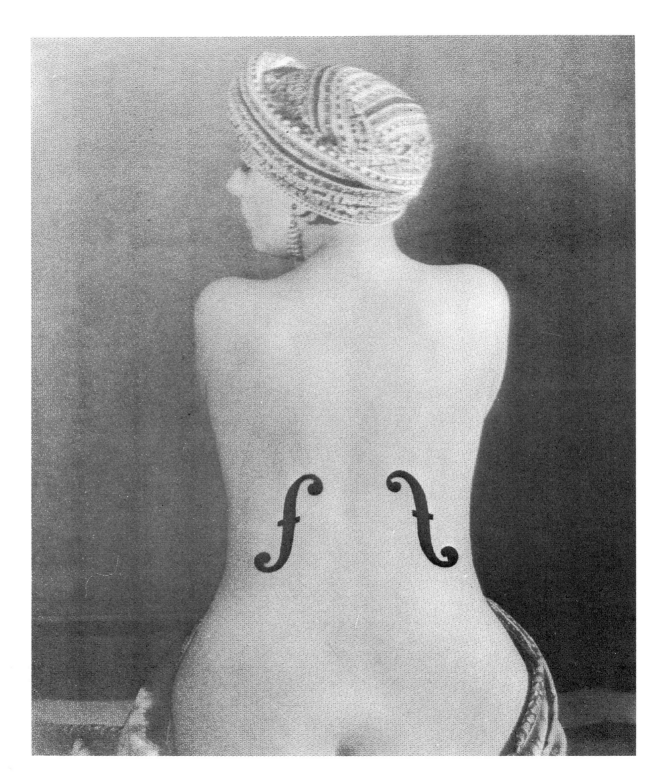

# CHAPTER 24

# *Introduction to Early Twentieth-Century Music*

*LISTENING PREVIEW Experimentation with all aspects of musical expression became even more widespread in the early decades of the twentieth century. Many composers retained a sense of tonality in their music, with traditional or new styles of harmony. Others experimented with harmonic styles that were not centered on a single tone. Listen to the opening section of the first movement of Hindemith's* Mathis der Maler *Symphony (side 10, band 4) and notice that while the overall harmonic sound is unusual when compared with earlier music, it is generally quite consonant and easy to assimilate. Contrast that with "Mondestrunken" from Schoenberg's* Pierrot Lunaire *(side 11, band 1), which does not emphasize a central tonality and seems to be based on a completely new harmonic language.*

## The Early Twentieth Century

### Material progress

In terms of material progress, the world began moving at a breathless pace at the beginning of the twentieth century. Practical inventions began multiplying late in the nineteenth century, and their proliferation has not yet ceased. Telephones, radios, electric lights, and automobiles were familiar to most Americans and many Europeans by the 1920s. Television, rocketry, and electronic computers followed soon after. In medicine, research opened the way to organ transplants, the discovery of hidden genetic factors, and cures for diseases that had once ravaged whole populations. Freud, Adler, Jung, and their successors explored the depths of the human psyche, discovering unconscious motivations behind human behavior. Einstein challenged the accepted version of physical reality as Freud questioned and revealed the workings of the interior world. The science of astronomy grew so rapidly that a mere decade or two into the second half of the century astronomers were probing the secrets of Mars and Venus, listening seriously for possible radio communications from non-human races in other solar systems, and finding hints that they

*Opposite Man Ray: Ingres's Violin, photo collage of 1924.*

might be looking at objects close to the edge of the universe. The world of space was no longer solely the realm of specialized science and mystical speculation; it was brought via television into the living room.

World wars

Still, scientific progress was hardly able to give the people of the first half of the twentieth century the peaceful paradise of which their ancestors had dreamed. World War I, the Russian Revolution, the Spanish Civil War, World War II, and the Chinese Revolution all took place in the years between 1914 and 1949. So did the development of the atomic bomb. After a half century of preparation for and fighting of world wars, humans had finally advanced to the point where they could destroy the entire planet.

Already before these developments, there had been a reaction to the introspection and emotionality of the Romantic age. The visual

Artistic movements

arts mirrored these political and scientific developments, almost as soon as they occurred. In 1907 Pablo Picasso painted the first Cubist work, *Les Demoiselles d'Avignon* ("The Young Ladies of Avignon"). Cubism fragmented its subject matter, presenting separate planes on one flat surface. In one way objective and adhering to a definite formal logic, it was nonetheless disorienting to the bourgeois world that was used to Romantic art. Another repudiation of ordinary reality was found early in the century in the paintings of Henri Matisse and his followers, a group called the Fauves (from the French word for wild animals). In Paris, Surrealist painters such as Joan Miró, Salvador Dali, and Max Ernst created endless images of anxiety and torment populating strange and fantastic landscapes. The Abstract Expressionist works of the midcentury carried the process still further, avoiding all semblance of a recognizable image. Similar trends could be seen in sculpture in the works of such artists as the English sculptor Henry Moore, who sought to portray the cosmic forces he found implicit in natural objects such as trees, bones, shells, and rocks.

Many of the artistic works of the early twentieth century were specifically created in rebellion against the crippling alienation artists felt in the newly technological world. Yet the increasing fragmentation of life found direct expression in the art of the time. Technology itself provided new means of artistic expression, most notably photography. Amid the welter of stock westerns, crime thrillers, and cheap romances, directors such as D. W. Griffith, Fritz Lang, Sergei Eisenstein, and Ingmar Bergman saw the artistic potential of the cinema and developed it brilliantly. Cinema was to prove an important medium for composers of many different styles.

Architecture and the applied arts took another route. The doctrine that "form follows function" was established at Walter Gropius's new art school in Germany, the Bauhaus, which started in 1919. The influence of the Bauhaus school extended not only to architecture but to industrial and advertising art, to interior design, and to the styling of small useful items such as dishes and perfume bottles. Other architectural pioneers of functional design included Alvar Aalto in Finland, Le Corbusier in France, and Frank Lloyd Wright in the United States.

**Literary movements**

In literature a multitude of new techniques was attempted. The experimental writing of Gertrude Stein and James Joyce's stream-of-consciousness narration in *Ulysses* and other works influenced the writers of an entire generation. *The Trial,* Franz Kafka's novel of 1925, introduced readers to a nightmarish bureaucratic labyrinth that has come to seem disquietingly familiar to the present generation. Common to both these works and many others, and related to Freud's discoveries, was a preoccupation with the relationship between outward and inner reality.

Playwrights also drew upon and sometimes satirized the temper of the time. George Bernard Shaw, Eugene O'Neill, and Jean-Paul Sartre were leading dramatists who used the theater as a pulpit to comment on the problems and meaninglessness they found in the real world. At times literature and music collaborated to produce such philosophical statements, as seen in *Die Dreigroschenoper* ("The Threepenny Opera") by Bertolt Brecht (1898–1956) and Kurt Weill (1900–1950), first produced in Berlin in 1928.

**Dance**

Dance, one of the oldest arts, also showed new vitality in the early years of the twentieth century. The interpretive power of traditional ballet received great stimulus from the entrepreneur Sergei Diaghilev. At the same time, a few pioneers, rejecting traditional ballet entirely, sought to return to the basic sources of movement and build a wholly new type of dance better suited to the modern spirit. Drawing upon

Martha Graham (b. 1894), a highly influential pioneer of modern dance in America. (The Bettmann Archive/BBC Hulton Picture Library)

ancient myth, folk custom, and modern psychology for insights (as did many artists and composers also), Martha Graham choreographed dances of rare dramatic power. She also made great use of music written for her by contemporary composers.

Both alone and in conjunction with the other arts, music participated in this early twentieth-century upheaval. Like the rest of the arts, it went in many directions and proclaimed many different ideas about its own role. Some of the paths taken have already seemingly turned out to be dead ends. Other are still, and will probably continue to be, of lasting importance.

## Trends in Early Twentieth-Century Music

### Impressionism

Straddling the nineteenth and twentieth centuries was the Impressionist music of Claude Debussy (1862–1918). Impressionism in music was allied to the Impressionist movement in French painting of the 1870s and 1880s, and to the Symbolist poetry of the same period. Rather than representing scenes or ideas musically or visually, Impressionist artists sought to evoke an impression or suggestion of the subject. Debussy's music avoided the precise narrative programs of the Romantic era, while being strongly influenced by Wagner's harmonic innovations. His own harmony was remarkable for its lack of tonal center; his melody and rhythm break new ground, being more atmospheric than lyrical. The lack of definition in his music is a fundamental factor in the music of the twentieth century, even though other composers were to react against his subjectivity.

Like the rest of society, composers were profoundly affected by the calamity of World War I. In the decades before the war, a sense of optimism, based largely on the improving material standard of living, had pervaded much of the Western world, though France and the dying Austro-Hungarian Empire also witnessed the pessimism of *fin-de-siècle* decadence. After 1918 the remembered carnage and futility of the war encouraged a widespread feeling of hopelessness. Not only did the prospects for a peaceful world seem bleak, but the tendency of industrial society to automatize the lives of individuals was increasing. Mass production, mass movements, even mass entertainment seemed to make personal creative efforts superfluous or impossible. People were increasingly divorced from the products of their labor and from their own inner lives. The gaiety and indulgence of the 1920s in America was in part a reaction against a growing sense of political uncertainty in a changed world, and of a spiritual void.

As a result, composers, like other artists, felt themselves deprived of any real social or economic role in society. This feeling prompted many of them to disassociate themselves from the music of the nineteenth century. The late Romantic passion of Wagner and his followers was rejected as pompous. The Impressionist concern for nature and sensuality was held to be overly subjective. A number of composers set out to rid their work of past encumbrances and to create a means of expression so new that their works might not even

Debussy in 1893, playing the piano at the house of a composer friend. (The Bettmann Archive)

be recognized as music by earlier standards. The pursuit of these goals by a number of major composers contributed to an unprecedented turmoil in musical style.

**Objectivity**

One of the most important new trends among composers in the years after World War I was an emphasis on objectivity. The trend, as already noted, was not peculiar to music. Artists in all fields began to aspire to a kind of detachment from their own works. It was as if aesthetic objects had gained an existence separate from the character and emotions of the people who gave them life. To the Romantic artist, art had been above all a projection of the artist's own creative imagination. To the twentieth-century objective artist, art was governed by rules inherent in the art form and in the techniques used to create it. In the latter case, the role of the artist involved a kind of service to the artistic medium—a shaping of the ideas at hand according to certain abstract rules. The Romantic concern with the expression of emotion was replaced by a new concern for structure, organization, and formal restraint.

**Primitivism**

Another artistic trend in the early years of the century was an interest in "primitive" art as a source of inspiration. Perhaps influenced by anthropological studies of non-Western societies, many artists came to associate what they considered primitive life with the

The Italian Futurist painter and composer Luigi Russolo with the "noise-intoners" he invented c. 1912/13 to produce what he thought should be the music of the future. This was to be based on noises of daily life produced by machines, rather than on notes played on musical instruments. Ravel, Milhaud, Honegger, Stravinsky and Varèse were impressed, but Russolo's radical ideas were not technically feasible until after World War II, with the beginnings of electronic music and musique concrète. (From L. Russolo: *L'arte dei rumori*, Milan, 1916; photo: Staatsgalerie Stuttgart)

freedom and spontaneity that Western civilization seemed to deny them. Eventually, a number of composers began to regard the late nineteenth-century works of Debussy and the other Impressionists as overly refined. Hoping to reinvigorate Western music, they turned to folk traditions outside the European mainstream. The energetic .rhythms of Africa had a great influence on postwar composers, as did the music of peasants in Asiatic Russia, the Balkans, and the Near East, and the blend of African and western elements that is jazz.

**Nationalism**

A new version of nationalism was espoused by some twentieth-century composers. Earlier composers motivated by nationalism had for the most part tried to incorporate individual folk idioms into their music. Their twentieth-century successors were more likely to use folk elements to expand tonal possibilities and create entirely new styles. Composers such as Bartók, Stravinsky, Prokofiev, and Shostakovich all made such experiments, although none of them can be classified simply as a nationalist.

**Futurism**

*Futurism* also made its appearance in the early twentieth century. Declaring that art needed a revolutionary aesthetic to make it compatible with the new world, the Futurists proclaimed that motion in the visual arts and noise in the auditory forms were the true objects of modern art. In an important 1913 manifesto, one Futurist composer, Luigi Russolo (1885–1947), wrote, "We must break out of this narrow circle of pure musical sounds, and conquer the infinite variety of noise-sounds." Some Futurists experimented with *microtonal composition*—music that uses an octave divided into more than the twelve half tones of the traditional scales. The French-American composer Edgard Varèse (1883–1965) was one of the outstanding adherents of this movement, which far outlasted Futurism.

Gebrauchsmusik

*Gebrauchsmusik,* or functional music, espoused by Paul Hindemith (1895–1963), was another important development. Reacting to what he considered "esoteric isolationism in music," Hindemith and several other German composers tried to write works that would be more easily understood and participated in by the general public. Hindemith also took into account the need that amateur performers had for an expanded repertory. Thus, Gebrauchsmusik represented a conscious attempt to meet the needs of all segments of society.

Light and satirical styles

Some composers reacted to the devastation of the war and the decline of Romanticism by writing light and even satirical music. Largely a French movement, it centered around Erik Satie (1866–1925) and a group of younger composers known as *Les Six* ("The Six"), the most prominent of which proved to be Arthur Honegger (1892–1955), Darius Milhaud (1892–1974), and Francis Poulenc (1899–1963). The turning toward irony and humor was felt to be a necessary antidote to both Impressionist obscurity and Romantic bombast.

Music of a machine culture

Since the composers of the twentieth century could no longer regard as their own the sources of imagery that Romantics had discovered in nature, many of them began to look instead to the products of industrialization as the symbols most relevant to the age. In particular, aspects of the accelerating process of urbanization found their way into the music of the 1920s. Satie's famous ballet score *Parade* (1917) included parts for typewriter and siren. At the same time, machine culture itself became a subject for art. The machine offered a powerful symbol of dynamic energy and motion—qualities that were sought by a number of early twentieth-century composers. Prokofiev's ballet, *Age of Steel* (1925–26), was just one of many works written in praise of engines and industry. Such works were often intentionally "dehumanized" in order to mirror what artists felt to be the depersonalizing features of modern life.

Jazz

The early years of the twentieth century also saw the evolution of jazz. Born not in Europe but in the United States, jazz was to become a major force in the music written on both sides of the Atlantic. Once it had become well established in America, European composers such as Hindemith, Weill, and Stravinsky began to take notice of it, borrowing both its techniques and its inspiration. The European interest in jazz peaked during the 1920s, with many composers adding elements of jazz in even their most serious works. This decade saw a high degree of cross-cultural influence especially between the United States and France.

Interest in folk and popular music also reached a new peak, due largely to wide dissemination through recordings, and to the gradual emergence of an increasingly affluent society. New popular styles developed every few years, such as blues, swing, bebop, and, in the second half of the century, rock.

One post-World War I movement seen in some of the works of

Stravinsky and Hindemith can be described rather loosely as *Neoclassicism*. The Neoclassicists were influenced by the techniques of earlier ages, especially by the Baroque emphasis on counterpoint and the Classical ideals of order and clarity of form. Many Neoclassical works combine such early techniques and forms with new aspects of twentieth-century style, such as new styles of dissonant harmony.

The composers of the early twentieth century introduced a number of new ideas to music that would have been unthinkable just a few decades earlier. One of the most important was *atonality*, which can be defined as a tendency to avoid referring to or creating any specific tonal center in a work. In order to achieve this, music has to abstain from harmonic and melodic patterns or phrases implying them. This was an outgrowth of Wagner's chromatic style.

Interest in atonal technique led to the twelve-tone, or serial, system of composition in 1923. As developed by Schoenberg and later refined and elaborated by his followers, *serialism* of pitch called for an equal emphasis on all twelve notes of the chromatic scale. The notes were to be used in a very systematic way following predetermined formulas. The system introduced a new means of maintaining structural coherence in a new harmonic language. Although serialism's formulas were revolutionary, the system nevertheless involved a clear set of procedures. Certain harmonic principles served as a blueprint for composition, much as the harmonic theory of the nineteenth century had served. The term *Expressionism* is often used to identify atonal and serial music, and a very general influence of Expressionist painters such as Oskar Kokoschka can be felt in some musical compositions of Arnold Schoenberg. Expressionist painters and composers developed bold, new methods for their artistic statements of strong, personal feelings.

Still other composers turned to electronic machinery as a new means of expression. In the later 1940s in Paris, Pierre Schaeffer (b. 1910) made experimental changes in musical sounds and noise by means of a tape recorder and other electronic devices. His work developed into a movement known as *musique concrète* ("concrete music" based on natural or man-made sounds, often changed electronically). Even greater advances in electronic music have been made since 1950.

Many twentieth-century composers have had teaching positions at colleges and universities, especially in the United States. Academic institutions, along with wealthy individual benefactors and foundations, have been very important patrons to all the arts in our century. Composers have often been influenced by their academic environments, in that their compositions have often been eclectic, associated with or influenced by other academic disciplines, or experimental in style. Other influences have been technological and political. Operas created for television and music for synthesizer are examples of the former. Music has also been influenced by the film industry, and, in recent times, by video tapes. Several works of Shostakovich were influenced by the Soviet regime of his time and Nazi Germany affected profoundly the lives and works of many composers, several of whom emigrated to the United States.

## *Melody and Rhythm*

### Melodic variety

The variety of melodic styles that developed in the music of the early twentieth century is enormous. Working from such models as plain-chant and Oriental music, a number of composers sought to obtain tighter melodic lines free of extraneous adornments and undue lyricism. Many composers, Stravinsky and Schoenberg among them, chose to build their melodies upon motives and phrases of irregular length, avoiding the highly structured quality and symmetrical phrases of earlier eras. Such melodies often featured large jumps through a broad pitch range. At other times, melodies were restricted to small movements in a narrow range. The latter choice was often used to create a very chromatic effect. Many twentieth-century melodies show a complete lack of tonal center. Others are vaguely or even strongly tonal. A wide variety of scales was used to form the basis of melody and harmony, among them the major, minor, chromatic, whole-tone see p. 418), and pentatonic scales, as well as the Medieval Church modes.

### Rhythmic innovations

Rhythm, certainly one of the most outstanding features of early twentieth-century music, showed a departure from previous practices at least equal to that of melody. Nineteenth-century composers were very interested in rhythmic variety and complexity, but their successors went much further. Inspiration for new rhythms came from a number of non-European sources. Great use was also made of

### Ostinato

rhythmic *ostinato*—a short, stubbornly repeated pattern, which was often used as a unifying force. Other composers employed rhythms that often avoided a strong, constant beat in order to allow the greatest possible latitude to the voice or voices involved. Debussy avoided a strong pulse, clear meter and prominently repeated rhythmic patterns in his music. Still other composers rediscovered and used older European rhythmic techniques. Among these were the isorhythmic principles of the later Middle Ages.

The renewal of old techniques and the invention of new ones made it possible for twentieth-century composers to create tense and powerful rhythms—irregular, unpredictable, and demandingly alive. Much of the power of the new rhythms was attributable to changes in the use of meter. In the eighteenth and nineteenth centuries, one meter ordinarily prevailed for a complete movement or section. In the twentieth century, however, this stability was renounced, and com-

### Frequent changes in meter

posers seeking a more pliant rhythm began to vary their meters frequently. In many of Stravinsky's works, for example, the meter shifts at almost every measure—a procedure that contributes much to the dynamic energy of the music. Moreover, the meters themselves were apt to be irregular, often containing five, seven or eleven beats in a measure. In a situation of this kind, it becomes almost misleading to speak of meter. Instead, the individual beat often becomes the basis of rhythm, generating short motives that multiply and combine to create exciting new patterns. Such formulas must necessarily avoid the traditional four-measure phrases and symmetrical rhythms of earlier music. Not all composers of early twentieth-century music were quite so innovative in rhythm. Yet many of the composers who continued to make use of more stable meters experimented with non-traditional phrasing and unusual meters. Odd numbers of beats to a measure became common even for stable meters, with the beats themselves frequently accented and subdivided in various ways. In many

It was probably Igor Stravinsky who, of all early 20th-century composers, had the greatest impact on the public mind. This photograph of him (seated) with Claude Debussy was taken by Eric Satie in 1910. (The Bettman Archive/BBC Hulton Picture Library)

cases the irregularity of the overall rhythmic pattern tended to counter-act any regularizing effect of the nominal division into measures.

## Harmony and Texture

**New harmonic techniques**

The harmonic structure of early twentieth-century music was also quite unlike that of any preceding era. More than ever before, dissonance came to be used for its own sake; consonance, as tra-ditionally perceived, was no longer obligatory. One of the new harmonic styles developed early in the century, *pandiatonicism*, was one that was essentially free of chromaticism and did not have the restrictions on chord progression usually found in major-minor har-mony. At the same time, Stravinsky, Copland (b. 1900), and others often achieved a dissonant effect by sounding two different chords together. The practice of superimposing two different tonalities was known as *bitonality* and was pioneered by Charles Ives (1874–1954). *Polytonality*, a technique involving the superimposition of more than two tonalities, was found to be less useful because the human ear cannot easily distinguish several tonalities played simultaneously. Another technique, *bimodality*, involved the superimposition of the major and minor modes.

A number of other early twentieth-century composers chose not to experiment with different tonalities but instead to reject tonality entirely. Different methods of achieving *atonality*, or the lack of tonality, will be discussed in Chapter 27.

**Renewed interest in counterpoint**

The music of the early twentieth century was also very much influenced by a renewed interest in counterpoint. A variety of contra-puntal textures was used, ranging from the traditional styles of earlier music to new textures that were very sparse and economical. Some-times single notes or short motives were presented in rapidly con-trasting registers, a texture referred to as *pointillistic*. (This term was originally applied to some Post-Impressionist paintings composed of tiny dots by such artists as Georges Seurat.)

Homophony and monophony, and various combinations of all textures, were used as well. While a number of composers continued to use the dense textures of late Romanticism, many others favored clearer and simpler textures. In a general sense, the most notable characteristic of early twentieth-century texture was probably its great variety.

## Timbre

A number of circumstances contributed to modifications of timbre in the early years of the twentieth century. One of the most important was the new feeling that sounds need not be pleasing to the ear in order to serve musical functions. This made possible the addition of previously unthinkable instruments such as wind machines and air-plane engines.

**Stress on percussive sounds**

Another important influence on timbre was the increased interest in rhythm, which led composers to stress percussive sounds at the expense of the lyric string and woodwind sounds of the nineteenth century. At times this was done by using traditional instruments in nontraditional ways. In Bartók's *Allegro barbaro* (1911), for example, the piano is used almost entirely as a percussive instrument, and in several other works violinists are expected to play with the wood of the bow, to tap the body of the violin with the bow, and to hit it with the hand. Composers also achieved a more percussive sound by adding such new instruments as the vibraphone and the wood block to orchestras and chamber groups. In some cases even wilder and more innovative sounds were sought through the use of rattles, thundersticks, and garbage cans. And a few composers, including Varèse, wrote chamber pieces for ensembles made up exclusively of percussion instruments.

**Use of electronic instruments**

As in earlier ages, changes in timbre were also brought about by technical advances. Electronic instruments were first devised in the 1920s and quickly put to use by the more progressive composers. A variety of electronic instruments developed later in the century added greatly to the composer's repertory of possible tone colors.

## Types of Compositions and Form

Composers of the early twentieth century continued to make use of many of the types of compositions developed in earlier centuries—symphonies, Masses, operas, and string quartets, among others. But some traditional types of compositions were treated so innovatively that they expanded the definition of their genres. Debussy's opera *Pelléas and Mélisande*, presented in 1902, challenged almost every operatic convention then current. New types of compositions also evolved at a rapid pace. Some were similar to older works but had new names that were in many cases programmatically descriptive. Others, as we shall see in succeeding chapters, were quite new. A number of these new works were for particularly innovative combinations of instruments, including purely percussion ensembles. At times some compositions defy easy classification as to the genre to which they belong.

Types of compositions were dictated to some degree by commissions from foundations, performing groups, and soloists. These commissions—the modern continuation of the patronage system—were sometimes specific, as when a pianist would ask a composer to write a sonata, but more often general, as when a foundation would ask for some sort of work for orchestra.

The twentieth century brought much more striking changes in form. With the early twentieth-century rejection of so many traditional musical techniques, form became a major problem. Classical forms had depended heavily on the major-minor system of harmony—a system that had been so largely abandoned. Much of the music of the twentieth century also involved totally new key relationships, distorted motives, and a general avoidance of complete restatements. Thus, although traditional forms continued to be used in many works, they were often so changed as to become virtually unrecognizable.

# Comparison of Romantic and Early Twentieth-Century Music

| Elements | Romantic Music | Early Twentieth-Century Music |
| --- | --- | --- |
| Melody | Often very lyrical<br>Phrases long and often irregular in length | Wide variety of styles and characteristics |
| Rhythm | Meters sometimes changed within movements<br>Great variety of meters and rhythmic patterns | Meters often changed within movements<br>Even greater variety of meters and rhythmic patterns<br>Rhythm both very prominent and occasionally complicated |
| Harmony | Major-minor system greatly expanded but remained the overall framework | Major-minor system used by some<br>Experimentation with new methods of creating tonal harmony<br>Atonal styles |
| Texture | Homophony and counterpoint both used<br>Texture often quite dense in works for large groups | Homophony, counterpoint and new textures such as pointillism all used<br>Range of textures from sparse to very dense |
| Timbre | Large orchestras, choirs, and bands<br>Small ensembles also prominent<br>Solo piano important | Earlier performing groups continued to be used<br>Bands grew in popularity<br>Increasing stress on percussive and electronically synthesized sounds |
| Important Forms | Forms of Classical period used and expanded in a variety of ways | Forms of all previous periods used, though changed in many ways<br>Freer forms developed |
| Important Types of Compositions | Types of compositions from Classical period, often expanded<br>Newly developed symphonic poem and solo song cycle | Types of compositions from all periods used and expanded<br>New types evolve |

A number of composers chose to avoid traditional forms and developed new freer forms. Compositions were often made up of a continuing series of ideas with brief recapitulations from time to time. Other works involved constantly changing themes or motives held together only by a repeated ostinato. No generally settled pattern emerged, and wide experimentation has continued to the present day.

## Trends in Twentieth-Century American Music

Most of the trends in western art music of the early twentieth century were the products of the ideas and creativity of European composers. Well into the century, American composers and performers were strongly influenced by European musical thought. During the first half of the twentieth century, American composers and performers began to reach a high level of accomplishment and maturity, increasingly independent of the Europeans. During this time, European-influenced and native musical ideas can be seen in different and sometimes curious mixtures and proportions. At the same time, American music for the first time began to exercise its own influence overseas. World War I proved a watershed for many aspects of American art and life, and not least for music. During the heady, affluent decade that followed the war, many American composers turned from the old German-dominated tradition to follow new paths and find new sources of inspiration in French music.

French influence

The general fascination with all things French that characterized the attitude of young American artists in the 1920s was particularly liberating to music. The French tradition encouraged the absorption of new influences in a way that German late Romanticism did not.

Griffes

Charles Tomlinson Griffes (1884–1920) was stirred by the Impressionism of Debussy. In his works for piano, orchestra, and chorus, Griffes achieved an Impressionistic, neutral tonality, making use of unresolved dissonance, bitonal ostinatos, and augmented chords. His last and probably greatest work was his *Piano Sonata.* (1917–18). But perhaps his most enduring and most popular work was his symphonic poem *The Pleasure Dome of Kubla Khan,* which he orchestrated in 1917. In the next generation, other young Americans were stimulated by their study of French music to become both more French and more American in their styles of composition. Having learned the new techniques, they set to work to apply them to indigenous American sources.

Influence of Nadia Boulanger

Many of the aspiring young American composers of the 1920s studied in Paris with Nadia Boulanger (1887–1979), whose influence as a teacher of composers, performers, and music scholars remains of considerable importance. From her the young composers acquired a grasp of the principles, not merely the surface appearance, of the new developments in French music. In particular they gained an understanding of the early work of Stravinsky. Many of them began to intermix exotic elements in their compositions. At the same time, a number of them and their French counterparts discovered and made use of the melodic, harmonic, and rhythmic wealth contained in American folk and ethnic traditions. From Oriental music they learned the uses of unusual scales, and when they looked back across the Atlantic to their own American heritage, they found the rhythms of jazz, folk music, and religious tunes. The result of all this innovation was not the founding of any one American school or sound but rather the subsequent development among twentieth-century American composers of quite dissimilar styles. Music historian Otto Deri has divided these twentieth-century styles into four groups, with some overlapping among them: Nationalists, Traditionalists, Progressives, and Experimentalists.

## Nationalism

### Gershwin

Like the Nationalist composers in Europe, those in America attempted, in varying degrees, to base their work on native folk styles. For the Americans this meant especially jazz, religious music and folksongs. One of many important nationalist composers was George Gershwin (1898–1937). Skillful at handling both popular and more complex styles, Gershwin wrote numerous successful popular songs and musical comedies as well as concert works such as *Rhapsody in Blue* (1924) and *Porgy and Bess* (1934–35), his great opera about people and life in black America. His great talent as a melodist allowed him to capture the spirit of an era in his popular songs and musical comedies from the 1920s. Perhaps more than any other composer, he possessed the ability to incorporate the techniques of jazz into concert music and opera.

The music of Aaron Copland (b. 1900) is at times very abstract and at other times strongly and clearly American. Many of his works quote traditional American melodies, and his musical style often seems evocative of the American spirit for less specific reasons. Copland's music will be discussed in more detail in Chapter 26.

## Traditionalism

### Neoromantics and Neoclassicists

The composers of the Traditionalist group are generally identified by their devotion to the music of the past. They can be divided into two very different subgroups. The Neoromantics favor a style that has evolved out of the Romantic tradition. The Neoclassicists, on the other hand, tend to place greater value on universal means of expression presented within rather strictly circumscribed forms.

### Barber

A composer who in many respects typifies the Neoromantic style is Samuel Barber (1910–1981). His music is generally lyrical and tonal but with unusual harmonies. *Adagio for Strings* (1936) and the earlier *Dover Beach* (1931) for voice and string quartet are popular examples of his work. *Knoxville: Summer of 1915* (1947) for soprano and orchestra is a superb example of Barber's lyricism at its peak. His *Concerto for Piano*, written in 1962, is a very engaging work featuring complex and driving rhythms. His opera *Anthony and Cleopatra* was commissioned for the opening of the new Metropolitan Opera House in New York in 1966.

Piston

The Neoclassical side of Traditionalism can be seen in the work of the New Englander Walter Piston (1894–1976). Piston studied with Nadia Boulanger in Paris and later taught music at Harvard, where he remained as an instructor and a major writer of textbooks until he retired in 1960. Piston composed almost exclusively for orchestra and chamber group. He wrote one ballet, *The Incredible Flutist* (1938), which is among his most highly praised works. His music is characterized by clearly defined melodies that display considerable variety of motion and mood. His harmony relies on a tonal foundation with a rich contrapuntal texture. And, as one might expect, he particularly favored Classical forms: his principal works include eight symphonies, sonatas, and concertos.

## Progressivism

Progressive composers have developed styles more modern than those preferred by the Traditionalists. Their techniques, however, have been largely those already developed to some extent by other composers—atonality, serialism, and new rhythmic devices, among others.

Sessions

One of the leading Progressives is the Brooklyn-born Roger Sessions (1896–1985). In 1925, after his early studies, he began a period of foreign travel that included trips to Italy and Germany. In 1933, he returned to the United States to teach. His compositions include operas and works for orchestra, piano, and chamber ensemble. Sessions' musical style has changed considerably through the years. Many of his early works exhibit extreme contrasts of mood, as can be seen in his incidental music for a play, *The Black Maskers* (1923), one of his best known works. He moved from a very Classical approach in the *Symphony No. 1* (1927) to a more chromatic style in the *Piano Sonata No. 2* (1946), and then to twelve-tone serial composition in the *Quintet for Strings* (1958). Other works that are atonal were usually a compromise between serial technique and freely structured chromaticism.

## Experimentalism

A fourth general group of twentieth-century American composers, the Experimentalists, have taken diverse paths in search of new methods, techniques, and materials. One of the earliest, most important and influential of these composers was Charles Ives (1874–1954).

Ives

Many of the works that resulted from Ives' remarkable combination of a highly imaginative temperament and complete professional freedom were quite extraordinary. Ives anticipated by decades some aspects of techniques that later became identified with Bartók, Hindemith, Stravinsky, and even Schoenberg—among them polytonality, atonality, and polyrhythm.

That Ives' early role as a musical innovator went unrecognized can probably be attributed to two main factors. The first was that he did not demand recognition. The other reason was that, unlike such composers as Hindemith and Schoenberg, he never organized his innovations into a system. Instead he roamed widely over whole new musical continents, seeking out and using new technical devices as they served to express the ideas he had in mind rather than as techniques for their own sake.

The extent of Ives' originality and stature has not yet been fully assessed. He was certainly one of the major tonal composers of the twentieth century. Accordingly, his work will be more fully discussed in Chapter 26.

**Cowell**

Another very important Experimentalist in the early twentieth century was Henry Cowell (1897–1965), born in California, the son of impoverished parents. In childhood Cowell had little chance to hear European concert music, but he did hear Medieval Church modes in music played by a local organist, the Oriental melodies of his Chinese neighbors, and the Irish folksongs of his own relatives. As a young man he began to compose, following his own intuition, and though he later acquired some formal training, the eclectic influences of his youth stayed with him. He became a writer as well, producing or collaborating on important works on twentieth-century music and making significant contributions to the study of non-Western music.

Cowell's compositions include works for orchestra, band, chorus, chamber group, piano, and voice. His melodies are based on a wide range of folk sources—American, Japanese, Indian, Persian, Celtic, and others. His harmonies include considerable dissonance, much of it unresolved. He was particularly fond of thick tone clusters.

**Experiments with the piano**

It was, however, in his expansion of the sound-producing capabilities of the piano that Cowell made some of his most fruitful contributions to modern music. Not content with the instrument's ordinary range of timbre, he began to experiment with direct manipulation of the strings and produced some startling new sounds. For example, one of his works, *The Banshee* (a Gaelic spirit who warns of approaching death by her appearance and wailing, 1925), calls for two players—one at the keyboard and the other standing at the crook of the grand piano. The player at the keyboard merely holds down a pedal while the other player sweeps, plucks, slaps, and scrapes the open strings with hand and fingernails, following a specially devised and very precise system of notation. The result is a shrieking, wailing, eerie sound entirely appropriate to the title of the work. In other works, the keyboard is used along with the manipulation of the strings. Such a technique is common today, but Cowell seems to have been the first to make serious use of it. His many experiments with new ways of organizing and representing musical sounds have had wide effect on numerous subsequent composers. Among other innovations, he collaborated in the invention of the rhythmicon (an electronic instrument which could play polyrhythms), and introduced elements of chance and improvisation into his music.

John Cage (b. 1912), who studied with Schoenberg and Varèse, is another composer who has experimented widely with new means and styles of musical expression. He has been one of the most significantly innovative composers of this century. His mature work is representative of the middle decades of our century and after, and it will be discussed in Chapter 28.

Composers whose works are viewed as part of the four trends in American music of the early twentieth century contributed greatly to the artistic growth of America's music. Examples of their compositions will be examined and discussed in subsequent chapters as they are appropriate to the aspects of music style being considered.

Debussy's orchestral work *Prélude à l'après-midi d'un faune* was first performed in Paris in 1894. The innovative spirit of the composition was matched by the choreography the great dancer Vaslav Nijinsky created to the music. This photograph shows him as the faun, in the Ballets Russes' first production of the ballet in 1912. (Victoria & Albert Museum, Crown copyright)

# CHAPTER 25

# French Music at the Turn of the Century

*LISTENING PREVIEW A number of different trends are apparent in late nineteenth-century music as composers sought new means of musical expression. The Frenchman Claude Debussy was one of the most innovative composers in the late years of the 1800s. He was influenced by many ideas of his predecessors, but he also frequently broke from traditional procedures of composition and explored new techniques. Listen to the opening section of his* Prélude à l'après-midi d'un faune *(side 9, band 5) and give special attention to the free sense of harmony and rhythm. Although the meters indicated in the score are very important to the performers, notice that it is nearly impossible for the listener to tell that the meter of the opening section alternates among $\frac{8}{8}$, $\frac{6}{8}$, and $\frac{12}{8}$. Debussy avoids a clear recurrence of regular pulses and creates a very fluid, rhythmic effect.*

## Impressionism

**Impressionist paintings**

The term *Impressionism*, now a respectable label for one of the most significant artistic movements of modern times, was first applied in derision to the work of a group of avant-garde French painters in the late nineteenth century. The revolutionary style of painting found in the works of Monet, Manet, Renoir, and others emphasized the play of light on a subject, using diffused outlines and subtly interwoven colors to suggest sentiments and moods. This fascination with light led to a preference for outdoor themes shaped and shaded by the changing sunlight at different seasons and different times of day. A fine example of the style is seen in Monet's *Water Lilies* (1917) shown in the art work presented on page 385.

**Symbolist poetry**

The literary counterpart of Impressionist painting was the Symbolist movement in French poetry. Led by Mallarmé, Verlaine, Rimbaud, and the Belgian Maeterlinck, it repudiated the moralism, sentimentality, and inflated literalness it found in late Romanticism. Symbolist poets delighted in atmosphere and nuance, shading their landscapes indistinctly in the manner of the Impressionist painters. They wanted readers to sense the emotion in their poetry, not be told about it. Their verses deliver their meaning subtly and with only the vaguest of assertions, relying on the suggestive possibilities of sound and metaphor rather than on definable meaning. Using words and phrases designed to arouse subconscious feelings, the Symbolists allowed no technical restrictions to interfere with the achievement of their goals. Traditional poetic forms and styles were often sketched, broken, or replaced by ambiguous, irregular structures.

## Impressionism in Debussy's Music

The composer who above all epitomizes Impressionism in music is Claude Debussy (1862–1918). It was one of his early works—a cantata entitled *La damoiselle élue* ("The Blessed Damoiselle," 1887–88)—that first drew the label of Impressionism to music. It was Debussy's mature work, however, that not only demonstrated but largely determined the very nature of Impressionism in music.

Debussy himself disliked the label "Impressionist" for his music, since he was not trying to imitate the Impressionist painters. Instead he was attempting to set French music free from the heaviness and formalism he perceived in the dominant German tradition. He wanted to return French music to its fundamental sources in nature—to allow it to find once again its own lighter, freer genius and express what he felt it was best fitted to express. In this sense he could almost be called a nationalist. And indeed he learned a great deal from the Russian nationalists who were his contemporaries, though he rejected their strongly folk-oriented style. His most immediate associations were perhaps with the Symbolist poets, whose subject matter he often used; he was a friend of Mallarmé.

Nonetheless, Debussy and the composers he influenced had much in common with the Impressionist painters. Like the painters, they sought to appeal to the senses rather than the intellect of their audiences. While Romantic music had generally tried to express well-defined emotions or ideas, the style developed by Debussy was more understated and less specific. Although Debussy used many Romantic devices—suggestive titles, colorful and changing timbres, motivic melodies—he used them in more subtle ways. The result was seemingly an unresolved harmonic style and a diffused sense of musical color and motion analogous to the luminous outlines and the play of light and color in Impressionist painting. In fact, some of the favorite images of the new painters—moving water, rustling leaves—lent themselves readily to Impressionist treatment in music.

Impressionist music is in many ways more difficult to define than earlier styles of music. Although Debussy himself had a clear goal in view, he deliberately tried to avoid falling into any predictable patterns. Above all he insisted on the freedom to use whatever compositional devices might best serve the needs of his current subject. Not all of Debussy's music is considered Impressionist. And those qualities that are considered Impressionist change significantly from piece to piece because he never ceased experimenting with new material and absorbing new influences.

*Influence of nature*

Certainly one major influence on Debussy's music was his great love of nature. The relationship he saw between nature and music is perhaps best expressed in his own words:

> I can imagine a music specially designed for the open air, all on big lines, with daring instrumental and vocal effects which would have full play in the open and soar joyfully to the treetops. Certain harmonic progressions which sound abnormal within the four walls of a concert hall would surely find their true value in the open air. Perhaps this might be a means of doing away with these little affectations of over-precision in form and tonality which so encumber music.

In a way, this sounds very close to some aspects of the early Romantic ideal. But the direction Romanticism had taken in its later years was as unacceptable to Debussy as was the passionate, often unlovely realism that had grown from it. Rejecting the overt realism of novelists such as Flaubert and Zola and their direct identification of art with life, he rejected also the programmatic explicitness and overpowering sound of Berlioz and Wagner. He created instead an ... rld of suggestion, delicately hinted at rather than boldly

... as a principal means by which Debussy achieved his ...se of harmony was perhaps his most revolutionary ...n traditional practice. While Classical and earlier Roman- ... had treated chords as functional elements in a har- ...ssion, Debussy and the Impressionists came to regard ...ness of a chord as separate from its context. The effect ...ecame an end in itself. If a certain chord seemed ...king, it might be repeated up and down the staff in the ...el motion that had been specifically forbidden in the ...e previous centuries. Parallel *chords* or *chord streams* ...ypical in Impressionist harmony can move by any ...en move by step, as in this passage from Debussy's *La ...nade* ("Evening in Granada," 1903):

*pp*    *pp*

*Increased dissonance*

By use of parallel chords and other similar techniques, Debussy weakened the traditional pull to the tonic note. He also introduced a number of other combinations of tones—triads with added ninths, elevenths, and even thirteenths—which often did not resolve as expected.

Debussy's harmony is also distinguished by the variety of scales he used. He is particularly identified with the *whole-tone scale*, which he found in the works of some other composers and in the music of the Far East. It is the basis for quite a number of his melodic and harmonic passages. The whole-tone scale divides the octave into six whole-step intervals rather than the seven half- and whole-step intervals of the conventional Western scale:

Whole-Tone Scale

Lacking the half steps of the conventional scale, the whole-tone scale is especially suitable if the composer is seeking to escape from the dramatic pull of major-minor tonality. Whole-tone harmony has a muted, ambiguous quality that greatly suited Debussy's purposes. He employed it often and quite imaginatively.

At times, Debussy also used the Church modes and the pentatonic, or five-note, scale common in Chinese music and in some Western folk music. One pentatonic scale results from sounding all the black piano keys in one octave. Pentatonic scales tend to avoid resolution and tonal centers. The chromaticism that had already become widespread in late Romantic music is likewise important in his work. In his desire to avoid predictability, however, he seldom depended completely on any one of these scales. In many of his works, he shifted back and forth among different scales in order to get just the tonal color he wanted.

The effect of Debussy's harmonic practice was not to destroy the concept of key but to expand it. In his works a new standard of consonance and dissonance evolved. Traditional dissonance often went unresolved, and even a final cadence was merely less dissonant than the chords that preceded it. A key was no longer a defined area in harmonic space with clearly identifiable boundaries. Instead it became an elusive entity, sensed as just a little bit out of reach but still somehow exerting an influence on the music.

Debussy's music is seldom explicitly contrapuntal, though occasional countermelodies do rise briefly out of the underlying chords. Often there seem to be several shifting layers of sound in his orchestral pieces, some static, some moving. His use of parallel motion and chord streams creates a generally homophonic style. At times, however, broken chords and other techniques help to establish a complex and lively polyphony. And at other times monophonic passages are heard, focusing the music temporarily into a clear, pure line. Texture is often as amorphous as the harmony, sometimes being a frequently changing flow of sound.

Debussy's melodies differ markedly from the strong, broadly articulated themes of his immediate predecessors. His melodies are generally built from short motives of narrow range freely combined, often repeated and changed. They use chromaticism frequently, often ambiguously. Whole-tone and pentatonic scales and Church modes are used to create unusual melodic and harmonic effects.

The beat in Debussy's music is often veiled by the use of syncopation and irregular subdivisions of measures. Rhythms thus seem to flow across metrical boundaries, and the pulses are seldom stressed. This indistinctness of meter contributes greatly to the desired effect of understatement and suggestiveness. In other works, however, Debussy used a clear, pulsing beat that is, at least for a short time, regularly recurring.

*Changes in timbre*

Debussy and his followers often composed for large orchestras, but they rarely sought the powerful, overwhelming effects of late Romanticism. Rather, the orchestral sound was veiled, and individual timbres were made to stand out delicately against it—the somber lower-register tones of flute and clarinet, the clear high notes of the violin, the muted voices of horn and trumpet. There were numerous solo passages for flute, oboe, and English horn. The harp was often featured, alone or with other instruments. And diverse percussion instruments—timpani, cymbals, glockenspiel, celesta, xylophone, and so on—added color to the orchestral sound. Debussy was also a highly accomplished pianist. His writing for piano makes sensitive use of the instrument's broad range of colors and effects. In his music timbre is always a central element of the overall effect.

*Freer forms*

Debussy disliked being bound by traditional forms and sought new, more flexible patterns. He believed that form should arise out of the subject matter of a work instead of being, in the older fashion, imposed upon it. In his larger works, he sometimes made general use of Classical structures, but always with much freedom, introducing motives and returning to them in obedience to the flow of musical ideas rather than according to preset patterns. While it is possible to discern the presence of contrasting sections in these works, the beginnings and endings of sections often overlap. Thus, in form as in all other elements of his music, Debussy tried to replace sharp definition and conclusive statement with suggestion and ambiguity. He wished to leave his listeners not with an answer but with an impression.

Many of the characteristics that contribute to Debussy's style of Impressionism in music are found in one of his early, best-known works, *Prélude à l'après-midi d'un faune*. A close examination of the work reveals how individual techniques and methods contribute to the style.

## *Debussy:* Prélude à l'après-midi d'un faune

In 1892 Debussy began work on a composition inspired by Stéphane Mallarmé's long poem *L'après-midi d'un faune* ("The Afternoon of a Faun"). Although Debussy intended to make his composition a long work of several movements, only the prelude was completed. The opening lines of the poem set the mood as the faun, light-footed and magical in his human shape with tiny horns and small goat feet, contemplates or imagines the airy nymphs:

Ces nymphes, je les veux
    perpétuer.
      Si clair,
Leur incarnat léger, qu'il
    voltige dans l'air
Assoupi de sommeils touffus.
    Amais-je un rêve?
Mon doute, amas de nuit
    ancienne, s'achève
En maint rameau subtil, qui,
    de meuré les vrais
Bois mêmes, prouve, hélas!
    que bien seul je m'offrais
Pour triomphe la faute idéale
    de roses
Réfléchissons …
    ou si les femmes dont
    tu gloses
Figurent un souhait de tes
    sens fabuleux!
Faune, l'illusion s'échappe
    des yeux bleus
Et froids, comme une source
    en pleurs, de la plus
    chaste:
Mais, l'autre tout soupirs,
    dis-tu qu'elle contraste
Comme brise du jour chaude
    dans ta toison?
Que non! par l'immobile et
    lasse pâmoison
Suffoquant de chaleurs le
    matin frais s'il lutte,
Ne murmure point d'eau que
    ne verse ma flûte
Au bosquet arrosé d'accords;
    et le seul vent
Hors des deux tuyaux
    prompt à s'exhaler avant
Qu'il disperse le son dans
    une pluie aride,
C'est, à l'horizon pas remué
    d'une ride,
Le visible et serein souffle
    artificiel
De l'inspiration, qui regagne
    le ciel.

*These nymphs I would*
    *perpetuate.*
      *So light*
*their gossamer embodiment,*
    *floating on the air*
*inert with heavy slumber.*
    *Was it a dream I loved?*
*My doubting, harvest of the*
    *bygone night, concludes*
*in countless tiny branches;*
    *together remaining*
*a whole forest they prove, alas,*
    *that since I am alone,*
*my fancied triumph was but the*
    *ideal imperfection of roses.*
*let us reflect …*
    *or suppose those*
    *women that you idolize*
*were but imaginings of your*
    *fantastic lust!*
*Faun, the illusion flows from the*
    *blue eyes,*
*icy as a spring of tears, of the*
    *one more chaste.*

*But that other one, all sighs, do*
    *you say she is different,*
*like a warm day's breeze ruffling*
    *in your fleece?*
*Ah, no! Through the motionless,*
    *oppressive swoon*
*that chokes with heat the cool*
    *morning if it struggles*
*no water flows save that which*
    *spills from my flute*
*onto the harmony-sprinkled*
    *thicket; and the only wind,*
*quick to breathe out through the*
    *twin pipes before*
*scattering the sound in a dry*
    *rain,*
*appears on the still*
    *horizon*
*like the seen, serene, and*
    *artificial breath*
*of inspiration, returning*
*heavenward.*

**Debussy:Prélude à l'après-midi d'un faune**

## LISTENING ANALYSIS

Debussy's *Prélude* is scored for three flutes, two oboes, an English horn, two clarinets, four horns, two antique cymbals, two harps, and strings. A solo flute presents the first theme—a theme made up of several juxtaposed motives:

First Theme

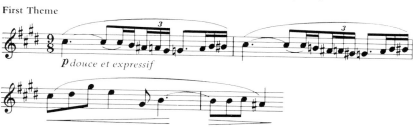

Harps, wind instruments, and muted strings enter to mark the end of the flute theme. The theme is then repeated and ornamented with irregular subdivisions of beats. This rhythmic irregularity, coupled with rather frequent changes in meter, creates a vague sense of beat and an easy, fluid rhythmic flow. Through much of the work, the strings are divided—the viola section, for example, is given two lines to play at the same time rather than just one. This division helps create a dense texture, but the dynamic level is generally low and the strings are often muted, so the effect is never overpowering. The prominence of flute and harp aptly reinforces the summery, pastoral quality of the work.

Harmony is quite chromatic, as can be seen in the accidentals of the first theme. The listener, however, is not strongly aware of dissonance because of the subtle nature of the music. While Debussy has clearly tried to avoid strong commitment to a particular key, there is nevertheless a slight emphasis on one note as the tonal center most of the time.

**Middle section** A contrasting middle section is introduced by a new theme in the woodwinds supported by a syncopated chordal accompaniment in the strings:

Second Theme

**Last section** The theme is extended with numerous changing and conflicting rhythms. The first theme then returns in a completely new setting.

While the work fits generally into a ternary pattern, the listener is much more aware of the use of timbre, motive, and rhythm than of any traditional formal structure. The *Prélude* has the vivid yet vague quality of a dream.

## LISTENING SUMMARY

Timbre: large orchestra of string and wind instruments and antique cymbals
Melody: opening theme, which is built from several motives, is most prominent; second theme features descending motion
Rhythm: basic $\frac{9}{8}$ meter with some changes; moderately slow tempo
Harmony: quite chromatic with a slight feeling of tonal center
Form: free ternary (ABA[1])

The singer Mary Garden who, at Debussy's request, created the female title role of *Pelléas and Mélisande* in 1902. (Bibliothèque Nationale, Paris; photo: Heritage of Music)

Debussy's innovative *Prélude* later provided inspiration for an equally innovative ballet. The work was first choreographed by the great Russian dancer Waslaw Nijinsky (1890–1950), who substituted stylized, two-dimensional movements reminiscent of a Greek frieze for the ordinary ballet steps. Like the music, the ballet was received with mixed feelings. Nijinsky's more conservative fellow choreographer Michel Fokine could scarcely bear to watch it.

Other works by Debussy

Among Debussy's other Impressionist works are two sets of preludes for piano, three nocturnes and *La Mer* ("The Sea," 1903–05), for orchestra, the opera *Pelléas et Mélisande*, a string quartet, and a number of songs. His piano pieces show that he wrote very effectively for that instrument. He was able to obtain from the piano a number of unique and highly innovative effects.

## Debussy: "Feux d'artifice," from Préludes, Book II

Debussy's twenty-four preludes for solo piano, in two books of twelve each, were composed during the years 1910 to 1913 and are miniature masterpieces in the Impressionist style. Each prelude bears a different descriptive title, such as "La sérénade interrompue" ("The Interrupted Serenade") and "La cathédrale engloutie" ("The Submerged Cathedral"), but the titles are placed at the end of each of the preludes in parentheses, suggesting, perhaps, that they should not be given too much importance. One of the most brilliant of the preludes is "Feux d'artifice" ("Fireworks"). This could well have been a subject for an Impressionist painting. It vividly suggest flashes of light created by fireworks against a dark sky, appearing singly first, then in greater, overlapping profusion to create more and more dramatic effects.

### LISTENING ANALYSIS

SIDE 9, BAND 6

"Feux d'artifice" comprises several sections that often contrast with one another in tempo, rhythm, tonal center, dynamics, and intensity. As in *Prélude à l'après-midi d'un faune*, however, form seems subordinate to other musical elements, and the sections flow easily from one to the next.

The opening section is built on a very rapidly repeated triplet pattern that creates a blur of sound in the middle register of the piano. The right hand plays occasional high notes, mostly in octaves, over the triplets. One can relate these short notes to single flashes of light at the beginning of a fireworks display. The section closes with a long glissando from very high to very low on the piano.

The next section begins with alternating notes between the right and left hands but then changes to rapid, short scale passages. In the third section a recurring figure in the right hand is heard over an ever quickly moving accompaniment.

Now the music goes suddenly softer. In the several short sections that follow, a quickly changing variety of rapid arpeggios, scale passages, and glissandos are heard, as well as a few varied repetitions of the rapid figure shown above. Although dynamics change within each of the sections, a general crescendo can be discerned as the piece progresses; the long crescendo finally culminates in a burst of harmonic color, played fortissimo, just before the final return to a slow tempo near the conclusion. The piece ends with two motives, played very quietly, from the French national anthem, *La Marseillaise*, closing a brilliant display of fireworks and pianistic virtuosity.

The rapid rhythmic motion throughout most of the piece sometimes serves as a foil for the periodic flashes of light suggested by the right-hand part. Sometimes both hands share in creating a show of virtuosity and a striking array of diverse harmonic sonorities. Changing meters, rhythmic patterns, and tempos, along with the chromatic harmony with frequently changing tonal centers, contribute to the free, sectional structure of "Feux d'artifice." The work is a spectacular finale to an extraordinary collection of musical images.

## LISTENING SUMMARY

| | |
|---|---|
| Timbre: | piano |
| Melody: | predominantly motivic with considerable rhythmic variety |
| Rhythm: | basic $\frac{4}{8}$ meter, with changes to $\frac{2}{8}$, $\frac{5}{8}$, and $\frac{6}{8}$; tempos range from very slow to moderately fast, with very rapid rhythms within these |
| Harmony: | very chromatic, with frequent changes of tonal center |
| Form: | freely sectional; seems subordinate to rhythm and harmony |

Debussy died in 1918, a victim of cancer. In his own lifetime, he was recognized as a composer of singular importance. He was admired throughout Europe for his almost Classical restraint and sense of proportion—qualities not always shared by the many composers who imitated his style. While his work may be said to mark the end of the Romantic style, it is more important as the beginning of a new age of musical style at the opening of the twentieth century.

Les Six, from left to right: Darius Milhaud, Georges Auric, Arthur Honegger, Germaine Tailleferre, Francis Poulenc, and Louis Durey. Seated at the piano: their "propagandist" and occasional librettist, the poet and novelist Jean Cocteau. (Roger-Viollet; photo: Lipnitzki-Viollet)

## Satie and Les Six ("The Six")

About 1916, six young French composers who opposed some of the ideals of the Impressionist style banded together to advocate the return to clarity and simplicity inherent in the contemporary Neoclassical movement. The group came to be called "Les Six," and included Georges Auric (1899–1983), Louis Durey (1888–1979), Arthur Honegger, Darius Milhaud, Francis Poulenc, and Germaine Tailleferre (1892–1983). Of these, Honegger, Milhaud, and Poulenc became particularly well known. Among Honegger's most important works are his oratorios *Le roi David* ("King David," 1921) and *Jeanne d'Arc au bûcher* ("Joan of Arc at the Stake," 1934–35). Poulenc established himself as a master of smaller compositions, particularly songs, as well as larger forms such as his opera *Les dialogues des Carmélites* (1953–56), which is about a group of nuns martyred during the French Revolution.

*Satie*

A mentor of "Les Six" in the early years of their association was the older French composer Erik Satie (1866–1925), a friend of Debussy, who had a keen sense of humor. Satire and whimsicality are apparent even in the titles of some of his works. An obvious example can be found in his piano piece *Trois morceaux en forme de poire* ("Three Pieces in the Shape of a Pear," 1903). In another work, the lighthearted ballet *Parade*, his style is especially concise and reserved, but still satirical. Like Debussy, Satie was influenced by his associations with poets. But these were the Surrealists and Dadaists, who deliberately fragmented words and ideas in the way the Cubists did visual images. *Three Pieces in the Shape of a Pear* is a surrealist title.

Satie and "The Six" attempted to write clear, neatly constructed pieces that would entertain and bring pleasure to their audiences. Aided by new dissonant harmonies, some of them wrote witty parodies of the highly passionate favorites of the past. These comic works served a dual function: they helped to purge certain antiquated musical techniques, and they also helped to express through satire the frustration and discontent of the new age.

## The Music of Ravel

Perhaps the best known of all twentieth-century French composers after Debussy, however, was Maurice Ravel (1875–1937). His music ranges from Impressionist as in his ballet *Daphnis et Chloé* (1909–12), to Neoclassical. No doubt the ballet *Boléro* is his best-known work, with its brilliant orchestration and its single rhythmic pattern repeated throughout. Two piano concertos exemplify his mature abstract style. The *Concerto for the Left Hand* (1929–30), written for the pianist Paul Wittgenstein (1887–1961), who had lost his right arm in World War I, is an unusual and vibrant virtuoso work. The second piano concerto, the *Concerto in G* (1929–31), is a very attractive, rather concise composition that demonstrates Ravel's knowledge and love of the instrument for which it was written.

Ravel (right) and Nijinsky playing the piano; Paris, 1914. (Bibliothèque Nationale, Paris)

### *Ravel:* Concerto in G

**First movement**

Ravel's *Concerto in G** is in three movements and is scored for piano and large orchestra with many percussion instruments as well as a harp. The harmony is tonal, but dissonance is both frequent and prominent.

The first movement is in sonata form with no development section. The movement begins with a quick tempo and agitated arpeggios in the piano supporting the first theme in the piccolo. Here the piano is clearly used as part of the orchestra, accompanying another solo instrument. The tempo then slows somewhat as the piano becomes the solo instrument. The second theme, played by the piano, is lyrical and at first rather slow moving. The bassoon repeats the theme, supported quietly by the rest of the orchestra and piano. The quick tempo then returns with the closing material of the exposition, throughout which the piano nimbly plays chordal and arpeggiated patterns. A brief scale passage for the solo piano functions as a transition to the recapitulation. Then the themes are repeated and developed in expected order. A unique characteristic of the recapitulation is that the piano plays the second theme as part of a solo cadenza, ornamented throughout with trills. A vivacious closing section follows, and the movement ends with a crisp, descending scale for the orchestra and piano.

**Second movement**

The slow, second movement provides melancholy contrast to the first. Its form is ternary. The first section features the piano by itself for many measures, playing a hauntingly lovely melody in triple meter:

First Theme

But while the theme is clearly in triple meter, its accompaniment in the left hand seems to be straining constantly toward a $\frac{6}{8}$ meter. The result is a very subtle rhythmic tension. The shorter middle section of the movement emphasizes arpeggios and scales in the piano. This leads to the final section, which begins with a repeat of the first theme played by the English horn and accompanied by the piano and other instruments.

**Third movement**    The third movement, cast in sonata form, returns to a fast tempo. The tempo is so quick, and the themes appear so rapidly, that it seems likely that Ravel was more interested in creating an impressive, virtuosic effect. Several themes appear in the exposition, each heralded by four sharply accented chords. The piano prepares for the first theme by playing a whirlwind pattern of chords alternating between left and right hands. Then the theme itself is introduced by the clarinet:

First Theme

The rhythmically surprising second theme is then played by the piano:

Second Theme

The third theme is played by the horns, then by the trumpets, in $\frac{6}{8}$ meter. The closing section of the exposition features a flashing succession of scales and arpeggios played by the piano.

A long crescendo builds throughout the development section. The sound begins quietly in the cellos and basses. Bassoons, harp, and other instruments are gradually added, playing parts of the first three themes. The recapitulation comes without pause or warning, as the piano suddenly begins the opening theme, which the clarinet had presented before. The other themes follow in the expected order, rising to a brilliant ending with the four accented chords from the exposition.

French music at the turn into the twentieth century provided some of the most vital and innovative trends in all of Western music at that time. Ideas of French composers influenced many composers in other countries, and the effects of their ideas continued well into the middle of the century.

# CHAPTER 26

# *New Styles of Tonality*

*LISTENING PREVIEW Composers in the early twentieth century found new ways to emphasize a central tonality in their music without using traditional harmonic progressions. They devised new harmonic progressions that were tonally centered, or they repeated a tone or motive to establish a tonal center. Listen to the opening section of the "Danse sacrale" from Stravinsky's ballet* Le Sacre du printemps *(side 10, band 2). Even though the harmony is purposely harsh and dissonant, notice that Stravinsky repeats a note, chord, or motive throughout a section, thereby creating an emphasis on one tone or a small group of tones.*

## Experiments with Tonality

Two main lines of development can be perceived in the music of the early twentieth century. While some composers experimented with radically new ways of using tonality, others chose to produce atonal works that avoided tonality entirely. For people familiar with the traditional musical styles of the Western world, the works of the first group of composers are generally easier to comprehend.

Many of the early twentieth-century composers felt that their music had to be based on some concept of tonality. A few continued to use the major-minor system of harmony to create tonal sounds. Others explored older modal systems and new harmonic systems, while retaining the emphasis on tonal centers.

Different styles of tonality

Among the most important composers of tonal music were Bartók, Hindemith, and Stravinsky. None of them can be easily categorized. Each explored, digressed, and experimented too much to fit under any single label. Stravinsky's works are especially varied, liberally mixing many different styles, rhythms, harmonies, and forms, and have had probably the greatest influence of any modern, tonal compositions on other composers. Bartók's works have a distinctive individual quality that makes them difficult to compare with other music. And Hindemith's works, although somewhat more systematic and consistent than those of Stravinsky and Bartók, show significant changes over the years. Two major American composers, Charles Ives and Aaron Copland, have in common with them an experimental outlook combined with a basic orientation towards tonality that distinguish their best-known works. All of these composers share a number of characteristics that set their works apart from those of the

Stravinsky playing *Le Sacre du Printemps*; drawing by Jean Cocteau.

more sharply revolutionary atonalists—the most obvious, of course, being their adherence to tonality.

## The Music of Bartók

### Influence of folk music

Several different influences can be seen in the works of Béla Bartók (1881–1945). In his youth he was caught up in the nationalist movement in his native Hungary, and he shared the typical nationalist interest in folk and peasant music. He traveled to rural areas of Hungary to discover the music of the peasants, rather than contenting himself with the more familiar and accessible gypsy music. He worked as an ethnomusicologist, collecting and transcribing into musical notation folksongs of Hungary and neighboring countries. The advent of the phonograph enabled him to record the material accurately for later analysis. Like a number of his contemporary composers, he found in folk music a key to new avenues of melodic and harmonic development. Most of his early works were based on folk melodies, some of which he had collected himself.

Bartók's interest in folk music was not limited to Hungarian melodies but encompassed a wide range of different European and Near Eastern styles. Romanian, Slovak, Arabian, Turkish, and Serbo-Croatian melodies can all be found in his early works. A certain Oriental quality is often heard, reflecting the Asiatic origins and affinities of many of the peoples of southeastern Europe. In this respect, Bartók's work can be considered a link between the music of the East and West.

Bartók also drew, indirectly, on the work of other composers. His string quartets have a textural richness reminiscent of Beethoven. His style of harmony and his orchestration both seem to have been influenced in minor ways by the works of Liszt and Richard Strauss. His driving, percussive rhythms show some influence of his great contemporary Stravinsky. However, it was the music of Debussy that most influenced his mature compositions. From a study of the works of the French Impressionist master, Bartók learned a great deal about modern orchestration and the effectiveness of transparent texture. He was surprised and delighted to find that Debussy used the pentatonic scale that he himself had earlier championed. He attributed the coincidence to their mutual interest in Russian folk music.

### "Night Music"

Finally, though perhaps less profoundly, Bartók responded to nature, the sounds of which sometimes provided him with both material and inspiration. In the five piano pieces of his *Out-of-Doors Suite* (1926), and in several other works as well, he tried to re-create the ambience of the night and its creatures. One of the movements, "The Night's Music," shows his unusual sensitivity to the sounds of the countryside. Against a pianissimo background of thick, dissonant chords, he set a melody that suggests the chirping and croaking of frogs and other nocturnal creatures. In other works, however, Bartók's ideas were much more abstract. In his early *Improvisations on Hungarian Folksongs*, for example, he used sounds that were probably derived more from his imagination than from close observation or imitation of real events.

In effect, Bartók achieved a synthesis of a variety of folk styles and older and newer elements of the Western art music tradition. Drawing on both these influences, he developed a number of original compositional techniques, many of which have become standard practice among twentieth-century composers. For this reason, and also because Bartók's music is of consistently high quality, a study of his works can serve as a useful introduction to contemporary music.

Béla Bartók during rehearsal with violinist Rudolph Kolisch for *Music for Strings, Percussion and Celesta.* Photograph (c. 1940)

Melody

Bartók's melodies tend to be fairly simple. They are often largely defined by the scales he used. These include not only the pentatonic, whole-tone, and various European folk scales but also three- and four-note scales derived from Arabic music, which contribute a certain exotic effect to his works. Occasional melodies make use of all twelve chromatic tones.

Octave displacement

One interesting melodic practice that Bartók often used is *octave displacement*—that is, the placing of successive notes of a melody in different octaves. Although the device is also used in the works of many of Bartók's contemporaries, he himself apparently learned it from peasant music. "Hungarian peasants do not devote much care to selecting a suitable pitch," he wrote. "Whenever a note is too high or too low for them, they transpose it by an octave, regardless of design and rhythmic conditions."

Bartók rarely ornamented his melodies, preferring to expand them by other means. One such means was harmony. His simplest melodies are often accompanied by especially exotic and complicated harmonies, as can be seen in his collection of folksong arrangements *For Children* (1908–09, revised 1945).

Rhythm assumes a special importance in Bartók's music. Other musical elements are often subordinated to it, and many of his works generate an overwhelming rhythmic energy. Sometimes this energy is the result of an insistent repetition of groups of notes accented by chords. At other times, energy is created through the use of asymmetrical and changing meters, dance and speech rhythms, or irregular subdivisions of beats. Most of these techniques are used in his *Mikrokosmos* (1926–39), a collection of graded piano pieces that can almost serve as an inventory of Bartók's compositional techniques.

Polyrhythms

Bartók also made much use of *polyrhythms*—a type of rhythmic counterpoint in which several different rhythms proceed simultaneously.

Many different harmonic techniques can be found in Bartók's works. The wide variety of scales he used made it possible for him to achieve new and complex effects without wholly abandoning the relationship to a tonal center. The tonal relationships in his works are often quite ambiguous. Even in passages suggesting traditional harmony, he systematically avoided any distinction between major and minor modes. In his more innovative works, he went considerably further, often introducing some degree of bitonality while remaining fundamentally concerned with the relationship of all the tones to a single tonality. He also made much use of *tone clusters*—very dissonant chords made up of several adjacent tones.

Tone clusters

Much of Bartók's music is contrapuntal. There are many passages of great richness, with each of the independent lines adding color and density to the sound. He also believed that the physical positioning of the different instruments on the stage played an important part in the proper rendering of texture. In *Music for Strings, Percussion, and*

*Celesta* (1936), for example, he stipulated that the two string orchestras involved should be separated by the other instruments.

Bartók's timbres are typical of twentieth-century music, with the range of tone colors extended in almost every possible direction. In his *Concerto for Orchestra* (1943, revised 1945), the use of a wide variety of solo and group sounds was one of his central goals. *Music for Strings, Percussion, and Celesta* calls for a double string orchestra with celesta, piano, harp, xylophone, timpani, and a number of other percussion instruments. (The *celesta*, invented in 1886, is a small keyboard instrument with steel bars that are struck to produce sound.) Because of his interest in rhythm, Bartók placed special emphasis on percussion instruments. He also used a number of other instruments, notably the piano, in a very percussive manner.

Bartók was also innovative in his use of form. Throughout his career he made use of the structural principles of earlier music, following at least the general outlines of such Classical forms as the sonata and rondo; but the manner in which he arrived at a formal plan was always fresh and imaginative. For instance, the last half of a piece sometimes took the form of a mirror inversion, making the piece a *palindrome* (e.g. ABCB'A'). In a general sense, he remained committed to traditional patterns of thematic contrast, development, variation, and recapitulation.

**Motivic development**

Form in much of Bartók's music depends greatly on his method of motivic development. He often built entire movements or works from motives or the smallest of phrases. A motive of perhaps only two or three notes is varied, developed, extended, and transformed continually in the course of a work. Thus a movement or composition seems to grow organically into its final shape and form, emerging out of material introduced at the beginning.

## Bartók: Music for Strings, Percussion, and Celesta

Bartók's *Music for Strings, Percussion, and Celesta** is one of his best known works. It can also be used to illustrate many aspects of his style. First performed in 1937, it was commissioned in honor of the tenth anniversary of the Basel Chamber Orchestra. The orchestra is of moderate size and includes the usual string section, harp, xylophone, cymbals, bass drum, timpani, side drums, piano, and celesta. Bartók specified in the score how the orchestra was to be arranged:

| | **Double Bass I** | **Double Bass II** | |
|---|---|---|---|
| **Violoncello I** | **Timpani** | **Bass Drum** | **Violoncello II** |
| **Viola I** | **Side Drums** | **Cymbals** | **Viola II** |
| **Violin II** | **Celesta** | **Xylophone** | **Violin IV** |
| **Violin I** | **Pianoforte** | **Harp** | **Violin III** |
| | | **Conductor** | |

*Béla Bartók, *Music for Strings, Percussion, and Celesta*. Copyright 1937 by Universal Edition; renewed 1964. Copyright and renewal assigned to Boosey & Hawkes, Inc. for the U.S.A. Excerpts reprinted by permission. Also reprinted by permission of Theodore Presser Company, sole representative in Canada and Mexico.

The work is in four movements of contrasting tempos and moods. A central tonality is clearly stressed in each movement, although little reference is made to traditional harmony.

### First Movement: Andante tranquillo; Fugue

The first movement is a neatly structured fugue. The subject, presented by the violas, immediately sets the character of the movement by its chromaticism and constantly changing meters:

Subject

The broken lines indicate subdivisions of measures, added to help performers in counting.

The subject is restated a number of times in different ways. The texture gradually becomes denser until eight parts are finally heard in the strings and celesta. After the climax of the movement, the subject is presented in inverted form in the second half of the fugue. The movement is centered basically around A, the starting and ending pitch of the movement, but Bartók's chromatic style avoids strong references to a tonal center in the course of the movement. The entrances of the fugue begin on pitches that are alternately a fifth higher and lower, starting from the first A and proceeding until E♭ is reached. Then the process is reversed until the movement returns to A for the close.

**Bartók: Music for Strings, Percussion, and Celesta, *Second Movement***

▸LISTENING ANALYSIS                                    SIDE 10, BAND 1

The second movement is cast in a rather straightforward sonata form. The main theme is introduced at once. It begins with a two-note motive that recurs throughout much of the movement.

Main Theme, Violin Part

Glissando

The line between the first two notes indicates a *glissando* or slide—an extremely rapid and sequential playing of all the tones between the two notes. Forms of the two-note motive close the exposition and are heard at the opening of and during the development section. All of the themes in the second movement are related to and seem to grow from the fugue subject of the first movement.

Bartók takes full advantage of instrumental color throughout the movement. The strings, for example, are played with a great variety of techniques—at times pizzicato, sometimes with a mute, occasionally close to the bridge at the center of the instrument to produce a dry and harsh sound, and at other times with harmonics, that is a partial depressing of the strings to produce a light and feathery sound. In certain places Bartók specifies the use of a strong pizzicato in which the string strikes the fingerboard; ordinary pizzicato is used in other places. Although the strings introduce much of the important thematic material, they sometimes seem to function almost as percussion instruments, presenting short motives in a dry, staccato manner. Bartók's unusual arrangement of the orchestra also adds to the effect. When the two groups of strings play in dialogue together, the percussion instruments are heard, not behind them, but between them.

**LISTENING SUMMARY**

Timbre: orchestra of moderate size with string instruments, percussion instruments, and celesta

Melody: several themes built from motives; disjunct motion favored; main theme features chromatic upward sweep

Rhythm: mainly $\frac{2}{4}$ meter with some other meters used as well; tempo Allegro (fast)

Harmony: tonal but dissonant at times; begins and ends with tonality centered on C

Form: sonata

### Third Movement: Adagio; Sectional Form

"Night Music"    The third movement quietly explores the sounds of the individual instruments and is a fine example of Bartók's "Night Music." It consists of six sections that relate to each other as follows:

A    xylophone and timpani accompany the viola that presents thematic material

B    violins and celesta present contrasting material

C    celesta, harp, and piano feature glissandos

D    a percussive section, the second half of which is a retrograde of the first

BC    melodic material of the B section and glissandos of the C section

A    melodic material and instrumentation of the first section return

The fugue subject of the first movement is the source of all melodic material in this movement, and motives from it also serve to link the sections.

### Fourth Movement: Allegro molto; Free Rondo Form

The final movement opens with a brief passage of sweeping pizzicato chords in the strings. The main theme is a transformation of the fugue subject, now cast in the Lydian mode (like a major scale with a raised fourth degree). Several sections contrast with the opening one.

Shortly before the close, the fugue subject returns in a form close to its original, but somewhat more diatonic. Changing meters, vital rhythms, and engaging counterpoint contribute to the effect of the movement.

## Other Works

Bartók was a noted pianist and teacher before his merits as a composer were widely recognized. By the 1920s, however, his works were well known in Europe and the United States. Like many twentieth-century composers, his life and career were disrupted by Nazism in Germany. He reacted earlier than most, banning all performances and broadcasts of his music in Germany and Italy in 1937. In 1940 he emigrated to New York. He never found professional security in America, though he received a grant from Columbia University and commissions for such major pieces as the *Concerto for Orchestra*. He died of an illness in 1945, leaving nearly completed his *Piano Concerto No. 3*.

Other major works by Bartók include the opera *Duke Bluebeard's Castle* (1918); *The Miraculous Mandarin* (1926, a ballet); Piano Concertos No. 1 and 2, and two violin concertos. Several chamber works, notably six remarkable string quartets, *Contrasts for Violin, Clarinet and Piano* (1938), and the *Sonata for Two Pianos and Percussion* (1937), are also important. He wrote many songs and folksong arrangements for solo and choral voices, and a larger choral work, the *Cantata profana* (1930). His major works for solo piano are the *Allegro barbaro* (1911), the *Sonata* (1926), and *Mikrokosmos*.

Bartók achieved a unique synthesis of artistic and folk elements in his music. As his style developed, his works became more and more complex in rhythm, texture, and harmony. But he never completely abandoned tonality. Throughout his career he devoted himself to writing in a clean, compressed, and economical style—a style that drives continuously forward with an especially dynamic vitality.

## The Music of Stravinsky

The works of Igor Stravinsky (1882–1971) are so wide-ranging and varied that any summary of his contribution to music must necessarily be incomplete. Never content to repeat past successes and always eager to continue the search for new techniques, Stravinsky moved from style to style throughout his life. His early pieces show many traces of the style of his first teacher, Rimsky-Korsakov. Especially attributable to Rimsky-Korsakov is Stravinsky's early use of Russian and Oriental melodies within a basically German-Romantic harmonic system. Other formative influences included Debussy and Scriabin. However, Stravinsky soon discarded most of their characteristics along with his early technique.

**Early use of folk music**   In the writings of his later years, Stravinsky linked his knowledge of Russian folk melodies with his youthful nationalist enthusiasm. Early in his career, he studied several collections of peasant music, including one prepared by Rimsky-Korsakov. Although he did not as a rule base his work explicitly on folk sources, many of his earlier pieces display undeniable folk characteristics. Three melodies in the *Firebird* (1910), one in *Les Noces* ("The Wedding," 1917), and one in *Petrouchka* (1911) were all intentionally taken from folk music. But in general, Stravinsky's works, like Bartók's, contain more exotic tendencies than overt folk elements, as is particularly evident in *Petrouchka* and the *Firebird*. Nationalism affected Stravinsky in much the same way that it did Bartók. It influenced his early works but soon diminished greatly as a source of inspiration, perhaps reflecting his exile from his home country.

**Early ballets**   The early years of Stravinsky's career were spent mainly in Russia. During this "Russian period," Sergei Diaghilev (1872–1929) commissioned him to write a number of ballets, some of which are now among his best known works. The *Firebird* was his first major success. Its initial performance was in Paris, where from 1910 he spent much time. He became an instant musical celebrity, and he gained the friendship and acclaim of Debussy, Ravel and other composers all over Europe. A year later he added to his success with *Petrouchka*. And two years later, in 1913, he produced a third ballet, *Le sacre du printemps* ("The Rite of Spring"), also premiered by Diaghilev's Ballets Russes. This last had a sensational impact. Now regarded as one of the most important works of the twentieth century, it roused the first-night audience to such violent reactions that the music could barely be heard.

The *Firebird Suite*, taken from the ballet, is distinguished by its brilliant use of timbre, orchestration, and texture. In place of the Romantic ideal of blended timbres, Stravinsky followed Rimsky-Korsakov and emphasized the contrast and opposition of timbres. Each instrument or group retains its unique sound. In Stravinsky's later works, this tendency toward separation of timbres became even more pronounced.

**Music and dance**   In his early ballets Stravinsky had to learn to cope with the special problems that confront the composer who writes music for dancers. In addition to the basic problems of creating new musical ideas and casting them in an appropriate format to be played by a desired performing group, the composer must be sensitive to the capabilities and limitations of dancers. If there is a program or narrative involved, how can it be best portrayed or suggested by the music? Is the music appropriate to the various types of movements of the dancers? Does the entire composition and its individual movements provide enough time and proper musical support for dancers to choreograph their movements? It is very helpful and usually essential to the composer to work with the choreographer of a ballet, so that they may coordinate the music and choreography. Diaghilev made it a policy to employ only the best designers and choreographers as well as composers. In Picasso, Fokine, Balanchine, Massine, and Diaghilev himself, Stravinsky found superb collaborators.

## Stravinsky: Le sacre du printemps

Stravinsky's third major ballet, *Le sacre du printemps*, or *The Rite of Spring*,* describes a pagan fertility ritual in which a young girl dances herself to death to appease the god of spring. The ballet is in two parts and consists of the following movements:

### Part 1  The Fertility of the Earth

Introduction
Dance of the Youths and Maidens
Dance of Abduction
Spring Rounds
Games of the Rival Towns
Entrance of the Celebrant
The Kiss of the Earth
Dance to the Earth

### Part 2  The Sacrifice

Introduction (The Pagan Night)
Mystic Circle of the Adolescents
Dance to the Glorified One
Evocation of Ancestors
Ritual Performance of the Ancestors
Sacrificial Dance

Costume design by Nicolas Roerich for the first performance of Stravinsky's *Le Sacre du Printemps*, Paris 1913. (Bakhrushin Theatre Museum; photo: Novosti Press Agency)

*Igor Stravinsky, *The Rite of Spring*. Copyright 1921 by Edition Russe de Musique. Copyright assigned 1947 to Boosey & Hawkes, Inc. Excerpts reprinted by permission.

Stravinsky's score, with a melodic, harmonic, and above all rhythmic inventiveness that surpassed even the boldness of his own earlier works, seemed to push music to the brink of anarchy. Stravinsky had long been willing to experiment with every compositional element to reach his expressive goals. In *The Rite of Spring*, his previous stylistic innovations crystallized.

**Rhythmic innovations**

Melodies in *The Rite of Spring* are very motivic, with each motive treated as part of a process of constant variation. But it is probably in the rhythm that the most startling innovations are found. Early in the work, Stravinsky introduced a new rhythmic device that soon became a favorite of many composers. It is the use of two quick beats that occur continuously, but in which the accent pattern changes and is often syncopated to the accompaniment. The result is a rhythm that generates surprising energy. Additional rhythmic devices used in *The Rite of Spring* include driving ostinato rhythms, frequent changes of meter, and polyrhythms. Another of Stravinsky's typical procedures, one that astonished listeners at the time, involves the rhythmic transposition of motives to different beats. A motive that originally began on the first beat of a measure might, when repeated, begin on the second beat or on any other later beat.

Unusual harmonies abound in *The Rite of Spring*. A variety of scales are used along with uncommon intervals and pandiatonicism. Frequent clashes of harmony are made possible by Stravinsky's clear definition of each tonality within the multitonal whole.

**Texture**

Texture in the work varies greatly, ranging from very sparse to extremely dense. A huge orchestra is needed. The brasses alone include eight horns, five trumpets, three trombones, and two tubas. The woodwind and percussion sections are even larger.

**Intricate score**

Like many other modern composers, Stravinsky included meticulous directions to the performers in the score. Dynamic and tempo markings abound. Stravinsky provided other helpful advice as well. In a note at the beginning of the score, for example, he explained that at least five timpani would be needed and suggested ways in which the timpani players could divide their labors. The music requires highly skilled players. Individual parts are very demanding; even counting beats is difficult since the meter changes so often. The work is an outstanding orchestral showpiece.

Form in *The Rite of Spring* is determined largely by the content and structure of the ballet. Musical form seems to grow out of the variation and evolution of motives and rhythms. Stravinsky's love of rhythmic invention is most apparent in the climactic last movement, the "Danse sacrale" ("Sacrificial Dance").

**Stravinsky: Le sacre du printemps**

**LISTENING ANALYSIS**                                                    SIDE 10, BAND 2

The movement opens with a series of chords played in irregular rhythms and constantly changing meters. The metrical pattern of the first twelve measures is shown as follows:

| 3 | 2 | 3 | 3 | 2 | 2 | 3 | 3 | 2 | 3 | 3 | 5 |
|---|---|---|---|---|---|---|---|---|---|---|---|
| 16 | 16 | 16 | 16 | 8 | 16 | 16 | 16 | 8 | 16 | 16 | 16 |

The rhythm continues to be unpredictable and driving throughout the dance.

Single chords and several different motives are explored. The most important motive in the first section (A) is heard near the beginning:

Prominent Motives

All of the instruments are used percussively in the dance. Indeed, the orchestra seems at times to function as one large percussion instrument. Even the strings, so often noted for their lyrical qualities, play short motives in a percussive manner.

A second, quieter section (B) continues to feature single, percussive chords, punctuated with a new motive.

The motive is developed and the section is expanded to some length before the crashing chords and motive of the first section reappear. Soon though, another contrasting section is heard (C), featuring brass (including the eight horns), timpani, and low strings. The opening chords and motive recur briefly before this section is expanded further. Finally they return prominently to bring the dance to a dramatic conclusion. Although the materials and sections tend to blend into one another, they generally relate to each other as ABA'CA'', and create a very free rondo form.

The music is tonal in that certain tones are stressed through repetition or through frequent reappearance. The harmony is generally quite dissonant when compared with earlier music, but it seems most appropriate to Stravinsky's goals.

**LISTENING SUMMARY**

Timbre: very large orchestra of string, wind, and percussion instruments
Melody: short repeated motives emphasized
Rhythm: meter changes frequently, often every measure; quick tempo
Harmony: tonal centers emphasized through repetition of central notes; dissonant harmony
Form: free rondo (A B A' C A'')

Stravinsky lived in Switzerland during World War I, where in 1918 he wrote *L'histoire du soldat* ("The Soldier's Tale"). It marks, according to Stravinsky himself, his final break with the Russian orchestral school. A brief stage work with a small ensemble, it resounds with angular, unblended timbres and percussive rhythms. Stravinsky's choice of instruments was influenced by his discovery of jazz, and the work seems to have been designed as a showpiece for unusual timbres. Throughout, Stravinsky pushed the instruments to the extreme limits of their ranges, emphasizing wide leaps and other virtuoso effects. We find characteristically complex rhythms with driving ostinatos as well as the increased use of counterpoint that became common in Stravinsky's Neoclassical period.

## Neoclassicism and later works

After World War I and the Russian Revolution, Stravinsky was never to return to live in Russia. From 1918 he lived in Paris for fifteen years. Still associated with Diaghilev's Ballets Russes, he was called upon in 1919 to orchestrate some eighteenth-century music by the Italian composer Giovanni Battista Pergolesi (1710–1736) for a ballet called *Pulcinella*. At first reluctant, Stravinsky soon became deeply involved in the project. He later recalled, "*Pulcinella* was my discovery of the past, the epiphany through which the whole of my late work became possible. It was a backward look, of course—the first of many love affairs in that direction—but it was a look in the mirror, too." Stravinsky had entered his Neoclassical phase.

The orchestra required for *Pulcinella* and for the suite derived from it is much smaller than that needed for *The Rite of Spring*. Stravinsky specified a number of solo string players, a small group of orchestral strings, and a small section of wind instruments. He also stipulated that the entire orchestra should consist of thirty-three players. While Stravinsky used much of Pergolesi's harmony, which today seems very consonant, he did inject occasional dissonances of his own. He also made use of eighteenth-century forms in *Pulcinella*.

Abstract principles of structure seemed to dominate Stravinsky's works thereafter. Neoclassical works such as the opera-oratorio *Oedipus rex* (1927) abound with references to other ages and styles, notably those of the Baroque and Classical periods. Responding to criticism that his music had become derivative and reactionary, Stravinsky wrote, "A real tradition is not the relic of a past irretrievably gone; it is a living force that animates and informs the present." The real purpose of Stravinsky's Neoclassicism seems to have been the establishment of discipline—not of form but of style.

*Oedipus rex*, set to a text by Jean Cocteau (1889–1963), offers a fine example of Stravinsky's fully developed Neoclassical style. He used text and melody sparingly, mainly to support other elements. The music is developed continuously, in such a way that each passage seems to unfold into the next. This type of construction contrasts with the basically Romantic structure of his early works, in which the music seemed to move in blocks or sections of form, timbre, and tonality. Finally, the work shows the repeated superimposition of contrasting harmonic materials and the resulting polychords and polytonality so highly favored by Hindemith.

Stravinsky's life was that of a major cultural figure. In Paris, his friends were outstanding artists in all fields. He moved to Hollywood

Stravinsky in his Paris studio, 1929. (Roger Viollet; photo: Lipnitzki-Viollet)

in 1940, and in 1945 became an American citizen. His associations with prominent literary figures—T. S. Eliot, W. H. Auden, Aldous Huxley, and Dylan Thomas, to name a few—led to collaborations of which the finest is the Neoclassical opera *The Rake's Progress* (1951), with a libretto by Auden and Chester Kallmann based on drawings by William Hogarth. Unlike Schoenberg, Stravinsky found acknowledgement and much success in America. He was honored by President and Mrs. Kennedy in 1962 and in the same year returned for a visit to Russia, where he was warmly received.

In sum, Stravinsky stands out among twentieth-century composers as one of the most versatile and certainly the least predictable. He explored a multitude of possibilities, from the paganism of *The Rite of Spring* to the solemnity of the *Symphony of Psalms* (1930) and beyond. For each work he established a unique harmonic and rhythmic framework. Many of his works confounded both critics and admirers. It seemed that his daring knew no limits, yet most of the techniques he adopted were in fact derived in some way from some previous composer or style. For a long time, it appeared that Stravinsky's approach to music was irrevocably opposed to serialism. But toward the end of his life, after the death of his neighbor Schoenberg (with whom he had no contact), he surprised his audiences with a group of serial compositions. (His works of this type will be considered, along with other modern serial works, in Chapter 27.) In spite of all the diverse sources he drew upon, Stravinsky's music is always thoroughly individual.

# The Music of Hindemith

The German composer Paul Hindemith (1895–1963) was one of the leaders of the twentieth-century attempt to make serious music more accessible to the general public. He was influenced by the Neoclassicism of Stravinsky and also by the atonal composers. But he felt that much modern music, especially the atonal styles, ignored the listener's desire for simplicity, directness, and personal involvement. Composers, Hindemith believed, had stressed virtuosity for its own sake and had proceeded without regard for principles of beauty. In doing so they had abdicated one of their basic responsibilities to their audience—they failed to communicate. As a result, Hindemith asserted, they could not expect their work to be of any lasting value.

**Gebrauchsmusik**

It was Hindemith's intention in the late 1920s to replace this compositional self-indulgence in "music for music's sake" with what he called *Gebrauchsmusik*, or "music for use." Following Gebrauchsmusik principles, a composer wrote music to suit the needs and level of understanding of the audience, and composed music for performance by amateurs. Composers had to bear in mind other factors, such as the place where the music was to be played and the abilities of the performers. Furthermore, Hindemith strongly suggested that to achieve a proper Gebrauchsmusik, composers had to adopt a rational, logical approach and base their music upon certain basic principles of order. To Hindemith, this insistence on logic and order in no way conflicted with the creative process. It comes as no surprise that he was a renowned teacher and theorist, as well as a professional violist.

While never abandoning his emphasis on order and logic, Hindemith did, as he grew older, become somewhat less rigorous in his adherence to the stern principles of his youth. The harsh demands that he placed on himself and his music softened, and his work grew in expressive power and lyricism. This mellowing process had the effect of introducing into his music certain Romantic elements that he

**Hindemith conducting a youth orchestra in 1932. (The Bettmann Archive/BBC Hulton Picture Library)**

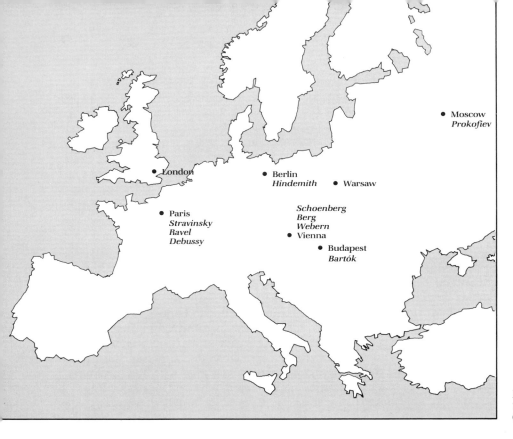

Major composers of the early twentieth century in Europe (*left*) and the USA (*right*).

had earlier rejected. After 1940 he gave increasing thought to the symbolic qualities of his music. He believed, along with the philosophers and mystics of many cultures, that the relationships of the elements in music were symbolic of a higher order in the spiritual universe. Thus in his song cycle *Das Marienleben* ("The Life of Mary," 1959), the various tonalities are given symbolic values. The basic key of E is associated with Christ, the dominant key of B is identified with Christ's earthly being, and the other keys are linked with spiritual ideas of greater or lesser importance, depending on how close they are harmonically to the key of E.

**Opposition to extreme harmonic innovation**

With his Classical bent for system and order, Hindemith objected strenuously to the harmonic experiments of some of his contemporaries. In his fifties he wrote:

> Yet, if anything seems to be of little reward, it is the search for originality in harmony. After a thousand years of research, experiment, and application, harmony has become thoroughly known; no undiscovered chord can be found. If we have to depend on novelty in harmony, we might as well write our last funeral march for the death of our own music.... there is only a limited number of harmonic and tonal combinations, and no matter how big this number is, it will be exhausted after centuries of continuous use. (*A Composer's World*, pp. 138–39)

He also accused his most important antagonists, composers of serial

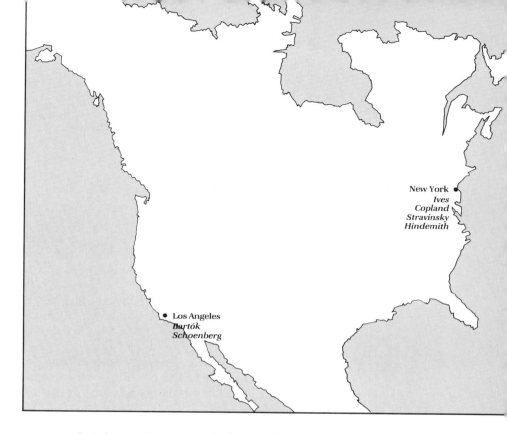

New York ●
*Ives*
*Copland*
*Stravinsky*
*Hindemith*

● Los Angeles
*Bartók*
*Schoenberg*

music, of violating the "natural" laws of sound. He likewise attacked other modern composers and in general objected strongly to new avant-garde systems.

Hindemith's own music includes works for large orchestras, small ensembles, and solo instruments. (Following the principles of Gebrauchsmusik, he wrote at least one sonata for each of the commonly used instruments.) His music is noted for its lean, uncompromising style. Even when the texture becomes occasionally complex, a sense of clarity prevails.

Harmony, as Hindemith himself recognized, was the point on which he differed most profoundly with other twentieth-century composers. In his *Craft of Musical Composition* (1937), he elaborated his theories, maintaining among other things the absolute necessity of tonality. The system that he developed was based on a threefold premise. First, there exists only a finite number of possible combinations for the intervals of the twelve-tone scale. Second, each interval has a natural, unchangeable relationship with all the others and with the central tonalities. Third, if these relationships are not preserved, music must necessarily descend into chaos.

Hindemith's own harmony, the result of the practical application of his theories, makes use of the twelve tones of the chromatic scale around a tonal center. He often uses triadic harmonies, or quartal harmonies, that is, harmonies based on the interval of the fourth.

Other passages seem modal in design, harking back to older scales—an element probably derived from his conservative training.

Critics have pointed out that Hindemith's assertion about the limited number of harmonic possibilities ignores certain elementary truths of composition. They maintain that the values and meanings of chords and intervals are not fixed but vary constantly according to the context in which they are used.

Hindemith emigrated to the United States in 1940, and taught at Yale until he settled in Switzerland for the last years of his life. While teaching (1940–1953) at Yale he directed an early music ensemble. His deep involvement with early music influenced his style, in that modal harmonies and other aspects of early music often appear.

For the forms of his compositions, Hindemith turned to the German musical heritage, making use of both Baroque and Classical models. He resurrected the concerto grosso, the toccata, and the fugue as well as the balanced structure of the Classical sonata. His *Ludus tonalis* ("Tonal Game," 1942) for solo piano includes excellent fugal writing and shows his knowledge of the great keyboard fugues of Bach. He also wrote duo sonatas for a number of different instruments. He developed a particular fondness for dance forms and was also one of the first European composers to become interested in jazz. All of his music, regardless of its inspiration or form, is classical in the widest sense. It has a logic of design and makes clear use of the basic principles of repetition and contrast. If Stravinsky represents the eclectic, radical side of tonal composition during the early twentieth century, Hindemith embodies its more conservatively innovative aspect.

## Hindemith: Mathis der Maler Symphony

Hindemith's most famous work is *Mathis der Maler** ("Matthias the Painter"), written in 1934. First presented as an opera, it is best known today in the form of a symphony excerpted from the original score. The full-length opera dramatizes the life and art of Renaissance painter Matthias Grünewald (? 1480–1528). Against the background of the Reformation and a peasant revolt, Matthias engages in a personal and moral struggle. Repudiating both his deep commitment to painting and the favor of a powerful patron, he decides to join the peasants. When the peasants are defeated, he flees with his newfound love, the daughter of the peasant leader, and endures trial, uncertainty, and disillusionment. At last, having relived in a vision the temptation of Saint Anthony, a subject from his greatest altarpiece, he devotes himself again to his art.

The opera centers on the question of how an artist can go quietly about his work while people are struggling and suffering all around him. For what reason does the artist create art that it should be pursued under such circumstances? The question is as relevant today

*Hindemith: "Mathis der Maler Symphony." Copyright 1934, B. Schott's Sohne. Copyright renewed 1962. Excerpts reprinted by permission.

as it was during the Reformation or in Hindemith's own time. It is significant that the opera dates from the early years of the Hitler era.

The *Mathis der Maler Symphony* is scored for an orchestra of moderate size. Included are pairs of flutes, oboes, clarinets, bassoons, and trumpets, four horns, three trombones, tuba, timpani, percussion, and strings. Apart from the trombones, tuba, and percussion, the orchestra is like one from the late Classical era. The melodies and harmonies of the symphony, and of the opera, were influenced by medieval modes, Gregorian chants, and popular religious songs of the Reformation.

The symphony has three movements. Each is derived from the opera score and named after one of the several panels in Grünewald's great Isenheim altarpiece, now at Colmar in France (one panel can be seen on page 83).

### First Movement: Ruhig bewegt (quietly moving); Ziemlich lebhaft (rather lively); Sonata Form

**Introduction**

The first movement, the overture of the opera, is entitled "Angelic Concert," in reference to the panel that shows angels singing a hymn at the birth of Christ.

---

**LISTENING ANALYSIS**                                    SIDE 10, BAND 4

In the introduction that precedes the sonata form, Hindemith features an early German chorale, *Es sungen drei Engel* ("There Sang Three Angels"). The melody of the chorale is first presented in moderate tempo by the trombones:

Introductory Theme Based on Chorale

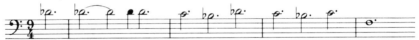

An active countermelody in the strings is woven around it.

**Exposition**

After the chorale tune is heard twice more, the sonata form begins with a quick theme in duple meter:

First Theme

Two other themes follow—one quiet and stately, the other more nervous and quick moving. The opening motive of the movement's first theme then returns to close the exposition.

**Development**

The development opens briefly with the first theme followed by the second. The two themes and motives from them are juxtaposed and tightly interwoven. The "Three Angels" chorale then returns broadly in triple meter in the trombones. It is then combined with the second theme and presented twice more as it builds to a grand climax.

**Recapitulation**

The first theme is recapitulated, but not at the original tonal level. The quickly moving third theme is then heard. The first and second themes are heard again before the movement closes with the first theme. Thus while Hindemith's use of the Classical sonata form is basically quite clear, he was obviously not bound by any predetermined order of themes within the structure.

**LISTENING SUMMARY**

Timbre:    orchestra of moderate size with string, wind, and percussion instruments

Melody:    German chorale melody used in introduction; three main themes in main body of movement

Rhythm:    introduction in $\frac{9}{4}$ meter, tempo Ruhig bewegt (quietly moving); main body of movement in $\frac{2}{2}$ meter, tempo Ziemlich lebhaft (rather lively)

Form:      sonata with introduction

### Second Movement: Sehr langsam (very slow); Ternary Form with Coda

The second movement, "Entombment," comes from the last scene of the opera and calls to mind the scene of Christ's burial. The mood is intense and restrained. Dissonant harmonies and changing meters contribute to the movement's great expressiveness. The first theme rises haltingly, and the second theme is somewhat more angular. The first theme returns, and the movement ends with a brief coda.

### Third Movement: Sehr langsam (very slow); Sehr lebhaft (very lively); Ternary Form with Coda

The final movement, "The Temptation of Saint Anthony," begins with a slow, dramatic introduction. The excitement of the opening section is created by a fast tempo and lively rhythms incorporated into the two themes. After a dynamic climax is reached, a slow, quietly contrasting section begins. There is a return to a quicker tempo and broader dynamics with some new thematic material and a repeat of the first theme. A return of the introductory material and a presentation of the Gregorian chant hymn "Lauda Sion salvatorem" ("Sion, Praise Thy Savior") constitute a concluding section or coda.

Theme Based on Gregorian Hymn

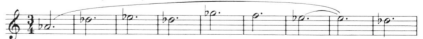

The final measures, preceded by a pause, are marked "Alleluia" in the score and provide a dramatic climax of broad chords. The ending seems to rejoice over both the saint's triumph and the painter's renewal of faith.

## Hindemith's Ideals

Hindemith's career was further linked to German art by his friendship with the painter Max Beckmann (1884–1950). The two men seem, like Picasso and Stravinsky, to have shared a common spirit. Both belonged to the humanist tradition, recognizing their responsibilities to others as well as to their art. Partly because of their political sympathies, their work was declared "degenerate" by the Nazis, and they were forced to leave Germany. Later both taught in the United States, where they received high acclaim for their achievements.

It was Hindemith's lifelong goal to reorient contemporary music in directions he thought consistent with historical traditions and the natural laws of music. Although his influence has varied from one decade to another and his harmonic system has been rejected by many composers, Hindemith is still regarded as one of the most important composers of the twentieth century.

## The Music of Ives

Innovation is a primary element in the music of the American composer Charles Ives (1874–1954). Ives was born in Danbury, Connecticut. His father was a bandmaster who combined an intelligent love of the classics with a passionate curiosity about all sorts of sounds. These enthusiasms he passed on to his son. At a time when polytonality had scarcely yet been thought of in Europe, Ives was learning to sing familiar songs in one key while his father accompanied him in another key. When chromaticism was still the furthest limit of daring for most American composers, Ives was hearing quarter-tone intervals on an instrument his father had invented. He was also trained by his father in the counterpoint of Bach.

Charles Ives; photograph by W. Eugene Smith. (CBS Records)

Ives studied music at Yale but decided not to make it his career. He knew that the kind of music he wanted to write would never earn him a living in his own generation. He remained an amateur composer all his life, while he ran a prosperous insurance agency for a living. As a very successful insurance agent, he made himself relatively secure against financial worries and was free to experiment musically as he would. However, he did serve briefly as organist for several churches, notably Central Presbyterian Church in New York.

Though he was often criticized for his lack of contact with professional concert life, Ives's freedom from traditions proved to be a great advantage. He was, in fact, so far ahead of his time that most of the conductors and performers to whom he occasionally showed his work considered it unplayable. Indeed, the greater part of his music remained unknown until after World War I. Significantly, one conductor who did express a willingness to present one of his symphonies was Gustav Mahler, but Mahler died before the project could be carried out. Ives himself seemed content to leave his work unknown and unplayed if the musical public showed itself disinclined to hear it, though he did publish some of his works privately.

Melody

Ives' treatment of melody was often surprising. He was very fond of quoting from hymns, popular songs, folk songs, or well known classics in order to establish a desired emotional context. Once this was done, however, he might alter and develop the melodies in unexpected ways—inverting them, turning them around, or expanding or diminishing the intervals.

Rhythm

His rhythmic techniques caused more conservative composers to consider his work "hopeless." He frequently used irregular meters such as $\frac{5}{8}$, $\frac{11}{8}$, or $\frac{7}{4}$, as Stravinsky was later to do. Occasionally he avoided metrical consistency altogether and instead simply added a bar line wherever he wanted to begin a new measure.

Harmony

In harmony and texture, he was equally complex. In fact, he seemed to disregard all preconceptions about the structure and function of chords. His music is full of polytonal and occasionally atonal passages. He also made much use of free, dissonant counterpoint—sometimes so dense that the ear can scarcely distinguish the lines. Some of the tone clusters in his music written for piano were unplayable by ordinary means, so he specified that a piece of wood be used to press all the necessary keys at once.

The sum total of this extreme harmonic dissonance and rhythmic irregularity was more than many listeners of Ives' day could understand. Many heard only clashing chaos. But Ives had something to say with this dissonance. He seems to have felt that each line of music, like each human being, had a certain right to an independent existence. If the various independences sometimes clashed—well, that was acceptable. He believed, and wrote, that music should concern itself with life's ideas and experiences, dissonance and all.

Antiphonal effects

One further device to which Ives' regard for musical independence led him was the use of antiphonal effects, in which different performing groups were stationed in different parts of the performing area. Such a technique was used in *From the Steeples and the Mountains* (1901), for brass instruments and bells, and in *The Unanswered Question* (1908).

In general, Ives' use of form was as free as his use of the other musical elements. Whether writing for orchestra, chorus, solo voice, piano, or chamber group, he used traditional forms only insofar as they served to express his ideas. He studiously avoided symmetrical and balanced construction, and within single movements he often allowed great disparity of mood and material. In his *Concord Sonata*, for example, passages of great difficulty and sophistication alternate with references to popular music. The unity found in Ives' works lies partly in his use of theme and structure and partly in his use of programmatic ideas.

## Ives: "Fourth of July"

Ives' "Fourth of July"* (1911–1913) is one of the four movements in an orchestral work entitled *A Symphony: Holidays*. This particular movement shows his adventurous style to good advantage. The other movements are "Washington's Birthday," "Decoration Day," and "Thanksgiving." The orchestration of the symphony is for large sections of wind, string, and percussion instruments.

Ives prefaced the score with the following brief description:

*Ives, "The Fourth of July." Copyright © 1959 by Associated Music Publishers, Inc. Excerpts used by permission.

It's a boy's "4th,"—no historical orations—no patriotic grandiloquences by "grown-ups"—no program in his yard! But he knows what he's celebrating—better than some of the county politicians. And he goes at it in his own way, with a patriotism, nearer kin to nature than jingoism. His festivities start in the quiet of the midnight before and grow raucous with the sun. Everybody knows what it's like. The day ends with the sky-rocket over the Churchsteeple, just after the annual explosion sets the Town-Hall on fire.

**LISTENING ANALYSIS**                                              SIDE 10, BAND 3

The work opens with a sustained and muted F♯ major chord in the low strings. At the same time, the first violins softly play the opening motive "Columbia, the Gem of the Ocean" in the key of C♯ major. The music thus begins with a clear example of the use of bitonality.

Opening Motive and Chord

In the second measure, suggestions of a new key in the second violin make the sound even more dissonant. String basses and tuba in turn play the opening motive in different, slow rhythms while a dissonant counterpoint is begun in one of the violin parts. The meter changes frequently—$\frac{4}{2}$, $\frac{4}{4}$, $\frac{7}{8}$, $\frac{4}{4}$, and so forth. Dissonance continues to grow as other instruments enter and the tempo and dynamic level gradually increase. Motives from "Columbia, the Gem of the Ocean" are heard again and again.

A climax approaches as the violin plays a brief excerpt from the "Battle Hymn of the Republic," followed by a motive from "The Battle Cry of Freedom" in the horn. Soon the horns and then the trumpets play a short passage from "Reveille":

Theme Based on "Reveille"

The mood then changes as the steady rhythm of a dissonant march begins. The piccolo, however, subtly slips in a phrase of "The Girl I Left Behind Me." The march is finally interrupted by a sudden explosive burst of sound, with tone clusters in the strings: the fireworks have started. Here as in many other passages, several different rhythmic patterns occur simultaneously, creating great rhythmic conflict and confusion. After this brief outburst, the mood becomes very quiet. Chromatic dissonance continues, and an altered version of "Columbia, the Gem of the Ocean" returns in the trombone part:

Chromatic Trombone Line

After the tune has been completed, there is a brief pause. Then furious activity breaks out in the entire orchestra, with dissonant chords, tone clusters, and glissandos in the strings. The sky rocket has obviously gone over the church steeple. The excitement then subsides toward a quiet, dissonant ending.

### LISTENING SUMMARY

Timbre:   large orchestra of string, wind, and percussion instruments and piano
Melody:   themes based on quotations from a number of popular tunes
Rhythm:   meter changes frequently; tempo slow at first, then faster
Harmony:  basically tonal, with chromaticism and dissonance; at times bitonal
Form:     free sectional form

Ives wrote four symphonies and an incomplete fifth, called "The Universe." He composed numerous keyboard works, including the vast *Concord Sonata* (1910–15) which was inspired by four prominent New England figures from the past. He also wrote other orchestral pieces, chamber music, choral works, and more than 150 songs. His music is unique, and his influence on younger American composers such as Copland, as well as on Cowell and other Experimentalists, was important. Ives was the first American composer to take music into new territory, rather than merely continuing to compose in the European tradition. Though figures like Mahler and Schoenberg perceived his genius during his lifetime, his music has not even now found the secure place it deserves in concert repertory.

Aaron Copland, photographed during rehearsal in 1967. (Photo: Erich Auerbach)

## The Music of Copland

The works of Aaron Copland (b. 1900) illustrate many of the trends apparent in American music during the twentieth century. Copland, who was born in Brooklyn of immigrant Russian-Jewish parents, early developed a strong desire to become a composer and in 1921 went to France to study with Nadia Boulanger. Upon his return three years later, he embarked on a career as a composer, as a proponent of new music, and as a concert organizer, lecturer, and conductor.

*Copland's styles*

Copland's early works use jazzlike rhythms, bold dissonances, and occasional Jewish melodies for programmatic and evocative effect. Later he turned away from this style, regarding it as superficial, and produced a series of nonprogrammatic, abstract works including his *Piano Variations* (1930). His works in this middle period were generally quite difficult and seemed most concerned with the working out of purely musical ideas. After 1935, sensing a public mission for composition in the crisis mentality of the Depression era, Copland began writing music for wider, less technically expert audiences. He wrote a number of ballet scores based on American themes of which the most frequently played music is from *Appalachian Spring*, written for Martha Graham in 1944. He also composed a number of scores for films, including the film versions of John Steinbeck's *Of Mice and Men* (1939) and *The Red Pony* (1948). Making frequent use of

American folk and popular music, including cowboy tunes, jazz, ragtime, and hymns, Copland appeared at this stage to be concentrating on communication and not on theoretical problems. The patriotic work *A Lincoln Portrait* (1942) was an extension of his public role into wartime.

**Melody**

The many different elements of Copland's ever-changing style, insofar as they can be identified, seem to be dominated by a desire for organization, clarity, and control. His melodies, flavored as they so often are with folk and religious tunes, are for the most part easily understood. They typically feature conjunct motion with occasional larger intervals. Copland believes that a long melodic line is indispensable and creates it by using repeated motives and adding new materials, so that the melody seems to grow out of itself. His melodies are both distinctive and very attractive.

**Rhythm**

Like most other twentieth-century composers, Copland has been much concerned with rhythmic vitality. Nearly all of his works have an unmistakable rhythmic drive. His earlier pieces are especially noteworthy for their use of percussive rhythms and ostinato. Various other contemporary devices, many of them introduced or made popular by Stravinsky, also appear in his works—among them the use of changing meters and the asymmetrical displacement of accents within the measure. By these and other means, he has achieved the syncopations that give his meters their characteristic unpredictability.

**Harmony**

In harmony Copland has remained rather consistently tonal. Within this framework, he has used a number of now standard modern methods such as polytonality and the deliberate confusion of the major and minor modes. It is true that in some of his more recent works, such as the *Piano Fantasy* (1957), he began to make use of the serial technique. Yet in the vast majority of his work he has retained the triad as the basis of harmony, using it regularly in order to suggest the simplicity and beauty of rural life. The texture of much of his music is rather transparent, with a stress on individual timbres, frequently in their upper ranges.

**Rodeo**

Copland's *Rodeo* is a striking example of the composer's prominent use of American tunes and settings in his works. It was commissioned by the Ballets Russes de Monte Carlo, which specified a ballet on western themes for the company's 1942–43 season; the choreographer Agnes de Mille was named collaborator with Copland. The first performance of *Rodeo* took place at the Metropolitan Opera on October 16, 1942.

Ms. de Mille created the story of the ballet and has described it as follows:

> Throughout the American Southwest, the Saturday afternoon rodeo is a tradition. On the remote ranches, as well as in the trading centers and the towns, the "hands" get together to show off their skill in roping, riding, branding and throwing. Often, on the more isolated ranches, the rodeo is done for an audience

that consists only of a handful of fellow-workers, womenfolk, and those nearest neighbors who can make the eighty or so mile run-over.

The afternoon's exhibition is usually followed by a Saturday night dance at the Ranch House.

The theme of the ballet is basic. It deals with the problem that has confronted all American women, from earliest pioneer times, and which has never ceased to occupy them throughout the history of the building of our country: how to get a suitable man.

Copland later compiled an orchestral suite (premiered in 1943), comprising four movements under the title *Four Dance Episodes from Rodeo*:

I.   Buckaroo Holiday
II.  Corral Nocturne
III. Saturday Night Waltz
IV.  Hoedown

Several American folksongs are incorporated into the score and may be found in most of the movements. A pseudo-rustic and popular quality results from the use of the folksongs and other folk-like themes throughout the score. It is scored for a very large orchestra—piccolo, two flutes, two oboes, English horn, two clarinets, bass clarinet, two bassoons, four horns, three trumpets, two trombones, bass trombone, tuba, timpani, xylophone, snare drum, wood block, bass drum, cymbal, piano, and strings.

## *Copland: "Hoedown" from Rodeo*

**LISTENING ANALYSIS**                                SIDE 10, BAND 5

The final movement, "Hoedown," depicts the Saturday night square dance. It is marked Allegro and is in duple meter, characteristic of most square dance music. The principal theme of this movement is based on a square dance tune called "Bonaparte's Retreat."

The form of "Hoedown" comprises several short sections, all maintaining an Allegro tempo and the key signature of D major. Contrast in this movement is achieved by orchestrating some portions for full orchestra and others for selected ensembles from its many instrumental timbres, and by considerable rhythmic variety. Frequent use of the open A and D strings in the violin and viola parts strongly suggests the style of square-dance music.

**LISTENING SUMMARY**

Timbre:   large orchestra with wind, percussion, and string instruments
Melody:   based largely on a square-dance melody
Rhythm:   $\frac{2}{4}$ meter; fast tempo
Harmony:  clearly tonal, key of D major
Form:     sectional

Other compositions by Copland are more abstract in style, without obvious reference to melodies or rhythms that are associated with traditional American music. Still, Copland has created an individual sound that can be heard in both his American and abstract works, in his conservative and progressive compositions. He has been a prolific and popular composer whose works seem to represent important aspects of the spirit of America.

## Tonal Music in England and Russia

**Britten**

In England the work begun by Elgar and Vaughan Williams was continued by a younger generation whose foremost composer was Benjamin Britten (1913–1976). Britten's music is in an attractively fresh tonal style. In works such as his opera *Peter Grimes* (1945) and his *Simple Symphony* (1933–34), he showed a particular ability to create very appealing melodic lines. He wrote many choral works, from children's pieces to the monumental *War Requiem* (1961).

**Prokofiev and Shostakovich**

The creation of tonal music continued in the Soviet Union as well. Those composers writing after the Revolution were very much affected by the Communist Party's opposition to "formalism"—that is, very progressive traits of style such as atonality. Composers were expected to adjust their styles so as to make them more accessible to the general public. Sergei Prokofiev (1891–1953) and Dmitri Shostakovich (1906–1975) were two outstanding Soviet composers who had to contend with the wishes of the Communist Party while developing their own styles. Prokofiev is remembered for a number of works, principally the *Classical Symphony*, the opera *Love for Three Oranges* (1919), *Peter and the Wolf* (1936, a children's tale) and his piano sonatas. The *Classical Symphony* (1917) is an early work that is one of his best known compositions in a very appealing Neoclassical style.

Sergei Prokofiev. This photograph was probably taken before he left Russia in 1918; not happy as an exile in Paris, he returned to his native country in 1933. (Novosti Press Agency)

### *Prokofiev:* Classical Symphony

Prokofiev's *Classical Symphony** was written for an orchestra of moderate size with the instrumentation of a late eighteenth-century orchestra. The symphony is in four movements, all of which are quite concise—again much in the spirit of a late eighteenth-century work.

**First movement**

The first movement, in sonata form, shows his skill in combining an older form and instrumentation with fresh melodic and harmonic ideas. The first theme grows from a rising D major arpeggio:

First Theme

The immediate repetition of part of the theme a step lower, beginning on C, offers an unexpected shift in harmony. The music soon returns to D major for the presentation of the second theme. Then after a modulation to A major, the third theme is heard:

Third Theme

But it is an A major that is almost immediately clouded and enriched by a shift to an F-major sonority. A brief closing section in the key of A major features arpeggios and scales.

A measure of rest separates the exposition and development sections. Parts of all the thematic materials from the exposition are developed at a variety of tonal levels. The recapitulation then begins with a return of the opening theme, but it is in C major rather than D major. The original key of D returns, however, with the second theme. The third theme is also in D, followed by the closing section, again based on arpeggios and scales.

**Last three movements**

In the last three movements, Prokofiev again combined traditional styles with harmonic innovations. The second movement is in ternary form, at the traditional slow tempo. A lovely, lyrical melody in the A sections contrasts with a more active middle section. The third movement is a gavotte, also in ternary form. And finally, the fourth movement presents a rollicking, vivacious conclusion to the symphony in sonata form. The symphony is a delightful synthesis of earlier forms and orchestration with fresh melodies and harmonies.

# The Early Twentieth-Century Sense of Beauty

***Cubism*** In both art and music, the early years of the twentieth century brought a multiplicity of different movements. Perhaps most important in the visual arts was the Cubist movement. Cubist artists sought to produce a new synthesis of mass and space, a vision of prismatic planes fluctuating in equivocal spatial relation. In part, they were seeking an artistic realization of new concepts of physics, of the twentieth-century discovery that solids and voids are always in ambiguous relation, never definitely one or the other. In Picasso's *Violinist*, the relationship of the forms seems to shift; now they appear in front of the picture plane, now behind it.

Pablo Picasso: *Violinist (Pretty Eva).* c. 1910. Staatsgalerie, Stuttgart.

Giacomo Balla: *The Hand of the Violinist – Rhythm of the Violinist.* 1912. London, Private Collection.

**Futurism**   The Cubist construction of a new reality was taken up and treated with special verve by artists of the Futurist movement in Italy. The Futurists optimistically, if intemperately, found a kind of salvation in modern physics and its discovery that the underlying reality of nature is energy. Futurist painters employed the shifting facets and multiple views of Cubism in works that attempted to represent the changing sensations, the frenzied tempo and pulse of modern life. Balla's *Hand of the Violinist* describes the "shock waves" of the musician's hand as it works on its instrument.

**Metaphysical and Surrealistic Art**   In the "metaphysical" art of de Chirico, a longing for a golden age and a desire for classic beauty are set against modern anxiety—the ideal and the everyday are juxtaposed in disturbing opposition. "Everything," said de Chirico, "has two aspects: the current aspect, which we see nearly always and which ordinary men see, and the ghostly and metaphysical aspect, which only rare individuals may see in moments of clairvoyance and metaphysical abstraction." De Chirico's *Nostalgia of the Infinite* is a visually disturbing reverie, combining the fantastic and familiar—extraordinary colors and deep shadow, the curious building and the two figures deep in conversation before it. Such painting laid the groundwork for the psychic speculations of Surrealism, in which, as Max Ernst wrote, we feel "the fortuitous encounter upon a non-suitable plane of two mutually distant realities."

Giorgio de Chirico: *The Nostalgia of the Infinite.* c. 1913–14. New York, Museum of Modern Art.

**Expressionism** Humanity's central role in the old Christian universe, challenged by the physical scientists of earlier ages, was struck a death blow by modern physics. Another assault on traditional beliefs came with the advent of modern psychology and its image of human beings fundamentally and irrevocably irrational. Freud's revelations of the subconscious world struck a responsive chord in Germany in the early years of the century. There Expressionist painters were eager to plumb the hidden depths of human emotion. They proceeded to create pictures whose subjects were psychological rather than physical, intangible instead of clearly apparent. In his *Impression III*, Kandinsky, a Russian who became associated with the German Expressionists, employed expressive distortion and hot colors to express the reactions of the audience at a concert.

Wassily Kandinsky: *Impression III (Concert)*. Munich, Städtische Galerie im Lenbachhaus.

Oskar Kokoschka: *The Power of Music.* 1918–19. Eindhoven, Holland, Stedelijk van Abbemuseum.

Oskar Kokoschka was another Expressionist painter who sought the psychological truth behind the outward appearance of his subjects. The bright, deep colors of *The Power of Music* are a visual realization of the intense effect music can have on its hearers.

Much of Marc Chagall's work is a reflection of his childhood and youthful experiences in a Jewish community in Russia. Here the fiddler and his apprentice in a Russian village exemplify these folk elements in his painting. Chagall's imagination transforms the reality of the scene, giving it a color and immediacy that almost convey the sound of the music being played.

Marc Chagall: *The Fiddler.* 1911. Düsseldorf, Kunstsammlung Nordrhein-Westfalen.

**Fantasy and the Metaphysical** Many artists of the early twentieth century produced work with no rational program. The art of Paul Klee is impossible to categorize: it has elements of the surreal, it is often strongly abstract, and (as here) it reflects the Cubist heritage. Klee was an artist profoundly affected by music, both within and outside his art. Line and color were of supreme importance in his work, and he used both most expressively to depict many musical subjects, sometimes with a humorous twist. He was himself an accomplished musician, and the rich colors of *Individual Measurements of the Heights of Layers* have a harmonious quality.

Paul Klee: *Individual Measurements of the Heights of Layers.* Bern, Kunstmuseum.

Manuscript page from Prokofiev's opera *The Flaming Angel*, composed 1922–25 in Paris. Among the early twentieth-century composers, Prokofiev was one of the most versatile, writing operas, oratorios, cantatas, ballets, and music for films as well as abstract instrumental works. On this manuscript page, note the constant use of accidentals and the many changes of meter. (© Copyright 1957, 1977 by Boosey & Co., Ltd. Used by permission of Boosey & Hawkes, Inc.)

Shostakovich is another major Soviet composer in the early to middle part of this century. His major works include his fifteen symphonies, fifteen string quartets, and opera *Lady Macbeth of Mtensk* (1934), which was strongly criticized in *Pravda* for its excessively "modern" characteristics. Ballets, film music, a piano concerto, and other piano and chamber music constitute Shostakovich's very impressive and important compositions. His symphony No. 5 is one of his most significant and appealing works.

## Music in Other Countries

The creation of important styles of tonal music has taken place in other countries as well. The preceding composers and their works were chosen for discussion because they represent some of the most significant and innovative styles of the early twentieth century. Other composers were also of importance, and their works should be studied in order to build a comprehensive view of styles in this period.

# CHAPTER 27

# *Atonality and Serialism*

*LISTENING PREVIEW One of the most innovative developments in harmony of the 1920s was Arnold Schoenberg's twelve-tone serial technique in which he avoided emphasis on one tone and gave equal emphasis to all twelve tones of the chromatic scale. In this system, Schoenberg devised a new, dissonant style of harmonic organization. Listen to the first movement of his Suite for Piano, Op. 25 (side 11, band 2), and observe that no single note is given priority over the others, except for very brief repetitions of a note from time to time. Remember your initial reaction to this harmonic style, and compare that with your impression of it after you become more familiar with serial technique and the sound of music based on it.*

## Atonality and the Second Viennese School

The growing interest in chromaticism during the nineteenth century continued to develop in the twentieth. It had started with the free use of tones alien to a given key—a technique that created new sonorities and tensions before returning to the security of a recognizable tonal center. By the twentieth century, however, even before 1913, the year in which Stravinsky's *The Rite of Spring* caused such a furor in the musical world, some composers were deliberately abandoning the security of a tonal center. At first the avoidance of one central tonality—*atonality*—was tried only in short passages. Later it was expanded to movements and entire works. A number of the more venturesome composers believed that such a path was the only one open for truly contemporary musical expression, and they undertook

Berg's opera *Wozzeck* was first performed in Berlin in 1925 and provoked a mixed reception, with opinions passionately in favor and against it. This drawing is one of the stage designs for this first production.

to create a radically new style. Important leaders in the endeavor were Arnold Schoenberg, Alban Berg, and Anton Webern, three Austrian composers who have come to be known as the "Second Viennese School" (the first being that of Haydn, Mozart and Schubert). These are the three composers whose works we will now consider.

## The Music of Schoenberg

Arnold Schoenberg (1874–1951) was the first and most important pioneer of atonal music as a style. His atonal works were the product of years of difficult labor on his part and at the same time a logical result of the development and transformation of harmony in the late nineteenth century. The music of first Brahms and later Wagner exerted a very powerful influence on Schoenberg. From Brahms he learned the important technique of using a motive for continuous development. From Wagner he derived an increasingly dissonant, chromatic harmony used for expressive purposes, as can be seen in his string sextet *Verklärte Nacht* ("Transfigured Night") of 1899. Schoenberg's early works are in a post-Romantic style—chromatic but still basically tonal.

Yet his approach left him dissatisfied. Over the years, his chromatic style changed, with a continual weakening of the old emphasis on a central tone. The last movement of the *String Quartet No. 2, Op. 10* (1908) was his first strongly atonal work. It also was revolutionary in that it used a singing voice in an instrumental chamber work. From 1910 on virtually all Schoenberg's compositions were atonal.

Schoenberg was closely associated with the Expressionist movement in German painting, and this was undoubtedly a factor in his shift away from the late Romantic style. He himself, however, always maintained he was continuing the German-Austrian symphonic tradition. Expressionism, like the Fauvism from which it was partly derived, discarded photographic realism and created intensely charged, highly introspective works that were meant to speak directly to the inner spirit. Sometimes the paintings were abstract; sometimes the objects in them were recognizable but distorted. The subjective reality of Expressionist paintings was seldom a happy one. It was akin to Freud's view of the unconscious in its fragmentation and irrationality. Max Beckmann's *Departure* suggested something of the unfathomable horror of Kafka's writings. Schoenberg himself produced some Expressionist paintings, and the direction his music took was greatly influenced by the works of Expressionist painter Emil Nolde. In addition, he was a good friend of Wassily Kandinsky, one of the most daring members of the Expressionist school. It is interesting to observe that Schoenberg abandoned the tonal system at almost the same time that Kandinsky abandoned the representation of any sort of recognizable concrete objects. His *Impression III (Concert)*, shown on page 460, provides a good example of this style. The artist was no longer to be the reporter or even the interpreter of reality. Instead he became the creator of a new reality.

**Influence of Expressionist painting**

Photograph (1911) of Arnold Schoenberg. (Städtische Galerie im Lenbachhaus, Munich; Gabriele Münter- und Johannes Eichner Stiftung)

## Early Atonal Works

Atonality literally means "without tonality," and it implies that all twelve tones of the chromatic scale are to be treated rather equally, without special emphasis on any one of them. In most of his early atonal works, Schoenberg relied on a combination of vocal texts with music to create meaning and lend form and continuity within the atonal framework. The texts tended to be brief descriptions of psychological states and were often intensely expressive, as in Schoenberg's song cycle *Das Buch der hängenden Gärten, Op. 15* ("The Book of the Hanging Gardens," 1909) and his monodrama *Erwartung, Op. 17* ("Expectation," 1909). Both works are examples of

**Expressionist style**

Schoenberg's Expressionist style. The music generally shows great changes of mood, with contrasts of tension and relaxation, loudness and softness, dense and sparse sounds.

Aside from the use of atonality, Schoenberg's early works also show other innovations. One of the more important is the use of the

**Sprechstimme**

*Sprechstimme* ("speaking voice") technique. This is a melodic style in which the singer sings only approximate pitches and slides from one to another. Rhythms, however, are precisely notated and sung. The result is a highly inflected type of recitation rather than song in the

**Klangfarbenmelodie**

usual sense. Another innovation was the *Klangfarbenmelodie* ("tone-color melody") technique, in which each note of a melody is given to a different instrument. This technique was used in a very obvious way in Schoenberg's *Five Orchestral Pieces, Op. 16* (1909).

## Schoenberg: Pierrot lunaire

*Pierrot lunaire, Op. 21** ("Pierrot of the Moon"), written in 1912, is another example of Schoenberg's Expressionist atonal style. It is a rather melodramatic cycle of twenty-one movements based on poems by the Belgian poet Albert Giraud. The work is scored for solo voice accompanied by piano, piccolo, flute, clarinet, bass clarinet, violin, viola and cello—an unusual grouping of instruments. Such small individual pieces and instrumental combinations were typical of early atonal works, in which Schoenberg was developing his ideas and techniques. While the voice is used in every movement, the instruments are never used all together but instead are grouped in different combinations in each movement.

---

**LISTENING ANALYSIS**                                    SIDE 11, BAND 1

### "Mondestrunken"

The first movement, "Mondestrunken" ("Moon-drunk"), is written for voice, flute, violin, cello, and piano. The piano begins quietly at a moderate tempo with a motive that is stated four times:

---

*Excerpts used by permission of Belmont Music Publishers, Los Angeles, California 90049. *Pierrot Lunaire, Op. 21*: Copyright 1914 by Universal Edition. Copyright renewed 1941 by Arnold Schoenberg.

Piano Motive

The wide leaps of register are typical of atonal melodies. The violin plays a simpler motive against the piano motive.

The vocalist performs the entire work in *Sprechstimme*. (The x's on the note stems indicate this.) The vocal part generally moves in small intervals but occasionally jumps very large ones. There is some repetition of motives, but more often one motive grows into the next.

First Line of Vocal Part

Den Wein, den man mit Au - gen trinkt

The three stanzas of text are all separated by short instrumental interludes, but otherwise the music seems to flow steadily without obvious sections. The overall form is quite free. Meters and rhythmic patterns change continually, avoiding any sense of beat and regularity. The dynamic level is very low, except for a sudden change to *forte* near the end. The piano closes the movement with the opening motive.

Text:

I   Den Wein, den man mit Augen trinkt,  
    Giesst Nachts der Mond in Wogen  
        nieder,  
    Und eine Springflut überschwemmt  
    Den stillen Horizont.

      *The wine one drinks with the eyes*  
      *The moon pours down in*  
        *waves at night,*  
      *And a spring tide submerges*  
      *The still horizon.*

II  Gelüste, schauerlich und süss,  
    Durchschwimmen ohne Zahl die Fluten!  
    Den Wein, den man mit Augen trinkt,  
    Giesst Nachts der Mond in Wogen  
        nieder.

      *Longings, terrible and sweet,*  
      *Unnumbered, swim the flood!*  
      *The wine one drinks with the eyes*  
      *The moon pours down in*  
        *waves at night.*

III Der Dichter, den die Andacht treibt

      *The poet, constrained by*  
        *devotion,*

    Berauscht sich an dem heilgen tranke,  
    Gen Himmel wendet er verzückt  
    Das Haupt und taumelnd saugt und  
        schlürft er  
    Den Wein, den man mit Augen trinkt.

      *Drunken with the holy drink,*  
      *Enraptured, lifts heavenward*  
      *His head and, reeling, sucks*  
        *and gulps*  
      *The wine one drinks with the eyes.*

**LISTENING SUMMARY**

Timbre:    ensemble of solo voice, flute, violin, cello, and piano  
Melody:    instrumental themes mostly disjunct; vocal themes more conjunct;  
             performed in *Sprechstimme* throughout

Rhythm:    meter alternates irregularly between $\frac{2}{4}$ and $\frac{3}{4}$, although not clear
           or important to the listener; tempo Bewegt (restful)
Harmony:   atonal
Form:      free, with repetition of some motives

The text of "Columbine," the second movement, is also in three stanzas. The vocal part again uses a variety of intervals, with an overall emphasis on small intervals. Flute, clarinet, violin, and piano accompany the soloist. Parallel, dissonant chords stand out in several passages. The overall dynamic level is quiet throughout. The form is quite free even though there is brief repetition of some motives.

In the remaining nineteen movements, a wide variety of instrumentation and effects are explored. Schoenberg was obviously trying to capture the spirit of each poem in a subjective and dramatically appropriate manner. The results are very arresting—the work seems to speak to us in a new musical language, bringing out the distorted fantastical visions of the text.

## Use of the Serial Technique

**Serialism or dodecaphony**

Schoenberg was convinced that the possibilities of tonal music had been exhausted. But he recognized that atonal techniques were not yet sufficiently developed to take its place. This situation led him into a ten-year period of reevaluation and experimentation during which he published almost nothing. Instead, he worked out a new method of organizing atonal harmony called *serialism* (or *dodecaphony*), in which the twelve pitches of the chromatic scale are arranged in a desired order and then used serially in that order throughout a movement or an entire composition. With this as a theoretical framework, he began to produce works that had a profound influence on later twentieth-century music.

Schoenberg's earliest compositions using the serial technique were written in 1923. All were quite brief, written for solo instruments or small groups. Later, as he gained confidence with his methods, he wrote longer works for larger ensembles, most notably the *Variations for Orchestra, Op. 31* (1928), the *Violin Concerto, Op. 36* (1936) and the *Piano Concerto, Op. 42* (1942). The works had a radically new sound, and the audiences who first heard them were seldom pleased.

**Twelve-tone row**

The underlying structure of Schoenberg's serialism and the rules that articulate it are based upon the atonal principle that all twelve tones of the chromatic scale must be treated with equal emphasis. In order to achieve this equality, a composer begins with a *twelve-tone row* (or "set" or "series"), in which each chromatic tone appears exactly once. The twelve notes may be arranged in any order that the composer chooses. Some tone rows, in fact, do suggest harmonic progressions found in tonal music, but more generally they do not. The only limitation, in the strict use of the system, is that all twelve notes must be played before any one is repeated. Only the organization of pitches is inherent in a tone row, and not the organization of other elements, such as rhythm. The composer may cast the notes of the tone row in any rhythmic pattern and in any register. Once the row is constructed, four different forms are possible: *original, retrograde* (in which the row is played backwards), *inversion* (in which the direction of each interval is reversed but the intervals are in the original sequence), and *retrograde inversion*. Examples are:

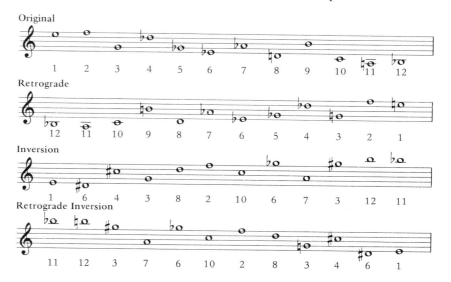

It can be seen that the retrograde form is produced by reversing the order of the notes, starting with the last note and ending with the first. The inversion is made by turning the intervals of the original row upside down. If, as in the example, the first two notes are originally E and F, they will become E and D♯. The retrograde inversion is produced by reversing the order of the inverted notes.

All four forms of the row can also be transposed so that they begin on any of the eleven other pitch levels. Thus there is a possible total of forty-eight different sequences of pitches from any tone row. These may be used melodically, contrapuntally, or to build chords, perhaps in support of a melody also derived from the row.

## Schoenberg: Suite for Piano, Op. 25

Schoenberg's first use of a tone row in an entire composition is in his *Suite for Piano** from the year 1925. It is notable that he chose the suite, an "old-fashioned" genre, for this otherwise very innovative work. His use of the tone row in the suite is very imaginative.

**LISTENING ANALYSIS**

SIDE 11, BAND 2

### First Movement: Praeludium; Rasch (quick); Free Form

The original tone row, on which the entire work is based, is shown below, as it appears at the beginning of the first movement, "Praeludium," played by the right hand. The four basic forms of the row are shown in the previous example.

Original Form of Tone Row

```
1   2   3    4    5   6   7  8    9      10  11   12
E   F   G    Db   Gb  Eb  Ab D    B      C   A    Bb
```

At the third tone, the left hand begins to imitate the right in a transposed form of the original row. The texture is momentarily contrapuntal, followed very soon by chords. Throughout the movement various forms and transpositions of the original row are used, both contrapuntally and chordally, creating a free formal structure. The meter is $\frac{6}{8}$, but rhythmic patterns vary so greatly that the sense of beat and meter is obscured.

**LISTENING SUMMARY**

| | |
|---|---|
| Timbre: | piano |
| Melody: | conjunct and disjunct; derived from tone row |
| Rhythm: | mostly $\frac{6}{8}$ meter with several changes near the end, but not necessarily clear to the listener; tempo Rasch (quick) |
| Harmony: | atonal, derived from tone row |
| Form: | derived from the use of various forms of the row |

The second movement, "Gavotte," is in duple meter. As in the first movement, rhythms change often, so that the characteristics of the old dance form—the gavotte—are not readily apparent. The original form of the row from the first movement is used, but the fragmented rhythms give it a completely different character:

Tone Row in Second Movement

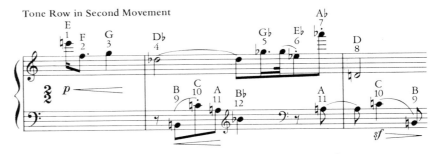

Notice how Schoenberg split the row into three segments: tones 1 2 3 4 in one segment, tones 5 6 7 8 in another, and tones 9 10 11 12 in still another. Having divided the row in such a fashion, he then proceeded to use the last four tones before the middle four.

The remaining movements in the suite are entitled "Musette," "Intermezzo," "Menuett," and "Gigue," and are also based on the same tone row. The "Musette" features the repetition of the note G throughout, producing a sound reminiscent of the bagpipe. ("Musette" is French for bagpipe.) The "Menuett" is classically structured with a minuet, a trio, and a repetition of the minuet. Schoenberg's use of such a traditional form represents a skillful blending of the old and the new.

## Schoenberg's Career and Influence

Schoenberg had little formal musical training. He began to teach theory and composition privately in Vienna, but found little recognition there for his own compositions. In 1926 he moved to Berlin to direct a composition master class at the Prussian Academy of Arts, but he was dismissed seven years later when the Nazis came to power. He thereupon rejoined the Jewish faith which he had left as a young man. In 1934 he moved to Hollywood where he remained, teaching privately and at the University of California, Los Angeles. One of his pupils was the American avant-garde composer John Cage (b. 1912).

Before 1908 Schoenberg had composed in a post-Romantic vein influenced by Wagner and Brahms. Important works from this period were *Verklärte nacht* and a huge cantata, *Gurrelieder* ("Songs of Gure," 1900–01). Two later works reflect his lifelong preoccupation with religious faith: the freely atonal oratorio *Die Jakobsleiter* ("Jacob's Ladder," 1917–22) and the serial opera *Moses und Aron* ("Moses and Aaron," 1932); neither was completed, though he began to revise the oratorio in 1944. The best known of his late works are instrumental except for the short, dramatic cantata *A Survivor from Warsaw, Op. 46* (1947), written in English for narrator, male chorus, and orchestra, and based on recollections of a resident of the Warsaw ghetto. It is notable that in his late works Schoenberg returned to tonal music without strict use of his serial techniques.

Schoenberg's most obvious influence was on his two most famous pupils, Berg and Webern. Many later composers also wrote serial music, in a great variety of more and less strict styles. Schoenberg's influence has thus been extensive. His works, especially from his tonal and Expressionist years, are now heard more frequently than they were in his lifetime. But his importance as an innovator is still far greater than public acceptance of his works.

## Serialism as an Art Form

The concept of the twelve-tone row was not completely new with Schoenberg. Several composers before him had written chromatic melodies using all twelve tones in a systematic way. Josef Matthias Hauer (1883–1959), another Austrian composer, had even developed a kind of twelve-tone serial process just before Schoenberg did. The great significance of Schoenberg's work, however, lies in his extensive development of the different forms of the tone row and the use of the row within a coherent system.

In the serial technique, we meet a completely new musical language—a radically different treatment of all aspects of music. Listening to serial music for the first time is much like hearing an unfamiliar language. At first the words make no sense whatsoever, but if we study the language for a time, we begin to grasp its meaning and become more and more comfortable with it. So it is with any new style of music. The more we hear it and study it, the more accessible it becomes. It simply takes time for people who are so conditioned by the tonal music of the eighteenth and nineteenth centuries to become comfortable with the atonal sounds of serialism.

It is important to remember that although serialism is strongly associated with atonality, the one may exist without the other. Music can be atonal, as we have seen, without using the twelve-tone serial technique. Schoenberg's *Pierrot lunaire* is an obvious example. And conversely, a composer may construct a tone row that may briefly suggest tonality, through the use, for example, of a prominent triad or two in the row.

It should also be noted that it is virtually impossible to tell simply by listening whether or not a work is based on a serial technique. Even if listeners know that a work is based on a tone row, they will have difficulty in hearing more than the most obvious characteristics of the row and its various forms.

The twelve-tone serial technique is rather like a set of tools. It is primarily a method that a composer uses to organize the twelve tones and bring order to a basically dissonant style. Every composer has used the technique in different ways—a fact that will become evident when we consider the works of two of Schoenberg's early students, Berg and Webern. Together these two composers were largely responsible for the propagation and development of serialism.

The work of Schoenberg and his immediate successors has had far-reaching influence. Nearly every composer of our time has at least experimented with serialism. Many have extended the principles of the system to govern other aspects of composition, using it strictly or freely and combining it with other techniques. The serial technique has thus proved a stimulus and a valuable asset, even though it has not become the almost universal musical language that major-minor harmony was in the past.

## The Music of Berg

Stress on lyricism

The Austrian composer Alban Berg (1885–1935) was an ardent disciple and a close friend of Schoenberg. Berg's style of composition was largely based on the serial technique, but it was tempered with a strong sense of lyricism. His works thus seem less removed than Schoenberg's from the late Romantic style, and are more accessible than many of his teacher's.

One of Berg's masterpieces is his Expressionist opera *Wozzeck* (1917–21). First performed in 1925, it raised a storm of protest from the public. The libretto was based on a frightening and tragic play by an early nineteenth-century dramatist, Georg Büchner (1813–1837). The plot concerns a pathetic soldier whose miserable life is almost totally determined by his political and social environment. Such a story was in many ways uncomfortably appropriate not only in a nineteenth-century play but also in an early twentieth-century opera. (Berg himself had been a soldier during World War I.) The music incorporates serial technique only sparingly, but the style is usually atonal. Berg's interest in past traditions is revealed in his use of traditional forms to provide a structural basis for the work. These

Berg posing with the portrait of himself (1910) by Arnold Schoenberg. (The Bettmann Archive/BBC Hulton Picture Library)

forms function behind the scenes for the most part and are not usually perceived by the listener.

Two other outstanding works by Berg are his *Violin Concerto* (1935) and a second opera, *Lulu* (1937), left unfinished at his death but completed from Berg's sketches. Both make great use of serial technique, but the *Violin Concerto* includes tonal writing as well. It even quotes from a Bach chorale at the beginning of the third movement, showing the flexibility of the serial method. Throughout his works, Berg used both tonal and atonal harmony, choosing one or the other according to the dramatic purpose of the individual work. In this way he achieved a style that he found personally valid and convincing. Many of his works allude symbolically to events of his own life, reinforcing the Romantic aspects of the music itself.

## Berg: Lyric Suite

Berg's *Lyric Suite** clearly shows many characteristics of his music. The work is a string quartet with six movements alternating between fast and slow tempos. It is rather freely based on several different tone rows.

**LISTENING ANALYSIS**

SIDE 11, BAND 3

*First Movement: Allegretto gioviale (rather fast and jovial); Binary Form*

The opening movement begins with a very brief chordal introduction. This is followed by the first tone row, which is presented as the main theme by the first violin:

*Lyric Suite* by Alban Berg. Copyright 1927, Universal Edition. Excerpts used by permission of the publisher. Theodore Presser Company, sole representative United States, Canada and Mexico.

First Tone Row

|  | 1 | 2 | 3 | 4 | 5 | 6 | 7 | 8 | 9 | 10 | 11 | 12 |
|---|---|---|---|---|---|---|---|---|---|---|---|---|
|  | F | E | C | A | G | D | A♭ | D♭ | E♭ | G♭ | B♭ | B |

**Hauptstimme and Nebenstimme**

In the usual manner of serialist composers, Berg indicated this phrase and certain others with the symbol H⌐, meaning *Hauptstimme*, or principal part. He also used the symbol N⌐, meaning *Nebenstimme*, or secondary part. These marks were added to help performers see more quickly and easily which parts to emphasize. A second, more tranquil thematic statement, also derived from the row, follows. Thereafter, both thematic materials are freely recapitulated, resulting in a binary (AA′) form. The movement closes with a brief coda.

While the use of the tone row is sometimes obvious in the first movement, it is more often hidden in contrapuntal and chordal passages. Both conjunct and disjunct motion are heard, with greater stress on the latter. Rhythmic patterns are quite varied and changing, and the meter alternates rather frequently between $\frac{4}{4}$ and $\frac{2}{4}$. The texture is largely contrapuntal, with the four instruments of the string quartet often moving independently of one another. A wealth of performance directions are given in the score, with special attention paid to dynamics.

**LISTENING SUMMARY**

| | |
|---|---|
| Timbre: | string quartet |
| Melody: | largely disjunct; derived from tone row |
| Rhythm: | meter alternates between $\frac{4}{4}$ and $\frac{2}{4}$; tempo Allegretto gioviale (rather fast and jovial) |
| Harmony: | atonal, derived from various forms of the tone row and their use |
| Form: | binary (AA′) |

The other five movements are entitled "Andante amoroso," "Allegro misterioso," "Adagio appassionato," "Presto delirando," and "Largo desolato." The descriptive movement markings reflect the very expressive qualities of the music. While the movements are organized rather clearly and traditionally in sections, melody and harmony are organized serially in a fresh, at times very dramatic, manner.

Half a century after Berg completed the *Lyric Suite*, its secret program was discovered. Berg left a notated copy of the score which revealed its private allusions to an extramarital relationship. After his widow's death, the details of his musical symbolism were published.

## The Music of Webern

Anton von Webern (1883–1945), who, like Schoenberg and Berg, was born in Austria, was trained as a musicologist, composer, and conductor. He was a devoted student of Schoenberg who avidly explored the possibilities of serialism. While Berg injected serial music with a somewhat Romantic spirit, Webern's style was much more Classical in its careful organization and economy of means.

Webern's music does not use many notes. He usually wrote for solo instruments or small ensembles, and his style was particularly lean and sparse. Some claim that melody simply ceased to exist with Webern—that it became completely merged with harmony. Certainly there is little relation to any traditional melodic style in most of his works. His melodies are characterized by very small and very wide leaps, and he frequently used octave displacement. He also fragments the melodic line by allocating its various portions to different instruments. The rhythms in his works vary. Some are quite steady, while others are very irregular and so syncopated that they completely hide any feeling of the basic beat.

Webern's use of a tone row was usually quite strict, though he sometimes repeated a note within the row or divided the notes of the row into parts that were used rather independently. His textures are, like his melodies, quite sparse, often made up of a single note or a very short motive followed immediately by one in another part and in a higher or lower register. Within very short passages he employs a large variety of tone colors. This type of texture has often been called "pointillistic" as it has been compared to the paintings of the Pointillists such as Georges Seurat—paintings in which images are built up out of innumerably tiny, distinct points of unblended color. Webern often used the outlines of Classical forms, but he effectively concealed them from the listener by his highly novel style. All of his works are exceptionally brief, even by the standards of atonal works. One movement of his *Five Pieces for Orchestra* lasts only nineteen seconds.

Although most of Webern's compositions were for small ensembles, he also wrote a few orchestral works, several sets of songs, and two cantatas. The title of his *Symphony, Op. 21* is somewhat misleading; the work is scored for a small chamber ensemble instead of a larger symphony orchestra.

**Pointillistic texture**

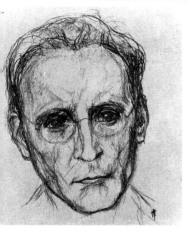

**Drawing of Webern by the poet Hildegard Jone. (Universal Edition, Vienna)**

## *Webern:* Symphony, Op. 21

Webern's *Symphony, Op. 21** (1928) displays many of his most characteristic techniques. It was written for a small ensemble made up of clarinet, bass clarinet, two horns, harp, first and second violins, viola, and cello. The work has only two movements and takes only ten minutes to perform. In effect, the *Symphony* is a skillful miniature—a study in contrast and exploitation of timbre and in control over pitch through the use of the row in its various forms.

---

**LISTENING ANALYSIS**                                          SIDE 11, BAND 4

*First Movement: Ruhig schreitend (calmly striding); Sonata Form*

**Almost from the beginning of the first movement, several different forms of the tone row are used. We clearly hear the first four notes of the original and inverted forms in the horns:**

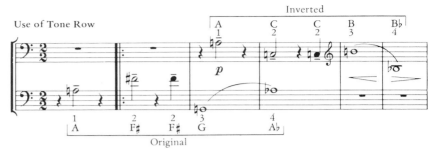

Use of Tone Row

Another form of the row is then started in the other instruments, and from this point on the various forms are constantly intertwined. Webern was not interested in having the forms heard individually; instead he used them to create a general effect.

The wide leaps within and between parts contribute to the characteristic pointillistic texture, that is, quite sparse and made up of notes and motives in rapidly changing registers. In most cases, an instrument plays only one note, or two at the most, before another instrument takes over. The $\frac{2}{2}$ meter remains constant throughout the first movement, but no steady sense of beat is set up, and thus the duple meter is not apparent. Nor is the form obvious. It is definitely a miniature sonata form, but this becomes clear only with thorough knowledge of the music. In the score, repeat signs indicate that the exposition and then the remainder of the movement are each to be repeated.

### LISTENING SUMMARY

| | |
|---|---|
| Timbre: | small chamber ensemble of string and wind instruments |
| Melody: | merged with harmony |
| Rhythm: | $\frac{2}{2}$ meter, but not clear to listener; tempo Ruhig schreitend (calmly striding) |
| Harmony: | atonal, derived from the use of several forms of the tone row |
| Texture: | sparse and pointillistic |
| Form: | sonata form, but not readily apparent to listener |

**Webern: Symphony, Op. 21, Second Movement**

### LISTENING ANALYSIS

SIDE 11, BAND 4 (FOLLOWING FIRST MOVEMENT)

*Second Movement: Sehr ruhig (very calmly); Theme and Variations Form*

The second movement is made up of a theme and seven variations. The theme, which is in inversion of the tone row of the first movement, is presented by the clarinet and then split up into less continuous groupings of notes, which are played by other instruments.

Theme

Note how Webern repeats most of the tones in the theme to give them more emphasis.

The variations tend to flow rhythmically, one into the next. No emphasis seems to be placed on recognition of the tone row, although it is always present. The texture continues to be quite sparse in this movement.

The variations are most easily distinguished by changes of instrumentation:

Variation 1: strings
Variation 2: wind instruments and harp
Variation 3: entire ensemble
Variation 4: entire ensemble
Variation 5: strings and harp
Variation 6: wind instruments
Variation 7: entire ensemble

### LISTENING SUMMARY

| | |
|---|---|
| Timbre: | small chamber ensemble of string and wind instruments |
| Melody: | theme is inverted form of original tone row |
| Rhythm: | $\frac{2}{4}$ meter, but not clear to listener; tempo Sehr ruhig (very calmly) |
| Harmony: | atonal, derived from the use of several forms of the tone row |
| Texture: | usually sparse; somewhat pointillistic |
| Form: | theme and seven variations |

The music of Schoenberg, Berg, and Webern represents one of the most significant, innovative trends in music in the first half of the twentieth century. Their work has had and continues to have far-reaching influence on the techniques and methods of many subsequent composers.

## The Evolution of the Symphony

Until the end of the nineteenth century, the history of the symphony was one of ever-increasing magnitude. Over the years, new instruments were added, parts were written for solo singers and choral groups, texture became denser, and dynamic range expanded to enormous proportions. The twentieth century brought an   end to the general expansion, with composers writing symphonies for groups of varied sizes, often with very nontraditional instrumentation.

Listen to selections from symphonies of four different periods—those listed below from the record set that accompanies the text, or other selections.

| | | |
|---|---|---|
| **Classical:** | Mozart's *Symphony No. 40 in G Minor*, First Movement | **Side 4, Band 3** |
| **Romantic:** | Brahms' *Symphony No. 3 in F Major*, First Movement | **Side 7, Band 5** |
| **Late Romantic:** | Mahler, any symphony, First Movement | |
| **Modern:** | Webern, *Symphony, Op. 21*, First Movement | **Side 11, Band 4** |

What musical qualities make it possible to identify the periods in which the symphonies were written? In what ways does each work reflect the spirit of its time?

# CHAPTER 28

# *Music in the Later Twentieth Century*

*LISTENING PREVIEW Composers in the later twentieth century have avidly sought new means to express their musical ideas. Among the numerous innovations of recent decades is the development and use of electronically synthesized music, which has provided many new challenges and solutions to composers. The spectrum of possible musical sounds has been enormously enlarged by the synthesizer. Listen to Mario Davidovsky's "Synchronisms No. 1" for flute and taped electronic sounds (side 12, band 1). Identify those specific aspects of the electronic sounds that are completely new and different from sounds made by traditional instruments.*

## The Early Postwar Years

The onset of World War II caused a reduction in musical activity, particularly in Europe. By the time the war had ended, the musical scene had changed considerably. Just before and during the war years, a number of composers, including Schoenberg, Bartók, Hindemith, and Stravinsky, had emigrated to the United States, where they were subsequently to exert great influence. The work of Schoenberg and Stravinsky has had an especially notable effect. In Europe, the development of twelve-tone music, censored during the war by the Nazis, was continued by a whole new generation of young composers. Many composers experimented with a variety of older and new styles. The major trends will be described.

## Influence of Messiaen

Immediately after the war, Paris was once again the scene of lively musical activity. Many members of the European avant-garde were attracted to the harmony classes of Olivier Messiaen (b. 1908) at the Paris Conservatory. Work there included the analysis of the scores of such important modern composers as Debussy, Schoenberg, Berg, Webern, and Stravinsky, as well as music of earlier composers. Messiaen himself was and has continued to be highly influential as both a composer and a teacher. His thorough study of the rhythms of Hindu music and Oriental music has had a major influence on his compositions. Some of his works contain rhythmic palindromes—that

Olivier Messiaen, May 1986. (Photo: Clive Barda)

is, rhythmic patterns that are the same forward and backward—as well as rhythmic canons and a variety of other interesting rhythmic devices. Messiaen is also an expert ornithologist and has traveled all over the world notating various birdcalls. Some of his most exciting and colorful works are those that incorporate such calls. *Oiseaux exotiques* ("Exotic Birds"), written in 1956, offers a particularly fine example. The music is scored for piano, wind instruments, and percussion instruments, and makes use of forty different birdcalls. In the preface of the work, Messiaen has listed each bird and its native habitat.

## The Expansion of Serialism

Some of Messiaen's young students were especially intrigued by the serialist works of Webern. They noted that while much of Schoenberg's music has an almost traditional structure in phrases and overall form, Webern's forms seemed to grow directly out of his use of the twelve-tone method. This they felt was the direction in which they should move. They were unsure, however, exactly how to proceed.

In 1949 Messiaen provided a possible answer in his *Modes de valeurs et d'intensités* ("Modes of Values and Intensities"), one of a group of piano pieces. In his use of the term "Modes," Messiaen was referring specifically to a melodic mode of thirty-six pitches, a rhythmic mode of twenty-four durations, a "loudness" mode of seven intensities, and a performance mode of twelve different kinds of attacks, or ways in which a note may be struck. Within Messiaen's work the modes are organized so that a given pitch is always associated with the same duration, intensity, and manner of attack.

The *Modes* introduced the idea of structuring each element of music—rhythm, dynamics, and so forth—in the same way that the twelve pitches are structured in the serialist, twelve-tone system. Thus, the concept of *multiple* (or *total*) *serialization* was importantly extended. The concept of multiple serialization was probably first used by American composer Milton Babbitt in his *Three Compositions for Piano* (1947) in which he serialized aspects of rhythm and dynamics, as well as pitch. The term "serial music," as it is used today, therefore, may refer not only to music in which there is serialized use of a tone row but to any piece in which there is a systematic ordering of pitches and/or other musical elements. The ordering of these elements will determine various aspects of the composition according to what operations and transformations the composer chooses to apply to them. "Serial music" is thus now a term of general description. A twelve-tone composition is just one specific type of serial music.

*Multiple serialization*

## Boulez

One of Messiaen's students, Pierre Boulez (b. 1925), undertook the development of Messiaen's ideas in his *Structures* (1952, 1956–61), a work for two pianos. Boulez serialized durations, intensities, and attacks as well as pitches in this composition. For the rhythm of his piece, he devised a sort of rhythmic row of twelve different durations,

A leading avant-garde composer, Pierre Boulez is also an outstanding conductor, and has run I.R.C.A.M., a research and experimentation center for modern compositional techniques in Paris, since 1976. This photograph shows him at a rehearsal in the Royal Albert Hall, London, in 1985. (Photo: Clive Barda)

ranging from a single thirty-second note to the combined duration of twelve thirty-second notes (the equivalent of a dotted quarter note). The twelve values were ordered in a manner similar to that used for the twelve pitches of the chromatic scale. The two rows and their forms were then used independently in such a way that each note of the tone row was associated in turn with each value of the rhythmic row.

Boulez' system was at once more flexible and more varied than that of his teacher. In Messiaen's *Modes* each tone is associated with the same duration, intensity, and attack throughout. But in Boulez' *Structures*, the duration, intensity, and attack of every pitch are constantly and systematically changed.

In 1955 Boulez wrote *Le marteau sans maître* ("The Hammer Without a Master"), a work that Stravinsky later hailed as a masterpiece. The work is a setting of three poems by René Char, a Surrealist poet much admired by Boulez. It is scored for flute, viola, guitar, alto voice, and a number of percussion instruments, including a *vibraphone* (an electrified *marimba*) and a *xylorimba* (an instrument of wide range that includes the low-pitched bars of the marimba and the high-pitched bars of the xylophone). The music is divided into nine movements, five of which are purely instrumental. The other four are settings of the three poems, with one of the poems set in two different versions.

Many influences can be seen in Boulez' *Le marteau*, including that of Oriental music. Boulez became familiar with Oriental music when he traveled to Japan as the music director of a European theater company. *Le marteau* differs from Boulez' earlier *Structures* in that it does not make use of multiple serialism. Instead there are groups of intervals that appear in various permutations and transformations throughout. The work vacillates between a flowing lyricism and a stark abrasiveness—a contrast that is especially noticeable in the second movement.

## Stockhausen

Karlheinz Stockhausen (b. 1928), a German who was for a year a student of Messiaen, has also made extensive use of serial techniques in his works, determining such things as density, register, and tempo changes by serial means. An example can be found in his *Zeitmasse* ("Time Block," 1956), a piece for five woodwinds in which systematic changes in tempo are serially controlled. Many of the accelerations and decelerations in tempo are quite complicated. At a certain point, for instance, one instrument accelerates, another slows down and a third maintains a steady tempo. In the work, Stockhausen was not trying to achieve a traditional ensemble of instruments. Rather, he sought to stress the independence of each instrument. The effect is one of great fluidity and freedom.

In his *Gruppen* ("Groups"), a work for three chamber orchestras written in the mid-1950s, Stockhausen explored some of these same ideas on a large scale. In a performance of the work, the three orchestras led by three different conductors are often called upon to play in different tempos. As Stockhausen explained, in this work "sound-groups should be made to wander in space from one sounding body to another and at the same time split up similar sound-structures: each orchestra was supposed to call to the others and to give answer or echo."

Stockhausen has also explored electronic music. In 1953 he began experimenting with electronic sounds at the Cologne radio station. (In Europe, a number of government radio stations have installed facilities for electronic music.) At Cologne, Stockhausen produced his *Gesang der Jünglinge* ("Song of the Youth," 1955–56), one of the classics of electronic music. The work is essentially the combination of electronic sounds with the sound of a child's voice reading a biblical text.

## Stravinsky's serial works

In the United States, twelve-tone music has taken as many paths as there are composers writing it. Composers as different as Copland, Sessions, and Stravinsky have made use of twelve-tone methods in their works. The individuality seen in the many compositions is evidence that serialism can provide a framework large enough for the expression of a multitude of ideas.

Stravinsky's development as a serialist composer has been one of the most discussed events of modern music. Serial techniques are found only in his late works, beginning with his *Cantata*,* written in 1952. The work is a setting of some anonymous lyrics of the fifteenth and sixteenth centuries for soprano, tenor, female chorus, and a small instrumental ensemble. The instrumentation, some of the rhythmic motives and cadential harmonies, and the crossing of voices are all reminiscent of certain techniques found in late Medieval music.

The "Ricercar II" in Stravinsky's *Cantata* opens with a short phrase sung by the tenor:

The phrase, made up of eleven notes, many of which are repeated, is treated in serial fashion. The eleven notes are stated in retrograde, inversion, and retrograde inversion just as the notes of a twelve-tone row would have been.

In later works, Stravinsky developed his own very personal method of using the twelve-tone system. His first piece to rely completely on

(*Top*) Karlheinz Stockhausen experimenting with electronic devices in his home near Cologne in Germany, 1985. (Photo: Clive Barda)

twelve-tone serial techniques is *Threni* for soloists, chorus, and orchestra (1957–58). He commented in particular on his *Movements for Piano and Orchestra* (1958–59), also a serial work, calling it "the most advanced music from the point of view of construction of anything I have composed." The work is a very engaging example of Stravinsky's dodecaphonic music.

**Stravinsky: Movements for Piano and Orchestra**

Stravinsky's *Movements for Piano and Orchestra** is very specifically scored for thirty-eight instruments, including piano, woodwinds, brass, strings, harp, and celesta.

**LISTENING ANALYSIS**                                                    SIDE 11, BAND 5,

The five movements are all quite brief, with frequent changes of meter. On the first page alone the following meters appear, and thus no recurring meter is apparent to the listener.

| | | | | | | | | | |
|---|---|---|---|---|---|---|---|---|---|
| **4** | **3** | **3** | **4** | **3** | **4** | **5** | **7** | **6** | **5** |
| **8** | **8** | **32** | **16** | **8** | **16** | **16** | **16** | **16** | **16** |

The music is based on a twelve-tone row that is used to create myriad motivic materials as well as to provide an overall sense of unity. Occasional, brief repetitions of a note or chord provide momentary tonal centers. A number of the motivic ideas feature specific intervals. An interval of a fifth, for example, is heard in the two trumpets near the beginning of the first movement and again in the third movement:

Interval of a Fifth

First Movement                                    Third Movement

In other cases Stravinsky combined both pitch and rhythmic factors in motives that appear several times. The ascending leap of a minor ninth in the first flute, heard at the beginning and end of the first movement and again at the opening of the fourth movement, is a typical example.

Texture throughout the work is sparse, at times pointillistic. Melody and harmony seem merged into one, and form is quite free, evolving as it does from the use of the tone row and from the repetition and imitation of motives.

The fifth and final movement has a special function. Many of the motives heard earlier in fragmented form or in combination with other elements are now separated out and presented clearly, even insistently. The last movement thus provides both a climax and a clarification of the entire work.

**LISTENING SUMMARY**

Timbre:     piano and orchestra of string and wind instruments, harp, and celesta

| Melody: | generally quite disjunct; seems to merge with harmony |
|---|---|
| Rhythm: | no repeated meter apparent to the listener; varying tempos |
| Harmony: | based on a twelve-tone row; tonality sometimes suggested by a repeated note or chord |
| Texture: | generally quite sparse; sometimes pointillistic |
| Form: | five movements; form of movements evolves from the use of the tone row and motives |

As many critics have noted, Stravinsky's serial music still has the "Stravinsky sound." One of the hallmarks of his style is the use of exact repetition, both on a small scale to generate rhythmic movement and on a larger scale as a unifying device. Schoenberg had devised the twelve-tone system partly to avoid the obvious use of repetition, but Stravinsky's twelve-tone serial music makes as effective use of repeated elements as his earlier music does. Stravinsky's adoption of the twelve-tone method thus showed that the polarity between tonal and atonal music was not an unbridgeable gap.

**Babbitt**

The American Milton Babbitt (b. 1916) has been outstanding both as a composer and as a theorist of serial music. His work has included the analysis of the serial procedures of Schoenberg and Webern and the exploration of a number of different ways of using the twelve-tone method to organize rhythm. His rhythmic theories are in many ways quite innovative. Drawing a parallel between two pitches in the tone row and the duration between two attacks—that is, the time between the beginning of one note and the beginning of the next—he has derived intervals of duration. As mentioned earlier, Babbitt was the first to serialize the use of rhythmic duration and other aspects of music. He has written a great variety of music, including works such as his *All Set* (1957) for jazz ensemble, *Composition for Four Instruments* (1948), *Partitions* (1957) for piano, and four string quartets. Since his complex musical ideas call for very precise realization in performance, he has turned more and more in recent years to electronic music.

**Electronic Music**

Varèse

The term *electronic music* generally refers to any music composed with the use of electronic equipment. As early as the 1910s, composers were envisioning the use of electronic instruments. By the early 1920s French composer Edgard Varèse (1883–1965) was urging the development of specific equipment with which he felt he could realize his musical ideas. But the technology was not yet sufficiently developed. The first concerts of electronic music in the United States were not held until after World War II. Today, however, there is wide interest in electronic music among both composers and listeners.

One of the reasons that so many composers have turned to electronic music is found in the limitations of traditional instruments. Most of the instruments now in use were perfected during the eighteenth and nineteenth centuries and are thus especially suitable for playing the music of that period. Many of them are largely restricted to the notes of the chromatic scale. Although new playing techniques are being developed, many composers find that only electronic instruments offer the completely new sounds they want.

A related problem found in nonelectronic music is the limited precision possible with live performers. Certain very rapid and complex rhythmic patterns that are perceptible to the human ear are, for example, virtually impossible for human performers to play. Such patterns can, however, be produced with ease by electronic means. In addition, an electronic work can be fully realized by the composer alone. The composer retains complete control of the final sound and does not have to rely on the interpretation of a performer. Not all electronic composers, though, wish to exercise such complete and invariable control; indeed, elements of improvisation and spontaneity are important to many electronic compositions. Some of the most effective electronic works combine live performance with taped sounds.

There has been great speculation about the potential resources made available to music by modern technology. After a century or more in which art was popularly regarded as more or less irrelevant to human progress, many composers have been pleased to find a point of contact between art and the front ranks of science.

At the present time, composers working in the electronic medium can proceed in one of two ways. On the one hand, they can record and modify instrumental sounds or sounds from the natural environment. Their other choice is to generate sounds directly by electronic means. The first method produces what French composers have called *musique concrète*, or, as it is often called, *tape music*.

### Musique Concrète or Tape Music

To modify sounds recorded on tape, composers can do a number of things. They may, for example, play the tapes backward, lower the pitch by slowing the speed of the tape player, fragment the tapes by splicing them, or form tape loops in order to create a repeating rhythmic ostinato. Most tape studios offer additional equipment for modifying sounds, including filters of various kinds that are similar in principle to those found on stereo preamplifiers but much more sophisticated.

### Synthesized Sounds

Musique concrète, the earliest form of electronic music, was soon followed by the development of equipment that could produce sound directly by electronic means. Oscillators and sound synthesizers of other kinds have made it possible for composers to obtain sounds of almost any timbre, intensity, and pitch, while maintaining direct control over the sounds produced. The exciting possibilities arising from this technology led, in the 1950s, to the establishment of several studios in the United States and Europe. In Europe, they are typically affiliated with radio stations; most in the United States have been connected with universities. The first was the Columbia-Princeton Electronic Music Center, established at Columbia University in 1959. Since then other studios have been established at many universities throughout the country.

Composing electronic music is a laborious process. Each sound must be generated separately, and a great deal of editing and splicing is necessary to create even a short piece. The RCA Mark II synthesizer installed at the Columbia-Princeton Electronic Music Center was developed to speed up some of these operations. The machine combines all the equipment of an elaborate tape studio with sophisticated sound-generating devices.

Recently, many smaller sound synthesizers have been produced for purposes ranging from composition to the live performance of electronic music. Most of them have been designed with emphasis on particular features, so each has its own combination of advantages and limitations. The synthesizers with keyboard are designed specifically to fill the needs of rock bands, with which we so often hear them.

### Use of Computers

Another important innovation in electronic music in recent years has been the use of computer programming. The computer calculates a series of numbers representing every sound in a composition and then converts these numbers into sound by means of a data translator coupled with a synthesizer. The composer, however, must still plan the composition and specify the sounds in it. The computer may be thought of as another kind of musical instrument, a means whereby a composer's work may be performed or realized repeatedly with precise accuracy.

The computer and, in fact, all the electronic devices discussed here demand more effort from the composer than writing for traditional instruments does. To produce the final tape of an electronic work, which is actually a performance of the work, the composer must determine dynamic values, tempo, phrasing, and all the other variables that are usually subject to some interpretation by a performer. In effect, composer and performer become one.

**Davidovsky: Synchronisms No. 1**

Among the most interesting and virtuosic of electronic works are the seven *Synchronisms* by Mario Davidovsky (b. 1934), an innovative Argentinean-American composer. Each of the six works combines electronically generated sounds, which are contained on tapes and one or more instruments played live. "Synchronisms No. 1"* (1962) is written for flute and a prepared tape of electronic sounds.

**LISTENING ANALYSIS**

The electronic sounds in "Synchronisms No. 1" are used particularly as extensions of the flute timbres. Several different timbres can be produced by the flute itself, depending on the fingering technique used and the way the flutist blows into the mouthpiece. A performer can, for example, make very precise and minute fluctuations in pitch, add noise elements to the sound, and attack sounds gently or percussively. By extending and enlarging upon these variations in the taped sounds, Davidovsky created a strong unity between the instrumental part and the electronic sounds. The example below shows the first part of the score:

Excerpt from "Synchronisms No. 1"

The lower staff in each set of staves shows the flute part. The two upper staves provide necessary cues for the flutist and the person operating the tape recorder. The extreme complexity of the electronic part means that it cannot be written out in traditional notation.

The flutist must maintain exact synchronization with the tape, which, unlike another live performer, is an inflexible element. The tape is stopped at certain points, both to provide sections of solo work for the flute and to keep the synchronization as precise as possible.

In addition to extending the flute timbres, the electronic sounds also imitate some of the flute passages and motives. The motive shown at the beginning of Tape Cue 2 is, for example, quite similar to some of those found in the flute part. While flute and electronic sounds are sometimes heard as separate units in a kind of contrapuntal relationship, they are at other times heard as one combined whole.

"Synchronisms No. 1" is quite short, lasting only about three minutes. The music seems to fall into three main sections. Each of the first two sections finishes with a short part for tape alone; the third section is almost entirely for solo flute, with the electronic sounds entering very briefly at the end. In the first two sections, climaxes are achieved by accelerandos and crescendos in which flute and electronic parts seem to merge. At these moments, it is no longer possible to hear particular "notes" or the distinctions between the two parts. The total effect is very striking.

**LISTENING SUMMARY**

Timbre:   flute and electronically synthesized sounds
Melody:   often widely disjunct with unusual effects in the flute part; wide new spectrum of sounds of definite and indefinite pitch in the electronic part
Rhythm:   no repeated meter apparent to the listener; varying tempos
Harmony:  generally atonal in the flute part; no traditional concept of harmony in the electronic part
Form:     three sections; form evolves freely

Morton Subotnick (b. 1933) is another one of the many composers who have worked extensively with electronic music, especially as a part of multi-media presentations. He has combined electronic music with conventional instruments and films, and is noted for his music created for dramatic productions. Numerous composers continue to explore the boundless possibilities in electronic music.

*New Sonorities with Traditional Instruments*

The interest in timbre that led to the development of electronic music has stimulated musical endeavor in many other areas as well. The repertory for traditional instruments is being expanded rapidly, and even the techniques and styles of playing these instruments are changing. This is in part because electronic music has so greatly influenced what we might call the "sound ideal" of mid-twentieth-century music.

The flute has especially fascinated modern composers because of its great range of sound. Although most flutists learn only about thirty or forty different fingerings, far more are possible. Even more sounds can be created by varying the way the flutist blows into the mouthpiece. A pioneering work for flute, *Density 21.5*, was written by Varèse in 1935. It is one of the earliest works to make use of new flute techniques, often requiring, among other things, that the keys be struck very hard to produce abrupt percussive sounds. As already mentioned, the music written for the flute in Davidovsky's "Synchronisms No. 1" incorporates the use of a number of new techniques. Flutter-tonguing and the use of extremes of range and dynamics expand sonorities traditionally heard on the flute. Luciano Berio (b. 1925), Kazuo Fukushima (b. 1930), and Harvey Sollberger (b. 1938) are other composers who have written very innovatively for it.

# John Cage

Another composer who has done much experimental work with instruments—and, in fact, with almost every aspect of music—is the American John Cage (b. 1912). Cage's ideas about music and the other arts have had considerable influence on artists in a number of fields. For him, art is not something separate from life; art is life and life is art. Thus part of his work as a composer has been to make people aware of all the sounds around them. "Wherever we are," he says, "what we hear is mostly noise. When we ignore it, it disturbs us. When we listen to it, we find it fascinating."

As a young composer in the 1930s, Cage followed the lead of Varèse in developing new forms of percussion music. His *First Construction* (*in Metal*), written in 1939, calls for the use of automobile brake drums, cowbells, and sheets of metal as well as more conventional percussion instruments. The work consists of a series of rhythmic units, combined and repeated in a systematic way, to form a symmetrical rhythmic structure. Cage's aim here was to devise a structure based not on melody or harmony but on rhythm alone.

### Prepared Piano

In 1938 Cage devised his *prepared piano* for use in a modern dance score. His invention grew out of the work of one of his teachers, Henry Cowell, whose piano string technique was discussed in Chapter 24. In a prepared piano such as the one Cage created, the strings are muted at a number of points with pieces of wood, metal, rubber, or glass. This alters the timbre as well as the pitch of the strings. A piano must be prepared differently for each piece, in accordance with the specific directions of the composer. The work is then played from an ordinary score, resulting in completely unconventional sounds.

Cage has remarked that "Art should imitate Nature in her manner of operation." He has tried, as much as possible, to let things be themselves and to get beyond the usual ideas about self-expression. One critic has interpreted Cage's philosophy thus: "Only by getting out of the imprisoning circle of his own wishes and desires can the artist be free to enter into the miraculous new field of human awareness that is opening up, and thereby help others enter it as well."

In 1952 Cage tried to sharpen his listeners' awareness of all the sounds around them by means of his so-called "silent piece," a work entitled *4′ 33″*. When the work was first performed, the pianist sat at a piano in silence for precisely four minutes and thirty-three seconds, opening and closing the keyboard cover three times to indicate the

Page from the score of Cage's *Music of Changes*. Cage's own notes about its performance include the following directive: "It will be found in many places that the notation is irrational; in such instance the performer is to employ his own discretion." (Copyright ⓒ by Henmar Press Inc., 373 Park Avenue South, New York, N.Y. 10016. International copyright secured. All rights reserved.)

beginning and end of the work's three movements. The "composition" was in actuality made up of all the sounds that occurred by chance in the auditorium during that time.

Cage's experiments have pioneered several other developments in music, some of which will be discussed later in this chapter. His work with new sonorities has influenced a number of contemporary composers. George Crumb (b. 1929) has been very innovative in his writing for piano to be played from the strings as well as the keyboard.

## Krzysztof Penderecki

Other composers have emphasized the development of new techniques for different instruments. Polish composer Krzysztof Penderecki (b. 1933), in particular, has created striking new sounds for strings. He is known widely for a number of major instrumental and choral works, such as his *Threnody to the Victims of Hiroshima* (1960) and *Passion according to St. Luke* (1963–65). His latest major work is the *Requiem Mass* (1985).

## Penderecki: Polymorphia

Written in 1961, Penderecki's *Polymorphia* is scored for twenty-four violins, eight violas, eight cellos, and eight double basses. Because conventional musical notation and symbols were not adequate to convey a number of new performance techniques to the players, Penderecki devised numerous new symbols to give instructions quickly, such as ||||, which means to play an arpeggio on the four strings between the bridge and tailpiece. A list of symbols and their meanings appears in the front of the score. In performance, the duration of measures is to be timed in seconds with a stop watch, following timings given in the score.

---

**LISTENING ANALYSIS**                                        SIDE 11, BAND 6

New string techniques

*Polymorphia* opens with a single, low, sustained chord in the bass register, that grows very slowly but determinedly. The bass note grows into a slightly larger sound mass, after which a new, sustained sound is added in the upper strings, followed quickly by a wandering layer of activity in the middle register. The performers play glissandos, at any speed they wish, between two given pitches or between the highest note on each instrument and some indefinite low note. After a climax is reached, these sounds taper off. They are followed by a section in which the players pizzicato as fast as possible. A number of different pizzicato effects are explored. Then fingertips are used to tap the instruments, and the palms of hands used to hit the strings. A second, main climax is reached. A section follows in which bowed, sustained and sliding sounds are explored, growing again to another climax. The effects created are very fresh, unconventional, and often surprising. Perhaps most surprising is the final resolution of the very dissonant work in a startlingly pure-sounding C-major chord at the end.

Melody in *Polymorphia* is generally subsumed under the greater preoccupation with harmony. No clear sense of meter is apparent to the listener. A

Krzysztof Penderecki conducting a rehearsal in 1983 of his *St. Luke Passion*, an oratorio composed in 1963–66 which met with immediate public success. As with the instruments, Penderecki makes the most surprising use of the human voice in this piece. (Photo: Clive Barda)

wide variety of rhythmic activity takes place, along with several changes of tempo. The texture often changes gradually from sparse to very dense, then back to sparse; it is sometimes built from two or three layers of activity.

Form is very free and evolutionary in *Polymorphia*. Several sections of different types of effects can be discerned. Perhaps most engaging in the work are the exploration of sustained and changing dissonance, the subtle and interesting changes of texture, and the fresh techniques used with the string instruments.

### LISTENING SUMMARY

| | |
|---|---|
| Timbre: | orchestra of string instruments |
| Melody: | not present in traditional sense due to sliding pitches and tone clusters |
| Rhythm: | no clear meter; varying tempos; much rhythmic variety; measures timed in seconds by stop watch |

| Harmony: | dissonant and generally atonal until C major chord at end |
| Texture: | gradual change from sparse to dense to sparse; at times two or three layers of activity |
| Form: | quite free, evolving from use of textures, dissonance, and string techniques |

### New Use of Percussion

In addition to experimenting with string and wind instruments, modern composers have increasingly varied the use of percussion instruments, leading to some of the most attractive and exciting developments in contemporary music. Percussion instruments are no longer used only for special emphasis or coloristic effects. They have often become an integral part of the whole, and there are now a large number of compositions for percussion only.

This development began early in the present century with the dazzling percussion parts Stravinsky wrote for *Les noces* ("The Wedding") and *L'Histoire du soldat* ("The Soldier's Tale"). At about the same time, in Italy, the Futurists were proclaiming their allegiance to the noise-music of shipyards, steel foundries, and railroads.

Edgard Varèse played an important part in the development of the new percussion music. His *Ionisation* (1929–31) was written for percussion alone. In this work and in others, he showed great sensitivity to the pitch level or register of the many percussion instruments of indefinite pitch. Bartók's *Sonata for Two Pianos and Percussion* (1938) is a remarkably original and outstanding work that features percussion instruments.

The new role of percussion instruments points up a very important aspect of modern music. Dynamics, timbre, and rhythm are no longer subordinated to pitch. Today composers are treating them as important structural elements in their own right. George Crumb, Karlheinz Stockhausen, William Kraft (b.1923, himself a percussionist), and many other composers have been creatively exploring new ideas in writing for percussion instruments.

### New Vocal Techniques

Innovations in vocal techniques are very much tied to the development of a sense of theater in contemporary music. This trend was apparent as early as Schoenberg's *Pierrot lunaire*. While making effective use of *Sprechstimme*, Schoenberg's work also requires that the singer have considerable histrionic ability. Today's singers may be asked to shout, whisper, groan, or murmur nonsense syllables, creating effects that range from the humorous to the macabre. They and instrumentalists may be asked to add theatrical gestures even in a concert piece; the gap between music and theater has been intentionally blurred in several recent vocal pieces. Many singers, including Cathy Berberian and Jan de Gaetani, have chosen to specialize in new music, and some very interesting works have been written for them.

Berio    *Circles* (1960), written by Luciano Berio (b. 1925) for his wife Cathy

Berberian, illustrates especially well a number of the demands made on singers by these contemporary scores. The work is a setting for voice, harp, and percussion of three poems by e.e. cummings. The singer must have a very wide range and must be able to execute a variety of vocal gymnastics in addition to singing. Timing must be perfect, both to sustain the dramatic tension and to maintain close coordination with the instruments. The sounds of syllables and even of letters are as important as the meaning of the words and are an integral part of the timbre. The percussion instruments are used to punctuate and emphasize the singer's line. A sibilant word in the text, for example, may be matched by a tingling buzz from a cymbal, or a sudden shout may be enhanced by an abrupt crash.

**George Crumb**

George Crumb in the early 1980s. Many of his works show the tremendous influence of the imagery created by the Spanish poet Federico García Lorca (1899–1936). (Peters Edition Ltd.)

A collection of works similar in spirit to Berio's is the four books of *Madrigals* by George Crumb (b. 1929). The madrigals were written in the period of 1965–69, and each of the four books contains three madrigals. The twelve pieces are all based on poems by the Spanish poet Federico García Lorca (1899–1936), whose works have had great attraction for Crumb and whose poems he has used in several other compositions. The texts of the madrigals deal with the subjects of life, death, love, and aspects of nature. The texts chosen by Crumb for each madrigal are brief, and so are the pieces themselves.

The madrigals are written for soprano solo, accompanied in each book by a different, small ensemble: Book I—vibraphone and contrabass; Book II—alto flute (doubling flute in C and piccolo) and percussion; Book III—harp and percussion; Book IV—flute (doubling piccolo and alto flute), harp, contrabass, and percussion. The percussion instruments in all four books are colorful and varied, including vibraphone, antique cymbals, glockenspiel, two timpani, marimba, bongo drums, three timbales, very small triangle, two suspended cymbals, glass chimes, and tubular bells. Crumb asks the singer and instrumentalists to perform in a variety of different, specific ways. The soprano is directed to sing at different times passages with no vibrato, coloratura passages, in quarter tones, to perform *Sprechstimme*, and to whisper. The instrumentalists are given copious directions, many of which are traditional in nature about dynamics, harmonics, and phrasing; others are unusual, such as one that tells the percussionist to scrape a coin over the surface of a cymbal in a single stroke. Crumb's use of instruments and voice shows a careful and sensitive choice of effects that add very convincingly to his overall musical plan. The madrigals in Book IV show many of Crumb's techniques and their effective use in composition.

**Crumb: Madrigals, Book IV**

In the madrigals of Book IV the soprano is accompanied by flute (doubling piccolo and alto flute), harp, contrabass, and percussion (glockenspiel, marimba, two suspended cymbals, glass chimes, and tubular bells). The instrumental ensemble is the largest of the groups in the four sets of madrigals. Rather extensive performance notes precede the score, suggesting the positioning of instruments and explaining details of performance practices. The first six of these instructions show Crumb's careful concern about how his music is to be performed.

Performance Notes (from score published by C. F. Peters)
1) The performers read from score.
2) Each note is preceded by an accidental, except in case(s) of an immediate repetition of pitch or a pattern of pitches.
3) All *glissandi* occupy the total duration of the note to which they are affixed. The *portamento* effect (a "delayed *glissando*") is always specifically indicated in the score.
4) The metronome indications are approximate and may vary slightly, depending on the acoustics of the hall.
5) All whispered sounds must project! The soprano may slightly voice the whispered passages if the acoustics of the hall require this.
6) The alto flute part is transposed for the convenience of the player; it will sound a fourth lower than written. The piccolo is notated in the conventional manner (sounding an octave higher than written). The abbreviation "Flzg." indicates flutter-tongue. Flute harmonics of the third partial are used in this work; the lower note shows the fundamental fingering, the upper note the actual pitch of the harmonic. The "Speak-flute" effect (on page 9) should be carefully studied so that both the Spanish words and the flute pitches are distinctly heard.

Crumb further explains some unusual marking he uses in the Madrigals, such as: ⌐7·⌐ = 7 seconds (approximately), 4̨ = a quarter note lower than written pitch, and 4̧ = a quarter note higher than written pitch.

---

**LISTENING ANALYSIS** SIDE 12, BAND 2,

### First Madrigal

Flute, harp, contrabass, and glockenspiel open the madrigal with a dissonant chord played percussively and permitted to die away; it is repeated seven seconds later. The contrabass (tuned *scordatura*, that is, with an unusual tuning) and harp are asked to play harmonics through much of the madrigal, that is, to play with very high, light pitches. The flute is also to play harmonics at times, and to be played with flutter-tonguing in two passages.

Text:
¿Por qué nací entre espejos?
El día me da vueltas.
Y la noche me copia en todas sus estrellas.

Why was I born surrounded by mirrors?
The day turns round me.
And the night reproduces me in each of her stars. (Translation from score)

The voice presents the first phrase of text in a detached, disjunct style. Motives in the first phrase are retrogrades of each other—the two-note motive after the opening chord is immediately presented in retrograde; the five-note motive heard next is built on retrograde, pivoting around the middle note; and the two-note motive that follows is immediately repeated in retrograde. The extensive use of retrograde is obviously related to the mention of "mirrors" in the text.

The following flute passage proceeds to the F in the middle of the passage and is then a retrograde of the first part of the passage. The voice then repeats the first phrase of text, set to a melody that is a free, inverted retrograde of the melody of the first phrase.

The harp is featured in the following phrase which begins a slightly slower section. As the soprano sings the second and third phrases of text, beginning in a half-sung style and fading to a whisper, a very soft contrabass appears with music that mirrors itself. Moreover, the C♯ in the middle of the phrase is also the middle of the entire piece.

The music thereafter is a retrograde of the pitches heard in the first half of the piece, although instrumentation is changed from the first appearance of the pitches to provide variation. The use of retrograde was suggested to Crumb by the text, and he used the concept subtly and well in his music to support the sense of the text. Retrograde is probably most clearly affirmed to the listener when the madrigal closes with the two chords with which it opened.

The harmonic language in the madrigal is dissonant and does not stress a tonal center, but the use of the small ensemble is delicate and highly expressive. Only in this madrigal and one other, the first of Book III, does Crumb use techniques, such as retrograde, that give obvious clarity to their structure. In both instances the techniques were suggested by the texts. In the other madrigals, structure is generally more freely evolutionary.

### LISTENING SUMMARY

| | |
|---|---|
| Timbre: | Soprano solo, flute (doubling piccolo and alto flute), harp, contrabass, and percussion |
| Melody: | Generally disjunct and detached |
| Rhythm: | No meter marked in the score nor clear to the listener. A variety of short motives are prominent |
| Harmony: | Dissonant, with no clear tonal center |
| Texture: | Sparse, rather pointillistic |
| Form: | Results from the use of retrograde on large and small levels |

### Other Madrigals of Book IV

The second madrigal, "Through my hands' violet shadow," features the ensemble, especially the tubular bells and flute. The soprano enters just before the end to present the text, first using glissando, and then fading to whisper.

The third madrigal, "Death is watching me," presents a drone in the contrabass throughout the work, basically on D♯ and G♯. As the piece unfolds these two pitches are changed a quarter tone higher and lower by the player turning the tuning pegs of the instrument as directed in the score. The singer presents the text dramatically with sung notes, shouted syllables, and in "speak-flute," Crumb's direction to the singer to speak certain words over the mouthpiece of the alto flute while specific pitches are fingered. At the close the contrabass drone fades from *ppppp* to nothing.

### Other Works of Crumb

Crumb's *Ancient Voices of Children* (1970) is another very effective work. It is a cycle of songs, also based on texts by Lorca. The music is set for mezzo-soprano, boy soprano, oboe, mandolin, harp, electric piano, and a large group of percussion instruments, including Tibetan prayer stones, Japanese temple bells, and tom-toms. Singers and instrumentalists create fresh sounds with unusual techniques. At one point, the mezzo-soprano sings into the amplified piano to produce what Crumb calls "a shimmering aura of echoes." The pianist is at times called upon to apply a chisel to the piano strings to change their pitch.

Among other significant works by Crumb are his four volumes of *Makrokosmos*, from the early 1970s, for amplified piano or two amplified pianos and percussion. In these works he expands the technical capabilities of the piano in new and engaging ways. While many of his ideas and techniques are unorthodox, they seem always to have a strong and clear sense of musicality and artistry.

## Microtonal Composition

Unusual intervals and divisions of the octave into more than twelve portions have been a feature of some twentieth-century works. Although most easily realized electronically, these practices have also influenced the use and treatment of acoustic instruments. In the United States, Harry Partch (1901–1974) created new acoustic instruments tuned in new ways and capable of playing microtones to realize his compositions. His innovations have influenced composers of many styles, including LaMonte Young and other "minimalists" (see page 503). George Crumb, as mentioned above, asks his performers in several compositions to perform quarter tones. It will be interesting to see if the concept is developed further in decades to come.

## New Principles of Structure

Many composers have sought new ways of structuring musical sounds, and fresh solutions have been found. Concurrently, composers have focused attention on performance itself, and elements that cannot be incorporated into a score. Improvisation and chance elements have thus acquired a role in the compositional process.

## Chance or Aleatoric Music

John Cage has explored the element of chance, or indeterminacy, in some of his work. The chance, or *aleatoric*, methods he has used vary greatly from work to work. In 1951 he composed *Music of Changes*, a work for piano, by using the *I Ching* ("Book of Changes"). This is an ancient Oriental book that describes a method of throwing coins or marked sticks to obtain chance numbers. Almost every aspect of the composition is determined by this method. One coin toss might determine the duration of a note, another its pitch, and so on.

*Chance elements in performance*

In recent years, Cage has used aleatoric methods less to determine the aspects of a composition and more as a means of leaving decisions up to the performers. Many of his latest works are made up of instructions to performers that may be interpreted in almost any way. *Variations II* (1961), for example, is a work for any number of performers using any sound-producing means. The score consists of six transparent sheets, each containing a single straight line, and a seventh sheet containing points. The sheets are laid out in random order, and perpendiculars leading from the points to the lines are measured. These measurements serve as a free guide for the performers, to be interpreted into sound in any way the performers wish.

Of course these instructions give the performers such great freedom that they virtually compose the piece, or rather a possible version of it, themselves. One recorded version of Cage's *Variations II* makes use of an amplified piano played by pianist David Tudor (b. 1926). Tudor produces rich and varied sounds, not only playing the keys but also stroking the strings with objects attached to contact microphones and phonograph cartridges.

Cage's attitude toward music and all the arts is an experimental one. He is interested more in the process than in the finished product. His concern is not so much with the operations by which people can manipulate their environment but with the fact that people and their environment together form a unity.

Cage's concept of art as a process that makes use of chance elements has definite parallels in the fine arts. In the works of the Abstract Expressionist or "action" painters such as Jackson Pollock, the fortuitous path taken by thrown or dripping paint is an important part of the work. One critic has commented, "By making art out of materials not usually familiar to art, Cage, along with his friend Marcel Duchamp, also provided ... precedents for pop art, found objects, industrial sculpture, and much else." Composers, too, responded to his ideas. Both Stockhausen and Boulez were influenced by Cage to introduce indeterminate elements into some works.

**Brown**

During the late 1940s and early 1950s, Cage became well known in New York, and a group of composers and painters began to gather around him. Notable among the composers was Earle Brown (b. 1926), who has since made much use of chance elements in his own music. Brown has been particularly interested in providing opportunities for spontaneous decisions during the performance of a work and the freedom to change the order of musical sections. He regards the performance of one of his works as "process rather than static and conclusive." His *25 Pages,** written for piano in 1953, was inspired by Alexander Calder's mobiles, in which, Brown has stated, "there are basic units subject to innumerable different relationships of forms." The twenty-five pages of work may be played in any order, and each staff may be read as either a bass or a treble clef. Each page may also be performed either side up: accidentals and dynamic markings are provided on both the left and right.

**Brown's use of time notation**

The excerpt from Brown's *25 Pages* that appears below shows the composer's use of *time notation*. To interpret the score, the performer must decide on a basic tempo and then determine how long to hold each note on the basis of its visual length.

Excerpt from *25 Pages*

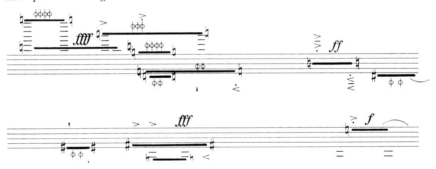

A great many other composers have incorporated chance elements into their compositions to a greater or lesser extent. Lukas Foss (b. 1922)—outstanding conductor, pianist, and composer—has written a number of works, such as *Elytres* (1964) that feature aleatoric techniques. His *Time Cycle* (1960) is a suite for soprano and orchestra that includes a number of improvisations of a small jazz group.

**Elliott Carter**

A number of composers have continued to search for yet other methods of structuring new music. Composer Elliott Carter (b. 1908), among others, has stressed the need young composers have for finding a new approach to structure. He believes that this need is

*Earle Brown, '25 Pages' (1953). Excerpt reprinted by permission: Universal Edition, London

much more important than the development of new styles of harmony or innovations in other musical elements. Problems of musical continuity, Carter feels, must be rethought today, just as ideas about harmony were revised and changed at the beginning of the twentieth century. Carter himself has developed a number of new ways of handling rhythmic and textural continuities. With his technique of metric modulation, for example, the basic pulse of one part of a work changes by first being introduced with a conflicting rhythmic pattern before it becomes the new basic pulse in the following section. Some of these new methods can be found in his *Double Concerto for Piano and Harpsichord*.

The structure of Carter's *Double Concerto* (1961) is essentially determined by the interplay of rhythm and texture. The texture is made up of several different layers, which often move at different speeds. The differentiation and interrelation of the various textural elements through rhythm is one of the hallmarks of Carter's style.

In a performance of the work, the two solo instruments, the piano and the harpsichord, are placed on either side of the stage, each with its own small orchestra of two percussion players and six other instrumentalists. Carter explained this arrangement in the following manner: "Primarily, both groups were chosen to suggest and reinforce the sonorities and character of the two soloists.... Each group ... also contains elements of the opposing group to weld the entire sound into one." The harpsichord's percussion group, for example, contains wood blocks, triangles, and cymbals, while the piano's percussion group is made up of drums. The harpsichord is also supported by brass instruments to compensate for its smaller dynamic range.

The *Double Concerto* is divided into seven contrasting sections:

| | |
|---|---|
| Introduction | |
| Cadenza for Harpsichord | Presto |
| Allegro scherzando | Cadenzas for Piano |
| Adagio | Coda |

The symmetrical structure of the work is striking. The slow middle section is surrounded by the two quickest sections. These in turn are surrounded by cadenzas, which are bracketed by an introduction and a coda. The overall structure thus depends in large part on changes of tempo and instrumentation.

Carter has often characterized his works in dramatic or poetic terms. Of his *Double Concerto* he has written: "The idea that there is always a large world going on from which items are picked out, brought into focus, and allowed to drop back, is one of the fundamental conceptions of the piece."

Other important works by Carter include his *Concerto for Orchestra* (1969) and three string quartets (1950–51, 1959, 1971), the last two of which won Pulitzer Prizes. Carter's significance and reputation are very wide. He has received numerous honors and commissions in the United States, and his works have found a wide-spread audience.

## Minimalism

Another solution to the problem of how structure can be best achieved in contemporary music can be seen in the works by several composers who began writing with very minimal resources in the 1960s. Eastern philosophies, then becoming popular in the West, were one inspiration in this direction. Composers LaMonte Young (b. 1935), Cornelius Cardew (1936–1981), and other American and English composers have composed works with very few melodic, rhythmic, and harmonic materials, treating and extending them with repetition, of motive on a small level and of larger rhythmic patterns as well. Young and others made intensive studies of Indian and other Asian music, and began to experiment with unequally tempered tunings. The music of Terry Riley (b. 1935) and Steve Reich (b. 1936) explores these ideas further, while showing influence of jazz, Asian music, ideas of Erik Satie and John Cage, and still other factors. Numerous repetitions of tiny motives and groups of motives in the music of composers who adhered to these principles have led to their music being described as "minimal" music or "systems" music. It is in one sense antithetical to other avant-garde styles, in that it leaves no aspect of the performance to chance. In recent years the composer who has come to be most widely known for his development of this musical style is Philip Glass (b. 1937), whose works have received considerable notice and acclaim. Glass is also known widely for the ensemble named after him—the group specializes in playing his music and music by other "minimalist" composers.

*Glass*     The music of Glass often uses highly amplified ensembles of keyboard instruments, winds, and voice. One of his chief goals is to create music that can be experienced "as a pure medium of sound freed of dramatic structure." Repetition and slow, subtle changes of the repeated motivic material is a fundamental characteristic of Glass's minimal style. The gradual lengthening of material during repetition is characteristic of some works. Glass has written for a variety of media. His opera *Einstein on the Beach* (written with Robert Wilson, 1977) is probably his most widely known work. *Satyagraha* (1980) is an opera about the life of Mahatma Gandhi. He has written many works to be played by chamber ensembles, such as the film score *North Star* and *Modern Love Waltz* (both 1977).

### Glass: Modern Love Waltz (arr. by Robert Moran)

The "Modern Love Waltz" was commissioned by the Da Capo Chamber Players, a group that specializes in playing new music, and was included as part of their tenth anniversary concert in Alice Tully Hall (New York) on 23 March 1980. It was inspired by *Modern Love*, a novel by Constance De Jong (with whom Glass collaborated on *Satyagraha*). The waltz is scored for flute, clarinet, violin, cello, and electric piano, and is a light, rather intimate expression of the minimal style.

## Glass: Modern Love Waltz

### LISTENING ANALYSIS

The structural basis of "Modern Love Waltz" is a progression of two arpeggiated chords in the bass, a minor second apart—the first is on A without a third, and the second is a B-flat seventh chord. The progression is played by the electric piano in a detached manner.

This progression is repeated constantly throughout the entire work. In its first appearance the right hand of the piano adds a short, descending, arpeggiated motive that begins one measure after the progression in the left hand. This motive, as well as most other motivic material that follows, moves quickly in eighth notes in A major, over the moderately quick basic progression in $\frac{3}{4}$. It is repeated with the next few repetitions of the basic progression, but it, and all other subsequent motives, are always subordinate to the basic progression. In the third presentation of the progression, the clarinet and flute enter with subtle, new arpeggiated motives, and then the violin joins the ensemble with the fifth appearance of the progression. The violin soon becomes a little more prominent when it presents a slower motive, but quick, nervous motion continues around it. As the repetitions of the basic progression continue, new, short motives creep in and out of the texture, enhancing the basic progression. The resulting harmony is always in the major mode. Syncopation plays a subtle role at times. Toward the end the texture, never very dense, thins out as the tempo increases slightly. Repetition of the basic progression stops, after seventy-three appearances, as the electric piano plays simple, arpeggiated versions of the chords one last time and ends on the A chord. The essence of the waltz is, thus, the constant repetition of the basic progression with repetitions and subtle changes in the motives added to decorate it. The straightforward tonal harmony is a feature of minimalist works.

### LISTENING SUMMARY

Timbre:   Instrumental chamber group of electric piano, clarinet, flute, violin, cello
Melody:   Numerous short motives are presented, repeated, and changed
Rhythm:   $\frac{3}{4}$ meter of the waltz is quite regular; quicker rhythmic motion over the basic meter; some syncopation
Harmony:  Two chords are repeated throughout, A and B-flat seventh
Form:     Results from the constant repetition of the basic harmonic progression and other motives added to enhance it

## Music of the Present and the Future

The musical situation in the second half of the twentieth century is unique. There is an unprecedented variety of styles and a tremendous independence of outlook among composers. It is interesting that much of the emphasis in contemporary music is on aspects of construction, perhaps in part because traditional forms are no longer easily accepted as models. Each composition, to a large extent, must therefore create its own form if conventional solutions are not followed.

Even with all their independence, composers today have more of a chance to influence and be influenced by one another than ever before. The new music is notable for its internationalism. This, of course, is due partly to the development of the long-playing record and tape, which can make any piece of music available all over the world. Broadcasting of new music also plays a significant role. The phonograph record and stereophonic sound have had other effects as well. Several compositions have been commissioned especially for records and written to fit in one or two record sides.

Ironically, at a time in history when there are more media than ever before for the dissemination of new music, very little of this music has reached the general public. The new developments have taken place, on the whole, outside of the symphony orchestras and other performance groups of the music establishment, though some organizations have instituted residencies for composers, whose works are thus guaranteed performance. Still, the average concertgoer hears very little contemporary music. Such a situation is unprecedented. The public at the time of Mozart and Beethoven, for example, heard most new works almost as soon as they were written. There are, however, some encouraging signs that the audience for contemporary music is steadily growing, and it is to be hoped that this trend will continue.

**Increasing role for women**

Another very important aspect of modern music is the increasing participation and acceptance of women, not only as performers, but also as conductors and composers. While women have been active in the writing and performing of music for centuries, their role has grown enormously in the twentieth century. Female singers have enjoyed great prominence and prestige ever since the seventeenth century, but women composers and conductors have rarely enjoyed the success and popularity of their male counterparts, most often due to social restrictions. In recent decades, Margaret Hillis (b. 1921), conductor of the Chicago Symphony Chorus, and Sarah Caldwell (b. 1928), conductor to the Opera Company of Boston, have been acclaimed for their particular genius. English conductors Jane Glover (b. 1949) and Iona Brown (b. 1941) have recently enjoyed a great deal of recognition and success. Composers Thea Musgrave (b. 1928), Esther Williamson Ballou (1915–1973), and Pozzi Escot (b. 1933) have all gained international repute. Ellen Taafe Zwilich (b. 1939) became the first woman composer to win the coveted Pulitzer Prize for music in 1983. Hopefully the barriers to recognition of female composers and conductors will all soon fade.

This is an era of almost unparalleled possibilities for musical exploration. For the listener, the new music represents a challenge and an invitation to an enormous variety of musical experiences. Our new music is reflective of our times, and it is enlightening to observe how the ideas of our age are incorporated into the many different types and styles of music that surround us.

# CHAPTER 29

# *American Popular Music*

*LISTENING PREVIEW All types of popular music have developed in the twentieth century at an extremely fast pace, due in large part to their wide dissemination by the recording industry, radio, and television. Jazz, an art form that is a native American creation, has undergone numerous changes in style since its birth. Yet one major characteristic is central to all jazz styles—improvisation, that is, the ability of a performer to create new musical ideas spontaneously, usually based on an existing melody or chordal progression. Listen to* West End Blues *(side 12, band 4) which features the great trumpeter Louis Armstrong. Notice the free, imaginative style of each of the soloists as they improvise on a given melody and harmonic progression.*

## Sources of Popular Music

Folk music, soul music, jazz, country, rock—whatever the style, popular music plays an overwhelming part in the daily lives of most Americans. The origins of any popular music are deep in the human spirit, and its history reaches back to the earliest ages. Today, it has a far greater commercial market in America than does "classical" music, and it has a significant role in the film industry. Through video, popular music is also closely allied to visual arts, and it is at the edge of emerging computer technologies. In some areas, distinctions between popular and "art" music are becoming blurred or even irrelevant.

Popular music in America has been influenced by folk traditions around the world. Over the years the millions of immigrants who came to this country brought with them the music they knew and loved. At times this music has been sustained virtually intact. Croatians still do round dances to traditional music in Detroit. German songs are heard in Milwaukee. And Chinese music abounds around Grant Street in San Francisco. Often, however, the music has changed in America, being blended and mixed with other traditions to create "American" folk and popular music. Often, too, folk traditions have served as a basis for distinctly new types of music. This can be seen most clearly in the black folk music roots of blues and jazz.

Because of the great importance of folk music both as a style in and of itself and as a source of other popular styles, we will begin our discussion of popular music in America with an examination of the two major folk traditions: Anglo-American folk music and black folk music.

Jazz trumpeter Miles Davis in action, 1986. An early proponent of cool jazz (1950s) and jazz-rock (1970s), he has long been part of the avant-garde and continues to surprise. (David Redfern Photography; photo: Suzi Gibbons)

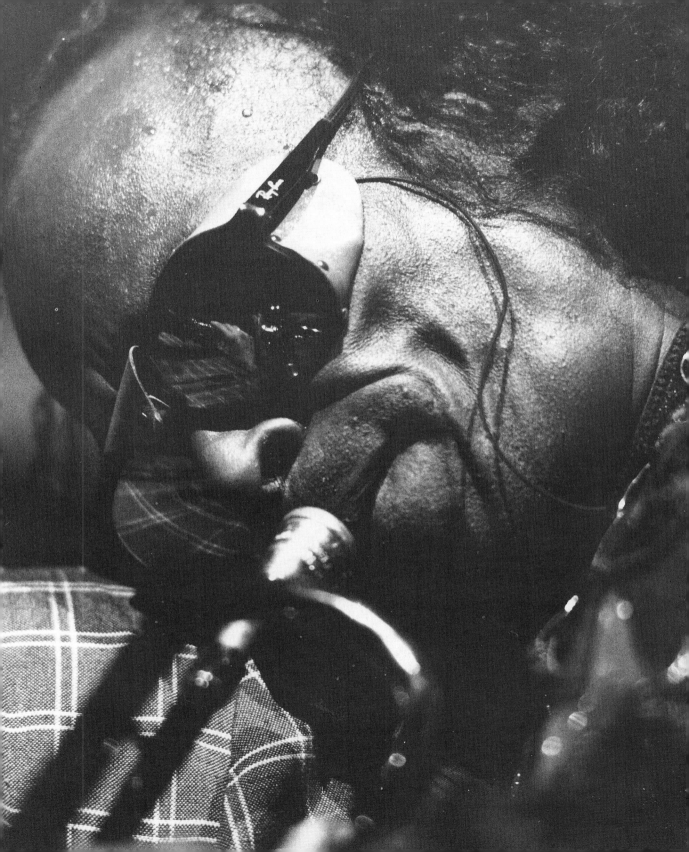

# Anglo-American Folk Music

Anglo-American folk music is strongly rooted in the English and Scottish styles brought to the New World in the seventeenth and eighteenth centuries. In these early times singing and dancing were among the most popular forms of informal entertainment in the colonies. Folksongs were sung daily in homes, at work, and of course on festive occasions. Often unaccompanied, they were at other times sung with the support of household instruments such as the guitar and the *dulcimer*—one of the most widely used folk string instruments in this country. Songs were devised by young and old and passed on orally from one generation to the next. Most remained unwritten, were thus prone to variation, and were easily responsive to outside influences.

**General characteristics**

Stylistically, Anglo-American folksongs share a number of basic characteristics. The music is generally uncomplicated, which allows it to be easily passed on orally from one person to another. Melodies are usually conjunct and organized into phrases of equal length, although singers sometimes add an extra measure or two at will. Rhythm and meter are derived to some extent from the words of the songs. Texture is generally homophonic, as the melodies are supported by the chordal accompaniment of guitar or dulcimer. Form is normally symmetrical and strophic. Repeated phrases occur, helping to delineate the structure more clearly. This simple and direct style, however, contrasts with and accentuates the profound ideas that the lyrics often convey, and permits rich variety in style of performance by individual singers.

**Ballads**

Some of the most important characteristics of Anglo-American folk music come from the English *ballad*, or narrative song. The typical ballad is made up of several stanzas with a recurrent refrain. The themes are generally sentimental, social, or political. A large part of the folk heritage of the British Isles was transmitted through the years by ballads, and when the English, Scots, and Irish came to America, their ballads came with them.

The English ballad tradition remained strongest in New England and Appalachia, areas not easily penetrated by changing styles. The ballads of these regions, like their antecedents, ordinarily recount the outlines of a tragic story, sometimes with refrains unrelated to the rest of the narrative. Their lyrics combine American colloquialisms and more refined literary English. Many New World ballads originally had no accompaniment or relied on the support of a single repeated chord strummed on a guitar, banjo, or dulcimer.

**Occupational songs**

Another type of Anglo-American folk music, derived more or less from the ballad, is the *occupational song*. The lyrics generally concern such things as the perils, loneliness, humor, or joys of mining, farming, cowherding, railroad building, and the many other jobs that went into building America. Some of the songs highlight serious accidents and tragedies. Others make a joke out of hardship. An example of the second type is found in the lyrics of a song about tarriers, or railroad laborers:

> ... *one day a premature blast went off;*
> *And a mile in the air went big Jim Goff;*
> *And drill, ye tarriers, drill....*

> *Next week, when payday came around,*
> *Jim Goff a dollar short was found.*
> *When he asked what for, came this reply:*
> *"Yer docked fer the time you was up in the sky!"*
> *And drill, ye tarriers, drill....*

One special type of occupational song, the *sea chantey*, was at first borrowed from other countries, but was gradually remolded to reflect the spirit of American sailors.

**Instrumental music**

Purely instrumental folk music supplied a background for dancing and marching. The *square dance*, patterned after the English rural jig and the French cotillion and quadrille, was a New World invention that required no more accompaniment than a lone fiddle and clapping hands. *Marches* were also often played on only fife and drum. As in vocal music, economy of style was a basic factor. One or two instruments had to suffice, although more could be added if they were available.

**Other types of folk songs**

A number of other types of folksongs were also patterned after British prototypes. *Patriotic songs* were widespread. During the Revolution, many such songs were written to convey news of battles, celebrate victories, boost morale, bolster courage, and even to make jokes about the enemy. Children's *play songs* such as *Skip to My Lou* were abundant. *Lovesongs* such as *I Gave My Love an Apple* and *lullabies* were somewhat rarer.

One uniquely American type of folksong related *tall tales* about life in the new World. Although musically similar to English songs, their lyrics manifested the peculiarly American penchant for self-deprecating humor and exaggeration found perhaps most clearly in the Paul Bunyan legends. As we have seen, this penchant often carried over to occupational songs.

Relatively pure versions of English folk music are still found in the remoter regions of Appalachia and the southern hill country. Scattered inhabitants of these areas have entertained themselves for generations with songs handed down by memory. In other areas, marked by a steady influx of immigrants from Europe, Africa, and elsewhere, the prevailing Anglo-American folk style has incorporated

**Use of styles from other nations**

many foreign elements—among them the folk styles of Germany, France, Poland, and Russia. Some foreign songs, such as the French *Alouette* and *Frère Jacques* and the German *O Tannenbaum*, have survived intact, even retaining their original non-English lyrics. Others, especially children's songs, have been translated into English to become lasting favorites.

In the hands of professional folk singers, the singing of Anglo-

American folksongs has today become more of a self-conscious art. Singers are generally trained artists, such as Joan Baez (b. 1941) and Judy Collins (b. 1939), who often present not the original folk songs but formally composed songs in folk style. However, many of these professional singers, Pete Seeger (b. 1919) in particular, are very well acquainted with the history of their art. Although they regularly alter traditional songs to please their audiences, they try to encourage public interest in authentic folk music and folklore. They have also set out to update the genre, as in many songs of protest written in the folk style during the 1960s. At that time there began also a tendency to combine folk idioms with rock and other popular music.

## Black Folk Music

Of all the ethnic influences that have gone into the creation of popular music in America, probably the most important has been that of black Africa. West African music, though very different from European music in many respects, shared with it certain basic characteristics of harmony. Thus, when the two traditions were brought together in America by slavery, it was possible for them to blend. Black folk music was just the first of many important and widely influential results.

Generally pressed into slavery by European adventurers on the west coast of Africa, the hundreds of thousands of blacks who began arriving in America in 1619 brought with them a highly developed musical tradition and a habit of incorporating music into virtually every activity of life. Religion, dance, and work were some of the main functions it served. Much of their music came to America intact. Once here it was gradually altered to meet new needs. The banjo, unique to America, is thought to have African roots. The use of drums, the most important instrument of West Africa, was continued in the New World.

American blacks developed a wide repertory of songs, both secular and religious. One early type of secular song, perhaps the closest of all to African prototypes, was the *field holler* that slaves often sang while working. A field holler was the yearning cry of a slave working alone, a sound midway between a yell and a song, whose words determined the tone. It began with a high, long-drawn-out shout and then glided down to the lowest note the singer could reach. Such songs were characterized by falsetto tones, swoops and slides from note to note, complicated and unexpected changes of rhythm, and an occasional line of melody from Anglo-American ballads or hymns. They were heard not only in the fields but wherever a black man or woman worked at hard, lonely tasks. When slavery ended, the songs were taken onto the docks, into the railroad camps, and onto the Mississippi River.

**Group work song**  Related to the field holler was the *group work song*. This, too, was close to African sources, for whenever Africans worked together at a task they found it natural to pace their labor with a song. Field hands

**Field holler** (margin note)

sang as they hoed or picked the cotton. Rowing songs were used to time the strokes on the flat-bottomed boats of the South. Later on, work songs were chanted by chain gangs and by railroad workers, whose backbreaking, dangerous labor was regulated by the rhythmic chanting of the song leader. The leader played a very important part in the group work song, choosing the song to be sung, setting the pace, adjusting it to the feel of the work being done, and improvising catchy lyrics and musical byplay to fire the energies of the other workers. A good song made the work go faster and better and relieved the weary monotony of it.

Although there was great variety in their lyrics and uses, the earliest work songs were almost entirely African in sound and structure. They made use of the African call-and-response pattern, expressive African vocal techniques such as those used in the field holler, and occasional syncopated African rhythms built around a steady meter. Most work songs were sung with the leader and chorus responding to each other, but some were performed almost in unison, with incidental improvised variants. Also typical of the early work songs was the implied use of tonic harmony, with little sense of the dominant or subdominant chords. Gradually, however, the songs picked up melodic and harmonic elements from Anglo-American ballads and hymns and evolved toward a style that anticipated the blues.

**Ring shout**    Another musical style that closely resembled its African counterparts was the *ring shout*, a shuffling dance with chanting and handclapping. To an African, dancing was a natural part of worship, but as the Bible was thought to prohibit dancing in church, slaves had to be content with a short shuffling step executed counterclockwise in a ring. This circular movement was accompanied by excited clapping and a kind of *shout song* that provided more rhythm than melody. Biblical stories supplied the words for the shout songs, which were chanted in the customary leader-chorus fashion. Starting slowly, the music gathered speed and intensity with the hypnotic repetition of body movements and musical phrases.

**Song sermons**    In many black religious services, the sermon also took on some of the qualities of a song, generally with a driving, hypnotic rhythm. Delivering such a *song sermon*, the preacher would at different times speak, chant, or sing, steadily increasing speed and passion as the song proceeded. The congregation, caught up in the pulse of the rhythm, would interject rhythmic cries or abbreviated lines of melody, using words such as "Amen!" or "Yes, my Lord!" Starting with a fixed text and then improvising, with a slow crescendo in the repeated phrases, an accomplished preacher could generate tremendous energy and fervor. Such sermons can still be heard today.

**Lining out**    *Lining out* was a technique borrowed from white colonial churches. In many of these churches hymnbooks were in short supply; in others many of the people of the congregation were illiterate. Thus, it was common practice for the preacher to sing each line of a hymn or psalm and then wait for the congregation to repeat it. This technique adapted itself perfectly to the African call-and-response pattern. In their own use of lining out, blacks added the African repertory of swoops, slides, shouts, and other ornaments to their responses, so that at times there was a splendid cacophony of multiple versions going on all at once.

## The Blues

Bessie Smith on stage in 1928. (The Bettmann Archive/BBC Hulton Picture Library)

The invention of the *blues* represents a major contribution of black folk music. Its influence on popular music has been notable, even since 1960. The blues style is characterized by distinctive *blue notes* produced by slightly bending the pitch of certain tones of the major scale, generally the third and seventh. The style was somehow right for plaintive songs of sadness. A whole repertory of such songs grew up, created by unrequited lovers, prisoners, lonely people far from home, and thousands of others who needed to ease their pain by expressing it.

As it was later harmonized, the usual blues song is based on the I, IV, and V chords. Generally the music is cast into twelve-measure units, divided into three lines of four measures each, resulting in an overall AAB form for each twelve-bar unit. The first half of each line is sung, while the second half is a *break*—a short musical passage played on one or more of the accompanying instruments. In the lyrics, the first two lines are always the same, made to rhyme with the third. Thus, the old African call-and-response pattern persists, now between singer and instrumentalists, and also between the lines of the text. The result is an easily identified, resilient structure open to multiple repetition and variation. It was very adaptable to jazz styles and ultimately to other styles as well. The blues style itself reached a peak of popularity in the early years of the twentieth century. Two of the greatest blues singers of the era were the unforgettable Bessie Smith (1894–1937) and Gertrude "Ma" Rainey (1886–1939), both of whom were recorded.

## Black Spirituals

In many respects, the religious counterpart of the blues was the *spiritual*. Developed largely in rural areas in the mid-nineteenth century, spirituals did not receive much public attention until they were made popular after the Civil War by groups who performed harmonized arrangements such as the Fisk University Jubilee Singers. *Nobody Knows the Trouble I've Seen* and *Steal Away* are among the most familiar examples. The black spiritual was superficially similar to spirituals written early in the nineteenth century during the Protestant "Second Awakening." However, it is the black spiritual that has remained important to the present day. The music of the black spiritual was in effect an extremely successful mixture of church melodies and harmonies and West African rhythms and styles of performance.

As originally performed, black spirituals underwent a great deal of improvisation. Practically all the elements of a spiritual—melody, rhythm, form, and text—were altered with each singing. The later, written versions could only capture the text and the basic melodies. The spirit and embellishments added during the performances elude transcription into notation.

Nevertheless, certain aspects of the spiritual style remain constant in all the songs. As with the blues, the melodies are generously adorned with sliding pitches. Rhythm is enlivened liberally with syncopations: not only the now familiar shift of accent from the customary first and third beats in a $\frac{4}{4}$ meter to the second and fourth, but also more minute shifts within subdivisions of normal beats. Texture, which appears monophonic in transcribed versions of the melodies, was in fact homophonic and even polyphonic in performance, when improvised parts were added. In form, spirituals often followed the call-and-response pattern, alternating line with a short refrain.

## Gospel Hymns

The *gospel hymn* rose to popularity after a Protestant revival movement in the 1850s. Gospel music is not strictly a part of the black or white folk tradition because it was generally written by songwriters, but the music written was quickly assimilated into black folk music. The hymns were first performed in huge tents during revival meetings. After World War I, they were introduced in black churches, where the congregations greatly embellished both the melody and rhythm of the songs. The result, as presented in recent years by such singers as Mahalia Jackson, is a joyous music with an insistent beat that contributes much to the overall flamboyant, pulsating effect.

## Minstrel Shows and Vaudeville

Black folk music has unquestionably had a major influence on the music of twentieth-century America. Perhaps less well known is the very significant effect it had on the popular music of the nineteenth century. Stephen Foster, the most famous composer of black-inspired songs for white Americans, has already been mentioned. His songs were sung in parlors in homes all over the country. The straightforwardly sentimental lovesongs and plantation melodies (by white composers purporting to write black music) of Stephen Foster and others continued to be extremely popular beyond the middle of the nineteenth century. *My Old Kentucky Home* and *Oh Susanna* are two of Foster's many songs that are now part of the American folk tradition. Such songs also became part of a typically American form of entertainment, the *minstrel show*. Based on the music and humor of blacks as understood by whites, the first minstrel shows featured white performers who masqueraded as blacks by darkening their faces with burnt cork. After the Civil War, however, blacks often played the roles themselves. The shows relied on a standard routine of jokes, slapstick, dancing, skits, and music all presented by a group of performers who sat in a semicircle. The dancing featured the buck-and-wing, the ancestor of tap dancing, while the skits generally parodied a popular play such as *Uncle Tom's Cabin*. A grand cakewalk finale caricatured the courtly elegance of southern aristocracy. Minstrel shows also capitalized on patriotic, sentimental, and topical themes and ultimately provided the format for *vaudeville*, the variety show of the early twentieth century.

## Jazz

Jazz, one of the few distinctly American types of music, was derived from a variety of sources. Its rhythms were strongly influenced by the complex rhythms of West Africa. Its basic harmonic structure was taken from the European tradition. And many aspects of its melody and harmony were adapted from nineteenth-century American folk music, especially from black folk music. Among its direct ancestors are black work songs, field hollers, the blues, military marches, dance tunes, and the popular songs and minstrel show music of the nineteenth century. Several types of religious music also contributed to its birth, most notably ring shouts, song sermons, and lining out. Other types of religious music, including variants of European church melodies and black spirituals, were also influential.

**General characteristics**    In general, jazz is distinguished by its emphasis on rhythm, especially syncopation, and its use of improvisation. The performers usually begin by introducing a theme and its accompanying harmony. A meter is clearly established, and syncopated patterns are superimposed on it. The work as a whole takes form through a series of melodic and rhythmic improvisations on the theme and harmony. Each new section brings further elaboration. The result, especially in highly embellished pieces, is a theme obscured by variations. Eventually the variations appear to bear no relation at all to the original statement of the melody even though the underlying chords usually remain the same. Typical methods of variation include ornamenting a theme, replacing the theme or part of it with new melodic material, and embellishing the theme by means of contrapuntal techniques.

**Ragtime**

**Joplin**    The development of jazz depended to a large extent on a style of music that was developed in the 1890s. *Ragtime*, or "ragged time," was derived from military marches and from the banjo tunes played to accompany jigs and cakewalks in the minstrel shows. Scott Joplin (1868–1917) played a large part in the development of ragtime and became one of its greatest composers. During its heyday, from about 1897 to 1917, ragtime became a national craze and was by far the most popular kind of music in America. Primarily piano music (but also written for voice and as dance music), ragtime adheres to a strict $\frac{2}{4}$ or $\frac{4}{4}$ meter and is clearly divided into sections. The left hand establishes the harmonies and maintains a rhythm that emphasizes accented beats. Meanwhile, the right hand ornaments this chordal foundation with syncopation, runs, and arpeggios.

## Early Jazz Styles

The creators of jazz were mainly black Americans, though there are many noted white jazz musicians. The first important center for jazz was the notorious red-light district of New Orleans called Storyville.

Louis Armstrong ("Satchmo," seated at the piano) with his Hot Five band at the time of their first recording in 1926/27. Despite appearances, Armstrong played the trumpet; his partners (left to right): Johnny St. Cyr (banjo), Johnny Dodds (clarinet), Kid Ory (trombone), and Armstrong's wife Lil Hardin (piano). (Jazz Music Books)

Morton

There at the beginning of the twentieth century, musicians such as composer-pianist "Jelly Roll" Morton (1885–1941) worked together to transpose the ragtime style into what came to be known as jazz, by blending it with elements of popular music and the blues. Among the outstanding musicians heard in Storyville were players such as Buddy Bolden (1877–1931), Joe "King" Oliver (1885–1938), and the young Louis Armstrong (1900–1971). At first they simply called their style ragtime played "hot."

When Storyville was closed down in 1917 by the federal government, the main center of jazz shifted to Chicago. A city controlled by criminal gangs which sold liquor during prohibition with a large, concentrated black population, it provided a ready audience. There the small New Orleans ensemble, often made up of only three featured instruments—cornet or trumpet, clarinet, trombone—with percussion backup, grew larger. It was also in Chicago that white players first began to take any major part in jazz performances, beginning with the first great white soloist, the cornetist Bix Beiderbecke (1903–1931).

The popularity of jazz was a social phenomenon as well as a musical one. In the years after World War I, middle-class white Americans were turning to a more leisured way of life. Their tastes widened to include jazz and other black-originated art forms, making what had been the music of a subculture into mainstream entertainment. The "jazz age" of the 1920s was one of economic expansion (which was to end with the stock market crash of 1929), and loosened social restraints. Dancing—to jazz—became a craze.

**Jazz combos**

In both New Orleans and Chicago, jazz musicians generally performed in small ensembles, or *combos*. A front line of several solo instruments—a trombone, clarinet, one or two trumpets, and later a saxophone—improvised collectively on the melody while the rest of the group provided a background of harmony and rhythm. The rhythm section consisted of some combination of tuba, banjo, guitar, piano, string bass, washboard, and drums. Bass and snare drums were always used, and tom-toms, cymbals, and other percussion instruments were often added.

The melodic and harmonic practices of the New Orleans and the early Chicago styles were generally similar. Thematic improvisations very often remained recognizably related to the original theme, with arpeggios and scalelike material commonly used to vary the theme. Methods of embellishing the melodies were influenced by the blues. Phrases were generally two and four measures in length, often followed by a break—a short improvised cadenza. Harmony tended to stay within the major mode, and chord progressions were made up chiefly of the I, IV, and V chords. There was some chromatic harmony, but it was rare.

The rhythms of early jazz were based on a steady duple meter (often in 2 in the Chicago style and 4 in other styles) defined by the percussion instruments. Superimposed over this was a series of syncopations that accented normally weak beats of the measure. A twelve-bar blues progression or a thirty-two-bar popular song structure generally served as a framework, with breaks and longer solos giving opportunity for variety and contrast.

## Armstrong: West End Blues

Louis Armstrong (1900–1971) was one of the great men of jazz from the early decades of the century through the 1960s. In a 1928 recording of *West End Blues,* written by Clarence Williams and Joe Oliver, his great skill at improvising on the trumpet is very evident.

**LISTENING ANALYSIS**                                    SIDE 12, BAND 4

The piece begins with an introductory trumpet solo by Armstrong and thereafter follows the blues form very closely, presenting five twelve-bar sections. Different instruments are featured in each of the sections: trumpet in the first, trombone in the second, clarinet and voice in the third, piano in the fourth, and all of the instruments in the last. The work, a classic in its own time, offers a good illustration of many of the characteristics of jazz in the 1920s.

**LISTENING SUMMARY**

| | |
|---|---|
| Timbre: | small combo featuring trumpet, trombone, clarinet, voice, and piano |
| Melody: | rather simple, singable tune; improvisation adds to it and replaces it |
| Rhythm: | duple meter; moderate tempo |
| Harmony: | major mode; much improvisation over repeated chord progression |
| Form: | after opening trumpet solo, twelve-bar blues form presented five times |

## The Big Band Era

**Henderson and Ellington**

By the late 1920s a new Chicago city government was stamping out the illegal cabarets and dance halls. Jazz was again on the move, with New York becoming the next great center of activity. This was due in part to the influence of Fletcher Henderson (1898–1952) and Duke Ellington (1899–1974)—the latter probably the greatest single figure in jazz history. New York saw the development of the "big band" or "swing" style, a style that rose to its greatest heights in the decade between 1935 and 1945.

In the early 1930s, Kansas City also became an important center for jazz, with bands such as the one headed by Count Basie (1904–1984). Basie's famous broadcasts from the Reno Club in Kansas City made it the heart of jazz for a time.

**Written arrangements**

Big band music was for the most part written down, a major departure from earlier jazz practice. The written arrangements provided a more reliable background against which soloists could improvise. At the same time, professionally trained musicians gave the music a more polished and sophisticated sound.

The earliest of the big bands had eleven or twelve instruments, usually including three saxophones of different sizes, two or three trumpets, one or two trombones, and four rhythm instruments—piano, tuba, banjo, and drums. In most bands the tuba was later replaced by the string bass, while the banjo was replaced by the guitar. By the 1950s, the typical big band included fifteen to eighteen players, with five saxophones, four or five trumpets, three to five trombones, piano, string bass, and drums.

**Changes in style**

The big bands altered the elements of jazz in many ways. Melodic improvisation became "cooler" as musicians began to avoid the excitement of earlier styles and opted instead for variations and rhythms that were somewhat more restrained. Yet their melody, harmony, and rhythm often became more sophisticated, and novelties such as variations of the harmonic structure were introduced. Among these harmonic departures were the use of unusual chords and a much greater interest in chromaticism. The written arrangements led to a more controlled form and style. The thirty-two-bar, AABA structure of the popular song became the most common form, although the twelve-bar, AAB blues form was still in use. The famous band of the era was Benny Goodman's. When the sale of liquor was legalized again in 1933, a new jazz audience was created; Goodman and other bandleaders became celebrated.

## Goodman: King Porter Stomp

Fletcher Henderson's arrangement of Jelly Roll Morton's *King Porter Stomp*—an arrangement made famous by clarinetist Benny Goodman (1909–1986)—is an outstanding example of big band style. The music was intended for dancing, and the size of the band made it necessary to write out all the parts: three trumpets, two trombones, one clarinet, four saxophones, piano, guitar, bass, and drums.

SIDE 12, BAND 5

**LISTENING ANALYSIS**

Based on the thirty-two-bar form and a repeating harmonic pattern, the piece presents solos in turn from trumpet, saxophones, clarinet, trumpet, and saxophones. Some degree of improvisation is apparent in all the solo sections. As in Armstrong's version of "West End Blues," the instruments join together to close the piece. This style of jazz is controlled and refined.

**LISTENING SUMMARY**

| | |
|---|---|
| Timbre: | large band |
| Melody: | basic melody widely varied and replaced by other material |
| Rhythm: | duple meter; quick tempo |
| Harmony: | major mode; use of repeated harmonic pattern |
| Form: | based on thirty-two-bar form |

**Small groups**

Along with the commercially successful dance music of the big bands were a number of smaller groups. These were centered in small clubs in midtown Manhattan. Their music was more serious than that of the big bands at first. Later the big bands themselves formed small groups.

## Bop

**Parker**

In the 1940s a number of jazz musicians began breaking away from big band swing and evolved a style called *bebop*, or more commonly *bop*. One factor in this trend was increasing frustration of black musicians, who were denied racial equality and rejected the commercialized music that attracted white audiences. One of the key figures in the development of bop was Charlie Parker (1920–1955), an alto saxophonist, and, along with Louis Armstrong, one of the most brilliant improvisers in jazz history. Dizzy Gillespie (b. 1917), who also played trumpet, was another major figure.

In bop, instrumentation was again reduced to small ensemble size. The group usually included a trumpet, a saxophone, and sometimes a guitar, while the rhythm section, which played a more important role than in the past, was made up of piano, guitar, bass, and drums.

The melody and harmony used in bop were more complex than that used in its predecessors. Improvisation came to be based increasingly on the harmonic structure of the music. In the 1950s a number of musicians made great use of ornamental tones, which often remained unresolved at the end of a phrase. The frequent occurrence of altered or substitute chords also expanded the melodic possibilities. Many bop artists, including Parker and Gillespie, used the basic chords from standard popular songs and improvised upon them. In addition, the intricate phrasing that had become widespread in the 1940s was continued. Phrases were less often organized into predictable lengths, and their length and structure varied considerably.

**Use of the rhythm section**

Bop was rife with rhythmic diversity and formal unpredictability. The rhythm section no longer functioned merely to set up a solid beat. Instead, each instrument was assigned a specific task in support

Saxophonist Charlie Parker in performance with Tommy Potter. Parker died prematurely in 1955, aged 35, but by that time he was already a legendary figure. (David Redfern Photography; photo: William Gottlieb)

of the solo melody and rhythm. The drummer might work for a legato effect, playing the beat lightly on the cymbal, in contrast to the prominent role of the bass drum in the Swing Era, and concentrating elsewhere on the creation of counterrhythms. The pianist usually played single-note solos with the right hand and complemented the basic harmonic structure with occasional chords in the left. Even the bass, though still concerned mainly with keeping time, sometimes forsook this role for a melodic role, playing more nimbly and contrapuntally. The addition of the electric guitar to the ensemble provided a new solo instrument. Furthermore, all the rhythm instruments now played solos. As a result of all these innovations, the bop structure became much less formalized, differing greatly from work to work and incorporating important elements from such differing musical traditions as symphonic music, popular music, gospel music, and the blues.

### Parker: "Ornithology"

An outstanding example of the bop style is found in Bennie Harris's "Ornithology," based on the chord changes of the popular song *How High the Moon*. Parker on alto saxophone, Fats Navarro (1923–1950) on trumpet, and Bud Powell (1924–1966) on piano are supported by drums and bass.

**LISTENING ANALYSIS**

After a brief introduction by the piano, the melodic line that forms the basis for the piece is played by Parker. Heard first in the home key, the tune is soon clouded with chromaticism. The piece proceeds with lengthy, freely improvised solos played by saxophone, trumpet, and piano in turn, leaving the original melodic line far behind.

**LISTENING SUMMARY**

| | |
|---|---|
| Timbre: | small combo of alto saxophone, trumpet, piano, drums, and bass |
| Melody: | simple melody (with some chromaticism) widely varied and replaced with improvised material |
| Rhythm: | duple meter; quick tempo |
| Harmony: | major mode; basic chord pattern widely varied |
| Form: | several sections of contrasting instrumentation |

## *Jazz in the Later Twentieth Century*

**Davis and cool jazz**

In the late 1940s, Miles Davis (b. 1926) and a number of other young jazz musicians began to move into more experimental types of jazz. The "cool" style blended the rhythms and harmonies of bop with a more lyrical melodic approach. The arrangements were usually written down and were characterized by understated variations, relaxed rhythms, and contrapuntal style. Venturing beyond the basic bop ensemble, cool jazz experimented with the use of horn, flute, oboe, cello, and tuba, as well as Latin American and other more exotic instruments. Cool jazz harmonies were at times complex, leading to protests from some critics that jazz was becoming cerebral and unemotional. Rhythm, too, became more complex, yet at the same time more relaxed. Among the innovators, Dave Brubeck is especially noted for having introduced unusual time signatures such as $\frac{5}{4}$ in his "Take Five." Experiments with form were also made, with many jazz composers using earlier forms such as rondo and fugue. Gerry Mulligan (b. 1927), Stan Getz (b. 1927), and the Modern Jazz Quartet were among the many important exponents of the cool jazz style.

**Third Stream**

In the late 1950s yet another important jazz style developed. Combining jazz and the traditional styles of serious music, it came to be known as "Third Stream." The music is well represented in the works of John Lewis (b. 1920) and Gunther Schuller (b. 1925).

**Recent trends**

While it is difficult to summarize all the many trends in jazz in the 1960s and 1970s, several distinct traits can be seen. One of the most basic and obvious characteristics of jazz in this period has been its eclectic nature. It has drawn from all the jazz styles of the past, as well as from rock, electronic music, traditional serious music, and the music of other cultures. Miles Davis, who ushered in the cool style in the early 1950s, helped set the tone for the 1970s with his fusion of electronic and rock styles with jazz. Some of the most important innovators in recent years have been John Coltrane (1926–1967), Ornette Coleman (b. 1930), Herbie Hancock (b. 1940), Gary Burton (b. 1943), Toshiko Akiyoshi (b. 1929), and Weather Report.

## Broadway and Musical Comedy

**Herbert and Romberg**

In the late nineteenth century, light opera, or *operetta*, made its debut in the United States and quickly became very popular. A number of transplanted European composers—Victor Herbert (1859–1924) and Sigmund Romberg (1887–1951), in particular—captured Broadway audiences with works that combined sentimental plots, fast action, picturesque settings, and attractive tunes. Their operettas were patterned after the European comic operas of the time, but employed lighter melodies, spoken dialogue, and more frivolous plots. Herbert's were among the most popular, with such titles as *Babes in Toyland* (1903) and *Sweethearts* (1913), and songs such as "Because You're You" and "I'm Falling in Love with Someone."

**Cohan**

In the early 1900s, a fast-talking, aggressive Irish-American showman and producer named George M. Cohan (1878–1942) popularized a new art form, the *musical comedy*. Really a play with music, this was a combination of minstrelsy, burlesque, farce, pantomime, vaudeville, and operetta. Like jazz, musical comedy was an American invention. It differed most clearly from comic opera in that its music, dances, lyrics, and spoken dialogue more closely reflected the current moment. It differed from the early minstrel shows and vaudeville by its adherence to a plot and, as it matured, by the integration of all its parts into a unified, elaborately produced whole.

Cohan borrowed from a multitude of sources and added a kind of drive and ingenuity that have characterized American musicals ever since. He enchanted Broadway audiences with *Little Johnny Jones* (1904), the first real musical comedy, *George Washington, Jr.* (1906), and other similar productions, highlighted by such catchy songs as "Yankee Doodle Boy," "Give my Regards to Broadway," and the very patriotic "Grand Old Flag."

**Berlin**

Irving Berlin (b. 1888) later took up the somewhat scattered threads of early musical comedy and tried to create more stylistically unified theatrical works. Berlin's first attempts included a "syncopated musical show" called *Watch Your Step* (1914), for which he wrote both music and lyrics. Its stars were the celebrated dancing team of Irene and Vernon Castle. Two of Berlin's most important contributions to American musical theater were *Face the Music* (1932) and *As Thousands Cheer* (1933), both with lyrics by Moss Hart (1904–1961). As in many other musicals of the 1920s and 1930s, the librettos were highly satirical with numerous allusions to contemporary political and social events. The climax of Berlin's Broadway career was the enormously successful *Annie Get Your Gun* (1946).

**Kern**

Jerome Kern (1885–1945) was perhaps the first to truly integrate all the different elements of musical comedy: story, songs, dances, costumes, and sets. In the 1920s the typical show was a collection of good tunes and a passable plot, pieced together to form a rather loosely organized work. Kern's *Show Boat* (1927), with lyrics by Oscar Hammerstein II (1895–1960), did much to change this. It was an extraordinarily well organized and successful production, on a legitimately American subject, with excellent songs such as "Ol' Man River." Critical comments ranged from "almost a folk opera" to the accolade that "no other American piece of its vintage left so large a permanent musical legacy and certainly no other surpassed it in quality." Other well known musical comedies of the period were Vincent Youmans' *No! No! Nanette* (1925), George Gershwin's *Strike Up the Band* (1930), and Cole Porter's *Anything Goes* (1934).

**Rodgers**

Musical comedy reached its maturity in the 1940s and 1950s. The combined genius of composer Richard Rodgers (1902–1979) and writer-lyricist Oscar Hammerstein II produced a number of strong and vividly memorable works. Their shows were based on literary classics, deep-rooted folk themes, or contemporary events, with music both immediately attractive and of lasting worth. The songs frequently helped to advance the plot; there was thus a reason for their existence beyond the mere function of breaking up the dialogue at regular intervals. The show *Oklahoma!* (1943) marked one of the great moments in Broadway history. It had a genuinely American setting with all the standard American virtues: it was friendly, good-humored, colorful, clean, and fast-paced. In *Carousel* (1945) and *South Pacific* (1948), Rodgers and Hammerstein dealt with more serious themes and offered a more complex treatment of human character than had been customary in the average Broadway show. *The Sound of Music* (1959) also dealt with a serious theme in the retelling of the saga of the singing Trapp family. Another masterpiece of the period, written very much in the tradition of Rodgers and Hammerstein, was *My Fair Lady* (1956) by Alan Jay Lerner and Frederick Loewe.

**Bernstein**

The production of *West Side Story* (1957) by Leonard Bernstein (b. 1918) epitomized a new kind of Broadway show, one in which the word "musical" was decisively severed from the word "comedy." A few "serious" musicals had been introduced before, mainly by classically trained composers such as Kurt Weill (1900–1950) with *Knickerbocker Holiday* (1938). *Porgy and Bess* (1935) by George Gershwin (1898–1937) was a great work that fused the Broadway stage with serious opera. But *West Side Story* began something of a trend in serious musicals. It dealt with grave contemporary problems such as juvenile delinquency and gang warfare on New York City streets, blended into a love story based on *Romeo and Juliet*. The show had a dramatic impact with tragic overtones. Everything fit, with Jerome Robbins' balletlike choreography conveying what the unpolished, often inarticulate characters were unable to say in words. Bernstein's jazzy and musically sophisticated score quite effectively captured the wildness, ecstasy, and anguish of the dramatic situation.

**Recent trends**

After the precedent set by *West Side Story*, the horizons of the musical were greatly broadened. A cross-fertilization seemed to take place between opera, musical theater, and the concert stage, yielding such varied new works as the rock musical *Jesus Christ Superstar*

Scene of the culminating fight between the two warring gangs in the first production of Bernstein's *West Side Story* on Broadway in 1957. (Vandamm Collection, Theater Collection, New York Public Library)

Ethel Merman making one of her spectacular entries in the first performance of Berlin's Wild West musical *Annie Get Your Gun* on Broadway in 1946. (Vandamm Collection, Theater Collection, New York Public Library)

(1970) by Andrew Lloyd Webber (b. 1948), Bernstein's *Mass* (1971), *A Little Night Music* (1972) by Stephen Sondheim (b. 1930), *Annie* (1977) by Charles Strouse (b. 1938), and *La Cage aux Folles* (1983) by Jerry Herman (b. 1933). In the late 1970s and early 1980s the English composer Andrew Lloyd Webber has enjoyed extraordinary success with his musicals *Evita* (1978), *Cats* (1981), and *Starlight Express* (1984). The wide variety in type of subject matter and musical styles is one of the most striking aspects of the musical of the last decade.

## Country and Western Music

Today's country and western music is directly descended from the folk ballads brought to the southern part of this country by the earliest settlers. The ballads long retained their original form and flavor in sparsely populated, ethnically homogeneous sections of colonial America. But eventually the southern Appalachian region became the last preserve for a strong heritage of these transplanted folk ballads.

Formerly a church, the Grand Ole Opry House was the home of country and western music from 1941 until 1974 (The Bettmann Archive/BBC Hulton Picture Library)

Western styles

Even in Appalachia, the New World environment brought a number of changes in the original models. The music was played on different instruments—on the fiddle, the guitar and the banjo, for example—and it was sung in a distinctive high-pitched, nasal style. Moreover, new subjects were added. All ballads by their very nature deal with topical themes. The southern Appalachian ballads concentrated on typical American frontier themes—hard work, hard times, evangelical religion, migration, violent life and death, along with the usual love and loss themes. Religious emotionalism—one of the cornerstones of the poor white southerner's existence—spilled over into this secular music. And at the same time, southern blacks introduced their white neighbors to blues singing and guitar and banjo picking.

Until the coming of radio, country music remained isolated in the southern Appalachians, the deep South, the Mississippi Delta, and eastern Texas. It was performed at home, or for local events. However, by 1922 there were eighty-nine radio stations in the South, giving country musicians a new platform and a chance at a far wider audience. In 1925, WSM radio in Nashville, Tennessee, inaugurated the Grand Ole Opry, now the oldest continuing radio show in the United States devoted to country music. The Opry featured fiddlers, guitarists, banjo players, singers, comedians, yodelers, and even barn dancers. Reigning over this scene was the Carter Family, the epitome of the traditional southern Appalachian singing family, and Jimmie Rodgers (1897–1933), the prototype of the country boy who makes it big singing about his kind of life.

Due largely to the influence of radio programs, country music found an audience in the North. During the Depression years, people found in the songs of the rural South expressions of the downtrodden hopelessness then spreading throughout the country.

Meanwhile, many southeasterners were migrating to the Southwest and to California, adapting their music to new influences they met along the way. A *western swing style* developed in Texas; it was a style that emphasized fiddles and was made for dancing. From labor camps and oil fields came the loud sound of *honky-tonk*. In Hollywood, Gene Autry (b. 1907), Tex Ritter (1905–1974), and Roy Rogers (b. 1911) glamorized the *singing cowboy* on a national scale, with Dale Evans and Judy Canova later adding the singing cowgirl. New instruments and new techniques for playing them were added. Country singers back in the East felt the effects of the new western branch of their music and began dressing in gaudy cowboy and cowgirl outfits. Eventually, the word "western" was grafted onto the designation "country" to produce country and western music.

Although country and western music had already infiltrated northern airwaves, many of the performers themselves moved north during World War II. At the height of the war, nearly two hundred out of the total of about six hundred recording artists in the United States were country performers. The big names were Roy Acuff (b. 1903), Ernest

Tubb (1914–1984), and Bob Wills (1905–1975), and they were trying to win the war in their own way with country songs about patriotism and coming home.

**Country blues**

In 1949 "Lovesick Blues" by Hank Williams (1923–1953) helped to popularize a new variant style known as *country blues*. Williams' music was of a kind very popular in the early 1950s just before the advent of rock and roll. The singing was nasal, the accompaniment was a whining steel guitar, and the lyrics very sentimental.

**Pop-country music and bluegrass**

In the mid-1950s, country and western music was almost eclipsed by the sudden emergence and enormous popularity of rock and roll. It did not make any sort of national comeback until the late 1960s. By then its styles were many and varied. *Pop-country* star Glen Campbell (b. 1936) had considerable success with a song called "Wichita Lineman;" other popular figures were Chet Atkins (b. 1924), and Roger Miller (b. 1938). The largely instrumental, virtuoso *bluegrass* style also came to the fore. But perhaps the biggest star of the early 1970s was Johnny Cash (b. 1932), many of whose songs seem to be drawn straight from the life of the poor dirt farmer in the southern hills.

**Recent trends**

In recent years the Grand Ole Opry has continued to broadcast the many sounds of country and western music: the honky-tonk style of George Jones (b. 1931) from eastern Texas, gunfighter ballads by Marty Robbins (1925–1982) from the Mexican border, Hank Williams, Jr.'s Cajun music from Louisiana, the mountain spirituals of the husband-and-wife duo Wilma Lee (b. 1921) and Stoney Cooper (1918–1977), and Tex Ritter's cowboy songs. Performance standards have become more professional than they were in the early days. Guitars and fiddles, played with great expertise, are often augmented or replaced by an orchestra. A group of background singers often supports a solo vocalist. The lyrics still deal with familiar country themes, but the music displays ever greater sophistication.

Country and western music has also continued to make new inroads into the mainstream of American popular music. Singers such as John Denver (b. 1942) and Kris Kristofferson (b. 1937) have gained a nationwide audience while Kenny Rogers (b. 1941) and Dolly Parton (b. 1946) have become full-fledged media celebrities. Robert Altman's hit movie *Nashville* (1975) reflected the continuing wide interest in the music and musicians of Nashville.

# Rock Music

The appearance of *rock and roll* in the 1950s was as much a social phenomenon as a matter of musical expression. The astonishing popularity of rock and roll can scarcely be understood without reference to the unusual cultural context of its birth. The rapid population growth after World War II dramatically altered the age balance of the American people so that by 1960 about half the population was less than twenty-five years old. This major demographic shift gave young people unparalleled social and political importance. In addition, the almost uninterrupted prosperity of the postwar decades gave tremendous purchasing power to young Americans, making them an inviting market for consumer goods of all kinds. Discs tended to supplant other forms of musical entertainment, and they were easily affordable to the newly affluent generation.

One of the first indications of a youth movement was the popularity in the 1950s of cult figures, such as James Dean, who projected the image of the rebellious, cruising "hood." Simultaneously, a Bohemian revolt that had been gathering strength underground for many years began to emerge. Its adherents, the "beat generation" or beatniks, loudly proclaimed their disenchantment with the values and goals of the prosperous American society. Instead they favored less materialist philosophies, drug use, and sexual freedom.

**Early style**

Into this milieu of changing economic patterns and intermingling subcultures came "rockabilly" music. It was aimed at white audiences and began as a mixture of blues and country music. After acquiring a large following, it was rechristened "rock and roll," a term used in several blues songs. Many black musicians became leaders in rock and roll, among them such important early stars as Little Richard (b. 1935), Fats Domino (b. 1928), Chuck Berry (b. 1926), and Bo Diddley (b. 1928).

Rock and roll was basically dance music. Its slangy lyrics usually described the pains and pleasures of young love or other trials of adolescence. Among its most important stylistic elements was the use of the electric guitar, which made possible certain startling experiments with timbre. Other instruments in the rock and roll combo were drums, a bass, a saxophone, and usually a piano.

Elvis Presley, rock music idol from the mid-1950s onwards, in performance. His rebellious style, adapting black forms for the first time, had an enormous impact on the development of American popular music. (The Bettmann Archive/BBC Hulton Picture Library)

Melody was simple and repetitive, sometimes accompanied by a rhythmic series of nonsense syllables that came to be known as the "doo-wop" sound. The heavily accented four-beat measures took their basic rhythms from the blues. Harmony consisted mostly of elementary tonic-dominant chord progressions. A commonly used structure was an alternation of verse and chorus, the pattern and length of which changed somewhat from song to song. The twelve-bar blues form also continued in use.

At its outset, rock music was performed most often by males for a female audience. Among the groups that helped establish this pattern was Bill Haley (1925–1981) and the Comets, whose jaunty "Rock Around the Clock" (1955) became the first hit rock song. It was not Haley, however, who came to epitomize rock music. The king was Elvis Presley (1935–1977), who ruled popular music in the 1950s with a series of hits that began with "Heartbreak Hotel" (1956). Presley's directness, his intense energy, and his sexual suggestiveness enabled him to perfect the tough "hood" image that so many rock singers later copied. This combination of brashness and lack of sophistication became standard for the rest of the decade.

The time between Presley's peak in the late 1950s and the "British

The Beatles at rehearsal in 1963, the time of their first big successes. Their early songs were often the result of collaboration and their influence on popular music worldwide is unprecedented. (BBC Hulton Picture Library)

invasion" of the early 1960s was a transitional period. Most of the rock performers of the period showed no striking innovations. Instead they preferred to continue the prevailing rock style found in the music of teen idols such as Pat Boone (b. 1934), Frankie Avalon, Fabian, Paul Anka, Bobby Darin (1936–1973), and Ricky Nelson (1940–1985). However, one group from those years was more adventurous and did exert some influence in the 1960s. This was the Everly Brothers, whose catchy lyrics and unusual harmonies were very much in evidence in the early Beatles' songs.

**Beatles**

The Beatles—Ringo Starr (b. 1940), John Lennon (1940–1980), Paul McCartney (b. 1942), and George Harrison (b. 1943)—began the British invasion with a sensational impact in England in 1963 and in the United States in 1964. They were the first English rock group to achieve success in the U.S., and they continued to be extremely influential for some time. Together with the other English groups that followed, they reworked American country, rock, and blues, revived Presley's singing style and came up with a fresh, more sophisticated model of rock and roll. This synthesis came to be known simply as *rock*. The Beatles' first two hits, "Love Me, Do" and "I Wanna Hold Your Hand" (both 1964), evidence something of the directness and idealism that tended to characterize certain aspects of the youth rebellion of the 1960s. Like Presley and his contemporaries, the British rock composers of the 1960s were for the most part self-trained. Many were drawn from the lower classes of Liverpool and other English cities. Ironically, their music became the hallmark of prosperous American middle-class youth. Their music and its American counterpart were very closely linked to the youth movements of the age.

The Beatles' instrumental ensemble served as a model for most of the new rock groups. By the mid-1960s the standard rock combo consisted of three electric guitars—lead, rhythm, and bass—and drums. Rock musicians were much more reliant on electric and amplified instruments than their rock-and-roll predecessors. The music was generally characterized by I–IV–V chord harmony and an uncompromising beat. Elements of country and western music appeared regularly, while a number of groups borrowed extensively from the Mississippi Delta blues singers.

**Rolling Stones**

During the 1960s, a schism developed within rock music between the raunchy "bad guys," represented especially by the Rolling Stones, and more clean-cut "boys" such as the Beatles. Divergent tendencies in their music paralleled the disparities in their public images. The Rolling Stones maintained an approach and style that was looser, less polished than the Beatles. Their style revealed a greater influence of the blues. Other rock stars of similar style began to emerge, notably the great Janis Joplin (1943–1970) and Jimi Hendrix (1942–1970).

**Folk-protest song**

The *folk-protest* song, a survival from the Depression years, renewed its popularity during the 1960s, especially as the civil rights and antiwar movement grew. Its direct, personal style, pictorial imagery, and often plaintive tunes offered the singers particularly good means for delivering deeply felt, serious messages. Joan Baez' "Birmingham Sunday" is a haunting example. Later folk-protest songs were increasingly merged with rock. In the *folk-rock songs* of Bob Dylan (b. 1941), the poetic and musical voice of the youth counterculture was vividly expressed. He continued to be at the forefront of developments, initiating *country rock* in the late 1960s.

It was also during the 1960s that the hippie movement began to affect rock music. With its slogans of "Flower Power" and "Tune in, turn on, drop out," this new offspring of the beat generation spread across the country from San Francisco. Hippies preached a mixed message of opposition to the Vietnam War, sexual freedom, togetherness, and mysticism. Rock music, fusing almost inevitably with the movement, carried the creed to the masses of middle-class youth. Rock groups on the West Coast, such as Jefferson Airplane and the Grateful Dead, and some other groups retained the hard, rhythmic center of the music but experimented with aspects of folk music, new electronic techniques, more chromatic harmony, new instruments, and even new styles such as the orientally inspired *raga rock*. The

**Raga rock**
**Acid rock**

style known as *acid rock*, with its slower tempo and more relaxed mood, tried to create musically some of the effects felt under drugs.

**British progressive**

A style known as *British progressive* developed in the late 1960s and early 1970s. Bands concentrated on producing sophisticated music that incorporated some nineteenth-century orchestral techniques. Leading groups that developed and fostered this style were Yes; Procol Harum; Pink Floyd; Emerson, Lake and Palmer; and the American group Kansas.

**Rock operas**

*Rock operas,* or *rock musicals*, made their first appearance on Broadway during the 1967–68 season. *Hair*, subtitled "An American Tribal Love-Rock Musical," was among the first and remains perhaps the most famous. It featured music by Canadian rock-jazz composer Galt MacDermot and was built around a framework that permitted certain improvisations. *Hair* soon came to be recognized as a major, innovative work. *Tommy* by Pete Townshend (b. 1945) of the British rock group The Who was a very successful and significant work from 1969. *Jesus Christ Superstar*, in stage and film versions, was another highly successful and popular rock musical from 1970. Generally, however, rock and musical theater appeal to different audiences.

**Soul music**

*Soul music* traded influences with rock throughout the 1960s. Soul music, based essentially on black folk and gospel music, had already contributed greatly to the development of early rock and roll. In the 1960s it formed a musical counterpart to the growth of black nationalism and black power and was enthusiastically received by a large part of the black and white youths. James Brown (b. 1933), Aretha Franklin (b. 1942), Otis Redding (1941–1967), and Ray Charles (b. 1930) headed the list of soul singers. The Supremes and The Temptations were two groups that helped to bring Motown Records in Detroit to great prominence.

**Jazz and disco**

Rock styles were combined with jazz in the 1970s by leading performers such as Miles Davis, Weather Report, and Herbie Hancock, and rock and soul music were major influences on the development of disco music, a style that came from dance clubs. *Disco music* emphasized technical, studio effects rather than the live performer, resulting in a rather slick sound that began to wane in the late 1970s.

**Punk rock**

*Punk rock* developed in England in the mid-1970s and represented the ideas of youth in the working class who were angry, violent, antiestablishment, and politically inspired. The songs were short, and melodies and harmonies were simple and basic. The group as a whole was much more important than individual stars. The Sex Pistols defined the style. Although punk rock achieved less outstanding success in America than some earlier styles, it did act as a catalyst on the work of many existing groups as well as that of new artists, adding a harder edge to their music. These changes were typified by the short, fast, aggressive songs of New York groups like the Ramones, and individual artists such as Patti Smith, whose harsh voice and poetic lyrics heralded the new wave music which followed.

**New Wave rock**

*New Wave rock* also features the economy of material and antistar sentiments, but it is more controlled, intellectual, and eclectic, drawing on some 1960s techniques, as well as ideas from Reggae, African, and black styles. Leading New Wave performers are the Talking Heads, Blondie, and Elvis Costello.

**Heavy metal rock**

Very high volumes and highly distorted guitar sounds are characteristic of *Heavy metal*, another style of the 1970s. Great sonic impact is basic, while rhythm is steady and regular, and harmony is not complicated. Led Zeppelin, Cream, and the Jimi Hendrix Experience formulated the style, which has flourished in huge stadium concerts. Groups in the early 1980s, such as Journey and Asia, have started from this style and added new ideas to it.

What changes have taken place in mainstream rock seem, from the very short perspective it is possible to have on music in the 1980s, to involve more a mixing of influences than the emergence of any single, quantifiable trend.

**Bruce Springsteen**

The remarkable popularity of Bruce Springsteen, and the excitement generated by his live performances, have proved that there is still an enormous demand for the sort of rock ballad of American life that derives from the work of Bob Dylan. In Springsteen's case, these songs are given an entirely new vitality by allying the powerful use of melody with a driving beat borrowed from hard rock. His themes, however, remain those of the wistful but rebellious teenager so popular in the 1960s. The tracks on two of his best albums, *Darkness on the Edge of Town* and *Born in the U.S.A.*, clearly show this combination of influences, combining gentleness and recklessness to powerful effect.

**Michael Jackson**

An entirely different set of influences shaped the work of Michael Jackson whose album *Thriller* broke all previous records in 1982. Originally part of the family group, the Jackson Five, he developed as a phenomenally popular solo artist at the end of the 1970s, his high, pure voice combining with a type of electronic disco music that still had echoes of an earlier Motown sound. His songs proved the perfect vehicles for the increasingly popular music videos which, by the mid-1980s, have to some extent taken over from live performance.

**Video**

Video has undoubtedly had a great effect on the way music reaches its audiences, and many artists have been quick to take advantage of its appeal. Performers whose style and presentation seem perfectly suited to the medium include Cyndi Lauper, Prince, and Madonna. All three play effective disco dance music; all employ flamboyant public images and suggestive lyrics, and have done much to inject new vitality into the rather tired pop-disco market, with new, sharp melodies and up-beat rhythms.

And yet, traditional rock styles continue to be popular. The Beatles are still greatly loved and copied, and the Rolling Stones are still influential. A strong element in this has been the recording industry, which has a businesslike conservatism of outlook. More experimental artists rely on an informal, loose network of tapes and radio stations. The video industry has accentuated this polarization, with its sophisticated production techniques and high costs. Yet new ideas are finding a mainstream appeal, together with new techniques such as the use of synthesizers and computers in rock music. Rock, in its many different guises, has proved to be one of the freshest aspects of music in the later twentieth century.

# PART SEVEN

# Music around the World

# CHAPTER 30

# *Aspects of Music in Some Non-Western Cultures*

*LISTENING PREVIEW Musics of non-Western cultures have distinctive sounds because of the use of different musical instruments, varying constructions of elements of music such as melody, rhythm, and harmony, and because of aesthetic ideals that are often unique to each culture. Listen to* Wild Geese Landing on the Sand Beach *(Side 12, Band 9), an example of traditional Chinese music played on a cheng (a 16-string, plucked Chinese instrument of the zither family). Identify specific characteristics of the sounds you hear and the way they are created that are not common in traditional Western music.*

## Music as a Cultural Phenomenon

There are even more different musical styles in the world than there are cultures. The people of one culture prefer vocal music, those of another prefer dance, and those of still another prefer instrumental music. Why is there such a wide range of musical traditions from one part of the globe to another? No single answer can be given. Both environmental conditions (geographical, political or social) and group philosophies, however, help to determine, or at least to influence, the music developed by each cultural group. Music has vital functions in many societies throughout the world. Some of its main uses are as part of religious rites, dances, and many different types of ceremonies. In many cultures, it is also a form of popular entertainment.

In this chapter, we will survey briefly some aspects of several important musical traditions from around the world. To describe any one of them in detail could, of course, result in a very lengthy study. We can only suggest some of the main features of each tradition and, in some cases, the underlying attitudes that have caused the music of one culture to develop differently from that of another. Suggested listening items for each culture discussed are given at the end of the section. It is important to listen to as many musical examples as

This 18th-century Indian miniature shows a lady musician playing sitar, very likely in a performance at a noble court. At this time the instrument became a solo instrument of classical music in parts of the Indian subcontinent. (The Metropolitan Museum of Art, Rogers Fund, 1958)

Nairobi tribal dancers in Kenya. Drums have been an essential accompaniment to African tribal dances for many centuries. (Frederick Ayer III, Photo Researchers, Inc.)

possible in order to form a general concept of the musical style of people in a culture different from our own.

We will begin with a look at the music of Africa south of the Sahara. North African nations such as Morocco and Algeria are culturally part of the Arab world, and their music is correspondingly Middle Eastern. For purposes of this chapter, therefore, "Africa" will refer to areas south of the Sahara with non-Arab musical traditions.

## Music of Africa

In African tribal societies, music is an essential part of daily life. Typically, there is special music for working in the fields, entertainment, news dissemination, gossip, and legal dealings. Each ceremony—celebrating birth, puberty, marriage, healing, the hunt, the new year, the new moon—has its own songs and dances. A god may be asked to aid a personal or communal project, to bring rain, or to give protection against fire and danger. Young people often learn the traditions of the culture and the "facts of life" through song. Thus, in many African cultures, music and dance serve as unifying forces.

*Bantu music*

The music of the Bantu-speaking peoples of central Africa is in many ways representative of the musical traditions of sub-Saharan Africa. The Bantu-speaking area is quite large, stretching from Kenya and Tanzania in the east to the Republic of the Congo in the west. Although there are many different Bantu languages and societies within the region, all share a similar cultural heritage.

Many Bantu rulers have traditionally had official orchestras, such as the royal drums of the Watutsi, which accompanied them wherever they went. The court bard, too, was and still is an important figure in many communities, composing and singing songs of the peoples' history. But music has in no way been the exclusive privilege of the nobility. Nearly everyone participates in some ways.

One of the distinctive aspects of Bantu music is related to the "tonal" nature of Bantu languages. The meaning of a word depends partly on the pitches at which the syllables of the word are spoken. This naturally has an effect on music. Melodies are apt to be greatly influenced by the speech tones of the words being sung. A song would sound ludicrous if, for example, a syllable meaning "dog" at a relatively low pitch were sung at a high pitch that changed the meaning to something entirely different. Another result of the tonal nature of Bantu languages is that instruments can be used to convey verbal meanings. This is the basis of the so-called talking drums, which send formulaic messages swiftly over long distances.

Much of African music, and Bantu music in particular, is built on short melodic phrases, which are repeated, alternated, and varied to make up longer melodies. *Responsorial singing* is common: each phrase is sung by a leader, then answered by a chorus. Variations on the basic phrase are improvised.

## *Work Song from Burundi*

One example of the responsorial style is found in a *Work Song from Burundi*, sung while moving a heavy tree.

**LISTENING ANALYSIS**                                    SIDE 12, BAND 7

The song is sung by a group of male workers while doing a strenuous task. Thus the song is not complicated, and its rhythms probably fit some aspect of the workers' bodily rhythms while moving the tree. The leader of the group sings a motive or short phrase which is answered by the group of workers—thus, a responsorial style is created. The basic motive sung by the leader is descending in shape. It is often repeated exactly before it is changed a little in words and rhythm. The leader's motives could be outlined as: *a a a1 a2 a3 a3 a a* etc. The workers' answering motive is simply a two-syllable, repeated-note response. The resulting texture of the entire example is basically monophonic, but there is some overlap of the singing of the leader and the answering group.

**LISTENING SUMMARY**

| | |
|---|---|
| Timbre: | male singers |
| Melody: | based on motives or short phrases; largely descending; responsorial |
| Rhythm: | patterns repeated |
| Texture: | mainly monophonic, with a little overlap of leader and chorus |
| Form: | derives from phrases sung and repeated by the leader; each phrase is answered by a motive sung by the chorus |
| Text: | concerns the work of moving a large tree |

Harmonic techniques

A general similarity between European and Bantu music is found in the fact that both cultures make use of harmony. Bantu songs are sometimes sung in *parallel motion*, with the voices singing simultaneous notes that are always a constant, specific interval apart. There are also songs that make use of *imitation*: the second voice imitates the first, somewhat in the fashion of western rounds. Another polyphonic texture is created when one voice holds a long *drone note* while the other sings a phrase. The first voice may then perform while the second holds the drone note, and so on in alternation. Counterpoint may also be performed by groups of singers and instrumentalists may repeat a short phrase over and over again, while the singers perform melodies based on the same short phrase.

**Rhythmic polyphony**

To the Western ear, the most distinctive feature of central African music is probably its rhythm. We are familiar enough with its American offspring jazz, but the original is even more impressive. In ensemble playing, several different rhythmic patterns may be used at the same time. This creates a kind of *rhythmic polyphony*, with perhaps one drummer maintaining a duple meter, another a triple meter. Sometimes, in fact, a single performer will play one rhythmic pattern on a drum while singing another.

## *Ibihubi*

Intense and contrasting rhythms can often be heard in the music of the Bantu peoples. In "Ibihubi," for example, five large drums and one small one are used.

**LISTENING ANALYSIS**                                     SIDE 12, BAND 8

A quick, regular beat is quite clear in the low drums throughout the piece. Changing rhythmic patterns complement the beat in the high drum. These two levels of rhythmic activity are clearly apparent in the piece. The more complex rhythmic patterns in the higher drum are sometimes repeated, but the rhythmic organization of the higher drum part evolves freely in an improvisatory manner.

**LISTENING SUMMARY**

Timbre:   five large drums and one small drum
Rhythm:   a basic beat with several complementary rhythmic patterns
Texture:  at least two layers of different timbre, pitch, and rhythm
Form:     free, with different rhythmic patterns played over a basic beat

The great variety of types and styles of native African music have only been suggested and sampled here. A study of African music will reveal many of the subtle details that make it unique, engaging, and representative of its people.

## *Suggested Listening*

**African Musical Instruments** [Folkways 8460]
**Music of Black Africa** [Everest 3254]
**Western Congo Folk Music** [Folkways 4427]

## *Music of the American Indian*

A number of distinct geographical areas can be identified in the study of American Indian music. We will consider only two of the areas, and only two cultures within each area. The Plains-Pueblo region, including the entire central part of the United States and the Southwest, has been chosen because its music is in some respects typical of early North American music. The Inuit (Eskimo) Northwest Coast region has been chosen because it includes some of the most complex and imaginative music of the continent.

## *Music of the Plains*

Among the peoples of the Plains are the Sioux, Comanche, Blackfoot, Crow, and Arapaho. Traditionally, these groups were buffalo hunters, following the migrating herds. During winter they lived in small family groups, but in summer larger groups joined together for a great hunt and for the social and religious celebrations that went with it. War, like the hunt, was highly esteemed. It was fought as much to win honor as to kill enemies. To "count coup"—that is, to touch an armed enemy in battle without trying to kill—earned a warrior the highest credit of all. Horses were the mark of wealth, and raiding parties were forever slipping into camps under cover of darkness to make off, if they could, with the enemies' mounts. Visions, dances, and spirits were of great importance in the religious and social life of the people.

In the traditional songs of the Plains, melodies cover a wide range, often beginning quite high and moving downwards, often in a terraced fashion. Rhythm is complex and changing. Voice quality is very tense and pulsating.

The songs are generally short. The text for the first half of each song is frequently made up of meaningless syllables. Singers may then vary the rest of the text—expanding or condensing it and changing words to bring it up to date or add a personal or topical reference. **Incomplete repetition** The musical form is often the kind known as *incomplete repetition*: ABCBC or AABCABC, for example.

Ceremonial dances play an important part in the life of the Plains peoples. The sun dance is especially important. Among the Sioux, it is performed by four dancers, repesenting four different animals, around a tall pole that symbolizes the sun. The singers repeat melodic phrases in unison, mostly in descending motion.

**Pueblo Indians celebrating the Green Corn ceremony; gouache (c. 1935) by Awa Tsireh. This ancient Maydance is the most important of the summer season dances. You can see the male drummer and choir on the right. (Museum of Modern Art, New York, Abby Aldrich Rockefeller Fund)**

## Pueblo Music

Southwest of the Plains area live the Pueblos, settled farming people who speak a number of different languages. They include the Hopi, Zuñi, Taos, and several other groups, some of which have farmed the same land for centuries. The Hopi village of Oraibi, for example, is the oldest continuously lived-in settlement in the United States, dating at least from the early thirteenth century. As members of a basically peaceful group, most of the Pueblos have been willing to let the rest of the world go on its way undisturbed. In contrast to the Plains people, the Pueblos tend to be suspicious of aggressive individuality and, as a group, place greater value on moderation. Religious and ceremonial practices figure largely in their way of life. This is especially true among the Hopi, who regard themselves as a specially chosen, almost priestly people.

Pueblo songs are much more complex than those of the Plains. They are longer and more varied, based on six- or seven-note scales. Although both groups share the same vocal tension and terraced, descending melodic style, Pueblo singers tend to favor the use of a low, growling voice, in contrast to the high-pitched voice of Plains singers. There are special songs for all the group ceremonies as well as for those of the many secret societies. Most complex, and perhaps best known to outsiders, are the Kachina dance songs, performed by masked dancers impersonating gods and ancestors.

## Inuit (Eskimo) Music

To the north of the Plains-Pueblo region is the Inuit-Northwest Coast region. While living conditions of the Inuit have hardly encouraged an elaborate culture, their music is highly developed in many ways. It is rhythmically complex, with a variety of contrasting accents and meters. Melodies tend to undulate back and forth, generally moving in small intervals within a limited range. Some are very short, using only a few notes. A declamatory or *recitative style* of singing is common. Inuit music includes dances, which vary from simple and relatively stationary solos to much livelier round dances with torches.

Singing and drum-surging Inuit of the Cap Barrow region, Alaska, photographed by Laura Boulton in 1946. To this day, Inuit in Greenland use drum-surging competitions as a means of settling differences. (Laura Boulton Foundation)

**Music of the Northwest**

To the south, along the Pacific Northwest Coast, live a number of groups including the Kwakiutl, the Nootka, and the Sitka. These groups early enjoyed highly developed cultures. The sea provided abundant food; the land teemed with berries, nuts, and game for the taking. Consequently, the Northwest Coast peoples literally had wealth to throw away—and they did just that. The famous potlatch was an enormous feast at which powerful people tried to shame their rivals by giving away more wealth than anyone else did. When even giveaways were not spectacular enough, property was destroyed. Food, oil, robes of fur, and carved canoes went into the flames. Among some groups, slaves might be killed. The prestige gained by the winner of one of these consumption battles was great enough to make all the sacrifice worthwhile.

A custom grew up in some Northwest Coast groups whereby many songs and dances were owned by individuals. Only the owner of a song could perform it. Greatly valued, such a song could be bought or inherited. It could even be acquired by murder, if the murderer could validate the claim afterward with an impressive potlatch. Other songs belonged to secret societies. These, together with the privately owned ones, were performed during the ten holy days of the great winter feast. At more light-hearted moments, there were the usual everyday songs and dances, sometimes comic and satiric.

Northwest Coast music differs from all other American Indian music in one way: it includes rudimentary part singing. Either a drone or parallelism at various pitch intervals may be used. There are also intricate, percussive rhythms and clear, rhythmic swings in the melodies. The words of the songs are often bold, confident, even threatening:

> Do not think for a moment that you can defeat us, for we have slaves from all the other tribes, even from the coast tribes to the north.

Many different instruments are used among the Northwest Coast peoples, and the melodies and singing styles are, in general, bolder and more expressive than those of the Plains.

**Suggested Listening**

**Authentic Music of the American Indian** [Everest 3450]
**Eskimos of Hudson Bay and Alaska** [Folkways 4444]
**Indian Music of the Southwest** [Folkways 8850]
**Music of the Pacific Northwest Coast** [Folkways 4523]

# Music of India

Like many other ancient peoples, the people of India felt that music and religion were closely connected. The vibrations of musical sound were believed to be directly related to the laws of the universe. Therefore, correct performance helped bring harmony between people and the world around them and was even thought to contribute to the stability of the universe itself. Presumably, this idea was associated with the discovery of the octave and other intervals. About

510 B.C., the Greek theorist Pythagoras developed a similar idea, and it is quite possible that there was contact between the two civilizations in this period. In any case, Indian classical music developed over centuries to a very high degree of complexity.

**Ragas**    Indian music is based on melodic formulas called *ragas*. Each raga offers a number of different melodic possibilities, which are explored and developed through improvisation. There are literally hundreds of ragas, but most performers use only about fifty. Improvisation requires years of study and is done within elaborate guidelines. One improvised piece can last for several hours.

**Talas**    There is also a set of rhythmic formulas called *talas*. These are repeated patterns of basic time units—units that are more or less equivalent to beats. The beats in a tala may number anywhere from three to over a hundred and are arranged in patterns of equal or unequal length. Talas and ragas together form the basis of the improvisational performance that is so important in Indian music.

Indian music makes little use of harmony in the Western sense. It does, however, use a drone note or chord. This may be the continuous sounding of either the tonic note, a 1–5–8 chord, or a 1–4–8 chord throughout the performance of a particular raga. To the untrained listener, this may sound monotonous. But in Indian musical theory, all notes are believed to take their meaning and effect from their relation to the tonic. Therefore, it seems logical to have this note constantly available for reference. Against the drone chord, the melody may be elaborately developed.

The voice is primary in Indian music, for it is thought to be the most perfect blending of the physical and the intellectual. The singer tries not so much to produce a rich tone quality as to obtain perfect accuracy of pitch. (The pitch, however, may not correspond to any used in the West. Intervals are often much smaller than a semitone, the smallest in general use for western music, and Indian intonation often sounds strange to western ears.) Here, again, we may see the influence of the metaphysical theory relating music and the universe. Northern India has developed some purely instrumental music, but in the older tradition of southern India, all music is fundamentally based on song, with instruments functioning mainly as accompaniment.

**Sitar**    Groups performing instrumental music, or vocal and instrumental music, are generally small. The instruments used may include strings, drums, flutes, and reed instruments similar to the oboe. One of the best-known Indian instruments is the *sitar*, a large, plucked string instrument of the lute family of instruments. Modern concert sitars usually have movable frets, a large resonating gourd at the top of the neck of the instrument, five strings for playing melodies, two drone strings, and twelve or more sympathetic strings. The sitar has become very widely known outside of India because of the superb playing of Ravi Shankar (b. 1920), a virtuoso performer on the sitar who has played concerts with his small ensemble all over the world.

Ravi Shankar in concert. Sitar music is passed on by aural tradition rather than musical notation. (Photo: Clive Barda)

The *tambura* and *tabla* are two of the many other instruments of India. The tambura is a plucked string instrument, also of the lute family. It usually has four strings and a movable bridge, and it provides drone accompaniments to other instruments and voices. Tabla are one of the several types of drums used in Indian music. They are single-headed, tuned with thongs. The smaller drum is made of wood, and the larger of clay or copper. Tabla are used with voices and other instruments and play a very expressive and significant role in Indian music.

The excitement of the performance of an Indian ensemble is likely to derive in part from a sort of contest that often develops among the participants. The drummer will introduce all kinds of complicated elaborations within the tala, while the singer or other leader does the same with the raga. Since the audience is quite aware of what is going on, a considerable amount of tension may be built up. When the performers finally, in perfect unison, reach the first note of the following tala, the sense of release can be clearly heard and strongly felt.

**Suggested Listening**

**Classical Indian Music** [Nonesuch 72014]
**Indian Folk Music:** Vol. 13 of *The Columbia World Library of Folk and Primitive Music* [Columbia 91 A02021]
**Religious Music of India** [Folkways 4431]
**Traditional and Classical Music of India** [Folkways 4422]

## Music of China

Chinese music is at least as old as that of India. Because of the traditional Chinese passion for setting things in order and keeping records, we have a great deal of information about the theory and importance of music under the ancient dynasties. The great philosopher Confucius (551–479 B.C.) wrote extensively about music, since he considered it an essential part of moral life as well as a source of entertainment.

In China, as in India, music was believed to be related to the cosmos. Its function was to imitate and uphold the proper harmony between heaven and earth. Each note was thought to be associated with some natural element and some group in society. Correct pitch was so important that it was customary for each new emperor to order a rechecking of the pitches in use so that a true foundation note could be established. Use of the right note was considered important in keeping the land stable and prosperous. There was even a government office of music, set up to regulate and standardize pitch throughout the empire. The effect of all this on popular music was probably limited, but for the music at court, it was of great importance.

Ya-yueh and Su-yueh music

Traditional Chinese music falls into two different categories. *Ya-yueh music* is refined, elegant, and polite. Historically, it has been the music of cultivated people and philosophers. The music is mono-

Musicians at the time of the T'ang dynasties (618–907) in China; at this period, the Chinese royal family kept 10 orchestras in their employ, and performances of music outside the court began to take place. (New York Public Library Picture Collection)

syllabic (one note to a syllable) and is not strongly rhythmic. *Su-yueh music*, on the other hand, was once considered vulgar and common, especially by educated people. It has many notes to a syllable, with complex melodies sliding from one note to another.

Pentatonic scales

The *pentatonic*, or five-note, *scales* used in Chinese music are derived from a series of twelve notes that were traditionally produced by blowing on a series of bamboo pitch pipes, each precisely related in size to the preceding one. If middle C is used as the foundation note, the twelve notes fall into the following order:

Twelve-Note Series

Two of the scales derived from the twelve notes are shown below:

Pentatonic Scales

Quite early, a system of musical notation was developed in China, and thus music could be preserved in notated form. Composed pieces, in turn, helped to enable the use of large orchestras. But music for soloists and small ensembles has always been common as well.

Instruments have traditionally been grouped according to the material from which they are made—metal, stone, silk (that is, silk-stringed), bamboo, gourd, clay, skin, or wood. Each material was thought to have a characteristic sound, and all materials had to be represented in a full orchestra. Chinese music does not use chordal harmony. However, the Chinese ear is very sensitive to the interplay of timbre and overtone harmony that is heard when a melody is played in unison by all the different instruments.

In any history as long as China's, there are bound to be several stages in the development of musical tradition. After the early formative period, lasting more or less through the fourth century A.D., there were several centuries of political disunity. During this time, the music was greatly affected by foreign influences coming mainly along the great trade routes to the north and west. Eighth-century records show that at one time there were no less than ten different kinds of music, most of them foreign. The office of music is likely to have had a hard time maintaining the purity of ya-yueh in those years.

**Chinese opera**

Through the centuries, the court lost much of its dominance over music. Regional and popular styles came to the fore, particularly the styles collectively known as *Chinese opera*. At least three hundred varieties of Chinese opera are known. Most of them are small and local, emphasizing folk drama; several, however, are highly developed art forms. The latter are generally associated with particular regions and named after a region's major city—Guangzhou, Shanghai, or Beijing. Beijing opera is probably the best known to people in the West. Its stylized vocal conventions—the rasping voice of the hero and the high, thin singing of the heroine—take some getting used to but can be very effective. Instrumental accompaniment varies according to the scene. Battle and military scenes, for example, call for a variety of percussion and wind instruments.

Many musical instruments contributed importantly to all aspects of traditional music of China, such as the *hsiao*, a vertical flute made of bamboo, and the *sheng*, an instrument made with a gourd and a number of small, vertical bamboo pipes fitted on top of it—it is actually a type of small, mouth-pipe organ. String instruments have also been prominent. Important examples are the *p'i-p'a*, a pear-shaped, four-string, fretted lute that is plucked with the fingers, and the *ch'in*, a seven-string type of plucked zither, one of the most venerable Chinese musical instruments whose history goes back 3000 years. The *cheng*, dating probably from the third century B.C., is also a type of plucked zither, with sixteen strings. The instrument has a range of three octaves and is tuned to a pentatonic scale. It has been used as a solo instrument and in ensembles for a variety of kinds of entertainment.

## Wild Geese Landing on the Sand Beach

That the *cheng* is capable of producing a wide range of sonorities is shown well in "Wild Geese Landing on the Sand Beach," taken from Chun Tsao Tang's music book which was written during the reign of Emperor Kang Hsi (1662–1722 A.D.).

**LISTENING ANALYSIS**                                                    SIDE 12, BAND 9

The piece is based on a pentatonic scale. The opening motive is strong in character, because of the octave leaps and the ornamented note, indicated by    .

The motive is immediately repeated and then followed by new motivic material. Several other motivic ideas are presented as the piece unfolds in a free structure. The motives are usually repeated, often with changes. One motive heard several times, especially at cadences, returns to the beginning note; it is often changed in its repetitions.

A motive that includes several repetitions of the same note is also heard several times. In it, and in the other motives, rhythms are flexible and fluid. Some of the motivic ideas might be thought of as reminiscent of the honking of geese and the flapping of their wings. Toward the end, rhythmic motion becomes faster. The final note, a major sixth lower than the opening note, is repeated several times calmly to reinforce the conclusion.

**LISTENING SUMMARY**

| | |
|---|---|
| Timbre: | solo *cheng* |
| Melody: | several prominent motives, most of which are repeated |
| Rhythm: | flexible and fluid |
| Harmony: | based on a pentatonic scale |
| Form: | evolves freely from the repetition and changing of motives |

The musical life of mainland China changed dramatically after the formation of the People's Republic of China in 1949. Most of the traditional styles were modified to conform with the ideals of the revolutionary leaders. Music, it was believed, should serve the people rather than the elite, and it should be capable, through its emotional content, of teaching new values and discouraging old ones. Collective composition was favored over individual creativity and a number of new works were signed by groups of composers. Interest was also revived in the many regional folksong styles, that were interpreted by groups trained in Russian-based styles of music. During the Cultural Revolution beginning in 1966, artistic policies became increasingly severe. Much traditional Chinese music was ignored, and the playing of Western music was banned. In more recent years, these restrictions have been greatly relaxed, but leaders still maintain considerable interest in musical performance and composition. Modern leaders seem to be following Confucius' belief that the value of music extends far beyond mere entertainment. In the 1980s, China has been increasingly receptive to musical influences from the West. Cultural exchanges are possible on a wider scale. It will be interesting to observe the effect of these changes on the music of China in future.

**Suggested Listening**

**China's Instrumental Heritage** [Lyrichord 792]
**Chinese Classical Masterpieces** [Lyrichord 7182]
**Exotic Music of Ancient China** [Lyrichord 7122]
**The Cheng** [Lyrichord 7262]

# Suggested Readings

## General Histories of Music

BORROFF, EDITH. *Music in Europe and the United States: A History*. Englewood Cliffs, N.J.: Prentice-Hall, 1971.

CROCKER, RICHARD. *A History of Musical Style*. New York: McGraw-Hill, 1966.

GROUT, DONALD JAY. *A History of Western Music*. Third edition with Claude V. Palisca. New York: Norton, 1980.

JANSON, H. W., and JOSEPH KERMAN. *A History of Art and Music*. Englewood Cliffs, N.J.: Prentice-Hall, 1969.

LANG, PAUL HENRY. *Music in Western Civilization*. New York: Norton, 1941.

ROSENSTIEL, LÉONIE (ed.). *Schirmer History of Music*. New York: Schirmer, 1982.

ULRICH, HOMER, and PAUL PISK. *A History of Music and Musical Style*. New York: Harcourt, Brace, and World, 1963.

## General Anthologies of Music

DAVISON, ARCHIBALD T., and WILLI APEL. *Historical Anthology of Music*. Cambridge, Mass.: Harvard University Press, 1966.

KAMIEN, ROGER (ed.). *The Norton Scores: An Anthology for Listening*. Third edition. 2 vols. New York: Norton, 1977.

LINCOLN, HARRY B. and STEPHEN BONTA. *Study Scores of Historical Styles*, Vol. I. Englewood Cliffs, N.J.: Prentice-Hall, 1986.

PALISCA, CLAUDE V. (ed.). *Norton Anthology of Western Music*. 2 vols. New York: Norton, 1980.

PARRISH, CARL, and JOHN F. OHL. *Masterpieces of Music before 1750*. New York: Norton, 1941.

STARR, WILLIAM J., and GEORGE F. DEVINE. *Music Scores Omnibus*. 2 vols. Englewood Cliffs, N.J.: Prentice-Hall, 1974 (Vol. I, second edition), 1964 (Vol. II).

## Pictorial Histories of Music

LANG, PAUL HENRY, and OTTO BETTMANN. *A Pictorial History of Music*. New York: Norton, 1960.

PINCHERLE, MARC. *An Illustrated History of Music*. London: Macmillan, 1962.

## Musical Instruments

BAINES, ANTHONY. *European and American Musical Instruments*. New York: Viking Press, 1966.

BAINES, ANTHONY. *Musical Instruments through the Ages*. New edition. New York: Walker, 1976.

BESSARABOFF, NICHOLAS. *Ancient European Musical Instruments*. Boston: Harvard University Press, 1941.

BRAGARD, ROGER, and FERDINAND DE HEN. *Musical Instruments in Art and History*. London: Barrie and Rockliff, 1967.

DIETZ, BETTY WARNER, and MICHALE OLATUNJI. *Musical Instruments of Africa*. New York: John Day, 1965.

MARCUSE, SIBYL. *Musical Instruments: A Comprehensive Dictionary*. Garden City, N.Y.: Doubleday, 1964.

MARCUSE, SIBYL. *A Survey of Musical Instruments*. New York: Harper and Row, 1975.

MERSENNE, MARIN. *Harmonie universelle: The Book on Instruments*. Transl. Roger E. Chapman. The Hague: Martinus Nijhoff, 1957.

MUNROW, DAVID. *Instruments of the Middle Ages and Renaissance*. London: Oxford University Press, 1976.

SACHS, CURT. *The History of Musical Instruments*. New York: Norton, 1940.

SADIE, STANLEY (ed.). *New Grove Dictionary of Musical Instruments*. 3 vols. London: Macmillan & Co., 1984.

WINTERNITZ, EMANUEL. *Musical Instruments of the Western World*. New York: McGraw-Hill, 1967.

## Early Music

ABRAHAM, GERALD (ed.). *The Age of Humanism: 1540–1630*, Vol. IV of *The New Oxford History of Music*. London: Oxford University Press, 1968.

APEL, WILLI. *Gregorian Chant*. Bloomington, Ind.: Indiana University Press, 1958.

BLUME, FRIEDRICH. *Renaissance and Baroque Music*. New York: Norton, 1967.

BROWN, HOWARD M. *Music in the Renaissance*. Englewood Cliffs, N.J.: Prentice-Hall, 1976.

HOPPIN, RICHARD. *Medieval Music*. New York: Norton, 1978.

HUGHES, ANSELM (ed.). *Early Medieval Music up to 1300*, Vol. II of *The New Oxford History of Music*. London: Oxford University Press, 1954.

HUGHES, ANSELM, and GERALD ABRAHAM (eds.). *Ars Nova and the Renaissance: 1300–1540,* Vol. III of *The New Oxford History of Music.* London: Oxford University Press, 1960.

REESE, GUSTAVE. *Music in The Middle Ages.* New York: Norton, 1940.

REESE, GUSTAVE. *Music in the Renaissance.* Revised edition. New York: Norton, 1959.

ROBERTSON, ALEC, and DENIS STEVENS (eds.). *Ancient Forms to Polyphony,* Vol. I of *The Pelican History of Music.* Baltimore: Penguin, 1960.

ROBERTSON, ALEC, and DENIS STEVENS (eds.). *Renaissance and Baroque,* Vol. II of *The Pelican History of Music.* Baltimore: Penguin, 1963.

SEAY, ALBERT. *Music in the Medieval World.* Second edition. Englewood Cliffs, N.J.: Prentice-Hall, 1975.

## Baroque Music

ABRAHAM, GERALD (ed.). *The Age of Humanism: 1540–1630,* Vol. IV of *The New Oxford History of Music.* London: Oxford University Press, 1968.

BLUME, FRIEDRICH. *Renaissance and Baroque Music.* New York: Norton, 1967.

BORROFF, EDITH. *The Music of the Baroque.* Dubuque, Ia.: William C. Brown, 1970.

BUKOFZER, MANFRED F. *Music in the Baroque Era.* New York: Norton, 1947.

DEAN, WINTON. *Handel's Dramatic Oratorios and Masques.* London: Oxford University Press, 1959.

DENT, EDWARD. *Opera.* Revised edition. Baltimore: Penguin, 1966.

GEIRINGER, KARL, and IRENE GEIRINGER. *Johann Sebastian Bach: The Culmination of an Era.* New York: Oxford University Press, 1966.

GROUT, DONALD JAY. *A Short History of Opera.* Second edition. New York: Columbia University Press, 1965.

HOGWOOD, CHRISTOPHER. *Handel.* London: Thames and Hudson, 1984.

HUTCHINGS, ARTHUR. *The Baroque Concerto.* New York: Norton, 1965.

NEWMAN, WILLIAM S. *The Sonata in the Baroque Era.* Fourth edition. New York: Norton, 1983.

LANG, PAUL HENRY. *George Frideric Handel.* New York: Norton, 1966.

LEWIS, ANTHONY, and NIGEL FORTUNE (eds.). *Opera and Church Music 1630–1750,* Vol. V of *The New Oxford History of Music.* London: Oxford University Press, 1975.

PALISCA, CLAUDE V. *Baroque Music.* Englewood Cliffs, N.J.: Prentice-Hall, 1968.

ROBERTSON, ALEC, and DENIS STEVENS (eds.). *Renaissance and Baroque,* Vol. II of *The Pelican History of Music.* Baltimore: Penguin, 1963.

SMITHER, HOWARD. *The Oratorio in the Baroque Era,* Vol. I of *A History of the Oratorio.* Chapel Hill, NC: University of North Carolina Press, 1977.

ULRICH, HOMER. *A Survey of Choral Music.* New York: Harcourt Brace Jovanovich, 1973.

## Classical Music

BLUME, FRIEDRICH. *Classic and Romantic Music.* New York: Norton, 1970.

BURK, JOHN. *Mozart and His Music.* New York: Random House, 1959.

CUYLER, LOUISE. *The Symphony.* New York: Harcourt Brace Jovanovich, 1973.

DENT, EDWARD. *Mozart's Operas: A Critical Study.* Revised edition. London: Oxford University Press, 1947.

FERGUSON, DONALD N. *Image and Structure in Chamber Music.* Minneapolis: University of Minnesota Press, 1964.

GEIRINGER, KARL. *A Creative Life in Music.* New York: Doubleday, 1963.

GIRDLESTONE, C. M. *Mozart's Piano Concertos.* London: Cassell, 1948.

GROUT, DONALD JAY. *A Short History of Opera.* Second edition. New York: Columbia University Press, 1965.

GROVE, GEORGE. *Beethoven and His Nine Symphonies.* London: Oxford University Press, 1948.

HUTCHINGS, ARTHUR. *A Companion to Mozart's Piano Concertos.* London: Oxford University Press, 1948.

LANDON, H. C. ROBBINS. *Haydn Symphonies.* Seattle: University of Washington Press, 1969.

MASON, DANIEL GREGORY. *The Quartets of Beethoven.* London: Oxford University Press, 1947.

NEWMAN, WILLIAM S. *The Sonata in the Classic Era.* Third edition. New York: Norton, 1983.

PAULY, REINHARD. *Music in the Classic Period.* Second edition. Englewood Cliffs, N.J.: Prentice-Hall, 1973.

RATNER, LEONARD G. *Classic Music: Expression, Form, and Style.* New York: Schirmer, 1980.

ROSEN, CHARLES. *The Classical Style: Haydn, Mozart, Beethoven.* New York: Viking, 1971.

SIMPSON, ROBERT (ed.). *The Symphony,* Vol. I: *Haydn to Dvořák.* Baltimore: Penguin, 1966.

SOLOMON, MAYNARD. *Beethoven.* New York: Schirmer, 1977.

ULRICH, HOMER. *Chamber Music.* Second edition. New York: Columbia University Press, 1966.

ULRICH, HOMER. *A Survey of Choral Music.* New York: Harcourt Brace Jovanovich, 1973.

WELLESZ, EGON, and FREDERICK STERNFELD (eds.). *The Age of Enlightenment 1745–90,* Vol. VII of *The New Oxford History of Music.* London: Oxford University Press, 1973.

YOUNG, PERCY M. *The Concerto.* Boston: Crescendo, 1957.

## Romantic Music

ABRAHAM, GERALD (ed.). *The Age of Beethoven, 1790–1830,* Vol. VIII of *The New Oxford History of Music.* London: Oxford University Press, 1983.

BARZUN, JACQUES. *Berlioz and the Romantic Century.* Third edition. New York: Columbia University Press, 1969.

BLUME, FRIEDRICH. *Classic and Romantic Music.* New York: Norton, 1970.

BROWN, MAURICE J. E. *Schubert Songs.* Seattle: University of Washington Press, 1967.

CUYLER, LOUISE. *The Symphony.* New York: Harcourt Brace Jovanovich, 1973.

FERGUSON, DONALD N. *Image and Structure in Chamber Music.* Minneapolis: University of Minnesota Press, 1964.

GILLESPIE, JOHN. *Five Centuries of Keyboard Music.* New York: Dover, 1972.

GROUT, DONALD JAY. *A Short History of Opera.* Second edition. New York: Columbia University Press, 1965.

HALL, JAMES H. *The Art Song.* Norman, Okla.: University of Oklahoma Press, 1953.

HORTON, JOHN. *Brahms Orchestral Music.* Seattle: University of Washington Press, 1968.

KIRBY, FRANK E. *A Short History of Keyboard Music.* New York: The Free Press, 1966.

KLAUS, KENNETH B. *The Romantic Period in Music.* Boston: Allyn and Bacon, 1970.

LONGYEAR, REY M. *Nineteenth-Century Romanticism in Music.* Second edition. Englewood Cliffs, N.J.: Prentice-Hall, 1973.

NEWMAN, ERNEST. *The Wagner Operas.* New York: Knopf, 1949.

NEWMAN, WILLIAM S. *The Sonata since Beethoven.* Third edition. New York: Norton, 1983.

PLANTINGA, LEON. *Romantic Music.* New York: W. W. Norton, 1984.

SCHONBERG, HAROLD C. *The Great Pianists.* New York: Simon and Schuster, 1963.

SIMPSON, ROBERT (ed.). *The Symphony,* Vol. I: *Haydn to Dvořák.* Baltimore: Penguin, 1966.

STEIN, JACK M. *Poem and Music in the German Lied from Gluck to Hugo Wolf.* Cambridge, Mass.: Harvard University Press, 1971.

ULRICH, HOMER. *A Survey of Choral Music.* New York: Harcourt Brace Jovanovich, 1973.

VAUGHAN WILLIAMS, RALPH. *National Music and Other Essays.* New York: Oxford University Press, 1963.

WARRACK, JOHN. *Tchaikovsky Symphonies and Concertos.* Seattle: University of Washington Press, 1969.

## Early Twentieth-Century Music

AUSTIN, WILLIAM W. *Music in the Twentieth Century.* New York: Norton, 1966.

COOPER, MARTIN (ed.). *The Modern Age 1890–1960,* Vol. X of *The New Oxford History of Music.* London: Oxford University Press, 1974.

DERI, OTTO. *Exploring Twentieth-Century Music.* New York: Holt, Rinehart and Winston, 1968.

HANSEN, PETER S. *An Introduction to Twentieth-Century Music,* Second Edition. Boston: Allyn and Bacon, 1967.

LEIBOWITZ, RENÉ. *Schoenberg and His School.* New York: Philosophical Library, 1949.

MACHLIS, JOSEPH. *Introduction to Contemporary Music.* Second edition. New York: Norton, 1979.

MARTIN, WILLIAM R., and JULIUS DROSSIN. *Music of the Twentieth Century.* Englewood Cliffs, N.J.: Prentice-Hall, 1979.

PALMER, CHRISTOPHER. *Impressionism in Music.* London: Hutchinson, 1973.

PERLE, GEORGE. *Serial Composition and Atonality.* Berkeley, Cal.: University of California Press, 1963.

RETI, RUDOLPH. *Tonality, Atonality, Pantonality.* New York: Macmillan, 1958.

SALZMAN, ERIC. *Twentieth-Century Music: An Introduction.* Second edition. Englewood Cliffs, N.J.: Prentice-Hall, 1974.

SCHOENBERG, ARNOLD. *Style and Idea.* New York: Philosophical Library, 1950.

SLONIMSKY, NICHOLAS. *Music since 1900.* Fourth edition. New York: Scribner, 1971.

STEVENS, HALSEY. *Life and Music of Béla Bartók.* Revised edition. New York: Oxford University Press, 1967.

VALLAS, LÉON. *The Theories of Claude Debussy.* New York: Dover, 1967.

WHITE, ERIC W. *Stravinsky: The Composer and His Works.* Second edition. London: Faber and Faber, 1979.

## American Music

BARZUN, JACQUES. *Music in American Life.* New York: Doubleday, 1956.

BÉHAGUE, GERARD. *Music in Latin America: An Introduction.* Englewood Cliffs, N.J.: Prentice-Hall, 1979.

BROWN, CHARLES T. *The Art of Rock and Roll.* Englewood Cliffs, N.J.: Prentice-Hall, 1983.

EDWARDS, ARTHUR C., and W. THOMAS MARROCCO. *Music in the United States.* Dubuque, Ia.: William C. Brown, 1968.

GREEN, STANLEY. *The World of Musical Comedy.* New York: Ziff-Davis, 1960.

HAMM, CHARLES. *Music in the New World.* New York: Norton, 1983.

HITCHCOCK, H. WILEY. *Music in the United States: A Historical Introduction*. Second edition. Englewood Cliffs, N.J.: Prentice-Hall, 1974.

HODEIR, ANDRÉ. *Jazz: Its Evolution and Essence*. New York: Grove, 1956.

MILLER, JIM (ed.). *The Rolling Stone Illustrated History of Rock and Roll*. Revised and updated. New York: Random House/Rolling Stone Press, 1980.

NANRY, CHARLES (ed.). *American Music from Storyville to Woodstock*. New Brunswick, N.J.: Transaction Books, 1972.

NETTL, BRUNO. *Folk and Traditional Music of the Western Continents*. Englewood Cliffs, N.J.: Prentice-Hall, 1965.

ROACH, HILDRED. *Black American Music, Past and Present*. Boston: Crescendo Publications, Inc., 1973.

SCHULLER, GUNTHER. *Early Jazz: Its Roots and Musical Development*. New York: Oxford University Press, 1968.

SHAW, ARNOLD. *The Rock Revolution*. New York: Macmillan, 1969.

SOUTHERN, EILEEN. *The Music of Black Americans: A History*. New York: Norton, 1971.

TANNER, PAUL O. W., and MAURICE GEROW. *A Study of Jazz*. Fourth edition. Dubuque, Ia.: William. C. Brown, 1981.

TIRRO, FRANK. *Jazz: A History*. New York: Norton, 1977.

## Contemporary Music

BABBITT, MILTON. "An Introduction to the RCA Synthesizer" in the *Journal of Music Theory*, Vol. VIII, 1964.

BRINDLE, REGINALD SMITH. *The New Music: The Avant-Garde since 1945*. London: Oxford University Press, 1975.

CAGE, JOHN. *Silence: Lectures and Writings*. Middletown, Conn.: Wesleyan University Press, 1961.

COPE, DAVID. *New Directions in Music*. Second edition. Dubuque, Ia.: William. C. Brown, 1976.

DERI, OTTO. *Exploring Twentieth-Century Music*. New York: Holt, Rinehart and Winston, 1968.

ERNST, DAVID. *The Evolution of Electronic Music*. New York: Schirmer, 1977.

GRIFFITHS, PAUL. *A Guide to Electronic Music*. London: Thames and Hudson, 1979.

GRIFFITHS, PAUL. *Modern Music: The Avant-Garde since 1945*. London: J. M. Dent, 1981.

HOWE, HUBERT S. *Electronic Music Synthesis*. New York: Norton, 1975.

JUDD, F. C. *Electronic Music and Musique Concrète*. Chester Springs, Pa.: Dufour, 1961.

MACHLIS, JOSEPH. *Introduction to Contemporary Music*. Second edition. New York: Norton, 1979.

RUSSCOL, HERBERT. *The Liberation of Sound: An Introduction to Electronic Music*. Englewood Cliffs, N.J.: Prentice-Hall, 1972.

SALZMAN, ERIC. *Twentieth-Century Music: An Introduction*. Second edition. Englewood Cliffs, N.J.: Prentice-Hall, 1974.

SCHRADER, BARRY. *Introduction to Electro-Acoustic Music*. Englewood Cliffs, N.J.: Prentice-Hall, 1982.

TRYTHALL, GILBERT. *Principles and Practice of Electronic Music*. New York: Grosset and Dunlap, 1973.

WITTLICH, GARY E. (ed.). *Aspects of Twentieth-Century Music*. Englewood Cliffs, N.J.: Prentice-Hall, 1975.

## Music of Other Cultures

DENSMORE, FRANCES. *The American Indians and Their Music*. New York: The Woman's Press, 1926. Reissued by Finch Press Reprints, Ann Arbor, Mich.

MALM, WILLIAM. *Music Cultures of the Pacific, the Near East, and Asia*. Second edition. Englewood Cliffs, N.J.: Prentice-Hall, 1977.

NETTL, BRUNO. *Music in Primitive Culture*. Cambridge, Mass.: Harvard University Press, 1956.

NETTL, BRUNO. *North American Indian Musical Styles*. Austin, Tex.: University of Texas Press, 1954.

NKETIA, J. H. KWABENA. *The Music of Africa*. New York: Norton, 1974.

POPLEY, HERBERT A. *The Music of India*. New Delhi: Y.M.C.A. Publishing House, 1966.

WADE, BONNIE C. *Music in India: The Classical Traditions*. Englewood Cliffs, N.J.: Prentice-Hall, 1979.

WARREN, FRED, and L. WARREN. *The Music of Africa: An Introduction*. Englewood Cliffs, N.J.: Prentice-Hall, 1970.

WELLESZ, EGON (ed.). *Ancient and Oriental Music*, Vol. I of *The New Oxford History of Music*. London: Oxford University Press, 1957.

WIANT, BLISS. *The Music of China*. Hong Kong: Chinese University of Hong Kong, 1965.

# Glossary

**accelerando**  Gradual quickening of tempo.

**accent**  Stress on a note.

**accidental**  Sharp, flat, or natural sign before a note indicating that the pitch is not to be played as it normally would be in a given key, but is to be altered according to the sign.

**acid rock**  Rock style in a slow tempo and relaxed mood, emphasizing improvisation and non-realistic words, predominantly of 1960s San Francisco.

**adagio**  Slow tempo.

**aerophone**  Any instrument that produces sound by the vibration of a column of air in a tube.

**aleatoric music**  See chance music.

**alla breve (cut time)**  Meter in which a measure consists of two beats, and a half note has a value of one beat.

**allegretto**  Moderately fast tempo.

**allegro**  Fast tempo.

**allemande**  Dance in duple meter and moderate tempo used in keyboard and ensemble music of the late Renaissance and Baroque periods.

**alto**  See contralto.

**andante**  Moderate tempo.

**andantino**  Slightly quicker moderate tempo.

**antiphonal**  Style of performance in which two groups alternate.

**aria**  Elaborate solo song found primarily in operas, oratorios, and cantatas. Three important types: strophic-bass, with melody in each stanza varied over a repeated bass line; ostinato, with lengthy melody over a short constantly repeated bass line; da capo, in an ABA form.

**arioso**  Vocal style found primarily in operas and oratorios; more melodic than the recitative but less rhythmically regular than the aria.

**arpeggio**  Chord whose tones are played in succession rather than simultaneously.

**art song**  Elaborate solo song, usually with piano accompaniment.

**atonality**  Tendency to avoid referring to or creating any specific tonal center in music.

**augmentation**  Compositional technique for varying a theme in which note values are lengthened in the repetition of the theme.

**authentic cadence**  Cadence consisting of a dominant chord that resolves to a tonic chord (V-I).

**authentic modes**  Four basic Church modes used in Medieval music.

**ayre (Fr. air)**  Term used in English and French Renaissance and Baroque music to denote a song or an instrumental composition of a song-like nature.

**ballad**  In folk music, a narrative song dealing with topical themes.

**ballade**  (1) Medieval French secular song based on a poetic form; (2) lyrical piano piece of the nineteenth century.

**ballata**  Medieval Italian secular song based on a poetic form.

**ballet**  Artistic dance or series of dances.

**balletto (Eng. ballett)**  Italian and English Renaissance part song, simpler in style than the madrigal, rhythmically regular, and usually with a "fa-la-la" refrain.

**bar lines**  Narrow vertical lines on a score, used to separate the measures.

**baritone**  Male voice that lies between the tenor and bass in range.

**bass**  Male voice with lowest range.

**basso continuo**  Baroque practice in which the bass line in ensemble music is played by a low melodic instrument (cello, viol, or bassoon), while a chord-playing instrument (organ, harpsichord, or lute) also plays the bass line and adds chords above it as indicated by figured bass. Also called thoroughbass.

**basso ostinato**  See ostinato.

**beat**  Pulse underlying most rhythmic patterns.

**bel canto**  Italian Baroque vocal style emphasizing beauty of sound.

**bimodality**  Simultaneous use of the major and minor modes.

**binary form**  Two-part form in which the second part often seems to answer the first.

**bitonality**  Simultaneous use of two different tonalities.

**blue note**  Note of the major scale, generally the third or seventh tone, played with a slight flatting of the pitch.

**blues**  Style of American music with origins in rural black folk music, usually consisting of a twelve-measure unit divided into three lines of four measures each. The texts generally express sadness, longing, or complaint.

**bop**  Small-ensemble jazz style popular in the late 1940s, requiring extensive knowledge of harmony and accomplished instrumental technique.

**break**  In jazz, a short, improvised passage.

**bridge**  Passage of secondary thematic importance played between two major sections, during which modulation usually takes place.

**bunraku**  Japanese puppet theater.

**cabaletta** Short song in opera written in a popular style; closing section of an aria, in a quick tempo.

**caccia** Fourteenth-century Italian canon for two upper parts, often supported by a lower part with notes of longer duration.

**cadence** Harmonic formula that brings a musical idea to a close. Common types: authentic, with movement from the V chord to the I chord; plagal, with movement from the IV chord to the I chord.

**cadenza** Elaborate passage for the soloist in a concerto, interpolated near the end of a movement, and often not written out by the composer but left to the performer to create.

**canon** Composition for two or more voices in which one voice enters after another in exact imitation of the first. A round is the simplest and best known type of canon.

**cantata** Vocal composition developed in the Baroque period for chorus and/or solo voice(s), based on secular or religious texts, including several movements, and accompanied by an instrumental ensemble.

**canzona** Italian instrumental work of the sixteenth and seventeenth centuries, derived from the vocal chanson.

**castrato** Male soprano or alto, prominently used in Italian Baroque opera.

**cavatina** Short, lyrical song.

**chamber music** Music for a small ensemble, usually with one performer to each part, and no conductor.

**chance music** Music into which the composer deliberately incorporates the effects of chance, either using chance methods to determine one or more elements of the composition or allowing the performers to introduce chance variations into the performance.

**chanson** French term for "song," used for secular song throughout the centuries.

**chant** See plainchant.

**cheng** Chinese plucked zither with 16 strings and moveable bridges.

**ch'in** Chinese plucked zither with seven strings without bridges.

**chorale** Hymn of the German Protestant church.

**chord** Three or more tones played simultaneously.

**chordal progression** Movement from one chord to another.

**chordophone** Any instrument that produces sound through the vibration of strings.

**chord stream** Series of parallel chords, ascending or descending.

**chromatic scale** Scale made up of twelve half steps in an octave.

**chromaticism** Use of notes that do not belong to the basic scale of a composition.

**church modes** In plainchant and chant-derived music, four scale patterns, each of which spans an octave and occurs in two versions (authentic and plagal), resulting in eight modes. Four additional modes were added in the Renaissance. Most of the modes differ from the major and minor scales in the location of the half steps.

**clavichord** Small keyboard instrument used in the Renaissance and Baroque eras in which small, metal tangents strike the strings when the keys are depressed.

**clef** Sign at the beginning of a staff that indicates the pitches of the lines and spaces. Common clefs: treble (G), bass (F), alto and tenor (C).

**coda** Closing section of a composition or movement, usually reinforcing the final cadence; in some, nineteenth-century works in sonata form, the coda becomes long enough to be considered a contrasting section in its own right.

**color** See timbre.

**coloratura** Elaborate style of singing, usually including fast scales, arpeggios, and ornaments; often associated with a light, high soprano voice, particularly in opera.

**combo** Jazz term for small ensemble.

**common meter** Hymn structure consisting of a four-line stanza with lines of eight, six, eight, and six syllables, respectively.

**common time** Meter in which a measure consists of four beats and a quarter note has a value of one beat.

**concertato style** Baroque style emphasizing contrast, with performing groups playing or singing in alternation with one another.

**concertino** Solo group (usually two violins and continuo) in a Baroque concerto grosso.

**concert master/concert mistress** First (principal) violinist in an orchestra.

**concerto** Work for solo instrument or instruments accompanied by orchestra, usually with three movements.

**concerto grosso** Baroque concerto in which a small group of soloists (concertino) plays against a small orchestra (ripieno).

**conjunct motion** Melodic movement by small intervals.

**consonance** Term used to refer to pleasing sounds, in contrast to dissonance.

**consort** Renaissance term for a family of instruments.

**continuo** See basso continuo.

**continuo madrigal** Late Renaissance madrigal with relatively few voices and basso-continuo accompaniment.

**contrabassoon** Larger bassoon pitched an octave below the bassoon.

**contralto** Female voice with lowest range.

**cornetto (Eng. *cornett*, Ger. *Zink*)** Late Renaissance and Baroque wooden wind instrument, having a cup-shaped mouthpiece.

**counterpoint, contrapuntal** Texture in which two or more voices proceed relatively independently.

**countersubject** Secondary melody in a fugue.

**countertenor** Very high tenor or falsetto voice with a range of an alto.

**courante** Baroque dance, usually in triple meter and a fast tempo. Italian version called corrente.

**crescendo** Gradual increase in volume.

**cross rhythms** One type of rhythmic pattern placed against a dissimilar one, such as duple against triple.

**crumhorn** Late Renaissance and Baroque wooden wind instrument curved at the bottom, played with an enclosed double reed.

**cut time** See alla breve.

**decrescendo** Gradual decrease in volume. Also called diminuendo.

**development** (1)) Growth of a musical idea through change or transformation; (2) second section in a sonata form.

**diatonic scale** Any major or minor scale, without chromaticism.

**diminuendo** See decrescendo.

**diminution** Compositional technique for varying a theme, in which the note values are shortened in the repetition of the theme.

**discantus** Medieval polyphonic style in which the tenor and other voices move in similar rhythms.

**disco** Rock style that emphasizes technical, recorded effects rather than live performers, with a strong, steady beat in duple meter, intended for dancing.

**disjunct motion** Melodic movement by large intervals.

**dissonance** Musical sounds that create a feeling of tension, often disagreeable to the ear.

**divertimento** Late eighteenth-century composition in several movements for a small instrumental group, usually in a light, entertaining style and often including dance movements.

**dodecaphony** See serialism.

**dominant** The fifth degree of a major or minor scale.

**dotted rhythm** Uneven rhythm produced when notes are dotted and played half again as long as the original note value.

**double stopping** Playing two strings at a time on a violin or other string instrument.

**drone note** Tone held throughout a musical work or a section of it.

**duplum** Second voice added to a tenor line in Medieval polyphony.

**dynamics** Intensity of sound; the various levels of loudness and softness in music. For specific dynamic markings, see chart on page 52.

**electronic music** Music in which sounds are created or modified with an electronic synthesizer.

**embellishment** See ornament.

**Empfindsamer Stil** German transitional style, leading to the Classical style, in which the complexities of the Baroque era were rejected in an attempt to present emotions freely and subtly.

**English horn** Alto oboe, pitched a fifth below the oboe.

**ensemble** Small group of performers, or a composition written for such a group.

**episode** Passage of freely invented counterpoint separating statements of the subject in a fugue.

**equal temperament** See temperament.

**étude** Literally a "study"; composition stressing the development of technical performance skills; in the nineteenth century, a short piece for piano or other instruments.

**exposition** The first section in a fugue or sonata form, in which the main melodic material is presented.

**Expressionism** Early twentieth-century style in the visual arts, often associated with atonal and serial music.

**fantasia** Composition in free form, often including difficult passages for the performer.

**fasola** Early American and English system of sight singing that depends primarily on the syllables *fa, sol,* and *la.*

**figured bass** Form of musical shorthand used in the Baroque period, in which the chordal accompaniment is indicated by numbers above or below the bass line, with some freedom of interpretation left to the performer.

**flat** Sign indicating that a pitch is to be lowered by a half step.

**form** Overall structure of a composition.

**French overture** Type of overture in late seventeenth- and early eighteenth-century music used by composers in France and other countries, usually in two sections—slow-fast.

**frequency** Rate of vibration of any medium, such as a violin string or a column of air, that determines the pitch of a musical sound.

**fugal** Having some characteristics of a fugue, usually involving imitation.

**fuguing tune** Imitative psalm setting used particularly by some eighteenth-century American composers such as William Billings.

**fugue** Contrapuntal composition of the Baroque and later period, based on a main melody, called a subject, that is presented in turn by each voice—usually three to five in number—and then repeated in different keys before ending in the original tonic.

**Futurism** Early twentieth-century movement featuring "noise music," especially the use of sounds derived from modern industrial society.

**gagliarda, galliard** Renaissance and Baroque dance, in triple meter and fast tempo.

**Gebrauchsmusik** Literally "music for use"; a style of twentieth-century music written principally for the use and pleasure of amateur performers.

**Gesamtkunstwerk** German for "unified art work"; a term used by Wagner to describe the interdependence and balance of all the arts used in a music drama.

**gigue** Baroque dance, usually in a compound meter and a quick tempo.

**glissando** Very rapid scale, played on the piano by sliding the fingernail quickly over the keys, or on a string instrument by sliding a finger up or down a string.

**grace note** Very short added note used to embellish a principal note; often approaches the principal note by step just before the beat.

**grand opera** Nineteenth-century French opera style that placed great emphasis on elaborate spectacle.

**grave** Very slowly and solemnly.

**great staff** Combination of the treble and bass staves placed one above the other, with an empty space between for the ledger line of middle C. Most piano music is written on the great staff.

**Gregorian chant** See plainchant.

**ground bass**  See ostinato.

**harmonic rhythm**  Speed at which chords change.

**harmony**  The sounding together of two or more tones.

**harpsichord**  Keyboard instrument used in the sixteenth through eighteenth centuries in which small plectra pluck the strings when the keys are depressed.

**heavy metal rock**  Rock style of the 1970s that emphasizes very high volume, distorted instrumental and vocal sounds, and noise.

**homophony, homophonic**  Texture made up of a melodic line and chordal accompaniment.

**hsiao**  Chinese vertical flute made of bamboo.

**hymn**  Religious song intended for congregational singing, usually in strophic form.

**idée fixe**  Literally "fixed idea"; a melody in the music of Berlioz, associated with a nonmusical idea and repeated throughout the work.

**idiophone**  Any instrument whose sound is produced through the vibrating of the whole body of the instrument.

**imitation**  The immediate repetition of a theme by different voices, either exactly or with small changes.

**imitative counterpoint**  See imitation.

**Impressionism**  Artistic movement of the late nineteenth century characterized by an understated approach and designed to appeal to the senses rather than the intellect; represented musically by much of the music of Debussy and those whom he influenced.

**impromptu**  Short composition, usually for the piano, designed to sound like an improvisation; chiefly popular in the nineteenth century.

**improvisation**  Composing music while performing it, either without a written score or by variations on a score.

**incidental music**  Music incidental to the action in a play: e.g., a musical setting for a love scene, or dance music for a ballroom scene; sometimes also overtures and music played between the acts of a play.

**instrumentation**  Parts assigned to particular instruments in an ensemble or orchestra.

**interval**  Musical and mathematical distance between two pitches.

**inversion**  Compositional technique in which a theme is repeated upside down.

**isorhythm**  Technique common in fourteenth-century music in which a rhythmic pattern is repeated throughout, often with a repeated melodic pattern of the same or different length.

**Italian overture**  Type of overture in late seventeenth- and early eighteenth-century music used by composers in Italy and other countries, usually in three sections—fast-slow-fast.

**jazz**  Indigenous American musical style of the twentieth century, distinguished by highly improvisatory performance and complex rhythms.

**key**  The basic scale of a composition, named for its tonic note and indicated on the score by a key signature.

**key signature**  Sharps or flats placed at the beginning of each staff of music to indicate the key used.

**Klangfarbenmelodie**  Technique used by Schoenberg and his followers in which each note or small group of notes in a melody is given to a different instrument.

**lai**  Medieval French secular song based on a poetic form.

**largo**  Very slow and broad tempo.

**lauda (pl. laude)**  Italian devotional hymn, especially in the Middle Ages and the Renaissance, that influenced the development of the oratorio in the Baroque period.

**ledger lines**  Short lines on which notes are placed above or below the lines of the staff.

**legato**  Smooth, connected manner of musical performance.

**Leitmotiv**  Melodic, rhythmic, and/or harmonic motive associated with a person, thing, or idea in the music dramas of Richard Wagner.

**lento**  Slow tempo.

**libretto**  Text of an opera or oratorio, often in poetic form.

**Lied (pl. Lieder)**  German for "song"; German art song, especially of the nineteenth century.

**lining out**  Practice in which each line of a song or hymn is sung by a leader and immediately repeated by the group.

**lute**  Fretted, plucked string instrument of the sixteenth through eighteenth centuries, shaped like half a pear.

**lyric opera**  Nineteenth-century French style of opera that was a compromise between grand opera and opéra comique.

**madrigal**  (1)) Secular composition, usually for two or three voices, in fourteenth-century Italy; (2) secular composition for four or five voices in Italy and England in the sixteenth and early seventeenth centuries.

**major scale**  Scale consisting of the following pattern of whole and half steps, beginning with the lowest pitch: whole—whole—half—whole—whole—whole—half.

**ma non troppo**  "But not too."

**march**  Music designed to accompany walking, in duple meter and a moderate tempo.

**Mass**  In music, usually a polyphonic setting of the Ordinary: Kyrie, Gloria, Credo, Sanctus, Agnus Dei.

**mazurka**  Polish dance in $\frac{3}{4}$ time, incorporating rhythmic features of Eastern Europe; used especially by Chopin in the early nineteenth century as a basis for his numerous piano pieces.

**measure**  Rhythmic group of beats with an accent on the first beat in each group, and sometimes a secondary accent on a later beat; each measure is set off in written music by vertical lines called bar lines.

**melismatic**  Having many notes per syllable of text.

**melody**  Succession of tones that assumes a recognizable musical shape in conjunction with a rhythmic organization.

**membranophone**  Any instrument in which sound is produced through the vibrating of a membrane such as a drum head.

**meno**  Less.

**meter**  Pattern of accented and unaccented beats. Common types: duple meter, with two beats, one accented and one unaccented; triple meter, with three beats, one accented and two unaccented.

**meter signature** Pair of numbers placed at the beginning of a score: the upper number indicates the number of beats per measure; the lower number indicates the type of note that has the value of one beat.

**metronome** Device invented in the early nineteenth century to indicate the exact tempo of a composition.

**mezzo-soprano** Female voice that lies between the soprano and contralto in range.

**microtonal composition** Music making use of an octave made up of more than twelve tones.

**minimal (systems) music** A musical style of the later twentieth century that makes use of a very limited number of musical materials which are repeated extensively in a work, often with subtle changes.

**Minnesinger** Courtly singer-poet of late Medieval Germany.

**minor scale** Scale consisting of the following pattern of whole and half steps, beginning with the lowest pitch: whole—half—whole—whole—half—whole—whole. The sixth and seventh degrees of the scale can be altered to create two additional forms of the minor scale, the harmonic and melodic.

**minuet** Dance of the seventeenth and eighteenth centuries, in triple meter and moderate tempo; often used with a trio in the third movement of a Classical symphony.

**Missa** Mass.

**Missa brevis** (1) In the Renaissance, a simpler and shorter setting of the five parts of the Ordinary of the Mass; (2) in the Baroque period, a setting of the Kyrie and Gloria used in the Lutheran Church.

**mode** (1) Scale such as the major or minor; (2) often used to refer to scales in non-Western music. See also Church modes.

**moderato** Moderate tempo.

**modified strophic form** Form in vocal music in which all stanzas of a text are sung to music that is basically the same but with some changes in the repetitions.

**modulation** Change of key or tonic note in a composition.

**molto** Very.

**monody, monodic** Style consisting of a melody and a simple accompaniment; used in early seventeenth-century Italian music.

**monophony, monophonic** Texture that is made up of a single line.

**motet** (1) Prominent type of composition of the thirteenth century, usually for three voices, often combining religious and secular texts; (2) an unaccompanied choral composition of the fifteenth and sixteenth centuries, written in contrapuntal style, usually for four or five voices, generally with a religious text.

**motive** Short melodic-rhythmic figure, generally consisting of from two to five notes, used as a unit in a composition.

**movement** Relatively independent part of a large composition, usually having a clear beginning and ending.

**musique concrète** Twentieth-century style in which conventional sounds are altered electronically and recorded on tape to produce new effects.

**natural** Sign indicating that a note is to be played without sharping or flatting; used only as an accidental, never in the key signature.

**Neoclassicism** Twentieth-century style that borrows certain characteristics of earlier periods—such as form, melody, instrumentation—and combines them with other elements used in a new way.

**neumatic** Having several notes per syllable of text but not as many notes per syllable as in the melismatic style.

**neume** Symbol used for a note or a small group of notes in Medieval notation.

**new wave rock** Eclectic rock style that began in the early 1970s, characterized by an economy of material and a controlled, intellectual style.

**nocturne** Literally "night piece"; a piano composition of the nineteenth century.

**note** Visual representation of musical sound.

**octave** Interval in which the higher pitch has twice as many vibrations per second as the lower.

**octave displacement** Technique in which the successive notes of a melody are placed in different octaves.

**Office** The form of daily common prayer in monastic and other religious communities, consisting mainly of psalms, hymns, and Scripture readings; usually divided into several services or "hours" distributed throughout the day.

**opera** Drama expressed through music, with dialogue generally sung rather than spoken; developed first in Italy in the seventeenth century.

**opera buffa** Italian comic opera.

**opéra comique** French comic opera.

**opera seria** Italian serious opera.

**operetta** Light opera with spoken dialogue, often with frivolous plot.

**opus (abb. op.)** Latin for "work"; used by composers beginning in the Baroque era to indicate the order in which their compositions were written, e.g., Opus 1, Opus 2.

**oratorio** Religious or secular work for solo voices, chorus, and orchestra developed in the Baroque period; usually presented without staging or scenery.

**orchestration** Use of instruments in orchestral music to achieve a variety of effects.

**Ordinary** Those parts of the Mass in which the text always remains the same; principally the Kyrie, Gloria, Credo, Sanctus, Agnus Dei.

**ordre** See suite.

**organum** Earliest Western polyphony, beginning in the ninth century, based on melodies borrowed from plainchant.

**ornament** Note or group of notes added to a basic melody to embellish or decorate it.

**ostinato** Melodic and/or rhythmic motive or phrase that is repeated persistently, often in the bass.

**overture** Instrumental introduction to a vocal work or orchestral suite. Common Baroque types are the French overture and Italian overture. Common Romantic types: one-movement instrumental introduction to a vocal work; independent programmatic work written for concert performance. Latter type often called concert overture.

**pandiatonicism**  A diatonic tonal style without the restrictions of traditional chordal progressions.

**parallel chords**  Chords of the same or similar structure that ascend or descend without a traditional resolution.

**parallel motion**  Movement of voices that remain a specific interval apart as they ascend or descend.

**paraphrase technique**  Compositional method that produces an elaboration of an existing melody in a new work.

**partita**  See suite.

**pavane**  Slow, processional dance of the Renaissance and Baroque periods, in duple meter. Also called padouana.

**pentatonic scale**  Scale of five tones.

**phrase**  Relatively short portion of a melodic line with a clear beginning and end, similar in length and function to a line of poetry.

**pianoforte (piano)**  Keyboard instrument that developed from the harpsichord around 1700, with a mechanism that causes the strings to be struck with small hammers when keys are depressed, and capable of producing a variety of intensity between soft and loud, depending on the amount of pressure applied to the keys.

**piano quartet**  String trio (violin, viola, cello) plus piano.

**piano quintet**  String quartet plus piano.

**p'i-p'a**  Chinese, fretted, four-string lute, shaped like half a pear.

**pitch**  Sound of a tone, relatively high or low, determined by the number of vibrations per second.

**più**  More.

**pizzicato**  Manner of playing a string instrument by plucking instead of bowing the strings.

**plagal cadence**  Cadence consisting of a subdominant chord that resolves to a tonic chord (IV-I); often set to the Amen at the end of hymns.

**plagal modes**  Four Medieval Church modes, each related directly to one of the four authentic Church modes. The name of each is preceded by the prefix "Hypo-"; the authentic Dorian mode, for example, shares some characteristics with the plagal Hypodorian mode.

**plainchant**  Monophonic church music of the Middle Ages, sometimes called Gregorian chant after Pope Gregory I. Also called chant.

**poco**  Little.

**pointillistic texture**  Sparse texture often made up of a single note or very short motive followed immediately by one in another part in a higher or lower register.

**point of imitation**  A section of music, especially of the Renaissance, where most or all voices enter in turn with the same melody in imitation.

**polonaise**  Polish ceremonial dance in triple meter and moderate tempo; used by Chopin in the early nineteenth century for piano compositions.

**polyphony, polyphonic**  Texture in which two or more voices proceed relatively independently.

**polyrhythm**  The use of several contrasting rhythms at the same time.

**polytonality**  Several tonalities occurring simultaneously.

**prelude**  (1) Free-form type of composition intended as an introduction; (2) in the nineteenth century, an independent short composition, usually for piano.

**prestissimo**  Extremely fast tempo.

**presto**  Very fast tempo.

**prima donna**  Italian for "first lady"; a female lead in an opera.

**program music**  Instrumental music associated with nonmusical ideas that are often drawn from nature, art, or literature.

**program symphony**  See symphony.

**Proper**  The parts of the Mass in which the texts change according to the particular rites of the day.

**punk rock**  Rock style that developed in the mid-1970s, characterized by short melodies and simple harmonies, representing the ideas of the angry, violent working-class youth.

**raga**  Melodic formula in Indian music.

**ragtime**  Precursor of jazz, in duple meter, with liberal use of syncopation.

**rallentando**  Gradual slowing of tempo.

**realize**  To play a chordal accompaniment from a figured bass score.

**recapitulation**  (1) Section of thematic restatement; (2) the third section in a sonata form.

**recitative**  Declamatory type of singing developed in the Baroque period, used particularly in opera and oratorios. Emphasis is on free rhythm, uncomplicated melody, and clarity of text. Two types: secco ("dry"), accompanied only by continuo; accompagnato ("accompanied"), accompanied by ensemble or orchestra.

**recorder**  Vertically held, end-blown flute prominent in the fifteenth through eighteenth centuries.

**relative major and minor scales**  Major and minor scales that share the same key signature, but have tonal centers a minor third apart.

**Requiem Mass**  Mass for the Dead in the Roman Catholic liturgy.

**resolution**  Movement from dissonant to more consonant sound.

**responsorial singing**  Vocal technique in which a chorus answers phrases sung by a leader.

**rest**  (1) Period of silence in music; (2) sign used for notation of such silence.

**retrograde**  Compositional technique in which a theme is presented backward.

**rhapsody**  One-movement work in the style of a free fantasy, generally of heroic or romantic inspiration, popular in the nineteenth and twentieth centuries.

**rhythm**  Organization of sound in time, governed by such aspects as tempo and meter.

**rhythmic polyphony**  Polyphonic texture created by interweaving of different rhythmic patterns.

**ricercar**  Imitative, contrapuntal instrumental piece of the sixteenth and seventeenth centuries, similar in style to the Renaissance motet.

**ring shout** In black religious music of the pre-Civil War South, a shuffling step with chanting and handclapping used in prayer meetings.

**ripieno** Orchestral group in a Baroque concerto grosso.

**ritardando** Gradual slowing of tempo.

**ritornello form** Baroque form with alternating ripieno and solo passages, in which the ripieno returns to modified versions of the opening theme, while the soloist elaborates on the opening theme or contrasts with it in virtuoso fashion.

**Rococo style** Highly ornamented style in music and the other arts in the early to middle eighteenth century.

**rondeau** Medieval French secular song based on a poetic form.

**rondo form** Form prominent in the Classical period, in which a main theme, always in the tonic key, alternates with subordinate themes in contrasting keys.

**round** See canon.

**rubato** Technique in which very small displacements in rhythm are introduced for expressive purposes; literally, "robbing" time from one note and giving it to another.

**sackbut** Early form of the trombone, used in the fifteenth century and later.

**sarabande** Baroque dance, in triple meter and a slow tempo.

**scale** Arrangement of tones, usually within an octave, used as the basis of a composition.

**scherzo** Literally "joke." (1) A movement of a symphony, sonata, or quartet that replaced the minuet in the nineteenth century; (2) sometimes an independent composition. In both cases, usually written in a light and rapid style.

**scordatura** Unusual tuning of a string instrument.

**section** Portion of a musical work.

**sequence** (1) Repetition of a melodic motive or short phrase at different pitch levels; (2) a part of the Proper of the Mass.

**serialism** Systematic ordering of pitches, durations, and/or other musical elements, so that they always appear in a predetermined order; originally associated with the twelve-tone system.

**sforzando** Sudden, sharp increase in loudness.

**shape-note notation** Early American type of notation making use of four notes of different shapes—generally triangular, round, oblong, and diamond-shaped.

**sharp** Sign indicating that a pitch is to be raised by a half step.

**shawm** Double-reed ancestor of the oboe, used in Western music from the thirteenth through the seventeenth centuries.

**sheng** Chinese instrument made with a gourd and a number of small, vertical pipes fitted on top of it.

**sinfonia** Instrumental work that developed into the Italian overture of the Baroque period.

**Singspiel** German comic opera of the eighteenth century, in which dialogue was usually spoken rather than sung as in Italian opera.

**sitar** Indian instrument of the lute family, having a long neck, moveable frets, and three to seven strings.

**sonata** Instrumental composition of the seventeenth through the twentieth centuries; Baroque trio sonata for two melody instruments and continuo; sonatas also written for one melody instrument and keyboard, as well as for single instruments.

**sonata-allegro form** See sonata form.

**sonata cycle** Three- or four-movement structure of compositions such as the symphony, sonata, quartet, and concerto of the eighteenth through twentieth centuries.

**sonata da camera** Baroque chamber sonata, usually comprised mainly of dance movements.

**sonata da chiesa** Baroque church sonata, usually slow—fast—slow—fast in structure and often influenced by dance forms.

**sonata form** Form developed in the mid-eighteenth century, consisting of an opening section called the exposition in which major themes are presented, a middle section called the development in which thematic material undergoes a variety of alterations, and a third section called the recapitulation in which the material of the exposition is restated.

**sonata-rondo form** Form combining characteristics of both the sonata and the rondo forms.

**song cycle** Group of songs with a unifying theme.

**soprano** Female voice with highest range.

**soul music** Popular style of American music, based on black folk and gospel music.

**spiritual** American religious folk song, developed by blacks and southern rural whites.

**Sprechstimme** Literally "speaking voice"; vocal technique falling somewhere between speech and song, used frequently by Schoenberg and his contemporaries; in notation, an X is sometimes placed through the stem of a note, indicating that the pitch should not be sustained.

**staccato** Literally "detached"; a manner of performance in which each note is made very short and clipped; indicated by a dot placed above or below the note.

**staff (pl. staves)** Series of horizontal lines (five in modern notation) on which musical notes are written.

**stanza** One of several sections in a poem that are usually identical or similar in length and structure.

**stile rappresentativo** Representative or theatrical style in the early seventeenth century, based on the belief that music should be subordinated to the expression of ideas and emotions in the text.

**string quartet** String ensemble made up of two violins, one viola, and one cello.

**strophe** See stanza.

**strophic form** Form of vocal music in which all stanzas of the text are sung to the same music.

**subdominant** Fourth note of a major or minor scale.

**subject** Primary melody in a fugue.

**suite** Composition consisting of a number of dance movements, loosely linked. In Baroque music also called ordre or partita.

**su-yueh music** Traditional Chinese common music.

**swing** Big-band style of jazz, intended for dancing, and popular in the late 1930s and 1940s.

**syllabic** Having one note per syllable of text.

**symphonic poem** Programmatic symphony in one movement; also called a tone poem.

**symphony** Orchestral composition, usually consisting of four movements, that originated in the eighteenth century. In the nineteenth century, the abstract symphony generally retained the Classical emphasis on purely musical expression while the program symphony was associated with nonmusical ideas as well.

**syncopation** Use of an accent on a beat that is not usually accented.

**synthesizer** Electronic instrument used to generate sounds.

**tala** Pattern of basic time units in Indian music.

**temperament** System of tuning. Equal temperament, devised in the seventeenth century, divides the octave into twelve equal intervals, enabling a keyboard instrument to play in tune in any key.

**tempo** Speed at which a composition is performed. For specific tempo markings see chart on page 29.

**tempus imperfectum** Imperfect or duple time, as referred to in late Medieval and Renaissance music.

**tempus perfectum** Perfect or triple time, as referred to in late Medieval and Renaissance music.

**tenor** (1) Highest of the ordinary male voice types; (2) in Medieval and Renaissance polyphony, the voice that includes a borrowed melody on which a composition is based.

**ternary form** Three-part form in which the third section is often a restatement of the material in the first.

**terraced dynamics** Sudden changes in dynamic level, characteristic of Baroque music.

**text painting** Direct association of musical ideas with words or a phrase in the text of a vocal work; e.g., a rising scale for the phrase "rise above us."

**texture** The number and relationship of musical lines in a composition. Main types: monophonic, consisting of a single line; polyphonic or contrapuntal, with two or more lines, each relatively independent; homophonic, consisting of melody with chordal accompaniment.

**theme** Principal melody in a composition.

**theme and variations form** Form consisting of a theme followed by a number of variations on the theme.

**third stream jazz** Style of jazz that developed in the late 1950s that combines jazz elements with traditional styles of art music.

**thoroughbass** See basso continuo.

**timbre** Tone color or specific quality of sound that distinguishes one instrument or voice from another.

**time notation** Notation in which duration depends on the visual length of the notes as determined by the performer.

**toccata** Virtuoso composition in free form, usually for keyboard.

**tonality** Aural effect of music centered around one note or based on a particular key.

**tone cluster** Dissonant chord made up of several adjacent notes.

**tone poem** See symphonic poem.

**tone row** Basis of structure in twelve-tone serial technique, using (in strict form) the twelve notes of the chromatic scale only once in an order decided by the composer.

**tonic** Basic or home note of a scale, frequently called *do*.

**transverse flute** Horizontally held, wooden or metal flute, used widely since the Middle Ages.

**tremolo** Rapid repetition of a single note, or rapid alternation between two notes, a chord, or slight variation of pitch around a central tone.

**triad** Chord consisting of three tones with a specific intervallic relationship to one another.

**trill** Ornament, usually indicated by the abbreviation *tr* or a wavy-line symbol, in which the written note is played in rapid alternation with the note just above it.

**trio** (1) Composition for three performers; (2) the second section of a minuet or scherzo movement.

**triplet** Beat subdivided into three parts.

**troubadour** Courtly singer-poet of the twelfth and thirteenth centuries in southern France.

**trouvère** Courtly singer-poet of the twelfth and thirteenth centuries in northern France.

**turn** Ornament consisting of a group of four or five notes that "turn around" the note given in the notation.

**tutti** Literally "all." (1) Direction given in a composition when the entire group is to perform together; (2) term for the combined orchestral and solo groups in a Baroque concerto grosso.

**twelve-tone system** Twentieth-century system of composition based on a tone row.

**variation** Compositional technique in which musical ideas are repeated with some changes.

**viol** General name for a family of fretted, bowed string instruments used chiefly in the sixteenth to the eighteenth centuries.

**viola da gamba** Fretted, bowed, six-string group of instruments held between the legs, in popular use from the sixteenth to the early eighteenth centuries.

**viola d'amore** Unfretted, bowed treble viol with sympathetic strings under the playing strings, used in the late seventeenth and eighteenth centuries.

**virelai** Medieval French secular song based on a poetic form.

**vivace** Very fast tempo.

**voice** (1) The human voice; (2) a part in an instrumental composition.

**waltz** Dance popular in the nineteenth century, in triple meter and a moderate tempo.

**whole-tone scale** Scale in which the octave is divided into six whole-step intervals.

**ya-yueh music** Traditional Chinese court music.

# Index of Musical Compositions

# General Index

| | 1750 | 1800 | 1825 | 1850 | 1875 |
|---|---|---|---|---|---|
| **MAJOR COMPOSERS** | Stamitz<br>Gluck<br>C.P.E. Bach<br>Haydn<br>Mozart | Beethoven<br>Schubert | Weber<br>Schubert<br>Berlioz<br>Mendelssohn<br>Chopin<br>Schumann<br>Donizetti | Liszt<br>Wagner<br>Rossini | Verdi<br>Brahms<br>Mussorgsky<br>Tchaikovsky<br>Bruckner<br>Smetana<br>Bizet |
| **MUSICAL EVENTS** | Development of string quartet<br>Mannheim Orchestra's greatest influence<br>Haydn's first symphonies<br>Mozart's *The Marriage of Figaro* | Opening of La Scala in Milan<br>Beethoven's *Symphony No. 5* | Berlioz' *Symphonie fantastique*<br>Founding of New York Philharmonic Society and Vienna Philharmonic | Liszt's *Les Préludes*<br>Wagner's *Tristan und Isolde* | Verdi's *Aïda*<br>Bayreuth Theater opens<br>Invention of phonograph |
| **MAJOR POLITICAL, SOCIAL, AND CULTURAL FIGURES** | Voltaire<br>Franklin<br>Rousseau<br>Frederick the Great of Prussia<br>Kant<br>Gainsborough<br>Catherine the Great of Russia | Jefferson<br>Goya<br>David<br>Blake<br>Schiller<br>Napoleon<br>Constable | Goethe<br>Byron | Delacroix<br>Balzac<br>Darwin<br>Dickens | Bismarck<br>Marx<br>Tolstoy<br>Manet<br>Whitman<br>Cézanne<br>Gauguin |
| **POLITICAL, SOCIAL, AND CULTURAL EVENTS** | First volumes of French *Encyclopédie*<br>Seven Years' War<br>Rousseau's *Social Contract*<br>Pompeii excavations Begin<br>Industrial Revolution<br>American Declaration of Independence<br>French Revolution | | First railroad built in England<br>Invention of photography | Reign of Victoria<br>Marx' *Communist Manifesto*<br>Darwin's *Origin of Species*<br>American Civil War<br>Unification of Italy<br>Franco-Prussian War<br>Unification of Germany | First Impressionist exhibition |